AN INTELLECTUAL HISTORY OF CHINA

He Zhaowu, Bu Jinzhi, Tang Yuyuan and Sun Kaitai
Institute of History
Chinese Academy of Social Sciences

Revised and Translated by
He Zhaowu

FOREIGN LANGUAGES PRESS BEIJING

First edition · 1991

Hardcover ISBN 7-119-00003-9
ISBN 0-8351-1880-0
Paperback ISBN 7-119-00006-3
ISBN 0-8351-1881-9

Copyright 1991 by Foreign Languages Press

Published by Foreign Languages Press
24 Baiwanzhuang Road, Beijing 100037, China

Distributed by China International Book Trading Corporation
21 Chegongzhuang Xilu, Beijing 100044, China
P.O. Box 399, Beijing, China

Printed in the People's Republic of China

Contents

TRANSLATOR'S PREFACE
TO THE ENGLISH VERSION

The Chinese have one of the oldest and at the same time one of the longest continuous civilizations in the world. In the long course of her development of more than four thousand years, China has not only created a most splendid culture but has also preserved a collection of abundant historical documents. Viewed from these aspects, she possesses a position almost unique in the world both in history and in historiography. Yet because throughout her long history she has been relatively isolated from the rest of the world, her ideology and culture have not been fully recognized, nor has she made her due share of contributions to world civilization.

The present work aims at introducing to readers the development of the Chinese ideology from the earliest to modern times. It is not an exposition in detail; what it affords is no more than a brief account by way of introduction. But it does endeavour to give a general description about what constituted the characteristic features of the main currents of thought in each historical era and what the chief contributions of the most outstanding thinkers were in various fields of the Chinese ideology, how thought came about as a product of its specific historical background and how it influenced the development of history itself. Hence it will not assume the form of a record of specific thought, or of the narration of certain philosophical or scientific concepts, but will be an attempt at a comprehensive survey intended to summarize all the main intellectual elements in the history of China.

Chinese ideas are usually characterized by their close connections with the ethical practices in daily life. In their search after truth, most of the Chinese thinkers focus on the perfection of personal morality and the maxim of social ethics. The over-emphasis on the moral and the ethical has made Chinese ideas in some aspects of pure thinking appear not so salient as those of the modern Occident. Nevertheless, this does not mean that China has not made immense contributions to the fields of intellectual activity. For instance, a comparison between the pre-Qin Dialecticians and the ancient Greek Sophists demonstrates how strikingly their ideas and arguments resemble each other. Some of their propositions are even identical in phraseology and content. This seems to indicate that in just the same golden age of the classical civilizations (about 4th century B.C.) the high speculative level reached simultaneously both by China and by Greece really amounted to a historical phenomenon, or a competition in brilliance and splendour between the East and the West. In a similar comparison, it is very probable that it is just because the Chinese laid over-emphasis on human relationships that throughout her history there had never been a religion or a theism dominating the whole sphere of spiritual activities as was seen in the mediaeval Chritianity in the West. Indeed Buddhism was introduced to China from abroad, yet in course of time it gradually but thoroughly became indigenous or sinicized until at last it lost its original religious flavour. The flow of Chinese ideology and its comparison with others, especially with those of the West, is a complex and extensive area of historical studies. Full exploration of all aspects is hardly possible within the space of a short volume, we do hope the present work may help lead readers to further interest and further research.

The mediaeval era lasted in China for more than two thousand years, while the mediaeval period in the West lasted only one thousand or so. This prolongation of the mediaeval period makes it possible for China to furnish the world a typical model of mediaevalism. For example, the peasant wars in China with their grand scale and frequent outbreaks were rare in the history of other peoples and hence afford a typical model for the ideology of peasants' wars. This mediaeval prolongation also made China lag behind the West in modern times. From an intellectual and cultural viewpoint, Chinese sciences and ideas, undoubtedly at a high level throughout the mediaeval period in world history, had begun falling behind the West since the Renaissance. Hence, the central theme of the modern history of China has been to learn, to equal and to compete with the West so as to become modernized and to have a foothold in the modern world. In the transformation from a mediaeval ideology into a modern one, China has made tremendous efforts in modern times and paid greatly and dearly. China in ancient times had produced brilliant ideas and a culture which rivalled that of Greece and India, and again in the Middle Ages she had produced ideas and culture which rivalled that of the Arabs when the Occident still remained in their so-called "Dark Ages". There would be sufficient ground to expect that in modern times she would also be able to create advanced ideas and culture second to none of the world. But in order to create new ideas and culture, it is impossible to discard the past; for without the past as a starting point, there can be neither the present nor the future. Nor can the present be understood without a knowledge of the past. No ideology whatever in the world can ever come into being by neglecting the past tradition, especially in the case of such an immeasurably rich historical legacy as that of the intellectual history of China. It was with this knowledge in mind that we began to undertake the work on the present volume. It is our hope that through our present work readers might be brought to understand more about the intellectual history of China and to make further research on it.

The present work was written in the years 1977-79, the first part (the Pre-Qin Period) by Sun Kaitai, the second part (from Qin to Tang) by Bu Jingzhi, the third part (from Song to middle Qing) by Tang Yuyuan and the fourth part (modern times) by myself. The arrangement of the joint work and the publication was done by Tang Yuyuan, while the revising, polishing and editing of the whole work was entrusted to me. Though the first draft of each part was written by separate authors, the whole book as it appears in its present form was discussed, modified and unanimously adopted in collaboration as outlined above. In the process of writing, we tried for a compact and coherent form so as to bring various aspects of the Chinese ideology into a general perspective in the light of historical development. Since the authors are for the first time to make such an effort and works of a comprehensive nature treating the intellectual history of China are still rare, there are unavoidably some problems in this book. One of the defects we find is that there is more plain narration than overall and pene-

trating analysis through a historical perspective. To write an intellectual history in a more perfect way, to make it reflect in true
depth the spirit of the age (or Zeitgeist, as the Germans term it)
in the light of the interaction and the intermingling of different
ideas, that is, to work out an intellectual history which really
deserves its name, this is an ideal to be fulfilled in the future.

For many years the authors have worked in the Institute of
History, Academia Sinica, and devoted themselves to research in
the field of intellectual history under the tutorship of Prof. Hou
Wailu, who with his outstanding scholarship and academic achievements has contributed much to this discipline for decades. As his
long-time pupils and assistants, we should like to take this opportunity to pay our hearty homage to his guidance and instruction
which enabled us to make such tentative research as the present
work; but needless to say, any fault or defect that may appear in
this book will be our own. Prof. Yang Xiangkui of our institute
was kind enough to give many valuable suggestions in its writing
and in its compilation. Mr. Meng Qingyuan of the Youth Publishing House rendered his generous services for its publication. For
the present English version, The Foreign Languages Press has
given us encouragement and valuable help. In the course of translation, I have kept constant contacts with the other three authors
and consulted with them in detail. As for the scholars, living and
dead, whose achievements are absorbed or assimilated in this book,
though there are too many to have their names and works enumerated one by one within the space of this brief preface, we acknowledge here our sincere gratitude to all of them.

As for the present English version, it should be appropriate
here to remark that by agreement with the authors as well as on
the part of the press, I decided on a free translation of the original
text of our work *History of the Development of the Chinese
Ideology* rather than a literal word-by-word one. I followed the
contents closely without any alteration or supplement which was
not consulted with or agreed to by the authors. For the quotations
from ancient works, except what were my own, I adopted freely
the translations from various sources, the list of which would seem
too tedious to be mentioned in the footnotes.

My thanks are due to Dr. Wykoff for his translation of parts of Chapters 23 and 24 which appeared in the American journal *Chinese Studies of History* and which I adopted with revisions and supplements in the present English version.

He Zhaowu
Institute of History
Beijing (Peking), 1985

Part I
IDEOLOGY OF
THE PRE-QIN PERIOD

INTRODUCTION TO THE SOCIETY AND
IDEOLOGY OF THE PRE-QIN PERIOD

When the pre-Qin period is referred to, it means in general the historical period before the unification of the six states by the Qin Dynasty. There were comprised in it the succeeding epochs of the Xia, the Shang and the Zhou dynasties and the Warring States Period. It marked the beginning of the development of Chinese civilization and ideology.

Even in the primitive era before the establishment of the earliest dynasty of Xia, our ancestors through their age-long labour had not only formed societies but also had developed their thinking powers, thus bringing to life the earliest elements of human thought.

Later, with the growth of social productivity, it became possible for people to enjoy surplus products and with this the idea of private property began. Then classes and states came into being. According to legends, this transition took place with the founding of the Xia Dynasty (about 21st-16th century B.C.).

The Xia Dynasty was followed by the Shang Dynasty (16th-11th century B.C.). By that time reliable written records had appeared. After the fall of the Shang Dynasty came the Zhou Dynasty (11th-8th century B.C.) which marked the stage of the development of slavery. As an economic institution, land ownership began according to the "nine-squares" system (i.e. one square of land divided into nine smaller ones, the outer eight being allocated to slaves, who had to cultivate the central one for their lord) and enfeoffment (i.e., investing the nobility with hereditary titles, domains and slaves). In political institutions, the Zhou differed from the Shang Dynasty mainly in its adoption of the primogeniture upon which the patriarchal clan system was formed. On this basis Duke Zhou (named Dan), the leading statesman of the early Zhou, "instituted the rites" and then a rather complete superstructure based on slavery was established.

In the sphere of ideology, the religious superstitions inherited from the primitive societies further developed. This was because of the low social productivity and because people were unable to resist natural disasters or to find out a rational explanation for them, which led to the worship of supernatural powers. Also, it was because people were being brought into a class society and suffering from both natural and even more severe social forces.Under these double suppressions people mistakenly saw their destinies being dominated by a superhuman power. Thus began a growing superstition in gods and in heavenly beings. With the collapse of the primitive communes and the growth of the slave state, the religious worship of natural objects (polytheism) was gradually turned into the worship of one supreme God, called Di or Shangdi (monotheism). This God was regarded as the supreme dominator of both heaven and the human world; and all natural phenomena and human affairs were thought to be under the control of his will. Such a belief was the reflection of the ruling power of the earthly majesty in human minds, once it was established and strengthened on earth. Thereupon, the ideological content of religious superstition was no longer the mere worship of the supernatural powers as in the primitive society but was replaced by the content of class suppression. The ruling class of the Shang slave society thus depended on the authority of God to maintain dominance over the human world. Therefore, offering sacrifices to God was a matter of cardinal importance in the political life of the state, with all major human activities needing the socerers for omens or prayers to heaven for help.

Later on, the ruling class of the Zhou Dynasty inherited the Shang's idea of the Mandate of Heaven (i.e., God's will) with the aim of maintaining their own dominance. At the same time, a serious lesson was taught by the fact that "the vanguards [of the Shang slaves] while on their march suddenly turned their spearheads backward" and thus brought about the fall of the Shang Dynasty. The Zhous as a result were deeply impressed with "the inconstancy of God's will"[1] and began to realize that it would be impossible to maintain their rule by simply professing the mysterious God's will. In order to compensate for the insufficiency of God's will, they put forward the idea of "virtue", or a kind of divine power. In their opinion, the fall of Shang was a result of its later kings having "failed to venerate the virtue". Therefore, it was taught that a ruler should uphold a virtuous policy, that is, he should care about what means he was to adopt for his rule. It was only then that he could hope for the blessing of God and "praying to Heaven for his eternal mandate".[2] The emergence of the idea of virtue reflected the fact the Zhou rulers were beginning to doubt the will of God and turning their attentions more and more to the human world.

By the later years of the Western Zhou (9th-8th century B.C.), as the disintegration of slavery reached a crisis the ruling class sensed its authority wavering. From their experiences of immense sufferings from natural calamities and from social and political injustices, the people came to realize that both God and their long-worshipped ancestral spirits seemed to have lost their magic, and thereupon they began to doubt the traditional belief in Heaven (God). They blamed their God for having failed to exercise his divine power and their ancestral spirits for their incompetence. God and the Mandate of Heaven, though not yet completely discredited in their minds, no longer assumed the supreme and absolute authority they once had. In some chapters of the *Book of Odes*, the suffering of the people and the social disorders were attributed not to the will of God but to the behaviour of man. As the poet lamented: "The misfortunes of the people did not come from Heaven; people said good-sounding words and then turned their backs with hatred, all these were the result of human actions."[3] From this we may trace an expression of suspicion about God, almost approaching the negation of God—an expression which might be looked upon as the germination of the earliest materialistic and atheistic tendency.

With the introduction of oxen and iron implements in farming, social productivity had accomplished much progress since the Spring and Autumn Period (770-476 B.C.). Along with the official "nine squares" land ownership, a large quantity of private land ownership came about as a result of opening up wastelands. The growth of private land ownership led to the ruin of the "nine squares" system and hence to the collapse to the very foundation of slavery. In the 15th year of the reign of Duke Xuan of Lu (594 B.C.) was proclaimed "taxation on the farmland for the first time"; to tax private farmland meant to acknowledge the legitimate existence of private land property, which marked the emergence of the feudal productive system.

The further development of this trend directly promoted the reform movements in almost all the states during the period of the Warring States and thus brought China into a new historical stage, i.e., that of feudalism.

Important changes in class relations went hand in hand with the appearance and development of feudal productive relationships. Besides the existing class of slaves and that of slave owners, there came into being the newborn landlord class and the peasants. In addition to these, numerous handicraftsmen and merchants also formed a new social force.

The changes in the economic basis and class relationships of necessity brought about a very complicated structure in the field of politics as well as in that of ideology. Hence from the Spring and Autumn Period, and especially during the Warring States Period, different schools of thought representing different social interests and viewpoints were born and flourished here and there; they argued with one another and thus an intellectual prosperity, called "the Contending of the Hundred Schools," began to rise.

In the sphere of ideology, with the growth of productive forces and the marked progress of scientific knowledge (especially that of astronomy) as well as with the decline of the authority of the ruling slave-owning nobility, an advanced current of thought came forth, characterized by its refusal to recognize "Heaven"and paying more attention to man and human affairs. Also by this time appeared a naive materialism based on the principle of Yin (the negative) and Yang (the positive) and on the five elements. What was more noteworthy was the fact that Confucius broke with the Western Zhou's tradition that "learning dwells only in the officialdom" and created the earliest private school—the Confucian School. On the ideological basis of "venerating the virtues and protecting the people" of the Zhou Dynasty, Confucius propounded a Confucian ideology with "ren" (humanity) at its core. Imbued with a conservative and reformist air, it was an ideological transition corresponding to the change from slavery to feudalism in the later Spring and Autumn Period.

With the violent social turbulence in the Warring States Period, a great schism within the camp of the Confucian School occurred, mainly between the school of Zi Si and Mencius and that of Xun Zi.

Along with the Confucian School, there was then a galaxy of eminent personalities: Lao Zi, Mo Zi, Yang Zhu, Xu Xing, Li Gui, Wu Qi, Shang Yang, Song Xing, Yin Wen, Hui Shi, Gongsun Long, Han Fei, Zou Yan and others who successively participated in the great debates of the age, professing earnestly their own doctrines, either with their writings or by their instructions. And with them emerged different schools of thought reflecting the interests and viewpoints of different social classes, strata and groups. Among the "hundred schools", the most important were the Confucians, the Taoists, the Mohists, the Dialecticians, the Legalists, the Strategists, the Agriculturalists, the Yin-Yang School and the Eclectics. Each of them held their own causes and reasoned in their own way; they differed yet influenced each other and thus brought forth a most lively situation which was generally known as "the Contending of the Hundred Schools". This proved to be an unprecedented impetus to the prosperity of learning and thinking. Indeed, it proved to be one of the most brilliant and flourishing periods in the history of the development of Chinese ideology.

By the end of the Warring States Period, in correlation with the historical trend of the unification of the whole nation, "the hundred schools of thinkers" were gradually tending to merge together. And finally with the establishment of the centralized feudal autocratic empire, the Qin Dynasty, "the Contending of the Hundred Schools" came to an end. However, this contending scene marked a most important stage in the intellectual history of China and a historic significance that could perhaps be only rivalled in the ancient world by the classical culture of Greece. Its influences on the Chinese ideology of the later generations were too great to be overlooked in any way.

Chapter 1

CHINESE IDEOLOGY FROM THE EARLIEST TIMES TO THE SPRING AND AUTUMN PERIOD

1. THE GERMINATION OF IDEOLOGY IN THE PRIMITIVE SOCIETY BEFORE THE XIA DYNASTY

China is located in the east of Asia with a wide expanse of territory and a long tradition of culture. Since about one million B.C., the ancestors of the Chinese people had labored, lived and prospered on this vast land. Like other peoples of the ancient world, the Chinese had undergone a stage of primitive society before the Xia Dynasty when their lives were led in the form of communal labouring and expenditure, that is, in a primitive communism with no exploitation or class.

The development of ideology was at first interwoven with the material activities and relationships of the people and with the language used in their daily life. Labour had both created the human society and given birth to the thinking and understanding of men. In the long course of their struggles against nature (that is, in the course of their labouring), people had reformed not only the natural world but also their own physiological organs and their own nature. As was necessitated by their communal labouring, they learned step by step how to express their intentions and ideas by means of complicated sounds and tones; and with the development of their vocal organs, the human language came into being. Both labouring and language led to the gradual transformation of the human brain together with consciouness and thinking, which in turn pushed forward the development of labouring ability and language. As their reflective capacity about the surrounding world was strengthened, people began to possess the power to abstract the common essence of the surrounding objects and identified them with certain terms, that is, concepts. This was the origin of the earliest human thinking.

In the long course of their primitive communal life, though people were almost entirely subjected to the spontaneous forces of the natural world, they were nevertheless constantly making progress in their way of understanding and mastering the natural forces, that is, from knowing nothing to knowing something and from scant knowledge to more knowledge about their environment as well as about themselves. In ancient documents and records there might be found many legends about the learning and knowledge of the ancient people—legends which, though not of a scientific or historically authentic nature, explained vividly how the ancients re-formed their natural as well as their social world. One of the ancient legends had it that there was a sage by the name of "House-Maker" who "built houses to protect people from harm";[1] another sage by the name of "Fire-Maker" who "made fire by drilling flints in order to get rid of stinking odours";[2] another sage by the name of Fu Xi who "used ropes to make nets for hunting and fishing";[3] and another sage by the name of "Faery Farmer" who "made farming tools with wood"[4] and "taught people the art of plantation".[5]

All these legends, though intermingled with the imagination of later generations, were in the main a reflection of the real background of ancient life, showing the evolution of the understanding and thinking of the ancients. They indicated that people through their long practice of labour were able to accumulate their experiences in the struggle against nature and to cultivate certain knowledge about natural phenomena and even to understand a few simple natural laws. This knowledge furnished the people not only the weapons with which they struggled against nature for the betterment of their material welfare but also obliged them to contradistinguish themselves from the outside world, which they came to realize as something outside and independent of mankind. And they could hope to know and to master it only by learning strenuously step by step. It was thus that the ancient ideology underwent an important stage in the long course of its development.

Among the ancients there were also such legends as Nü Wa smelting the stones to mend the heaven, Pan Gu separating the heaven and the earth from the chaos, and Hou Yi shooting down nine scorching suns in the sky. Though these stories were but fancies, they represented the wish of the people to conquer and to control the natural forces in an imaginary way. They were a reflection of the endeavours of the ancient labouring people who, with the progress in their production, had strengthened their ability to struggle with nature. In a certain sense, the above legends were based on historical fact. The belief in people's ability to conquer nature laid down the foundation for the growth of atheism in ancient China. These tales drew their origin from the oral tradition of the primitives and crystallized the wisdom of the ancients. Subsequently they were modified and embellished by later generations. From the inscriptions on the pottery excavated at Banpo in Xi'an, which belonged to the Yangshao culture that flourished 6,000-7,000 years ago, the origin of the earliest writings and characters might be observed. They were among the earliest ideograms in the world and they enhanced the thinking power of the ancients.

Possessed only with crude knowledge of the natural world, the ancients still remained under the domination of the natural forces and in a state of extremely low social productivity, and so were unable to provide correct interpretations either of themselves or of the world surrounding them. This state of affairs gave rise to the predominant role of religion. Religion, as a rule, was engendered from the erroneous ideas which people held either about their own nature or about the nature of things outside of themselves. When people knew nothing of their own psychological structure and could not explain the reason for their dreams, they came to believe that they were endowed with souls apart from their bodies and consequently that thinking and sensation were not a part of their bodily activity but a special function of the soul that dwelt temporarily within the body but would leave it after death. Hence was engendered the idea of the immortality of the soul. Various productive instruments and articles in daily life, such as flints, stone pearls and animal teeth found in the tombs of the primitives excavated at Zhoukoudian near Beijing showed that they believed they would continue their daily activities after death. Clearly, they embraced the worship of the spirits of their ancestors.

As they could not understand the reasons for such natural

phenomena as winds, storms, thunder and earthquakes and often felt astounded when these natural phenomena occurred; so they conceived in their minds the religious illusion that there was a supernatural power. Thus they embraced the worship of the deities of nature. For instance, it was recorded in the *Zuo's Chronicles*: "the disaster of the drought, the rain and the epidemics belong to the charge of the deities of the mountains and rivers; and we should pray to them. The disorders of the snows and storms belong to the charge of the deities of the sun, the moon and the stars; and we should pray to them."[6] All these were but the fanciful reflections in the human minds of the external forces which dominated daily life. It was through these reflections that even human forces assumed the forms of the superhuman. Ancestor worship combined with nature-worship (animism) formed the origin of religion in ancient China. When mankind entered class society, the ruling class of slave-owners began consciously to modify and to utilize the primitive religion, turning it into an effective spiritual instrument to enslave the people.

Artistic ideas were also in germination in primitive society. Shandingdong people at Zhoukoudian near Beijing had already learned to use perforated animal teeth, fish bones, shells and red-tinted stone pearls for their decorations. They had already cultivated their own aesthetic preferences. On occasions after hard labour or victories in war, they rejoiced with songs and dances. It was said that Zhuan Xu, who, according to legends, was a direct descendant of Huang Di, first introduced singing and dancing. The pottery Xun (an ancient egg-shaped pipe instrument with holes) found in archaeological excavations is evidence of the early date of primitive music. The coloured pottery excavated in ancient tombs represents primitive works of art of both artistic and practical value. On these were painted various styles of plants or geometric designs, some symbolizing the undulation of waves, others the artistic weavings of nets and textiles. These arts, as an expression of ideology, reflected the productive practice of the ancients.

Moral ideas already existed in primitive society. Though there was not yet any systematic ethical theory, in their daily life, people were cultivating common moral criteria, which served to modulate relationships between the members of the same clan or among different clans and tribes. Labouring in common, mutual cooperation, equal distribution, obedience to common decisions, obligation for consanquine revenge, courage in war and love of fellow members —all these constituted the moral standards obligatory to primitive people. In the last analysis, these standards were determined by common sharing in their productive relations.

The legend had it: "The Faery Farmer never promulgated decrees but the people were in obedience[7] ... he ruled without punishment and reigned without arms,[8] ... people slept in peace and worked in ease with no intention to harm others."[9] These legends indicated that in the primitive society there was neither class oppression nor any coercive force of the ruling power and everything went naturally in accordance with the common moral criteria. All the members of the clan joined in common labour and lived in peace and equality. A famous passage in the *Book of Rites* which recalls the communal society before the Xia Dynasty reads: "When the great Tao (the Way) was being carried out, the world was common to all; men of talents, virtue and ability were elected [democratic election of the clan chieftains]; sincerity was emphasized and friendship was cultivated. Therefore men did not love only their parents, nor did they treat as children only their own sons.... Men had their proper work, and women had their homes. They hated to see the natural resources undeveloped, but also did not hoard wealth for their own cause [common ownership of property]. They hated not to exert themselves, but also did not exert themselves only for their own benefit [from each, according to his ability]. Thus selfish schemings were repressed and found no development. Robbers, filchers and rebellious traitors did not show themselves, and hence the outer doors were left open. This was called the Great Harmony [Da Tong]."[10]

This morality of primitive communism was gradually changed with the transition from primitive society to class society. Starting in the Xia Dynasty, when Chinese society entered into the stage of slavery, the will of the slave-owner class began to become the governing morality of the society.

Although the above-mentioned ideology was conditioned by the extremely low level of productivity of that time, it was the earliest origin of the history of thought. Ideology in a more developed sense could come forth only under conditions of a much higher level of productive forces.

2. IDEOLOGY FROM THE XIA DYNASTY
TO THE SPRING AND AUTUMN PERIOD

The ideology in the slave society was closely related to the theory of Heavenly Mandate (that is, the will of God) because political ideas at that time were closely connected with religious superstitions. Therefore, the political thought and the religio-philosophical thought were so mingled together that it would be hard to distinguish the one from the other. In the present section, consideration of both will be given simultaneously.

The Idea of Heavenly Mandate from Xia to
the Western Zhou and Its Decline

Judged from the ancient legends, China entered the slave society after the founding of the Xia Dynasty. In political regulations, the Xia Dynasty for the first time in Chinese history instituted the hereditary system from fathers to sons in place of the former practice in primitive society of abdication of the sovereign to some one regarded as a talented person. It was by then that fortresses and city walls were built, armed forces organized[11] and punishment for crimes prescribed (for example, the Criminal Law of Yu).[12] The blood relationship of the former clan commune broke down and in its stead was created state power on a territorial basis. The *Zuo's Chronicles* had the record: "The immense vastness of Yu was divided into nine prefectures", that is to say, the regime of the state was eventually established.

As a reflection of this change in ideology, there was a record in the *Book of History*: "The Xia Dynasty accepted the Mandate from Heaven."[13] In the *Book of Rites* there was also a record that Confucius once said that the Xia Dynasty reigned over the people by the Mandate of Heaven. This idea of the Heavenly Mandate in the Xia Dynasty was in reality a form of theism.

The reason why that idea was generally accepted in the minds of the people should be attributed to the low productive forces as well as to the under development of scientific knowledge. People knew very little about the cause of natural disasters and of social disparities, so they were easily convinced that there was a God who arranged and disposed everything in the world. The theory of the Heavenly Mandate coincided with the interests of the slave owner class who in consequence firmly believed in it and employed it to justify the rationality of their political control. Fooled as the slaves and other labouring people might have been, in the course of their productive and social struggles they began to realize something which made them discontented with their miserable lots. They began to doubt the justice of God and gradually even went so far as to doubt the very existence of God. In the *Book of History* there was a record: "The king of Xia exhausted his people with ceaseless toil and ruled his kingdom with cruel punishment" and thus compelled "the populace to join in open revolt".[14] During the reign of Jie(18th century B.C.), the last king of Xia, the slaves rebelled against the throne with the outcry: "Let the sun be perished so that we might be able to die with you together."[15] Jie had assumed his rule as the eternal sun, but the slaves hated him so much that they would rather perish together with the sun. Such a rebellious outcry pitted the ideas of the slave class against the Heavenly Mandate. The fact that the slaves even dared to pray for the total extinction of themselves together with their rulers should be regarded as an audacious challenge to the theory of the Heavenly Mandate.

The ideology of the Shang Dynasty inherited and developed that of the Xia Dynasty. In political thought, the Shang rulers were dominated by religious superstitions. It was recorded in the *Book of Rites* (Dai the Junior's version): "The Shangs venerated the deities and led their people to the same worship; they gave priority to their spirits over the rites."[16] From these words it might be seen how superstitious in relation to deities and spirits they were. They resorted to witchcraft in order to drive the slaves to war or to hard labour in the name of deities. And often the slaves were made human sacrifices in funerals and religious offerings. In the bone inscriptions of the Shang Dynasty, extensive records about the escape of slaves and pursuit by the slave owners were found. In company with their religious superstition, the Shang regime preferred the rule of force to the rule of virtue. Among the oracle inscriptions during the reign of

Wu Yi and Wen Ding, kings of the late Shang Dynasty, one reads: "The king instituted three camps for his armed forces: the right, the middle and the left." This was the origin of military organizations in the form of three armies of the later generations. By the end of the Shang Dynasty, Wei Zi once said: "The common people were rising up in hostility against the government."[17] This showed to what extent the class struggle was then going on. Obviously, the strengthening of the armed forces was aimed against the revolts of the slaves.

The ideology of the Western Zhou (11th century-770 B.C.) differed from that of the Shang in the following two aspects: 1. the God of Shang was monist while the God of Zhou was dualistic; 2. the Shangs preferred the employment of brute force while the Zhous favoured the idea of "venerating the virtues and protecting the people".

The Shangs identified their gods with their ancestors. When the Zhou regime replaced the Shang, the idea of Heavenly Mandate suffered a severe stroke. And the Zhous were so deeply impressed with "the inconsistency of God's will",[18] that they elaborated the idea of "virtue" as a supplement to the theory of the Heavenly Mandate. They preached: "The supreme Heaven prefers not anybody, but only helps the virtuous."[19] Because the Shangs "did not venerate the virtue", they lost the favour of God; whereas the Zhous "manifested their virtues", therefore God let Zhou come forward to substitute for the regime of Shang. In the Book of History, the Zhous were recorded as having said: "Not that a small nation like ours ever dared to replace the mandate of Shang, but that Heaven would not grant it to them."

Duke Zhou, the preeminent statesman in the beginning of the Zhou Dynasty, who was a son of King Wen and a brother of King Wu, seeing that the Shangs in maintaining their regime were much too dependent on brute force and cruel punishment, worked out a policy of "venerating Heaven and protecting the people" for the purpose of carrying out more moderate control. He advised King Cheng of Zhou: "Don't employ cruel punishment too frequently on the people, nor put them to death at will."[20] This measure, compared with the ruthless suppression of the Shang Dynasty, seemed more humane, though its essence remained the theory of the Mandate of Heaven. In fact, the so-called "venerating the virtue" had its root in the idea of the Mandate of Heaven, while "protecting the people" embodied that same idea by proclaiming that the Zhou rulers were endowed with the power to rule the slaves in accordance with the will of Heaven. As cited above, the *Book of Odes* once asserted: "The misfortunes of the people did not come from Heaven, ... all these were the results of human actions."[21] Here the role of Heaven (or God) was greatly lowered; and the dominance of Heaven over human affairs was even negated. There were many passages in the *Book of Odes* expressing hatred for and complaints about Heaven, some lamenting: "The Mandate of Heaven is unreliable",[22] some complaining: "Why Heaven is too unjust",[23] others even blaming: "Heaven is mischievous."[24] It became apparent that towards the end of the Western Zhou (8th century B.C.) the idea of the Mandate of Heaven was beginning to decline.

The Early Theory of the Five Elements and the Thought in the *Book of Changes*

From Xia to Western Zhou, two doctrines ran in contradiction with the idea of the Mandate of Heaven: 1. The naive materialistic theory of the Five Elements as expressed in *Hong Fan* (the *Grand Norm*); 2. The naive dialectic theory of the Yin and Yang and the Eight Trigrams (a trigram is a combination of three whole or broken lines originally used in divination, thus: ☰ , ☵, etc.) in the *Book of Changes*.

According to tradition,[25] the *Hong Fan* was written by the Shang nobleman Ji Zi, while a captive answering questions put to him by King Wu of Zhou concerning the topic of the Way of Heaven. Scholars had differed in their opinions about the author of this book. But even if the book was written at a much later date, it is without question that the germination of the theory of the Five Elements appeared first in the Shang Dynasty. The passage of the first item in the nine categories of the *Hong Fan* might perhaps be attributed to the ideas of Ji Zi.

The original theory of the Five Elements looked rather simple. It consisted of the idea of the five directions: the east, the west, the south, the north and the central; and of the idea of the five materials: water, fire, wood, metal and earth. There seemed nothing mysterious in it. The Five Elements in the *Hong Fan* signified water, fire, wood, metal and earth. The entire material world was, in the last analysis, summed up into five elements which were characterized thus: "Water moistens, fire burns, wood straightens, metal cuts and earth harvests."[26] (And each of them had its own peculiar flavour in taste.) This statement coincided with the five elements in the *Book of History* in which it was recorded that when King Wu of Zhou waged war on the Shangs, he camped in a suburb of the enemy's capital. The soldiers sang and danced through the whole night, chanting: "Water and fire are what people need in preparing foods and drinks; wood and metal are what people need in their daily life; earth is what everything needs in its growth and is of great use to mankind." As might easily be seen, the five elements here meant the five kinds of materials necessary to human living, each with its peculiar usage. This idea represented a naive materialistic concept of the natural world in ancient times. It was at the same time a conceptual formulation of the natural knowledge of the ancients.

The doctrine of the Five Elements was then still kept in its primitive form without any philosophical or diagrammatical (mystical) implication. It looked roughly the same as the doctrine of the five elements described in *Zuo's Chronicles* and the *Sayings of the States*. In *Zuo's Chronicles*, it was recorded that Zi Han of Song once said: "Nature affords five materials which people make use of. Not any of them can be dispensed with."[27] Here the five materials signified metal, wood, water, fire and earth. Again *Zuo's Chronicles* recorded: "In heaven there are three celestial bodies (sun, moon and star) and on earth there are five elements."[28] The five elements here referred to were the five materials. Again it recorded that Xi Que of Jin once said: "Water, fire, metal, wood, earth and crops are called the six resources."[29] The five materials plus the crops made up six kinds of resources from which the world was constituted.

In various ancient documents, the five materials were roughly the same. In the *Zuo's Chronicles*, the physician He was recorded as having spoken of "the five flavours"[30] which Du Yu explained as: "Metal tastes hot, wood tastes sour, water tastes salty, fire tastes bitter and earth tastes sweet." They were identical with the "five flavours" in the *Hong Fan*. The physician He had also mentioned the "five colours" and the "five sounds".[31] In the records of *Zuo's*

Chronicles, Cai Mo once enumerated "the officials in charge of the five elements" as: "the official in charge of wood is Ju Mang, that of fire is Zhu Rong, that of metal is Ru Shou, that of water is Xuan Ming and that of earth is Hou Tu."[32] It may be seen that the doctrine of the five elements by that time had become more elaborated than that described in the *Hong Fan*. In the *Sayings of the States*, Shi Bo was reported having said: "Our ancestral kings had combined and intermingled metal, wood, water, fire and earth to make up all things",[33] the five material elements being considered as what constituted the basic matter of all things in the world. This was a cosmogony which may be taken as an ancient form of naive materialism. By this time, the doctrine of the five elements began to bear a philosophical implication. Shi Bo flourished during the reign of King You (8th century B.C.) of Zhou, and the "ancestral kings" he referred to should of course be dated before the Western Zhou. This means that before his time the doctrine of the five elements had already undergone a long process of development. Hence its root should be traced as far back as the transition from Shang to Zhou (11th century B.C.).

The *Book of Changes* is originally a book on divination, comprising the text and its commentaries. The text was the oracles in augury or divination and the commentaries were their annotations and expositions consisting of ten sections which were hence termed "the Ten Wings" or "Appendices".

As the legend had it, it was the ancient sage-king Fu Xi who invented the eight trigrams which were further multiplied into sixty-four (eight by eight) by King Wen of Zhou. The *Book of Changes* was apparently written in the transitional period from Shang to Zhou (11th century B.C.). The Shangs manipulated their divinations by having the tortoise shells or animal bones burned, and they foretold their fortunes by observing and interpreting the cracks thereupon. This procedure was very complicated. The Zhous in its stead used yarrows in different permutations so as to make up different pairs of trigrams, and then interpreted them. This procedure was much easier to practise and hence was called Yi (meaning "easy" as well as "change"); and because it was invented by the Zhous, so it was called also the Zhou Yi. Its commentaries or "Appendices" were written at a much later date, about the time from the end of the Warring States to the interval between Qin and Han

(3rd, 2nd century B.C.). It was not a work by any individual writer but a collection of the interpretations on the *Book of Changes* prepared by the Confucians from generation to generation.

Although the *Book of Changes* was devoted to superstition in divination, its theological ideology included some of the naive materialistic elements as well as the naive dialectical elements of ancient times.

The eight trigrams symbolized the eight elements which constituted the material world. The commentaries or "Appendices" interpreted them as: "Qian symbolizes the heaven, Kun the earth, Zhen the thunder, Xun the wind, Kan the water, Li the fire, Gen the mountain and Dui the river."[34] This passage was written undoubtedly at a much later date, but explained fairly well the meanings of the eight trigrams that symbolized the eight kinds of matter out of which the world was supposed to be composed. It is a vivid description of how the world was generated from these materials. The commentaries also stated that all things in the world were engendered by the interactions of the Yin (the negative) and the Yang (the positive). The heaven and the earth were likened to the parents and the thunder, wind, water, fire, mountain and river to the children of the parents; and the children in their turn helped their parents to generate all things. Such was the naive materialistic world picture described in the *Book of Changes*.

The naive dialectic ideas in the *Book of Changes* were shown in the trigrams and their interpretations. The basic symbols in them were "—" and "--", called respectively the Yang Yao (the positive line) and the Yin Yao (the negative line). They represented a pair of basic contradictions in a state of antagonism. Three Yaos (lines, broken or unbroken) formed a "normal trigram". There were altogether eight normal trigrams ($2^3 = 8$). The combination of two normal trigrams formed a "corollary trigram" which were sixty-four in number ($2^3 \times 2^3 = 64$), indicating thirty-two pairs of contradictions. With each change of the line in every trigram (i.e. the change of the Yang Yao into Yin Yao, or vice versa), there would be a new trigram. The *Book of Changes* took the changes in the trigrams to signify the changes in the objective world and thus tried to probe the laws of change and movement in it.

The *Book of Changes* had, in an intuitive way, touched upon the relationship of the mutual transformations of opposites in contradiction. In one of the interpretations it affirmed: "There is no plane without a slope, there is no going without a coming; insistence in hardships will bring you good luck."[35] In such statements as "by the extremity of the worst, the best begins",[36] there were obviously comprised in it some elements of naive dialectics. But the author of the book understood the laws of changes only in a cyclic way without the idea of development from the lower to the higher in a spiral way. Thus the changes, by being isolated from their concrete conditions and backgrounds, were made known to the author or authors in a somewhat mysterious and abstract fashion. After all, the law of changes in the world was something beyond the capacity of human understanding. Therefore people were ultimately unable to master their own fate and had to resort to the deity for the prophecy of their own fortunes.

Atheism and Naive Dialectics in the Spring and Autumn Period

In the Spring and Autumn Period (770-476 B.C.), the idea of the Mandate of Heaven was strongly shattered under the pressures of naive materialism and naive dialectics. One of the most important consequences in the political and philosophical ideas at that time was the emphasis on the role of the people and the development of atheism. In the early years of Zhou there was engendered the idea that it was the people rather than Heaven that should receive more attention. In the Spring and Autumn Period, this idea further developed, as reflected in the words of Ji Liang: "The people are the master of the deities."[37] The deities, though still remaining, were put in a secondary position, while the people were promoted to predominance. Hence there was the saying: "The sage-kings engage themselves first to keep their people and then to deal with their deities."[38]

It was in this way that many of the natural phenomena got even more correct interpretations. In the spring of the year 645 B.C. (the 16th year of the reign of Duke Xi of Lu), five meteorites fell in the kingdom of Song, which was documented not as a wonder but as "falling stars". And when six birds flew in a backward fashion over the capital of Song, they were considered as blown by the strong wind into a reverse direction. Shu Xing considered such natural phenomena as having nothing to do with the fortunes of human affairs and forwarded the proposition: "Fortunes and misfortunes are caused by men alone",[39] thus leading to the denial of superstition toward deities. In the same tone, Min Zi Ma also proposed: "there is no other cause of fortunes and misfortunes except that they are brought about by men."[40] In the year 640 B.C. (the 21st year of the reign of Duke Xi of Lu), there was a serious drought in the kingdom of Lu; as people thought it was due to the malevolence of the witch Wang, Duke Xi was about to burn the witch alive as a way of praying for rain. On this occasion Zang Wenzhong expressed opposition, arguing that this was not the way to meet the issue of the drought and that if it was indeed the witch who had brought about the drought, then the drought would become even more serious if he were to be burnt alive.[41] Here Zang denied the supernatural powers of the deities.

This atheistic attitude was manifested strongly in the thought of Zi Chan. Once in the kingdom of Zheng, the inundation became uncontrollable and some people suggested making offerings to the dragon. Zi Chan stood in opposition, saying: "I have nothing to deal with the dragon, nor the dragon with me."[42] He did not take the dragon as something sacred but considered it as having nothing to do with the inundation, nor with any human affair. He also opposed the explanation of human affairs by reference to astrology He did not agree with the belief then in vogue that the appearance of the planet Mars in the evening would bring about a conflagration. He asserted audaciously: "The heavenly ways are far away while the human ways are near by; they have nothing to do with each other."[43]

The naive materialistic ideas mentioned above went hand in hand with the atheistic current of the Spring and Autumn Period, and both helped greatly to shatter the theory of the Mandate of Heaven at its very foundation.

With the shattering of the ruling idea of the Heavenly Mandate, there began a most fourishing era in the intellectual history of China. Of the dialectical thoughts then coming to the front, that of Shi Mo might be regarded as typical. In the year 510 B.C. (the 32nd year of the reign of Duke Zhao of Lu), the Duke was exiled by the House of Ji and died abroad. Zhao Jian Zi of Jin had discussed the matter with Shi Mo, who thought that the rulers of Lu had indulged in luxurious enjoyments for generations and done nothing good for the people, while the House of Ji worked earnestly and this was the reason why the people had forsaken their rulers and turned to uphold the House of Ji. Saying that no one would have pity on the Duke Zhao of Lu even as he died in his exile, Shi Mo drew his conclusion thus: "There is no eternal reign in a country, there are no eternal positions for rulers and subjects; this has been a truth ever since the old times." Hence in the *Book of Odes* it reads: "The high peaks became ravines and ravines became mountains."[44] He had noticed that thrones and regimes, the ruling and the ruled, were constantly changing their positions just like peaks and ravines in the natural world were constantly transforming into each other.

3. CONFUCIUS AND THE EARLY CONFUCIANS

The real name of Confucius (551-479 B.C.) was Kong Qiu with the cognomen Zhongni. A native of the kingdom of Lu at the end of the Spring and Autumn Period, he was born in a family of the waning nobility and had in his youth served as a low-ranking official in charge of the store-houses and herds. Because of his knowledge of the rites of Zhou, he was sent by Duke Zhao of Lu to the royal court of Zhou to learn rites from the royal historian. When civil strife burst out in Lu, Confucius went to the kingdom of Qi but he was little honoured there. He then returned to Lu, engaging himself in teaching and in sorting out historical classics.

During the reign of Duke Ding of Lu, Confucius had been appointed the mayor of Zhongdu and later the minister of justice, "taking part in the politics of the state for three months".[45] After that, Confucius travelled widely from one kingdom to another in company with his disciples for more than ten years. He successively visited the kingdoms of Wei, Song, Chen, Cai and Chu; but nowhere was he in a position of being able to carry out his political ideas. In his later years he returned to Lu, where he continued to study the ancient classics. The book *Analects*, (*Lun Yu* or *Sayings of Confucius*), a compilation of his teachings and remarks by his disciples, afforded the most important sources about him.

The Ru (or what had once been generally known as the Confucian or Confucianist) School, had already come into being long before the time of Confucius. They were the people whose profession it was to practice rites for others on ceremonial occasions. Besides, they possessed certain knowledge about astronomy, geography, etc. In accordance with their birth and education, they might be divided into the so-called "gentleman scholar" and the "little-minded scholar".[46] But the school of the Ru (or the Confucian or Confucianist) scholars was first founded by Confucius. It was said that Confucius "was never weary in learning and never tired in instructing others."[47] Undoubtedly he should be ranked among the greatest teachers and thinkers of all ages. His ideas exerted a tremendous influence upon later generations.

Political Ideal of Confucius

Confucius spent his life in the great social upheavals at the end of the Spring and Autumn Period when the ruling power of the royal house of Zhou was falling into the hands of the princes of various states. And in the principalities, the nobles did not obey the princes and sometimes even the vassals of the nobles became strong enough so that "it was the vassals who took over the sovereignty of the state".[48] As to this, Confucius once remarked: "When the world is in good order, practicing rites and making wars are held in the hands of the royal throne; when the world is not in good order, practicing rites and making wars are held in the hands of the princes."[49] He expressed sharp opposition against the downward transference of political power and against the usurpation of the ritual institutions by the princes and nobles of his time. In his opinion, political power controlled by the princes could hardly last more than ten generations; political power controlled by the nobles could hardly last for more than five generations; and political power controlled by the vassals of the nobles would certainly be lost within the span of three generations.[50]

In the year 513 B.C., the criminal code of the kingdom of Jin was made public by having it cast on a bronze tripod. Confucius stood in opposition by asserting that such a practice would be no less than having the ancestral institution of the kingdom of Jin discarded and the regulations on the distinctions between the nobles and the commons ruined. Chen Heng (i.e. Tian Heng), of the kingdom of Qi murdered Duke Jian—a fact which was termed in historical writing as "the replacement of the Qi regime by the House of Tian". On hearing the news, Confucius went solemnly to the court, asking Duke Ai of Lu to despatch an expeditionary force against Qi.[51] The vassals of the three noble families of the Ji Sun, the Shu Sun and the Meng Sun in the kingdom of Lu became so powerful that they assumed the control of the three capitals of Fei, Hou and Cheng. The three noble families also intended to make an effort to limit the powers of their vassals. Always inspired by the possibility of enlarging the power of the government of the royal house, Confucius endeavoured to make use of the existing conflict among the three and took an active part in planning for the "destruction of the three capitals".[52] From the above-mentioned stories it is apparent that Confucius tended to be conservative in his political attitude.

This conservative tendency was clearly reflected in his stand concerning the issues of the "rites" and the "rectification of names". According to the book *Explanations of Characters*, a famous ancient dictionary, the etymological meaning of the word "rite" was to "worship the deities in praying for blessings."[53] Hence it meant a relationship between human beings and deities; and its close connection with theocracy led to the demand for a strict demarcation between kinship as well as between social strata in a hierarchical system under the rule of the nobility. It aimed at maintaining the age-old ceremonies, customs, manners and moral code, including sacrificial, funeral, diplomatic, warring and marital affairs. In reality, it consisted of the totality of the regulations and institutions of the old social order.

Confucius held the institutions of the rites of the Western Zhou as the perfect model, because it was designed with specific reference to the rites of the foregoing Xia and Shang dynasties. Of the rites of Zhou he spoke repeatedly with veneration: "Zhou enjoyed the advantage of surveying the former two dynasties. How refined its culture was! It is the rites of Zhou that I'd like to follow."[54] And again: "If I were placed in power, I would create another Zhou in the east."[55]

Nevertheless, Confucius did not and could not reconstruct the rites simply upon the old model of the Western Zhou. He scrutinized the rites of all the previous epochs and realized that all three former dynasties (Xia, Shang and Zhou) had carried out their own reforms and modifications in their practices of rites. So he intended to preserve the old social order by means of reforms, provided that the basic interests of the ruling class would not thereby suffer any harm. Such a reformist attitude was clearly shown in his endeavour to complement the insufficiency of "politics" and "punishments" with the help of "virtues" and "rites". He said: "Guided by policy and coerced by punishments, the people would be obedient but shameless; guided by virtue and coerced by rites, the people would be regulated by a sense of shame."[56] This was his way to reconcile the contradictions between the governing and the governed. He also urged to "select talents"[57] to take part in the government so far as it did not come into contradiction with the principle of "priority in kinship" as prescribed by the rites of Zhou. It was only by doing so, he argued, that the "people will obey";[58] otherwise the "people will not obey". Further, he proposed "the governing should be frugal and love the people; make use of the people at the appropriate time"[59] and "get benefits by benefiting the people".[60] All these propositions were aimed at moderating sharp social contradictions.

As to the rites, Confucius admitted the necessity of making some modifications in order to accomodate them to the changed social reality, so long as the essence of the rites could be kept unchanged. For instance, hats made of linen conformed to the rites of the Zhou but would cost more labour. The prevailing mode then was to have them made of silk. Confucius approved it because it cost less.[61] He was very discontented with the actual observances of the rites at that time, since they paid more attention to formality than to sincerity. Upon this he remarked: "In ceremonials, it is better to be simple than to be lavish; and in the rites of mourning, heartfelt distress is better than mere observances of details."[62] And again: "'Ceremonials!' they say 'Ceremonials!' Can mere gems and gowns be called ceremonials? 'Music!' they say 'Music!' Can mere bells and drums be called music?"[63] This practical attitude towards the rites showed that he wished to carry out some reforms on the social realities without harming the fundamental interests of the ruling class.

The conservatism of Confucius was embodied predominantly in his advocacy for the "rectification of names". In the time in which he lived, it happened not infrequently that courtiers murdered their princes and sons their fathers. Confucius realized it was a time when the traditional rites became destroyed and the traditional music corrupted. To meet the social crisis, he advocated for the rectification of names. When he and his disciples were on their itinerary by way of the state of Wei, one of his disciples Zi Lu asked him: "As the Prince of Wei is now awaiting you, Sir, to take charge of his administration, what will you undertake first, Sir?" To this, the Master (Confucius) replied: "The one thing needed is the rectification of names."[64] The rectification of names meant to employ the hierarchical names in the rites of Zhou to rectify the social relationship being destroyed by the social mobility in the Spring and Autumn Period.

Confucius thought that if all people and all things were rectified by the regulations in conformity with the rites of Zhou, that is, if the social order were so reconstructed as to "let the prince be prince, the courtiers be courtiers; let the father be father and the son be son" after his idealized pattern of the rites of Zhou, then the world would be all right. He tried to regulate the social realities by their names but not to derive the names from the realities. Names were given the primary place, and realities the secondary. Such a view on the relationship of names and realities represented the idealistic viewpoint of Confucius. In his opinion, the social turbulences of the time resulted from the incongruity of names with realities; therefore he tried to solve it by means of the rectification of names. This conservatism obviously ran counter to the currents of the social and political developments of the age.

The kernel of the political ideas of Confucius consisted in the observance of the rites and in the rectification of names; the former, while upholding the old social order, had more or less admitted certain measures of improvements and reforms, whereas the latter, possessing a more conservative character, ran utterly against the current of that time.

The Ethical Ideas of Confucius—"Ren"

The idea Ren (human-heartedness or benevolence) formed the most important constituent in the thoughts of Confucius and one from which all his ethical teachings were derived. As a philosophical category, Ren began with Confucius, though its etymological origin might be traced to a much earlier era. After all, then, what did the term Ren mean? The authoritative ancient linguistic work *Explanations of Characters and Interpretations of Words* explained it thus: "Ren means dearness or intimacy, and the word is composed of two components: man and two."[65] Ruan Yuan, the famous Qing scholar, interpreted "the two components: man and two" as "the pairing of man and man",[66] i.e., the relationship between man and man. Therefore, Confucius identified Ren with "the love of other people", that is, people should love each other. The famous saying of Confucius: "My teaching contains one all-pervading principle"[67] meant that his main doctrine consisted of Ren and its realization.

According to the interpretations of Zeng Shen, one of the famous disciples of Confucius, "Our Master's teaching is Zhong (conscientiousness or loyalty) and Shu (toleration or altruism) and nothing else."[68] Thus the realization of Ren was summarized in Zhong and Shu or "the teaching of loyalty and toleration". Then, how could "the love of other people" be realized? In Confucius' opinion, it required, on the one hand, that "desiring to maintain oneself, one sustains others; desiring to develop oneself, one develops others";[69] and on the other hand, "do not do to others what you do not like yourself".[70] Zi Gong, another disciple of his, said: "I do not do to others what I do not like others to do to me."[71] The first requirement in the above proposition meant loyalty; and the second, toleration.

As to the relation of "benevolence" and "rites", Confucius said: "Benevolence (Ren) is the denial of self and response to the rites";[72] so that for the embodiment of Ren one should practice self-control in conformity with the requirements of the rites. With this purpose in mind, Confucius even asked people "Do not see anything that is not in conformity with the rites, do not hear anything that is not in conformity with the rites, do not speak anything that is not in conformity with the rites, and do not do anything that is not in conformity with the rites."[73] He thought that once someone had put Ren (benevolence) into practice, all the people would admire and follow his example.

From what was stated above, it appeared that the rites should be taken as the criteria of benevolence. An action could be accorded benevolence only when one acted in accordance with the regulations of the rites. But there were times when Confucius described benevolence as something purely subjective, i.e., a kind of internal cultivation, asserting: "Benevolence has its source in one's self; is it forsooth derived from others?"[74] It was just because benevolence was a kind of mental cultivation on the part of the inner self that Confucius considered its realization no difficulty. So he affirmed: "So soon as I desire benevolence, benevolence is there."[75] With such a teaching he asked all people to cultivate benevolence for the purpose of maintaining the rites of Zhou (i.e., the traditional social order) in their minds.

Confucius proclaimed: "The people are in need of benevolence more urgently than that of water and fire."[76] This implied that the principle of benevolence should be applied to the governing as well as to the governed. Again he said: "When the gentleman are earnest to their kinsmen, the people will be inspired with benevolence."[77] Hence in the opinion of Confucius, the people were not only required to have benevolence but also were possessed with the capacity to practice it.

The well-known slogan of Confucius: "The benevolent loves other people" was in its essence a supra-class slogan. In a society in which people were divided into classes, there could be no such thing as the universal love of mankind. The love of one class always invariably meant the hostility to another, for the interests of different classes always clashed with each other. The aim of Confucius' advocacy: "The benevolent loves other people", was to reconcile the social contradictions of the age—both the internal contradiction within the governing class itself and that between the governing and the governed. As a far-sighted thinker, Confucius surpassed other members of his class in that he came to realize the intensifications of the contradictions during his time, especially the impending clash between the ruling class and the common people which was approaching the point of explosion and threatening the very existence of the ruling class itself. The slogan of "the love of others" propounded by him served to alleviate the sharp class contradictions of the time. But for the oppressed, this slogan could only mean deception. Confucius said: "If you love the people, how can you leave them not to work?"[78] Therefore it might appear that the lip service to "love" aimed only at urging the people to work for the ruling class.

Furthermore, he advocated that filial piety and fraternal duty made up the foundation of benevolence. When these ideals were exercised in full, the people would no more revolt against their rulers, or as his disciple You Ruo so clearly expressed it: "It is rare that those who conduct well in filial piety and fraternal love are prone to offend their seniors or superiors; and there is none who is not prone to offend his seniors or superiors and is yet prone to make revolts."[79] Once this is apprehended, many seeming contradictions in the book *Analects* will be resolved. For instance, Confucius said on the one hand: "The people will be inspired with benevolence", but on the other hand, he saw in practical life that the people were not so interested in "benevolence" as he advocated it, nor were they able to practise it; so he lamented, "there are gentlemen who are not benevolent, but there is no little-minded man who is ever benevolent."[80] This vindicated the class character of the "benevolence" of Confucius.

Nevertheless, the fact that Confucius posed the slogan "to love other people" in order to amend the more austere postulate of the "denial of self and response to the rites", reflected the progress of the idea of "caring for the people" ever since the time of the Western Zhou. Such an idea underscored the changes in the social status of the labouring people as well as the attempt to amend the former idea that slaves were no more than speaking instruments. This should be rightly regarded as a step forward in the intellectual history of ancient times.

Philosophical Ideas of Confucius

In the ideas of Confucius, that portion concerning the Mandate of Heaven and deities looked rather ambiguous. He said: "One can pray for nothing when punished by Heaven for his crimes",[81] a statement which implied that heaven possessed supreme authority like that of a God with volition and personality, or like that of a lord in Heaven who disposed everything in the world, including the fortunes of human beings. Therefore, he said: "A gentleman (or superior man) holds three things in awe. He holds the Mandate of Heaven in awe; he holds the great man in awe; and he holds the precepts of the sages in awe."[82] Obviously this was to demand that the governed be content with their social lot in perfect subjection to the will of the governing without the least intention of resistance. Again he said: "If my principles are going to prevail, it is through Fate. If my principles are going to fail, it is through Fate."[83] That is to say, the success or failure of his principles is to be determined by Fate (i.e., the will of Heaven), and people are powerless to change or to impede it. In this respect, Confucius was basically upholding the traditional idea of the Mandate of Heaven.

On the other hand, he also said: "Heaven says nothing. The seasons move in their turn, all things grow up. Heaven says nothing."[84] Heaven here meant simply nature without any supernatural implication. Again Confucius said: "I make no complaint against heaven and lay no blame on men, for though my studies are lowly, my mind soars aloft. And that which knows me, is it not heaven?"[85] Though there still lingered in his mind the shadow of the Mandate of Heaven, it included in it a positive element that demanded one to do one's vocation. At the death of his beloved disciple Yan Yuan (or Yan Hui), Confucius lamented mournfully: "Alas! Heaven has bereft me! Heaven has bereft me!"[86] Such a lamentation bore a tone of complaining about heaven. In truth, he was often self-contradictory in his interpretations of the Mandate of Heaven. The wavering of the belief in the Mandate of Heaven in the last years of the Western Zhou also affected the thought of Confucius.

The attitude he held towards deities was somewhat akin to that he held towards the Mandate of Heaven. He praised the Great Yu for "paying his filial piety to the deities"[87] and said: "It is a mere flattering to offer sacrifices to the spirits who are not entitled to enjoy them."[88] Hence it might be seen that Confucius supported the practice of offering sacrifices to the spirits and believed in them, but somewhat differently than the traditional way. He advocated: "While respecting the spirits, keep away from them";[89] and again: "Being still unable to do your duty to men, how can you do your duty to the spirits? ... not knowing life, how can you know death?"[90] Furthermore, he even "would not discuss prodigies, prowess, lawlessness or the supernatural".[91] To a certain degree, this meant he felt suspicion about the supernatural deities and laid more emphasis on the human aspect.

The epistemology of Confucius was imbued with an air of eclecticism. He remarked: "Superior are those who are born to know, next to them are those who know by learning, again next to them are those who learn through hardships, and inferior are those who do not learn at all in their hardships."[92] And again: "Only the wise superiors and the stupid inferiors remain unmoved."[93] Hence, according to his theory of knowledge, people were divided into four grades or ranks. Both the wise superiors and the stupid inferiors were born by nature and hence incapable of being changed. It implied that knowledge for some people was inborn and there was no need for them to learn or to practise, a doctrine which was apparently idealistic apriorism.

At the same time, it should be noted that Confucius did not acknowledge himself as a man with inborn knowledge. He said: "I am not one of those who are born with knowledge";[94] and again: "There are people who act without knowing, but I am not one of them."[95] Many a time he acknowledged he had committed errors and vowed to make corrections. And he never called any one a genius. In fact, the grade which he called "those who are born to know" was only a fictitious one or an empty class which to a certain degree modified his idealistic apriorism. When the empty class is made known, the second class, i.e., "those who know by learning" becomes more significant. What Confucius emphasized was substantially that kind of knowledge which came through learning. He urged people "learn a great deal; make choice of what is the best in it and hold it fast".[96] This statement furnished a fine commentary on his idea of "to know by learning". And he persuaded people to "read a lot and memorize it".[97] He denied himself a genius and what he tried to do was to "learn a great·deal", to "make choice", to "read a lot" and to "memorize it", that is, to undergo the whole process of diligent learning. It was evident that in his epistemology idealism and materialism were mingled together, or rather materialistic elements were contained in a body of idealism. Therefore, concerning the characteristics of his ideas, concrete analysis should be made carefully.

The Educational Ideas of Confucius

In connection with his conservative tendency in politics, there might be found also a conservative vein in his educational ideas. The content of his teaching consists mainly in the rites, music, classics (notably the *Book of Odes* and the *Book of History*) and moral precepts; but he opposed his pupils learning any technical or productive knowledge. Nonetheless, through the long years of his educational activities he reached a series of conclusions which tallied the objective laws of the development of human understanding and should be valued for their lasting significance.

Confucius taught his pupils a stick-to-the-fact attitude in their pursuit of knowledge, saying: "What you know you should acknowledge you know, and what you do not know you should acknowledge you do not know,—this means knowledge."[98] As to the learning method, he advised frequent repetitions, saying: "Is it not a pleasure to learn and often to review?"[99] And again: "You'll learn new knowledge by reviewing the old."[100] While stressing the individual effort in learning, he rejected any intellectual prejudice or preconcieved ideas, saying: "Never be opinionated, never be prejudiced, never be stubborn and never assume self-infallibility."[101] On the relation of learning and thinking, he proposed an appropriate union of both of them by saying: "Learning without thinking makes one puzzled and thinking without learning makes one endangered."[102] He knew fairly well the importance of learning from predecessors and taught that it was only through following their footsteps that one could hope to make progress, or as he put it: "You can not be led into the house of the master unless you follow his steps."[103] This attitude of respecting the objective facts and opposing the subjective prejudices was strongly emphasized in his methodology of learning.

Confucius formulated his method of teaching by means of enlightening on the basis of individual talents. He preferred to let his pupils think independently and would not prompt them unless they could not think it out after repeated speculations. And his pupils were asked to be able "to reflect upon the three others when the one is hinted".[104]

Confucius held the most important place in the history of education in China. By initiating and propounding his private teaching among the people he destroyed a long-standing intellectual monopoly which decreed that "learnings reside in the offialdom"[105] and thus paved the way for the "contending of the hundred schools" in the Warring States Period. In his teachings, Confucius recommended the practice of "teaching all people equally without discrimination toward ranks or social status",[106] a practice which greatly enlarged the sphere of education among the comparatively lower social strata. It was said that the disciples of Confucius totalled three thousand among whom there were seventy-two well-trained in the "six arts"[107] —i.e., the rites, music, shooting, harnessing, the classics and mathematics. His whole life was spent in teaching pupils and studying ancient classics. It was said also that the Five Classics (the *Book of Odes,* the *Book of History,* the *Book of Rites,* the *Book of Changes* and the *Spring and Autumn Annals*) were all selected and edited by him. They added a precious cultural heritage to the treasury of civilization in China and the world.

In his own time, the doctrine of Confucius was not much honoured by the ruling class. But later, after feudalism was well established, the landlord class began to revise and modify it so as to meet their own needs and made it into a systematic ideology of the feudal landlords. Confucius was then raised to the height of "the Supreme Sage and the Foremost Teacher" and the Confucian writings were honoured as classics. Thenceforth, Confucianism assumed the role of the spiritual support of the feudal society and exerted a tremendous and lasting influence upon the later history of China.

Chapter 2
IDEOLOGY IN THE WARRING STATES PERIOD (I)

1. IDEOLOGY OF THE EARLY MOHISTS

The great social upheaval taking place during the transitional period from the Spring and Autumn Period to the Warring States Period (6th-5th century B.C.) brought about a great change in class relationship. Schools and doctrines representing interests of different classes, strata and groups all swarmed to the forefront. The rising landlord class, in order to consolidate its rule, professed itself the representative of all the people, but it never did nor could represent the interests of the labourers. In the time of the Warring States, the schools that reflected the interests of the labouring people were the Mohist School founded by Mo Zi, the school of Yang Zhu and the Agricultural (or Physiocrat) School headed by Xu Xing . Owing to the differences in the classes, strata and groups they represented, these schools differed from one another in their theories as well as in their practices. Roughly speaking, the Mohist School was the ideological representative of the small craftsmen, the school of Yang Zhu was that of the small land proprietors and the Agricultural School was that of the poor peasants.

Life and Teachings of Mo Zi

Mo Zi (about 480-420 B.C.), named Di, was born in a family emigrated from the kingdom of Song and long settled in the kingdom of Lu. He had in his youth "studied the professions of the Ru and learned the arts of Confucius",[1] but later he forsook the Confucian School and founded his own Mohist School. Mo Zi came from a declined noble family and first served as an official in Song; later when his social position became lowered to that of a labourer, he took a job as a craftsman and hence was known as "a man from the low grade".[2] *Lü's Spring and Autumn Annals* described Mo Zi as "a savage from the north",[3] a term which showed his low social position. Most of his disciples belonged to the labourers of the lower social ranks too, they "dressed in leathers, with wooden or straw slippers on the feet, toiled day and night, and took self-suffering as their life ideal".[4] Often Mo Zi spoke from the standpoint of the "people on the farms and in the workshops". Xun Zi has pointed out that the doctrine of Mo Zi was "the doctrine of the labourers".[5] The above facts help to illustrate the political and social attributes of the Mohists.

The Mohists formed a strictly organized and well-disciplined body. Their leader was called Ju Zi (the Great Master) who executed the disciplines of the Mohists. According to the record of *Lü's Spring and Autumn Annals*, "There was a man named Fu Tun who was the leader of the Mohists. When he lived in the kingdom of Qin, his son killed somebody. King Hui (337-311 B.C.) of Qin said to him: 'You are old, Sir, and have no other son, and so I have already given orders not to punish your son. You must obey me on this matter.' Fu Tun replied: 'According to the law of the Mohists, he who killed someone must die, and he who wounded someone must receive corporal punishment. This is done to prevent murder and injury. For not to kill nor to injure others is the great duty in the world. Even if Your Majesty were to relieve him by giving orders not to punish him, I could have no choice but to carry out the laws of the Mohists.' Thereupon he did not accede to the king's offering, but had his son executed."[6] This story revealed strikingly the severity of the laws and disciplines that governed the Mohists. Because of this spirit, they were well known as good fighters in battle with the morale of those "whom the leader could have ordered to enter the fire or to tread on knife blades and whom even death would not have prevented from following one another".[7]

Mo Zi was a scientist and a technician; and the Mohist School was a body composed of scientists and technicians. In the field of mathematics, physics, medicine and logic, they made outstanding contributions which held a prominent place in the history of ancient science.

The Book of Mo Zi is a collection of his remarks and about his activities recorded for the most part by his disciples or the disciples of the second generation. It affords the main source for the study of his thoughts. Of this book, the "Canons (former part)", "Canons (later part)", "Expositions of the Canons (former part)", "Expositions of the Canons (later part)", "Major Illustrations" and "Minor Illustrations" are the writings of the later Mohists, while the "Loving of the Talents", "Cultivation of the Self" and others are probably works fabricated by the Confucians.[8]

Mo Zi posed ten main theses; they are: "universal love", "anti-militarism", "agreement with the virtuous", "agreement with the superior", "the Will of Heaven", "belief in spirits", "anti-music", "anti-fatalism", "frugality in expenditure" and "frugality in funeral ceremony".[9] These principles would be applied so as to accommodate themselves to different circumstances. For a country falling into tumult or disorder, "agreement with the virtuous" and "agreement with the superior" would be given prior attention; for a country which was poverty-stricken, "frugality in expenditure" and "frugality in funeral ceremony" would be given prior attention. These ten theses characterized the essence of the thought of Mo Zi.

Political Ideas of Mo Zi

Influenced by the interests of the small producers, Mo Zi advocated the theory "to love universally and to benefit mutually"[10] which constituted the nuclei of his doctrine. He considered that tumults, wars and social disasters were all engendered by the fact that people "did not love one another";[11] therefore he claimed the necessity of "universal love". By "universal love" he meant "to look upon other nations as one's own, to look upon other families as one's own and to look upon other persons as one's self".[12] When one loved and benefited others, others would do the same in return. Thus the equality between man and man would become a fact, or, as he put it, "a love without differentiation in gradation".[13]

The advocacy of "love others" by the Confucians and that of "universal love" by the Mohists seemed to sound the same; but their actual bearings ran counter to each other. The Confucians professed the "priority in kinship" (or the endearment of the dear), that is, the love of others should be differentiated in gradations according to their intimacy in kinship; whereas the "universal love" of the Mohists taught people to benefit mutually without regard to the different grades in intimacy. Confucius himself "very seldom spoke of benefits or interests"[14] and thought that only the little-minded men would be motivated by benefits and interests. With regard to this topic, the viewpoints of the Confucians and the Mohists were in sharp contrast to each other. At the roots of their respective theories, the Confucian "love of the people" started from the interests of the governing class, while the Mohist "universal love" from that of the small producers, with the intent of resisting exploitation and oppression.

However, the so-called "universal love" was, after all, something utopian which turned out to be impractical and unrealistic. A good-sounding ideal like that of "universal love" was impossible in any society in which people were divided by contrary interests. Mo Zi made no distinction between the ruling class (princes, dignitaries and gentlemen) and the "peasants and craftsmen"; and consequently he did not propose the abolishing of classes and social hierarchy. His "universal love" was saturated with a desire for class reconciliation. As a matter of fact, the small producers themselves were powerless to carry out any fundamental reform of the existing social conditions and hence were obliged to take a wishful thinking position of maintaining the status quo so that their private properties might be kept safe and the various social forces kept in a state of peaceful co-existence. This was a reflection of the class character of the small producers in the Mohist theory of "universal love".

From his idea of "universal love", Mo Zi was led logically to the conclusion of "anti-militarism". The wars of annexation and invasion that so frequently happened in the time of the Spring and Autumn and the Warring States Periods he viewed as unjust, because they ran contrary to the principle of "universal love". He pointed out: "When the war happens in the spring, it will deprive the people the opportunity of sowing and planting; and when it happens in the fall, it will deprive them of the opportunity of reaping and harvesting"; in short, "it deprives the people of their opportunities and their benefits."[14] But it should also be noted that Mo Zi did not oppose wars in general but only those of aggression. He supported whole-heartedly all defensive wars, a well-known example of which was his help to the state of Song in defending the invasion by the state of Chu. The small producers were earnest in their opposition against the destruction of their small-scale enterprises and eagerly wished to ensure their lives and properties in peace and safety. This attitude was formulated into Mo Zi's doctrine of "anti-militarism".

Closely connected with the idea of "universal love" were Mo Zi's theses of the "agreement with the virtuous" and the "agreement with the superiors". As a new social force, the small producers emphatically demanded the elevation of their political positions. And Mo Zi taught that it was unjust and unjustified that some people should enjoy political and economic privileges on the sole ground of their high birth. He pointed out that those who were born noble and wealthy were noble and wealthy with no justifiable reason whatsoever. So he put forward his proposal of the "agreement with the virtuous", the principle of which he asserted as: "Whoever is talented should be chosen, even if he comes from the peasants and the craftsmen", and "the officials should not always be high and the people should not always be low", and "whoever is competent should be chosen and whoever is incompetent should be dismissed".[15] Here the Mohist principle of the "agreement with the virtuous" was much more thorough-going in its efforts against social hierarchy based on blood lineage than the "selection of the talents" preached by the Confucians.

This doctrine of the "agreement with the virtuous" of Mo Zi went even so far as to maintain that the royal throne should be committed to the virtuous or the talented. He propounded a political theory to the effect that before the emergence of the state everyone had his own criterion of what was right and what was wrong, and since there was no unified opinion, the world fell into disorder. Mo Zi reasoned that "the person of virtue and talent and of wisdom and intelligence should be elected the Son of Heaven under whom the standards in the world might be unified",[16] Then from among the virtuous and the talented, the Son of Heaven (i.e. the sovereign) should choose the leading people of various echelons with whose help the Son of Heaven might unify the thoughts and wills of the whole people. This meant the agreement with the "Will of Heaven" which was for him no other than "universal love". When this principle of "universal love" was carried out by everybody, the world would enjoy the full blessings of peace. At that time, this ideal of his could remain only a fancy. Nevertheless, it needed a centralized autocracy which had not yet arrived politically but was inevitable in future historical development.

Religious Ideas of Mo Zi

The "Will of Heaven" and the "belief in spirits" in Mo Zi constituted the theoretical foundations of his doctrine of "universal love". In them the religious ideas of Mo Zi reached full expression. He said: "All states in the world, no matter how large or how small they may be, are the domains of Heaven; and all the people in the world, no matter how old or young, how noble or how low they may be, are all the subjects of Heaven."[17] He treated all states and all peoples equally without discrimination. He said repeatedly: "The Will of Heaven abominates the large state which attacks small states, the large house which molests small houses, the strong who oppress the weak, the clever who deceive the simple-minded and the noble who condemns the humble; these are what Heave abominates. But more than this, the Will of Heaven wishes those having energy to work for others, those knowing the right way to teach others, and those possessing wealth to share with others."[18]

For Mo Zi, Heaven possessed the authority to reward the good and punish the evil-doers: "Those who obey the Will of Heaven, practise universal love and benefit others, will as a rule be rewarded. Those who oppose the Will of Heaven, being partial and unmerciful and harming others, will as a rule incur punishment."[19] And further: "Those who love and benefit others will be blessed by Heaven; and those who hate and harm others will be ruined by Heaven."[20] From all these, there shines a stronger religious connotation in Mo Zi, implicitly as well as explicitly, than in any other thinker of ancient China.

Mo Zi used the "Will of Heaven" as a scale for measuring all men from the princes and dignitaries down to the common people. "When applied to the nobles, it can be used as a measure of the policies and jurisdictions of the princes and dignitaries; when applied to the common people, it can be used as a measure of the writing and talking of the people."[21]

The Heaven of Mo Zi differed from the traditional Heaven in that it was engendered by the fancy of the small producers and represented their interests. The traditional Heaven which defended the interests of the rule of the slave-owning nobility was now confronted by the Heaven of the labouring people who were striving for equal rights. The idea of Heaven, being thus modified, was turned to serve a different kind of doctrine and was rendered more easily accessible to the people.

"The belief in spirits" was also manipulated by Mo Zi in such a way that the spirits might serve to help Heaven in "rewarding the good and punishing the evil-doers".

The Will of Heaven in Mo Zi differed fundamentally from the Mandate of Heaven of the Confucians in that Mo Zi while advocating the Will of Heaven, professed also "anti-fatalism". The Confucians held that human fortunes and misfortunes were destined by fate and hence were irresistible and invariable. This theory was refuted by Mo Zi with his "anti-fatalism". He pointed out the dangers in believing fate, saying: "If people do believe in fate and rely on it, then the princes and dignitaries would become weary of their judicial and political activities, the officials weary of their administrations, peasants weary of their farming and planting and women of their weaving."[22] It would unavoidably lead to a situation of universal disorder and poverty. Thereupon Mo Zi posed the idea of "labour" in confrontation with fate.

Mo Zi professed that human fortunes and misfortunes were dependent not on fate but on human labour; and "he who depends on his own labour will survive, and he who does not depend on his own labour will not survive".[23] In this proposition was implied his sentiment that whoever did not labour should not share the harvest. He stressed the subjective effort on the part of human beings and termed it "hardship", asserting: "Through hardship good order will result, while through the lack of hardship social disorder will result", "hardship will result in being honorable while the lack of it will result in being dishonorable", and "hardship will bring in wealth, while the lack of it will bring in poverty".[24]

It is interesting to note that his Will of Heaven was closely united with his anti-fatalism. He taught that Heaven would be pleased with those who tried their hardest and would invariably reward them with success. That is to say, so far as one tried his utmost, he would as a rule be successful. This theory strongly reminds one of that of John Calvin in the 16th century. Both of them regarded the mundane efforts of man as a vindication of Heaven, but with the difference that Mo Zi tried hard to liberate the small producers from the bondage of the slave-owning nobility, while Calvin tried hard to liberate the bourgeoisie from the bondage of the feudal nobility. It is no wonder that they bore a striking similarity in the logic of their arguments. Nevertheless, the ancient small producers were far weaker than the bourgeoisie of the early modern times and were finally doomed to failure in their activities. It is really a pity to see that their religious ideas, which were originally for the interests of the labourers, were ultimately utilized by the governing class as a narcotic to lull their fighting spirit.

Epistemology of Mo Zi

Since the class of the small producers engaged themselves in productive labour and as a matter of necessity accumulated experiences through their practice, so it was but natural that their epistemology as expounded by Mo Zi was that of materialistic empiricism. The Mohists held that knowledge came from experiences of the senses and all existence of material objects ought to be tested by senses such as seeing and hearing. This implies that what can be seen or heard exists and what cannot be seen or heard does not exist.[25] It means also that experiences from the senses are the reflections of the objective existence. Though in a certain sense it affirmed that knowledge came from practice, it still bore all the limitations of parochial empiricism.

Concerning the relationship between the "name" and the "reality", Mo Zi held that "name should be given on the basis of reality", that is, concept is derived from the real object to which it refers. Hence, the "reality" is the primary and "name" the secondary. This materialistic understanding of the relationship between the name and reality was in sharp opposition to the "rectification of names" held by Confucius, who took the names as the primary and taught that all reality was determined or ought to be regulated by names.

One of the great contributions Mo Zi made to the development of epistemology was his "method of the three tests", which afforded a valid criterion both of knowledge and of judgment. Test here means criterion or standard (Yi). He expounded this in the following way: "What are the three tests? Mo Zi said: 'its basis, its verifiability and its applicability'."[26] And he further amplified: "On what is it to be based? It should be based on the deeds of the ancient sage-kings. By what is it to be verified? It is to be verified by the senses of hearing and seeing of the common people. How is it to be applied? It is to be applied by adopting it in government and observing its benefit to the country and the people. This is what is meant by the three tests in judging every doctrine."[27]

Although Mo Zi's epistemology, like Confucius', is in the last analysis reduced and confined to the narrow sphere of political practicality and neglected natural knowledge, by his method of the three tests Mo Zi had presented a very advanced theory for his time. And he employed this materialistic epistemology and methodology in criticizing the fatalism of the old times. But it should be pointed out meanwhile that this doctrine was much too limited to the functions of the senses only and hence knowledge for him remained on the whole at the level of perceptual knowledge without being able to raise itself to that of rational knowledge. It was due to this shortcoming that much one-sidedness and superficiality existed, from which wrong conclusions were drawn. For instance, based on the story that someone had once indeed seen the spirits, Mo Zi tried to prove the existence of the spirits. Here lies the historical limitedness of Mo Zi, who was after all far from being a thorough-going materialist.

2. THE IDEOLOGY OF YANG ZHU

Yang Zhu (circa 395-335 B.C.) was a contemporary of Mencius and Xu Xing, though a bit earlier. He was said to possess "a farm about three mu [about 0.2 hectare]"[1] and seemed to be a small landowner by his social position. The time in which he lived was one of great social upheavals. In the course of two centuries and half —that is, from the middle Spring and Autumn Period (when Duke Xuan of Lu in the year of 594 B.C. proclaimed "taxation on the farmland for the first time", thus acknowledging the private owner-ship of land) to the middle Warring States Period (when the anti-quated nine squares system finally collapsed with the introduction of reform by Shang Yang)—there had sprung up a great number of small landowners or landholding peasants who formed a rather influential social force and demanded politically as well as socially the protection of their rights and properties. Yang Zhu and his school were the representatives of these small landowners.

From the very small number of documents now in existence concerned with Yang Zhu, it might be seen that the propositions "everyone is for himself"[2] and "accord priority to self"[3] in opposition to "the conquering of things" constituted his main doctrine. Mencius said of him: "The principle of Yang Zhu is 'everyone for himself'. Though he might have benefited the whole world by plucking out a single hair, he would not have done it."[4] And Lie Zi said too: "There were ancients who would not benefit the whole world by plucking out a single hair."[5] Both statements referred to the doctrine of Yang Zhu. Han Fei said of Yang Zhu: "He would not have a single hair plucked out from his leg for the great benefit of having the whole world,"[6] and conversely Lie Zi said of him: "He would never consent for the world to serve him."[7] From these assertions it was apparent that the view point of Yang Zhu included the idea of not harming others. Therefore the thought of Yang Zhu might well be summed up in two propositions: "It is precious to preserve the self" and "It is unworthy to conquer things."[8]

"To preserve the self" means "everyone for himself"—a propo-sition Yang Zhu positively advocated; and "to conquer things" means plundering or intruding on the property of others, which he firmly rejected. It should be stressed here that the denial of the conquering of things means no more than one should do no harm to others. In the past, much of the research on Yang Zhu wrongly interpreted his "for the self" or "accord priority to the self" and described him as a hedonist or a sensualist. Such a valuation seems unjust to him.

In Yang Zhu's opinion, men were born "with avidity and de-sires". By affirming "accord priority to life", what was really meant by him was the appropriate satisfaction of human desires. Yang Zhu claimed: "It is out of the human passions that the ear desires

variegated sounds, the eye variegated colours and the mouth variegated flavours."[9] If one could not get appropriate satisfactions, life
would be no better than being dead. Here the importance lay in that
what Yang Zhu accorded priority to was not desire but life. He
commented: "The ear, the eye, the nose and the mouth are in the
service for life; though the ear desires the sound, the eye the colour,
the nose the fragrance, the mouth the flavour, if they are harmful to
life, they should be discarded."[10] As a matter of fact, indulging too
much in sensual enjoyments would often be harmful to life; so that
in order to live long and to enjoy long, one should control one's
desires. He went on to propound: "Be always moderate so as to be
able to control your desires",[11] that is, one should come to a stop
whenever and wherever one's desires were satisfied appropriately, the
criterion being their benefits to life. Contrary to the age-old and very
popular impression of him, Yang Zhu was far from being a hedonist
or sensualist.

The thought of Yang Zhu reflected the demands of the small
landowners of his time. "Everyone for himself" and "accord priority
to life" were in their essence only the striving for equal living rights
by the people, that is, every one should have the right to satisfy his
own desires to a rational extent as opposed to the suppression under
the waning slavery era and the exploitation of the newborn feudalism. His doctrine was meant as a criticism of the deceptive propaganda of "checking the desires" on the part of the ruling class. His
formula "everyone for the self" did not mean becoming wealthy by
exploitation; it was for the sake of protecting one's own fruits of
labour from being robbed by others. More than a proposal, it was a
protest against the violation of the private ownership of the small
landowners.

The political ideal of Yang Zhu was to build a society in which
"everyone does not lose a hair and every one is not interested in
having the world".[12] It was said that he had discussed "how to rule
the world" with the king of Liang. Han Fei once said that Yang Zhu,
just like Mo Zi, was endowed with the talent to govern a state.[13] Yang
Zhu opposed the worship of the ancient kings[14] and flavoured the
building of a new society. This political idea was begot from his view
on life and living. He proclaimed: "If everyone does not lose a hair
and everyone is not interested in having the world, then there will

be the reign of peace in the world."[15] This saying amounts simply to that if everyone does not let a hair be plucked out from his leg for the great benefit of having the whole world, then the world will enjoy the reign of peace. That is to say, if every one is concerned only with himself, with no intention to intrude upon the possession of others, then all will be well.

The above reasoning of Yang Zhu naturally led to the ideal of the reign without a sovereign, so that Mencius said of him: "The principle of Yang Zhu is 'everyone for himself', which is to be without a sovereign."[16] For Yang Zhu, one's life and living was more precious than being a sovereign capable of enjoying the whole country; because once life was lost, all things would be in vain. Concerning the relationship between the individual and the state, he said: "The essence of truth consists in the maintenance of one's life; and next to it, one may do something for the state in his leisure."[17] Obviously he put the interest of the individual above that of the state. Hence Mencius blamed him severely: "Without a sovereign—that would be the same as being a beast."[18] Han Fei also said of him that if his doctrine was to be accepted, then "it will be impossible to urge the people to dedicate their lives to their superiors or sovereigns".[19] Thus both the Confucians and the Legalists were in sharp contradiction with Yang Zhu's theory of the reign without a sovereign.

How, then, should an ideal society be governed? His answer was that those governing a society should be virtuous and talented with the humility of "doing what is virtuous without assuming himself to be virtuous"[20] and all the members of the society should be prudent in their conduct. There was a well-known story of Yang Zhu weeping at the crossroad which illustrated quite well this mentality. *The Book of Xun Zi* recorded that once when on his way Yang Zhu happened to come to a crossroad, he sighed: "At this very spot if one step is directed in the wrong, it would lead to a mistake for thousands of miles."[21] And not knowing where to go, he wept bitterly, because once the wrong way was selected in life, it would result in infinite disasters.

Each member of the society should be asked both "for the self" and at the same time "not to conquer things". But to fulfill both requirements at one and the same stroke was no easy thing. It exacted serious deliberations at each step in life. This long-circulated story mentioned above reflected the unstable economic position and the wavering political attitude of the small land proprietors in the early feudal society.

In fact, it is certainly impossible to build up a society in which everyone is for himself and at the same time not to encroach on others. This was a wishful thinking on the part of the small landowners. Han Fei in his criticism of Yang Zhu pointed out that sophisticated as Yang Zhu's doctrine was, it did not correspond to social reality and was hence impracticable.[22]

Lie Zi criticized Yang Zhu by saying: "Yang Zi is wise but does not know fate." By fate he meant the Mandate of Heaven. Yang Zhu inherited the anti-fatalist tradition of the Spring and Autumn Period not only in his world view but also in his view on daily life. For instance, he did not believe that the sick would get well by praying to the deities and said: "Now, the more people go to pray to the deities and ask for oracles, the more they fall in illness."[23] This atheistic idea formed an important element in his own ideology as well as in that of his age.

There were naive dialectic ideas as well. Han Fei in his writings narrated the following story.[24] Once when his brother Yang Bu went out dressed in white but came back dressed in black, the dog did not recognize him and barked at him. Thereupon Yang Zhu told his brother that if the positions were changed, if the dog going out looked white but coming back looked black, then his brother, too, would be mistaken. This story showed how Yang Zhu realized that things in the world were in constant change, so that we should observe them carefully and searchingly without being puzzled by their mere appearances. Similar was his view on the issue of life and death. Though he advised people to enjoy their lives as long as possible, he did not think anyone should be able to live forever. He asserted: "A long life does not mean an unbroken continuance of a short life but only a better accomplishment of its duration",[25] that is to say, the duration of one's life has its limitations.

Though the viewpoints of Yang Zhu remained in a rather coarse form, they influenced his time immensely. Mencius said: "The doctrines of Yang Zhu and Mo Zi prevail all over the world. The doctrines held by the world either approach those of Yang or those of Mo."[26] Zhuang Zi thought that the influence of Yang Zhu could be "compared with that of the dialecticians[27] ... which brought the world into a great tumult".[28] He even shouted: "Let the mouths of Yang Zhu and Mo Di be shut up."[29] From the fact that Yang Zhu was always mentioned together with Mo Zi, it may be seen how widely his theory prevailed at that time.

In the Warring States Period, various schools had criticized Yang Zhu in various ways from which some of the essence of Yang Zhu's thought might be depicted. At first sight, it seemed that there were some similarities between Yang Zhu and the Taoists, but in reality they were not that much as they looked. The Taoists held the slogan: "To accord priority to the body" which in contrast with Yang Zhu's "to accord priority to self" or "to accord priority to life", aimed at achieving "the forgetfulness of the self" and at searching for a state of "the equalization of life and death and the identification of the self with others".[30] This Taoist ideal ran counter to the materialism of Yang Zhu. The Taoists advocated the negative inactivity of life while Yang Zhu advocated the positive activity of life, so they ran in opposite directions. Therefore Yang Zhu should not be listed with the Taoists nor be regarded as one of the founders of Taoism as people are always apt to think, although both of them preached "completeness of living and preservation of what is genuine".[31]

Mencius in the middle of the Warring States Period attacked Yang Zhu violently on his doctrine "for the self" from the Confucian political point of view but entirely neglected his "completeness of living and preservation of what is genuine". For Mencius, "So far as the doctrines of Yang and Mo do not cease to be ... the doctrine of Confucius will be unable to become manifest." And this was the reason why Mencius engaged himself so energetically in attacking Yang Zhu and Mo Zi. Mencius was even convinced that it was only by doing so that one would prove oneself to be worthy of "a follower of the Sage [Confucius]".[32]

The doctrine of Yang Zhu in its defending of the interests of the small individual labourers was detrimental to the rule of the newborn landlord class, and so Han Fei, the greatest of the Legalists, launched an attack on it and pointed out in particular: "A man who values his life so much ... that he is obliged not to remain within a besieged city nor to join the army, nor even to pluck out a hair from his leg for the great benefit of having the whole world",[33] would not be able to do anything useful nor to render any service to his country (of course, a feudal legalist country).

There were some things in common between the doctrine of Yang Zhu and that of Mo Zi, yet there were also evident differences. Both of them "valued the body", but Mo Zi laid more emphasis on "valuing the obligations".[34] They were also diametrically opposed to each other in that Mo Zi was for "universal love" whereas Yang Zhu was "for the self". In regard to their views on deities, the School of Yang Zhu was atheistic whereas the Mohist School was theistic. These are the points which deserve careful study when one makes a comparison of the two representative schools of the labouring people in ancient times.

In the early and middle Warring States Period, the School of Yang Zhu, just like that of Mo Zi, was generally acknowledged as one of the most influential schools. Thus in the ideological sphere at that time a tri-lateral confrontation between the Confucian School, the Mohist School and the School of Yang Zhu appeared. And hence Mencius assumed it his duty to resist both the School of Yang and that of Mo. But the School of Yang Zhu did not last long, being even more short-lived than the Mohist School. This was because the small landowners who came to the fore during the transition from the collapse of slavery to the emergence of feudalism were in a precarious condition; and with the acceleration of social polarization, a small number of them were raised to the rank of the newborn landlords while most of them were soon reduced to poor peasant. As soon as the social basis of this school disappeared, their doctrine was doomed to disappear along with it.

3. THE IDEOLOGY OF MENCIUS

In tradition, Mencius had ever been held as the greatest Confucian sage, next only to Confucius himself. Undoubtedly, Mencius represented the most important development of the Confucian School in the Warring States Period.

According to Han Fei, after the death of Confucius, his school was divided into eight sects: "There were the Confucian followers respectively of Zi Zhang, Zi Si, Yan Shi, Mencius, Qi Diao, Zhong

Liang, Xun Zi and Yue Zheng."[1] In fact the followers of Zi Si, Mencius and Yue Zheng belonged to the same sect, i.e. that of Zi Si-Mencius, which with the sect of Xun Zi formed two most influential Confucian sects in that historical epoch.

Zi Si (circa 492-431 B.C.), named Kong Ji, was the grandson of Confucius and a disciple of Zeng Zi, though some regarded him as a disciple of Zi You. It was Zi Si who composed *Zhong Yong* (*The Doctrine of the Mean*), one of the Four Books in the Confucian classics.

The idea of sincerity (cheng) and, in close connection with it, the doctrine of the Five Elements, constituted the main theory of this sect. Sincerity was both the basic concept in their ideology and at the same time their highest moral norm. Zi Si said: "Sincerity is the way of Heaven."[2] Here "the way of Heaven" meant no other than the Mandate of Heaven. And again he said: "What Heaven mandates is called nature. To follow this nature is called the Way [Tao]."[3] That is to say, sincerity is at the same time the trinity of the Mandate of Heaven, Nature and the Way (Tao).

Again Zi Si said: "Sincerity is both the beginning and the end of all things. Without sincerity there would be nothing at all"[4] and "The quality of sincerity does not consist simply in perfecting one's self; it is that whereby one perfects all other things."[5] Thus, cosmologically "sincerity" was identified with the creator of all things in the world; and if there were no sincerity, there would be left only nothingness. This means that the subjective "sincerity" was what was primary and essential from which the objective world was derived. In other words, this doctrine endeavoured to explain the world and its development by means of a subjective spirit which was termed "sincerity".

The thought of Zi Si was permeated with a strong mysterious vein by endowing sincerity with a miraculous power, or as he himself put it: "The utmost sincerity is something divine...."[6] The way of the utmost sincerity can foretell the things to come; when a nation is about to flourish, there would certainly be something propitious; when a nation is about to fall, there would certainly be something devilish."[7] Here sincerity was considered in direct communion with Heaven and deities. So far as one possesses this utmost sincerity, he is able to foretell fortunes and misfortunes.

Zi Si taught that the way to sincerity (i.e., the communion of Heaven and man,) was simply to develop one's nature to the utmost, saying: "It is only he who having the utmost sincerity in the world can develop his nature to its utmost. Able to develop his own nature to its utmost, he can do the same to the natures of other men. Able to develop the natures of other men to their utmost, he can do the same to the natures of things. Able to develop these to their utmost, he can assist the transforming and nourishing of the operations of Heaven and Earth. Capable of assisting in these transforming and nourishing operations, he can form a trinity with Heaven and Earth."[8] This is just what Mencius called "exercising the mind to the utmost, ... knowing nature" and "knowing Heaven" whencefrom a mysterious state of "the communion of Heaven and man" could be reached. This idea of "the communion of Heaven and man" exercised a great influence on later generations, especially on Dong Zhongshu in the Han Dynasty and on the Neo-Confucians in the Song Dynasty.

The idea of sincerity expounded by Zi Si bore an epoch-making significance in the intellectual history of China. As explained in the above chapter, Duke Zhou, giving an explanation of why Zhou replaced Shang, propounded the idea of "venerating the virtue" as a means to revise and to amend the antiquated idea of the Mandate of Heaven. In the later Spring and Autumn Period when the idea of the Mandate of Heaven was already tottering, Confucius came forth to propound the idea of "Benevolence" as a moral code in his endeavor to reconcile the contradictions between men. Though "benevolence" had nothing to do directly with God or Providence, Confucius did not abrogate the place of God or Providence altogether. Then Zi Si propounded the idea of sincerity, the function of which it was to substitute for the place of God or Providence, and by doing so the worship of God was transformed into a pantheism. It enlarged the pomp of the ethical ideas of Confucius into a broader, a more sophisticated and more idealistic doctrine of religion. An important stage in the development of the Confucian ideology was accomplished by the Zi Si-Mencius School, which eventually laid down the philosophical and metaphysical foundation of Confucianism.

The sincerity of Zi Si was closely connected with the doctrine of the Five Elements. Cheng Xuan (the famous classical scholar in the Han Dynasty) in his annotations on *The Doctrine of the Mean* commented that the proposition "what Heaven mandates is called nature" as "wood sanctified was benevolence, metal sanctified was obligation, fire sanctified was rite, water sanctified was intelligence, and earth sanctified was honesty"; that is to say, embraced in this proposition were the contents of the Five Elements. Zhang Taiyan, the famous classical scholar in the early 20th century, identified them with the ideas of Zi Si.[9] It should be noted that what was termed sincerity here was named honesty or the way of the mean. Among the five elements, the earth held the place in the center, hence honesty meant the middle way or the way of the mean. In the writings of Zi Si, though no word on the five elements (metal, wood, water, fire and earth) ever appeared, the doctrine of the five elements nevertheless always remained in spirit.

In *The Book of Mencius*, the doctrine of the Five Elements was more salient. In the lost ancient books recently unearthed in December 1973 from the Han tombs No. 3 at Mawangdui in Changsha, Hunan, eight moral norms, were mentioned: wisdom, sageness, righteousness, far-sightedness, intelligence, benevolence, rites and musicality,[10] which were in turn formulated into four elements: benevolence, righteousness, rites and intelligence, or into five: benevolence, righteousness, rites, intelligence and sageness. They were the same eight moral norms which Zhuang Zi opposed. Jia Yi of the Han Dynasty said in his book: "There are human behaviors of benevolence, righteousness, rites, intelligence and sageness." These are the five elements which plus music make up the six elements. From them one can get a better understanding about what Mencius affirmed: "What benevolence is to the fathers and sons, what righteousness is to the sovereigns and subjects, what rites are to the hosts and guests, what intelligence is to the talented and what sageness is to the way of Heaven are all dominated by fate." Here the five virtues are just the same as the five elements mentioned above.

In may seem that the exposition on the five elements recently found in the books long lost since the old times were just what was expounded in *The Book of Mencius*.[11] Then what does the term sageness mean? It could mean no other than sincerity. Mencius said: "What the sage is to the way of Heaven"[12] is closely related to "Sincerity is the way of Heaven."[13] Hence sincerity and sageness were for him identical and interchangeable. In *The Doctrine of the Mean*, it was said: "He who takes the way of the mean modestly is a sage", a proposition which means just the same as Mencius'. Therefore it is obvious that sincerity is but honesty or the way of the mean which in a cosmological sense corresponded to the central position of the earth.

The doctrine of the five elements of the Zi Si-Mencius School thus underwent a process of development. Sincerity as a metaphysical concept was first elaborated by Zi Si and was assigned the central place in the five elements. Mencius inherited it from Zi Si and developed it into the concept of sageness, which modelled the five elements into a definite pattern of benevolence, righteousness, rites, intelligence and sageness—a pattern which continued to prevail in later generations.

This new theory of the five elements transformed the essence of the old theory of the five material elements (metal, wood, water, fire and earth) and substantiated it with a thoroughly metaphysical character. The naive materialistic doctrine of the five elements was completely transformed and idealized by the Zi Si-Mencius School.

Mencius (circa 390-305 B.C.), also named Meng Ke, was a native of Zou (now in Shandong Province) and a descendant of the Meng-suns, the royal family of Lu. He was a second generation disciple of Zi Si and was the foremost representative of the Confucian School in the middle Warring States Period. In an earnest attempt to realize his political ideals, he travelled widely in the kingdoms of Qi, Song, Lu, Teng, Wei and other states for the purpose of influencing their sovereigns; but nowhere did he succeed. In his later years, he came back to his native Zou, where he wrote *The Book of Mencius* with his disciples Gongsun Chou, Wang Zhang and others.

Political Ideals of Mencius

Mencius lived in the middle Warring States Period when feudalism had already been established in all the major principalities for more than a hundred years, except in Qin. The landlord class had seized power in these principalities and continued to strengthen its regime. The small land proprietors who had emerged from the ruins of the ancient nine squares system were losing their small land properties by the violent annexation of lands; and frequent wars of annexation resulted in tremendous suffering by the people. The main social contradiction in feudalism, i.e., that between the landlords and the peasants, was becoming acute. Under such circumstances, Mencius evolved a theory representing the interests of that part of the landlord class which was begot from the old slave-owner nobility. In order to moderate the contradiction, Mencius elaborated his doctrine of a benevolent government.

Mencius inherited this doctrine from Confucius and applied the Confucian idea of benevolence to the political field, forming his own theory, the main idea of which might be summed up in his well-known proposition: "[In a state], the people are the most important, the land and the grain are secondary, and the sovereign is the least." The reason that he laid so much emphasis on the role of the people was that he realized it was by relying on the people that the reign of a sovereign might be ensured. And it was with this reason in view that he urged the sovereigns to maintain a benevolent government and to share the joys and sorrows of the people. A tyrant who conducted his policies contrary to what was required of a benevolent government should deservedly be exiled or even put to death. Hence concerning the case of King Wu of Zhou waging a war against the ruthless King Zhou of Shang, Mencius said: "I have heard of the execution of the bad fellow Zhou, but never heard of anything of a regicide."[14] In his opinion, King Zhou deserved not to be treated as a legitimate sovereign, because he was a mere bad fellow. Of course, Mencius' assertion did not and could not run against the fundamental interests of the ruling class; but it still bore with it a very significant implication in the progress of democratic ideas in China.

As for the practical measures of his benevolent government, he designed, first of all, the regulation of the proprietary of land. Each peasant was to be given a farm of a hundred *mu* (about 6.67 hectares) together with house land of five *mu* for the realization of his idealized nine squares system, thus: "A square *li* (half a kilometre) covers nine squares of land which totalled nine hundred *mu*. The central square is the state-owned field, and eight families, each having its private hundred *mu*, should cultivate the state-owned field collectively."[15] The hundred *mu* of farmland given to each peasant was a kind of hereditary property which was not permitted to be sold or bought. On the one hand, such a system acknowledged the legitimacy of the peasants' proprietary and thereby set a hindrance to the annexation of lands; while on the other hand, it also bound the peasants to their farmlands by their hereditary status.

Secondly, Mencius stressed the importance of protecting farming and the alleviation of taxation. In addition, enlistment for the army and the governmental corvée should not be exacted so as to harm agricultural production. He advocated the adoption of the tithe and the labour rent and advised there should be no taxation on the commodity storehouses. He thought this was a measure which would bring profits to the ruling class in the long run.

Thirdly, he paid more attention to education than to judicial and criminal punishment. The aim of education consisted in the "clarification of human relationships", that is, "There is intimacy between fathers and sons, there is obligation between sovereigns and subjects, there is distinction between husbands and wives, there is order between the elders and the youngsters and there is honesty between friends."[16] In a society so well-regulated, people would not run the risk of joining rebellions, and thereby the rule of the feudal hierarchy would remain secure.

In order to ensure the practice of his ideals, Mencius proposed the veneration of the sage, which implied that a benevolent government should be run by the sage. The sovereigns should venerate the sage. And the culmination of this veneration of the sage would manifest itself in the intention of the sovereign being ready to abdicate his throne to a sage. But Mencius limited his doctrine of the veneration of the sage. He insisted that only those who were gifted with special talents could be so entrusted, without paying regard to their status or their birth; while as a general rule, the appointment of officials should be kept strictly to the principle of hierarchy. He upheld the reservation of the privileges of the hereditary nobility and considered that relatives and kinsmen of royalty should keep themselves in a powerful position. He even advised: "[In politics] one should avoid to offend the dignitary houses."[17] This showed the eclectic and conciliatory character of his doctrine of venerating the sage.

In his demand for a benevolent government, he opposed vehemently wars of aggrandizement and annexation and preached the employment of "an army of benevolence and justice that would have no interest in killing others"[18] so as to win over the people and to make possible the unification of the whole of China, which was already becoming an irresistiable historical current. The wars of aggrandizement and annexation launched by the newborn landlord class he condemned as scrambling for power and wealth. In their stead he preached the unification of the world through peaceful means. This reflected his own reformist political stand in opposition to violent struggles between the states. To a certain degree it represented the desires of the common people, who suffered in the constant feudal wars and longed for peace and for a unified country.

The doctrine of a benevolent government served him as a political means to moderate the class tensions between the landlords and peasants as well as to win the hearts of the people. His famous statement that "the people are the most important" and "the sovereign is the least" followed the advanced ideological legacy of the Western Zhou, which more or less acknowledged the place and the role of the people. If the people were over-exploited by the ruling class, then they might possibly endure no more and rise up in arms. And his proposal of a benevolent government was aimed at a long-term arrangement for the benefit of the ruling class. However, Mencius paid too much attention to the preservation of old and antiquated ideas, which made his theory look "pedantic and far from reality."[19] It turned out to be impractical in his time.

On the Goodness of Human Nature

Mencius' doctrine of the benevolent government was founded on his theory of the goodness of human nature. He taught that there were beginnings of goodness in every human being, declaring: "The feeling of compassion is the beginning of benevolence (or humanheartedness). The feeling of shame and aversion is the beginning of righteousness. The feeling of modesty and humility is the beginning of rites (or propriety). The sense of right and wrong is the beginning of intelligence (or wisdom)."[20] Among these, the most important is the feeling of compassion, by which he meant "every one has a feeling which cannot bear [to see the sufferings of] others". He went on to make a famous parable: "If now men suddenly see a child about to fall into a well, they will without exception experience a feeling of alarm and distress. This will not be as a way whereby they might gain the favour of the child's parents, nor whereby they might seek the praise of their neighbours and friends, nor that they are so because they dislike the reputation [of being unvirtuous]." They would hasten to his rescue solely because of the innate goodness of human nature.

Then, why were there evils in human nature? To this, Mencius argued that mankind was endowed with good, and when people did evil it was because they indulged in sensual desires which prevented that goodness from developing. This thesis of his was later adopted and greatly amplified by the Neo-Confucians of the Song Dynasty.

Mencius compared the innate goodness of human nature to an exuberant tree which could not flourish if chopped with an axe day after day. Therefore he advised people to preserve "the restorative influence of the night",[21] that is, though people did something evil in the daytime, in the stillness of night they might yet be able to reflect upon their evildoings and wish to correct them through their feeling of shame; just like the tree chopped by an axe might yet sprout out new branches after being moistened by rain and dew. But those who could not preserve "the restorative influence of the night" would degrade themselves to a position akin to that of the beasts and never be able to rediscover their conscience. Hence Mencius affirmed that "everyone might be a sage as Yao or Shun (the ancient sages)",[22] provided they were not involved in material desires and were able to develop their potential in full.

Thencefrom derived the theory of the benevolent government of Mencius. He taught that there was a feeling of compassion in everyone from which benevolence might germinate; and when it was developed and applied to politics, it would serve as the basis of a benevolent government.

As it was so well pointed out by Karl Marx: "The human essence is no abstraction inherent in each single individual. In its reality it is the ensemble of the social relations"; Mencius's doctrine of the goodness of human nature had turned the issue upside down and mistook the social nature of human beings for an a priori abstraction. Although he professed that everyone possessed the beginnings of goodness, nevertheless, he claimed that only the "gentlemen", i.e., the ruling class, were able to expand and develop goodness and the common people were unable to do so.[23] This argument furnished a theoretical basis for the hierarchical distinctions in feudal society.

The Idea of the Mandate of Heaven

Heaven as expounded by Mencius was namely God. Heaven was the supreme being which he characterized as "what is done, though no one does it, is by Heaven".[24] Therefore Heaven was endowed by him with supernatural powers. Further, he argued that the sovereign was the son of Heaven, or the representative of God on earth, chosen by Heaven. The power of Heaven was irresistible, and "whoever obeys it will survive and whoever resists it will perish".[25]

The idea of the Mandate of Heaven in Mencius was somewhat different from the traditional one in the Western Zhou. In it he paid due attention to the role of men in their relationship with Heaven. Preaching the divine right of kings as he did, he acknowledged, nevertheless, that they should in their turn be sanctioned by the will of the people. Sometimes he even assigned to Heaven an implication of natural laws; for example, he said: "Heaven is high, the stars and planets are far; but if only we seek for the causes [of their movements], the winter solstices of a thousand years to come can be deduced from wherever we sit."[26] However, this implication held only a secondary place in the theoretical system of Mencius.

Mencius also preached fatalism, saying: "What comes, though no one contrives, is fate."[27] For him, the lives and fortunes of human beings were predetermined by a fate to which men were obliged to submit passively. He taught that everyone's endowment was predestined and that was the reason why there were distinctions in social ranks among men. Every one should be content with his lot, resigning himself to Heaven, that is, one should not try to rebel against the established social order. Obviously, such a theory served to uphold the rule of feudalism.

To a certain extent, Mencius taught people to develop their subjective capacities; he said: "Weal and woe are never but self-sought."[28] But the subjective activities could be given play only within a certain range and their eventual success and failure would depend on the Mandate of Heaven, that is to say, human efforts were in the last analysis disposed by Heaven.

Mencius advocated that so far as one would give full play to his innate goodness he would be capable of knowing both human nature and the Mandate of Heaven, thus attaining a mysterious state of "the communion of Heaven and man". By "knowing Heaven" he meant the acknowledgement of the intention of Heaven and the avoidance of resisting the heavenly will. In other words, it meant an endeavour to attain a spiritual liberation through imaginative thinking about the will of the supernatural Deity. The formula of his "communion of Heaven and man"—or as he put it: "He who goes to the bottom of his heart knows his own nature; and knowing his own nature he knows Heaven"[29]—served to lead people to scrutinize their innermost hearts rather than to urge them to fight against the social injustices and to search after the objective truth of the world .

The Epistemology of Mencius

In Mencius' theory of knowledge, such perceptive organs as eyes and ears were incapable of thinking and prone to be misleading when in contact with external objects. Mencius proclaimed: "To think is not the office of the eyes and the ears, and they are easily blinded by things. Anything [i.e., the eye or the ear] that is handed over to things is guided by them altogether. To think is the office of the heart. It gets by thinking, and without thinking it does not get. All that we are is the gift of Heaven. Once a man stands upon the great in him, he cannot be robbed of it by his littleness."[30] It is note-worthy that here Mencius made a fine explanation of thinking by asserting "to think is the office of the heart". But he set the great (the office of the heart) against the little (the office of the sense organs), as though they were mutually exclusive or even antagonistic; and thus he was led to the logical conclusion that all rational knowledge was independent of perceptual knowledge.

Rationalism in the Mencian sense is wholly idealistic, because the object of his knowledge consisted not in the external world but in an internal world in which "all things are complete within me".[31] For him, rational knowledge was something innate or a priori and hence was segregated from perceptual knowledge. Epistemologically, this gave rise to his mysticism, which permeated his whole world view.

There was something sophisticated and penetrating in Mencius' theory of self-cultivation. But by denying the validity of perceptual knowledge he was bound to the confines of introspection or introversion, completely divorced from any practical or empirical element. Mencius laid special emphasis on "the cultivation of the heart" the best way to which, as he asserted, was to "keep few desires",[32] or to decrease the bodily desires to the minimum—a theory which the Neo-Confucians of the Song Dynasty brought into full sway. As to the concrete means for "the cultivation of the heart", Mencius proposed "the preservation of the restorative influence of the night[33] . . . the feeding of the boundless spirit",[34] "keeping the heart unaffected"[35] and "seeking peace of mind".[36] By means of such introspective "cultivation of the heart", one was enabled to attain the highest state of the spirit whereby "all things are complete within me".[37] Here Mencius fell into his own idealistic self-intoxication; and as a past master in this respect he greatly influenced the development of idealism of the later generations, especially that of the Neo-Confucians.

This preaching of the Mencian idealistic rationalism was welcomed and supported by the feudal ruling class. Since the "office of the heart" was considered as "the great" and the "office of the sense organs" as "the little", Mencius came to the conculusion that "those who are led by the great in them are great men, and those who are led by the small in them are small (or little-minded) men", while answering the question: "We are men all alike, why then is some one a great man and some other a small man?"[38] The distinction between the great man and the small man was none other than that between the governing and the governed. The following are among the most often quoted lines from Mencius: "There is work for great men and work for small men (or little-minded people)", because "some toil with their heart, some toil with their strength; those who toil with their heart rule men, those who toil with their strength are ruled by men; those who are ruled by men feed men, the rulers of men are fed by men."[39] Nowhere did Mencius apologize for the exploitation of the governed by the governing more straightforwardly than in the above lines. Since then, it has afforded an important theoretical ground for feudal exploitations for thousands of years.

4. THE IDEOLOGY OF XUN ZI

The thought of Xun Zi marked the last stage in the development of the Confucian School during the Warring States Period. Xun Zi (fl. 298-238 B.C.), named Kuang, with the cognomen Qing, also called Sun Qing, was a native of Zhao at about the end of the Warring States Period. He had travelled widely in the states of Zhao, Yan, Chu, Qin and Qi. When he stayed in the state of Yan during the reign of King Gui, he was not honoured there. In the state of Qi, he remained a long time in the Academy of Ji Xia of which he had been three times appointed the dean. In the state of Zhao, he had discussed military affairs with the Duke of Linwu in front of King Xiao Cheng. In the state of Qin, he had made investigations on its policies and politics. In the state of Chu, he had served the Duke of Chun Sheng as the mayor of Lanling (now in Shandong). It was there he composed his book in his later years with his disciples.

His Political Ideals of "Following the Later Kings"

Xun Zi divided the people into three ranks, saying: "The superior Confucians can be made kings or the three dukes; the inferior Confucians can be made nobles, prefects or officials; the ordinary men can be made labourers, farmers or merchants." But his standard of distinguishing the social ranks was not the antiquated Mandate of Heaven, nor the blood kinship of nobility, but individual talent. He advocated: "The most talented should be made the three dukes (the highest dignitaries), the less talented should be made the nobles and the least talented should be made the prefects and officials." Such a theory apparently served to strengthen the new feudal hierarchy as opposed to the old one based on blood lineage. But Xun Zi did not wholly throw away the antiquated convention of "ennobling the nobles". This incoherence in his doctrine resulted from the limitations of the class to which he belonged.

One of his great contributions to Confucianism lay in his radical modification of the conventional rites. The rites modified by him differed very much from those propounded by Confucius. He forwarded his proposal as follows: the descendants of the princes, nobles and ministers not conforming to the standards of the rites should be demoted to the common people; while the descendants of the common people conforming to the standards of the rites should by promoted to the ministers and magistrates.

With this purpose in view, he made new explanations of the rites by uniting them with the law. He proclaimed: "What is called rite is the great functioning of the law, it is the unifying principle of the classes." And again: "To go contrary to the rites is the same as to be without the law." Thus the rites were given the implications of the law, which was in urgent demand by the landlord class then arising in that era. In this fashion, the thought of Xun Zi typified the transition from the rule of the rites proposed by the Confucians to the rule of the law proposed by the Legalists.

At the same time, Xun Zi was also the founder of a doctrine of autocracy for feudal times. For him, the rites constituted the standard of ruling. A sovereign who mastered the rites would have in his hands the possession of absolute authority. So he remarked: "Treat those who are good and come to you according to the rites; and treat those who are not good and come to you with punishment." That is to say, whoever conforms to the standard of ruling is considered good and should be treated according to the rites; otherwise punishment should be employed. This idea was the forerunning doctrine of autocracy in China. His disciples Han Fei and Li Si further amplified it, thus laying down the theoretical foundation of the absolutism of the Qin Dynasty. Ever since then, this theory had been inherited by nearly all the emperors in the later ages.

During the periods of the Spring and Autumn and the Warring States, each of the hundred schools used to hold up the banner of some ancient sage-king for the sake of propagating their own doctrines. But the legendary ancient sage-kings that each school upheld differed greatly from one another. The Confucians "never speak anything without mentioning the names of Yao and Shun", while the Taoists uplifted the legendary Huang Di who was supposed to be even earlier than Yao and Shun. Xun Zi criticized them severely as "invoking the ancient kings in order to deceive the stupid people", and in their stead he advocated his proposition of "following the later kings".

What did Xun Zi really mean by "following the later kings"? The term "later kings" was an antithesis of the "ancient kings", as he remarked: "The Way (Tao) which antedates the three dynasties (i.e., Xia, Shang and Zhou) is vague; the law (method) which is different from that of the later kings is not fine." For him, the time of the later kings did not exceed that of Xia, Shang and Zhou. Among the three dynasties, he referred especially to Zhou, because the times of Xia and Shang were far more antiquated. So he said: "To give up the later kings and follow those of the extremely ancient times is like giving up one's own prince and serving another's prince", and further he advised: "If you wish to know the ancient times, then examine the Way (Tao) of the Zhou Dynasty." Hence "the later kings" were meant by Xun Zi "the Way of Zhou", i.e., that of King Wen, King Wu and the Duke of Zhou.

The slogan of "following the later kings" in Xun Zi also implied "returning to the ancients"; and he even asserted definitely that resorting to the later kings meant returning to the way of the Zhou Dynasty. He declared: "All music that is not fine should be totally abandoned. All colours that are not in accordance with the old fashion should be totally dispensed with. All utensils which are not of the ancient sort should be destroyed. This is what is meant by returning to the ancients. And this is the institution of a king." Thencefrom it is clear that the following of the later kings in Xun Zi did not differ very much from the following of the ancient kings advocated by Mencius.

Of course, the returning to the ancient kings in the doctrines of Mencius included in it a demand for reformation under the pretext of resorting to the ancients; the following of the later kings in Xun Zi included not only a simple returning to the way of Zhou but rather a theoretical innovation for the sake of strengthening the newly established feudal institutions of the landlord class. On the other hand, It should be pointed out as well that "the following of the later kings" did not mean the same thing as in the historical perspective of Han Fei, the Legalist, who "does not wish to follow the ancients nor observe any permanently correct way".

Xun Zi himself did not completely get rid of the Confucian tradition of "following the ancient kings", but his innovation of "the following of the later kings" undoubtedly influenced greatly his disciples Han Fei and Li Si, both the greatest representatives of the Legalist School in their opposition to the age-old tradition of the returning to the ancients. Herein lies the historical significance of Xun Zi's idea of "following the later kings". It played an intermediate role in the transition from Confucian School, which demanded a return to the ancient kings, to the Legalist School, which demanded a thorough breakup with the old institutions.

Xun Zi's View on the Way of Heaven

Xun Zi's view on the way of Heaven epitomized the materialistic ideologies of the pre-Qin time. In his "Essay on Heaven", he discussed in detail the relationship between Heaven and man, and placed himself in contradistinction to both Confucius and Mencius. With him, the idealistic Heaven in the tradition of the Confucian School was remodelled and transformed into a materialistic Heaven.

With Xun Zi,the term Heaven was but a collective noun for all natural phenomena, as clearly shown in his statement: "The fixed stars make their rounds; the sun and moon alternatively shine;the four seasons come and go in succession; the Yin and Yang go through their great mutations; the wind and rain widely affect things; all things acquire their germinating principle and are brought into their existence; each gets its nourishing principle and develops to its completed state." All these occurred naturally, as Xun Zi thought, without any mysterious implication. Heaven was for him purposeless and aimless; it brought forth everything naturally: "To produce without acting and to obtain without seeking, this is what is meant by the office of Heaven." With this doctrine he launched a forceful critique on the traditional theistic idea that everything was dominated by the Mandate of Heaven.

Heaven was for him but objective existence and moved according to objective laws, independent of any will, human or divine. So he proclaimed: "Heaven has a constant regularity of action. It does not exist for Yao, the ancient sage-king, nor extinguish for Jie, the ancient tyrant"; and moreover: "Heaven does not suspend the winter because men dislike the cold; the Earth does not suspend its spaciousness because men dislike distances." He taught that one "should know the offices both of Heaven and man" and criticized the mysterious doctrine of the "communion of Heaven and man" of the Yin and Yang School.

Stressing the role of subjective activity, Xun Zi forwarded his brilliant proposition of "adopting oneself to the appointments of Heaven and making use of them"; that is to say, by making use of natural laws to their own advantages, people were capable of transforming the natural world. With his idea that "man overcomes Heaven (nature)", Xun Zi forcefully refuted the ancient fatalism. In his handling of the relationship between Heaven and man, Xun Zi pushed forward pre-Qin ideology to a high level.

The emergence of Xun Zi's materialistic viewpoint on the Way of Heaven was facilitated both by the development of social productivity and by the progress of science and technology in the Warring States Period. Progress in tranforming the natural world by men provided the material condition for the birth of his new point of view on the Way of Heaven, which in a certain way reflected the ideology as well as the self-confidence of the landlord class at its ascending stage in history.

However, the viewpoint of Xun Zi on the Way of Heaven still bore its limits. His materialism in the main was only intuitive without the necessary speculative depth. And at times Heaven for him was not entirely devoid of the divine volition; for example, he said: "Though Heaven produced all men, it fell to their lots that there were distinctions whereby they took their different positions in life." A statement like this indicated some of the residues of the ancient belief in a volitional Heaven. He also adopted a compromising attitude towards religious superstitions and even consented to preserve the antiquated sacrificial ceremonies merely to make fools of the people.

The Epistemology of Xun Zi

The epistemology of Xun Zi was strongly characterized by a materialistic tendency. He stated his main position in these words: "To know the knowable belongs to the human faculty and what is knowable belongs to the laws of the material world"; that is, men are gifted with the ability to know the objective world and the objective world is knowable to men. People got their knowledge about the external world by means of their sense organs (the ears, eyes, mouth, nose and touch) which Xun Zi called "the heavenly (natural) organs". And the heart was considered by him as the thinking organ which he called "the heavenly (natural) sovereign". Through the function of the heart, the sensations received by the sense-organs were organized into knowledge. People then began to apply different terms in naming different objects, and thereby formulated and developed their common language for mutual understanding. In this way, Xun Zi formed his theory of names (terms) and realities (objects) in which the most outstanding feature was its materialistic theory of reflection.

In the process of knowing, Xun Zi paid balanced attention to both the perceptions of the senses and the function of thinking. Hence his epistemology had overcome both the one-sidedness of Mo Zi, who emphasized merely the perceptions of the sense organs, and that of Mencius, who emphasized merely the function of the thinking heart. In his assertion: "Not having learned the knowledge is not as good as having learned it; having learned it is not as good as having seen it; having seen it is not as good as understanding it; understanding it is not as good as doing it. Scholarship reached its end and goal in doing it." He thus set doing as the goal or perfection of knowledge. The notion of doing in his theory of knowledge had not as yet reached the meaning of practice in its modern sense, but nonetheless, it might be regarded as an important contribution to the treasury of ancient materialism.

Xun Zi's Theory of the Evilness of Human Nature

Xun Zi's theory of the evilness of human nature formed the theoretical foundation of his political doctrine; it was expounded as the antithesis of the theory of the goodness of human nature held by Mencius. In their essence, both theories started from the abstract and transcendental view on human nature, although human nature in its last analysis is but a social product, not something a priori. In their theories of human nature, Xun Zi and Mencius adopted different approaches in their argumentation, but they aimed at the same thing —the justification of the rationality and neccessity of the feudal rule.

The fundamental proposition of Xun Zi on human nature reads: "Human nature is evil; its goodness is artificial (i.e., acquired by training)"; or in other words, human nature is evil a priori, its goodness comes only by being remodelled a posteriori. According to his theory, human nature is no more than mere naturalness or a sort of raw material, and artificiality means giving a treatment to the raw material. Without human nature, there would be nothing left to be treated with; without artificiality, human nature could not become good by itself.

Xun Zi argued that men were born with desires such as "seeking profits" and "repugnant to the bad", preferring enjoyment to hard labour, etc.; and there was no such thing as what Mencius called "the beginnings of goodness" in human hearts. He proceeded to argue that the rule of rites and righteousness adopted by the ancient sage-kings was a matter of necessity for correcting the evils of human nature. Since human nature was inherently evil, human desires could never be satisfied. If free rein were given to human desires, then, to be sure, endless strife and social disorders would ensue. With a view to avoiding such social disasters, the ancient sage-kings instituted the rule of the rites. Such was Xun Zi's answer to the question on the origin of the rites: "Whence does the rule of the rites arise? Men by birth have desires. When desires are not satisfied, they cannot but seek for satisfaction. When this seeking for satisfaction is without a proper measure or limit, then there can only be contention. When there is contention, there will be disorder; when there is disorder, then there will be poverty. The ancient sage-kings hated this confusion, hence they established the rule of the rites in order to set limits to this confusion, to educate and nourish men's desires, to give opportunity for this seeking for satisfaction, in order that desires should never be extinguished by things, nor things should be used up by desires; that these two should support each other and should continue to co-exist. This is whence the rule of the rites arises."

This appears indeed a very elaborate theory concerning the issue of the origin of the state—of how mankind came out of the "state of nature" and entered the "civil state". This theory strikes us by its similarity to the contract theories of the Western thinkers of the 17-18th centuries. But there is this difference to remember: the modern thinkers of the West wanted to justify a civil state ruled by the newborn bourgeoisie while Xun Zi wanted to justify a civil state ruled by the newborn feudal landlords.

Xun Zi went on to expound: "To be honored as the emperor, to be as wealthy as to own the country—this what men desire all alike. But if men's desires are given a free rein, then their authority could not be endured, and things would not be sufficient to satisfy them. Hence the ancient sage-kings invented the rule of the rites and righteousness for men in order to make differentiations among them, such as the classes of the noble and the base, the disparity between the aged and the young, and the distinction between the wise and the stupid, the able and the incompetent: all to cause men to assume their duties and each to get his proper position; then and only then can the amount and grade of their emoluments be made fitting to their positions. This is the way of living in society and of enjoying harmony and unity." This theory developed by Xun Zi was to meet the need of the feudal hierarchy to which the modern theory of natural rights was in turn evolved as its antithesis.

In his viewpoint on the Way of Heaven, Xun Zi proved himself worthy of the name of a materialist; but in his theory of human nature he resorted to the rule of the sage-kings by whom the rule of the rites and righteousness was instituted and the development of history itself was activated. His viewpoint on history so exaggerated the role of the sage-kings as to deny both the initiatives of the masses and the role of material forces.

Xun Zi lived at the end of the Warring States Period when people suffered immensely from the ceaseless wars and feudal regimes of the local principalities and longed desperately for a unified country under a unified control. In the meantime, economic and social progress made unification an inevitable historical trend. Because of the reformation carried out by Shang Yang, the state of Qin became the most powerful and, on that account, was qualified to play a leading role in the fulfillment of the historical mission of the great unification. It was under such circumstances that "the contending of the hundred schools" was tending towards an ideological summarization. And the thought of Xun Zi came forth to proclaim the beginning of this new epoch in history.

As the foremost thinker representing the interests of the newborn feudal landlords, he remodelled the traditional and very pedantic Confucian doctrine of Confucius and Mencius into a fresh and lively materialism. In accordance with the will of the newborn landlords, he transformed and integrated the rites of Confucius with the spirit of the rule of the law. Xun Zi had lived and remained active for a very long time in the Academy of Ji Xia, the greatest centre of learning at that time, where he was much influenced by various schools then prevailing and critically absorbed much from each of them. In his thought one may well find the traces of the beginning of the fusion of the "hundred schools". He excelled also in literary writings and initiated the form of rhymed prose known as Fu which became an important style in later generations. He should be rightly ranked as one of the great teachers, along with Confucius and Mencius. And as mentioned above, the famous Legalist masters Han Fei and Li Si were among the most prominent of his disciples.

5. THE IDEOLOGY OF THE YIN-YANG SCHOOL

Originally the Yin-Yang School was engendered out of the art of prophecy based on the calculation of numbers and figures (divination) in the Warring States Period. Down to the Han Dynasty, the study of numbers and figures was divided into six branches: astronomy, the calendar, five elements, oracles, augury and geomancy. So the Yin-Yang School members were required to possess a certain knowledge of sciences, including astronomy, the calendar and agriculture, all of which were mingled unavoidably with large amount of witchcraft, necromancy and superstitions. Sima Tan, the father of the famous historian Sima Qian in the Han Dynasty (2nd century B.C.), criticized them for "keeping the people always restrained and in fear".[1] Another famous scholar in the Han Dynasty, Liu Qin pointed out too that "they give up human affairs and believe in spirits".[2] This school was strongly affected by the Zi Si-Mencius School and shared their idea of "the communion of Heaven and man".

The foremost Yin-Yang expert in the Warring States Period was Zou Yan (4th-3rd century B.C.), who was a native of the state of Qi and lived a bit later than Mencius. Articulate about celestial affairs, he was known by the name "Yan, the good talker on celestial affairs".[3] For a certain time he had spent his life in the Ji Xia Academy of Qi, and then travelled widely in the states of Wei, Zhao and Yan, where he was venerated by all of their princes. The king of

Yan built the Jieshi Palace for his entertainment and honoured him as a great master.[4] In the states of Zhao he was said to have refuted the theory of "a white horse is not a horse" of Gongsun Long in a confrontation. It led, so the story went, to the dismissal of the latter from the courts.[5]

Most of Zou Yan's works were lost. In the *Records of the Historian*, Sima Qian reported that the works he wrote amounted to as many as 100,000 words. *The History of Han* recorded that *The Book of Zhou Yan* consisted of forty-nine chapters and *The Transmutations of Zou Yan* fifty-six chapters. Judged from the statement of Sima Qian that "the disciples of Zou Yan wrote about the fate of the transmutations of the five virtues (power)", the book *The Transmutations of Zou Yan* might probably be composed by his disciples. Sima Qian mentioned Zou Yan as having composed an essay entitled "Zhu Yun" (the "Mastery of the Fate") which might perhaps be a chapter from *The Book of Zhou Yan*.

Zou Yan was closely related to the Confucian School. His doctrine was summarized as an exposition of "benevolence, righteousness and frugality, and the relationship between the sovereign and the subjects, the upper and the lower as well as that among the kinsmen",[6] the topic of which appeared very much in conformity with the main teachings of the Confucian School. It was said that "Zou Yan tried to persuade the sovereigns with Confucian teachings but failed; and then he elaborated his own theory of changes and transmutations which earned him a great fame".[7] So it seemed that he was first a Confucian and later became a Yin-Yang expert. His teachings on the transmutations of the five virtues (powers) was evolved from the doctrine of the five elements of the Confucian (Zi Si-Mencius) School.

The theory of Zou Yan consisted mainly of the following three aspects:

First, his celestial theory. He dealt widely with astronomy and the calendar, lecturing on the history of the natural world from its very beginning and "discussing the heaven and earth since their creation" and even "went as far as beyond the beginning of the heaven and earth and scrutinized the inscrutable (the state of the primordial chaos)".[8] But concerning this aspect of his teachings, no material now exists.

Second, his historical viewpoint of the transmutations of the five virtues (powers). His treatise "The Mastery of the Fate" dealt specifically with this topic. He idealized the Zi Si-Mencian doctrine of the five elements, which was originally a remoulding of ancient naive materialism. The "five virtues (powers)" designated the miraculous powers of metal, wood, water, fire and earth, each of which was supposed to be correlated with the fate of the reign of a certain dynasty. The destiny of a certain dynasty was said to be dominated by its corresponding virtue. The course of history developed stage by stage according to the order by which one virtue succeded the other in their cycles. Thus, the great Shun became king by his virtue of the earth; the wood subdued the earth and so it was the Xia Dynasty by its virtue of the wood to reign instead of Shun; the metal subdued the wood and so it was Shang by its virtue of metal to become kings instead of Xia; the fire subdued the metal and so it was Zhou by its virtue of fire to become kings instead of Shang. According to this theory of the "reinforcement and counteraction of the five virtues", Zou Yan prophesied that "it has to be water that will come to replace (the reign of) fire",[9] that is to say, the dynasty which would come in succession to Zhou would be one gifted with the virtue of water.

Zou Yan proclaimed that when a new dynasty would come to reign, Heaven would be sure to reveal a certain premonition beforehand, which was called the evidence of a prophesy (or a symbol). The legend had it that before the reign of the Great Yu of the Xia Dynasty the momentum of the virtue (power) of the wood had become so strong that even the plants and herbs did not whither in the fall and winter; this evidenced (or symbolized) that the Great Yu was going to reign by his virtue of wood. To the respective dominating virtue of each dynasty, there should be also a corresponding colour of dress. The Xia Dynasty reigned by its virtue of wood, the colour of which was green, so that Xia adopted the green colour for their dress. The Shang Dynasty reigned by its virtue of metal, the colour of which was white, so that Shang adopted the white colour for their dress. The Zhou Dynasty reigned by its virtue of fire, the colour of which was red, so that Zhou adopted the red colour for their dress.

In the light of Zou Yan's theory of the transmutations of the five virtues, history never remained unmoved but underwent a constant process of changing in cycles. To reduce the complexity of the moving forces of history into an esoteric theory involving the reinforcement and counteraction of the five elements: this represented an ideological effort on the part of a capricious thinker to devise a formula which, to a certain extent, predicted the historical trend towards a great unification. And the real meaning of his theory was its relation to the demand in that epoch for a great unification by the newly arisen landlord class. The First Emperor of Qin, after his unification of the whole country, took over the theory of Zou Yan and professed that the Qin Dynasty reigned by its virtue of water. He promulgated a series of decrees and institutes that corresponded to the virtue of water, including the adoption of the black colour for their dress.[10] Zou Yan's philosophy of history, though possessing its own historical significance in his own time, later became a constituent part of the ruling theories of the feudal sovereigns: that their reigns were ordained by the heavenly powers or, in other words, by the grace of God.

Third, the geographical theory of the nine great continents. Sima Qian commented as follows: He (Zou Yan) regarded the Middle Kingdom (China)—that was what the Confucian scholars called it —as occupying one of the eighty-one parts of the whole world (literally all that is below heaven). He called the Middle Kingdom the Red-Territory-Spirit-Subcontinent within the boundary of which there were nine provinces, i.e., the Nine Provinces which the Great Yu had demarcated. Besides the Middle Kingdom, or the Red-Territory-Spirit-Subcontinent, there were still eight others all alike in size, which altogether were called properly the nine Great Subcontinents; and they were encircled by seas which neither men nor birds nor beasts could ever cross. And they made up one great area or one great continent. There were altogether nine such great continents, encircled entirely by a great outer sea where heaven and earth merged together.[11] This doctrine, of course, represented merely a conjecture of the world in which the whole Middle Kingdom (China) was only a small part. But by his capricious imagination, Zou Yan enlarged the world picture in human minds and brought significant progress in their attitude toward the outside world.

Of the three aspects in Zou Yan's theory stated above, the most influential had been the transmutations of the five virtues which showed the endeavour of the Yin-Yang School to get an overall comprehension of the entity of both the natural world and human society. The communion of Heaven and man was a fictitious bridge erected by the Yin-Yang School, designed to mingle the natural and the human into a synthetic whole, as if to say the world should be a unified one, and so should be our knowledge of it.

The idea of Yin (the negative) and Yang (the positive) and the five elements embraced some naive materialistic factors as well as the superstitious and mystic ones. Therefore after the Qin and Han dynasties, this school began to differentiate along two directions. The one tended to merge with natural science, as was clearly shown in the medical theory of the Yin and Yang and of the five elements. The other tended to further develop superstitious and mystic factors which resulted in an absurd theology derived from the doctrine of the communion of Heaven and man.

6. THE IDEOLOGY OF THE LEGALIST SCHOOL

In the slave society, "It was blood lineage that served to demarcate the high and the low."[1] Social ranks were as a rule inseparably connected with wealth, and so the slave-owning nobility possessed both high rank and property. As private land property appeared in large quantity during the middle and the late Spring and Autumn Period, the landlord class began its formation. With the increase of their private land properties, they were economically growing, but in the political arena they were for the time being still powerless in general. A class which obtained its superiority economically was sure to attempt to gain political power. In order to protect their properties against the extravagances of the nobility, the landlords demanded that reforms be carried out and laws instituted; in other words, they were preparing to take the political place of the old nobility. Their foremost ideological representatives were the Legalists. In the three states of Han, Zhao and Wei (or the three Jins—so called because all of them had been a part of the state of Jin), feudalism developed much earlier than in other states, so it was there the Legalists were concentrated. Among the representatives of the early Legalist School were Li Kui, Wu Qi, Shang Yang, Shen Buhai and Shen Dao; and of the later Legalist School the greatest representative was Han Fei.

The Early Legalists

Li Kui (circa 455-395 B.C.), a native of Wei, had served the Marquis Wen of Wei as the governor of Beidi and then as his minister. In the year 453 B.C. the three houses of Han, Zhao and Wei overthrew the royal house of Zhi in the state of Jin and paved the way for the rising landlords to step forward onto the political stage. In the year 403 B.C. the three states of Han, Zhao and Wei assumed the titles of principalities, which marked the establishment of the newborn landlord regime. The Marquis Wen of Wei appointed Li Kui as his minister to carry out reforms. Li Kui abolished the hereditary status of the old nobility and in its stead enforced measures rewarding and punishing each according to what he personally deserved.[2] For the sake of developing the feudal economy and protecting the landlord class, he wrote Fa Jin (*The Book of Laws*) in six chapters in which he stressed; "Nothing is more important for the reign of a king than the prevention of robbers",[3] a proposition which intended to ensure the property of the newborn landlords from being violated. The content of his work embodied the will of the landlord class in opposition to both the nobility and the peasants. The Book of Laws was the first feudal code in a more or less systematic form. It laid down the foundation of the feudal jurisdiction before the Qin Dynasty.

Wu Qi (circa 440-381 B.C.), a native of Wei, was well reputed as a strategist and a statesman in the early times of the Warring States. He was appointed the governor of Sihe by the Marquis Wen of Wei to assist Li Kiu in his reforms. Later, he went to the state of Chu and served King Dao of Chu in his reforms. He recommended "to make the laws and decrees clear"[4] and revised the old hereditary system by limiting the succession of a hereditary title to three generations. His reforms struck a blow at the old nobility of Chu, who contrived against him and murdered him soon after the death of King Dao. However, it was due to his reforms that the poor and weak state of Chu became wealthy and powerful.

Shang Yang (?-338 B.C.), a native of Wei, spent most of his life in a career of reformation for the state of Qin. Before his reforms, the old nobility of Qin held a powerful sway in that country and slavery still prevailed. Compared with other states in the east, the state of Qin appeared rather backward. Under the patronage of Duke Xiao of Qin, he twice initiated large-scale reforms. He abolished the hereditary system of the old nobility based on blood lineage and adopted the practice of rewarding military merits.

Among other measures of reform, he carried out a system of registry of the inhabitants within the realm, a unified responsibility system for any offender against the law, the encouragement of farming and weaving and of the small farming economy (in opposition to the large-scale farming adopted under slavery), the abolishment of the nine-square farms, the cultivation of criss-cross paths in the countryside, unification of weights and measure, institution of the Qin laws and prohibition of travelling scholars. Although, like Wu Qi, he did not escape the fate of being murdered by the old nobility, the reforms introduced by him were still enforced in the state of Qin after the death of Duke Xiao, because they suited the needs of social development at that time. The solidification of feudalism in Qin brought that poor and backward state in almost a single surge to the forefront of the most advanced and most wealthy and powerful, thus laying down the foundation for the future unification of the whole of China.

The theoretical ground of the reforms launched by the early Legalists was their evolutionary view of history. Shang Yang explained the course of history in this way: "During the time of Hao Ying (a legendary sage-king), people earned their living by lumbering and hunting", and "during the time of the Faery Farmer, peoples' food depended on the farming of men and their dresses on the weaving of women; the society was then well governed without any administration and the king reigned with no use of arms",[5] The times of Hao Ying and the Faery farmer might be roughly equated to that stage of primitive society when there was already a division of labour between men and women, but not yet a state nor an army nor punishment. Later, the state appeared and together with it the rituals between the sovereigns and the subjects, fathers and sons and husbands and wives, hence "there were penalties and punishments within the state and arms and armours outside the state",[6] that is, suppression within and waging wars outside.

At any rate, this provided a progressive view relating to the evolution of history and had a historical background. Such a viewpoint was employed by Shang Yang as an ideological weapon to refute the doctrine held by the old nobility that "It is always no fault to observe the old ways and it is always no evil to follow the old rites".[7] For the Legalists, history was always developing and changing, so the rites and laws that governed a state should never remain unchanged. Therefore Shang Yang advised people "not to observe the old ways" and "not to follow the old rites".[8] Such was the theoretical basis upon which the Legalists demanded reforms.

In their effort to attack the old nobility with their reforms, the Legalists needed to win the patronage of the sovereigns. In the cases of Li Kui, Wu Qi and Shang Yang, they were all determined to exalt the position of the sovereign and to reinforce his power. In order to serve this purpose, they elaborated theories on law, on statecraft and on power.

Shang Yang laid emphasis on law, asserting that a sovereign had to hold the law as his standard. He argued that a state could certainly be well governed, provided it was governed by law. And the law should be clear and easy to understand,[9] so that when the people once learned it they would not ignore it; otherwise the sovereign would endanger himself. If the laws were not unified, the society would fall into disorder. If the laws were unified, then "the administration need not listen to the indications of the sovereign and the people need not follow the officials in their actions",[10] because everything would be then settled by the rule of the law.

On the one hand, Shang Yang advised the sovereign to concentrate his power by employing the law to prevent the old nobility from committing all kinds of outrages. And on the other hand, the law served to suppress the labouring people and to prevent them from any violation of the prestige and privileges of the rising landlord class.

The thought of Shen Buhai contributed to the Legalist theory mainly with respect to statecraft. He was originally a man from the lower stratum in the state of Zheng but later owing to his mastery of the study of statecraft he was appointed by Marquis Zhao of Han as his minister. His works have been lost, but in *The Book of Han Fei Zi* some paragraphs of his dialogues with Marquis Zhao on the topic of statecraft have been preserved.

He interpreted statecraft as the political tactics with which a sovereign should and could rule over his subjects. He asserted: "Statecraft consists in awarding offices according to the functions required and in exacting actualities in accord with the names. It consists in keeping in the sovereign's hand the power over others' lives and in examining the abilities of the officials. All these are what should be kept tightly in the sovereign's grasp."[11] Such practices were considered able to strengthen the power of the sovereign and to prevent the subjects from usurpation or rebellion.

The thought of Shen Dao made its contribution to the Legalist theory mainly with respect to the study of power. He was a native of Zhao and lived somewhat earlier than Shen Buhai and Han Fei. He had spent some time in the Academy of Ji Xia in Qi and was appointed an official in the year 325 B.C.[12] His complete works have been lost since early in the Song Dynasty. Of the three editions of his writings now extant, the one from the Shoushange Library edited by Qian Xi Zuo was generally acknowledged as the best. In it were collected seven of his essays together with seventeen pieces from his fragments.

Shen Dao laid special emphasis on the importance of power for the sovereign. Han Fei quoted his words as follows: "Yao the Sage as an ordinary man would have been unable to govern three people, whereas Jie the Tyrant as the Son of Heaven was able to bring the whole empire into tumult. From this I know that it is power and position that should be relied upon, whereas talent and wisdom are not worthwhile to be respected."[13] As a parable, he cited the story of Li Zhu (or Li Lou in *The Book of Mencius*,) who was said to be able to discern the slightest hair at a distance of hundreds of yards away but was unable to see anything whatsoever under water. The reason for that, he explained, "is not that his eyesight was not good enough but that his position prevented him from seeing them."[14]

Hence the conclusion he reached was that the position and power held by the sovereign was of cardinal importance. He considered it unneccessary for a sovereign to be talented and wise; so long as the sovereign grasped in his hands the necessary power or authority, he could do everything he ordered or deny what he prohibited. By advocating "all administrations follow authority and all officials follow the sovereign,"[15] he tried to concentrate the political powers in the hands of the sovereign alone. Obviously, this doctrine was advantageous to the autocracy of a centralized feudal regime.

The laws advocated by Li Kui, Wu Qi and Shang Yang, the statecraft advocated by Shen Buhai and the power advocated by Shen Dao were all essentially in the service of the establishment of the autocratic despotism of the feudal landlords,—each in its own way and with its own arguments. And the historical task of formulating a systematic Legalist ideology through a critical absorption of all the three branches of the early Legalists fell to the lot of the past master of the pre-Qin Legalist School, Han Fei.

The Later Legalist Han Fei

Han Fei (circa 280-233 B.C.) was born in an old noble house of the state of Han and in his youth "took interests in the study of punishments, names, laws and statecraft, while basing his doctrine on the founders of Taoism, Huang Di and Lao Zi".[16] Both he and Li Si were disciples of Xun Zi, the last master of the pre-Qin Canfucian School. Many a time Han Fei advised the King of Han to carry out reforms for the strengthening of the nation but his advice was declined. Thenceforth he engaged himself in his writings. When the King (later the First Emperor) of Qin read his works, he enjoyed them so much that he invited Han Fei to come to Qin. After Han Fei arrived there, he was framed by Li Si with fabricated accusations and finally committed suicide in prison.

Using as a basis the ideas of the three groups of the early Legalists, Han Fei elaborated his own political doctrine by coordinating and unifying law, statecraft and power.

Han Fei held that all these elements were indispensable for the effective rule of a sovereign. He criticized Shang Yang for not understanding the importance of statecraft (political tactics and manoeuvering), so that though Qin became strong and wealthy by his advocacy of the rule of the law, there were still no effective ways and means to detect what ambitions the high officials were embracing. Hence the power and wealth of the state of Qin resulted merely in the growth of property and influence of the high officials. He also criticized Shen Buhai's emphasis on statecraft (political tactics) as "neither good at ruling by law nor at unifying the decrees, so that there sprout out lots of disastrous problems":[17] Therefore Han Fei said: "Both of them [Shang Yang and Shen Buhai] were imperfect in treating law and statecraft";[18] for "if the sovereign be without statecraft, it would cause weakness above; if the ministers be without the law, it would cause confusion below".[19] And Han Fei had law, statecraft and power combined together, with the rule of law at the core of his ideology.

Han Fei compared the law to the instrument employed by the carpenter in straightening crooked wood, that is, the law should serve as a standard to unify the ideas of all the people. He affirmed definitely: "All speeches and actions that do not observe the law have to be prohibited."[20] Since laws were to be observed by everyone, they "should be codified in written form, preserved in the governmental offices and proclaimed publicly to the people",[21] so as to make them well known to everyone all over the country. And since the laws were what all the subjects should follow, he argued: "Education should consist of the laws, and the tutors should consist of the officials."[22] By this identification of ruling and instructing, he set forth an ideal model for the reign of despotism in the history of China.

The sovereign was advised to be good at discerning the tricks and treachery of his ministers and officials by means of statecraft. Han Fei said: "Statecraft should lay deeply hidden in the bosom of the sovereign, so that he may rule over them in extreme secrecy."[23] This statecraft was also termed "the art of punishment". And he made an exposition of it in these words: "In order to prevent any treachery, the ruler of men should make his judgment by combining the punishments and the names."[24] By "names" he meant the speeches and by "punishments" (xing,) the affairs or deeds. That is to say, the sovereign should appoint his officials to take charge of the affairs they proposed and should then pass his own judgments on them. If they had done their affairs fairly well as they had promised, they should be rewarded; if not, they should be punished. This is what Han Fei described: "It is the sovereign who holds the names and the officials who are to bring forth the effects."[25] This is what he meant by "the examination of actualities (shi,) according to their names."[26]

The rewards and punishments constituted the two cardinal vehicles of power in the hands of the sovereign and were also called "the two handles",[27] or "the handle of life and death".[28] If the sovereign was skillful in using the "art of punishments and names" and held tightly in his hands "the handle of life and death," then "all his inferiors would be kept in constant fears ... the ministers would be prevented from usurping power and his kinsmen and relatives would not dare to make any bargain".[29]

Han Fei taught that it was by means of power that laws and statecraft were capable of being enforced; in other words, power (or the position of power) was the prerequisite of the enforcement of the law and statecraft. In this respect, Han Fei inherited and further developed Shen Dao's doctrine of power. By "power" he meant the sovereign's supreme position with all its authority. So he asserted: "Power is the means for maintaining supremacy over the masses";[30] and again: "It is with his authority (power) that a sovereign with ten thousand warring chariots might come to dominate the world and to conquer all other principalities."[31] Hence power was meant as an instrument by which a sovereign was to rule his country as well as to wage wars upon others.

Han Fei drew a bitter conclusion on the relationship between man and man. He pointed out that there were always sharp contradictions between the sovereign and his inferiors and between the sovereign and his relatives and intimates. He believed that the submission of the subjects to their sovereign was not because there was any intimacy between them but solely because the subjects were under the constant restraint of the sovereign and were obliged to be so.[32] This political view of his, together with his view on human nature, was essentially akin to that of Niccolo Machiavelli, or rather let us say it was a kind of Machiavellianism in ancient oriental form. In fact, the more one reads Han Fei, the more one is reminded of Machiavelli. Both of them lived at a time when political intrigues and treacheries prevailed, and both of them longed for a powerful sovereign with keen insight into the depth of human nature who might manage to build a strong and prosperous country by the rule of very cunning statecraft. And what is more important, both of them shared the same pessimistic view of human nature as something intrinsically base and bestial.

Starting from this point of view, Han Fei went on to say: "Each day there were hundreds of wars between the superiors and the inferiors" in the court, and "the reason that the officials do not as yet murder their sovereign is simply because their treacherous clique is not yet well organized".[33] Once they discover the necessary conditions to do it, they are sure to usurp the throne. Hence in order to consolidate the position of the sovereign, it is necessary to get the political powers centralized within the grasp of the sovereign alone, or as Han Fei himself put it: "Events occur each day all over the country, but the essential among them should be centred to the judgment of the sovereign. When the sovereign grasps the essential, all the country would pay homage to him."[34] This doctrine of his contributed directly to the establishment of the centralized feudal regime of the Qin Dynasty.

The Qin Dynasty was built after the theoretical model of Han Fei, who among other proposals on the necessity of a centralized autocracy strongly advocated the unification of ideologies. He affirmed: "The ice and the burning charcoal cannot co-exist long within the same pot, the cold and the hot weather cannot dwell together at the same time; so a country cannot be orderly in its reign with different schools of learning in opposition and contention."[35] He insisted on the necessity of upholding solely the Legalist School to the exclusion of all other schools. With the help of his doctrine, the First Emperor of Qin accomplished the historical task of the great unification of the whole of China—an accomplishment which might well be attributed to the thought of Han Fei.

However, his doctrine was, after all, too cruel and ruthless to be practicable and at the same time too incomplete in its comprehension of human nature and human society; or perhaps one may say of him that he did not see life steadily nor see it whole. What is noble and ennobling in human nature was completely ignored by him; and by doing so the human relationship was reduced to a matter of personal speculation and mutual utilization—it was indeed "a war of each against everyone" in the Hobbesian sense. And some ancient writers had already criticized him to that effect.

The fact that soon afterwards the great peasant uprising overthrew the reign of the short-lived Qin Dynasty proved the bankruptcy of Han Fei's ideology. The tragedy of the Legalists lay in the fact that they depended merely on the personal patronage of the sovereign but not on the wills and wishes of the populace.

Han Fei stressed: "The law does not flatter the dignitaries", meaning "punishments do not evade ministers and rewards do not leave out the common people".[36] This was the antithesis to the privileges of the old nobility. It benefited the newly-rising landlord class and played an active role in history at a pivotal period. And his demand for a centralized autocracy was in keeping with the historical tendency towards full unification.

But his emphasis on statecraft afforded a theoretical implement for all kinds of political schemes and intrigues in feudal power struggles for the ruling class of the later generations. It should be admitted that a very large part of his thought constituted a deep-rooted tradition in the ideology and in the practices of age-old feudal political tricks and treacheries. This feudal autocractic ideology of his has remained one of the lasting influences of the Legalist School on the history of China.

In his historical viewpoint, Han Fei inherited and developed the ideas of Shang Yang. Shang Yang divided the course of history into three successive stages: "In the archaic antiquity people loved their relatives and were fond of what was their own, in the middle antiquity they honoured talent and enjoyed virtues, and in recent epochs they valued noble ranks and respected the governmental offices."[37] Han Fei agreed with him on the proposition that each stage had its own specific problem so that in different epochs there were different problems for people to solve and the methods adopted should be different. Hence, with the progress of history, the social and political institutions were always changing. Therefore he asserted: "When the epochs differ, the issues differ; and when the issues differ, the procedures to solve them also change."[38] With this view in mind, he proceeded to oppose the dictum "follow the ancient kings", or return to the ancients, as professed by the Confucian School. Upon this topic he cited a well-known parable: "Once there was a man of Song tilling his farm in the midst of which stood the stem of a tree; and one day a hare in full course rushed against that stem, broke its neck and died. Thereupon the man left his plough and stood waiting at that tree in the hope that he would catch another hare. But he never caught another hare and was ridiculed by the people of Song." The conclusion he reached was: "If you wish to rule the people of today with the methods of the governments of the ancient kings, you would do exactly the same thing as that man who waited for a hare by his tree."[39]

Compared with others, Han Fei's division of the stages of historical evolution was a far more advanced one. It not only acknowledged the changes and developments in history, but also endeavoured to probe the reasons for them. For example, he mentioned that the growth of population would cause a scarcity of material wealth and hence cause contentions in human society, and remarked: "In the archaic antiquity people competed in virtues, in the middle antiquity people competed by intelligence, and nowadays people strive after forces."[40] Confronting the situation of striving after forces, or power, he urged the rule of the law as the sole efficient means to make a nation strong and wealthy.

Yet, hard as he tried to interpret the development of history in the light of material causes, the limitedness of his world view nevertheless prevented him from realizing the real motives and moving forces in the making of history. He paid no attention whatever to the role of the masses and even went so far as to assert: "The wisdom of the people is just the heart of a baby upon which you can never trust."[41] For him, the people were of no significance at all because after all history was created only by a small number of heroes.

Han Fei developed Xun Zi's theory of the evilness of human nature and employed it fully in his socio-historical viewpoint. He taught that each one seeking his own interest makes the relationship between man and man no more than a clash of personal interests. For instance, the relationship between the sovereign and his inferiors was but a bargain in which the inferiors did all they could for the sovereign who in his turn rewarded them with high ranks and handsome pensions as an exchange.[42] As for the usefulness of the people, the sovereign recognized it only by hurling them to the battle front in times of war and exacting from them labour and taxes in times of peace.[43] Even among the members of the royal house, there were always sharp conflicts of interest as well. So it was of the utmost importance for a sovereign to safeguard himself from usurpation or regicide by his skilful mastery of statecraft. And this relationship holds valid also among the common people. Cartwrights of the luxurious carriages wished that more people would become wealthy in order to enjoy their products, while coffin makers wished people would die earlier. All men are motivated by their own interests, independent of their personal moral qualities.

Upon this theory of human nature were founded his political doctrines, such as the rule of the law, the application of severe penalties and harsh punishment, "the art of punishments and names", etc. Once such a theory was applied to the field of politics, its class character in favour of the landlords was exposed in its full nakedness. At the same time, it also exposed the hypocrisy of the traditional ideas and ceremonies in the slave society by openly declaring that the relation of the ruling class to the people was but cruel suppression and exploitation and no more than that. It showed how the landlord class in its rising stage dared to face the bitter reality of social life with a realistic spirit. Since all his viewpoints were for the establishment of centralized feudal autocracy, they invariably and inevitably incited the resistance of the people. This explained why the historical role of his progressiveness was either ignored or short-lived.

Along with his reform theory, his philosophical ideas on the Way of Heaven and on epistemology should be considered the most advanced of the pre-Qin period. Variegated as the origin of his thought was, the influence of his master Xun Zi appeared most manifest. He had also absorbed the thought of the Taoist and the Mohist Schools as well as some of the materialism of the Ji Xia Academy.

His view on the Way of Heaven was expounded in his interpretation of the doctrine of Lao Zi. He reinterpreted the Tao (the Way; or what seems a better translation, the Logos) of Lao Zi in his own way. The term Tao literaly means the Way or the Word. The Gospel of St. John reads: "In the beginning there was the Word." Here the term "Word" in the Greek version of the New Testament is "Logos". It seems that the Tao of Lao Zi bears just the same connotation as the "Word" in the sense that "in the beginning there was the Word (Logos). The Word was with God and God was the Word". But Han Fei transformed it by explaining: "Tao is that by which everything becomes what it is"[44] and "Tao is that by which everything is completed or accomplished".[45] Thus the idealistic conception of the Tao of Lao Zi was recast materialistically into the idea of a general principle or a material origin of the world.

Another important concept elaborated by Han Fei was the

Principle (Li). He remarked: "The principles are the lines along which things are completed."[46] The term "principle" here may roughly be equated to specific laws of specific things. Again he said: "There is nothing without a rule";[47] so the principle also corresponded roughly to the rule of things. In other words, things are to be understood by getting hold of their laws or rules. To do things in conformity with their laws one would succeed; otherwise one would fail. It was the first time in the intellectual history of China that by the category of "principle" both the general laws of the world and the specific laws of specific things were explicitly involved. Credit should be attributed to Han Fei.

Moreover, the principle (li) is by no means unchangeable but is in a state of constant changing, so he asserted: "The fixed principle emerges and perishes, exists and dies out, flourishes and declines."[48] When applied to the political field, this idea would lead to the conclusion that every political institution is, as a matter of fact, always changing. It was the philosophical basis for his demand for political reforms.

His view of the Way of Heaven put Han Fei in direct opposition to the belief in the Mandate of Heaven and deities. He explained fairly well that the idea of the spirits originated at a time when people fell ill or suffered hardships. If people were not threatened by diseases or disasters, they would have no need of belief in spirits at all. Against the superstitions prevailing at the end of the Warring States Period, he wrote an essay advocating atheism. He considered superstition toward the Mandate of Heaven and spirits to be signals of a nation approaching the brink of collapse, saying: "Belief in the choice of the dates, adoration of the spirits, reliance on auguries and indulgence in sacrificial offerings—all these signify that the nation is going to fall."[49] This atheistic attitude showed the self-reliance of the rising landlords on their own strength.

In epistemology, Han Fei contributed his doctrine of "comparison and test". He taught the use of a series of comparisons to see whether an opinion or a statement was correct; and that it should be tested by facts to see whether it was in conformity with reality. This is what he called: "To decide the right and the wrong by examining the names and the reality, and to judge the statements and propositions by using comparisons and tests."[50] This assertion touched upon an essential issue in the history of epistemology, i.e., to hold practice as the criterion in the test for truth. On this account, Han Fei opposed any kind of a priori knowledge, which he identified with groundless conjectures.[51] In his works Han Fei cited many vivid examples illustrating the fact that truth could only be proved or verified by practice. For instance, whether a sword was sharp or not could hardly be judged by its colour or shape alone, even by an expert craftsman, but by using it to butcher livestock everyone could easily draw a correct conclusion.[52]

Han Fei developed the materialistic epistemology of the pre-Qin philosophers. But his epistemology was inextricably entangled with his "art of punishments and names". For him, the judgment of what is right or wrong should be examined by "comparisons and tests", but the final standard of the "comparisons and tests" consisted in the laws and decrees. And after all is said and done, what conforms to the laws and decrees is right, and what does not is wrong. And thus the theory of knowledge in the quest of truth was vulgarized by him so as to serve only a pragmatic basis for the execution of laws and the decrees. Han Fei advocated unification by the sovereign of the thoughts of the people by laws and decrees, and his theory itself furnished an ideological implement for this unification of thoughts by the sovereign. His materialistic epistemology was thus stamped with the narrowness and shallowness of the newborn landlords; for, after all, truth is something that exists by its own right and ought not to be judged by reference merely to its immediate political or social effects.

Chapter 3
IDEOLOGY OF THE WARRING STATES PERIOD (II)

1. THE IDEOLOGY OF THE TAOIST SCHOOL —LAO ZI, SONG XING AND YIN WEN

The founder of the Taoist School was Lao Zi who lived by the end of the Spring and Autumn Period. Down to the Warring States Period, this school had been differentiating in the main along two directions, one of which was represented by Song Xing and Yin Wen, the other by Zhuang Zi.

The Ideology of Lao Zi

It is hard to make certain the basic facts about the life of Lao Zi. According to *Records of the Historian*, his family name was Li and his personal name was Er with the cognomen Dan. He was a native of the Ku district in the state of Chu (now Gui De, in Henan Province), and lived at about the same time as Confucius, but seemed an elder to him. It was said that he had served as an official historian to the royal house of Zhou and became well known for his versatile learning; and that Confucius had inquired from him about the rites of Zhou.

The ideology of Lao Zi was set forth in *The Book of Lao Zi*, or *Dao De Jing*. It should be admitted that *The Book of Lao Zi* was written at a much later date, roughly about the middle Warring States Period, that is, not much earlier than *The Book of Zhuang Zi*. In the year 1973, in the Han tombs No. 3 excavated at Mawangdui, Changsha, Hunan, there were found two versions of the manuscript of *The Book of Lao Zi* which differed from the prevailing edition both in their arrangements, the *De Jing* being put before the *Dao*

86

Jing, and in their chapter orders and wordings. It was ascertained by experts that the newly found versions were closer to the original texts of *The Book of Lao Zi*.

As evidenced in his political theory, Lao Zi was well versed with the rites of Zhou and knew its hypocrisy deeply. "The rites (propriety) is the thiness of loyalty and honesty, and the beginning of disorder,"[1] said he. In view of the collapse of the ancient rites and music, a trend which had become dominant since the Spring and Autumn Period, Lao Zi went against the adoption of the rule of the rites. And at the same time, he also developed a deep hatred towards the rule of the law. He remarked: "When the law and decree become more conspicuous, there will be more robbers and thieves."[2] Hence he stood in opposition to both the Confucians and the Legalists.

He exposed many acute social contradictions of his time and pointed out: "The palace is kept clean and nice, and the fields are full of weeds and the granaries are quite empty."[3] And again: "The people are starving; because the man on top devours too much tax, so they are starving."[4] That is to say, the starvation of the people was caused by the heavy taxation of the governing class. Such an exposure should be ranked among the most penetrating in ancient times. He even attacked the sovereigns, comparing them to the chieftains of robbers who "wear embroidered clothes, carry sharp weapons, are satiated in food and drink and have excessive treasures and goods."[5]

Lao Zi taught that both the rule of the rites and the rule of the law had proved ineffective and that the best method of governing in their stead was the rule of "non-activity", or the rule of non-ruling. And conversely, non-activity means also non-inactivity, for inactivity—i.e., making up one's mind never to do anything—means also an activity; so that non-ruling implies that nothing is unruled. In this argumentation from activity to non-activity and from non-activity to non-inactivity, we find in him on a higher level than all the previous thinkers.

In fact, this position of Lao Zi reflected a passive attitude of a decadent mentality of a declining class. And his penetrating exposure of social irrationality was, to a certain degree, to give vent to his dissatisfaction with the new feudal institution from the standpoint of the antiquated nobility. The non-activity—and it should be borne in mind that non-activity is identified with non-inactivity—proposed by him was at its bottom another method of governing the people. So he emphasized: "I do not act and the people reform themselves; I love tranquillity and the people rectify themselves; I employ non-activity and the people become prosperous; I have no desires and the people become simple by themselves."[6] This proposal was in reality no more than to ask the rulers to adopt milder measures so as to make the people obey their rule more willingly. His doctrine of the rule of non-activity afforded the rulers, so to speak, an invisible rope to bind up the people by rendering them into a state of inertia and depriving them of any reason to resist or rebel.

Furthermore, Lao Zi invented an obscurantist policy for making fools of the people. He remarked: "The reason why the people are hard to govern is only that they know too much,"[7] and therefore "the ancients who were good in practising the Way [Tao] did not teach the people with intelligence but kept them in ignorance".[8] Being ignorant, the people would be kept "void of knowledge and desire"[9] and thereby it would be easy for the rulers to govern.

Under the guidance of this idea of non-activity, Lao Zi designed his ideal social model of "a small country with few inhabitants" in which "though there be boats and carriages, no one will ride in them; though there be armours and weapons, no one will exhibit them" and "the neighboring states will be so close that they can see each other and hear the sounds of the neighbors' roosters and dogs but the people will grow old and die without having visited each other".[10] This vista, almost like a return to primitive society, was the source from which Lao Zi drew his inspiration.

This political doctrine of Lao Zi was founded on a view of the Way of Heaven which was no more than a metaphysical exposition of his theory of non-activity. In his view of the Way of Heaven, he discarded the traditional idea of the Mandate of Heaven (or of God), and in its stead he elaborated the idea of Tao (Dao, the Way or rather Logos) as the source of the world. For him, Tao is formless, invisible, untouchable, soundless and tasteless; it was something indescribable in chaos or trance, trans-temporal and trans-spatial and in eternal immobility. Tao was regarded by him as "the forefather of all things",[11] i.e., the lord master of the world. It even "preceded God"[12] and "existed before Heaven and Earth";[13] and all things in the world were generated by it. Thereupon he expounded a cosmogony with a semi-poetic and semi-philosophic expression in these words: "Tao begets One. One begets Two. Two begets Three. Three begets all things."[14] This paragraph of his might be interpreted: Tao, the Logos, begot the entity (or being) which was divided into two: the Yin (the negative or the passive) and the Yang (the positive or the active). The interaction and the intercourse of the Yin and the Yang generated all things in the world. So he remarked again: "All things in the world are generated by Being, and Being is generated by Non-being."[15] Here the proposition "Being is generated by Non-being" is equivalent to that of "Tao begets one"; Being is equivalent to one and Non-being to Tao. That Being is derived from Non-being (Tao) and all things in the world are generated by Being (One) implies that Tao (the Logos) is the essential or the transcendental from which the actual world is derived. By Tao is meant not the material substance but the Absolute Spirit, or rather the Logos (the Word) indeed.

From this idealistic system Lao Zi deduced his aprioristic epistemology. He asserted: "Without going out of doors, one can know the whole world. Without looking out of the window, one can see the Tao of Heaven. The farther one goes, the less one knows. Therefore, the Sage does not go and yet knows, does not see yet names, does not act yet completes."[16] This is an extreme extension of his metaphysical theorizing in the field of epistemology. He proclaimed that men were born with innate knowledges which depended neither on the experiences of the senses nor on any kind of practice, social or scientific. He advised people to "block the passage and shut the door",[17] that is, to blockade all the sense organs without any contact with the outside world. Not only did he deny the possibility of any perceptual knowledge, but he even refused to recognize the role of any rational thinking. He taught that any genuine knowledge into the nature of things could only be obtained through a mystic intuition. So he remarked: "Attain the ultimate emptiness, maintain the absolute tranquillity. All things move and grow; and I observe their return."[18] This means that all things start out of emptiness, all movements out of tranquillity; therefore though all things move and change, they will ultimately return to the Non-being. Thus by mere speculation, one might get true knowledge from contemplating the comings and goings of all things. Therefore he radically opposed any study or learning, declaring: "The pursuit of learning increases daily, while the pursuit of Tao decreases daily."[19] That is, the more one learns, the more the Tao suffered. This theory led him to his policy of making fools of the people.

Idealistic as his theory is, there are yet embraced in it many naive dialectic elements. From his own observations he learned that social life was ever changing and so also were all things in nature. The social and natural changes as he witnessed them gave birth to the dialectic elements in his thoughts.

Lao Zi acknowledged that all things were composed of two opposite sides in a unity of contradiction, such as having and having-not, hard and easy, long and short, strong and weak, honour and shame, fortune and misfortune, large and small, life and death, intelligent and foolish, victory and failure, etc. The two opposite sides are by no means isolated and independent in itself but are interdependent mutually. So he observed: "Being and Non-Being beget each other; hard and easy complement each other"[20] and so forth: propositions like these show that Lao Zi was well aware of the unity of opposites in a contradiction.

At the same time, Lao Zi also observed some phenomena relating to mutual transformation of contradictory opposites. He asserted: "Good fortune lieth within bad, bad fortune lurketh within good",[21] thus pointing out that things may transform into their opposites. But in his comprehension (or rather miscomprehension) of them, such transformations were taking place unconditionally. This way of thinking opened the road to the theory of relativism, which was later developed to its culmination in the thoughts of Zhuang Zi.

Lao Zi had made some very good observations on the quantitative nature of things in their course of development. He observed: "A tree as big as one's embrace originates from a root-let, a nine-storey terrace begins with a heap of earth, a thousand-*li* journey starts from beneath one's feet."[22] But this germination of his developmental viewpoint was stifled under the burden of his idealistic system. The development of things as comprehended by him remained in a simple cyclic form of repetition instead of a spiral and upward form, or as he put it: "Returning is Tao's motion."[23] He considered that things would return toward their original position after arriving at their extremities; and so he advocated not pushing things to develop ever further but rather preventing them from developing and restraining or stopping them by keeping them in a moderate state so as to avoid their transformation into their opposites. Hence he proclaimed: "The rigid and stark are disciples of death, while the supple and weak are disciples of life."[24] For him, to be kept in a state of being supple and weak is the way to avoid death and to win victory over the strong.

This idea of Lao Zi was further developed into a philosophy of deception in dealing with the people; as he taught: "About to destroy it, let it be first advanced. About to snatch it, let it be first given away."[25] The statecraft or political tactics of Han Fei, the foremost spokesman of the Legalist School, was much influenced by this doctrine. The strategists made use of it in dealing with their enemies. And the sovereigns of the later generations absorbed part of it for their method of governing the people.

The Ideology of Song Xing and Yin Wen

During the Warring States Period, the Academy of Ji Xia was founded outside the western gate of Lin Zi, the capital of the state of Qi; and the scholars who swarmed there were generally called "the scholars of Ji Xia" or "the School of Ji Xia", who were said to amount to "more than one thousand"[26] in its most flourishing days. Among them, "seventy six were given houses and designated as senior officials who did not hold administrative duties but made proposals and advice".[27] Some of the most noted scholars of this period, such as Zou Yan, Chunyu Kun, Tien Bing, Shen Dao, Huan Yuan and others, had spent part of their lives there. Learning at the Ji Xia Academy with its ups and downs had lasted a century and more till the downfall of the state of Qi. Although it seemed that various schools of learning were incorporated in it, it was the Taoist School that reigned supreme.

There the followers of the Taoist School developed the ideology of Lao Zi in three lines, each with its own characteristic features. One group was represented by Song Xing and Yin Wen, the other by Tien Bing and Shen Dao, and another by Guan Yin (i.e., Huan Yuan). It was said that *The Book of Lao Zi* was arranged and revised by Guan Yin, who had reserved in it much of the ideas of Non-activity of Lao Zi. The group of Tien Bing and Shen Dao advocated "reforms in conformity with Tao"[28] the ideas of which approached those of the Legalist School. But the most important of these three groups was that of Song Xing and Yin Wen.

Song Xing was also named Song Keng or Song Rong Zi or Zi Song Zi, and Yin Wen was his pupil. It is very hard to ascertain the basic facts about their lives and activities. It was said that Song Xing was a native of the state of Song. According to the records in *The Book of Mencius*, Song Xing had discoursed with Mencius, who addressed him with the honourable title Sir and called himself in a modest way by his own name Ke. Very probably Song Xing was his senior and flourished in the reigns of the Kings Wei and Xuan of Qi (in the later half of the 4th century B.C.). Yin Wen was a native of the state of Qi and lived a bit later than Song Zing, at about the reigns of the Kings Xuan and Min (in the early years of the 3rd century B.C.), because in *Lu's Spring and Autumn Annals* there was a record of the dialogue between Yin Wen and King Min of Qi.

Both Song Xing and Yin Wen had stayed quite a time in the Ji Xia Academy. But owing to the fact that their writings had long been lost, their doctrines had never been paid due attention by later scholars. It was only some decades ago that scholars began to note that some chapters in *The Book of Guan Zi (The Book of Guan Zhong*, or rather the book attributed to Guan Zhong) were in fact the posthumous works of Song Xing and Yin Wen;[29] since then it has become possible for the world of learning to give an appropriate valuation to their places in the history of ideas.

The famous Han historian Ban Gu said the work of Song Xing, i.e., *The Book of Song Zi*, "amplified the doctrine of Huang Di and Lao Zi"[30] and listed it under the heading of the Taoist School. However, the doctrines of Song Xing and Yin Wen were evidently much more imbued with an eclectic tone. For example, their main propositions that "they checked aggression and proposed disarmament in order to save their generation from war" and that they "desired few things" sounded very much like the teachings of the Mohist School; hence Xun Zi placed Song Xing together with Mo Zi. Nonetheless, the ideas of Song Xing and Yin Wen were not the same as the Mohist School, because they upheld "benevolence and righteousness", which came closer to the Confucian School. Zhuang Zi spoke of them: "By warmth of affection they sought the harmony of joy in order to harmonize the world."[31] It meant probably that they intended to harmonize the Taoists with the Mohists and Confucians. At any rate, it might be ascertained that the doctrine of Song Xing and Yin Wen was the product of a transitional era and constituted an intermediate link between different schools of the Warring States Period. They had influenced both Mencius and Xun Zi of the Confucian School and the Legalist Han Fei. For a more penetrating study of the ancient history of ideas, it is worthwhile to study anew the ideology of Song Xing and Yin Wen and to revaluate them in a new historical perspective.

In their political viewpoints, Song Xing and Yin Wen discarded the backward-looking ideal of "a small country with few inhabitants" preached by Lao Zi, and inclined more towards the Legalist line.

Song Xing developed the "rule of Non-activity" of Lao Zi into a new theory that "Non-activity is the way of the sovereigns while activity is the way of the inferiors"[32] by which he tried to introduce a new kind of relationship between the sovereign and his subjects. Song Xing taught that a sovereign should behave himself in accordance with the principle of Non-activity, or in conformity with nature; and he called it "the way of tranquillity without any enforcement".[33] Also, he put it in a figurative way, saying: "A sovereign can neither gallop instead of a horse, nor fly instead of a bird";[34] so that he should not and could not try to do what his inferiors should or could do, but ought to be contented only to give rein to them. This theory was inherited by Han Fei, who made it one of the guiding principles for the sovereign in governing his inferiors, or what he termed "statecraft".

Concerning the issue of the relationship between the sovereign and his inferiors, Song Xing and Yin Wen were among the opponents against the old traditions of the old nobility. They asked: "When an inferior assumes power in place of his sovereign, it is called usurpation. Then how should an act of usurpation be praised as in the case of King Wu of Zhou [who overthrew the reign of the Shang Dynasty]?"[35] Hence, it was not necessarily an act of usurpation that an inferior took the place of his sovereign. This idea was similar to that of Mencius in his treatment of the relationship between the sovereign and his inferiors. It provided a theory to the advantage of the rising landlords for their seizure of power from the waning slave-owner sovereigns.

Instead of the old hierarchy, Yin Wen urged the necessity of establishing a new one based on feudal principles. In his discourse with King Min of Qi on the topic of what constituted the virtuous, he affirmed: "There are persons who are virtuous and there are persons who are not, therefore the sovereign [as the virtuous] ought to be venerated high and his ministers and officials graded low; it is the promotion of the virtuous and the demotion of the vicious that leads to the differentiation of the upper and the lower."[36] In other words, Yin Wen urged building a new hierarchy based upon the feudal principle of the distinction of the virtuous and the vicious. In this respect, he came nearer to the Confucians than to the Legalists.

As exponents of the rising landlords, Song Xing and Yin Wen preached the Tao and De (virtue) like the Taoists, the rites and righteousness like the Confucians, and the rule of the law like the Legalists. They proclaimed: "Every thing is regulated by law, law is generated from authority, and authority is generated from Tao";[37] that is to say, the law should be taken as the criterion in judgments, but the law itself was ultimately derived from Tao. The identification of the law with Tao showed the close connection between the Song-Yin School and the Legalist School. But they evaluated punishments and rewards differently from the Legalists; they taught: "Mere rewards are not enough to induce goodness and mere punishments are not enough to prevent wrong-doings."[38]

From what is stated above, it might be seen that the Song-Yin School was a branch split off from the Taoist School but impregnated with an eclectic tendency, while their main political ideas approached the rule of the law. Han Fei was greatly nourished by the doctrine of Song Xing and Yin Wen. In short, the Song-Yin School formed an intermediate stage in the transition from the Taoists to the Legalists, or even a group of the earliest Legalists.

In the field of political and social ideas, Song Xing and Yin Wen entirely abandoned Lao Zi's point of view; and in the field of philosophy they reformed Lao Zi's idea of Tao. For Song Xing and Yin Wen, Tao is "void and formless[39] ... moves but cannot be perceived",[40] and "it has no roots, no leaves and no flowers";[41] that is, Tao is wholly imperceptible. But in addition, they propounded the idea of Qi (air) and identified it with Tao. Qi was constituted by the slighter and finer substances called Jing (essence). Jing and Qi, or essence and air, are considered as the source of all things in the world. They proclaimed: "When a man is born, Heaven furnishes his essence and earth his body, the union of which makes up a man."[42] here the essence (jing) denotes the air of the essence (jing qi) and the body the air of the body (xing qi).

They further asserted: "[The air] produces crops on earth and becomes stars in heaven; and when it circulates between heaven and earth, it is called the spirit and when it hides in the bosom of a man, it is called the sage."[43] That is to say, both the material world and the spiritual world are produced by the movements of one and the same essence-air. They asserted that all things in the world were begotten from the air, which never changed in itself. With them, Tao ceased to be an abstract spiritual reality or the Logos, but turned into a material substance, though so slight and refined as to be barely perceptible. In this theory we may get a glimpse of the earliest atomism in China, which may fairly be compared with that of the ancient Greek atomists Leucippus and Democritus, who were incidentally contemporary with Song Xing and Yin Wen.

But some logical shortcomings in their theories were also apparent. With regard to the relation of the body and the spirit, they claimed: "The air is transformed into life by Tao; with life there is thinking, and with thinking there is knowledge."[44] Yet in claiming so, they segregated the spiritual life from the material life by assuming that human spirit has its own existence independent of its body. It was this immaturity in their theory that was employed and transformed by Mencius into his "moving force (or moving air)". Later Xun Zi criticized and mended this immaturity in the theory of essence and air by pointing out that the spirit and the body were mutually interdependent and inseparable, and that each could have no existence of its own independent of the other.

Some of the writings of Song Xing and Yin Wen concerning the theories of knowledge played an important role in the development of the epistemology of various schools in the Warring States Period. Song Xing and Yin Wen paid special attention to the function of the mind in human knowledge, saying: "Everyone wants to know, but does not understand how knowledge is to be obtained. The object is something outside of one's self, but the obtaining of it is within one's self."[45] By this assertion they meant that people always wanted to obtain correct knowledge without examining first how correct knowledge could be obtained. And it is the function of the mind that enabled people to obtain correct knowledge. Their famous chapter on "Xin Shu or the Function of the Mind" (appearing in The Book of Guan Zi) discussed this topic in detail. For them, objects could only be known by the mind, for "within the body the mind holds the place of the sovereign" and "the eye and the ear are the organs of seeing and hearing".[46] Furthermore, "if the mind is disturbed by desires, then the eye sees not even when the object passes by and [the ear] hears not even when the sound thrills".[47] So it is only by the right cultivation of the mind that the good functioning of the sense organs could be ensured; and "if this [mind] is not cultivated, how can one hope to know that [object]?"[48]

In the opinion of Song Xing and Yin Wen, the way of the cultivation of the mind dwells in "emptiness" and "tranquillity". By emptiness is meant "no hiding" of anything in the mind and by tranquillity is meant keeping the mind in peace. They taught that as in the case with a human sovereign, the mind as the sovereign of the body, "should be kept unmoved by external objects in order that their laws might well be observed; for once moved, it will lose its place. And only in tranquillity will it regain or reassure itself".[49] When the mind wavers, one is unable to observe things correctly. The mind should learn to know external things just like the process of "an image imitates a figure or an echo responds to a sound";[50] it should reflect the external world objectively as a mirror does.

Based on this idea, they expounded their theory of names and realities. They asserted: "All objects have their proper shapes, and all shapes have their proper names", and that "this means that the name should not go so far as to exceed the reality, nor should the reality surpass the name";[51] that is, the name and the reality should correspond to each other. Further, they taught that "all correct names will naturally be followed, while all incorrect names will naturally be abandoned."[52] This theory of corresponding names and realities should deservedly be considered as one of the most outstanding and the most valuable in the early stage of development of ancient epistemology.

Another intellectual innovation in their epistemology was their theory of "the discernment of limitedness".[53] They proclaimed: "In the perception of things one should start from the discernment of one's own limitedness"; or in other words, in order to know something one should start by overcoming the narrowness or one-sidedness in his own mind. An interesting story cited by them[54] tells that once there was a man in the state of Qi who stole golden articles from a gold shop in broad daylight and was caught in the act. The shopkeeper asked him: "How dare you take them in front of the public?" And this man replied: "I have not seen the people there, I have seen only the gold pieces." Song Xing and Yin Wen drew the conclusion from this story that "people do not know until they have made a discernment of their own limitedness".

Though in their theory of knowledge they recognized that human knowledge by its nature was a reflection of the external world, they took such a reflection purely as a passive one and hence were led naturally to the neglect of the subjective and initiative elements in human knowledge. Due to this reason, it unavoidably bears a mechanistic character.

However, as an important intermediate stage in the development of the theories of human knowledge, the historical place of Song Xing and Yin Wen ought not to be undervalued. Mo Zi emphasized the role of the experiences of the senses in human knowledge but neglected that of rational thinking. Song Xing and Yin Wen overcame the one-sidedness of Mo Zi's empiricism and emphasized the role of the mind in human knowledge to the extent of neglecting subjectivity in human knowledge. Then Mencius in his turn re-emphasized the subjective side of human knowledge and arrived at an idealistic subjectivism. And last, Xun Zi inherited from Song Xing and Yin Wen in the main and criticized Mencius while at the same time assimilating the rational elements of Mencius' assertion of the important role of human subjectivity. Thus, the epistemology of Xun Zi brought pre-Qin philosophy eventually to an unprecedented height.

2. THE IDEOLOGY OF THE TAOIST SCHOOL—ZHUANG ZI

Zhuang Zi (369-286 B.C.) was a contemporary of Mencius but a bit later. According to *Records of the Historian*, Zhuang Zi, named Zhou, was a native of Meng, originally within the realm of the state of Song (now Caozhou, in Shandong Province), so it was always said that he was a native of Song; although since the middle Warring States Period Meng had already become a part of the state of Wei. He held a small official post at Qiyuan in Meng[1] and led a life so poor that he had to borrow his daily grains from others.[2] On the occassion he went to visit the king of Wei, he was poorly clad, with shoes so worn as to have them fastened on his feet with flaxen strings.[3] A good friend of Hui Shi, he refused to hold a high post as Hui Shi did. When King Wei of Chu (339-329 B.C.) sent a messenger inviting him to be his minister, he declined the invitation.[4] From the above-mentioned story, it might be conjectured that in social status he belonged to the waning nobility.

As regards his works, *Records of the Historian* said: "His writings, which run to over 100,000 words, are for the most part allegorical."[5] According to the *History of the Han Dynasty*, The Book of Zhuang Zi consisted of fifty-two chapters[6] of which now only thirty-three are extant, including seven "Inner Chapters", fifteen "Outer Chapters" and eleven "Miscellaneous Chapters". It has been generally acknowledged that the Inner Chapters were his own writings and the Outer and the Miscellaneous Chapters those of his followers. Nevertheless, the Outer and the Miscellaneous Chapters may also be regarded as the main sources in the study of his thought.

Zhuang Zi's Political and Social Ideas

Zhuang Zi described his ideal society as "the world of perfect virtue" in which there was no distinction between the gentlemen and the small or little-minded men. People who were "without knowledge" and "without desire" lived in company with the beasts; and being in a state of "letting alone the world"[7] there was no need of any government where people lived by nature itself without any restraint of artificiality; because there was nothing whatever that was artificially made or invented. He compared the "governing of the world" to "putting a string through a bullock's nose," saying: "horses and oxen have four feet. That is natural. Put a halter on a horse's head, a string through a bullock's nose,—that is artificial".[8] And he insisted: "do not let the artificial obliterate the natural",[9] or the Tao would be hurt. This is a step further than Lao Zi's propostition: "To rule a large nation is as to cook a small fish" (i.e., never try to turn it over); it recommended strongly never to intervene in the natural course of the world. It aimed at returning to the primordial chaos wherein: "The universe and I come into being together, and I, and everything therein, are One."[10] Then there would be no more distinction between the subject and the object, nor between the ego and the world around him. It meant a step further backward than Lao Zi's ideal of "small countries with few inhabitants". In fact, it was a complete negation of the social life. In the opinion of Zhuang Zi, people should lead their lives in the most ignorant way and any artificiality, no matter how slight, would mean a violation of the Tao in its naturalness. Thus he asserted: "Tao is obscured by our want of grasp."[11]

Starting from such a point of view, Zhuang Zi went firmly against any kind of social progress and social reform. In his book he cited the following story: "When Zi Gong (one of Confucius' disciples) was on his way back to the state of Jin from going south to the state of Chu, he passed through Hanyin. There he saw an old man engaged in making a ditch to connect his vegetable garden with a well. He had a pitcher in his hand with which he was bringing up water and pouring it into the ditch—hard labour with very little result. 'If you had a machine there', cried Zi Gong, 'in a day you could irrigate a hundred times your present area. The labour required is trifling as compared with the work done. Would you not like to have one?' 'What is it?' asked the gardener. 'It is a contrivance made of wood,' replied Zi Gong, 'heavy behind and light in front. It draws up water as you do with your hands, but in a constantly overflowing stream. It is called a well-sweep.' Thereupon the gardener flushed up and said 'I have heard from my teacher that those who have cunning implements are cunning in their dealings, and that those who are cunning in their dealings have cunning in their hearts, and those who have cunning in their hearts cannot be pure and incorrupt, and those who are not pure and incorrupt are restless in spirit, and those who are restless in spirit are not fit vehicles for Tao'."[12] Therefore Zhuang Zi recommended: "Away with wisdom and knowledge", and "split measures and smash scales".[13] All these ideas reflected his discontent with the social reality of his age, yet he could find no way out and was doomed only to try to safeguard himself. In this sense, he represented the ideological tendency of the waning nobility of the ancient world.

Zhuang Zi's Theory of Knowledge

The relativistic way of thinking led Zhuang Zi's theory of knowledge toward idealistic agnosticism.

In his interpretation of the unity of contradictions, Lao Zi entirely neglected the specific conditions necessary for the transformation of opposites and thus opened the door to relativism. From this starting point, Zhuang Zi led astray the naive dialectics of Lao Zi to a relativistic conclusion which was nowhere in the ancient literature more explicitly expressed than in his "Treatise on the Identity of Contraries".

Zhuang Zi taught that there were in the world no such contradistinctions as truth and falsity, good and evil and beauty and ugliness. Such controversies, in his opinion, would remain forever and could never be solved. "Hence there were the affirmatives and negatives of the Confucian and Mohist Schools, each denying what the other affirmed and affirming what the other denied."[14] The Confucian School took the grand burial ceremony as goodness, but the Mohist School took the simple one as goodness. So was the case with the issue of beauty and ugliness; for instance, "Mao Qiang and Li Ji were famous for their beauty in ancient times, but at the sight of them fish at once plunge deep down in the water, birds soar high in the air, and deer hurry away",[15] because these animals did not think them good-looking. Here the relativity of the values of things became so exaggerated by him that all things in the world became equivalent without any difference in their qualities.

By negating the qualitative differences of things, he was logically led to the denial of the existence of the objective world. Therefrom he concluded that there was no such thing as the objective world at all and human knowledges was only what was subjective. "From the point of view of sameness (identity), all things are One (identical, or equivalent)".[16] And therefore he did not acknowledge the possible existence of any criterion for truth nor any objective truth at all. For example, he argued it was utterly meaningless to speak of "the proper dwellings", since apes lived comfortably in trees while people lived within their houses. Since there could not exist any truth in the objective sense, he considered it impossible to judge whether human knowledge was correct or not.

As this scepticism was carried to its extremity, Zhuang Zi even began to doubt his own existence. In his book, there was a well-known and often-quoted allegory which reads: "Once upon a time, I, Zhuang Zi, dreamed I was a butterfly, fluttering hither and thither, to all intents and purposes a butterfly. I was conscious only of following my fancies as a butterfly, and was unconscious of my individuality as a man. Suddenly, I awoke, and there I lay, myself again. Now I do not know whether I was then a man dreaming I was a butterfly, or whether I am now a butterfly, dreaming I am a man."[17] This allegory typically illustrated how far his agnosticism and scepticism went. Yet it was an agnosticism and scepticism as full of brilliant philosophical insight and logical depth as was ever thought of by an ancient genius. The fundamental issues of all philosophies, such as what is the "ego" and what is "reality", were for the first time not only touched upon but penetratingly scrutinized by Zhuang Zi, though in an abberant fashion. Sometimes in the history of human knowledge, the proposing of questions was by no means less valuable than the solving of them. It is in this sense that Zhuang Zi ought to be listed among the most marvellous of the ancient thinkers.

Seeking untiringly for knowledge as he actually did, he was nonetheless theoretically opposed to the search for knowledge. He affirmed: "My life has a limit, but my knowledge is without limit. To drive the limited in search for the limitless, is fatal; and the knowledge of those who do this is fatally lost."[18] This is a theory which ridiculed both his theoretical effort and his own doctrine of the equivalence of all affirmative and negatives; because after all there is something (i.e., the wisdom of life) in the world which seems more preferable.

Zhuang Zi's Philosophy of Life

From his relativistic theories Zhuang Zi deduced his philosophy of life. He recommended that the key to the philosophy of life lay in the eliminating of any thing opposite or contrary and thereby all contradictions might be avoided. This he called "the axis of Tao"[19] upon which one could rotate freely so as to accomodate various possible circumstances—that is, an attitude of escaping from the reality in life. He said: "The true sage, while regarding contraries as identical, adopts himself to the laws of Heaven. This is called following the two courses at once";[20] in addition, "he judged not the rights and wrongs of mankind, and thus lived quietly in his generation".[21] It must be noted that this attitude of muddling along brought with it some significant effects on the daily life and manners among the literati of the later generations.

Zhuang Zi went even so far as to advocate forgetting oneself. The way to reach such a state was by "sitting in forgetfulness". And under the name of Yan Hui, he declared: "I have abandoned my body and discarded my knowledge, and so have become one with the Infinite. This is what I mean by sitting in forgetfulness."[22] He thought that when one is completely unaffected by all outside happenings or events and even forgets his own existence, he would attain his greatest freedom, i.e., a freedom which is unconditional. Such an ideal man or "perfect man" would be more free than the Roc, because the Roc, though it can fly high and far, is not perfectly free, but has to be conditioned by the wind, the climate, etc.

Apparently this philosophy of life was nothing but self-hypoptism in its desperate endeavour to escape the social reality which after all is inescapable for anyone and everyone and Zhuang Zi himself was eventually obliged to come to a compromise with inescapable reality. Politically he advocated a returning to the primordial state of chaos, yet he had to admit the inescapability of the relationship of the sovereign and the inferiors in social reality. He remarked: "A subject's allegiance to his sovereign is duty"[23] (though he put the saying under the name of Confucius); and admitted that this sort of duty is after all inevitable in society.

The ideology of Zhuang Zi, like that of the Confucian School, has afforded the Chinese a lasting spiritual support in their lives and sufferings. It immensely influenced the metaphysics of the Wei and Jin Dynasties as well as the general life-view of later ages.

The passive and the decadent aspects in the thought of Zhuang Zi, of course, deserve our serious criticism. But in the history of ideas, he held a significant place. In addition to his unparalleled belles-letters, his contributions in the field of inquisitive thinking were among the most remarkable of the ancient thinkers. Many topics, though treated by him in a negative and incorrect way, have greatly inspired later generations. And without them, the history of ideas would have been less deepened and developed.

3. THE IDEOLOGY OF THE DIALECTICIANS

The Dialecticians, or the School of Names or, in what seems a better translation, the Sophists, were also called the School of Forms (jurisdiction) and Names[1] in the Warring States Period. The scholars of the Han Dynasty called them the Dialecticians[2] and that title has persisted ever since. Scholars of this school engaged themselves in inquiring about names and concepts.

The violent social changes and transformations of the Spring and Autumn Period and especially of the Warring States Period had made the old concepts out of date and apparently inappropriate for the expression of new things and new ideas; and the newly emerged concepts were still in need of being generally accepted. The discordance between the names (concepts) and the reality (facts) was then becoming an acute social problem and various schools were trying to solve it. Confucius, representing the conservative tendency of his time, has tried hard to regulate or to confine the changed social reality within the model of the old concepts by means of his "rectification of names". On the contrary, the Mohist School tried to give new names to the new things and new orders according to their real properties and to throw away the old names, which had ceased to conform to the changed reality—this was known as giving names in accordance with reality.

The emergence of the School of Names was also connected with the promulgation of the written laws, whereupon there appeared a group of people whose job it was to argue or to defend cases on the ground of the articles in the law, similar to that of professional lawyers. The term xing (form) also meant jurisdiction (xing) and hence the Dialecticians were called the School of Forms (jurisdiction) and Names. In the Spring and Autumn Period, Deng Xi was the most famous among the representatives of this school.

The ideological basis of this school had originated by the end of the Spring and Autumn Period, while the Dialecticians as a school flourished in the middle of the Warring States Period, engaging in the study of the problem of names and reality. At that time the most notable representatives of this school were Hui Shi and Gongsun Long whose analyses of concepts and terms had made great contributions to the development of logic and methodology in ancient times. Meanwhile, they also dealt with many problems valuable in the field of natural sciences, especially Hui Shi. But sometimes they indulged in mere playing with ideas and fell into sophism, especially Gongsun Long. Hui Shi and Gongsun Long represented the two main groups of the School of Names and their viewpoints were directly opposed to each other.

Hui Shi's Doctrine of the "Unity of Similarity and Difference"

Hui Shi (circa 370-318 B.C.) was a native of the state of Song and had served in the state of Wei as a minister for more than a decade. He worked on legislation for the state of Wei which "was welcomed by the people".[3] After the defeat of Wei in the Battle of Maling by the army of Qi, he plotted the union of Wei and Chu to defeat Qi.[4] Then, he arranged the reconciliation between Wei and Qi and made the Duke of Qi and the Marquis of Wei assume the title of "king" through mutual recognition. He was also an organizer of the anti-Qin alliance and hence suffered the calumniations of Zhang Yi, the organizer of the pro-Qin alliance, and was expelled by Wei; so he went to Chu. The King of Chu sent him to the state of Song. Afterwards, he returned to Wei and was sent as envoy to Chu and Zhao.[5]

Zhuang Zi said of him: "Hui Shi was a man of many ideas, and his works would fill five carts";[6] and once "an eccentric fellow in the south, named Huang Liao, asked why the sky did not fall and the earth not sink; also, whence came wind, rain and thunder. Hui Shi was not backward in replying to these questions which he answered unhesitatingly. He went into a long discussion on all creation and talked away without end; though to himself he seemed to be saying very little. He supplemented this with most extraordinary statements".[7] It is really a pity that his works were almost entirely lost, for they would surely have been placed among the most valuable scientific legacies in the history of China. Fortunately, in *The Book of Zhuang Zi* there were preserved ten propositions of Hui Shi which have afforded the main sources for the study of Hui Shi's thought. In addition, there were also some fragments of Hui Shi preserved in *The Book of Xun Zi, The Book of Han Fei Zi* and *Lü's Spring and Autumn Annals*.

The ten propositions of Hui Shi were permeated with his idea of "the unity of similarity and difference". He asserted: "A great similarity differs from a little similarity. This is called the little similarity-and-difference. All things are in one way all similar, and in another way all different. This is called the great similarity-and-difference."[8] What he was in search of by this proposition was the relativity of the similarities and differences of things. For example, the horse. According to his argument, all animals belonging to the species of horse are included in the concept of horse, hence there is a great similarity in them. At the same time, each individual horse has its own specific features in colour, shape, etc., hence there is little similarity (that is, with many differences as well). The general notion of horse and the specific notion of each individual horse are different from each other. Viewed from the aspect of similarity, all of them are horses. From this it may be deduced that all things have something in common, i.e., similarity. But viewed from the aspect of difference, all horses are different from each other. From this, it may be deduced also that all things have something dissimilar to each other, i.e., differences.

He taught that all things have their similarities as well as their differences. And the similarities and differences are but relative. They all consist in a unity (or entity).

But Hui Shi stressed that the differences of things are relative and their similarities absolute. From this, he drew his conclusion that things in the world are "all similar". Thus all things, whether similar or different, are comprised into a unity—of course, only in an abstract way, that is, in human conceptions. He reached the conclusion: "Love all beings (or things) equally; the universe is one."[9] *Lü's Spring and Autumn Annals* interpreted this statement as: "The universe with all things in it is a whole body; this is called the great similarity."[10] This idea is very akin to that of Zhuang Zi's "all things are One".[11] But the doctrine of Hui Shi should not be identified with the relativism of Zhuang Zi, who denied any qualitative difference of things and virtually negated the existence of the external world. Hui Shi never went so far as to agree with the subjectivism of Zhuang Zi.

The object of Hui Shi's study, as shown in his ten propositions, is the objective world outside of us. In the relationship between the name and the reality, he started from the stand point of the existence of reality, acknowledging that reality was the primary whereas the names, as the reflection of reality in human minds, the secondary. Herein lies the divergence of Hui Shi and Gongsun Long, a difference which is worthy to be noted.

Gongsun Long's doctrine of "Separating Hardness and Whiteness"

Gongsun Long (circa 320-250 B.C.), a native of the state of Zhao[12] at the end of the Warring States Period, lived later than Hui Shi and was contemporary with Zou Yan. He had been a favourite guest of the Prince Pingyuan[13] and had persuaded King Zhao of Yan and King Hui-wen of Zhao to agree to his proposal of disarmament and pacification,[14] probably under the influence of the doctrine of pacifism of Song Xing and Yin Wen. He was engaged in political activities during the war of Zhao against Qin. After prince Xinling of Wei, at the request of Prince Pingyuan, came to the rescue of Zhao and defeated the invasion of Qin, some one asked a fief for Prince Pingyuan; on learning the news Gongsun Long hastened to him at midnight, advising him not to accept it. Afterwards, Zou Yan on his way through Zhao refuted Gongsun Long's famous argument that "a white horse is not a horse". Gongsun Long was then expelled[15] and died in exile. As regards his works, the *History of the Han Dynasty* recorded that there were in *The Book of Gongsun Long Zi* fourteen articles of which only six are now available.

Judged from his life and activities, he seemed to be conservative in his political attitude. Zhuang Zi quoted him as saying: "When I was young I learned the Tao of the ancient sage-kings; when I grew up I knew all about the practice of benevolence and righteousness."[16] This shows that he was at first connected with the Confucian School. He stressed the necessity of the maintenance of the old names and orders, proclaiming: "How perfect were the ancient sage-kings who examined the names and realities and took care about what they said. How perfect were the ancient sage-kings."[17] Such a proclamation revealed how he enjoyed reminiscing about the old names in their ancient splendour.

According to *The Book of Huai Nan Zi* the philosophical doctrine of Gongsun Long consisted in "dissociating similarity and difference" and "separating hardness and whiteness". In sharp contrast to Hui Shi's doctrine of the "unity of similarity and difference", he broke away from all perceptual knowledge and concentrated entirely on the logical analysis of concepts; and his teachings bore a strong metaphisical colour. In the study of logic, his contributions are of first-rate historical significance.

His argument of "separating hardness and whiteness" started from the logical analysis of a hard and white stone. He asserted that by sight people knew the stone was white without knowing its hardness, and by touch people knew the stone was hard without knowing its whiteness. So he concluded that hardness and whiteness did not exist in the stone itself but each had its own existence independent of the stone.[18] This is the argument of his doctrine of "separating hardness and whiteness" which separated the attributes of things from their corporeal existence and isolated them one by one to the entire negation of their unity. Or in more philosophical terms, it means that the universal does not consist in the particulars but has its own separated and independent existence. The sophist character of this doctrine was most obviously expressed in his famous proposition that "a white horse is not a horse".

The argument of this famous proposition runs thus: "The word horse denotes a shape and the word white denotes a colour. What denotes a colour does not denote a shape. Therefore, I say that a white horse is not a horse."[19] The term "horse"—so he argued —denotes the shape of a horse, and all that possess the shape of a horse are termed "horse". The term "white" denotes the white colour and whatever possesses the white colour is termed "white". Now a white horse is the shape of a horse plus the white colour, or a horse shape in white colour. Since the "horse" and the "white horse" are two different concepts, it is evident that "a white horse is not a horse". This argument proceeded from the discernment of the logical implications of the concepts.

Also, he argued from the standpoint of the logical extension of concepts. He stated: "When a horse is required, yellow and black ones may all be brought forward; but when a white horse is required, a yellow or black one will not do."[20] The logical extension of the term "horse" consists of all horses, including the yellow and the black ones; but the logical extension of the term "white horse" is limited only to the horses of white colour, excluding the yellow and the black ones. Since the concept of "horse" and the concept of "white horse" differ from each other, it ought to be admitted that "a white horse is not a horse".

His argument proceeded also from the relationship of the universal and the particular. He asserted: "What is white is not namely a horse. A white horse is a 'horse' together with 'white', or 'white' together with a 'horse'. Therefore I say that a white horse is not a horse."[21] That is to say, the term "white" applies to all that is white, not only to horses that are white; and the term "horse" designated the universal sum of all horses regardless of the colour. A white horse requires the universal of the white colour plus the universal of the horse. Therefore a white horse is not a horse.

On the topic of logical and conceptual analysis, Gongsun Long was unrivalled in the intellectual history of ancient China. But the fallacies in his analysis led him into sophism. He did fairly well in his discernment of different concepts, especially in that of the universals and the particulars. But he exaggerated their difference so much that the two were utterly separated and made absolute. Eventually he was led to the complete denial of the existence of the particulars and acknowledged only the existence of the universals which he turned into something existing in itself and independent of the particulars. Hence the conclusion of his objective idealism that only what is conceptual exists.

It was recorded in his book that when he witnessed the tumult and disorder in the relation of names and realities effected by the great social transformations of the age,"he endeavoured to extend his argument (of the doctrine that a white horse is not a horse) so as to rectify the names with their realities, and thus to reform the whole world".[22] In ancient times, a logical proposition, no matter how sophistic it might look, was deemed to be closely interconnected with the political and social actualities of the age. So was the case with Gongsun Long's theory of the white horse which must not be regarded as a mere logical play of words but an algebraic formulation of the contemporary political and social issues. As is known, in ancient Greece Socrates died not for political reasons but under the accusation of his preaching of sophism.

Gongsun Long propounded: "rectification means to rectify the actualities. To rectify what designates an actuality means to rectify its name".[23] By this he meant both to rectify the unrectified (actuality) by the rectification (of names) and to test the rectification with the unrectified. The rectification of the names was not fulfilled until the social actuality was rectified. Here the names are primary and the actualities secondary. His aim was to rectify the social actuality by the old names, that is, to redress the already changed social realities by the old traditional ideas.

Besides the logical propositions of Hui Shi and Gongsun Long, The Book of Zhuang Zi had recorded twenty-one propositions which were respectively correlated to the theories of the Dialecticians. Among them, the proposition "a fowl has three legs"[24] belongs to Gongsun Long, who had recorded it in his own book. The proposition "the shadow of a flying bird never moves"[25] might also belong to him. It means that at any given instant a flying bird may be regarded as staying at one spot unmoved. This proposition provoked a very minute search into the nature of motion unprecedented in the intellectual history of China; though it expanded a partial truth into an entirety and thus led to the denial of any possibility of motion.

The School of the Dialecticians was a product of the great social transformation of the age. All tried to rectify the names from their respective positions. Both Hui Shi and Gongsun Long exaggerated one side of the process of knowing; Hui Shi stressed solely the side of the unity of things, whereas Gongsun Long stressed solely that of the difference of things. Each elaborated a highly sophisticated theory in his respective sphere and each was confined by the one-sidedness of his respective metaphysical way of thinking.

Nevertheless, the contributions of the School of the Dialecticians should not be undervalued. They resembled the ancient Greek Sophists to a striking degree, and many of their propositions were similar or even identical word by word; for instance, one may readily compare the proposition that "the shadow of a flying bird never moves" with that of Zeno of Elea (5th century B.C.) that "a flying arrow never moves". It is interesting to note that both the School of the Dialecticians and the School of the Greek Sophists engaged in the same sophistic theoretical activities at about the same time, one in the Occident and the other in the Orient. Both of them participated in the historic social transformations of their times, and with the penetrating depth of their theories greatly promoted the advancement of human thinking. It was really one of the most significant phenomena in the history of human civilization.

4. THE IDEOLOGY OF THE STRATEGISTS —SUN WU, WU QI AND SUN BIN

During the frequent wars of the pre-Qin era, there was obviously an urgent need for strategists, so many of them emerged to meet the military situations, whether in civil wars, power struggles or in offensive and defensive wars against other states. For the sake of winning wars, some of their foremost representatives "took advantage of the circumstances to mend the state of affairs"[1] and studies the strategic theories of how "to overwhelm the enemy and to triumph immediately"[2]. Among them the most prominent were Sun Wu, Wu Qi and Sun Bin who all had their own works entitled "Art of War".

Sun Wu, a native of Qi, living at the end of the Spring and Autumn Period, was the forefather of the strategists. He was born in a noble family and later came to the state of Wu in the lower Yangtze valley; and by recommendation of the famous statesman Wu Zi Xu he visited He Lu, the King of Wu, and earned the king's great admiration for his military talents. He was appointed the commander-in-chief of the army, and in the war against Chu he defeated the enemy's troops of 200,000 with an army of 30,000 and occupied the capital of Chu (Ying), thus "menacing the states of Qi and Jin in the north and his name becoming widely known to all kings and princes."[3] Henceforth, the state of Wu enjoyed a period of prestige and prosperity.

His work *Sun Zi's Art of War* consisted of thirteen chapters, about six thousand words in all. In the year 1972 in the archaelogical excavation of the Han tombs at Yinque Hills in Linyi, Shandong, five other chapters of *Sun Zi's Art of War* which had long been considered lost were found. These chapters provided new materials for the study of Sun Wu's thought.

In *Sun Zi's Art of War*, he made an excellent summarization of the knowledge and experiences of wars in ancient times, and laid down the foundation for later strategic theories. It was not only the earliest military writing, but an excellent work which exerted tremendous influences on strategic theories not only in China but all over the world.

Wu Qi (circa 440-381 B.C.) was a native of Wei, living at the beginning of the Warring States Period. In his youth, he went to the state of Lu and learned after Zeng Shen, the famous Confucian, but he soon turned away from Confucianism to the study of the art of the war. As a general of Lu, he defeated the army of Qi. During the reign of Marquis Wen of Wei, Wu Qi had stayed for twenty-seven years in Wei, holding the governorship of Sihe where he carried out a series of military, political and economic reforms, making "the troops of Qin daring not to peep eastward at Wei, and the states of Han and Zhao to keep good terms courteously with Wei"[4] and so "the territory of Wei was widened by thousands of li in all derections",[5] thus laying down the foundation of the hegemony of Wei. But later he was framed by the courtier Wang Cuo and was compelled to lead an exile's life in the state of Chu. King Dao of Chu appointed him to an important position for carrying out reforms in Chu, but finally Wu Qi was murdered by the nobilities of Chu. His book *Wu Qi's Art of War* was written during his governorship in Sihe. It combined his rich experiences in war with penetrating theoretical studies. His book, now extant in six chapters, may be regarded as his own writing, though revised through later generations.

Sun Bin, a native of Qi in the middle Warring States Period, was a descendent of Sun Wu. He studied the art of war together with his friend Pang Juan who later became a general in Wei. Realizing himself much inferior to Sun Bin, Pang Juan called Sun Bin to Wei in secrecy and arrested him illegally. But with the help of the envoy from Qi, Sun Bin managed to escape from Wei to Qi, where by the recommendation of the famous general Tien Ji he was appointed the Chief of the General Staff by King Wei of Qi. It was through his planning that Qi won a series of victories; the most illustrious were the Battle of Guiling between Qi and Wei in 353 B.C. and the Battle of Maling to rescue Han against Wei in 341 B.C. The fatal defeats of the powerful Wei Army by Qi brought the prestige of Qi to a new height and "the kings and princes turn eastward to pay their homage to Qi".[6]

According to the record in the *History of the Han Dynasty*, *Sun Bin's Art of War* consisted of 89 chapters, but all of them had been lost before the Sui Dynasty (6-7th century), for it was not mentioned at all in the *History of the Sui Dynasty*. Since the time of Song (11th century), many scholars doubted whether Sun Wu and Sun Bin had each written his own work separately or they were but one and the same book. It was not until the archaelogical excavations at the Yinqiao Hills in the year 1972 that among other military works there were found both *Sun Wu's Art of War* and the *Sun Bin's Art of War*, thus bringing to light again the book of Sun Bin, which had been lost for more than a thousand years; and the long unsettled question was answered. Soon afterwards, *Sun Bin's Art of War* was edited and published in thirty chapters, totalling 11,000 words. It developed the military theories of his predecessors Sun Wu and Wu Qi and summarized the abundant experiences of the middle Warring States Period in a unique fashion.

As a treasury of military ideas, the works of the pre-Qin strategists held a predominant place in the intellectual history of China. All of them had a good comprehension of the significance of war. Sun Wu proclaimed: "War constitutes the cardinal issue of the state; it concerns the problem of life and death of a nation as well as the way of its survival, which no one can afford to neglect examining."[7]

Wu Qi advocated that Chu ought to "strengthen her arms and armies so as to be able to win the world in times appropriate and opportune".[8] Sun Bin taught: "Be able to win the battle in war and to stand with might in peace—this is the way to ensure you the obedience of the world."[9] These views illustrated the dauntless yet realistic spirit of the rising landlords in face of the issue of war.

As a prerequisite in war, Sun Wu laid special emphasis on the role of Tao (policy) which, he urged, ought to be given priority over all other considerations in waging and winning war. With a keen insight into the relationship of war and politics or policy, he realized that victory in war came only from the support of the soldiery and the people, asserting: "Tao is that which makes the people in agreement with their superiors, so that they will be fearless in living together and dying together with their superiors."[10] This priority given to policy was a most valuable point of view in the history of military thought which was inherited later by both Wu Qi and Sun Bin. Wu Qi taught that to make herself stable and strong a nation ought to "refine policies within her boundary and prepare her arms towards the outer world".[11] He tried hard to find out the social origins of war and to distinguish just wars from unjust ones, making a great advance in understanding the nature of war.

In strategic and in tactical ideas, all of the strategists made contributions which were taken by later generations as models. Sun Wu for example, advocated that in strategy one should be encouraged by "great boldness", despising his enemy, while in the concrete guidance of his operations one should be as careful and prudent as possible. In all their writings, it was apparent that preparations for war were always given paramount importance.

In warfare, Sun Wu emphasized strategic offensive. Sun Bin further developed this idea into his famous proposition: "Be always on the offensive and never on the defensive"[12] which might be regarded as a reflection of the aggressive mentality of the social forces then in their ascendancy. Sun Wu held that in war one should try first to attract the enemy with false impressions and then to ambush and annihilate them. Wu Qi further expounded the same idea. During the famous Battle of Maling, Sun Bin lured the enemy and suddenly smashed them with his ambush. The enemy followed him in a seeming victory as far down as Maling, where the defeated enemy commander-in-chief Pang Juan committed suicide and the enemy Prince was taken captive. This was a brilliant example of a great victory won by the dexterous employment of Sun Wu's method in warfare, the guiding principle being taking initiative to place oneself in an advantageous position over the enemy.

Sun Wu was the first to propound the idea of the employment of the situation. This idea was further developed by Sun Bin, of whom it was said "Sun Bin valued the situation above all"[13]. In the Chapter discussing "the Employment of the Situation" in *Sun Bin's Art of War*, he investigated in particular the topic of how to make the situation favourable to oneself and unfavourable to the enemy.

Sun Wu expounded the principle of defeating the enemy by surprise, or as he put it: "Attacking where the enemy has made no preparation and assaulting when the enemy has not thought of it."[14] And he taught further that the employment of this principle in warfare should be flexible, or, in other words, "one should triumph over his enemy by the ingenious utilization of changed conditions on the part of the enemy".[15]

Wu Qi furthered this idea and taught that determinations and decisions in military operations should be made according to different concrete conditions. Therefore he did not approve sticking to dogmas. An example is his discussion on the besieging of cities. Sun Wu in his *Art of War* considered the besieging of a city an unclever act, whereas Sun Bin emphasized the importance of besieging cities. This change in military thought reflected the historical fact that the economic growth of the middle Warring States Period heightened the significant role of the cities, so that the focus in war was turned to the occupation of cities. Meanwhile, progress in technology also provided the material for armaments for taking cities. This viewpoint of Sun Bin showed how he developed strategic ideas to meet a new era.

On the topic of battle arrays, both Sun Wu and Wu Qi talked very little; but Sun Bin gave a full exposition of the ten battle arrays in all their varieties and complexities. It reflected the fact that in the middle Warring States Period the scope of warfare was getting much more broadened and therefore large-scale military plans and operations were more necessary than ever before.

The strategists formulated many important rules and laws of

warfare in their works. Sun Wu in his book wrote: "Know the enemy and know yourself, and you can fight a hundred battles with no danger of defeat."[16] This observation deserves to be ranked among the most excellent propositions ever evolved in the science of war. Again he observed: "Avoid the enemy when he is in a dashing spirit and strike him when he is tired and withdraws."[17] Principles like these were frequently made use of in later ages. Wu Qi from his own experiences in war had studied various conditions of how one should make sudden attacks and how one should avoid enemies. Sun Bin formulated the principle that one should disperse the enemy forces as much as possible while concentrating his own forces to attack them. Until the enemy forces were dispersed, one should never attempt to launch an assault but should keep himself from throwing his forces into the battle. This originated from Sun Wu's postulate: "Always avoid the enemy's strong points and take advantage of his weak points."[18] The above ideas of the strategists illustrate the depth of their understanding in the art and science of war.

Sun Wu taught that to keep well informed about the enemy, one should never resort to superstitious methods like auguries or divinations, but should obtain correct information about the enemy from those who had true knowledge of them. This teaching showed the atheistic spirit of the strategists, which was so necessary in war. Wu Qi noted the importance of developing human initiatives to their utmost. He taught that a general should be good at mastering all kinds of military arts so as to deal with all possible varieties of circumstances, otherwise he would be doomed to failure and even to death. In this idea was manifested Wu Qi's denial of the theory of the Mandate of Heaven that "life and death are all predestined".

On the relationship of the forms and the names, Sun Bin asserted: "the name is given after the form is fixed";[19] that is to say, names should be given in accordance with the concrete formation of things. And therefrom he postulated that the outcome of the war "will be determined by the formations of both sides"; [20] in other words, it was decided only by the antagonism of the two hostile forces, not by divine intervention.

In directing a war, the strategists were always opposed to any kind of subjective conjecture. They laid special attention to knowledge of georaphy, of investigation and information about the enemy, and taught that it was through a good knowledge of the distribution of the enemy forces that one was able to choose the weak points of the enemy and to launch an attack. In all these teachings, it was apparent that their scientific spirit outweighed conventional superstitions.

To a certain degree, the strategists realized that things were in constant contradiction and in mutual transformation. Sun Wu mentioned that "order and tumult", "courage and cowardice", "strong and weak", "difficulty and ease" could all be mutually transformed into their opposites under certain conditions. Wu Qi taught that in a life-and-death struggle only those who dared to give themselves up valiantly in fighting could hope to win and to survive, and those who dared not to do so were doomed to bring about their own fall. On the issue of the magnitude of forces, he pointed out that it sometimes happened that the side of the few by creating a favourable condition became able to overcome the side of the multitudinous. He personally created a typical example in war by defeating the Qin army of 500,000 with a force of only 50,000 plus 500 chariots and 3,000 cavalry. The idea of the transformation of the opposites was further developed by Sun Bin, who was known for his skill in creating favourable circumstances to overwhelm the enemy. Thus in various ways, the ideas of the strategists had greatly enriched the ancient intellectual history with their research in the field of warfare.

With regard to the principles concerning military administration, the strategists, as a rule, recommended the practice of strict rewards and punishments and of promotion of personnel based on their individual merits and talents, as Sun Wu advocated "to train the army with education and to rule them with enforcement";[21] by education he meant political instruction, and by enforcement the enactment of strict discipline. Wu Qi taught that an army would "win the war only through its enactment of strict discipline",[22] but at the same time "the orders and regulations should be easy to understand and not very complicated"[23] so that all personnel could easily execute them. Sun Bin valued highly the role of man, saying: "between heaven and earth, there is nothing more precious than man."[24] He used to choose his personnel strictly and train them hard to heighten the fighting quality of his troops.

The theoretical works of the pre-Qin strategists and their military practices helped pave the way for the historic task of the ultimate unification of China, and also had influence on the ideas of the later ages. But inevitably limited as they were by their epoch and their class, all of them in various degrees exaggerated the role of the individual commander while having little confidence in the soldiery; so they held a policy of keeping the soldiers in ignorance and thus led themselves to the idealistic view that history was in the final analysis created only by a handful of heroes, and the role of the masses, if any, was too small to be noticed. Here and there in their works one may find traces of the feudal delusions. So their irrational elements ought to be carefully distinguished from the rational and rationalistic and should be treated separately in the light of scientific analysis.

It is very unfair that the thoughts of the strategists should have been generally neglected so long in nearly all the works dealing with the history of ideas; so it seems only appropriate for us here to restore their true value and their proper place in history.

5. THE MERGING OF THE HUNDRED SCHOOLS AND THE *LÜ'S SPRING AND AUTUMN ANNALS*

The violent social changes during the Spring and Autumn and the Warring States periods as reflected in the sphere of ideology, brought forth the lustre of the hundred schools in their contention. Between the hundred schools there existed an extremely complicated relationship; there were confrontations of ideas yet there was also a mergence of ideas. More often than not, it happened that one school did not represent precisely the interests of a certain social class, stratum or group; and it is hard to combine the whole richness and complexity of the Pre-Qin ideologies into a ready-made formula.

During the rise and development of the hundred schools, by the end of the Spring and Autumn Period (about 6th century B.C.) there was opposition and contention between the two predominant schools, the Confucian and the Mohist. Down to the early and middle warring States Period (5th-4th century B.C.), there emerged a tripartite confrontation between the Confucians, the Mohists and the School of Yang Zhu.

In the early Warring States Period, there developed in the Ji Xia Academy the School of Ji Xia, with the Taoist ideology as its main current; but it was as late as the middle Warring States Period that Zhuang Zi, who was a bit later than Mencius, developed the doctrine of Lao Zi and brought the Taoist School to an influential position.

The early Legalists engaged themselves mainly in reform movements within the political and economic sphere. Their theoretical confrontation with the Confucians was not yet acute and their role in the sphere of ideology had not yet prevailed. Therefore the main opponents to Mencius then were the schools of the Mohists and of Yang Zhu.

By the end of the Warring States Period (3rd century B.C.), Han Fei came forth summarizing the judicial theory of Shang Yang, the statecraft theory of Shen Buhai and the power theory of Shen Dao, thus bringing the Legalist doctrine to its perfection. It was the role of Han Fei to carry out the systematic criticism on Confucianism from the standpoint of the Legalists; and it was only then that the so-called confrontation of the Confucians and the Legalists escalated considerably for a time. With the great unification of China by the Qin Dynasty and, soon after it, the establishment of the Han Dynasty, the Confucian and the Legalist Schools began gradually merging together until at length there was no trace whatever left of the confrontation and contest between them.

In the course of the contention of the hundred shools, there had been the contests between the Confucians and the Mohists, between the Confucians and the Legalists and between the Confucians and the Taoists. On the one hand, they argued vehemently for their own causes against the others; while on the other hand they influenced and even permeated one another in the very course of their contention. Ban Gu, the official historian of the Han Dynasty, described this situation involving the pre-Qin schools and scholars as: "Their opinions though were as different as fire from water, destroying each other, they were nevertheless generating and generated by each other. Like benevolence and righteousness or veneration and reconciliation, they were contrary and yet were complementary to each other."[1]

With the formation and growth of their respective ideologies, they criticized yet supplemented each other. For instance, the most important figures of the Legalist School derived their origin from the

Confucian School and later they transformed the ideas of Lao Zi by turning his idealistic Tao (the Logos) into the materialistic Tao (the objective laws) and making it a constituent part of their ideology. Xun Zi was the last and the greatest pre-Qin Confucian, but he endowed the traditional "rites" of the Confucians with the sense of "laws" in order to meet the requirements of the ascending landlords; and the most eminent Legalists Han Fei and Li Si were both the disciples of Xun Zi. These facts might show that the Confucian School and the Legalist School were not so diametrically opposed to each other as though they were ever in a state of absolute contradiction (as some had been prone to assume a few years ago). On the contrary, they were gradually merging together in their historical development.

Even within the same school, it might be observed that there were different groups and sects contending with each other, such as that between Mencius and Xun Zi. Xun Zi criticized as well as reformed and absorbed the ideas of Mencius.

Xun Zi was the key figure in the merging of the Confucian and the Legalist schools, which were eventually integrated into one in the Han Dynasty. He was also the first to begin the task of summarizing the hundred schools.

Han Fei launched a systematic criticism on the Confucian School, but that did not mean an irreconcilable struggle between two different lines, because in criticizing the Confucians he also criticized the Mohists, Yang Zhu and the Taoists, from each of whom he had absorbed something in forming his own thought. Following the undertaking of Xun Zi, Han Fei further summarized the hundred schools, while systematizing the Legalist theory.

The last chapter entitled "The World" in *The Book of Zhuang Zi* was written during the end of the Warring States Period and the author of it (a devoted follower of Zhuang Zi) gave a compact criticism to each of the prevailing schools of the pre-Qin times from the standpoint of the Taoist School.

Xun Zi, Han Fei and the author of the chapter "The World" had each in his own way summarized the hundred schools and elaborated their own theories by adapting the merits of various other schools. But the case seemed somewhat otherwise with the book *Lü's Spring and Autumn Annals*, compiled under the editorship of the famous premier Lü Buwei of the state of Qin at the end of the Warring States Period. This book, by its "combining of the Confucians and the Mohists and uniting of the Dialecticians and the Legalists"[2], had led to a great blending among the hundred schools. The appearance of such a book reflected in the sphere of ideology the political trend resulting from the contests of various states towards unification.

Lü Buwei (b. between 290-80 B.C. and d. 235 B.C.), a native of Puyang in the state of Wei (now in Henan Province), ran a commercial business in Yangdi (now Yuxian in Henan) and accumulated large wealth. He then turned his commercial manoeuvring to speculation in the political field. With wealth and with a beautiful woman, he first managed to make an acquaintance with a Qin Prince, named Zi Chu (or Yi Ren) born by a concubine of the king. Lü Buwei stored him up as a kind of precious commodity, and then bribed the Queen of Qin to take Zi Chu as her adopted son and then to make him the Crown Prince. After the death of the King Xiaowen, Zi Chu succeeded the throne as King Xiang, and Lü Buwei was appointed the prime minister and made a marquis "with a fief of 100,000 families in his domain at Luoyang ... having a thousand household servants".[3]

In the year 247 B.C., King Xiang died and his young Crown Prince Ying Zheng, who was known later by his assumed title Shi Huang (i.e., The First Emperor) succeeded to the throne. Since the king was too young, political power fell into the hands of Lü Buwei. When the king came of age, he seized power and executed the influential eunuch Lao Ai with whom Lü Buwei was connected. Finally Lü Buwei was expelled from office and compelled to commit suicide on his way to exile in Sichuan.

During his premiership in Qin, Lü Buwei had gathered three thousand guests in his court, asking "each of them to write down what he knows... in order to prepare a perfect compilation of the knowledge of all things, whether in heaven or on earth, whether ancient or modern".[4] This resulted in the compilation of the book of *Lü's Spring and Autumn Annals* which was arranged under a very strict schedule, including 140 chapters in 26 volumes, totalling more than 200,000 words. When the book was finished, so the legend had it, it was proclaimed on the city gate of the capital Xianyang that anyone who could revise any word in it would be rewarded with a thousand pieces of gold, the purpose being to show how solemnly and seriously this book was prepared.

It is strange to observe that though *Lü's Spring and Autumn Annals* was well ordered in its schedule, it had no ideology of its own, except a medley of the various doctrines of the hundred schools. Viewed from this persepective, the book looks rather like a collection of documents drawn from the various schools of the pre-Qin Period. Therefore, the History of the Han Dynasty listed it under the heading of the Miscellaneous School which "combined the Confucians and the Mohists and united the Dialecticians and the Legalists".[5] Wang Zhong, famous scholar of the Qing Dynasty, said of it: "With the appearance of *Lü's Spring and Autumn Annals*, all the doctrines of the ancient scholars and schools were comprised in it."[6] It was a representative work of the Miscellaneous School indeed.

In this book some of the guiding principles of the editor were of necessity reflected. In one place it mentioned; "One who is good at learning borrows the merits of others to compensate his own shortcomings, therefore he who is good at borrowing from others will win the world."[7] From this saying it might be seen that the editor of the book endeavoured to embrace all schools by absorbing their merits and thus to unify public opinion in preparation for the coming of a great political unification. But in truth it failed to elaborate a new ideology from the basis of summing up the hundred schools and succeded only in mixing up various doctrines into an eclectic medley. Hence the book inevitably bore such defects as the following:

First, repetition. The story of Wu Qi being framed by Wang Cu and obliged to assume exile was repeated in two chapters roughly in the same wording.[8] Another two chapters wrote about the same content dealing with the communion of heaven and man.[9]

Second, self-contradictions. One chapter in it opposed the "anti-musicalism" of Mo Zi,[10] one opposed his "anti-militarism";[11] whereas another chapter was slanted toward the viewpoint of Mo Zi.[12] In another part, one chapter advocating the Confucian emphasis on the solemn funeral ceremony[13] was put together with another which reflected just the opposite Mohist viewpoint.[14] It seemed that the editor aimed badly in evaluating the Confucians and the Mohists.

Such self-contradictory viewpoints also manisfested themselves over the big political issues: on the one hand, the book upheld the great unification, professing "when unified, the world would be in good order; when divided, the world would be in disorder";[15] but on the other hand it advocated the old system of enfeoffment, professing "the more the enfeoffment is under way, the longer will be the fortunes of the enfeoffed principalities and the more illustrious their fame".[16]

It is no accident that the *Lü's Spring and Autumn Annals* as the representative work of the Miscellaneous School was produced by the end of the Warring States Period. After the long years of the feudal separatist rules as well as constant wars of annexation, the demand for a great political unification had already become the trend of the age. Hand in hand with this political trend toward unification came an ideological trend toward unification. It was to satisfy this historical need that the eclectic ideology of the Miscellaneous School rose to the fore.

But in reality, *Lü's Spring and Autumn Annals* played no significant role in the task of establishing a unified autocracy. This perhaps should be attributed to the limits or the weakness of the theory itself, because it represented the political demands only of those landlords who had sprung from the old nobility and hence tended to be conservative. This also explains the reason why Lu Buwei on the one hand advocated unification and on the other hand proposed the practice of enfeoffment in an endeavour to preserve the privileges of the old nobility. This social group was in some way at odds with the ascending landlords. Though they demanded unification, after the establishment of the centralized feudal autocracy they were nevertheless dissatisfied with it, even proclaiming; "The world does not belong to any individual alone, it belongs to all the world."[17] This was an outcry against the limitations imposed on them by the centralized royal power of a great unified country.

With all its defects *Lü's Spring and Autumn Annals*, owing to the fact that it incorporated the doctrines of diverse schools, had after all preserved many ideological sources and documents of the pre-Qin times. Many lost writings and stories became known only through the records in this book. The writings of the great pre-Qin thinkers such as Yang Zhu, Song Xing, Yin Wen, Hui Shi and Gongsun Long had long been lost but some relevant material of theirs could be found in this book; and since it was written by the end of the Warring States period, a time very close to that of the ancient thinkers, it possesses a high historical value. And what is more, it contains a rich collection of sources on agricultural science and technology of the ancient times.[18]

Further, the eclecticism of Lu's Spring and Autumn Annals, by comprising various schools, reflected the trend toward the merging of the Confucians and the Legalists. In it, the Legalist viewpoints were often mixed with Confucian elements. In one place it asserted: "It is appropriate to carry on reforms with the succession of the generations and the change of the times";[19] this sounds like a Legalist theory in nature. But it asserted again: "One may get to know the ancient by observing the present; the ancient and the present are one and the same"[20] and "the ancient and the present, the past and the future are one and the same";[21] these assertions differed greatly from that of the Legalists. Shang Yang advocated: "For the governing of the world one ought not to follow one and the same way, and for the convenience of the nation one ought not to follow the ancient";[22] Han Fei also advocated: "One should not expect to follow the ancient."[23] Obviously, the proposition in *Lü's Spring and Autumn Annals* that "The ancient and the present are one and the same"[24] was a product of the reconciliation between the Confucian School and the Legalist School. Another point worthy of mention is that there were some outstanding innovations in its arrangement of materials and its method of compilation which considerably influenced the editing and compiling of the encyclopaedic reference books of later ages, including the *Taiping Imperial Encyclopaedia* and others.

Chapter 4

ECONOMIC, SCIENTIFIC, HISTORICAL AND LITERARY IDEAS IN ANCIENT TIMES

1. ECONOMIC IDEAS IN ANCIENT TIMES

In the ancient literature, few records were found about economic ideas. There were some verses in the *Book of Odes* which described the agricultural conditions in the Western Zhou Dynasty and the Son of Heaven participating personally in the farming ceremony every year. In the management of public finance, the Zhou government followed the principle: "to limit expenditure in accordance with income."[1] *Rites of the Zhou Dynasty*, though the time of its composition is still an issue of controversy, had narrations about some of the economic measures which illustrated fragmentarily the economic ideas of that time. The primitive ideas about the importance of food and other commodities and of the division of labour in social life as conceived by the Shangs constituted the embryo of the economic doctrines of the Spring and Autumn and the warring States periods.

Among the most important economists in the Spring and Autumn Period were Guan Zhong, Ji Ran and Shan Qi; and among those in the Warring States Period were the representative figures of the Confucians and the Mohists, the author of *The Book of Guan Zi*, and the Legalists. They all influenced later developments in economic thought with their economic theories.

Guan Zhong's Theory of the Settlement of the Inhabitants by the Division of Professions

Guan Zhong (circa 730-645 B.C.), a native of Yingshang, now in Anhui Province), came from a house of the declined nobility. In his youth, he engaged in trade and accumulated a great deal of commercial experience. Later, he was appointed by Duke Huan of Qi, the first famous sovereign of the Five Powers of the Spring and Autumn Period, as the minister in charge of reform in Qi and in this office he won great success.

According to the legend, *The Book of Guan Zi* was composed by him. But since it included records of some historical events after him, scholars considered it a composite of the Warring States Period. Though *The Book of Guan Zi* was not the personal writing of Guan Zhong, some parts of it can be studied in comparison with related parts in other books, such as the *Zuo's Chronicles* (or *Zuo's Commentaries on the Spring and Autumn Annals*) and *Discourse on the States*. Combined, they afforded an important source about his thought.

From the measures of reform he adopted we may get a glimpse of his economic thought. Most outstanding was his doctrine of inhabitation according to the division of professions, whereby the gentry, the peasantry, the craftsmen and the merchants (i.e., "the four categories of the people") had each been allocated to their own settlements.

With the growth of social productivity, the ratio of the craftsmen and the merchants in the makeup of the whole population was increasing. The gentry were designated as the warriors whose duty it was to safeguard the interests of the ruling class. To ensure the predominance of the gentry in the society was a matter of cardinal significance to the states of the ruling class. For the first time in history, Guan Zhong formulated the theory of the division of the inhabitants by professions under the headings of the four categories mentioned above.

He placed the gentry at the head of the four categories and did not allow them to engage in any kind of labour so as to gaurantee them as professional warriors. He made the peasants settle in the countryside, the craftsmen in the official workshops and the merchants in the market places. With their status fixed by their professions, the inhabitants were assigned to their specific areas of settlement.

The whole country was thus divided into twenty-one counties, each being bound by the professions of its inhabitants under the control of the government. No one would be allowed to move outside of his settlement. The aim of such an arrangement was to make them accustomed to their occupations and to think no more of changing their jobs, and hence of changing their lots. The social order was established in such a way that "the descendents of the gentry will always be the gentry ... the descendents of the peasants will always be the peasants ... the descendents of the craftsmen will always be the craftsmen" and "the descendents of the merchants will always be the merchants".[2] This division and perpetuation of professions reminds one of the caste system in ancient India and of the similar division of the social classes designed by Plato in his Republic. It is interesting to note that all these theories and practices appeared roughly at the same time in ancient China, India and Greece.

As private landownership was gradually replacing the waning nine-squares system, Guan Zhong acknowledged the status quo and instead of the old measures, adopted a method of collecting rents and taxes in accordance with the productivity of the farmlands. This was called "taxation in accord with the fertility of the farmland"[3] which historically marked the beginning of feudal land rent.

At the same time, Guan Zhong carried out a series of reforms on trade and commerce and soon brought the state of Qi to prosperity and power. This furnished the material foundation upon which Duke Huan of Qi was able to assume hegemony among the principalities.

The Economic Theories of Fan Li and Ji Ran

With the cities flourishing in the later Spring and Autumn Period, commerce was greatly developed and the merchants as an important social force were in ascendancy. Often the wealthy merchants participated in practical politics; and the famous story of the merchant Xian Gao of the state of Cheng who by contrivance helped to induce the invading army of Qin to withdraw was an outstanding example. In the state of Yue, Fan Li and Ji Ran were renowned among the merchant-statesmen whose economic ideas reflected the interests of the merchants and tradesmen of their times.

Fan Li served King Gou Jian of Yue in defeating the state of Wu; later he engaged in commercial activities and "within the span of nineteen years he had three times accumulated thousands of gold".[4] Based on his experiences in commercial activities, he expounded his theory of "watching the time"; that is, grasping advantageous opportunities for economic activities. He taught that it would be a disaster to lose the "heaven-bestowed" good opportunity.

Fan Li learned from his master, Ji Ran, who came from a family immigrated from Jin to Yue. Ji Ran's economic ideas consisted mainly in:

First, his cyclic theory. He made an analogy between the harvests and the theory of the Five Elements, observing: "[There are] good harvests for six years and bad ones for six years, and then a great famine for every twelve years."[5] This cyclic doctrine influenced Bai Gui in the Warring States Period.

Second, his measure for stabilizing the grain price. He elaborated this measure to meet possible famines, observing: "The selling price of the grains at twenty coins per Dan would harm the farmers and at ninety per Dan would harm the merchants", and "if the price could be kept within the range between thirty and eighty, it would profit both the farmers and the merchants. This measure of stabilizing the grain price so as to keep the market lively is the way governing a state".[6] He proposed the institution of a market run by the government to regulate the grain price and to keep it in a stable state, no matter how the harvests might turn out. This idea was inherited and developed by the early Legalist Li Kui in the Warring States Period.

Third, his theory of price. Concerning the law of prices, he remarked: "Prices of commodities are dependent on whether they are abundant or scarce."[7] Again, he observed: "The price will fall when it rises to its highest, and will rise when it falls to its lowest."[8] By this observation he meant that a high price would stimulate people to produce more and more, and this in its turn would cause the price to fall; and vice versa. Ji Ran was the first among the ancients to work out the law of prices.

In his commercial practice, he was said always to "sell out his goods lavishly when the price is high, and buy in thirstily when the price is low".[9] By selling at high prices and buying at low prices, one might get great profits. This idea was further developed by the famous merchant Bai Gui into his principle: "Take in what others give out and give out what others take in."[10]

The Monetary Theory of Shan Qi

As regards monetary theory of ancient times, legends had it that there had already been the idea of capital and interest as early as the time of King Wen of Zhou. In the middle Spring and Autumn Period, King Zhuang of Chu "thought that the coins were too light" and intended "to substitute them with the bigger ones".[11] But it was Shan Qi who first expounded a monetary theory which considerably influenced the later generations.

Shan Qi, or Shan Mou-gong, had been a royal official under the reigns of King Jing and King Jing of Zhou in the later half of the 6th century B.C. In the year 524 B.C., when King Jing planned to cast bigger coins, he stood in opposition by proposing his monetary theory of "the correspondence of the heavy and the light". He argued that the function of money consisted in "measuring the value of commodities and in buying foodstuff to relieve the people". Here he dealt with the function of money both as a measurement of value and as a means of circulation of wealth. He found a close connection between the circulation and the value of currency. If the hard currency was too light, its purchasing power would become lower and lower and then the circulation would be impeded. So he proposed casting heavier coins for regulating the ratio between the heavy and the light so as to keep both of them in circulation in the market. When the heavier coins became inconvenient in daily use, it was necessary to have lighter ones supplied for circulation. This monetary theory of his was known to later generations as the theory of the correspondence of the heavy and the light—a theory which prevailed for a long time in history.

There were discussions on money in *The Book of Guan Zi*, typifying the monetary theory of the Warring States Period. It was asserted that "gold is for the use of measuring";[12] that is, gold served a measure of value as well as a counter of expenditure in public finance. And the proper amount of gold in circulation would help to keep the prices of commodities in conformity with the development of production. It seemed that *The Book of Guan Zi* had tentatively envisaged the regulative effect of the law of value upon the production of commodities.

Several other economic ideas in *The Book of Guan Zi* held a significant place in the history of Chinese economic doctrines. For instance, his economic interpretation of morality was rather influential on later ages. A well-known proposition of his reads: "One knows the rites and courtesies only after his granary is full; and knows the honours and disgraces only after he is well fed and dressed."[13] Thus he endowed abstract moral ideas with certain concrete contents, and considered ethical ideas not something supra-utilitarian but based on material welfare.

In his financial theory, Guan Zi advocated the policy of "light taxation" by "taking from the people within a certain scope"[14] and emphasized enlargement of financial income through the channel of the monopoly of the state and decrement in the exaction of taxes. This is a policy in the interests of the ascending merchants and landlords. In its treatment of wealth and labour, his theory held that land and labour constituted the sources of wealth. With a view to the role of the union of land and labour, it concluded: "The land will not produce without the people, and the people will not get rich without labour. All the products in the world come from labour and labour from manual work."[15] In this way, it affirmed that labour is the dominant factor in the creation of wealth. This idea was full of initiative and insight. Coming in the Warring States Period, it was far in advance of its time.

The Economic Ideas of the Confucians

The economic ideas of the Confucians exerted great influence on later ages in several ways.

Stressing righteousness and making light of profits formed one of the guiding principles of the Confucians. Righteousness designates the role of the moral norm while profits designate the search for material interests. Both Confucius and Mencius put morality in priority. Confucius taught: "At the sight of the profits, one should think the righteous first"[16] and "it matters to me only like a piece of floating cloud that I could become both rich and dignitary but without righteousness".[17] He despised from the depth of his heart becoming wealthy by ways of unrighteouness. Perhaps it might be admitted that he was justified in saying so; but he went so far as to place righteousness and profits in absolute opposition, affirming:

"The gentleman is persuaded by righteousness while a little-minded man by profits."[18]

Mencius went even further than Confucius in preaching righteousness versus profits. He said: "Enough will it be to have benevolence and righteousness; why do you need more to speak of profits?"[19] He was of the opinion that the search after profits would lead a nation to the danger of scrambling for wealth.

In this respect, Xun Zi differed somewhat from both Confucius and Mencius. He professed: "Both righteousness and profits are the desires of human beings."[20] But after all, righteousness outweighs profits; and when righteousness prevails, the world would be in good order, and when profits prevail the world would be in disorder. At bottom, Xun Zi did not break through the bounds of the Confucian view about righteousness and profits.

The emphasis on righteousness led the Confucians to look down upon manual labour. When his disciple Fan Chi asked to learn how to plow, Confucius blamed him as "a little-minded man".[21] Confucius taught: "Engaging in plowing, you will become hungry; engaging in studying, you will become a well-paid official."[22] Mencius even taught: "Those who labour with their brains govern others; those who labour with their brawn are governed by others. Those governed by others, feed them. Those who govern others are fed by them. This is a universal principle in the world."[23] And again: "If there were no gentleman, there would be no one to rule the countrymen. If there were no countrymen, there would be no one to support the gentlemen."[24] With this argument, he tried to justify the rationality of feudal exploitation and feudal hierarchy.

In line with their conservative attitude in politics, the Confucians also held a conservative attitude towards economic reforms. In the year 594 B.C. when Duke Xuan of Lu carried out the first taxation on farmlands, acknowledging the legitimate status of private land ownership, Confucius criticized it as not in conformity with the rites in *The Spring and Autumn Annals* which he edited. In the year 483 B.C., when the government of Lu levied military taxation on farmlands, Confucius also expressed opposition. Mencius lived in the middle Warring States Period when feudalism was well established. Aware of the antagonism between landlords and peasants as well as the serious problem of land annexation, he planned the reformation of the nine-squares system to solve the land problem of the peasants. He proposed to distribute the farmlands to the peasants while preserving the traditional forms of the nine squares system. Xun Zi made a similar proposal through which each peasant was to be rationed with "five mu of land for housing and a hundred *mu* for farming".[25]

As regards the issue of "enriching the people" and the "benevolent government", both Confucius and Mencius viewed it from the long-term interests of the ruling class and did not approve over-exploitation. Confucius was in favour of a more generous policy, saying: "You will win the people by your generosity."[26] When discussing politics with his disciple Ran You, Confucius insisted that it was important "to enrich the people" by asserting: "When the people are abundant, how can the sovereign be not abundant; when the people are not abundant, how can the sovereign be abundant?"[27] Confucius advised earnestly "to take interest in what is the interest of the people".[28] At the same time, he advocated that "taxes should be levied as light as possible"[29] and "to recruit the labour forces at the appropriate time"[30] so as to make possible a moderate livelihood for the people. To the ruling class Confucius also preached: "Prodigality leads to insolence and frugality to stability",[31] asking them not to be prodigal but frugal. Another maxim of his was: "Stick to economy and love the people."[32] Herein lies the Confucian idea of benevolence in its application to the economic sphere. Later, Mencius developed it further and propounded the theory of "benevolent politics" in a definite form.

Influenced by the theory of "benevolent politics" or "benevolent government" of Mencius, Xun Zi shared roughly the same economic ideas; though Mencius appeared more conservative by his adoption of the traditional form of the nine-squares system. In addition to his proposal that each peasant was to be rationed with "five *mu* of land for housing and a hundred *mu* for farming", Xun Zi further advocated that "the customs should be strict but not to charge any tax; the mountains, woodlands and rivers are opened and closed at proper times but not to impose any duty[33] ... taxes on the countryside should be light, the exaction of goods and the recruitment of the corvee should be seldom as not to defer the time for farming"[34] and "schools should be run for the education of the people".[35] His basic economic thesis was: "Without wealth one cannot cultivate the mentality of the people; without education one cannot enlighten the nature of the people."[36] All these were obviously in the tradition of "enriching the people" and "educating the people" of Confucius.

In course of time, the Confucian doctrines had undergone a process of changing. Confucius at the end of the Spring and Autumn Period tried to carry out some reforms in order to maintain the rule of the declining nobility. Mencius in the middle of the Warring States Period tried to remodel the doctrine of Confucius so as to meet the demand of his own time, yet to preserve the old tradition. Xun Zi at the end of the Warring States Period realized that the historical current toward a great unification was becoming inevitable and irresistible and tried to transform the Confucian doctrine to accommodate it to the requirements of the ascending landlords.

The Economic Ideas of Xu Xing

In contrast to the Confucian School, whose economic ideas represented the demands of the upper class, the Mohists and Xu Xing belonged to another pattern representing, to a considerable degree, the interests of the lower class. As mentioned in the preceding chapters, the Mohists insisted on "the economy of expenditure" and "the economy in funeral ceremonies". Mo Zi asserted: "When a sage governs a nation, the wealth of that nation may be doubled."[37] And again: "To double its wealth does not depend on aggrandizing its territory, it is enough to double it by cancelling the useless expenditure of the nation."[38] The wealth of the nation was always the goal the Mohists strove for. In their view, financial expenditures should be so arranged as to ensure benefits to the people. Hence Mo Zi asserted: "A sage-king never increases his expenditure that does not bring benefits to the people."[39] Therefore, Mo Zi expressed violent opposition against the extravagant funeral ceremonies which reflected the Confucian ideas of a strict hierarchy.

Xu Xing's economic ideas came very near to that of the Mohists but with his own characteristic features. Xu Xing (circa 390-315 B.C.), a native of Chu, was a contemporary of Mencius and an outstanding representative of the Agriculturalist (or rather let us say, the Physiocrat) School in the Warring States Period. In *The Book of*

Mencius there was a record about his life and teaching. Some identified Xu Fan, one of the second-generation disciples of Mo Zi, with Xu Xing, the former being mentioned in *Lü's Spring and Autumn Annals*,—a supposition which lacks authentic evidence. Xu Xing and dozens of his disciples led an extremely simple life and earned their livings by such manual labour as shoemaking and mat-weaving. They wandered from place to place and finally arrived at the state of Teng in the hope of settling down there by engaging in farming. The teachings of Xu Xing became so influential that the brothers Chen Xiang and Chen Xin even gave up their Confucian discipline and took Xu Xing as their master. So far as we know now, the teachings of Xu Xing consisted of the following two points:

First, "the sage-rulers cultivate farmlands together with their people and govern them while eating what they themselves produce."[40] He was recorded having said: "The Prince of Teng is indeed a worthy prince. Nevertheless, he had not yet heard the true Way", because "now the Prince of Teng has his granaries, treasuries and arsenals, which are nothing but oppressing the people to nourish himself. How can he be deemed worthy?"[41] There was a legend that Shi Zi once said: "The Faery Farmer cultivated the farmland and had his daily meals in common with his people in order to persuade them to work in the farm."[42] Shi Zi was named Shi Jiao who was, as the legend went, a native of Lu and the master of Shang Yang. The doctrine of Xu Xing, which looked very much like that of Shi Jiao, might perhaps have some connections with it.

Second, "there should be no two different prices in the market".[43] Obsessed by the social division of labour, Xu Xing proposed direct exchanges of farm products with handicraft products, i.e., a barter system, the principle he had in mind being: "Linen and silk of the same length would be the same in price. So would it be with the prices of hemp and silk, these being the same in quantity; with the five kinds of grains, these being the same in amount; and with shoes that were of the same size."[44] That is, so far as the same products were concerned, there should be the same price for the same quantity; and the prices of all commodities in the market would be thus kept in uniformity.

The teachings of Xu Xing reflected the interests and demands of the poor peasants of that time. The ideal that sovereigns should

cultivate the farm together with their people represented an equalitarian vision of the lower peasantry. This ideal of his was forever to
remain a fancy, incapable of being realized; but the thesis that each
one should be a labourer supporting his own living was in sharp
contrast to the Mencius doctrine that "those who labour with their
brains govern others; those who labour with their brawn are governed by others. Those governed by others, feed them. Those who
govern others, are fed by them". And Xu Xing's theory of price
echoed the protest of the poor peasants against the exploitation of the
merchants in the market.

Xu Xing was more radical than Yang Zhu; the latter represented
the interests of the small proprietors who demanded only to preserve
what was their own, while the former represented that of the poor
peasants who had nothing of their own except their manual labour.

Owing to the limitations of his age, Xu Xing was unable to
formulate a good theory about the division of labour and the problem
of price. Mencius' theory of the division of "those who labour with
their brains" and "those who labour with their brawn", to a certain
extent, followed the historical trend of the growing enlargement of
the social division of labour and hence bore positive implications in
the history of ideas. But Mencius went so far as to hold this necessity
as "a universal principle in the world" to apologize for the rationality
and eternity of the feudal exploitation system. It was theoretically
wrong, and in practise served the interests of the exploiting class.

Xu Xing's theory of price took care only of the quantitative
aspect of the commodity and neglected entirely its qualitative aspect.
He understood almost nothing about the factors which determined
the price of a commodity; so his theory of price was built on fictions
and could not be carried out in practice. By contrast, Mencius laid
emphasis on the qualitative differences of the same kind of products
and the differences in the labour necessitated in producing them. So
he affirmed: "If the way of Xu Xing is to be followed, falsities
will ensure one after another; then how could the nation be well
governed?"[45] Here he exaggerated the faults of Xu Xing's theory and
even misrepresented the author's original meaning. Nevertheless, his
care about the qualitative aspect of products made his theory of price
a step more advanced than that of Xu Xing.

The Economic Ideas of the Legalists

Among the ancient economic doctrines, the doctrine of the Legalists was the most outstanding and the most influential. Farming and warring constituted the nuclei of their ideal. Early in the Spring and Autumn Period, Guan Zi had proposed that soldiery should be rooted in the peasantry, an idea which might be regarded as germinating from the Legalists' emphasis on the combination of farming and warring. By the time of the early Warring States Period, "Li Kui taught the people to utilize the farmland to its utmost",[46] and to encourage warring, he decreed that convictions in civil disputes were to be decided by the contest of the shooting art performed by the clients. During his reforms in Chu, Wu Qi inherited Li Kui's idea and proclaimed the policy of "farming and warring" and "instructed the people to engage both in farming and in warring at one and the same time."[47] Thus the business of farming and of warring were eventually brought into one.

Since the middle Warring States Period, Shang Yang and other Legalists developed greatly the idea of "farming and warring". Shang Yang affirmed: "It is farming-warring that makes a nation prosperous", and "it is from farming-warring that a nation becomes secure and it is from farming-warring that a sovereign becomes respected."[48] Since the rise and fall of a nation depended on farming-warring, he elaborated a policy of (1) "Valuing the peasants and repressing the merchants" and (2) "encouraging the military merits". He favoured the private propriety of the small farmlands of the peasants in order to keep them concentrated on the activities of farming and warring, and at the same time he excluded any other channel of obtaining ranks in officialdom except through merits in farming and warring. All activities other than farming were levied with heavy taxes so as to guarantee priority of the policy of farming and warring.

This idea reached its culmination in the theory of Han Fei, who considered all professions other than farming and warring as the causes of social disaster and tried hard to abolish the privileges of the old nobility, who engaged neither in farming nor in warring. Han Fei's central proposition was: "A nation is enriched by agriculture and is able to resist the enemy by the armed forces";[49] hence the policy of farming and warring would lead to the way of wealth and power, which constituted what he called "the capacity to reign", that is, the qualification for the task of the great unification of all the nations.

It was Han Fei who first expounded the motto: "Agriculture is the essential, and handicrafts and commerce are the incidental"[50]—a motto which obviously dominated the Chinese mentality for ages to come. Such a concept as "the people engaged in farming and warring fall into hardships while the people engaged in the incidental occupations [i.e., commerce] make profits"[51] was in his opinion a signal of the decline of a nation. To encourage agricultural labour, Han Fei opposed measures of heavy taxation and corvee, and upheld a policy of "reducing the disparity between the rich and the poor by means of appropriate regulation and employment of governmental taxation";[52] yet he also opposed the adoption of methods "to tax the rich and to give alms to the poor".[53] Such a position showed his concern for the interests of the landlords, to whom he himself belonged. This concept of farming and warring of the Legalists played a significant role not only in the establishment of the new regime of the landlords but also in strengthening their cause of the great unification of the whole of China.

2. SCIENTIFIC IDEAS IN ANCIENT TIMES

In the pre-Qin period a developed agricultural society was well under way and various branches of natural sciences were of necessity in close connection with agricultural production. Planting and harvests were going on seasonably, and there was always an urgent need for an exact calendar to guarantee that agricultural activities would be duly on schedule. As calendars were prepared, astronomy developed very early to meet their practical needs.

The Xia Dynasty had already worked out a calendar; and it was recorded in *The Analects* that Confucius intended to employ the calendar of Xia. Perhaps he was of the opinion that the calendar of Xia was better than others. The calendar of Shang was a mixture of the solar and the lunar systems in which the method of using the Heavenly Stems and the Earthly Branches was introduced. The Heavenly Stems were composed of ten signs and the Earthly Brraches of twelve signs. By various possible combinations of the two sets of signs, with one being taken from each, there were formed sixty pairs to designate the years, months and days. In each month there were twenty-nine or thirty days in conformity to the phases of the moon. There were twelve months in an ordinary year and thirteen in a leap year so as to conform to the solar year. In the middle Spring and Autumn Period, the method of inserting seven intercalary months in every 19 years was adopted, a century earlier than that in ancient Greece. At some point before the 7th century B.C., defining the days of the solstice by means of measuring the length of the projection of the sun was in practice. As late as the 4th century B.C., the quarter-remainder calendar of the four solar terms (i.e., the two equinoxes and the two solstices) was already in common use, which predated by three hundred years that of the Julian calendar of the Roman Empire.

Astronomical observations were carried out very early in ancient China. Legend said that once during a solar eclipse in the reign of Zhong Kang (King of Xia Dynasty in the 20th Century B.C.) it happened that Xi He, who was the official in charge of the celestial observations, in his drunkeness failed to make a report of it in due time and was hence put to death.[1] The Zuo's Chronicles recorded a solar eclipse in the Xia Dynasty which was generally acknowledged as the earliest record in the world. In the bone inscriptions of the Shang Dynasty, records of eclipses were found, which were regarded as important events in ancient times. There were also records of the names of the stars for determining the days of the spring equinox and the summer solstice.

There were also ancient records about meteorological observation, such as winds, rains, snows, thunderstorms and rainbows. The Bamboo Chronicles recorded that in the tenth year of the reign of King Jie of Xia (circa 1580 B.C.) "stars rained down at midnight". This was the earliest record of meteors in the world. The Zuo's Chronicles recorded that in the fourteenth year of Duke of Wen (613 B.C.) "a star rushed into the Great Dipper". This was the earliest record of a comet in the world.

In the Warring States Period, it was found that the period of the movement of Jupiter was twelve years; and since then the way of chronicling the years was founded on the position of Jupiter, which was known as the star designating the year. Between the years from 360 to 350 B.C., Gan De, a native of Chu, wrote the *Astronomical Observations*, and Shi Sheng, a native of Wei, wrote *Observations on the Stars*, both of which were among the earliest star atlases in the world. Shi Sheng also did research on the causes of eclipses.

At the same time, the merchants made their contributions to mathematics. They applied the decimal system. The terms "compass" and "square" were found in the bone inscriptions, which showed that the ancient Chinese possessed implements to describe circles and right angles. The ruins of the buildings of the Shang Dynasty indicated knowledge of geometry. In the late Spring and Autumn Period, The book *Sun Zi's Art of War* mentioned the application of fractions; and some books of the Warring States Period mentioned the multiplication tables. Both Hui Shi and the Mohists were excellent mathematicians and physists. They explored the ideas of limits and variables.

In the sphere of productive technology, the ancient Chinese possessed knowledge of some of the main crops, such as rice, wheat and sorghum, and of irrigation works. The fact that the Shangs indulged themselves in getting drunk indicated the prosperity of the art of brewery. Among the handicrafts, those of bones, of jade, of pottery and of bronze had all attained a high level of craftsmanship. Bronze played a predominant role in all the material areas of development of the ancient society. It was prepared in the ratio of 15-20 per cent tin and 80-85 per cent copper that gave the metal the required hardness and casting was done on a large scale. The famous tripod of Si Mu Wu weighed 750 kg. would have had to be cast with a labour force of no less than hundreds of craftsmen. By the Spring and Autumn Period, iron began to come into use. In the early Warring States Period the technique of iron casting was invented, predating by about 1,800 years that in Europe. In the field of metallurgy, the technique of steel making and quenching invented then by the Chinese was the earliest in the ancient world.

Civil engineering had made great progress by that time. The book *Artificers Record* summarized knowledge in that field. In the Spring and Autumn Period, Sunshu Ao took charge of the construction of Shao Bei in Chu, the earliest large-scale reservoir and irrigation engineering in ancient China. Later on came the building of such well-known canals as Han Gou, Hong Gou and the irrigation system of Zheng Guo. By the end of the Warring States Period, Li Bing and his son completed the famous hydraulic and irrigation work of Du Jiang Yang at Chengdu in Sichuan province, then a part of the kingdom of Qin. It brought great benefits to the agriculture of the Chengdu Plain and marked the peak of technical expertise of that time.

The earliest physicians were magicians or sorcerers. The official physicians first appeared in the Shang Dynasty. Certain diseases and epidemics were studied and became known as early as in the Spring and Autumn Period. In the *Rites of the Zhou Dynasty*, there were records about medicine and surgery and even medical organizations as well. In some other pre-Qin books, there were detailed records about diagnoses, treatments and effects of different diseases. In the *Records of the Historian* by Sima Qian and other books, there were recorded such cases as Jian-Zi of Zhao in coma for five days and the crown prince of Guo falling in a state of shock. Both of them recovered through the wonderful cures of the famous physician Bian Que. Blood release, acupuncture, heat treatments, herb stews and tonic wines were common medical cures. As to surgery, medical powder and medical paste were already in use, and sometimes even operations were undertaken. All these laid down the foundation of medicine and pharmacology for later ages in China.

This scientific and technical body of knowledge and ideas was among the most advanced in the ancient world, and was fully qualified to compete with the glory of the scientific learnings of ancient Greece. Both contributed much to the advancement of the civilization of mankind, one in the Orient, the other in the Occident.

The Cosmography of the Ancient Times

The ancients described the cosmos by their conjectures. Some imagined that "the heaven is round like a cover and the earth is square like a plate".[2] This constitutes the main contents of the doctrine of the covering heaven which appeared as early as the Zhou Dynasty. From this doctrine stemmed Zou Yan's theory of nine great continents.

This doctrine was treated with suspicion because it failed to explain the phenomena of the revolutions of the celestial bodies. Zeng Sen (or Zeng Zi), one of Confucius' disciples, once remarked: "If the heaven is really round and the earth square, then the four corners of the earth would be left uncovered."[3] Nevertheless, the doctrine of the covering heaven was utilized by the ruling class in their political preaching that "the way of heaven is round and the way of the earth is square, so that the sage-kings in following it established the order of the upper and the lower".[4] Thus a doctrine of astronomy was turned to serve as an argument for the divine right of kings and a justification of the social hierarchy. Till the very end of the feudal society it was still prevailing just as the Ptolemaic cosmography in the West served the mediaeval theocracy as an official doctrine.

It was also in the pre-Qin period that the idea of a round earth was first propounded, which in many respects replaced that of a covering heaven. Shen Dao of Zhao in the Warring States Period proposed that "the celestial bodies are like catapult-balls".[5] Although he made no definite description of the round shape of the earth, the above proposition might lead directly to the conclusion of a round earth. Hu Shi, a bit later, remarked: "I know the centre of the world is located in the north of Yan (a nation in the north) and in the south of Yue (a nation in the south)."[6] Now it seems hard to define the exact implications of this proposition, but it might be regarded as a hint that the earth is round. Other related propostitions of Hui Shi were: "The south has no limit and yet has a limit"[7] and "the heaven is as low as the earth";[8] both of them might be regarded as providing a theoretical foundation of the doctrine of a round earth, which implied intrinsically a negation of the superiority of heaven and the inferiority of earth when understood in a social sense. Especially so was the propostition that "the heaven is as low as the earth".

Ideas of Time and Space

The Book of Shi Zi was written in the Han Dynasty, but it recorded some remarks of Shi Jiao, who was said to be the master of Shang Yang and lived in the middle Warring States Period. He was reported as observing: "The yu (space) includes all directions and the zhou (time) includes the bygones and comings"; that is, the cosmos (yu zhou) means no other but space plus time. Somewhat later, Zhuang Zi also remarked: "Existence without limitation is yu (space) and continuity without beginning or end is zhou (time)."[9] This proposition was in agreement with that of Shi Jiao.

The ancient Chinese thinkers and scientists considered the south as limitless; because the south was the place of the sun and hence of the light, while the north was the place of obscurity and darkness. Therefore the later Mohists, though excellent scientists themselves, mistook the movement of the earth as north-south instead of west-east. Nevertheless, they united the idea of movement with space and time to form their world picture and thus brought the ancient world view to a new level.

The cosmography of the ancients included the topic of infinity. Hui Shi observed: "The greatest has nothing beyond it, and is called the Great Unit."[10] This proposition concerned both the spatial limit of the cosmos and also the logical limit of human thinking (i.e., whether the limitless was thinkable to man). As regards the issue of time, Hui Shi had remarked: "I go to the state of Yue and arrived there yesterday."[11] Hard as it is to define exactly the paradoxical implication of this propostition, it apparently was intended conjecturally to touch upon the connection of movement and time.

Another propostition of Hui Shi reads: "The smallest has nothing within itself, and is called the Little Unit."[12] It might mean (1) that things were physically not infinitely divisible, and hence were constituted by the smallest indivisible particles or atoms: or (2) that he embraced logically the idea of the infinitesimal. The latter interpretation seems more in conformity with his other famous propostition that "if you take a stick a foot long and every day cut it in half, you will never come to the end of it";[13] that is to say, things were logically divisible infinitely. This theory concerning the concept of limit should be deservedly considered as one of the most brilliant intellectual achievements of ancient times.

Medical Ideas of Ancient Times

In the early times, sorcery and witchcraft exerted a considerable influence on medical science. When the Marquis of Jin fell ill, the sorcerer explained that it was due to the mischievous astrological omens. But the atheist Zi Chan refuted it, pointing out that it was simply due to his "misconduct in diet and indulgence in excessive emotions",[14] having nothing to do with the deities in heaven or on earth. This idea marked the beginning of the separation of medical science from superstitions, sorcery and witchcraft. Some of the illustrious ancient physicians were named in *Zuo's Chronicles* (or, *Zuo's Commentary on the Spring and Autumn Annals*) as well as in the *Records of the Warring States*.

The physician He made many contributions to ancient medical ideas. He was the innovator of the age-long tradition that applied the doctrine of the five elements to medical theory. He observed: "There are in heaven six airs (i.e., Yin, Yang, wind, rain, obscurity and brightness) which generate five tastes, five colours, five musical notes and, in the case of excess, six kinds of diseases."[15] It meant that tastes, sounds and colours are conducive to health but, in the case of excess, would also lead to illness. The excess of each air was considered the cause of a certain kind of disease. This medical theory constituted the basis of the traditional medical ideas in China. Further, he asserted that the six airs were connected and conditioned by the four seasons and the five elements. With the union of the six airs and the five elements, Chinese medical theory, or the five element theory of physiology, was formed.

In diagnosis, the well-known physician Bian Que laid down the foundation of the study of the types of pulse. The *History of the Han Dynasty* recorded that he had left his works in nine volumes of the *Inner Canons* and eleven volumes of the *Outer Canons*. Sima Qian said that Bian Que in treating his patients would look at their complexions, listen to their sounds and observe their actions and manners.[16] It was through him that the elementary outline of the study of diagnosis came into being.

During the Warring States Period, there was a fair knowledge about human physiology. It was known that good health depended on good physiological condition.[17] In *Lü's Spring and Autumn Annals*, there were passages dealing with ways to keep good health by moderation[18] and with analyses of various causes of diseases. It taught that men should moderate their desires, or they would certainly fall ill. And if one wished for longevity,one should keep himself away from any excess in sensual enjoyment, in emotional excitement or in hardships. With the repudiation of excess, everything in life could be constantly in moderation and there would be no more illness.[19] Thus began the study of sanitation in ancient learning.

The fact that, without physical exercise, men would become easily vulnerable to diseases, was paid due attention. Hence the proverb: "The running water never gets stale and the turning doorhinge never gets worm-eaten."[20] Thencefrom it was concluded that living too comfortably might lead to illness. All these medical ideas formed an integral part of the treasury of the intellectual tradition of China.

3. HISTORICAL IDEAS IN ANCIENT TIMES

The Chinese historiography is one of the oldest in the world. As early as the Shang Dynasty, official historians were appointed to take charge of the official documents. In the Zhou Dynasty, the official historians were also charged with recording the important speeches and events. This official post was hereditary from fathers and sons. In the Spring and Autumn and the Warring States Periods, many books on history appeared, among which the most notable were the compilation of official documents called the *Book of History*, such chronicles as *The Spring and Autumn Annals*, *Zuo's Chronicles* (or *Zuo's Commentary on the Spring and Autumn Annals*), *The Bamboo Chronicles*, and histories dealing with separate nations such as *Discourse on the States* and *Records of the Warring States*. These historical works afforded abundant sources for the famous historian Sima Qian's immortal work, *Records of the Historian*, which synthesized the methods and styles applied in the preceeding works.

The Spring and Autumn Annals was the history of the state of Lu, compiled by the official historians of Lu in chronological order and considered the earliest historical work now extant. According to the records in *The Book of Mo Zi*, there were at that time the Spring and Autumn Annals of the hundred nations. *The Book of Mencius* also mentioned the histories of various nations,—of Jin, of Chu and of Lu.[1] But among all of them, only *The Spring and Autumn Annals* was preserved and handed down to the later ages, mainly because it was revised and edited by Confucius and hence became a classic for the Confucians. It dealt with the history of the state of Lu within a course of 242 years, from 722 B.C. (the first year of the reign of Duke Yin of Lu) to 479 B.C. (the 16th year of the reign of Duke Ai of Lu), including almost all the important activities in various fields.

According to Sima Qian, the purpose Confucius had in mind in revising and editing The Spring and Autumn Annals was "to illuminate the way of the three ancient sage-kings and to discriminate the order of human affairs, to distinguish the truth from the doubtful, to show the right and the wrong, to determine the undeterminable, to praise the good and condemn the evil, to honour the righteous and blame the unrighteous". Sima Qian remarked: "For the rectification of a world in disorder, nothing could serve better than *The Spring and Autumn Annals*."[2] It was clear that by means of passing ethical judgments on past events Confucius had aimed at the rectification of names (i.e., the hierarchical orders) in the political and social sense. By the end of that period, the old social order and rites were collapsing, so Confucius attempted to rectify the disorders by drawing lessons from history. But in doing so, he was handicapped in doing justice to historical facts by deliberate digressions in his historical writing.

The accounts in *The Spring and Autumn Annals* were too simple to give the reader a clear idea of the historical realities of that time. For a detailed explanation of that book, three different versions of interpretations were worked out, namely *Gongyang's Commentary of the Spring and Autumn Annals*, *Guliang's Commentary of the Spring and Autumn Annals* and *Zou's Commentary of the Spring and Autumn Annals* (or *Zuo's Chronicles*). The authorship of *Gongyang's Commentary* was attributed to Gongyang Gao, a native of Qi in the Warring States Period, who was said to be a pupil of Confucius's disciple Zi Xia. It emphasized the "subtle exposition of the great justice", while *Guliang's Commentary* emphasized only the "great justice" with no regard to the "subtle exposition". The "great justice" consisted in the condemnation of the "usurpers and rebels", while "the subtle exposition" consisted in the "legislation for the later kings". By comparison, the historical idea in *Gongyang's Commentary* appeared more outstanding and exerted more influence upon modern thought.

Historical Ideas in *Gongyang's Commentary*

What appeared most outstanding in *Gongyang's Commentary* was its evolutionary outlook on history, i.e., its doctrine of the three historical epochs. It divided the history of the Spring and Autumn Period into three epochs in succession, namely "the decadent epoch", "the well-to-do epoch" and "the prosperous epoch of peace". The development of history was interpreted as a process from the decadent epoch to the well-to-do epoch and then to the prosperous epoch of peace, hence a process from the lower to the higher stage. This evolutionary outlook on history afforded the theoretical ground for the reform movements of the later ages. The theory of reform held by Kang Youwei at the end of the 19th century was formulated by unifying the theory of the three epochs expounded in the *Gongyang's Commentary* with the theory of the "Evolutions of Rites" in *The Book of Rites*.

Closely connected with the concept of the three epochs was its exposition of the idea of "the great unification".[3] *Gongyang's Commentary* proclaimed that the king of the Zhou Dynasty, by grace of Heaven, promulgated the calendar at the beginning of the year so as to let all nobles and commons observe it—an act symbolizing the great unification of the whole nation instead of the separatist rules of the local principalities. The idea of the great unification in *Gongyang's Commentary*, in opposition to the separatist rules of the Warring States, voiced the demand of the age for an overall unity and bore with it a considerable historical significance. The representative of the Gongyang School in the Han Dynasty, Dong Zhongshu amplified this idea of "the great unification" by asserting that the idea of the great unification outlined in *The Spring and Autumn Annals* was the constant way between heaven and earth as well as the universal justice throughout the past and the present; and the purpose of such an assertion was to strengthen the unification and the autocracy of emperor Wu of The Han Dynasty.

Gongyang's Commentary held that Confucius' compilation of *The Spring and Autumn Annals* was aimed at rectifying the disorders of that time by "setting up justice in this book and leaving it to the sages of the later ages",[4] that is, the compilation of the book was aimed at legislating for future generations. In this way, *The Spring and Autumn Annals* was closely interconnected with feudal politics. This idea was further developed by the later Gongyang School to such a degree as to bestow the title "uncrowned king" on Confucius, thus making Confucianism a religion with Confucius as its pontiff. This doctrine had great influence on the development of Confucianism as well as on intellectual and political history through the long course of feudalism in China.

The Historical Idea in *Zuo's Chronicles*

Zuo's Commentary of the Spring and Autumn Annals, or *Zuo's Chronicles*, appeared roughly at the same time as *Gongyang's Commentary*. In the opinions of modern researchers, it was worked out not by an individual writer but by many people and was eventually completed by the historian Zuoqiu Ming at about the early Warring States Period. There were always controversies about its authorship and the date of its completion, however.

Zuo's Chronicles recorded the history of various nations of the Spring and Autumn Period and was a unique achievement in ancient historiography. It further developed the Western Zhou's idea of the people in preference to the Heavenly Will. In it, the Way of Heaven, as compared to the way of man, was minimized, sometimes to the degree of the complete denial of the Mandate of Heaven and the deities. It provided a new interpretation of history, starting from the humanistic rather than the theistic point of view. It acknowledged the fact that the interaction of the people affected immensely the rise or fall of a nation and its triumph or defeat in war. It remarked: "He who has pity on the people is qualified to reign",[5] and if not, "the deities would get angry and the people would rebel, then how is it possible for him to last long?"[6] and "when the people rebel, how is it possible for him to wage a war?"[7]

In *Zuo's Chronicles*, one may find the traditional belief in deities much diluted by its emphasis on paying more attention to the people. The author observed: "When a nation is going to rise, the sovereign lends his ear to the people; and when she is going to fall, the sovereign lends his ear to the deities." Although the deities still admittedly had their role, they were obliged to "act in accordance with human beings", solely because the deities "are wise and upright in their integrity".[8] Hence in the relation between deities and men, the latter outweighed the former. In comparison with the traditional belief in the Mandate of Heaven and in deities, the viewpoint shown in *Zuo's Chronicles* was far more advanced. But during a time when "the main affair of the state consists in sacrificial offerings and warring",[9] *Zuo's Chronicles* was still unable to break entirely away from traditional superstitious beliefs.

In its social viewpoints, *Zuo's Chronicles* opposed the cruel practice of human sacrifices.[10] It represented the advanced current of thought of that time. During the decline of the royal house of Lu, the House of Ji expelled Duke Zhao, who died later in exile. *Zuo's Chronicles* commented in these words: "For generations the sovereigns of Lu followed the wrong way while the House of Ji followed the strenuous way; the people have long forgotten their sovereigns. Though the Duke died abroad, who was there to have pity on him?"[11] Here the author showed virtually an approving attitude towards the fact that in the Spring and Autumn Period the regimes were always in transition from the higher to the comparatively lower social strata. He acknowledged that society was constantly changing and hence "there is never constant reign in the realm, nor constant rank between the sovereign and vassals".[12] This ranks as an enlightened and progressive idea by the standard of that time.

In its accounting of the respective historical roles of the heroes and the masses, the book took a rather realistic manner and more or less objectively recorded the uprisings of the slaves and artisans of the age, such as that of the twenty-third year of the reign of Duke Xiang (i.e., 550 B.C.) and that of the seventeenth year of the reign of Duke Ai (478 B.C.).[13]

Of historiographical interest is the author's attempt to write an "authentic history" and to reveal the conflicts among the nobles, the sovereigns and the vassals, the royal house of Zhou and other principalities, and to depict a truthful picture of the social realities of the age. *The Spring and Autumn Annals* recorded that in the eighteenth year of the reign of Duke Xi (632 B.C.) "The Son of Heaven (i.e., the King of Zhou) went hunting at Heyang"—a fact which *Zuo's Chronicles* explained: "At that meeting the Marquis of Jin summoned the King just like ordering a subordinate prince and the King was compelled to go hunting."[14] It made plain the fact that

Confucius gave this account with "digressed writing" in order to rectify the names and their respective positions. The Marquis of Jin (i.e. Duke Wen,) was a vassal to the King of Zhou, who was the universal sovereign; and "it would give a bad precedent if the King was described as summoned by one of his vassals".[15]

Zuo's Chronicles paid due attention also to natural phenomena. It recorded thirty-seven solar eclipses, the appearances of comets, the times and places of earthquakes and other natural disasters, all of which provided invaluable sources in the field of history of science.

Complementary to Zuo's Chronicles was another book entitled Guo Yu (or Discourse on the States). In contrast to the style of Zuo's Chronicles, this book was compiled under the heading of each state. The section for Zhou was placed in the beginning and then in succession were the sections for Lu, Qi, Jin, Cheng, Chu, Wu and Yue respectively. This order of compilation showed that the author still took the King of Zhou as the universal sovereign and lined up other states in accordance with their importance and orthodoxy. But he had to admit that the King of Zhou as the universal sovereign was unable to maintain his supreme position any longer, and that the struggle for hegemony among the great powers was going on ruthlessly. The author did not approve the old patriarchal system and emphasized on the contrary "the employment of the talented". Such political proposals favoured the new classes then appearing on the horizon.

After the narration of an event, the author often made comments on its development and expressed his own view on it. The book recorded how cruelly King Li of Zhou supressed freedom of speech for fear that people might speak ill of him. It gave a detailed story of how Duke Zhao tried to persuade him that "it is even harder to prevent the utterance of opinions from the mouths of the people than to prevent the deluge from a river".[16] However, King Li would not listen to him, and the result was "within the span of three years, the King was dethroned and exiled to Zhi".[17] The story reflected the author's endeavour to sum up experience from past events for reference in the future. This method of historiography constituted an integral part of the tradition of Chinese historical writing and influenced the composition of the renowned work of Sima Guang in the Song Dynasty, Zi Zhi Tong Jian (History as a Mirror).

Each of these two books had its own character; *Zuo's Chronicles* was minute in its narration of events while *Discourse on the States* in its records of speeches. In fact, they were supplementary to each other. For the occurrence of any incident, there might be different versions recorded in these two books. *Zuo's Chronicles* gave more detailed accounts to the political and military aspects, while *Discourse on the States* stressed the economic aspects. For example, *Discourse on the States* mentioned that King Xuan of Zhou "did not attend the ceremonial farming". This was the earliest record of the fact that the nine-squares system was on the wane. Yet such a significant event was never mentioned in *Zuo's Chronicles*.

Each of these two books was an independent historical work, but there was something in common in their historical ideas. Both of them were still incapable of shaking off the heroic interpretation of history, yet their records preserved large amounts of historical resources, some of which did reflect rather objectively the forces and active roles of the common people.

4. LITERARY IDEAS IN ANCIENT TIMES

It seems strange that the ancient Chinese did not in their vast treasury of literature produce lengthy heroic epics such as the Iliad and Odyssey of ancient Greece or the Mahabharata and Ramayana of ancient India. Nevertheless, they did produce some of the best lyrics that the ancient world ever had. Though there were still no specific works on literary theory, literary ideas emerged in fragments among some of the very ancient literary compositions.

In addition to the lyric poetry, of which the best known were compiled in *The Book of Odes* and *Elegies of Chu*, there were some excellent examples of belles-lettres in the prose compositions of the ancient thinkers, as in *The Book of Mencius, The Book of Zhuang Zi, The Book of Han Fei Zi*, etc. The Confucians were especially concerned with literary theory. Among the disciples of Confucius, Zi You and Zi Xia were renowned for their versatile learning in various fields of literature. And the Confucians always tended to unite literature with their teachings and preachings.

Confucius spoke thus of *The Book of Odes*: "without learning poems, one would not know how to speak well."[1] During the Spring and Autumn Period, people often employed poems to express their intentions elegantly in court and on occasions of diplomatic intercourse. This is what is meant by the saying that "poems express one's will",[2] or as Confucius put it: "Poems are employed to express one's intentions";[3] for without the knowledge of poetry it would be hard to carry out political and diplomatic activities. Again Confucius said: "If one is able to recite three hundred pieces of poems but unable to fulfil the political missions nor to deal with other nations in his envoyship; then of what use is it, though he recites a lot of them?"[4]

Confucius taught that the learning of poetry would encourage people's aspirations, strengthen their ability of observation, make them familiar with the community, help them to give expressions to their passions, enable them to serve their parents and their sovereigns, and learn a great deal of knowledge about plants and animals.[5] At another occasion, he remarked: "If one does not learn the 'Zhou Nan' and 'Zhao Nan' [two groups of poems in *The Book of Odes*] one would be just like confronting a wall (and could find no way out)."[6] Confucius thought of poetry in terms of its practical value.

Speaking of literature, Confucius always put the Way (Tao) before the arts. Once he remarked: "One should learn literature after he has behaved well and is still energetic in his leisure."[7] Literature was mentioned in contrast with behaviour, and obviously the latter held priority over the former. Again he said: "The virtuous will certainly speak well, but a good speaker will not necessarily be virtuous."[8] Here virtue and speaking denote respectively the Way and literature. That virtue held priority over speaking (or language) meant that the Way held priority over literature. This was the origin of the age-long conviction of the Confucians that "literature serves to bear the Way".

Mencius' literary ideas inherited and developed those of Confucius. In the Spring and Autumn Period, poems were frequently recited on occasions of diplomatic activities; later in the Warring States Period, the scholars, especially the Confucians, used to cite poems to justify their arguments. Mencius forwarded his new interpretation on poetry: "To meet the intention of the author with one's own understanding." He claimed: "In explaining poems, one should not injure the language by their words, nor the intention by their language";[9] and "the true meaning can only be grasped by meeting the intentions of the author with one's own understanding".[10] Mencius himself interpreted poems in this way. He pointed out that poets in moments of the overflowing of their passions were apt to use exaggerated expressions which were not facts; therefore one ought not to submit oneself merely to the literal words and terms in interpreting poems. But this method of his sometimes led to pure subjective conjectures, even to the distortion of the original meanings of the author. Mencius himself was not able to avoid this kind of abuse, which brought harmful effects in later ages.

After all, Mencius was a critic with keen insight who pointed out penetratingly that one should learn to know where lay the shortcomings of a literary work by finding out its insincerity of expression.[11] Furthermore, it was he who propounded the famous proposition: "One should know the personality of the author and pass a judgment of his time."[12] He observed: "In reading his poems and studying his books, is it possible not to know the man? It is in this way that we are qualified to judge his time." Conversely, by understanding his time, one might get a better understanding of his works.

In his literary theory, Xun Zi followed the line sketched by Confucius and Mencius. He observed: "The author should make use of the right names and appropriate terms that might serve to clarify his intentions."[13] This demand for clarifying one's intentions also had a direct effect on the idea that "literature serves to bear the Way" of the later ages. Concerning the contents and effects of literature, Xun Zi urged that they should conform to the demand of the Way, that is, literature should take the ancient sages and their classics as its standard.

Xun Zi asserted: "What man is to literature is just like what jade is to carving and polishing."[14] He cited as an illustration the story that the famous jade of He before being carved and polished was just like other ordinary stones, but after being carved and polished by the craftsman it became a precious treasure. So was the case with men. He cited as examples the cases of Zi Gong and Ji Lu, the well-known disciples of Confucius, who were at first but ordinary people from the countryside, but after having learned literature and the code of rites became prominent scholars.[15] Like all Confucians, Xun Zi laid emphasis on the practical value of literature and tied it up with the

Confucian ideal of a benevolent government.

Generally speaking, literary ideas in ancient times emphasized the practical aspect in a rather crude way. The Legalists even despised literature. For example, Shang Yang considered that literary men would lead people "getting weary of farming and warring"[16] and hence the nation would fall into poverty and weakness. Han Fei, when speaking of literature, warned the sovereign "never forget the usefulness of a literary work while reading it."[17] It has ever been a characteristic feature of Chinese thought to lay special emphasis on practicality and to neglect the purely logical and esthetic aspects. So was it with literary ideas.

Part II
IDEOLOGY IN THE EARLY MIDDLE AGES

GENERAL SKETCH OF
THE EARLY MIDDLE AGES
(3RD CENTURY B.C.-A.D. 10TH CENTURY)

By the term of "the early middle ages" were included the periods of Qin, Han, Wei, Jin, the Southern and Northern Dynasties, Sui Tang and the subsequent Five Dynasties. It lasted more than 1,180 years, from the unification of the whole country by the Qin Dynasty (221 B.C.) down to the establishment of the Song Dynasty (A.D. 960). It was a period in which the feudal society grew out of its first buds into its full maturity. In both the socio-economic and the cultural and intellectual aspects, it accomplished greater progress than the pre-Qin period, while laying down at the same time the basis for transforming into the later middle ages.

(1)

With the unification of all the other six states under the sole reign of Shi Huang Di (literally the First Emperor) of Qin in the year 221 B.C., a multi-national, centralized, autocratic but unified empire was eventually founded for the first time in the history of China. The political and social model upon which it was founded had been later followed by all succeeding dynasties for more than two thousand years with all its far-reaching consequences throughout the later history of China.

Under the ruthless domination of the Qin Dynasty, there broke out the first nationwide peasant uprisings headed by Chen Sheng and Wu Guang; and the Qin Dynasty was finally overthrown.

After years of cruel suppression by the Qin regime and the subsequent civil war which lasted eight years, especially between Chu and Han, the social productive forces were seriously damaged, leading to the extreme destitution in social life at the early Han Dynasty.

For the purpose of consolidating the newly founded dynasty, it was of the utmost urgency for the Han rulers to maintain a stable political situation so as to make possible the recovery and development of the economy, or the material basis of the Han regime. Facing such a serious reality, the early Han rulers were obliged to learn from the lessons of the downfall of the Qin Dynasty. The Qin policy of "harsh decrees and severe punishments" accommodated itself no more to the demand of the time. So the Taoist ideology with its emphasis on "quietness and non-activity" replaced the Legalist stand as the guiding principle of the ruling class. The early Han government pursued the policy of "letting the people to have a rest". This indeed met the demand of the age and brought a positive effect on the economic recovery as well as on the stabilization of the regime. It was upon this basis that there emerged the good days of "the reign of emperors Wen and Jing" which provided the material strength of the later Emperor Wu.

For the sake of enforcing his domination and strengthening the centralization of his power, Emperor Wu gave up the Taoist ideology of non-activity and adopted in its stead Dong Zhongshu's proposal of "banning the hundred schools and up-holding the supremacy of Confucianism". Since then the orthodoxy of Confucianism came to power.

For the sake of giving the divine right of emperors a theoretical ground, Dong Zhongshu developed the idea of the communion of Heaven and Man into a theory of interaction of Heaven and Man, thus rendering the doctrine of Confucianism into an official theology.

While this new variety of Confucianism, with Dong Zhongshu as its spokesman, was taking shape and developing into a superstitious theology, there also emerged a current of naive materialism with such figures as Sima Qian, Huan Tan, Wang Chong and Zhong Changtong as its foremost representatives. The struggle between atheism and theological teleology constituted one of the main features of the ideological development of the Han period. This manifested itself not only in the sphere of philosophy but also in that of historiography and natural sciences. Philosophical ideas and scientific knowledge were in close connection and in a relation of mutual promotion.

Lively also were the social and economic thoughts of the time. Confronting the issue of how to consolidate the imperial central regime and its material strength, of how to meet the problem of land annexation and to moderate the ever-sharpening social contradictions, many thinkers tried to work out their proposals and programmes. Some of their ideas produced lasting influence on the later ages.

(2)

During the later period of the Eastern Han Dynasty (A.D. 2nd-3rd century), the once prevailing theological Confucianism, with all its vagueness and absurdity and under the smashing blow of the great Yellow-Turban Uprising of the peasants, had gradually lost its former dominance and lure as an ideology of the ruling class. Under this new circumstance, some representatives of the ruling class endeavoured to choose those parts of Confucianism, Taoism and Legalism which in a mixed fashion suited their need as an intellectual weapon for re-establishing the ruling order then in rapid decline. Hence in the late Eastern Han and the subsequent Wei and Jin dynasties (A.D. 3rd-5th century), there appeared successively the nominalistic-legalitic and then the metaphysical currents of thought. The later, in particular, dominated the intellectual stage in the Wei and Jin period. It was born and growing up with the increasing powers of the great nobilities as an official ideology in which were blended various elements from Confucianism and Taoism. In view of the failure of the former theological teleology of the Han Dynasty, it ceased to take an open form of theism but substituted the personified deity with a spiritual noumenon dressed in a highly sophisticated philosophical form.

The domination of the Confucian theology being shaken, the intellectual confinements laid by the traditional classical study were broken down and there appeared a situation of "intellectual liberation". As Lu Xun once said of it: "Since intellectual liberation had burst open obstination and stubbornness, so it became possible for people to absorb paganism and ideas from abroad with the result that

ideas other than the Confucian were introduced in a steady stream."*
As a result, in the time of the Northern and Southern Dynasties,
Buddhism and Taoism with the support of the great nobilities pre-
vailed throughout the country.

Running through the intellectual polemics of this period were
the pros and cons of metaphysical idealism and of Buddhism. Such
thinkers as Yang Quan, Pei Wei and Bao Jingyan launched sharp
criticism on metaphysical idealism. When Buddhism was in vogue,
there came forth also a number of atheists among whom the most
prominent was Fan Zhen during the Liang Dynasty. His famous
thesis "On the Mortality of the Spirit" carried the atheistic tradition
of Wang Chong forward to a new level.

In the sphere of intellectual activities, peoples' ideas were always
interconnected. Liberated from the confinements of the Confucian
classical studies, literature assumed its independence and works on
literary criticism and literary theory were tinted strongly with a sense
of self-consciousness.

During the period of great schism and tumult of the Wei, Jin
and Southern and Northern Dynasties, people of all strata emigrated
in large numbers from the north to the south, thus providing the
economic development of the south, especially the lower part of the
Yangtze valley, or south of the Yangtze as the area was usually
called, with advanced techniques and labour and bringing about a
great progress, economically as well as culturally, of this area. Soon
it excelled the formerly advanced areas such as the middle and lower
parts of the Yellow River valley and the Guanzhong (east of Tong-
guan Pass) Plain. So it was no accident that Lu Bao at that time wrote
his famous satire "On the God of Money" in which he sharply
mocked at the worship of money in the daily life of the people. It
reflected the social change caused by the growing commodity-money
relations. It was at that time too that there emerged the first idea of
the equalization of the farmland which was later put into practice to
a certain extent during the Sui and Tang dynasties.

In the field of natural sciences, the most prominent representatives of this time were Zu Chongzhi and Jia Sixie whose achieve-

---

*Lu Xun, "The Demeanour and Literary Style in Wei and Jin and Their
Relations with Medicine and Wine", *Collected Works of Lu Xun.*

ments had greatly promoted both practical technology and scientific ideas and should be in every way ranked among the best intellectual legacy of ancient China.

(3)

With the great unification of the whole empire under the Sui Dynasty (A.D. 581-618), the moderation of the contradiction within the landlord class found its ideological manifestation in the tendency of harmonizing the three different teachings of Confucianism, Buddhism and Taoism. The Tang Dynasty, founded on the ruins of the short-lived Sui Dynasty, was earnest in learning from the lessons of Sui's downfall brought about by the uprisings of the peasants. As civil wars greatly depopulated the entire country and production was seriously damaged, society was then in urgent need of recovery. The Tang regime adopted a policy of reconciliating the social contradictions with a view to developing social production. While doing so, the Tang regime also made wide use of religions. Both Buddhism and Taoism were brought to full flourish. It was then that different sects of Buddhism came into being and prevailed. Alongside with it, the government paid special attention to the preaching of the ethical norms of Confucianism and summoned erudite scholars for editing and compiling the Confucian classics, resulting in the promulgation of the Correct Interpretation of the Five Cassics. Hence came into being the co-existence of the three teachings of Confucianism, Buddhism and Taoism.

On the other hand, the anti-Buddhist tradition of Wei, Jin and the Southern and Northern Dynasties was carried on in the early Tang by Fu Yi, Lü Cai and others who applying naturalism as their theoretical weapon, launched criticism on theology and religious superstitions. In the middle Tang Dynasty, Han Yu started an anti-Buddhist and anti-Taoist movement from the standpoint of Confucianism. Yet the tendency of the confluence of Confucianism, Buddhism and Taoism had already laid down the theoretical foundation of the coming Neo-Confucianism of the Song Dynasty.

After the rebellion of An Lushan and Shi Siming in the mid-8th century, the Tang Dynasty declined rapidly with ever sharpening

social crisis and intense class antagonism. Political reform move-
ments then began to surge with the aim of solving the social crisis.
There also appeared an intellectual trend against feudal privileges.
The foremost representatives of this trend were the literary figures
Liu Zongyuan and Liu Yuxi who had contributed much to the
intellectual treasury of the Middle Ages.

By the end of the Tang Dynasty, there broke out a great torrent
of peasant uprisings, advocating for the first time in history the ideal
of naive egalitarianism which strongly influenced the revolutionary
ideas of the peasants in later ages. Closely connected with this torrent
were the ideas of some advanced thinkers such as Pi Rixiu and Tan
Qiao who criticized the feudal autocracy and expressed their sympathy with the sufferings and good wishes of the peasants.

In sum, the culture of the Tang Dynasty witnessed the glory and
splendour of mediaeval China and brought the intellectual activities
in various fields up to a new peak unparalleled in the cultural history
of the mediaeval world.

Chapter 5

IDEOLOGY IN THE QIN
AND HAN PERIOD

1. THE AUTOCRATIC IDEAS OF
THE QIN DYNASTY

In the year 221 B.C., the first unified, centralized and autocratic empire was founded by the First Emperor of Qin.

In the interest of the ascending landlord class and of the imperial power, the First Emperor strengthened his rule by continuing the Legalist policy which had proved so effective since the time mf Shang Yang. In the meantime, he adopted Zou Yan's doctrine of the "revolutions and transmutations of the Five Powers (or Virtues)" as an ideological support of his autocratic rule.

Li Si (?-208 B.C.), the last great Legalist of the age, was a native of Shangcai in Chu. He came from a plebian family and had served as an official in a prefecture. Later he became a disciple of Xun Zi and a learning-mate of Han Fei. His Legalist doctrine won the favour of the king of Qin (later the First Emperor) and he was promoted to the position of prime minister. With the help of Li Si, the First Emperor did his utmost to consolidate his centralized autocracy after the Legalist pattern and on the basis of the prefectural system under the direct control of the imperial court instead of the former practice of enfeofment.

The First Emperor began taking measures to strengthen the royal power and to deify the personal dignity of the sovereign. It was for the emperor himself to assume the sole credit of governing the whole country and his imperial reign was supposed to perpetuate to eternity. As a sign of his supreme power and authority, after the great unification of the whole country he did away with the title of "king" and substituted it with that of the "emperor", which became thenceforth a symbol of the centralized and autocratic empire assumed by all later dynasties.

In addition to the Legalist doctrine, the First Emperor also made use of the doctrine of the Yin Yang School as presented by Zou Yan. The doctrine of the Five Elements of the Yin Yang School, originally naturalistic in its nature, was transformed by Zou Yan into a mystic theory of the "revolutions and transmutations of the Five Powers (or Virtues)" by which the rise and fall of the succeeding dynasties were supposed to find an explanation. But this theory failed to show where lay the primum mobile of the powers of the Five Elements and had to attribute it to Providence. It was claimed that before the ascendancy of a certain Power (or Virtue, literally a divine force), Heaven was of necessity to show some of its propitious forebodings.

This mystic theory of Zou Yan had already been mentioned in the *Lü's Spring and Autumn Annals*. When the king of Qin assumed the title of emperor, somebody in Qi mentioned this theory to him, informing him that his ancestor Duke Wen had once hunted a black dragon, an omen of the Power of Water, some five hundred years ago. The First Emperor adopted this theory of the Five Powers and made the following regulations:

1. Winter was appointed the due season for the Power of Water, hence the tenth month of the year was stipulated as the first month.

2. The due colour of the Power of Water was black, so blackness was stipulated as the official colour for dresses, banners and flags.

3. The due number of the Power of Water was six, so the number six was stipulated as the standard number and all things should be counted by six.

4. According to the doctrine of the Yin-Yang School, the Water dwelt in the north and by its very nature bore with it cruelty and death; so the Qin Dynasty ran the country with ruthless and cruel penalty, or with "rigidity" and "harshness" instead of "benevolence and reconciliation". The political doctrines of the Legalist School was thus tightly united with the theory of the Five Powers of the Yin-Yang School in service of the feudal autocratic regime.

This combination was in its essence nothing else but an endeavour to assume a super-social and super-natural force in order to deify the royal authority. It was to justify that the First Emperor of Qin came to the throne as a result of the good omen of the Power of Water and that he was the genuine "son of Heaven" by grace of Providence from which all his authority was derived. In the last analysis, all this was but for the purpose of cheating the people and making them willingly subject to the dominations imposed on them. It was for this reason that this theory was perpetuated by all the subsequent dynasties. The truth is that it is not religion that creates men but men who created religious myths.

The First Emperor abolished the old practice of enfeofment and in its stead instituted a centralized and autocratic government controlling directly over a system of prefectures and districts. And for the sake of strengthening his policy of intellectual despotism, he banned all "private learnings" and repelled all schools (the Confucian and the Taoist included), while compelling people only "to learn from the imperial officials" following the Legalist line. And such a policy and its practice had eventually led to the well-known incident of "burning the books and burying the scholars".

In the year 213 B.C. (the 34th year of the Emperor's reign), at a banquet given by the Emperor in the palace, Chunyu Yue made his proposal to restore the practice of enfeofment of the old but Li Si came forth to oppose it, holding that such an idea would be a rejection of the present and a restoration of the past which would certainly leave the people in puzzle and create disadvantages in the execution of the government's decrees and edicts and should, therefore, be completely nullified. On Li Si's proposal, the Emperor ordered to burn the books of the classics, the hundred schools and the histories of all other states, except the history of Qin, the official documents and archives and such technological books as concerned with calendar, mathematics, medicine and forestry. Thus a catastrophe befell to many books of antiquity. In the next year when some alchemists failed to find elixirs of life for the Emperor and accused the Emperor for being despotic, the Emperor had all the scholars involved in the case arrested and more than 460 of them were buried alive in the surburb of the capital Xianyang. This was known in traditional historical writings as "the burning of books and the burying of scholars".

Such was the brutality resulted from the intellectual despotism and the totalitarian autocracy of the Qin Dynasty. It showed the essence of despotism in its cruelty and ignorance. The Emperor tried to control the thoughts of the people by means of extremely ruthless despotism and obscurantism. But things proved the contrary. With the brilliant ancient cultural legacies savagely devastated and the intellectual hightide of "the contending of the hundred schools" ruthlessly suppressed, the Emperor never attained his aim of despotic rule by a forced conformity of the people's thoughts, or by an intellectual unification. It sounds like an irony that such measures led only to the break-up of the internal relations within the ruling class and the weakening of its ruling forces. And the Qin regime fell and collapsed rapidly within only two decades.

Sarcastic as it happened, both Xiang Yu and Liu Bang who helped so much in overthrowing the Qin regime were no intellectual at all. They cultivated no literary learning whatsoever, nor did the rebel leaders of that time Chen Sheng and Wu Guang. The case with the First Emperor of Qin perhaps may help to show a fact so plain and so simple in history that no issue in the ideological sphere could be met with dictatorial or coercive measures.

In its execution of the Legalist policies, the Qin regime stressed especially on the side of harsh punishments and rigid laws. One of the characteristics of the Legalist line was the naked flaunt of its ruthless suppression and its shameless deception. From the bamboo sheets of the Qin laws recently unearthed, it might be perceived how cruel the Qin laws were. There were more than twenty statutes concerning the arresting of the people. In the criminal code there were listed the names of various kinds of corporal punishments beyond imagination, including numerous methods of putting people to death, to torture and to inhumane hard labour. All these were employed for the enslavement of the people, who were compelled at last to break the fetters imposed on them. During the last years of the Qin Dynasty, people violated the laws so often that "criminals blocked the roads and prisons everywhere were overcrowded".[1] The extreme exploitation and suppression of the people intensified the political and social contradictions, and soon peasant uprisings burst out under the leadership of Chen Sheng and Wu Guang. The rule of the Qin regime was overthrown and together with it came to an end the Legalist rule in the sphere of ideology. History finally proclaimed the bankruptcy of the effort of the First Emperor for an ideological uniformity and unification.

2. THE TAOIST IDEOLOGY IN THE EARLY HAN PERIOD

Under the tyranny of the Qin rule, the heavy burden of the innumerable corvées and taxations plus the ruthless criminal punishments seriously disrupted social productivity. It was followed first by peasant uprisings and then by civil wars among contending groups especially between Chu and Han. During the early years of the eventual establishment of the Han Dynasty, social economy was in a miserable state. There was a desperate lack of labouring forces in the countryside; and in the urban area the population was greatly decreased. It was said that "the population was only two to three tenth of the original".[2] For instance, the original population of thirty thousand households in the city of Quni (now in Hebei) was reduced to only five thousand. In some places there were even cases of cannibalism. The public finance was in such difficulties that even the emperor could not afford four horses of the same colour for his carriage and the prime minister was obliged to ride in an ox cart.

The task of top priority for the government was to stabilize the new born regime and maintain social order so as to guarantee the recovery and development of the economy upon which the government could finance the bureaucracy and the army. As was exacted by economic need, the rule by harsh punishment and rigid law gave way to the Taoist ideology with its stress on "quietude and non-activity" which played the role of the governing ideology of the early Han period.

The lot of an ideology always depends on the degree it could meet the social need. The Taoist School originated in the mid-Warring States period in the name of Huang Di. Later, it absorbed and transformed the doctrine of Lao Zi and formed an independent school. With its theme of "the rule of non-activity", it furnished the governing class with a set of theory and practice regarding political and social policies. The principle of "quietude and non-activity" did meet the urgent need of economic recovery fairly well. As regards the governing of the people, it did provide more flexibility than the Legalist School who knew nothing else than to resort to the cult of violence. This explains the reason why the Taoist ideology got the upper hand in the early years of Han Dynasty. From the time when the first emperor of Han, Liu Bang, marched into the capital of Qin, Xianyang, and made "an agreement in three articles" with the people by adopting the Taoist doctrine to alleviate the brutal exaction of the Qin regime, down to the early years of the reign of Emperor Wu who began to employ the Confucians for his rule, there had been five emperors in succession—Gao, Hui, Wen, Jing and Wu—who reigned altogether for more than sixty years with Taoist teaching as their guiding principle.

The famous prime minister Cao Can of the early Han Dynasty was at first the prime minister to the king of Qi. By that time, the whole country was just being settled after long years of upheavals. Cao sent for a Taoist Gai Gong to take the position of his adviser who proposed to him to adopt the Taoist policy of "quietude and non-activity in order to keep the people in repose". Within a period of nine years the state of Qi became well governed and Cao Can, renowned as an excellent prime minister. After the death of Xiao He, the first prime minister of the Han Dynasty, Cao Can succeeded him and continued his Taoist policy. It was said of him that "by bringing about quietude he has kept the people in peace". In the Records of a Historian, it was written that "after the people had got rid of the cruelty of the Qin regime, Cao Can brought them quietude and non-activity, therefore all the world came to praise him".[3]

During the succeeding reigns, Emperor Wen with wife Dou and their son Jing were all great admirers of Taoism. And the famous prime minister Chen Ping, successor to Cao Can, was also an upholder of the Taoist policy. It was not until the reign of Emperor Wu (later 2nd century B.C.) that the imperial policy took a turn. Emperor Wu was an ambitious man and fond of entrusting the Confucians for his administration. Hence there broke out some political clashes between the Emperor Wu and his grandmother, Empress Dowager Du.

The main point of the Taoist policies in the early Han Dynasty consisted in not to disturb or to burden the people too much, so as to be able to keep a relatively stable situation under which the people might be permitted to have a chance to thrive. And this led to the development of the social economy and to the consolidation of the Han regime. It was surely not due to their personal preferences or kindheartedness that the early Han rulers adopted the Taoist doctrine as their guiding principle. The real reason for it lay in the fact that after long years of war the people were reduced to such a miserable state as to have nothing left for being exploited any more, and thereupon the ruling class was obliged to lighten the burdens of the people. Oppression and exploitation in a lighter degree had proved more profitable to the ruling class than limitless exactions.

Though the rulers of the Former Han (or Western Han) upheld the Taoist teaching, they had never repudiated the hundred schools. So the pre-Qin "private learnings", once the prey of Qin's intellectual policy, were then gradually reappearing, and so did the pre-Qin thoughts of various schools. Some outstanding thinkers of this period such as Lu Gu, Jia Yi and Sima Qian, endeavoured to sum up the ideas of the hundred schools into a synthesis, though the Taoist doctrine as the main stream of the age was still held supreme. The famous statesman and writer Jia Yi was essentially a Confucian, but he also upheld Taoist teaching. He maintained that Tao constituted the basis of all things and that rulers should always keep in mind the Taoist principle of non-activity. It should be noted that non-activity meant merely that the government should not trouble or burden the people too much. Roughly speaking, the Former Han Dynasty reigned with this Taoist policy rather successfully and smoothly.

Lu Gu (cir. 240-170 B.C.) had been a member in the staff of Liu Bang. After the establishment of the Han Dynasty he was ordered to write a book summarizing the experiences of the downfall of Qin and the success of Han. He often lectured Liu Ban on the Confucian classics. The latter declared, "I won the country on my horseback, of what use are those books to me?" To this Lu answered: "You won the country on your horseback, but is it possible to rule it also on your horseback?"[4] In Lu's opinion, for the sake of having a country well-governed, both means should be made use of, one being the armed forces and the other the ideological indoctrination; and the reason of Qin's rapid downfall was due to its cult of sheer force while neglecting the other. In his book A New Treatise, he remarked, "The more the Qin government took actions, the more the country fell into disorder.... It was not that the Qin government did not want to keep the country in good order, but what caused it to fall was that it exacted too much and resorted too often to punishments."[5] Reviewing the lessons of Qin's downfall, he advised the Han Dynasty to follow the Taoist lines to let the people have a rest, so that the social economy might get nourished and the imperial rule become more stable. Therefrom he concluded, "In non-activity lies activity."[6]

The Taoist teaching did meet the demand of the age considerably and hence brought its positive effects on both the development of the social economy and the stability of the political situation.

3. DONG ZHONGSHU AND THE SPREAD OF THEOLOGICAL IDEAS

As the Former Han (206 B.C.-A.D. 8) entered the middle stage of its reign, the ruling ideology began turning away from the Taoist line of non-activity and heading towards the orthodoxy of Confucianism with Dong Zhongshu as its foremost representative.

Through a period of sixty years of recovery and development the Han Empire was getting stronger under the reign of Emperor Wu who was enabled to provide an armed force to attack the Huns beyond the northern border, abolish the disobedient princes and suppress the peasants' rebellions. The Taoist ideology was then becoming out-of-date and distasteful to the imperial rulers, because it ceased to meet the requirement of the new situation. So the Confucian ideology propounded anew by Dong Zhongshu stepped to the fore as the official ideology which had since then dominated all the later ages as the orthodoxy.

Dong Zhongshu (179-104 B.C.), a native of Guangchuan (now in Hebei), was a great master of the Gongyang School and the founder of the New Text School in classical studies. Of his writings the best known was the Exuberant Dew of the Spring and Autumn. In the year 104 B.C. he was appointed by the Emperor to the post of prime minister of a local principality and years later to the same post of another principality. As the foremost spokesman of the new orthodoxy of Confucianism, he had been the undisputed Dean ever since that time.

With the great unification under the Han Empire, all scholars and all schools were contending to win the favour of the imperial power with their teachings and proposals, and hence it became necessitated for them to reform or remould themselves so as to adjust to the new situation. The ideology propounded by Dong was already not the original pre-Qin Confucianism, but one recast and remoulded to meet the political needs of the unified empire. Dong elaborated a new theological ideology that comprised the Communion of Heaven and Man of the pre-Qin Confucianism, the totalitarian ideals of the Legalists and the theory of the revolution and transmutations of the Five Elements of the Yin-Yang School. The Confucian classics were thus remodelled into a theological system by his introdution of the Interaction between Heaven and Man with the "three cardinal guides and the five constant virtues" at its nucleus.

While recommending the idea and ideal of the Great Unification to Emperor Wu, he emphasized the importance of intellectual uniformity. He worked out new interpretations on traditional classics. *The Spring and Autumn Annals*, he affirmed, was written by Confucius with the intention of accomplishing the Great Unification. Meanwhile, he also drew from the Legalist School the idea of a centralized autocracy and combined it with the idea of Great Unification. He advocated that it was only in case where the uniformity of thought was realized that there could be "uniformity of the governing measures and clear-cut administration of justice".[7] Hence he made the suggestion to Emperor Wu, "All that are outside of the scope of the Six Arts of Confucius should be totally banned and given no room to thrive."[8] By advocating the adoption of political coercion, he advised the Emperor Wu to do away with the hundred schools and to uphold only Confucianism in supremacy, so that Confucianism might play the role of the sole instrument not only to concert the ruling groups internally but also to intensify its intellectual control over the people externally. Besides, he suggested that the whole country should be unified under the rule of the emperor and the local principalities should be given no right of enfeoffment or hereditary territory. This provided the imperial power with a theoretical ground to strengthen its centralized control.

The theory of the divine rights of emperors was more polished by his doctrine of the Interaction between Heaven and Man. Inheriting and developing the theory of the Mandate of Heaven of the pre-Qin Confucian school while incorporating the mystic power of the Five Elements of the Yin-Yang School, he made Heaven the supreme Deity that created and ruled both the natural world and the human society by his divine will. The emperor was said to be the son of Heaven who accepted the Mandate of Heaven and represented the authority of Heaven on earth. Therefore, the authority of the emperor was sacred and inviolable.

Both Heaven and Man were possessed of the same temperament and emotion; and in consequence of this, there was of necessity the interaction between Heaven and man, or "what is between Heaven and man will come in one",[9] as he described it. To obey the imperial edict would mean to subject to the will of Heaven. On occasions when the imperial reign was successful or about to fall, Heaven would show propitious omens or natural disasters. When the emperor behaved well, there would appear unicorns, phoenix, never-withering plants and sweet heavenly dews as the symbols of heavenly rewards; conversely when the emperor behaved foul and the state was about to decline, then there would appear landslips, earthquakes, eclipses and so on as symbols of the fury or warning from Heaven.

Throughout Dong's theological ideology there was threaded the metaphysical theme: "The great sources of Tao derives from Heaven; Heaven never changes, nor does the Tao." Here by Tao was meant the ruling orthodoxy, or the whole set of political, social and ethical principles and norms of feudalism which were supposed to be postulated by Heaven. Since Heaven is eternally unchanging and unchangeable, so also the rule of Tao. To Dong, the ruling order of the existing institution was something eternally solidified and no change whatever could ever happen. His metaphysical thesis: "Heaven never changes, nor does Tao"[10] served an argument for the reign of feudal order to all later ruling classes as an invariable credo. Social reality begets ideas and ideas in their turn serve the social reality. Feudalism begot Dong's doctrine and and Dong's doctrine served feudal rule.

The historical conception of Dong was that of cyclicism. By absorbing Zou Yan's theory on the successive rotation of the Powers of Five Virtues, he elaborated a theory of Three Reigns and Three

Beginnings by which he asserted that each new dynasty coming to the throne should adopt a new colour (black, white and red in succession) and a new beginning for the calendar year. Thus Xia Dynasty belonged to the reign of the black with the first lunar month as its primary calendar month; Shang Dynasty the white with the twelfth, and Zhou Dynasty the red with the eleventh. Now it was the Han Dynasty's turn to undergo again the reign of the black. With this theory he tried to illustrate on the one hand how the changes of the successive dynasties took place, while on the other hand why the reality of the feudal rule should remain untouched. Hence his proposition: "The sovereigns may sometimes be carrying out institutional reforms in name, but in reality they never make any change on the Tao."[11] That is to say, a new regime in place of the old serves only to remedy the wrongs committed by the old to the Tao, but never to change the Tao itself, i.e., the fundamental ruling order.

In correspondence with the idea of Tao was his theory of human nature which he classified into three categories: the sovereigns and the sages belonged to the top category and were gifted by Heaven with extraordinary talents; landlords and the gentry to the medium category who had to be cultivated by the sages; since the peasants and labourers were supposed to be born ignorant and stupid, they had to be subdued to the rule of the sovereigns and sages.

The most widely spread thesis of Dong was his doctrine of the three cardinal guides and the five constant virtues. The three cardinal guides included that the sovereign should be the guide of his subjects, the father that of his children and the husband that of his wife. The five constant virtues consisted of benevolence, righteousness, propriety, intelligence and good faith by which the three cardinal guides were maintained and harmonized. Furthermore, "the origin of the three cardinal guides in a good polity may be traced to Heaven",[12] so Heaven served once more a guarantee for the existing ruling order. The deification of the feudalistic principles thus came to its completion by being aggrandized into a basic cosmic law. And thus was laid down the feudalistic ideology as the spiritual fetters imposed on the people. It should be noted that in this ideology the ancient Confucianism was recast and reinterpreted by combining various elements from both the Legalists and the Yin-Yang School. It was but the logical product of the age and, as a matter of course, assumed the status of the official orthodoxy.

After the reign of Emperor Wu, as social contradictions steadily sharpened, Dong's theological doctrine became increasingly mingled with religious superstitions. Particularly the *Book of Changes* and the *Spring and Autumn Annals*, being studied along the line of the New Text School, became the main sources for superstitious analogies. Noted scholars of that time, like Xiahou Changming, Xiahou Sheng, Liu Xiang, Kuang Heng, Xiao Wangzhi and others were all promoted to high positions for being good at explaining political affairs by applying the idea of Providence.

By the end of the Western Han, during the reigns of Emperors Ai and Ping (6 B.C. to A.D. 6), the imperial government under the blows of the upsurging peasants' rebellions and frequent natural disasters, sought religious superstitions for its rescue. In order to fool the people with the will of the Providence, the learning of prognostication and apocrypha combined with the study of classics in a superstitious mood became a vogue.

The so-called Chen (prognostication) refers to the prophecy supposed to be found in the esoteric teachings, and Wei (apocrypha), the interpretation of the classics by prognostication. When Wang Mang (A.D. 9-23), the founder and emperor of the short-lived Xin Dynasty, was attempting to usurp the royal throne, many scholars hurried to prepare the Chen and Wei (prognostication and apocrypha) for him. During the civil wars by the end of the Western Han, all political leaders like Liu Xiu and Gongsun Shu competed in fabricating prognostications and apocrypha to prove that they were ordained by Providence.

Liu Xiu (A.D. 25-58) became the first emperor of the Eastern (Later) Han Dynasty. In the year A.D. 56, he issued an imperial edict proclaiming a set of theological prognostications, which later became established as the official orthodoxy. In this way Confucianism was further made both a religion and a theology. In the year A.D. 79, Emperor Zhang (A.D. 76-88) summoned many scholars to a conference presided by himself at the White Tiger Temple to discuss the classics. The documents of this conference was compiled by Ban Gu, the renowned historian, into *A General Treatise from the White Tiger* which along the line of Dong's doctrine, mixed prognostications and apocrypha with the Confucian classical studies in its explanation of social, political and ethical institutions.

As the feudalistic code of the ruling class, *A General Treatise from the White Tiger* focused its theory on how to consolidate and heighten the centralized power of autocracy. In its exposition of the Five Elements, it gave special prominence to the element Earth, asserting that Earth was supreme among the elements. Its proposition "the earth resides in the centre" implies that the imperial power should rule over all others, because earth symbolizes the royalty. Even the revolutions of the planets were treated with a reference to the relationship between sovereigns and subjects.[13]

Dong's doctrine of the three cardinal guides and five constant virtues was expanded by *A General Treatise from the White Tiger* into three cardinal guides and six disciplines. Suffice it to say that the very first suggestion of the idea of the three cardinal guides might be found in *The Book of Han Fei*, but Dong manipulated it in a theological way by stipulating a sovereign-subject model in human relationship or as he put it: "The Yang is the superior and the Yin the inferior." Thereupon the human relations were channelled into the feudal hierarchy by the six disciplines.

4. WANG CHONG AND THE IDEOLOGICAL CURRENT OF THE LATER HAN DYNASTY

At the same time when Confucianism represented by Dong Zhongshu was heading for superstition and theology, the current of naturalism was also taking its shape. Sima Qian, a contemporary of Dong, in his work had already taken a critical attitude towards the mystic theory of the Five Elements. Sima held that Yin and Yang and the succession of the four seasons were governed by irrevocable natural laws to which people should only comply but never superimpose any superfluous superstitions, which could only make people "restrained and afraid".[14] In the last years of Western Han, Yang Xiong (53 B.C.-A.D. 13) in his book *The Model Sayings* held the view that nothing in the world was divine disposition and all things were but the natural products of heaven and earth. His view opposed directly to Dong's. He also embraced certain atheistic elements with which he confronted various kinds of superstition, necromancy and divination.

In the early Eastern Han period, Huan Tan (cir. 40 B.C.-A.D. 32) stood in open opposition to Dong's theological teleology and had almost cost his life under the accusation of his "sacriligiousness and lawlessness". The significant contribution of his teaching lay in its exposition on the relation of body and spirit. It reads: "The spirit dwells within the body just like the fire in the burning candle" and "without the candle the fire cannot exist alone in the void".[15] By this proposition he intended to show that there could be no existence of the spirit without the body and hence no spirit could ever dispose the body. Huan Tan represented the polemic character of the advanced ideological currents of the age against the prevailing prognostication and apocrypha and had a direct impact on Wang Chong.

Wang Chong (A.D. 27-97), a native of Shangyu (in Zhejiang), came from among the lower social strata. In his youth, he had studied in the Royal Academy at the capital Luoyang and had been a disciple of the great scholar Ban Biao. He was well trained in various doctrines of the hundred schools. His main work entitled *Discourses Weighed in the Balance* consisted of eighty-five chapters, totalling more than 200,000 words. In launching an unrelenting ideological struggle against the prevailing theology of prognostication and apocrypha, he supported his arguments with the knowledge of natural sciences of the age as well as with the advanced social thoughts of the past. With him atheism in ancient China reached a new peak.

He formulated a naturalistic theory of the primordial ether. For him, both heaven and earth were the physical reality which, with all things in it, was composed of this primordial ether. The ether manifested itself both in its diffusive state as the cosmic ether and in its coherent state as the ether of the five elements. Though their forms might differ from each other, their essence would always remain one and the same. "All things are generated from this ether"[16] through a natural process "by which the heaven crowns above and the earth burdens below; the ether below evaporates above and the ether above sinks below; all things are generated in a natural way".[17] Beyond the primordial ether (an idea akin to matter), there is no creator nor any supernatural will.

With this naturalistic theory, he forcibly refuted Dong's theological teleology based on the theory of the Communion and Interaction

. of Heaven and man. Wang proclaimed: "Some scholars taught that man is generated by Heaven and Earth. This is wrong. It is by the fusion of the ethers of heaven and earth that man is spontaneously generated, just as by the union of the ethers of husband and wife, the child is spontaneously generated."[18]

For Wang, heaven is but a material object without any sensation or consciousness, so there can be no communion or interaction whatsoever between heaven and man. "Man knows nothing of what heaven does, then how can it be that heaven knows what man does?" Furthermore, "since heaven is but ether, how can it be that ether, something like mist or smoke, listens to man?"[19] For reasons like these, he denounced the theory of the premonitary natural disasters and propitious omens by pointing out that all eclipses, natural disasters and changes of climates were but natural consequences of the natural world which had nothing to do with any divine or human affair. He proclaimed: "Eclipses appear by constant periods and have no relation with politics",[20] "inundations and droughts are but caused by the ether of the seasons"[21] and "since the four seasons are not caused by politics, the changes of cold and warm weather should never respond to any politics".[22] In this way he concluded: "Natural disasters do not mean evils, nor propitious omens good fortunes".[23] The Han theologians were fond of myth-telling such as the virtue of a sage-king might cause the appearance of the phoenix or unicorn and bring peace and prosperity to the world. To these teachings Wang held a contrary position: "The knowledge of the birds and animals has nothing in common with that of the human beings, how can they come to know whether a state is well governed or not?"[24] The theory of the propitious omens on the occasion of the coming enthronement of a certain virtuous emperor so pompously propagated by the Han theologians, was thus reduced to the mere fiction of theocracy. By negating the theory of the propitious omens, Wang dealt a crushing blow on the divine rights of emperors.

On the issue of the spirit versus the body, Wang insisted the standpoint of the mortality of the spirit against the idea of its immortality. He taught that the spirit was a product of the body and functioned by its dependence on the body, and that when the body perished, the spirit ceased to exist. He followed Huan Tan by employing the analogy of candle and fire to illustrate the dependence of the spirit on the body, saying: "Since there is no fire without a candle, how is it possible in the world that there can be a spirit independent of the body?"[25] Herein lies the firm ground of his radical atheism that spirit is always dependent on coporeal bodies. Confronting the prevailing notion of the immortality of the spirit he stressed: "When a man dies, his blood exhausts and his spiritual ether perishes; and when it perishes, his body decays and becomes ashes; then how can he ever become a ghost?" Since he opposed strongly all superstitious beliefs in magic, necromancy, devils and ghosts, he recommended simplified funeral ceremony against all sacrificial offers to deities and the dead. He was indeed one of the most audacious thinkers in history who confronted face to face the mode and the fashion of his own time.

In opposing the theological views of the age, Wang had also worked out his own theory of knowledge. Human knowledge, so he taught, was obtained by way of human sensations of the external objects, therefore "truth and fact must be testified by seeing and hearing" and "when one sees and hears nothing, one cannot know anything at all".[26] Hence "one can never know anything well until he sees with his own eyes and inquires with his own mouth". This provided an antithesis to the theory regarding the born sages who were said to have been born with inborn knowledges. In exposing the myth of the born sages, he made examinations on lots of facts and concluded: "Sages can never be so miraculous as to know everything beforehand." In the chapters under the titles of "Interrogating Confucius" and "Critiquing Mencius", he exposed the self-contradictions in the classics which had been held as sacred dogmas. Like other arguments of his, this came into a clash with the orthodoxy in his time.

As to his historical views, he took history as a course of continuous progress; so he remarked categorically: "Zhou [the much idealized dynasty in tradition] was by far inferior to Han [his own time]", —a view which contradicted sharply with the retrogressive historical view point of the orthodoxy which adhered to the line of "back to the ancients".

As for his political and social views, Wang should be remembered for his keen insight on the relationship between the rule of the government and the state of the people's daily life. He considered that the poverty of the people was the cause of their rebellion. In this, he was a follower of Guan Zi who once taught: "The people will know propriety only after their granaries are full and will know honour only after they are well fed and clothed." Wang went even so far as to condemn the hereditary nobilities in governmental posts in these words: "Once they hold high positions in governmental office, they annex farmlands and houses"—a common occurrence under the reign of the hereditary status.

Yet Wang's naturalism, a forcible weapon as it was against the theological teleology, had missed the distinction between the natural laws and the social laws; and he tried in vain to explain the social phenomena by directly applying the former to the latter. This led him to attribute the fate of the nation and that of the individual to the absolute role of natural necessities and accidents. So the logical conclusion he reached was unavoidably a desperate fatalism which in every way had to be regarded as a great fallacy of his theory.

Yet Wang deserved, after all, to be ranked among the foremost thinkers in history who dared to attack the orthodox ideology; and this was the reason why he had been regarded as a heretic and his book had long been suppressed.

During the last years of the Eastern Han Dynasty, with the ruling class becoming wantonly corrupt and the peasants' rebellions upsurging, there emerged an intellectual current among the literati assailing the government's policies and demanding reforms. This current was then being called "the critical opinions of the scholars" among whom the most outstanding representatives were Wang Fu, Cui Shi and Zhong Changtong.

Wang Fu (dates unknown), a native of Anding (now in Gansu), accepted Wang Chong's naturalistic conception of the primordial ether, propounding that all things in the world were the products of "the action of ether".[27] He proclaimed: "A noble-minded man is not necessarily in possession of wealth and power", "nor a small-minded man necessarily in poverty and misery".[28] With this idea, he came into open confrontation to the prevalent ideas of the feudal hierarchy.

Cui Shi (?-170), a native of Anping (now in Hebei) bravely assailed "the corrupt political practices, the sluggishness of the officialdom, the degeneration of morality and the deceitful lives in society".[29] He advised that to run a state was just like to keep the body in good health, one should always take care of keeping it in good condition when healthy and giving a good cure when in illness. He compared moral teachings to nutriment and punishment to medicine. To rule a society in disorder, he advocated the employment of "high rewards and severe punishments".[30]

Zhong Changtong (179-220), a native of Gaoping (now in Shandong), had for sometime served on the staff of Cao Cao, the renowned statesman in the last years of Eastern Han. Against the widespread superstitious beliefs of the time, Zhong forwarded his basic proposition: "The human affair is the essential while the superhuman Tao the accidental".[31] He openly negated the Providence, saying that this was to make use of "the pretext of the Providential authority" to fool the people. The sole reason of the decline and fall of a dynasty was not due to the arrangement of the Providence, but to the acts of the ruling groups who "were exploiting the fruits of the people's labour and exhausting their marrows". He demanded strongly for political reform and proposed that "all that once proved effective in the past but are no longer of any use to the present, should be modified".[32]

This current of reform was only an attempt to rescue the rule of the regime then in crisis, and hence did not exceed the limit of reforming it. But their objective significance surpassed their subjective intentions by exposing the darkness and corruption in the political and social life. In their writings one may sense the coming catastrophe, or as Cui Shi had once put it: "Now as hostilities were burning all over the country, is it not a cause for fear?"[33]

5. REVOLUTIONARY IDEAS OF THE PEASANTS' UPRISINGS IN QIN AND HAN

The earliest leaders in the great peasants' uprisings during the last years of Qin were Chen Sheng (?-208 B.C.), a tenant-farmer from Yangcheng (now in Henan) and Wu Guang (?-209 B.C.), a pauper from Yangxia (also in Henan). In 209 B.C., they were enlisted in company with some nine hundred other poor peasants and dispatched to Yuyang (near Beijing) to serve in the frontier garrison.

While on their way through the Great Marshes (in north Anhui), they were detained by heavy storms and could not reach their destination on time. For such a failure, they knew they should be put to death according to the laws of Qin. Facing the menace of being put to death, they deliberated: "If we are to escape, we are doomed to die; if we are to revolt against the government, we are all the same doomed to die. On either choice, death awaits us. Isn't it advisable to die for the country rather than for the self?"[34] Thus there sparkled out the first revolutionary ideas of the peasants.

Thereupon they killed the officers supervising them and encouraged themselves with those words: "If a hero is to die, let him die majestically with a renowned fame; the princes and nobilities, ministers and generals—are they born to be so?" As they took up their arms, they upheld their fighting mottoes: "Smash the unmerciful and annihilate the tyranny." Within one month, they won over a large part of the country and established their regime under the title Zhang Chu with Chen Sheng on the royal throne. This was the first nationwide peasant uprising in the history of China which led to the eventual collapse of the Qin Dynasty and set the earliest example for a long series of peasants' revolutions in later ages.

The revolutionary slogans and ideas of Chen Sheng, fragmentary as they were in the records of history, reflected nevertheless the poverty-stricken and helpless peasants demanding the change of their social status in their desperate resentment against the suppression of the feudal tyranny. They had embraced a vague sense that the social status of either the wealthy and powerful or the poor and powerless was never doomed irrevocable. It was not decreed by Providence. Consequently, the idea of the eternal rule of the hereditary nobilities was shaken. Chen's idea might be traced back, at least theoretically, as early as to Mo Zi who during the time of the hierarchy of the hereditary nobilities had said: "The dignitaries are not always on the high, nor the people always in the low."[35]

Chen, though expressed the idea of the variability of the social status, did not touch the real reason of the antagonism between the wealthy and the poor, nor of the tyranny of the royal regime. At the early stage of the feudal society, the peasants had not yet attained such a height of consciousness as to demand the total abolition of class distinctions in wealth, power or status. The initiative of their uprisings was only motivated by a spirit of struggling for subsistence. It might be said that the peasants were still in a spontaneous stage of striving for the right of personal existence.

Four centuries later, i.e., in the late Eastern Han period when the annexation of farmlands by the powerful nobilities and the corruption of the government plus continuous natural disasters rendered the peasants bankrupt or in exile, there appeared the panorama of "hundreds of thousands of people suffered from famine and lived in exile" and "death befell them one after another". It was then that the peasants' rebellion broke out on a large scale. And amid the peasants emerged the idea of the Great Peace of the primary Taoism. A vivid expression of this revolutionary idea might be found in a popular folk ballad of that time which read: "The common people are like chives, they will grow again after each cutting; their heads are those of chickens, they crow even after they have been severed; the officials are nothing to be afraid of and the people can never be despised." In A.D. 184, there burst the Yellow Turban Uprising, which soon turned out to be a conflagration all over the country. The leader of the uprising, Zhang Jiao, a native of Julu (now in Hebei) founded the Great Peace Sect, which propagated widely among the populace.

In the primitive Taoist classic, *Canon of Great Peace*, in addition to its teaching of theism and feudal ethics, there were also passages propagating the primitive Taoist idea of opposition to exploitation and oppression. In a section advocating the egalitarianism under the Great Peace, it demanded the abolition of all unequal social practices, urging a peace and equality in such a manner that all human beings should be nourished only by nature itself just like other things in the world. Starting from this principle, the *Canon of Great Peace* taught that since everyone was endowed with the ability for labour, so it was the obligation for everyone to engage in labour to subsist his own life. In the book we read; "Men are born with the ability for labour to subsist themselves; and he who dare spare his labour shall not be exempted from being condemned guilty."[36] It denounced the wealthy: "Those who accumulate great wealth for themselves but do not give any help to the poor and the needy, just sitting and watching them to die in hunger, shall never be exempted from being condemned."[37] It even compared the wealthy to the mice in the granary and openly asserted that the wealth in the royal treasury came from the wealth of the common people "who ought deservedly to have the right to spend them in case of necessity". Here its spearhead was already directed toward the sovereign. This signalled the earliest demand for common property.

This primitive Taoist teaching as expressed in the *Canon of Great Peace*, though unrealistic, inspired the people to rise up in arms to protest against social inequality and to pursue after an ideal society of equality. Therefore, it was later employed by Zhang Jiao and others to arouse and organize the populace for a great armed rebellion in the late Eastern Han. When the banner of rebellion was raised, Zhang heralded: "Dead is the blue heaven, and hail to the coming reign of the yellow heaven."[38] The yellow heaven symbolized the Yellow Turbans, and the slogan evidently bore the imprint of the mystic theory of the Five Elements. But it nevertheless reflected the revolutionary spirit for setting up a new "yellow heaven" in place of the vanishing Han regime.

Chapter 6
ECONOMIC THOUGHTS
IN THE HAN PERIOD

The period of Western and Eastern Hans marked the early stage of feudalism. The economic thoughts of this time were concentrated on the following issues: how to consolidate the economic basis upon which the centralized monarchy was built up, and how to meet the annexation of farmlands by the nobilities or the land property contradiction between the landlords of the upper strata and the free farmers. Most of the Han economists aimed at the relaxation of the ever-sharpening class antagonism.

1. THE ECONOMIC THOUGHTS OF
JIA YI AND CHAO CUO

Both Jia Yi and Chao Cuo were renowned essayists and ideologues during the reigns of Emperors Wen and Jing, both fought actively for national unification and in economic field both influenced their own age with their ideas.

After the Han Dynasty was founded, Liu Bang while continuing the prefecture system upon the model of Qin, had also carried out large-scale enfeoffment on his family members, relatives and followers as local princes. During the reign of Emperor Hui under the patronage of Empress Dowager Lü (194-179 B.C.), both the imperial government and the local principalities were busily engaged in the cause of economic recovery and political stabilization within their own realms. But by the reign of Emperor Wen (178-158 B.C.), as social economy was restored and developed, the contradiction between the imperial power and the local principalities began to come to the fore.

Jia Yi (200-168 B.C.), a native from Luoyang (in Henan), was a versatile scholar on the learnings of the hundred schools. Absorbing the Legalist and Taoist teachings, he upheld Confucianism in predominance but with certain naive materialistic ideas of his own. He had been appointed the royal secretary to the emperor who had once intended to promote Jia to the post of premiership. But owing to the objection on the part of the princes and dignitaries, Jia was finally banished to Hunan where he wrote his famous literary works *Elegy on Qu Yuan* (the famous ancient poet in exile) and *Ode on the Roc*. He died at the age of thirty-two.

Jia was one among the earliest of those who came to realize the impending menace of the local principalities to the Empire's unification. In his memorandum to the Emperor, he pointed out the serious situation the Empire was in and advised him to take measures "to diminish the powers of the local princes by increasing the number of enfeoffments",[1] for "when they are less powerful, it is more easy to command them; when they are much smaller, they are less ambitious".[2] Emperor Wen accepted his advice and divided the kingdom of Qi into seven fiefs and the kingdom of Huainan into three. These measures helped much to strengthen the unified imperial regime.

After a rather stable and peaceful reign for more than forty years in the early Han, the feudal land property became much developed along with the growth of social economy. The result was that on the one hand there appeared the large-scale forcible occupation and annexation of farmlands by the influential landlords, while on the other the bankruptcy and exile of the independent farmers. Jia was much irritated by all those potential crises and urged a reform by which agricultural production, the economic basis of the unified Empire, might be kept in safety. He followed the ancient tradition of "upholding agriculture and repressing commerce", taking the activities of the merchants and artisans as non-productive, so he deemed it necessary to repress them in order to get the agricultural production under way. Jia also proposed his famous theory of saving and accumulation, the realization of which, he argued, would provide the state with surplus provisions and wealth and enable it to become "invincible", "invulnerable" and "triumphant".[3] Here the pre-Qin idea of wealth was further developed.

On the issue of money and currency, Jia while pointing out the harms of private mintage, maintained that it should be monopolized by the central government. Such a monopoly could help to drive those people who were engaging in private mintage back to the farms for agricultural production, to stabilize the social economy and to increase the financial incomes to the government for armed resistance against the Huns. It paved the way upon which Emperor Wu was later capable to stipulate the unitary mintage under the imperial government. Jia also advised to set a system of standard money for legal tender and its circulation amount should be determined with respect to the fluctuation of its value. This contributed much not only to the monetary theory but also to the stabilization of market prices as well as to the adjustment of supply and demand.

Chao Cuo (200-154 B.C.), a native from Yingchuan (now in Henan), at his youth studied the Legalist doctrine and learned *The Book of History* from the renowned scholar Fu Sheng, and then served the Crown Prince who later ascended the throne and became known as Emperor Jing (157-141 B.C.). During the time of Emperor Wen, father of Emperor Jing, the crisis of splitting the newly founded Empire appeared not yet so impending, so that Jia Yi's moderate policy of "diminishing the powers of the local princes by increasing the number of enfeoffments" had its way. But by the time of Emperor Jing, this crisis reached a stage of antagonistic clashes; the armed rebellion headed by Liu Bi, Prince of Wu, was already well under way. So Chao advised the Emperor to abolish abruptly the hereditary territory of the local princes and to deprive their powers by sending imperial officials to take charge of the administrations of those local principalities. In this way the local principalities were reduced to the status of the imperial prefectures and the princes to the local landlords "depending on tenant rents as their sole source of income"[4] with no more political powers. Thereupon an open revolt of the princes against the imperial court broke out with the kingdoms of Wu and Chu at its head. Chao insisted on his original policy "in short of which the emperor could never be made supreme and the imperial reign never stable".[5] In confrontation with the rebellious princes, the Emperor first put Chao to death, pretending to show appeasement to them, but at the same time sent out a strong army to suppress them. Soon the rebellion was suppressed and Chao's policy was carried out in full with the result that the centralized imperial regime was at length firmly established.

Chao stressed the predominance of the agricultural production as the indispensable means to maintain the unification of the Empire, proclaiming: "in grain consist the cardinal function of the sovereign and the essential concern of the policy".[6] And his theory of "giving importance to grain", he argued, would lead to the prosperity of the sovereign, the decrement of rents on the people and the stimulation to agricultural production. Besides, he advocated that dignitary ranks might be bought with grain and guilts ransomed with grain. This measure would contribute to absorbing the surplus money in circulation and diverting it from buying too much farmlands, while the guilty when exempted might keep their status of free citizen, leading to the amelioration of class contradictions. In short, it did promote social productivity and strengthen the unifying imperial power; but at the same time it also opened the way for foul practices such as buying and selling official posts and of protecting the feudal privileges.

2. THE ECONOMIC THOUGHTS OF SANG HONGYANG

Sang Hongyang (152-80 B.C.), a native of Luoyang, was born in a merchant's family and later became the minister of financial and agricultural affairs of the Han Dynasty.

As an outstanding financier, Sang had been in charge of the imperial finance for more than twenty years during the reign of Emperor Wu. His measures played an important role in strengthening the imperial regime as well as in providing the material supports for Emperor Wu's expenses in political and military activities. The frequent wars with the Huns on the northern borders had brought the imperial finance into great difficulty. But soon after Sang was commissioned to take charge of public finance, he managed "to make the country rich without increasing taxes",[7] so wrote the famous historians Sima Qian and Ban Gu.

The economic thoughts of Sang succeeded that of Guan Zi and exceeded the confines of the tradition of "upholding agriculture and repressing commerce". He valued highly the role of crafts and commerce in national economy. He proclaimed: "When possessed with large fertile lands, the people are still poorly fed, it is because they are not furnished with proper instruments. When with the rich products from the land and the sea, the people are still poorly nourished, it is because they are not sufficiently provided with crafts and commerce."[8] From this, he concluded: "There are always more than one way to make a nation wealthy."[9] In his exposition of the significance of crafts and commerce to the wealth of a nation, he held a view which was more far-sighted than his predecessors.

With a view to the role of crafts and commerce, Sang urged that salt, iron and brewery should be monopolized by the government. Private manufacturers of these items should be condemned to penalty. With the government monopoly of salt, iron and brewery, he opened a new financial resource which enabled the government to overcome the financial crisis under the heavy burden of military expenses. Thus a contemporary writer Huan Kuan said of him: "The profit that iron and salt have brought in is enough to meet all requirements of the government, to afford the military expenses and to provide the resources in times of need; they support the government in many ways."[10] But what was more was that it served the political aims of Emperor Wu to repress the powers of the principalities and nobilities and to strengthen the imperial sovereignty. Hence Sang asserted: "The monopoly of iron and salt is not only for the benefits of the government's income, but also for the consolidation of the root [i.e., the centralized imperial sovereign] and the restraint on the tip [i.e., the principalities], the liquidization of political factions and the prevention of both the luxury and the annexation of lands."[11]

Sang expounded a specific theory of commercial circulation. He taught that the wealth of big cities where merchants concentrated was accumulated by the "managing ability" (i.e., the exchange of commodities at unequal prices) of "the wise"; in other words, it was multipled through the process of circulation of commodities. Hence his well-known proposition: "Wealth exists in the managing ability rather than in manual labour."[12] This proposition ought to be taken as one of the earliest versions of the theory of "enrichment by commerce". While advising the enrichment of the nation by means of trade and commerce, he instituted a system of balanced transportation and the equilibrium of market prices by which the government was to run the transportation and trade with a view to balance the supply of different commodities from one place to another all over the country. In addition, an agency was instituted in the capital for stabilizing the market prices there. This agency would "sell any kind of commodity out when its price is high, and buy it in when low".[13] The consequence of such a practice was that "the big merchants would have nowhere to earn their big profits"[14] whereas the government obtained a strong financial support. This policy laid down by Sang had since then undergone "five reigns of the Emperors Xuan, Yuan, Cheng, Ai and Ping, without alteration".[15]

3. THE ECONOMIC REFORMS OF WANG MANG

By the last years of Western Han, the social life was falling into such a miserable state that "the populace, thousands upon thousands, were dying on their way of exile or in pestilence, and there even occurred man eating man".[16] And the people, predominantly the peasants and state slaves, were compelled to rise up in arms. It was under this circumstance of acute social contradictions that Wang Mang (A.D. 8-23) usurped the royal throne and elaborated a series of economic reforms, the main contents being:

1. The institution of royal land system. In A.D. 9, Wang decreed, after the pattern of the nine-square system as recorded in *The Book of Rites*, that all farmlands in the country should be renamed the royal farmlands and a hundred *mu* were allocated to each couple, husband and wife, and not permitted to be sold. Wang was aware that land of private ownership would lead to free sellings and buyings of it, resulting in the annexation of land property; and he thought that once the land was owned by the state (literally the imperial government) and prohibited from buying and selling, land annexation would naturally come to an end. But contrary to his will, the feudal ownership of land property was then just established and developing with an unprecedented momentum, and any attempt to stop it would be destined to be a chimera in theory and a failure in practice. Or, in more general terms, any political action which aimed to run

contrary to the economic trend of the society would be doomed in front of that irresistable trend. The royal farmland system sponsored by Wang was in essence neither the reformist "limitation on land property" (as proposed by Dong Zhongshu) nor the peasants' egalitarian demand of land; so that it was opposed both by the influential landlords and by the poor peasants.

2. State control of market prices. With this measure Wang attempted to deal with the big merchants who were manipulating the market. Wang tried hard to hold the management of commercial business and with that the control of the market prices in the hands of the government. He instituted in Changan, Luoyang, Handan, Linzi, Wan and Chengdu, the six biggest cities at that time, the Wujun (officials in charge of supply-demand equilibrium) to keep control of the market prices. It was the duty of these officials to regulate and maintain a legitimate mean price. When the supply in the market surpassed the demand, they would take care to buy in the surplus commodities at normal price; and vice versa.

In addition, Wang Mang instituted also the Liuguan (the officials of the six governmental controls) in charge of iron, salt, wine, coinage, natural resources and the above-mentioned Wujun. The aim of these government-run businesses was "to keep equilibrium among the populace and to prevent annexation".[17]

These measures adopted by Wang Mang were but modifications of the economic policy of Western Han under the name of the stabilization of the market and the state management of salt and iron. A policy, no matter how well it sounded, when being carried out by a corrupted regime, would only help to accelerate the collapse of itself. So was the case with the newly founded Xin Dynasty of Wang Mang whose measures served a convenient means for the corruption and bribery of the officials in governmental posts.

3. Monetary reform. In the years A.D. 7-14, Wang Mang launched several monetary reforms, each time with ever more complicated coinages and exchange rates. These resulted in bringing extreme disorder to the monetary systems and bankruptcy to the money-holders. "With each time of his monetary reform, the people were rendered more impoverished",—so wrote Ban Gu in his *History of the Han Dynasty.*

All the economic reforms of Wang Mang afforded no solution

to the existing social contradictions but only aggravated them. Not only did the broad masses rise up against Wang's regime, but also a considerable part among the landed nobilities whose privileges were harmed by Wang's reform came into open clash with the Xin government. In the turbulences of political upheavals and the peasants' armed uprisings, Wang's regime eventually collapsed.

4. ECONOMIC THOUGHTS IN THE EASTERN HAN

The armed uprisings of the peasants in large scale by the end of the Western Han, culminated in those of the Red Brows, the Greenwooders and the Bronze Horsemen, had dealt a fatal blow at certain groups of the old nobility landlords; and the acute land problem was by then somewhat ameliorated. But with the founding of the new dynasty, the Eastern Han, and the re-establishment of social order, the problem of land annexation reappeared. How to deal with this impending problem constituted the main theme of the economic thinkers and social ideologues of that period. The most noted figures among them were Xun Yue with his theory of "plowing but not owning" and Zhong Changtong with his proposal of restoring the nine-square system.

Xun Yue (148-209), a native of Yingchuan (now in Henan), was the author of *The Record of Han* in thirty chapters and *An Exposition of the Precedents* in five chapters. Facing the serious situation of land annexation, Xun proposed the doctrine of "plowing but not owning",[18] recommending that the peasants might have the right to use the farmland but had no ownership over it, i.e., the farmland was not permitted to be bought or sold. "Let the people have the right to plow the land, but not the right to sell or to buy it", the aim being "to support the poor and the weak, and to prevent land annexation".[19] Yet this proposal of his failed to meet the problems of how to deal with the large amount of land property owned or occupied by the powerful landlords and how to turn the private property of the landlords to the state. This showed his position that while intending to solve the land problem for the peasants he nevertheless dared not hurt the fundamental interests of the landlord class. His proposal, even if realized, would be no more than an attempt to prevent further land annexation by means of interdicting the selling and buying of lands. Yet for the first time in the economic ideas in China, the conception of the right to own was distinguished from that of the right to use. And this deserved to be acknowledged as a novel idea.

Zhong Changtong attributed the cause of violent land annexation to the ruin of the nine-square system, proclaiming: "Ever since the decay of the nine-square system, the powerful began to engage themselves in commercial activities; so that their houses scattered all over the prefectures and their farmlands stretched from one principality to another."[20] The sole way out, argued he, was to restore the nine-square system which would serve to prevent the annexation of land and the sources of all kinds of social disturbances as well. But by the nine-square system he did not mean the idealized institution of Western Zhou in antiquity. What he really maintained was but the small land ownership, each family being given a quota of no more than a hundred mu of farmland while leaving the big land property untouched. Obviously this idea of his went no further than an utopia. Advanced ideologues, such as Zhong, realized the seriousness of land annexation but failed to meet it with any design which would not harm, as they expected, the basic interests of the landlords.

Closely connected with the annexation of land was the loss of large amount of labours. On this issue, we should not omit to mention the name of Xu Gan (170-217) and his theory of population. Xu was a well-known literary writer in the late Eastern Han and one of the "Seven Poets of Jianan Period" (196-219), and used to serve in the staff of Cao Cao. In his writings, he stressed the significance of the quantitative aspect of population (i.e., the labouring forces) in its relation to the consolidation of the regime. "The number of the people", remarked he, "means that by which the state is instituted and the household regulated."[21] It was upon the census, especially that of the peasants, that the government was to distribute the farmlands, to regulate the taxation, to arrange economic affairs, and to enlist civil corvées and military services. In other words, all regulations, in the last analysis, had to be dependent on the amount possible in exploiting the surplus labour of the dependent peasants. Therefore, he urged the imperial government to have a good mastery of the quantity of population upon which all policies of the administration relied. He advocated a hereditary system of division of labour which could in no respect be regarded as conducive to social progress, but his stress on the relationship between the numerical aspect of the population and the economics and politics of a country represented a profound insight no one had had before.

Chapter 7

SCIENTIFIC, HISTORIOGRAPHIC AND LITERARY IDEAS IN THE HAN PERIOD

1. SCIENTIFIC IDEAS IN THE HAN PERIOD

The Han was generally acknowledged as one of the two great periods of prosperity in mediaeval China (the other being the Tang) when, among others, sciences and technologies achieved a world high in the cultural history of mankind.

In the field of astronomy, there were detailed records on the eclipses. Sima Qian in his *Records of the Historian* ("The Book on Astronomy") had taken notes of all the constellations known at that time and of the movements of the five planets (Venus, Mercury, Mars, Jupiter and Saturn). During the reign of Emperor Wu, Sima and others were entrusted to draw up a calendar by the name of Taichu, one among the most renowned and long-standing calendars in Chinese history. In 1973, there was unearthed in Hunan a document on astronomical study by the name of "The Calculation on the Five Planets", written about the year A.D. 170 with the record of the celestial positions of Venus, Jupiter and Saturn in a span of seventy-three years from Qin to early Han as well as the computations on the periods of their revolutions and coincidences. The numerical value in their computation came very near to that of modern astronomy.

In the *History of the Han Dynasty* ("The Book on the Five Elements"), one may find the earliest records of the sunspots (in the year 28 B.C.) in the history of mankind. It revised the ratio of 365 1/4 days to a year to 365 335/1539 days to a year, thus coming closer to the real value. The preeminent astronomer of the time Zhang Heng expounded a more advanced theory of the cosmos and invented some of the most important astronomical apparatus in history.

Connected with the development of astronomy and calendar was that of mathematics. In the world-famous mathematical work, *Nine Chapters on the Mathematical Art*, there were included 246 exercises on application and operational methods of which many were among the most advanced in the world at that time.

In the year 105, Cai Lun greatly improved the method of paper-manufacturing by using barks and rags of worn-out linens and nets as raw materials. This invention of a better and less expensive kind of paper, known by the name of "Marquis Cai's paper", marked a significant progress in world culture. It reflected the high level of cultural development of ancient China and promoted greatly the spread of and the intercourse between different cultures of the world.

Hand in hand with the scientific and technological progress were the innovations of scientific ideas of many preeminent scholars of whom suffice it to mention only two names.

Zhang Heng's Scientific Ideas

Zhang Heng (78-139), a native of Nanyang (in Henan), was the foremost astronomer of the time and had been twice in charge of the royal observatory. Starting from a naive naturalistic view, he rejected all kinds of interpretations of nature by the approach of prognostication and apocrypha then much in vogue. He contended: "The data of the movements of the heavenly bodies should never be fabricated by imagination nor the truth substituted by falsity";[1] so he proposed to the government "the complete ban of all kinds of prognostication and apocrypha".[2] It was he who made the first seismograph in the world besides his renowned armillary sphere, which was similar to the modern celestial globe. And his main contribution to the history of ideas was his theory of cosmogony which afforded the best interpretation of the universe of that time.

As early as in the Zhou Dynasty, there was the theory of the vaulted sky, asserting that the sky was round and the earth square and that "the sky covers in the shape of a vault, and the earth copies the model of a plate". During the time of the Warring States, both Shen Dao and Gongsun Long had already embraced some germinal ideas of the global theory of the universe. It was upon this model that the renowned astronomer Luoxia Hong worked out his apparatus for astronomical observations.

Zhang knew well that the moonlight was the reflection of the sunlight and the eclipse of the moon was caused by the projection of the earth upon it. In ancient Greece, both Pythagoras and Aristotle had, from the projection of the earth on the moon during the eclipses, reasoned that the earth was round. Very probably it was by the same reason that Zhang came to know the round shape of the earth and carried further the global theory of the universe of his predecessors. He definitely proclaimed: "The celestial globe is like an egg, and the celestial bodies are like the balls". The earth is like the yolk suspended in isolation within. The sky is much larger whereas the earth much smaller. There are waters in and out of the sky, and the sky like an egg-shell encircles the earth. Both the sky and the earth are kept by the air and are floating on the waters".[3] This global theory of the universe was a step forward in comparison with the theory of the vaulted sky.

Zhang elaborated a naturalistic cosmogony. By accepting the idea of the primeval ether, he postulated that before the differentiation of the heaven and the earth there was only chaos from which was begotten the primeval ether; and then the ether differentiated itself into the clear and the dirty, the rigid and the fluid, by the actions of which the sky was formed without and the earth within. In contrast to the traditional theory of the divine creation of the universe, this cosmography of his took both the heaven and the earth as material substances.

Zhang had also embraced the conception of the infinity of the universe. The *Mohist Canon* of the time of the Warring States and *The Book of Shi Zi*, completed in Han, had expressed some definite ideas on the magnitude and duration of the universe. Zhang developed it by saying: "There is no limit on the extension of the space and no finity on the duration of time."[4] This idea of the infinity of the universe with respect to space and time was really one among the most advanced in the ancient world.

Yet Zhang failed to get rid of the brands of ancient astrology. In his writings, he still regarded the movements of the sun, the moon and the planets as the symptoms or the premonitions of the coming fortunes. As is well known, astronomy and astrology were, as a rule, inseparable in the ancient world. This shortcoming of his was more due to the limitations of the age rather than to that of his personal traits.

Besides the above-mentioned theories of the universe, there was still a third one generally known as the nocturnal theory of the universe (because these astronomers always worked late in the night) which had been recorded as early as in the second century. It held that the heavens had no definite shapes and all the stars were floating in a natural way in the void with no attachment to any celestial sphere. The existence of the solid celestial sphere being rejected, the supposition of the boundaries of heaven was broken through. This doctrine was indeed a very brilliant one in the history of man's knowledge about the universe. Another contribution of this theory consisted in its insistence that "all motions or state of rest" of the sun, the moon and the stars "are depending on the ether"[5] which filled up the space in the universe. It is also in the Han period that we may find the earliest record of the notion of the earth in constant motion.

Medical Ideas in the Han Period

The *Canon of Internal Medicine* usually attributed to Huang Di was essentially a summation of the ancient medical science. It employed the doctrine of Yin, Yang and the Five Elements to explain human physiology and pathology, laying down the theoretical basis of the Chinese medical science of later ages.

The *Canon* succeeded the ancient naive naturalistic view, taking the world with all things in it as a product of the interactions of Yin and Yang, the two primeval ethers. Thus human body was considered a part of the structure of the natural world whereby all human diseases were to be studied in the light of natural causes in a naturalistic way. It claimed: "Yin, Yang and the four seasons are that by which all things begin and end, and on which life and death depend. Whenever they are disobeyed, disasters will follow; and whenever obeyed, disease will disappear."[6] Although it showed no knowledge of the infection of diseases, it admitted the existence of certain ether, vicious and harmful, and pointed out that so far as the Yang (healthy) ether prevailed, the human body could resist the intrusion of the "vicious ether". These are the scientific elements in the study of pathology through empirical observations as expressed in the *Canon*. In medical treatment, the *Canon*'s principle was employing different remedies for different cases.

The *Canon* claimed that the five physiological organs of the human body were interdependent and mutually conditioned whereby different organs of the body constituted an organic whole, just like the five elements constituted the whole natural world. It advised the study of the interrelations between the physiological and psychical elements and taught people to control their emotions properly. But on the whole, the author of the *Canon* could not help from being limited by the scientific level of the age which was, to a considerable degree, merely intuitive in nature. Therefore there might be found in it erroneous explanations and even mystic elements.

Zhang Zhongjing (150-219) was also a native of Nanyang who combined the medical theory of the *Canon* with his own experiences in medical practice. His monumental work, *Treatise on Febrile and Other Diseases* in sixteen volumes, by far the foremost medical classic in Chinese medicine, summed up all the treasures of hitherto accumulated medical knowledge and he himself was laureated "the Sage of Medicine" by later scholars. His main contribution lay in the combination of the theoretical (the doctrine in the Canon) with the experimental (his long-time medical practice). In treating each case, he gave his prescriptions according to the concrete condition of the patient. In this way he improved greatly the scientific research as well as the methodology of the Chinese medicine which was unique in the world.

2. HISTORIOGRAPHIC IDEAS IN THE HAN PERIOD

The foremost historical writings of the time, or even of the whole traditional China, were Sima Qian's *Records of the Historian* and Ban Gu's *History of the Han Dynasty*. Both authors lived in the prosperous periods of Han, the former during the reign of Emperor Wu, the latter during that of Emperor Guang Wu (25-55) when conditions were ripe for their immortal works.

Sima Qian's Historiographic Ideas

Sima Qian (145-90 B.C.), a native of Hancheng (in Shaanxi), was generally acknowledged as the most remarkable literary figure of the age. His father was an official historian in the imperial court. Sima Qian had travelled far and wide over the country and learned a lot about the real life of the people. In 110 B.C. his father died and three years later he succeeded to his father's post. He studied extensively the rich collections of the national archives and governmental documents. In 99 B.C. when he was writing his immortal work, *Records of the Historian*, he was put into prison for defending the case of a defeated general; his sufferings helped to form his heretical tendencies. For nineteen years, he had been engaged in his work.

Records of the Historian narrated the whole story from the legendary Huang Di down to his own time (the reign of Emperor Wu), covering a length of more than three thousand years in an admirably refined style and including twelve Basic Annals, ten Tables, eight Treatises, thirty Hereditary Houses and seventy Lives which sketched comprehensively the whole course of historical development. As an unprecedented general history, it left us roughly the following legacies:

1. He examined the fate of a nation from the viewpoint of development and evolution. The purpose of his writing was summarized in these words: "To scrutinize the reasons of the rise and the fall of a nation" so as "to comprehend the evolution from antiquity down to the present".[7] He was not satisfied to leave his study on the level of mere narration of events but tried to find out the thread of change behind the historical phenomena. Both his conception of history and his historiographic methodology were the antitheses to the prevailing metaphysical way of thinking that "Heaven never changes, so nor does the Tao". Throughout his work, he rejected the idea of the interference of the supernatural on human affairs

2. He was an excellent scientist himself. In his comprehension of history, he gave priority to the role of the objective factors. He criticized severely the prevailing idea of the divine disposition in human affairs. For instance, on the tragic end of Xiang Yu who lost his battle to Liu Bang, Sima Qian commented: "While Xiang was about to die, he was still not aware of his own mistakes, and instead of blaming himself he was lamenting, 'It is Heaven that fails me, but not my own fault in battle.' Isn't it an absurdity?"[8] To place the interpretation of history on the humanistic basis rather than on

Providence,—here lies his remarkable insight rarely found in ancient historiography.

3. He made great efforts to explain the social and intellectual life in terms of its material conditions. For him, the economic activities of men was but a natural process, "just like the waters always flowing downwards unceasingly day and night, they will come without being summoned and appear without being sought after."[9] He succeeded Guan Zi's viewpoint in stressing the role of economic factor in social life and attributed the differentiation of the social ranks to the disparity in wealth. Here again his humanistic standpoint in upholding the people's right to live was in vivid contrast with the traditional moral preachings which denied the people their rights of material life only for the benefits of the ruling class.

4. Though Sima Qian gave detailed descriptions of the lives of the nobilities, he never overlooked the historical role of the people of the lower strata. Thus in his work the leader of peasants' uprising Chen Sheng was placed among the Hereditary Houses and the armed uprising led by him against the Qin regime was compared to King Wu of Zhou's campaign against the rule of Yin. Emphatically he remarked: "Although Chen Sheng died soon, the preeminent persons following him had eventually overthrown the Qin regime. This was due to his initiation."[10] In orthodox historical writings, one can hardly find such appreciations of the rebels as the innovators of history. In so doing, Sima Qian was of necessity to expose at the same time the cruelty of the ruling class and all the social disasters resulted therefrom. In his *Records*, he denounced the ruthless officials and praised the chivalrous personages. He showed his sympathies for the common people and thus in a certain degree had broken through the traditional ideological bonds, though he was yet not able to go beyond the confines of both the heroic and the cyclic conceptions of history. It was this progressive and advanced aspect in his historiography that led Ban Gu to criticize him as preaching "a truth that runs contrary to the teachings of the sages".[11]

Ban Gu's Historiographic Ideas

Another representative of the Han historiography was Ban Gu (32-92), a native of Fufeng (now Xianyang in Shaanxi). On the basis of the work of his father Ban Biao, a prominent historian of the age, he had within a course of twenty years completed the first dynastic history of China, the *History of the Han Dynasty*. It dated from 206 B.C. to A.D. 23, covering the whole course of Western Han and comprising four parts under the headings of Basic Annals, Tables, Special Topics and Lives respectively. It left to the later ages a model of the dynastic history, a collection of rich materials and a versatile record of knowledge.

In his conception of history, Ban Gu succeeded the theological ideology of the Western Han with the purpose of providing a theoretical ground for the divine rights of the emperors of Eastern Han by means of sanctifying that of the emperors of Western Han. Therefore his whole work was permeated throughout with a tint of theology, and the historical course was put within the model of a mystical cyclism. The rise and fall of the succeeding dynasties were identified with the cyclic turns of the powers of the Five Elements, and the rule of Han was attributed to the reign of the virtue of fire.

Yet Ban Gu was unavoidably influenced by his own age when after the great upheaval of the peasants' uprisings, the role of the idea of orthodoxy was declining rapidly; so that his work bore a strong eclectic tendency. In some parts of his book, the changes happened in history were attributed to Providence, while in other parts, social life and activities were explained in terms of natural and historical conditions which were more or less in conformity with reality. On the one hand, it described the history of Western Han as a history created by the leading heroic figures, while on the other hand, it made plain the evils of the ruling class and exposed the social disasters. The mixture of the positive and negative aspects in his thoughts as the guideline of his writing reflected his eclectic conception of history. After all, Ban Gu as well as Sima Qian had brought the historiographical ideas to a new height which as a classical model had been followed by almost all historical writings of the later ages.

3. LITERARY IDEAS IN THE HAN PERIOD

The flourish of the rhymed prose and verse in the Han period gave impetus to the literary views and ideas of that time, the most outstanding among which were the *Major Preface to the "Book of Odes"* and the works of Yang Xiong and Wang Chong.

Major Preface to the "Book of Odes"

Since the reign of Emperor Wu of Han, the Confucian doctrine had assumed supremacy not only in the political and academic realms but also in the literary sphere. In the Preface to the traditional classic the *Book of Odes* (or rather the Mao version of the *Book of Odes*, for it was edited by Mao Chang) were included two pieces, one being the *Major Preface* which dealt with literary principles while the other the *Minor Preface* which dealt with the historical backgrounds. As to the authorship of these prefaces, Zheng Xuan (the renowned classical scholar of Han) held that the Major one was written by Zi Xia, a disciple of Confucius, and the Minor by both Zi Xia and Mao Chang. But Fan Ye, the renowned historian of the Jin period, held that they were all written by Wei Hong. Very probably they were not composed by one hand at one time and only assumed their definite form by scholars in the Han period. The Major Preface amplified the ideas of Xun Zi and the *Book of Rites* and should be regarded as a summation of the poetic theories of Qin and Han.

The origin of poetry was given an exposition by the *Major Preface* in these words: "What makes up a poem is that which deals with our intentions. Intention is that which dwells in our hearts; when being spoken out it becomes a poem. When our emotion is inspired within us, it will find its outward expression in words. And when words do not suffice, one laments; and when lamentations do not suffice, one is involuntarily led to dances, gesticulating with hands and feet."[12] Here poetry was interpreted by the theory of spontaneity of emotions that were in close connection with music and dance. In the *Book of Rites* we may find such a comment on the origin of art: "All the musical sounds are caused by our hearts and the emotions in our hearts are caused by the outside conditions."[13] This theory of artistic reflection of the real life was incorporated by the *Major Preface* which taught the impetus on the emotion was produced by the outside world independent of which the emotion never existed in itself and by itself.

The *Major Preface* further explained the close relationship between the poetic art and the social reality. Different social conditions of different epochs would produce different styles and different contents of poetic arts. So it proclaimed: "Tranquil and harmonious sounds the poesy of a well-governed nation, because its politics is in good order; complaining and angry sounds the poesy of a nation in disorder, because its politics is in tumult; lamenting and sorrowful sounds the poesy of a downfalling nation, because its people suffer in misery."[14] In other words, the prosperity or decline of a nation and the good or bad governing of a country would be of necessity reflected in the poetical works which were the display of the social life of the people.

The *Major Preface* also paid attention to the social functions of the poetic works, pointing out that they both reflected the emotions of the people and at the same time reacted tremendously upon the people. It urged: "There is nothing more powerful than poetry in helping to correct the wrongs, to move the world and to inspire the spirits. It was by dint of this medium that the ancient kings regulated the family, nourished the filial piety, cultivated the social morals, modified the customs and regulated the manners."[15] Following the tradition of Confucius' and Xun Zi's conceptions of poetry, it emphasized the social and educational functions of the poetical art which was in its essence a representation of the demand of the ruling class to make literature and the arts serve the existing feudal order. In this respect, it naturally bore a strong feudalistic intent.

But in the meanwhile it also made some observations on the other side of the issue, i.e., besides the educational function of the poetry from above, the poetry also played its role of irony and satire from below; or, "the superior educated the inferior with their songs, while the inferior satirizes the superior with their songs too". Such a viewpoint on the function of poetry lent the people of later generations an ideological weapon for satirizing and criticizing the social reality.

Yang Xiong's Literary Ideas

Yang Xiong (53 B.C.-A.D. 18), a native of Chengdu (in Sichuan), was a famous philosopher and literary writer. In his early years he indulged in the composition of the rhymed prose then in vogue, he soon found its defects in mere formalistic extravagances which he criticized as "not what a manly man should do", so he turned to the study of philosophy.

In his criticism of the prevailing form of rhymed prose, he maintained his literary position of "amplifying the [Confucian] principles", "revering the sages" and "adhering to the classics". So in his literary writings he gave priority to the study of Confucian classics which, he asserted, all writings and speeches should take as an invariable norm. As regards content and form in literary writings, he stressed on the predominance of content over form, affirming that content should convey the principles of the Confucian classics. It was clear that Yang started along the routine of the Confucian teachings, but after all he had brought positive effects against the vogue of mere formalistic embellishments in literary works.

But his overemphasis on the Confucian principles had set a serious limitations on his own writings. Not only his main works *The Ultimate Mystery* and *The Model Sayings* lack originality and independent opinions but even their structure were imitations of the styles of the *Book of Changes* and *The Analect*. In sum, we may fairly say that his literary doctrine was basically a reflection of the role of Confucianism in the field of literature and, as such, had influenced the later literary writers, among them the famous Han Yu in the Tang period.

Wang Chong's Literary Ideas

Wang Chong's *Discourses Weighed in the Balance*, while expounding the naturalistic and atheistic ideas, advocated a fairly systematic view on the course of the progress of literature:

1. He esteemed highly the practical value of literature in serving society. "Of the writings that help to serve the world, hundreds would bring no harm; and of those that do not serve the world, even a single one would be useless,"[16] said he. Hence, he was against all writings that would have no social value at all, no matter how ornate a style they might assume.

2. He stressed the unity of literary form and content, demanding the match of literary content with its style. A good content plus an excellent style, he argued, would by its touching on the emotions

bring positive social consequences.

3. He advocated initiative and originality against cliché and imitation in literature. Hence he came in opposition to "reverence of the antique and disdain of the present" then in fashion, criticizing severely the conservative tendency in literary writings. He refused to take the model of the antiquity as the criterion of literary works and pointed out that a work of literature should only be judged by its own merits, intellectual and artistic.

4. He insisted his "abhorence to all kinds of falsity" and demanded "the return to plain truth"[17] against any pursuit of mere artificial exaggeration and superficial ornaments, urging that literary works should be written in a clear and easy-to-understand language by their unity of language and content.

Wang's literary views launched a critique on the formalistic fashion of his time and influenced Liu Zhiji of the Tang period and Zhang Xuecheng of the Qing period.

Chapter 8
IDEOLOGY IN THE WEI, JIN AND SOUTHERN AND NORTHERN DYNASTIES

1. POLITICAL THOUGHTS IN THE WEI AND JIN.

The Logico-Legalist Current

By the end of the Eastern Han, the Confucian theology represented by prognostication and apocrypha as the ruling ideology, was gradually in its waning. The great peasants' uprising of the Yellow Turbans had paralyzed the regime of the hereditary nobilities and brought about the collapse of the rule of Confucian theology. Face to face with this situation, the ruling class was in desperate need of a theory other than the Confucian tradition in the hope that it might afford them a new ideological weapon to support and stabilize the ruling order. And in company with it was the issue of how to choose the right people to safeguard the interests of the ruling class.

In order to consolidate his newly founded regime, Cao Cao was much concerned in repressing the strong nobility households and promoting officials from amongst the common people. He advocated the slogan: "appointing officials by their talents", the aim of which was to deal the hereditary nobilities a blow on their priviledges and to change their standard of choosing officials along the traditional Confucianist line.

Thereupon, some of the pre-Qin hundred schools once banned. by Emperor Wu of Han were now being revived among which were the Logician (or Dialectician) school and the Legalist. The significance of the Logicians, viewed in the light of practical politics of the time, lay not in their theoretical reasoning but rather in their method of appointing officials on their talents. The Legalists also advocated that "officials are to carry out their duties as they are required". It dealt not only with the issue of how to discover the talented but also with the issue of how to use them properly. In other words, the issue concerned the stability of the rule of feudal institution. Thus by the time of the late Han and early Wei (mid-4th century), there arose a current of Logico-Legalist thought supported by the newly founded Wei Dynasty. One may find records of it in the official history: "The present-day scholars are following Shang [Shang Yang] and Han [Han Fei] in admiration of their statecraft, seeking to outdo one another in their denouncing of the pedantry of the Confucians who are blamed as useless to the world."[1] A great number of writings following the lines of the Logicians and Legalists then came forth one after another. Their main contents were mostly dealing with the issue of how to assess the proficiency of the officials and how to pass judgments on their respective merits. Of those writings, the most prominent was Liu Shao's *Book of Personalities* which represented this current comprehensively.

These realistic considerations in close affiliation with political requirements, when being raised up to the height of abstract thinking, were turned into the inquiry of the universal nature of human beings and thencefrom to that of the nature of the world at large—a theme which later occupied the central place in the Wei and Jin metaphysics, or neo-Taoism as it was sometimes called. It was through this intellectual channel that the Logico-Legalist current became the germination of the metaphysical current that flourished from the 4th to the 5th century.

With the decline of the supremacy of Confucianism, all other schools of the pre-Qin period became in a certain sense active again, though in different ways. Of them we shall content ourselves by mentioning only two names.

Cao Cao and Zhuge Liang

Cao Cao (155-220), a native from Qiao (now Boxian in Anhui), was the most widely-known statesman of the time who in the course of his unification of the north and in his establishment of the Wei Dynasty, had undergone hard struggles against the separatist regimes of the hereditary nobilities. He imposed strict interdictions on the annexation of farmland and on the shift of taxes by the great landlords onto the peasants and their presumptuous exactions on corvées. He had put to death some officials with backgrounds from the hereditary nobilities and run the officialdom along the Legalist line by selecting officials "in virtue of their talents" with no regard to their birth. This meant a breakthrough of the monopoly of the officialdom by the households of the hereditary nobilities.

From Shang Yang, the Legalist master, Cao succeeded to the idea of "farming and warring". He proclaimed: "The statecraft consists in a strong army and sufficient provisions. Qin unifed the country by developing agriculture and Emperor Wu of Han pacified the western borders by having the garrison troops engage in farming there—these are the good examples of the former dynasties."[2] To meet the aftermath of continuous wars, he distributed the wasted land to the enlisted men and peasants. This measure both strengthened the centralization of his regime and restrained the social disorders and political corruptions since the late Eastern Han. And with the amelioration of the social contradictions, the economy was considerably recovered.

Cao himself had annotated the *Book of Sun Zi*, the foremost pre-Qin strategist. In his preface to that book, he forwarded the idea "let war stop war". He enacted a system of strict rewards and punishments, proclaiming: "Once orders are clearly defined, rewards and punishments must follow."[3] And on the relation of Heaven and Man, he openly professed himself "by nature disbelieving in Providence",[4] taking heaven barely as something in obedience to the laws of the natural world. In the same preface, he asserted: "There is no constant situation for the fighting forces, just as there is no constant shape for the water.... Any favourable situation is of necessity turning into the unfavourable".[5] In these observations he showed that the opposites in a contradiction were of necessity not unchanged and unchangeable, each tended to turn to the other's side. Therefore, while admitting the objective conditions as indispensable, he paid much attention to give full play to the subjective initiative of men. His basic view was stated in these words: "Of all between heaven and earth, it is man that is most valuable" and that "the war is determined rather by the part of ourselves than by the part of the enemy". In the Battle of Guandu in the year A.D. 200, Cao planned a strategic retreat at the outset and then attacked his enemy at their weak points with his partially superior force. It ended with an overwhelming triumph over his enemy. With thirty thousand men, he managed to defeat his opponent Yuan Shao's army of 100,000 strong, furnishing an illustrious instance of the application of his military thoughts and laying down the foundation for his unification of the north of the country.

Fu Xuan in his memorandum to the Emperor Wu of Jin (165-290) said: "Recently Emperor Wu of Wei (i.e. Cao Cao) was fond of studying statecraft, so all scholars turned to the study of the Legalists."[6] Yet Cao should not be simply identified with the Legalists, for his position in the last analysis was rather that of eclecticism. In 203, he promulgated an Edict on the Cultivation of Learning so that "the ways of the ancient sage kings [i.e. the Confucian ideals] should not be lost."[7] Then in 213 he again declared: "For the good functioning of a government, priority should be given to the [Confucian] rites, while for the policy of preventing turbulence, the first place should be given to the employment of strict punishments."[8] For him, both the rites and the punishments were required by the rulers. As to how to employ them, it should be left to the expediency of the situation.

Zhuge Liang (181-234), a native of Langya (now Yinan in Shandong), was one of the best-known statesmen in the history of China. For more than twenty years he was the prime minister of Shu Han founded by Liu Bei who assumed the title of emperor. In the year 207 when Zhuge was still in his recluse, he had already worked out a penetrating analysis about the impending political situation as well as a clear-minded evaluation of the national affairs, shown in his famous proposal to Liu Bei in which he expounded his idea of taking the southwest region as a base area, getting the internal affairs done and allying Sun Quan's forces in the southeast for the preparation of the final expedition to the north against Cao and for the unification of the whole country.

In the sphere of internal policies, Zhuge, like Cao, considered the rule of law accompanied by strict rewards and punishments to be "the essence of good governing". In confrontation with the caprice of the powerful households, he pursued strongly the line of "cultivating the rule of the law".[9] Along with this was his emphasis on selecting talents to the official posts. For the achievements of the rule of law, he enjoyed a great reputation both at his own time and in later ages.

He also employed his idea of the rule of law in military affairs and regarded a sound and strict regulation on rewards and punishments as a prerequisite of cardinal importance in times of war. A wide-circulated story told that once during the war against Wei, his favourite general Ma Su was executed by his own order for having lost the battle, while he himself was asking the Emperor to degrade himself, saying: "What made Sun [Sun Wu] and Wu [Wu Qi, both being renowned strategists in ancient times] won the world was their firm stand in carrying out orders and law."[10] In his study of warfare, he showed a scientific attitude concerning the comparison of the forces of the hostile camps and also their mutual yet ever-changing positions.

2. THE METAPHYSICAL AND ANTI-METAPHYSICAL CURRENTS IN THE WEI AND JIN

The Metaphysical Current

Since the reign of Emperor Wen of Wei (Cao Pi, son of Cao Cao, 220-226), the regime was turning to compromise with the influential nobility households by its measure of dividing the people into nine different ranks on the basis of which officials were appointed. Thereby the powers of the influential nobility households, once tottering under the heavy blow of the peasants' uprisings and then under the restriction imposed by Cao Cao, were again coming to the fore. Down to the Western Jin period (266-315), the rule of the nobility households was so firmly set up that "among the higher ranks there is no common folk, and among the lower ranks there is no nobility".[11] Metaphysics (or Neo-Taoism, or the study on the Ultimate), as the ideology of the nobility households of the Wei and Jin period, spread widely hand in hand with the development of their powers and influences.

The so-called Metaphysics of Wei and Jin derived its name originally from the study of the three ancient metaphysical writings: the *Book of Lao Zi*, *Book of Zhuang Zi* and *Book of Changes*; or strictly speaking, it tried to interpret the Confucian classic *Book of*

Changes in the Taoist terms of Lao Zi and Zhuang Zi. The metaphysicians of the age professed themselves to adhere both to nature (that is, to the Taoist "inactivity") and at the same time to the ethical teachings of Confucianism. Therefore its essence was a mixture of the Taoist and Confucian doctrines in a new and systematic form which represented a higher level of theoretization than the learning of prognostication and apocrypha of the former days. Above and behind the phenomenal world, it introduced a noumenon, persuading people to seek a more mystic and more obscure world of ideas. This theory marked an important stage in the development of idealism in history and played an immense role in the deepening of theoretical thinking.

At a time when the theology of the past—the preaching of the interaction between Heaven and man on the basis of prognostication and apocrypha—lost its attraction, the ruling class was compelled to make a change in the form of their ideology by elaborating a spiritual substance in a more sophisticated fashion in order to replace the outdated personified deity. The metaphysicians worked hard to reduce the real world to "emptiness" or "void" the effect of which was to lead people as far away from reality as possible. The metaphysical current began to emerge during the reign of Zheng Shi (240-249) with He Yan and Wang Bi as its earliest exponents.

He Yan (190-249), a native of Nanyang (in Henan), was a noted imperial minister and the author of *A Treatise on Tao and Its Virtues*, *Collected Annotations of the Analect* and *A Treatise on the Nameless*. Wang Bi (226-249), a native of Shanyang (now Xiuwu in Henan), was the author of the *Commentaries on Lao Zi* and *Commentaries on the "Book of Changes"*. Wang and He were intimate friends and their viewpoints were basically in agreement.

The metaphysicians were primarily occupied with the problem of the origin of the reality—whether it originated from Being or from Non-Being. Wang and He proposed their theory of non-being by professing: "All that are in heaven and on earth derive their origins from non-being."[12] But for them, non-being was not perfectly passive, because "it creates and works in its omnipresence",[13] that is to say, non-being was the creator of all things, i.e., the Tao (Logos). "Tao is that by which non-being is termed,"[14] "it is without shape or form and without sound or echo, so that nowhere does it not communicate, nowhere does it not penetrate and nothing does it not know".[15] It might be seen that such a super-sensual substance could be nothing else but an idea of the supernatural, and in this way the reality of the world was identified with the spiritual. The proposition "the Way [Tao] of heaven is natural and inactive" was interpreted by them in such a way that the development of the natural world was said to be but the development of ideas.

There was in this theory a political implication. On the one hand, these metaphysicians were frightened by the peasants' uprisings, so they preached "non-activity" in political affairs on the ground that "both heaven and earth are taking non-activity as the principle", persuading the people to keep the principle of non-activity and not to make too much trouble. On the other hand, by preaching the rule of inactivity, they tried to render powerless the sovereign Cao Fang, Prince of Qi (240-254) then on the throne, and at the same time to work out a theoretical ground for the reign of the nobility households headed by Cao Shuang and He Yan.

They combined the Confucian ethical code with the Taoist idea of naturalness and non-activity rather sophisticatedly by proclaiming that the Confucian ethical code came from nature or the Way (Tao or Logos). Thencefrom they went on to argue that the ethical code was also derived from non-being and hence was also an outcome of nature itself. Thus the rule of feudalistic rites was reduced to the exaction of nature.

After He and Wang, the foremost representatives of this current were Ji Kang and Ruan Ji. Both Ji Kang (223-262), a native of Zhi (now Suxian in Anhui), and Ruan Ji (210-263), a native of Chenliu (now Kaifeng in Henan) were closely affiliated to the Cao Shuang clique in opposition to the Sima clique. Their ideas reflected the interests of the middle and small landlords in contradiction with the upper ruling class. But by that time the power of the Sima clique was ascending and so political persecutions on their political enemies was well under way with the pretext of protecting the Confucian ethical code. Ji and Ruan were very much disheartened with the rule of the Sima clique, and adopted an attitude of passive opposition. Thereupon they indulged themselves all day long in talking about metaphysics in a new vein and never took any official post. Ruan Ji remarked: "Cruelty arises with the establishment of the royalty, treachery emerges with the appointment of officials, and the ethical code and rites are instituted for no other reason than for the restrictions on the people."[16] Ji Kang "blamed the King Tang of Shang and King Wu of Zhou, and despised the Duke of Zhou and Confucius",[17] while urging people to "transcend the ethical code and return to nature".[18] With these assertions, they raised up their feeble protest against the reign of the Sima clique and gave vent to their political disappointment.

In their philosophical views, they succeeded Zhuang Zi in segregating the subjective and the objective. By citing the example of the same piece of music which might sound pleasant to some while sad to others, Ji Kang came to the conclusion that human knowledge did not represent the objective reality—a conclusion which eventually led to relativism and scepticism. In reality, it reflected the pessimistic mentality of those who were still inclined to the old regime under the reign of the house of Cao.

The main representatives of the metaphysical school during the Western Jin (266-316) were Xiang Xiu and Guo Xiang, both natives of Henan. Xiang Xiu (227-277) wrote the *Commentaries of Zhuang Zi*, which was plagiarized and amplified by Guo Xiang (252-312) into an independent work. Xiang and Guo differed from the theory expounded by He Yan and Wang Bi in that they held their position that being could not originate from non-being. This assertion when expounded philosophically, led them inevitably to regard all existences as existences per se to the entire exclusion of any possibility of their transformations and hence their interconnections.

Politically, the metaphysical theory of Xiang and Guo served to defend the privileges of the nobility households. Because everything being ordained by nature, the social ranks were, among others, also destined to be absolute and invariable. Hence the people ought to be content with their own lots and their social status. Nowhere else did the reactionary character of the Wei and Jin metaphysics showed itself more manifestly than in its preaching of the submission to the existing political and social orders.

This kind of metaphysics prevailed in the Western Jin. But down to the times of Eastern Jin and the Southern and Northern Dynasties (4th-6th cent.), Buddhism was steadily taking the place of the ruling ideology, and the Wei and Jin metaphysics was gradually incorporated into the Buddhist system.

The Anti-Metaphysical Current

While the metaphysical thinking was much in vogue, there also appeared an anti-metaphysical current. Yang Quan (flourished late 3rd century), a native of Liang (now Shangqiu in Henan), succeeded Wang Chong and condemned metaphysics as an empty talk. He claimed that the world was made of primeval ether and human beings were given life by the ether. Once the ether perishes, one dies; just as when the woods are burnt out, the fire extinguishes. This doctrine of his was a critique on the prevailing metaphysics.

Pei Wei (269-300) wrote a book entitled *On the Primacy of Being*. He proclaimed that the world originated from being, not from non-being, and that being could not come from non-being. Different from Xiang Xiu and Guo Xiang, Pei acknowledged the variability of all existences. "It is being that begets being,"[19] said he. But in his opposition to metaphysics, he took the standpoint of the Confucian ethical code, considering that the upholding of non-being would be harmful to the maintenance of the ethical code and the existing social order upon which the ethical code was founded. He was still incapable of freeing himself from the tradition of ethical bonds.

The writings of Bao Jingyan (early 4th century) had long been lost. We can only find fragments of his teachings mentioned in the work of Ge Hong. Bao advocated an anarchical theory and attacked fiercely the prevailing metaphysics. Starting from his concept of nature that all things in nature were naturally equal, he proceeded to argue that natural equality should also reign in human society. He claimed both heaven and earth were made of ether (Yin and Yang) from which all things originated. Hence they were all material objects with no distinction of the superior and the inferior. Thencefrom he went on to refute the ethical teachings of the metaphysicians that "heaven is superior and earth inferior" or "sovereign is superior and subjects inferior". He pointed out that it was just owing to the existing social distinctions that the natural world was imposed with ethical attributes. Thus by revealing the social grounds of the ethical structure of the world fabricated by the ruling class, he provided one of the keenest social viewpoints in the intellectual history of China.

As a logical corollary of the above theory, he went on to oppose the doctrine of the divine rights of sovereigns, proclaiming that the stipulation of the relation of the sovereign and the subjects was but an outcome of the fact of the strong over the weak. Ever since there had been the sovereigns, so he asserted, the people had experienced endless disasters. So he proposed to build up such a society in which there would be neither the sovereign nor the subjects, with all people living in common prosperity and happiness. This ideal of his was apparently only an utopia, but it strongly reflected the visions of the populace and their protest against feudal oppression and enslavement. Here lies the progressive nature of his ideas.

3. BUDDHIST AND TAOIST THOUGHTS AND THE ANTI-BUDDHIST CURRENT

In the Western Han, Dong Zhongshu had made great efforts to turn Confucianism into a religion. The Confucian theology dominating the Western Han was in fact a combination of the Confucian ethical code and religious superstitions. Since the breakdown of this Confucian theology, the nobility households in the Wei, Jin and Southern and Northern Dynasties had elaborated on the one hand the metaphysics, and on the other hand some new kinds of religious superstitions in its stead. Their aim was to dress up the hierarchy under the sway of the nobility households in the name of the eternal truth in nature. He Shangzhi, an official in Song of the Southern Dynasties, had once made his proposal to Emperor Wen (424-453) that the propagation of Buddhism would help "to cultivate the good manners and customs of the people".[20] This meant no other than that the people once converted to Buddhist teachings would become content with their lots and status, inclining no more to rebel. The flourish of religions at that time was primarily due to the encouragement from the ruling class.

Besides, social conditions were ripe for the spread of religions. After the Yellow Turban uprising, there emerged a number of the local separatist regimes waging constant wars against each other. The people in their extreme distress and depression could find no hope for happiness in the present world and naturally looked for a superhuman power that might come to their rescue. Thus the way was paved for the introduction of Buddhism.

The Introduction and Propagation of Buddhism

In the late Western Han (the last years of the 1st century B.C.), Buddhism was introduced into China from India. The course of its development fell roughly into three periods: 1. The period of introduction (Eastern Han, Wei and Jin) which was mainly concerned with the translation of Buddhist literature. 2. The period of growth and propagation (Eastern Jin and Southern and Northern Dynasties). 3. The period of prosperity (Sui and Tang) when indigenous sects in China were founded.

In the Eastern Jin and the Southern and Northern Dynasties, most of the emperors, royal families and nobility households were converted to Buddhism. Prominent Buddhist monks like Buddhochinga and Kumaradjiva were honoured by the royal courts of the Northern Dynasties as the Pontifices of the State. In the Southern Dynasties, Buddhism was for sometime honoured as the state religion; and Emperor Wu of Liang (503-549) was a most superstitious Buddhist who had thrice given himself up to the Buddhist temple as a converted monk. According to historical records, during the Northern Wei (from the 5th to the early 6th century) there were as many as thirty thousand Buddhist temples within its realm with more than two million Buddhist monks and nuns. Under the reign of Emperor Wu of Liang, in the capital Jiankang (now Nanking) alone, there were five hundred Buddhist temples with more than one hundred thousand monks and nuns. These temples possessed large amounts of farmlands and labourers, constituting a special group of monastery landlords with the same privileges as the secular nobility landlords. As a matter of course, the multiplication of the religious landlords aggravated the exploitation of the people and led to economic crisis and growing rebellions. At the meantime, the contradictions between the religious and secular landlords was a constant cause of the anti-Buddhist campaigns.

In the course of the evolution of Buddhism, there had appeared various sects and schools, but as regards its teachings there were two main systems: the Hinayana (of the early Buddhism) and the Mahayana (of the later Buddhism). They both claimed the doctrine of the immortality of the spirit and of karma and retribution; their differences lay in that the Hinayana was mainly concerned with the doctrine of karma, sansara (the transmigration of the soul), the future incarnation, etc. in a stronger superstitious vein; while the Mahayana was more concerned with the logical analysis of philosophical ideas and preached their religious doctrine in a more theoretical way by arguing that all things were but illusions and so there was no reality whatever at all. During the period of Han, Wei and Jin, both schools were successively introduced into China and began to take roots.

At first, Buddhism was regarded as a sort of magic and necromancy and was hence incorporated into the prevailing doctrine of prognostication and apocrypha. Later in the period of Wei and Jin, under the influence of metaphysics of the time, Buddhism intermingled with the metaphysical current. Many noted monks lectured Buddhism in terms of metaphysics and explained metaphysics with Buddhist conceptions.

The Mahayana School then introduced into China belonged to the Kung (emptiness) Sect with their canon Pradjna Sutras (the Intelligence Canon). The term Pradjna denotes the intelligence in a mystic connotation. It means not the knowledge of the objective world, but a subjective identification with the spiritual noumenon. As this current was influenced by the metaphysics of the time, it differentiated into various sects, generally known as the "six schools and seven sects", depending on their different interpretations of "emptiness". In the main, they might be classified into three schools, i.e., the school of Original Non-Being (Benwu School,) represented by Dao An and Hui Yuan, the school of Matter As Such (Jise School,) represented by Zhi Dun and the school of Non-Being of Mind (Xinwu School) represented by Zhi Mindu. The most influential among them was the school of Original Non-Being.

The school of Original Non-Being headed by Dao An and Hui Yuan was basically in conformity with the non-being theory of He Yan and Wang Bi. On the basic issue of thinking versus existence, they held that the material world was illusory and only the spiritual entity the sole reality. They claimed: "Non-Being antecedes the primeval commencement, and Emptiness foreruns all kinds of nature",[21] and that above and behind the material world there was a higher world of spiritual noumena as its basis. In consequence of this, they urged that only by discarding the phenomenal world one could hope to attain a state of spiritual liberation called Nirvana (the ideal state of a Buddhist) in which the spirit would cease all and every kind of activity with no reaction to the outside world at all.

They expounded the Buddhist doctrine of karma in such a way that all the worldly fortunes or misfortunes were ascribed to the inevitable consequences of one's own actions. Therefore if one intended to liberate oneself from the sufferings of the chains of karma and retributions, one was obliged to repudiate and give up any strife for worldly purpose and to pursue the state of nirvana. Such a doctrine sounds more sophisticated than either the Confucian fatalism ("life and death are pre-ordained, wealth and honour are disposed by heaven"[22]) or the popular superstitions.

At the turn of Jin and Song (in the early 5th century), the noted Buddhist theoretician Kumaradjiva translated some of the Indian Buddhist classics of Nagarjuna into Chinese. One of his disciples Brother Zhao (384-414) developed the Pradjna theory in his wide-circulated works: *A Treatise on the Emptiness of the Unreal, A Treatise on the Immutability of Things, A Treatise on Pradjna Not Being Knowledge* and others. His theory was one among the most thoroughgoing idealism in the history of ideas. He completely denounced the reality of the existence of the objective world together with all changes and developments in it. As he was discontent with all the three schools of the Pradjna Emptiness prevailing at that time, he undertook to remould them from a more thoroughgoing idealistic position.

In the ontological viewpoint of his *Treatise on the Emptiness of the Unreal*, he did not repudiate the reality of the material world in a straightforward way. He admitted the variety of the phenomena of all things in the world, but denied their reality by asserting: "The things are not the real things" and "their appearances are not what they look like".[23] Again in his *Treatise on the Immutability of Things*, he did not make a flat denial of the changes and developments of things, but only repudiated the reality of them. For instance, he did not admit the present, the past and the future by holding that the present was no more than the present and so had nothing to do with either the past or the future. So all things and phenomena in the world were but "instantaneously appearing and disappearing" without any duration in time; they were only a sequence of independent and disconnected fragments. This extreme phenomenalistic interpretation led to the total negation of any idea of reality regarding the objective world with all the changes and developments in it. When people came to know the unreality of the world with their own lives in it, they would turn to seek their liberation only in their spiritual world. Such was the teaching of Brother Zhao.

Another noted Buddhist monk of the time was Zhu Daosheng (355-434) who brought a strong intellectual impact on his time by advocating the doctrine of "becoming a Buddha through instantaneous enlightenment".[24] He enunciated that Buddhahood existed no where else but within the very nature of everyone, so that everyone would become a Buddha whenever his nature was enlightened. Such an instantaneous enlightenment did not cost a long process of self-cultivation and good-working as required by the Hinayana school, nor a progression through various stages of intellectual awakening as taught by Zhi Daolin and others. Since all and everyone might attain Buddhahood and become a Buddha, it attracted the people who wished to enter a paradise cheap and ready and leaving all their sufferings in real life to oblivion. It was in this way that the Buddhist religion had become a spiritual drug to both the people who suffered deeply and the ruling class who looked for something more than their worldly enjoyments. This widely propagated doctrine formed the earliest germination of the Zen (or Chan) Buddhism of the Tang period.

4. THE FORMATION AND PROPAGATION OF TAOISM

Taoism as an indigenous religion of China emerged in the Eastern Han, though its origin might be traced to a much earlier time. It was related to some polytheist beliefs and magic of the ancients and absorbed some elements about the mental and physical cultivation of the pre-Qin Taoists as well as other elements from the necromancy and the prognostication and apocrypha. But it was not until the time of the strong influence of Buddhism that it assumed the definite shape of a religion with its own theories and rituals.

At its earliest stage, the Taoists professed their allegiance to Huang Di and Lao Zi, being called "the Taoists of Huang and Lao", and prevailed among the populace only. Of the primitive Taoism there were two main sects, one being "Five-dou-rice Taoism" and the other "Taiping Taoism". The former was so called for the reason that all their adherents were required to pay five dou of rice. It spread in Sichuan and southern Shanxi with Zhang Ling (or Zhang Daoling) and his descendants Zhang Heng and Zhang Lu as its earliest founders. Another branch of it was headed by Zhang Xiu in Ba (now Chongqing in Sichuan). The latter prevailed in the middle and lower valleys of the Yellow River with Zhang Jiao as its leader. During the great peasants' uprisings of the late Eastern Han, both Zhang Jiao and Zhang Xiu employed this primitive Taoism as a revolutionary weapon to mobilize and organize the masses.

The classic of the primitive Taoism was the *Taiping Canon* (originally entitled *The Book of Taiping Qingling*). Basically it preached the teaching of theism in combination with the traditional ethical code. But in certain parts, it exposed and blamed the political suppression and social corruption, reflecting more or less the demands of the people for the rights of living and equality and a vague vision of an ideal society in the future. It was for these parts in it that the Taoists promoted their ideas and activities among the people.

The primitive Taoism was concerned with curing patients and running social welfares, so that the Taoists were often affiliated with the peasants' movements. But by the time of the Three Kingdoms (in the 3rd century), Taoism was more and more coming under the control of the ruling class. Later in the Jin period, popular Taoism was finally remoulded into an official religion in service of the rule of the nobility households. Among the celebrated representatives of this current were Ge Hong and Kou Qianzhi.

Ge Hong (284-364), a native of Danyang (in Jiangsu), was known by the name of Bao Pu Zi (literally the Adherent to Simplicity) which was also the title of his work. The main theme of his study was how to attain immortality of the corporal life and become a fairy by dint of research on the elixir. With him, the medical practices of the primitive Taoism was turned to the search for the elixir of life. The primitive Taoist forms and contents usually utilized by peasants' uprisings were condemned by Ge as a black magic. And he attacked fiercely the armed rebellions led by Zhang Jiao and others. Such a transformation of the nature of Taoism suited the demands of the ruling class, because it would satisfy the nobilities' longing for their corporal immortality as well as for the eternity of their luxurious enjoyments. Thereupon the study of alchemy was becoming a fashion among the ruling class.

Ge Hong adopted some of the traditional Taoist terminology and took Xuan (the Ultimate, or the Indescribable, a term somewhat synonymous with Tao) as the source of all things and phenomena. Xuan was ascribed to the mysterious function of "the arch-patriarch of nature and the master of all varieties"; it "comes without being seen and goes without being caught".[25] Obviously it was not something material with an objective existence, but only a mental fiction. And it was said that once it was grasped, it might fulfil infinitely wonderful feats. Herein manifested the distinctive feature of Ge Hong as a fairy seeker.

In his *Bao Pu Zi*, Ge's political ideas showed a mixture of Confucianism and Legalism. Starting from the experience of the suppression of the peasants' uprisings, he remarked that too much rituals and ceremonies would turn out to be useless and only harsh punishments would meet the requirements in time of disturbances.

But as a scientist, Ge's contribution should by no means be undervalued. He was one of the foremost alchemists and physicians in Chinese history. As an alchemist, he formulated all the alchemical knowledge hitherto accumulated and studied various kinds of minerals and their reactions with one another, and thus contributed much to the primitive chemistry in the history of China. As a physician, his medical writings were among the precious legacies of traditional medical science.

The most celebrated Taoist master after Ge Hong was Kou Qianzhi (?-448) in the Northern Wei. Kou assumed the title of "the Heavenly Master" and refined Taoism by cancelling the popular elements in the primitive Taoism. He taught that "one should not rebel against the sovereign nor plan to set up a new regime" nor "be disloyal to the king".[26] He asked people to be content with their sufferings and to behave in obedience to the existing ethical norms. Thus the Confucian ethical code was infiltrated into Taoism in the stead of its original, much more popular constituents. For this reason, it obtained the favour of the ruling class. Emperor Tai Wu (242-451) of the Northern Wei proclaimed Taoism the state religion and Kou the state patriarch. It was with Kou that popular primitive Taoism was eventually turned into a state religion for the benefits of the ruling class. Under the support of the nobility households, Taoism like Buddhism became much in vogue for a long time.

In their mutual competition for supremacy, Taoism and Buddhism had sustained a long series of polemics and controversies. The ruling class sometimes upheld the one against the other and sometimes vice versa, depending on the political expediencies of the time. After all, the fluctuations of their relative positions were but different manifestations of the contradictions within the camp of the ruling class. At bottom, both served the ruling order of the nobility households, the one as well as the other.

Fashionable as these religions were, Confucianism still always held its rein in the ideological sphere. Royal academies were then instituted where studies and discussions on traditional classics were held. A tri-partite co-existence of Confucianism, Buddhism and Taoism was then in the forming with their constant intellectual influences and controversies among one another.

The Anti-Buddhist Campaign

During the period of the Southern and Northern Dynasties when religious ideas were overflooding, Fan Zhen in the naturalistic and atheistic tradition of Xun Zi, Huan Tan, Wang Chong and He Chengtian (a forerunner of the anti-Buddhist current), worked out his famous writing *A Treatise on the Mortality of the Soul* which hurled a sharp critique on the Buddhist teaching of karma and the migration of the soul.

Fan Zhen (450-515), a native of Wu Yang (now Miyang, in Henan), in his youth "was fond of high-sounding speeches which often irritated his fellow literati".[27] When he was at his post as the governor of Yidu, he interdicted the people from going to the Buddhist temples for worship.

Once in the face of Xiao Ziliang, Prince of Jingling and prime minister of Southern Qi, Fan Zhen alleged there was neither the Buddhahood nor the karma in the world. Xiao asked him: "Then why are there the rich and the poor, the dignitary and the down-graded?"[28] At this, Fan pointed out to the flourishing blossoms in the courtyard and replied that people in the world were just like the flowers falling in the wind, some of them fell on the floor of a magnificient hall and others into a manure pit; it was all owing to accidental circumstances, how could it be attributed to the result of karma?[29] Then Xiao brought up Buddhist scholars and monks together to argue with Fan, but still of no avail. Thereupon Xiao promised to grant him a high official post if only he would be willing to give up his anti-Buddhist polemic. But Fan refused "to sell his view point at the price of an official post".

Fan's *Treatise on the Mortality of the Soul* was publicized at a time when Buddhism was already proclaimed the state religion by Emperor Wu of Liang; so he was confronted with fierce attacks from the nobilities in power, clerical and secular. There broke out a great debate over the issue of the mortality versus the immortality of the soul. More than sixty dignitary monks and officials with more than seventy of their theses launched a campaign against Fan's theory of the mortality of the soul; but Fan never surrendered. At length, his opponents were obliged to acknowledge that they "could find nothing to refute his piercing argument".

The Buddhist teaching of karma was founded upon the theory of the immortality of the soul: the spirit (the soul) when segregated from the body, had its own existence independent of the body. In confrontation with it, Fan based his theory of the mortality of the soul on the unity of the body and the soul, declaring: "The spirit consists in the body and the body consists in the spirit; hence the spirit exists whenever and wherever the body exists, and perishes whenever and wherever the body vanishes."[30] And further: "The body is the substance of the spirit and the spirit the function of the body."[31] For a clearer exposition of this standpoint of his, Fan cited the relationship between the sword blade and its sharpness as an analogy: "What the spirit is to its substance is just like the sharpness to the sword blade.... People never heard that the sword perishes while its sharpness subsists; then how is it possible that the body perishes while the spirit alone subsists?"[32] For him, the spiritual was, and could only be, dependent on the material or the corporal. This was the earliest systematic exposition and explanation of the unity of the two opposites of the body and the soul in their interdependence and differentiation. In his refutation of the Buddhist assertion of the immortality of the soul, Fan transcended the logical shortcomings of his predecessors who took the spirit as something totally different from and independent of the body.

From this standpoint Fan proceeded to argue that every spiritual activity had to rely on certain physiological organs. Seeing and hearing had to rely on eyes and ears, and passing judgments on truth and falsity had to rely on the thinking organ which he mistook for the heart as did all the ancients. He distinguished human cognition into two stages: "knowing" and "thinking", the former referring to knowledge by perception and the latter to rational thinking. By sense organs man would acquire perceptual knowledge, and then through the process of thinking he would reach a higher level of the rational knowledge. With this argument in view, Fan rejected the Buddhist theory of segregating the body and the spirit as well as their teachings on the innate or a priori knowledge.

The social significance of Fan's theory was in its exposure of the deception of the religious fatalism which taught people to obey all existing social hierarchies as though they were pre-ordained. He criticized Buddhism for its spiritual enslavement on the people and the Buddhist monks of higher ranks for their luxurious way of life. "Buddhist teaching is harmful to good politics and Buddhist monks are corrupting the good manners and customs," so he proclaimed. Such was his position in the campaign against the intellectual rule of the religion.

Fan Zhen's *Treatise* was a significant contribution to the naturalistic current of ancient and mediaeval China. He succeeded to the tradition of Wang Chong and exercised profound influences on the naturalistic and atheistic thoughts of the later ages. But like all other naturalistic thinkers of the past, Fan in his understanding of the social phenomena was still maintaining the traditional view that sages surpassed the common people in their morality and intelligence because of their superior inborn gifts. In this respect, he fell into naive mechanism. He was not able to get rid of the Confucian bonds and had in some places made concessions to the rule of religion. But all these rather belonged to the limitations of his age than to his personal traits and inclinations.

Chapter 9

ECONOMIC THOUGHTS IN THE WEI, JIN AND SOUTHERN AND NORTHERN DYNASTIES

The period of Wei, Jin and the Southern and Northern Dynasties underwent a long series of political disunity and social disorder. It lasted almost four centuries, beginning with Emperor Wen of Wei's enthronement (220) in substitution of Han and ending with the unification of Sui (589). Except for a couple of decades under the unification of Western Jin (266-315), most of the period under discussion witnessed continuous wars and rivalries among various competing regimes and antagonism between the Northern and the Southern Dynasties. Naturally the main concern of the economic thoughts of the time was concentrated on how to maintain agricultural production through a better arrangement of land properties, so that the social substratum might be kept unshattered.

1. THE ECONOMIC THOUGHTS OF FU XUAN

Fu Xuan (217-278), a native of Niyang (now Yaoxian in Shaan-xi), was similar to his contemporary Yang Quan in philosophical views. He held that the natural world was in constant motion in obedience to the rule of the "ether" and that the world and the history of mankind were parts of the whole process of nature. With this naturalistic view, he criticized the prevailing theistic beliefs. And in the field of economic thoughts, he showed his originality on many issues.

During the constant wars in the period of the Three Kingdoms, large numbers of peasants were compelled to desert their own homes and became refugees. The unprecedented migration of population led to the serious breakdown of agricultural production, endangering directly the very foundation of the feudal rule. For the stabilization and recovery of production, Fu proposed a theory of division of labour by means of fixing the professions of the people. He advocated: "Let the gentry, the peasantry, the artisans and the merchants engaged in their respective professions.... The youth of the gentry should be educated in the royal academy.... The peasants should provide the country with their harvests.... The artisans should supply their manufactured articles.... The merchants should circulate the commodities"; and so "there would be no one in idleness".[1] The intention of his proposal was to get the refugees settled down and to set the society in order. He further explained it in these words: "By division of professions, each will engage in his own occupation; the division of professions will lead to order and, the engagement in one's own occupation will lead everyone to do his best."[2] By promoting the economic activity with such a measure, he supposed that social order might be guaranteed.

The characteristic feature of his theory consisted in the unprecedented proposal of the regulation on the ratio of "the gentry, the peasantry, the artisans and the merchants" in the whole population. The number of each category was to be adjusted by the social requirements of the time. Proposals like this, of course, often tended to be mere fancies. But in expounding his ideal, he launched severe attacks on the hereditary privileges of the nobilities of the time. He even advocated that all the surplus officials should be sent down to take part in the agricultural production. This, too, tended to be a fancy, but his audacious recommendation meant a breakthrough of the feudal hierarchy based on ranks and status, representing an opinion rarely found at that time.

In the sphere of finance, Fu proposed three principles in taxation, i.e., "fairness", "economy" and "regularity". By "fairness" was meant that taxes should be levied with a view to the circumstances of different people. By "economy" was meant that luxuries and squanderings of the government should be avoided by all means. Fu observed keenly that spending without restraint always caused the greatest harm to the nation, and hence he took moderate spending on the part of the rulers as the key to economy. By "regularity" was meant that a constant system of taxation should be instituted to the exclusion of capricious exactions, so that "the superior shall never levy extraordinary taxes and the inferior shall never pay extraordinary tributes".[3] Otherwise, so he taught, the security and order of the society would be jeopardized.

These principles had been treated separately by some of his predecessors, but none of them had ever combined them into a comprehensive theory. It would seem overcritical to say that he missed the fundamental point of the issue, i.e., how to prevent the encroachment and annexation of the privileged nobilities at its very root. After all, he made contributions to the social and economic thoughts of his age with his advises of minimizing the burdens on the people and of protecting the interests of the comparatively lower social strata.

2. LU BAO'S *ON THE GOD OF MONEY*

Characteristic of the spirit of the age was the pecuniary idea expressed in Lu Bao's outstanding satire *On the God of Money*. Lu Bao (flourished mid-4th cent.), a native of Nanyang (in Henan), was a hermit and his celebrated satire was the development of a work by Cheng Gongsui (231-273) bearing the same title.

In his work he made an exhaustive and penetrating analysis on the social role of money. It runs in these words:

"When you have no money, you will become weak and poor; and when you have it, you will be rich and powerful. Those who have more money will take the lead, and those who have less will follow behind. Those who are taking the lead will be the sovereigns and those who are following behind will be the subjects. Money is honoured without having any virtue, and is envied without having any official post."

"Where money dwells, danger is turned to safety and death to life; and where the money vanishes, the honourable is turned to the down-graded and the living to the dying."

"Life and death are not pre-ordained, and honour and wealth are not endowed by heaven." (An antithesis to Confucius' thesis: "Life and death are pre-ordained, and honour and wealth are endowed by heaven".)[4]

"What heaven is in want of, money will come to its rescue". Indeed, it was no accident that within a century's time there appeared successively two pieces *On the God of Money*. They were the by-products of the development of money economy. Ever since the unification of the currency by the First Emperor of Qin, the commodity-money economy developed rapidly. Even in the tumultuous years of the late Han and the Three Kingdoms when commodities tended to be bargained in kind, the Han currency was still in circulation. The popular superstitions in money and the greed for money showed how far-reaching the commodity-money economy had developed. While many prominent figures of the time were following the fashion of talking haughtily about metaphysical topics, they never forgot their pursuits on money. Wang Rong, one among the most noted figures of the age, owned large estates and farmlands, and was busy all day long in counting his incomes. Another noted figure Pan Yue in his writings boasted himself of how he made a good bargain of the products from his estates. The vogue of the extreme greed for money showed the fact that money fetishism had already permeated various aspects of social life. In mediaeval Europe, money was considered a destroyer of the economic and social order, but down to the beginning of modern times people began to turn to admire money and its power. Money fetishism was but the natural result of a certain stage in the development of the commodity-money economy. In the Western Han, Sima Qian had already suggested this money fetishism in social life, inciting such proverbs as "a young man from a rich family shall never be sentenced to death". The description of the miraculous role of money in Shakespeare's *Timon of Athens* is well known and frequently quoted:

> Gold! yellow, glittering precious gold! . . .
> Thus much of this, will make black white, foul fair;
> Wrong right, base noble, old young, coward valiant.[5]

About one thousand years before Shakespeare, Lu Bao had made the same observation and came very much to the point.

3. THE DISTRIBUTION OF FARMLAND IN WESTERN JIN

The programme of the distribution of farmlands as carried out by the Western Jin government marked another significant step on the part of the feudal regime to meet the impending land problem after the failure of Wang Mang's land reform.

Ever since the mid-Western Han, various programmes had been elaborated and proposed in order to cope with the acute situation of land annexation, including Dong Zhongshu's limitations of farmlands, Cui Shi's emigration to the under-populated areas, Shen Yue's interdiction of the bargain of land and the distribution of land on the basis of workforce and Zhong Changtong's restoration of the nine-square system. All these helped to prepare the way for the formation of the land distribution policy of the Western Jin government.

As a catastrophic aftermath of the constant wars during the late Eastern Han and the Three Kingdoms, the population decreased greatly and large areas of farmland were left in waste. But the nobility households never ceased their forcible annexation of land which led to the decrement of farmland and labourers under the direct control of the imperial government and hence of its financial income. Thus in addition to the sharpening antagonism between the nobility landlords and the peasants, there was also the acute conflict between the imperial government and the nobility households. For the sake of strengthening the government's control of land and labourers and thereby increasing the imperial taxes and corvées, in the year 280 Emperor Wu (266-290) of Western Jin promulgated an edict on the distribution of land which, under the prerequisite of not injuring too much interests of the nobility households while satisfying to a limited degree the peasants' demand for land, had moderated the social contradictions for some time.

The peasants were given farmland not exceeding a certain quota for which they were required to pay rents correspondingly. In the meantime, there was limitation on the largest permissible possessions of the farmland by the nobilities and government officials as well as on the number of their dependents exempted from the imperial taxes and corvees. The guiding principles of this system were as follows:

1. The feudal privilege of the nobility households for possessing large estates was officially affirmed and guaranteed by law. This reflected the essence of the Western Jin Dynasty as an autocracy of the nobility households. But on the other hand, the biggest among them, the royal house, placed certain restrictions on the possession of farmland to prevent land annexation. This system represented once more the endeavour of the ideologues since the Western Han to overcome the unsurmountable dilemma of guaranteeing both the exploiting and the exploited.

2. While the privileges of the nobility households were guaranteed by law, the peasants were allowed to possess farmland in proportion to their labouring forces. To a certain degree, this satisfied the land demand of the peasants and temporarily mitigated the social contradictions at the time.

3. A male adult was allowed to have seventy *mu* of farmland of which fifty were required to pay rents, and a female adult thirty and twenty respectively. This was a measure to encourage the peasants' initiatives by providing them with farmland and partial exemptions.

4. The distribution of land according to different gradation of labouring forces was a view already forwarded during the Warring States (for instance, by Mencius). But it was carried further in the Western Jin. The burden of taxes was regulated in proportion to the strength of labouring forces (the full or the subsidiary, the male or the female). This was a step more advanced than that in the former days when taxation was based on the area of farmland or on the number of labourers.

Thus, after a long period of war, there emerged "the prosperity of the Taikang period" (the reign of Emperor Wu of Western Jin) with the population doubling that of the preceeding years of the Three Kingdoms.

Yet the land problem could not be thoroughly and satisfactorily solved. Soon after the public land was distributed, this measure came to an end, as the government provided no stipulation on how the land could be returned from the peasants to the government. So this policy was no more than an expediency for the time being. It was not until the time from the Northern Wei to Tang that the land problem could find a more advanced way of solution.

4. THE FARMLAND POLICY OF NORTHERN WEI

Since the late Western Jin (early 4th century), the heartland of the country was intruded and plundered successively by various minorities from beyond the northern border, and the people there were compelled to desert their homes and leave the farmland in waste. When the north was again unified under the regime of the Northern Wei, the government came into possession of large areas of wasteland. In the process of their rapid feudalization, the nobilities of the northern hordes were transformed into new landlords; and new social problems arose. This obliged Emperor Xiaowen (471-499) to find out some effective measures. In the year 485, the Emperor adopted Li Anshi's proposal for re-distributing land by which the government-owned wastelands were distributed to the peasants on the basis of the number of the people in each family while leaving the landlords' ownership intact.

Li Anshi (443-493), a native from Zhaojun (now in Hebei), had a good knowledge of the situation of the forcible seizure of land by the nobilities, the misery of the homeless peasants and the government's control of large areas of wasteland. So he proposed that the individual occupation of the amount of land should "match the labouring force of the owner" in order that "the common folk may acquire their means of earning a living, and the powerful should be allowed no much surplus land".[6] As to the ownership of land still in dispute, he ordered to pass it "to the present owner".[7] With this system of land distribution, the ideas of the nine-square system and of the restriction on farmland occupation since the ancient times found their expression.

1. His measure laid down certain restrictions on the capricious annexation of land and seizure of labourers by the nobility households, with the intention of making "the powerful unable to monopolize the fertile land, while the weak being enabled to enjoy a part of his due".[8] In fact, it did not touch the feudal land ownership of the nobility households, and in some respects even protected them through a legal form. Therefore it was carried out without much difficulty.

2. Its main purpose was to find out a solution both for the land problem and for the income of the imperial government. It stipulated

that when the peasants obtained their land, they were obliged to pay their rents and taxes; and when their land were returned to the government, they were no longer obliged to do so. This combination of land utilization and tax payment was a further development of the land distribution of the former times. To a certain extent, it did meet the peasants' urgent demand of land. Besides, the increase of the small land proprietors helped to strengthen the economic foundation of the imperial reign by providing it with more revenues and more manpower. Later on, the Prefectural Military Service was evolved on this basis, affording the main military support of the Sui and Tang empires.

3. What proved more important was the fact that it enforced the peasants' personal dependence on and attachment to the land. Its initiator knew very well that the more the peasants were attached to the land, the more stable would be the feudal economy; hence the labouring forces were taken as the basis in land distribution. In order to get their shares of land, the peasants were ever more closely attached to the land they cultivated.

4. It reflected some new ideas in regard to its execution. It showed a deeper knowledge of the variety of land utilization. Except for land allocated for grain growing, there was specific land for vegetables, hemps, trees and housing; the part of land for grain growing was to be returned in due time, but the other parts were allowed to be inherited. The principle of land distribution was "the poor first and the rich later",[9] giving priority to the homeless peasants without a livelihood, so that the social economy might be recovered and stabilized more easily. It also paid due attention to the relationship between the migration and the density of the population in different areas, aiming at a more balanced distribution of the inhabitants over the country.

This system proved itself a more advanced land programme than all the preceding ones and played a positive role in the recovery of social productivity seriously damaged long since the late Han, Wei and Jin. Within a couple of decades in peace, the population and farmland were greatly increased. So the well-known book *Buddhist Temples in Luoyang* had it in these words: "By that time the people were leading a substantial life, with good harvests and in happy modes."[10] Since then, this guiding principle in land distribution had dominated the succeeding generations for about three centuries and greatly promoted the prosperity of the Sui and Tang empires.

Nevertheless, it should be noted that this programme went no further than a supplement to the feudal ownership of land property, beyond the limit of which it never effected. It was valid only under the given historical conditions with vast areas of wasteland. The imperial government placed restrictions on the annexation of land only in so far as the nobility households were not permitted to possess more than the legal maximun amount of their land properties and dependents. But it never afforded any effective means to counter the feudalistic practice of land annexation, legal as well as illegal. And the growth of population soon outburst the material condition of its own existence. On the whole, it accomplished its historical role intermittently only within a limited scope for an epoch which happened to be appropriate for its working.

Chapter 10

SCIENTIFIC, HISTORIOGRAPHIC AND LITERARY IDEAS IN THE WEI, JIN AND SOUTHERN AND NORTHERN DYNASTIES

Cultural advancements in this period were manifold, and their representative figures were numerous. In the present chapter we shall confine ourselves to name only a few of them in a brief survey.

1. SCIENTIFIC IDEAS

Liu Hui and Zu Chongzhi

The creative genius of the Chinese scientists in this period had found its expression not only in discoveries and inventions but also in innovation of ideas and ways of thinking. In the year 263, Liu Hui, the leading mathematician of the age, annotated the *Nine Chapters on the Mathematical Art*, a classical work dated before the early Western Han. The author of the book was unknown but it was generally acknowledged as the corner-stone of Chinese mathematical science. In his annotations to the book, Liu gave his proofs in words and diagrams with great originality. One of his greatest contributions was his calculation on the value of π. He opposed the habit of "following the ancients" and daringly pointed out the fault of the traditional belief that the value of π was 3. By using the "method of intersecting a circle" (i.e. by multiplying the sides of an inscribed polygon within a circle), he started from a hexagon and finally reached an inscribed polygon with 96 sides; and the approximate value of π was found to be 3.14. He taught that the more were the sides of an inscribed polygon, the closer it would come to coincide with the circle; or, as he put it: "The more it was intersected, the less will be the error; and by intersecting again and again until the unintersectable, it will coincide with the circle without any error."[1] This method of infinite intersection implies the concept of the infinitesmal and the limit in modern mathematics and represents the most advanced ideas of the age. As was generally known, it was not until the turn of the 17th and the 18th centuries that mathematicians in the West formally began to employ this method and opened the gate to modern mathematics.

In the field of mathematics and astronomy, another outstanding scientist after Liu Hui was Zu Chongzhi (429-500) who was an emigré in the Southern Dynasties from a family in Fanyang (now Laiyuan in Hebei). Zu studied in an exact and solemn manner, always preparing to overthrow the erroneous conclusions of his predecessors and to pronounce his own views with accurate proofs and measurements. Thus on the basis of his predecessors he was able to make new achievements.

Zu's greatest achievement was his furtherance of Liu's calculation on the value of π which by his computation should lie somewhere between 3.1415926 and 3.1415927. This numerical value was of world significance in the history of mathematics. Never before had any one calculated it as far as seven figures after the decimal point. This highly precise record was unbroken for almost one thousand years until 1427. For the sake of convenience, Zu formulated two ratios to show the value of π, the precise ratio being 355/113 (= 3.1415929 roughly) and the approximate ratio being 22/7 (= 3.1428571 roughly). The former ratio comes very near the precise value of π and deserves to be ranked among the greatest achievements in world mathematics. It was by far the earliest and the most brilliant result on this subject. In the history of mathematics, numerous mathematicians engaged themselves in search of the ever more precise value of π. If the preciseness of the value of π may be taken as the level of the development of mathematics of a nation, then the brilliant works of Zu should rightly be qualified to serve a mark of the highly developed mathematical science in China. Hence it was suggested that $\pi = 355/113$ should be laureated as the Zu ratio. It was really a pity that some other works of his had been lost.

Yu Xi, an astronomer of the Eastern Jin, discovered that the sun in the interval from the Winter Solstice of the first year to that of the next, did not return to its original point, so that he concluded the sun did not describe a celestial circle exactly in a year. By his computation he found that in every fifty years the vernal equinox and the autumnal equinox moved one degree westward on the ecliptic—a phenomenon called the precession of the equinoxes. Yu's research was adopted by Zu who, taking into account the precession of the equinoxes, attributed 365.2428 days to a tropical year and 27.21223 days to a nodical month—a value very close to the modern computation which gives 365.2422 and 27.21222 respectively. In addition, he made innovations on the calculation of the leap year. In the year 462 he recommended to Emperor Xiaowen of Song to promulgate a new calendar. But his recommendation met great obstruction from the conservatives who proclaimed the old calendar "an institution from the antiquity" and hence "inviolable" and at the same time abused him as a "blaspheme and renegade". But Zu was not frightened by all these and wrote the well-known *Refutation* against them.

In this *Refutation* he insisted that the heavenly bodies moved in accordance with fixed laws which were cognizable to man. He pleaded the case of his computation with the eclipses and concluded: "[The movements of the heavenly bodies] are not acted by gods and monsters, and can be checked by their celestial positions and calculated by mathematics."[2] This naturalistic view of the universe brought the scientific outlook of the age to a new height.

In the field of cosmography, there was a long train of prominent astronomers who with their new ideas enriched the knowledge of the universe and the natural world. During the time of the Three Kingdoms, Yang Quan developed the Nightly Theory of the Universe with his ethereal conception of nature. He forwarded the proposition: "The earth has its shape but the heavens have no definite body...."[3] The ether evaporated with their quintessence floating up in a flexible fashion which is called the Milky Way or the nebulae."[4] Here he expressed his idea of cosmogony intuitively. Zhang Zhan of the Eastern Jin proclaimed a similar view that not only was the heaven full of ether, but also the sun, the moon and the stars were made of ether that sparkled. This view was a development of the Nightly Theory of the Universe of the former times. Yu Xi in his cosmography dealt with the infinity of the universe which, he declared, "extends to infinity".[5] He also remarked that the movements of the sun, the moon and the stars were subject to invariable laws which were "as regular as the tides of the sea".[6] Even before him, Zhang Hua of Western Jin had said: "The universe is always in motion with the sun incessantly revolving and the earth ever floating."[7] One may fairly find in it the earliest buds of the idea of the rotation and revolution of the earth. All of them had made their contributions to the theory of the movement of the earth as well as to the advancement of the scientific ideas.

Jia Sixie and His Agricultural Ideas

Jia Sixie (the 6th century), the leading agronomist in the time of the Northern Wei, had been the governor of Gaoyang (now Zibo in Shandong). From 533 to 544, he worked on his famous writing *Important Arts for the People's Welfare* in which he summarized experience in agricultural production. He consulted more than 150 kinds of writings in this field, collected a great deal of productive knowledge from the peasants and examined all of them through his own observations.

Among others, his contribution to world science lay in his scrutiny of the relationship between agrarain production and natural surroundings. In agrarian production he stressed the importance of the local and climatic conditions, proclaiming repeatedly: "Obeying the climatic variations and taking into account the local conditions, one will reap more harvest with less labour; conversely, giving up to one's caprices regardless of the objective laws, one will labour harder with less harvest or even nothing at all."[8] He advocated farming with specific regard to seasonal and climatic variations as well as to the different qualities of the soil in different localities.

He studied minutely the past experiences in recovering and improving the fertility of the soil, especially in the measures of drought-relieving and moisture-preserving of the soil. He recommended the fallow system in farming. In particular, he carefully studied the system of crop rotation and worked out the application of green manure, i.e., to improve the fertility of the farmland by increasing the nitrides through the implantation of the legumes. This was a great innovation. It was not until the thirties of the 18th century that the English began to practise the same system.

Further more, Jia made detailed analysis of the nature of different crops and elaborated a relatively clear standard in the classification of the species and a system of seed breeding, leading to the knowledge of the role of artificial selection. He paid special attention to the variation caused by different local conditions and came to the first knowledge of heredity in relation to its surroundings. By treating the topic that the change of the surroundings would lead to variations in heredity, he came very close to the idea of the "heredity of the acquired character", a notion which was advanced in Europe as late as the 18th century, i.e., more than a thousand years later than Jia.

The above-mentioned achievements of his were in some way correlated with his social ideas. He emphasized the role of agricultural production in the national life, claiming: "The essence of good government consists in reassuring the people, and the essence of reassuring the people consists in the sufficiency of provisions, and the essence of the sufficiency of provisions consists in not interfering with the timely schedule of farming."[9] And this was the reason why he treated in details all that were concerned with farming.

He succeeded Xun Zi in upholding the belief "what man proposes will outweigh what heaven disposes", and gave priority to man's initiative in transforming the natural world. He cited many historical facts to show the truth that the power and wealth of a nation did not consist in the extension of its territory but in the full play of its human resources and their initiative. This idea made him an earnest advocate of the importance of the improvement of technology and the employment of advanced scientific methods. He had no faith at all in the inborn knowledge of the legendary sages. It was the experience of the labouring people in their age-long productive practices that he was concerned with. His creed "verification by practices" was saturated with scientific spirit of the age.

2. HISTORIOGRAPHIC IDEAS

By the time of Wei and Jin, historiography stepped into a new stage in its development and manifested more and more its prominent significance in the academic field. The Emperor Wen of Song had stipulated four topics in learning: the Confucian doctrine, the metaphysics (or Neo-Taoism), literature and history. Since then history attained its independence as a specific learning. Many scholars engaged themselves in writing histories not under the sponsorship of the government but by their own initiation. Among the historical writings of the time, the most noteworthy were the *History of the Later Han Dynasty* by Fan Ye, *History of the Three Kingdoms* by Chen Shou and Annotations to the *"History of the Three Kingdoms"* by Pei Songzhi.

Fan Ye (398-445), a native of Shunyang (now Xichuan in Henan), in the writing of his *History of the Later Han Dynasty* emphasized the predominance of the Confucian ideology. He taught that when people "talk about [the Confucian teachings of] benevolence and righteousness and follow the way of the sages", and "each one knows the key link between the sovereign and the subject and between the father and the son, and each family sticks to the right against the wrong",[10] then the imperial reign would be going on smoothly generation after generation. Hence he took the Confucian ethical code as the criterion in passing judgments on historical personalities and events. What was characteristics of his book was his innovation of the "biographies of the martyresses", the standard of whose enlistment was their compliances to the feudalistic norms. Those women who stuck to the feudal bonds to their death were held the most praise-worthy. This innovation of his reflected the strengthening of the spiritual enslavement imposed on the weaker sex by the feudal ruling class.

But in his book, there were also paragraphs that shed a light on atheism. And starting from the Confucian orthodoxy, he stood against the Buddhist ideas then in fashion. He declared decidedly: "There is no Buddhahood under the sun", and rejected the superstitious preachings of the Buddhists on the doctrine of karma and retribution. In close connection with it, he also showed his firm position against the teaching of prognostigation and apocrypha. He praised Huan Tan as "a great talent" and agreed with Huan's anti-apocrypha standpoint. But far from being a thorough-going atheist, his ideas were always vacillating among ideological contradictions.

More often than not, he expressed in his book his belief in the Mandate of Heaven as well as in other superstitious ideas, and asserted that some happenings were omens foreboding the turn of lucks.

3. LITERARY IDEAS

The Yellow Turbans' Uprising in the late Eastern Han had not only smashed the imperial reign but also shaken the rule of the Confucian orthodoxy. It became possible in Wei and Jin to break away from the ideological bonds of the past and to take a new direction of its own. Against this background, the study of the nature of literature was influenced by the new attitude of life and a new epoch of literary criticism began. There appeared some important works on literary theory which were of lasting significance to the literary works and literary ideas of the later ages.

Cao Pi's Literary Ideas

Cao Pi (178-226), son of Cao Cao, ascended the imperial throne in 220 and became the first emperor of the Wei Dynasty. During his reign he was much devoted to the promotion of literary careers and headed personally the literary circle at the capital. One of his main works *On the Literary Writings* was specifically concerned with literary criticism which served a landmark of the literary ideas of his time.

He made a high evaluation on the role of literature which he termed "a great affair of the state and a splendid career in eternity".[11] The place of literary writings was elevated to the same height as the academic learnings. Literary writings were then officially endowed with an independent worth of its own. This new awakening of literary self-consciousness signalled the new tendency of regarding literature as an art in itself.

His view on the nature of literature in some aspects surpassed by far his predecessors. He pronounced definitely his thesis: "Literary writings are not all of the same genre.... All literary writings are of the same substance but in variegated forms of expression."

He formulated them into eight categories of style and four kinds of expression. A pure formal classification as they were, they nevertheless represented a progress in literary ideas. In the pre-Qin period, literature and academic learnings were hardly distinguishable from each other; in the Han period, the dissimilarity of the two was beginning to be discerned. Cao Pi's classification marked another step forward. In particular, he pointed out: "The poetic diction attempts at magnificence."[12] Here by the term magnificence was meant the thinking in images (or imagination in contradistinction with either fancies or logical thinking) which in his view characterized the nature of literature. This discernment was somewhat analogous to Coleridge's[13] but antedated it by sixteen centuries.

He advanced the viewpoint that "a literary work is dominated by its spirit"[14] whereby he tried to show the connection between the spirit of the writer and his style of work. He considered the literary composition the reflection of its author's spirit. But he missed the point that a work of art was at the same time dominated by the background of society and of the age. He took the spirit of an author as the inborn gift by temperament and advocated him to write in his own style. At any rate, this view of his played an active part in promoting the freedom of literary expression.

He claimed that owing to the differences of inborn gifts, each writer would naturally have his peculiar merits and defects. He condemned the frivolous habit of the literary writers of "looking down on the defects of others from the standpoint of their own merits".[14] Assuming such an attitude, he passed his judgments on the "Seven Writers of the Jianan Period": Kong Rong, Chen Lin, Wang Can, Xu Gan, Ruan Yu, Ying Yang and Liu Zhen with concrete analysis on their respective merits and defects.

Another standpoint of his was his objection to the prevailing attitude of honouring the antiquity and the formalistic tendency in literary creation.

Liu Xie's Literary Ideas

Liu Xie (5th-6th century), the most celebrated literary theorist of that time, came from an emigré family in Jingkou (now Zhen-jiang in Jiangsu) and recieved both the Confucian and the Buddhist teachings in his youth. In his main work *A Scrutiny of the Spirit of Literature,* he summarized rather comprehensively all the preceding literary theories and criticized severely the formalistic tendency of his contemporary writers.

His literary ideas were noteworthy in the following aspects:

1. He succeeded Xun Zi and Yang Xiong in asserting: "Literature originated from the Tao."[15] In the chapter entitled "On Tao", he proclaimed that the Tao was but "the way of nature". Everything in nature was gifted with its own "literature", such as the glory of the sun, the charm of the landscape, the flourish of the plants and the sounds of the flowing waters. All these were the natural beauties, but with mankind "literature is found in the writings of their speeches".[16] They came out spontaneously by themselves as the expressions of "the way of nature". The aim of literature, so he held, was "to describe the splendour of the heaven and the earth, and to enlighten the eyes and ears of the people", so that a literary work should realistically represent the real life, its social function being to enlighten and to educate the people. This position of his afforded an antithesis to the prevailing formalistic tendency of writing.

But Liu's ideas were very much under the restrictions of the traditional Confucianism, so that his "way of nature" was inextricably entangled with the Confucian teachings. It seemed to him that "the way of nature" had to be made clear by the doctrines of the ancient sages, and that a writer was necessitated to learn from the ancient sages and especially the Confucian classics. It was on this ground that the first chapter of his book was entitled "On Tao", the second, "Consulting After the Sages" and the third, "Honouring the Classics", all of which illustrated the priority he gave to the learning of the traditional classics that provided in his opinion not only the sources of all literary writings but also the criterion of all literary measurements. It was no wonder that in his enlightened ideas there were mingled a strong tendency of feudal conservatism.

2. Against the formalistic style of pursuing the flowery language at the cost of the content, Liu proposed his argument on the interrelations of the literary form and content. He contended that

literary grace had to rely on the substance it was to deal with and conversely the substance should correspond to the literary grace for its expression. But the two were not on a par, for, after all, a literary work was determined predominantly by its content for which the literary form served.

Based on this principle, he laid down his proposition: "A literary piece is worked out for the sake of expressing the sentiment" instead of what he denounced as "the sentiment is worked out for the sake of composing a literary piece".[17] It was the expression of the sincere sentiment of the writer that should serve the aim, while the literary grace or skill only a means to that aim. By such a balanced treatment on the relation of the form and content in literary writings, Liu made a valuable contribution to the treasury of Chinese literary ideas along the realistic line.

3. As regards the interconnections between literary writings and their times, Liu expounded that literature was ever changing with the changes of times and that literary works of different ages reflected different social realities in their embodiment of different ideas and different artistic forms. Thus he explained the literary style of the Jianan period against the background of constant wars and social disturbances as well as against the sufferings of the people at that time. He concluded that all literary works were closely related with the social realities of their times. This was indeed a brilliant view, though sometimes he could not help from exaggerating the role of the sovereign in promoting literature.

4. Liu brought forth a far more comprehensive criterion in literary criticism than almost all of his predecessors. Prior to him, Wang Chong and Cao Pi had raised objections to the fashion of "honouring the ancient and despising the present" and of "the literati looking down upon one another"; but Liu made an overall comment, asking the critics to be qualified with broad cultivations and profound learnings, because "it is only after listening to thousands of songs that one comes to know music, and it is only after examining thousands of swords that one comes to know the weapon".[18] So was the case with literature. In evaluating a literary work, he demanded that the critics examine it by six standards: the idea of the theme, the rhetorical skill, the combination of the tradition and the individual talent, the modes of expression, the

mastery of the materials and lastly the musicality of the composition. This theory of literary criticism formed an integral part of Chinese literature and played a lasting role in the literary studies of the later ages.

Zhong Rong's Literary Ideas

Zhong Rong's *Judgment on Poesy* was the earliest existing work dealing with the specific topic of poetry. He passed his systematic judgments on more than 120 poets from Han to Liang, and classified their works into three grades: the superior, the medium and the inferior. Hence his work was also called *Criticism on Poesy*. His critical opinions about these poets are of enduring significance in the history of Chinese poetic ideas.

Zhong Rong (flourished early 6th century), a native of Yingchuan (now Changge in Henan), criticized the formalistic style of writing in his days and upheld a realistic view of literature. He was particularly concerned with the relationship of poetry and its natural and social backgrounds.

He made intensive inquiries into the origin and the role of poetry. In the preface to his work, he asserted: "The ether moves all things which in their turn move the human beings; therefore when human emotions are aroused, they find their expressions in dancing and singing";[19] in other words, poetry originated from human emotions stimulated by the external world. Different natural conditions or social surroundings would incite the poet in different ways.

In judging the works of different poets, he paid much attention to their lives and the influences of their surroundings on them. For instance, in commenting on Li Ling, he remarked: "There was so much bitterness in his works which belonged to the genre of the complaining". "Had he not suffered so much hardship, how could he write his works like these?"[20] To interpret the ideas and the characteristic styles of a poetic work with respect to the social surroundings and the life and suffering of the author, herein lay one of Zhong's most valuable insight in his literary viewpoints.

Zhong deemed the concrete contents and genuine emotions the indispensable requirements of a good poem, so he came to oppose the metaphysical style among the nobilities and the vulgar artificiality of poetic diction. He advocated "the style and the spirit of the Jianan period" with its unity of content and form as well as its natural poetic diction. His positive affirmation of the literature of the Jianan period promoted the literary current against the prevailing formalism and had an important bearing on the prosaic and poetic literature of the Tang period.

Chapter 11

POLITICAL AND PHILOSOPHICAL THOUGHTS IN THE SUI, TANG AND FIVE DYNASTIES

1. POLITICAL THOUGHTS IN SUI AND EARLY TANG

Throughout the Southern and Northern Dynasties (from early 4th to late 6th century), Confucianism had continued to hold its sway and the study of Confucianism never ceased, though Buddhism and Taoism were much in vogue. The tri-partite co-existence of the three beliefs was already in the formation, and they acted upon one another intellectually. With the unification of the whole country under the Sui Dynasty in 589, the internal contradictions within the landlord class were considerably alleviated. As reflected in the ideological realm, this new situation brought about a new tendency of reconciliation of the three teachings. After the Tang Dynasty was founded in 618, in view of the rapid downfall of the Sui Dynasty as well as of the urgent need of recovering the social economy, the imperial government pursued a more moderate policy. It was then that the tri-partite co-existence of the three beliefs was finally established.

Wang Tong and the Union of Confucianism, Buddhism and Taoism

The outstanding representative of this tendency of union was Wang Tong (584-618), a native of Longmen (now Jishan in Shanxi), who was renowned both for his career of teaching and for his work entitled *The Middle Sayings* or *Wen Zhong Zi*.

In his work he urged the necessity of the union of all the three beliefs. Once when a disciple of his asked him: "How about the three beliefs?" He answered: "Good politics had already suffered long under their polemical teachings."[1] And his disciple went on to ask: "Then how would it be if all of them are to be banned?" Such a violent measure, Wang replied, would be just like "to put out a fire by lending it a favourable wind".[2] The conclusion he came to was: "Now it is time for the three teachings to be united in one",[3] his intention being to reconcile the social contradictions intellectually as well as theoretically. But Wang's basic position remained Confucianism. He professed himself to be the master of the Confucian orthodoxy "in succession of Duke Zhou" and "in the direct line of Confucius".[4] He propagated the Confucian ethical code of the three cardinal guides and the five constant virtues, proclaiming "benevolence is the beginning of the five constant virtues" and "nature is the substance of the five constant virtues". But at the same time, he also appreciated the Taoist teaching: "When the superior keeps to non-activity, the inferior would be satisfied."[5] Consequently besides the rule of the Confucian rites, he resorted also to the Taoist non-activity doctrine with a view to imposing certain restrictions on the wanton extravagances of the ruling class. He knew well that it was only when the social contradictions were ameliorated that the political and social order might get stabilized.

Political Thoughts in Early Tang

Emperor Taizong of Tang (599-649) was the most brilliant sovereign ever since the First Emperor of Qin and Emperor Wu of Han. He and his circle had personally experienced the thunderstorm of the great uprisings of the peasants in the last years of Sui and witnessed the Sui regime being overthrown. They realized that in order to secure an enduring stability, certain restrictions should be imposed on the ruling class. Emperor Taizong compared the relation between the sovereign and his subjects to that between the boat and the water, saying: "Water can float the boat but can also capsize it."[6] He drew lessons from the rule of the preceding dynasties and pointed out: "The First Emperor of Qin conquered all the six kingdoms, and Emperor Yang of Sui (605-617) enjoyed all the wealth of the four seas; but with all their prides and comforts they fell down within a very short time"; so he confessed: "Each time when I think of the danger of falling, I give serious warnings to myself".[7] And in this vein he always give warnings to his sons and his ministers.

He realized that over-exploitation would definitely lead to the eventual ruin of the regime. "Under unrestrained taxation and exaction, the people will perish, and together with them the sovereign will perish too."[8] so remarked Emperor Taizong. He compared the greedy ruler to "a glutton who eats his own flesh", "when the flesh is eaten up, he himself is doomed to die."[9] And further: "Material desires lead to more expenses, more expenses lead to heavier taxes, heavier taxes lead to the distress of the people, the distress of the people leads to the precariousness of the nation and the precariousness of the nation leads to the fall of the throne."[10] Thencefrom he drew his conclusion: "The way of the sovereign has to dwell primarily on the subsistence of the people."[11] In other words, the exaction on the people should be confined within certain scope so as to keep them in a state of being able to maintain their simple reproduction. Otherwise, the ruling class would lose their people to exact upon.

He also realized the importance of winning the people's support. In the early years of his reign, there had been a controversy over the issue of how to rule over the peasants. Feng Deyi proposed the policy of severe suppression, but Wei Zheng came to his opposition by advising "to take [the fall of] Sui as a mirror" and asked for relative alleviation of the people's burden. The emperor adopted Wei's advise and said: "The world can never be won by sheer force.... The social disorder can never be stopped by violence."[12] He analysed the reasons of the downfall of Sui: first, heavy taxes and corvée services; second, the corruptions of the officials; third, the misery of the poverty-stricken populace. But for all these, so he taught, the people would never have raised up in revolt.

With the instance of the downfall of Sui in their view, the early Tang rulers strove hard "in regulating the way of governing", the main features of which included the following:

1. They laid down a series of policies along the line of "ceasing the war and cultivating the peace" with the idea that "once China being pacified, the minorities on the borders would naturally come to submit themselves".[13] The officialdom was so regulated as to meet the demand of both decreasing the number of the officials and

enhancing administrative efficiency. As the government's policies were executed rather smoothly, the political and social stability that followed provided favourable conditions for the development of production. Emperor Taizong innovated an imperial examination system through which the elites from the middle and lower social strata were given a chance of being absorbed into the government. It was an effective measure to break through the political monopoly of the hereditary nobilities and to strengthen the imperial reign.

Taizong himself was renowned in history as an emperor who was good at adopting advices from his inferiors. Wei Zheng used to forward to the emperor many advices and was remembered for his famous saying: "Listen to both sides and you will be enlightened, heed only one side and you will be benighted."[14] Thus in the early years of Tang, there was fostered a good mood in political affairs rarely seen in history. The practice of the policy of "light taxation and small corvée" had made the people possible to have a rest and at the same time stimulated their initiative in production. Meanwhile they pursued a policy of peaceful co-existence of the various nationalities within the empire, in consequence of which the multi-national empire was well developed.

Taking all these measures, the Tang regime aimed at a lasting reign by means of easing up the social contradictions. Compared with the tyrannical exaction of Sui, it did make substantial progress in many respects.

2. The way of governing conceived by the early Tang regime was also embodied in its intellectual control over the people to whom the three teachings were the main contents. Following the steps of Wang Tong, the early Tang regime knew well how to utilize these three teachings to their greatest benefits. On occassions of national ceremony, leading figures of the three teachings were summoned up for open debates in the court or public gatherings. And finally the tri-partite co-existence of them was established.

But Emperor Taizong also drew his lessons from the catastrophic results of the Buddhist worship in the courts of the Southern and Northern Dynasties. He realized that the Buddhist teaching was incompatible with the Confucian ethical code and that the clerical privileges contradicted with the imperial government over the issues of taxation, corvée and military services. Hence while paying homages to Buddhism, he upheld Taoism to counterbalance it. But what he was most fond of was still Confucianism. He openly declared: "Now what I am inclining to is but the way of Yao and Shun and the teachings of the Duke of Zhou and Confucius."[15] He gathered many Confucian scholars to compile the Confucian classics and enlarged the Royal Academy for Confucian Studies. By appointing Yan Shigu to edit the *Definitive Texts of the Five Classics* and Kong Yingda to compile the *Correct Meaning of the Five Classics*, he brought to an end the age-long controversy of various schools over the interpretation of the Confucian classics since the Eastern Han, such as the controversy between the Old Text School and the New Text School, between the teaching of Wang Su and that of Zheng Xuan, etc. By unifying people's ideas with these measures, the great unification of the empire was facilitated.

2. BUDDHISM, TAOISM AND THE ANTI-BUDDHIST CURRENT

By the time of Sui and Tang (from late 6th to early 10th century). Buddhism held its sway over the whole society and the clerical landlords formed an influential political and economic force. Immediately after the stormy years of the peasants' uprising at the end of Sui, the imperial regime was in need of a spiritual force to pacify the restless minds of the people, not to mention the religious sentiment deeply rooted in the hearts of the poverty-stricken and down-trodden people. It was against this background that Buddhism reached its zenith.

From different interpretations of the Buddhist teachings there sprouted various Buddhist sects, each with its own theoretical doctrine as well as with its clerical properties. The most prominent among them were the Tiantai Sect headed by Zhi Kai, the Dharmalaksana (or Ideation) Sect headed by Xuan Zhuang, the Huayan (or Garland) Sect headed by Fa Zang and the Zen (or Chan) Sect headed by Hui Neng.

1. The Tiantai Sect was founded by Zhi Kai (538-597) at the time between the Chen and Sui dynasties (second half of the 6th century), with the *Louts Sutra* and *The Mahayana Method of*

Cessation and Contemplation as its main classics, and hence it was also called the Lotus Sect.

The essential teaching of the Tiantai Sect was based on the Mahayana theory of the Pradjna of the Emptiness Sect, emphasizing the complete repudiation of the reality of the objective world. It started its argument not by directly cancelling the objective world, but by reducing it to a dichotomy, i.e., the world of ideas and the world of phenomena. Then it proceeded to argue that both ideas and phenomena were but mere illusions of the cognitive subject and that only the mind constituted the sole source and substance of the world, or as what they put it: "All the functions or laws of the world are caused by the mind."[16] In other words, all existences and happenings in the world were but derivatives of the mind. With this reasoning, Zhi Kai proposed his doctrine of cultivation through cessation and contemplation. By cessation was meant the attainment of a state of quietude of the mind by means of meditation and abstraction (Dhyana); and by contemplation, the self-reflection of the mind by itself. To put it in terms of daily expression, it meant the cultivation of the self-knowledge of the subjective spirit through which the wisdom of Pradjna (intelligence) might be attained. They proclaimed that by such a method one might be led to the cognition of the mind (the sole substance of the world), i.e., the highest spiritual state sought after by the Buddhists. To discard the life in the world and to pursue the truth within one's own mind, such, in short, was the essence of the teachings of this sect.

The Tiantai Sect prevailed in the early Tang but gradually declined since the middle Tang. Later on, in the intellectual field the Neo-Confucianism was formed under its influence. The famous Neo-Confucianist Shao Yong's emphasis on introversion was evidently related to the Tiantai teaching of cessation and contemplation.

2. The Dharmalaksana Sect, or the Ideation Sect or the Faxiang Sect, was founded by the most celebrated translator of the Buddhist classics Xuan Zhuang (600-664) and his disciple Kui Ji (632-682). Their representative writings were *The Doctrine of Completion Through Ideation* compiled by Xuan Zhuang and *The Commentaries on "The Doctrine of Completion Through Ideation"* by Kui Ji.

The Ideation Sect propounded their basic teachings by an exposition of their central theme: all are ideation. They claimed that only the ideation (consciousness) was real while all in the objective world were but illusions of that ideation. Through their manipulation of conceptual analysis, consciousness was reduced to eight categories: of the eye, the ear, the nose, the tongue, the body, the mind, the manas (or the seventh) and the alaya (or the eighth). Of them the first six concerned respectively with the cognition by seeing, hearing, smell, taste, feeling and knowing while the seventh with that by thinking, or rather a kind of internal self-consciousness. But all these would require the existence of a cognitive subject which served to realize these cognitions and without which all these cognitions would be impossible. And this cognitive subject was no other than the eighth or the alaya. "If there is not this cognition, then who would it be that would cognize the other cognitions"?[17] Hence it was only the eighth or the alaya that functioned categorically by its faculty of furnishing a common ground for the preceding seven, because in it, so they argued, there was a spiritual "seed" (Bijas). All were derived from this alaya which, as a spiritual substance, was everlasting and immortal. It might be seen that in the last analysis, this alaya or the eighth cognition was but a mutation of the immortality of the soul.

The peculiarity of the Ideation Sect dwelt in that their theoretical system assumed a more sophisticated form than that of other sects. It was because of the fact that it was too rigid an introduction of the scholasticism of the later Mahayana teachings in India without being accommodated itself to the requirements of the Chinese indigenous peculiarities, that after a short time of propagation it ceased to prevail and finally declined. But in their theoretical reasoning, there might be found valuable dialectic elements, and their logical inquiries still furnish a topic worthy to be studied carefully.

3. The Huayan Sect (or the Garland Sect) founded by Fa Zang (643-712) was so called because it expounded its classic Huayan Canon (Avatamsaka Sutra).

In its basic teaching, the Huayan Sect did not differ very much from the former two. Similarly, it took the objective world as the product of the subjective spirit. It claimed: "All phenomena have no quality by itself",[18] meaning that all phenomena were but the embodiment or manifestation of the subjective spirit and therefore had no independent existence of their own. Fa Zang alluded to the analogy of a golden lion, proclaiming that the golden lion was made of gold, but "the gold has no quality by itself" and was made into what it was made into, i.e., a lion. Since the golden article was what it made into, it followed that the golden article was nothing real in itself. So was it with all that were in the world. In other words, all were but the illusions of the subject.

Another fundamental thesis advanced by this sect was the idea of that "there was no barrier between the nounemon and the phenomenon". Here by the word noumenon was meant the ultimate spiritual substance, and by the word phenomenon all that were in the objective world. They taught that all that were in the objective world were but illusory and had to rely on the noumenon for their own existences which were nothing else than the manifestations of that noumenon. Consequently there was no barrier whatsoever between the two. Since phenomena were but manifestations of the noumena, so all in the objective world were thus led to merge into the subjective world. The social implication of this theory was simply that underlying all the variegated social phenomena there was at bottom no conflict nor contradiction. Thus it tended to justify the rationality of the social injustice and inequality, because all were but the different manifestations of the one and the same noumenon which was rational and just. As a matter of course, the only way out from the entangled life of the world was to seek one's extrication along the Buddhist line of giving up the real world and pursuing the self-sufficient spiritual world. For this reason, the Huayan Sect obtained the favourable support of the ruling class and flourished for nearly two centuries. It should also be mentioned that their theory on the relationship between the noumenon and the phenomenon influenced greatly the Cheng-Zhu School of Neo-Confucianism.

4. The Zen Sect (or the Chan Sect) was a product of the indigenous Buddhism of China, flourishing in the late Tang and the Five Dynasties (from 9th to 10th century). By that time, nearly all other sects were gradually declining, and the Zen Sect assumed predominance in Buddhism.

The flourish of the Zen Sect was tightly connected with the existing social circumstances. From the rebellion of An Lushan and Shi Siming to the peasants' uprisings in the late Tang, the whole society suffered incessant civil wars. In the extreme despair, frustration and languishment of a war-torn age, people were naturally prone to accept an easy way of self-deception of "attaining Buddhahood by instantaneous enlightenment".

The great master of the Zen Sect was Hui Neng (638-713), the founder of the Southern Zen Sect, who taught that whenever one's mind was so purified as to be capable of attaining an instantaneous enlightenment, the Buddha-nature was already there in him. This was the doctrine originally initiated by Zhu Daosheng who preached that the Buddha-nature was within everyone and might be acquired by mere internal consciousness.

It was said that Hong Ren, the legendary fifth patriarch of the Zen Sect, while intending to choose an heir apparent from among his disciples, asked each of them to write a hymn to illustrate the Zen teaching. One of his disciples Shen Xiu wrote:

> The body is like unto the Bodhi-tree,
> And the mind to a mirror bright,
> Carefully we cleanse them hour by hour.
> Lest dust would fall upon them.

Here he stressed the importance of cultivation and learning, or a step-by-step approach to the Buddha-nature. Upon reading his hymn, Hui Neng deemed it "not seeing the true nature", and wrote another hymn of his own:

> Originally there was no Bodhi-tree,
> Nor was there any mirror.
> Since originally there was nothing,
> Whereon can the dust fall?*

These hymns were recorded in *The Sutra* spoken by the Sixth Patriarch, the main writing of the Zen Sect, the sixth patriarch of the Zen Sect being Hui Neng.

Hui Neng criticized Shen Xiu for not thoroughgoing in his negation of the objective world and advocated that since all was within the very nature of man, no cultivation nor learning was required at all. In his epistemological theory, Hui Neng professed that all existences with their movements and transformations were but the phenomena of the subjective consciousness. For instance, once upon the occasion of a flag waving in the wind, he taught: "It

---

*Prof. D. Bodde's translation.

is neither the flag nor the wind that is moving, it is solely the movement of your mind."[19] Therefore, according to him, knowledge was to be acquired not by learning of the external world, but by self-reflection of the internal world. It was asserted that men were born with a cognitive faculty to know their own nature, and that "once when man comes to know his own nature, he might attain the Buddha-nature through an instantaneous enlightenment".[20]

This doctrine of a cheap and easy way of instantaneous enlightenment was in fact no more than dumping entrance tickets for paradise. It deceived the populace and allured the ruling class as well, so that no other Buddhist sect could rival it either in propagation or in duration. This theory of the inborn Buddha-nature and the innate wisdom came in conformity with Mencius' doctrine of the innate consciousness. It was no wonder that such an agreement of Buddhism and Confucianism afforded one of the sources for the formation of the Lu-Wang School of Neo-Confucianism later on.

Though with the spread of Buddhism, a new spiritual chain was forged upon the people, it should nevertheless be noted that through the medium of Buddhism the cultural intercourse between China and India and Central Asia was at the same time greatly facilitated. Learnings from abroad such as logic, phonetics, music, painting, sculpture and others were introduced into China while bringing with them a new impact on Chinese culture. It is no exaggeration to say that this was the greatest event of international cultural intercourse in the history of China before modern times.

Anti-Buddhist Current

Actions and reactions always went along in company with each other. On the one hand there was the widespread Buddhist teachings, while on the other there had always been the unceasing anti-Buddhist movements, the foremost exponents of which during this epoch were Fu Yi and Lü Cai.

Fu Yi (555-639), a native of Ye (now Anyang in Henan), was an outstanding scientist of the time. Standing on the position of upholding the traditional ethical code, he considered the spread of Buddhism a danger that would jeopardize both the feudal rule by its rejection of the social hierarchy and the feudal regime by its encroachment of the financial income of the imperial government. Time and again he made petitions, asking the emperor to expel Buddhism. In his compilation of anti-Buddhist literatures of the ages, he succeeded Fan Zhen's atheistic ideas. He declared: "Life or death and longevity or premature death are all the outcomes of nature"[45] which had nothing to do with the Buddhist faith.

Lü Cai (600-665), a native of Qingping (now Liaocheng in Shandong), was a scientist as well as an atheist. Most of his writings were lost, and his thoughts can only be glimpsed from some of the existing fragments.

He confirmed that the ether was the source of the world and that heaven, earth, planets and the changes of seasons were all complying with objective laws which might be known from the motions caused by the contradiction of Yin and Yang. He criticized fiercely all kinds of superstitious practice based on the belief of predetermination. He employed the very method of the fortune-tellers to study the fates of some prominent historical figures such as the First Emperor of Qin and Emperor Wu of Han, and showed that their real lots were quite different from what the fortune-tellers predicted they ought to be. He showed that the fortunes of men were not predestined by fate but were outcomes of human behaviours: But Lü was so much restrained by the Confucian orthodoxy that his criticism was mainly directed at popular superstitions rather than at the superstitions in the Confucian classics.

Taoist Thoughts

Since the Southern and Northern Dynasties, the ruling class were used to upholding one religion against another and vice versa. Hence the three teachings were being kept in a state of co-existence and balance of power, each serving in its own way. In the Sui and Tang period, Taoism became very active alongside with Buddhism. Emperor Wen of Sui honoured the Taoist monk Jiao Zishun with the title of Heavenly Master. The royal house of Tang under the strong bias of noble birth boasted themselves to be the descendants of Lao Zi whose family name happened to be Li, the same with that of the royal house. They honoured highly Taoism which according to legends was founded by Lao Zi. Emperor Xuan Zong of Tang

(713-756) dedicated to Lao Zi the title "the Supreme and Ultimate Emperor" and decreed that the affairs of the Taoist monks and nuns should be managed by the Bureau in charge of the Royal Household. In 741, the emperor instituted an academy for Taoist studies and the scholars trained therein were qualified to take part in the imperial examination.

Under the influence of Buddhism, the Taoists began to turn also to theoretical inquiries, though still engaging in their alchemical and magic studies and practices. Among the noted Taoist theoreticians were Sima Chengzhen and Li Quan.

Sima Chengzhen (647-735), a disciple of the third generation of the noted Taoist monk Tao Hongjing in the Southern Dynasties, won the favour of the Tang emperors. His doctrine consisted in the predominance of the subjective spirit over all others. "The mind," he proclaimed, "is the master of the body and the leader of all spiritual activities."[21] Quietude was said to be the way to wisdom, or "quietude begets wisdom";[22] so that he advocated a method of cultivation similar to that of the Buddhist cessation, contemplation and meditation. When one closed one's eyes and sat in quietude with no idea whatsoever, so he taught, one would be empty of thought and merged into the void. Then a mystic state would be reached wherein "the mind would be in one with the Tao", or, in other words, "when one's body identifies itself with the Tao, one would exist in all times; when one's mind identifies itself with the Tao, one would be in communion with all laws".[23] Then one would become an immortal. This emphasis on quietude as the basic method of the cultivation of the mind had its influence on Neo-Confucianism of which Zhou Dunyi's doctrine of "quietude originating from no desire" was a direct derivation.

Li Quan (flourished late 8th century) was the author of the *Harmony of the Seen and the Unseen* and *The Hidden Canon of the Venus*, treating primarily on military topics. His theological view found its expression in his synthesis of the three teachings of Confucianism, Buddhism and Taoism. But in those part of his work which dealt with military affairs, there were elements of a naive naturalistic tendency which ran contrary to his theological teachings.

The outcome of the war, so he taught, was predominantly determined by human factors, so that those who resort to superstitious beliefs for the directions of their actions and operations were doomed to fail on the battlefield. He doubted the existence of the supernatural forces such as Providence, gods and demons. In his theory of human nature, he did not acknowledge any inborn character and observed that human nature was acquired. He also made studies on the role of the subjective factors. All these were rarely found in other Taoist writings.

3. THE THOUGHTS OF HAN YU AND LI AO

Throughout this epoch, the anti-Buddhist and anti-Taoist campaigns from the Confucian camp had never ceased. This intellectual campaign reflected the contradictions between the lay landlords and the clerical. Yet it was at the same time that the confluence of the three teachings was finally taking shape and preparing the way for the emergence of Neo-Confucianism.

Han Yu (768-824), a native of Nanyang (in Henan), was most renowned as the founder of the literary movement for writings in classical style as well as the forerunner of Neo-Confucianism. In the anti-Buddhist campaign of the mid-Tang, he played a leading role.

Ever since the early Tang, the Buddhist monastery economy had been more and more aggrandizing. Down to the mid-Tang when the land system of the early Tang was ruined and the separatist local regimes were becoming ever more powerful, the imperial finance fell into great difficulty. Then the clash between the interest of the imperial government and that of the monasteries broke out. From the standpoint of upholding the Confucian orthodoxy, Han started an anti-Buddhist campaign. In the year 819 when Emperor Xianzong (806-820) prepared a welcome ceremony of the so-called relic of the bone of Buddha, causing a sensation in and out of the royal court, Han Yu presented to the Emperor "A Memorandum Against the Welcome to the Bone of Buddha" in which he advised the emperor to throw away the bone of Buddha and even asserted that it might be easily seen from historical precedents that all sovereigns who embraced the Buddhist faith were doomed short-lived. This infuriated the emperor and Han was banished from the capital to the distant Chaozhou (in Guangdong). But Han did not give up his anti-Buddhist position.

Han upheld the Confucian orthodoxy and condemned Buddhism as an import from the barbarians abroad and totally foreign to the traditional code. Further, the development of the monastery economy led to the multiplication of persons exempted from taxes and hence to the financial crisis of the imperial government. He proposed to confiscate all the temples and compel the Buddhist monks to reassume their secular lives.

In this anti-Buddhist campaign, Han resorted to the Confucian classics. He proclaimed that by the principles enunciated in "The Great Learning" in the *Book of Rites*, the supreme political ideal of pacifying the world was tightly bonded with the moral cultivation of the individual, the former being the embodiment of the latter. But the Buddhists taught the people to cultivate themselves in order to escape the world into a state of inactivity which ran contrary not only to the active political ideals but also to the ethical norms. This criticism, besides its anti-Buddhist significance, had a bearing on strengthening the royal power of the imperial government against the separatist regimes of the local warlords at that time.

The Buddhists had fabricated a theory of the Buddhist patriarchal succession. In direct confrontation with it, Han also fabricated a theory of the succession of the Confucian orthodoxy which was said to have come down from the legendary sage-kings Yao, Shun, Yu, Tang and Wen and Wu (of Zhou) to Confucius and Mencius. And he took it his own historical mission to restore this orthodoxy. In his famous *Treatise on the Tao*, he amplified the notion of the Confucian benevolence and righteousness, declaring that the faults of the Buddhists and the Taoists lay in their violation of the normal standard of daily life and tended to lead people to discard totally the society and the state with all the ethical code indispensable to them.

With this theory of the Confucian orthodoxy, Han advertised a heroic conception of history, giving prominence to the role of the sages who were said to be the creators or innovators of history. "Had there been no sages in ancient times, mankind would have long extinguished."[24] so he affirmed. Therefore he drew the conclusion that the people should subject to the rule of the sages and the sage-kings—this was an obligation exacted by the Tao itself since old. In case the people would not pay tributes to the rulers, they deserved to be punished. This doctrine of his was much appreciated by all orthodox ideologues and thenceforth constituted an integral part of Neo-Confucianism.

This orthodoxy was identified by Han with the embodiment of the will of Heaven which incarnated in the personalities of the sages. Hence it was everlasting and inviolable. This identification of Tao with Heaven made him the predecessor of the Cheng-Zhu School of Neo-Confucianism.

Han Yu succeeded Dong Zhongshu in propounding that men were endowed not only with human nature but also with emotion which had its basis in human nature. "Human nature is that which is born with men, and emotion is that which is generated by the contacts of human nature with the external objects."[25] The five virtues constituted human nature. But since each person was endowed with the five virtues in different degrees, so human nature fell into three grades: the superior, the medium and the inferior. As to the question of what constituted the human emotion, Han suggested there were seven items in it: pleasure, anger, sadness, happiness, endearment, resentment and desire, being called "the seven emotions". In correspondence to the different grades of human nature, human emotion, too, fell into three grades: the superior, the medium and the inferior. These grades were transcendentally stipulated and hence were unchangeable and insurmountable. Education should and could only be applied to those above the medium grade. Those of the inferior grade should and could only be harnessed by the coercion of the authority.

But Han's theory of the three grades of human nature was also employed for the repudiation of the Buddhist theory of the Buddha-nature. The Buddhists taught people to escape the ethical relationship, contending that so long as people were involved by emotions they would never be capable of witnessing the true nature, nor of attaining their Buddhahood. Opposed to it, Han advocated that by being given the ethical standards the people would be enabled to witness human nature. So the other-worldly view held by the Buddhists was reversed by the Confucian view. Yet Han's anti-Buddhist argument failed to strike it at its very root, because he attributed all social differentiations to the Mandate of Heaven instead of their social factors.

Li Ao (772-814), a native of Longxi (in Gansu), was a close

follower of Han Yu. But he was under strong Buddhist influences. In his philosophical work *An Essay on the Recovery of Human Nature*, he amplified the teachings of the *Doctrine of the Mean* along the line of Zi Si-Mencius School, while infiltrating into it with Buddhist ideas. The confluence of Confucianism and Buddhism was pushed a step further by him.

The *Doctrine of the Mean* was originally a chapter from the ancient Confucian classic *Book of Rites*, dealing with human nature and moral cultivation. It was said to be the writing of Zi Si, the grandson of Confucius. Li Ao claimed that ever since Qin the *Doctrine of the Mean* was neglected and that it was left to him to restore this learning.

On the topic of human nature, Li amplified Mencius' proposition that "the nature of all human beings is good". They were transcendentally in conformity with the moral standard and therefore everyone had the capacity to become a sage. On the relation of human nature and human emotion he agreed with Han Yu's viewpoint that human nature was the primary from which emotions were derived. Good and evil depended on the fact that emotions were "sometimes good and sometimes not". The evils in human nature were generated by the confusions of "the seven emotions" which caused the obscurity of human nature. He compared human nature to fire and water and human emotions to smokes and muds, claiming that when the water was mixed with muds it became turbid and when the smokes gathered the fire became dark. Instead of being perplexed by emotions, those who became sages were capable of manifesting human nature to its fullest extent, like water becoming clear after the muds were precipitated or fire shining again after the smokes were blown away. However, the fact was that most ordinary people were constantly indulging in their emotions and thereby losing their own nature; hence the result was that "there have been more troubled times in history than the well-ordered ones".[26] For the sake of bringing about the well-ordered times, it was necessary for the people to recover their nature by getting rid of their emotions.

From this, Li advocated "the recovery of the human nature" by cutting off all contacts with the external world and casting away all sensations and thinking. When one had "no thoughts and no cares at all", so he recommended, "emotion would not be aroused".[27] Then by a process of internal cultivation, one would attain the highest state of "supreme honesty", i.e., the perfect goodness and motionless quietude. This was what he meant by the recovery of human nature. Here the main theme of the Doctrine of the Mean ("honesty leads to enlightenment") was mystified as the intrinsic human nature which was said to be in communion with the cosmos. Obviously, this recovery of human nature by excluding all emotions was derived partly from the Buddhist teachings and partly from the Doctrine of the Mean. It marked the confluence of Confucianism and Buddhism.

In Li's theory, there might be found a strong element of asceticism which served to profit the feudal rule. Later on, the Lu-Wang School of Neo-Confucianism was much inspired by its emphasis on introversion and intuition.

4. THE THOUGHTS OF LIU ZONGYUAN AND LIU YUXI

Liu Zongyuan and Liu Yuxi, both famous literary writers and statesmen, lived at a time when the Tang Dynasty, after the rebellion of An Lushan and Shi Siming, was in rapid decline and the society, on the eve of the coming peasants' uprisings, was falling into tumults and disturbances. In the early Tang, the lower strata of the landlords-intellectuals without nobility status were beginning to form a political group, or rather an opposition party, in confrontation with the nobility households. A ceaseless political struggle thus ensued. The foremost proponents of the lower landlord strata against the privileged nobility households were Liu Zongyuan and Liu Yuxi.

The Thoughts of Liu Zongyuan

Liu Zongyuan (773-819), a native of Hedong (now Yongji in Shanxi), made acquaintance with Wang Shuwen, Wang Pi and Liu Yuxi in the capital Changan. In the year 805, Wang Shuwen and Wang Pi, the political leaders of the landlords of the lower strata, launched a reform campaign under the support of Emperor Shunzong in A.D. 805. Both Liu Zongyuan and Liu Yuxi took an active part in it. They carried out a series of reforms with the aim of meeting the demands of the lower strata and to deprive certain powers and privileges of the nobility households, the eunuch clique in the royal court and the local separatist warlords, so as to re-establish a strong imperial power. But the reform campaign lasted only five months and ended in a complete failure. All the partici-pants of this campaign were banished. In ten years time of his exile and degradation, Liu Zongyuan wrote many works on literature, politics, history and philosophy. In 815, he was summoned back to the capital and then again degraded and banished to Liuzhou (in Guangxi) where he died four years later at the age of forty-seven.

In his philosophical ideas, he developed the age-old monism of ether in his writings *A Treatise on Heaven*, *Answers on Heaven* and others, the first one being a polemic with Han Yu, the second an answer to *Questions on Heaven* by the ancient poet Qu Yuan. In both of them the author showed a clear-cut standpoint of his naturalism and atheism.

Liu pointed out emphatically that the cosmos was constituted by the primeval ether from which all existences were derived and that all variations and developments in the world were set forth by the mutual actions of Yin and Yang. Qu Yuan in his poetical work had asked: How was it that Heaven and Yin and Yang were combined? How all things changed? To this, Liu replied: Heaven and Yin and Yang were combined by the dominant action of the primeval ether which set in motion all variations and developments in the world. By this reasoning of his, the variety of the world was reduced to the primitive matter (the primeval ether) and its motions to the exclu-sion of any mystic or supernatural force of the beyond. The reasons of the natural world were to be sought solely within the natural world itself and nowhere else.

In his *Answers on Heaven,* he affirmed the infiniteness of the universe which extended beyond any measurement could reach. And he combined the idea of a global earth with that of the motion of the earth. Though this idea of his was still only a guess, it enriched greatly the mediaeval conception of the universe with his intuitions. He also forwarded another valuable proposition that Heaven and man "each go independently in their own ways without interfering with each other".[28] For him, heaven and earth, the primeval ether, and Yin and Yang were all but natural existences which had no volition at all. Therefore the success or failure of human affairs should not be attributed to any role of heaven. So he claimed it would be absurd to pray to heaven for its mercy on man. The natural world and the human world were separate and independent of each other. He attacked openly all beliefs in deities from an atheistic standpoint. He contended that all natural catastrophes and disasters so often considered to be signs of Providence were in truth but natural phenomena which had nothing to do with human affairs. He formulated his view in these words: "Those who possess sufficient force in themselves will appeal to men, while those who did not will appeal to heaven."[29] It was just because the evil rulers had no confidence in their own force that they turned to deities for help.

It was noteworthy that Liu Zongyuan made no criticism of Buddhism. On the contrary, he held an attitude of compromise toward it in a desperate effort to extricate himself from the spiritual depression resulting from his long degradation. This should be considered as one of his weak points.

In his socio-historical conception, Liu Zongyuan advanced the idea of "trend". Historical development, so he held, had its inherent trend independent of human wills and desires. His social theory was most explicitly expounded in his famous *Treatise on Feudalism* in which he declared the following thesis. In the antiquity, men lived together with animals in the forests. In order to maintain their own existence, men learned to use instruments and began to dispute with one another. Hence they were in need of one who might come to pass judgments over their controversies. The one who was to rule must have in his hand a coercive force which led to the institution of the sovereign. With the growth of the community, the principalities were multiplied, a trend which finally resulted in the establishment of the feudal hierarchy. This he regarded as a necessary trend of historical development instead of the innovation of any sage-king or Providence. In it we may find a rather subtle theory of the origin of the state which he tried to discover within the frame of the human society itself without resorting to any superhuman force. This dealt a blow to the traditional theory of the divine innovation of the sage-kings as expounded by Han Yu. Nevertheless, he was powerless to probe the fact of the suppression and exploitation of men by men, and so he was led to imagine that all the rulers in antiquity were intelligent and just.

The substitution of the pre-Qin feudalism by the imperial system of prefectures was, in his opinion, also necessitated by historical trend, for the latter was superior to the former in that it helped to consolidate the centralized political powers by directly appointing the local officials by the imperial government. In his view, feudalism was a hereditary system in which the superiors were not necessarily the just and the local powers always tended to set up separatist regimes to the disadvantage of the unification of the whole country. With arguments like these, he exposed the irrationality of the privileges of the nobility households as well as the harms of the separatist regimes of the local warlords of his age.

The Thoughts of Liu Yuxi

Liu Yuxi (772-842), a native of Pengcheng (now Xuzhou in Jiangsu), was an intimate friend of Liu Zongyuan in their common struggle against the privileged dignitaries and the theological ideology. They both took an active part in the reform movement headed by Wang Shuwen and Wang Pi.

In his *Treatise on Heaven*, he developed his friend Liu Zongyuan's ideas. Like his friend, he insisted the monism of ether, taking ether as the origin of the material world in which "all were produced by ether".[30] But he surpassed his friend in his treatment of the relation of space and matter. He proclaimed that emptiness was but the very subtle bodies beyond the reach of human sensations, hence it was not something in its own existence independent of material bodies but a manifestation of a much subtler matter. What was usually meant by "no shape" was only "no constant shape", because the form of a body was always changing. Therefore he concluded that there was no void nor emptiness in the world, a refutation of the teachings of the Buddhists and the Metaphysicians that took Emptiness or Nothingness as the origin of the world. This viewpoint of his with its profound scientific and philosophical insight deserves to be ranked among the best in the mediaeval history.

Ideologues prior to him, owing to their ignorance to make a distinction between the natural and the social, always tended to interpret the social phenomena in the light of natural laws. And in their emphasis on the universality and absoluteness of the natural laws, they were prone to neglect or obliterate the peculiarity of social life and human initiative and to fall thencefrom into some kind of historical fatalism or the theory of contingency. Thus Wang Chong of the Han period attributed the cause of social and political prosperity and decline to the vehicle of time, Fan Zhen of the Southern Dynasties considered the cause of fortunes and social ranks of man as an outcome of accidents and Liu Zongyuan, contemporaneous with Liu Yuxi, failed to see the role of man in his reaction to the natural world once when natural knowledge was mastered by man, while proposing his theory of non-interference between the natural world and human affairs. Liu Yuxi surpassed all of them in that he not only rejected the idea of Mandate of Heaven but also overstepped the level of parallelism between the natural world and the human world.

In his *Treatise on Heaven*, Liu Yuxi pointed out the distinction between the natural world and human affairs by asserting that each of them was governed by its specific laws. "The way of heaven [the natural world] consists in the reproduction of itself, and functions through the overcoming of the weak by the strong; while the way of man [human affairs] consists in the establishment of legal institutions and functions through the overcoming of the unjust by the just,"[31] so he proclaimed. Although what he termed "just" and "unjust" were still limited to their feudalistic connotations, his observations on the distinctions between the natural world and the human world as well as on their respective laws and functions were among the most brilliant in history. Nature was "to produce all things", while man was "to rule over all things"; that is to say, once when man mastered natural laws, he was capable of transforming or utilizing all natural things for the benefits of his own. Consequently he concluded: "What heaven is capable of, man is incapable of; but what man is capable of, heaven is sometimes also incapable of."[32] Here he made a distinction between "what heaven is capable of" and "what man is capable of"; but, what is more, he saw in them a relation of reciprocal overcoming and mutual serving to each other. They were opposed, yet linked up and functioned together. This doctrine of his reinforced the atheistic current against prevailing beliefs.

Liu Yuxi stated openly that the widespread of the religious superstitions was the consequence of the political corruption and that society might be set in good order only by the rule of law. When the rule of law could not be maintained, the political situation would go from bad to worse with the just people suffering and the unjust getting along all right. In such a condition people would lose any hope and confidence in themselves and turn to fate or the Mandate of Heaven for help. Here Liu offered a very good explanation of the origin of religion whereby the religious critique was linked up with the political critique. By revealing the social background of religious beliefs, he went on to criticize the rule by the privileged in social life. To be sure, he never trespassed upon the traditional ideal of the rule of the sage-kings and sagacious ministers, but he did expose the reality of the religious authority which served to uphold the rule of the privileged class. Liu's theoretical activities formed an integral part of the political reform movement of his time.

Liu further worked out an epistemological explanation on the religious authority. He claimed that when people came to know the necessity of things, they would have confidence in their own power to overcome the natural world, and then they would discredit the rule of Heaven. But conversely, when they were all at a loss about the external necessity and their own lot, they would then appeal to Heaven as a last resort. For this, he cited an instance of a boat sailing on a stream: when one sailed the boat safely on a tranquil stream, he was confident in his own power to manage the sailing and would not appeal to Heaven for help; but when on the rough sea in storms he was incapable of controlling his sailing in front of the blind force of nature which he did not understand, then he would turn to appeal to Heaven for help. Having made the epistemological explanation of the origin of theism, he went on to ask people to study the necessity in the objective world, so as to be able to develop the subjective capability to its greatest extent.

Liu Yuxi's knowledge about the external necessity as well as about the subjective initiative were no more than naive intuitions. He talked in an abstract manner about the rule of law which seemed to him the determining factor in history, but he made no research on the social background of it in any depth. Like his friend Liu Zong-yuan, he also held an attitude of compromise with Buddhism, an attitude which was conditioned by his long-time sufferings in his life of degradation. It was one of the weak points in his theory.

5. REVOLUTIONARY IDEAS AND PROGRESSIVE IDEOLOGUES

Huang Chao and the Peasants' Uprising

With the aggrandizement of large land properties in the last years of Tang, "the wealthy annexed tens of thousands of *mu* of farmlands, while the poor could find no place to set their feet".[33] The local warlords' independent regimes, the eunuch clique in control of the royal court, the factional struggles within the ruling camp and the continuous wars at the frontiers, all these accelerated the dissolution of the existing political and social orders. In the year 874, there broke out the great peasants' uprising, one of the largest in the history of China. It lasted ten years and swept almost all the country from the valley of Yellow River to that of the Pearl River. It captured the capital Changan and established the Da Qi regime.

The armed uprising was led by Huang Chao (?-884), a native of Caozhou (now Heze in Shandong), who was a salt pedlar. In 875 he joined the uprising army led by Wang Xianzhi. Wang died in 878 and Huang succeeded him as the leader. Some time before that, the peasants' uprising in eastern Zhejiang had demanded equalization of farmlands. This egalitarian demand became more evident in Huang's slogan. Both Wang and Huang included the word "equal" or "egalitarian" in their titles of reign. Opposing inequality between the wealthy and the poor, they demanded the equalization of wealth and status. But except for these slogans, no more recorded materials relevant to their doctrine and practice were left to us.

During the stormy years of the peasants' uprising, the ruling class itself was undergoing a process of differentiation. Part of the landlord intellectuals clear-headedly faced the reality. They learned more and more about the facts of social evils and turned to sympathize the lot of the common people. Some of them even took part in the armed uprising. The old ruling order was severely shaken, along with the old ruling ideology. Among these progressive ideologues we shall enumerate a few in a brief survey.

The Thoughts of Pi Rixiu

Pi Rixiu (834?-883?), a native of Xiangyang (in Hubei), was a renowned literary writer. About the year 878, he participated in the armed uprising of Huang Chao, and was killed after its defeat. As a sharp opponent to religious superstitions, he strongly refuted the common belief that Heaven possessed the power of retribution on good and evil. He illustrated his view by citing instances as the following. When a bad man was thunderstricken, then people would say it was due to the retributive punishment by Heaven. But Pi refuted it by posing a reverse question: if it were so, then why were there other villains left untouched? With arguments like this, after the fashion of Wang Chong, Pi affirmed that there was no such thing as the heavenly retribution. He exposed relentlessly the deception of the fortune-tellers and other superstitions. When one went to the fortune-teller, he contended, one would be certainly told that his physiognomy looked partly like a dragon and partly like a phoenix, etc. "When one was told that he looked like an animal, he would be pleased; but when one was told that his physiognomy did look like that of a human being, he would get angry and irritated"; because people were accustomed to the popular belief of the fortune-teller's nonsense that "one would get great wealth and high ranks when one looks like an animal, but would get poverty and low ranks when one looks really like a human being". With such arguments, he scathingly ridiculed the popular superstitions.

The progressive character of Pi's ideas was also shown in the importance he attached to the people's livelihood. He asserted that when the sovereign acted contrary to the wishes of the people, then it was appropriate and right for the people to strangle him, a rare view in the mediaeval times.

The Thoughts of Wu Neng Zi

The name and life of the author of the book *Wu Neng Zi* (literally the *Book of the Useless Master*) was unknown, but we are able to ascertain something about his background from his preface

to the book. It recorded that this Wu Neng Zi (The Useless Master)
lived during the time of the revolt of Huang Chao and wandered as
a refugee from place to place in poverty and misery. In 887, the third
year after Huang's defeat, he was in the capital Changan where he
worked out his book which comprised thirty-four chapters in three
volumes.

In his conception of nature, he belonged to the naturalistic
tradition of the ether theory, holding that "prior to the differentiation of heaven and earth, there was but the chaos of ether".[34] And
then by the motion of the ether, the two phases (Yin and Yang) were
differentiated. The lighter and cleaner parts ascended upwards and
formed the heaven, while the heavier and more turbid descended
downwards and formed the earth. With the emergence of heaven and
earth and the interaction of Yin and Yang, the species were begotten.
Heaven and earth were not reigning deities but insensible bodies.
"Heaven and earth have no mind nor consciousness, they cannot rule
over themselves. Then how can it be that they are able to rule over
all other things?"[35] The relationship between heaven and man, like
all others things in the natural world, was nothing mysterious; so
there was between them no distinction of the higher and the lower
or the superior and the inferior. By this naturalistic argument, he
categorically refuted the theoretical ground upon which the secular
and the clerical authorities rested.

From the standpoint that all things were generated by "the
communion of the Yin ether and the Yang ether", he attacked all
kinds of superstitions in catastrophic and propitious omens. Since all
were but products of nature, so "the phoenix does not necessarily
anticipates fortunes, nor the owl misfortunes"[36] as people were often
taught to believe. Such remark was a logical corollary of the equality
of all things and of all men. Thereupon he propounded a naturalistic
theory of the origin of the state thus: in the antiquity men were born
and living in a state of nature with no difference from other species,
but later on, the differentiation of social ranks and the institutions
of political coercion were devised by the strong and imposed upon
the weak. Such was the origin of the social inequality which resulted
in endless miseries and sufferings of the people. It was this view that
led him to launch a vehement attack on the "sages who forced the
provision of fine buildings and delicious food to incite the desires of

the people, forced the distinction of the dignitary and the down-
graded to stimulate their contentions, forced the moral teachings to
substitute their nature and forced punishments and wars to ruin their
lives".[37] What he called "sages" were but the sovereigns of the people.
He attributed the social evils to the innovations of the sages and thus
denied any rationality of the feudal hierarchy. But he made no
inquiry into the social basis upon which the sages emerged, though
he blamed the ruthlessness of the sovereigns as "to sacrifice the lives
of other people in order to satisfy their own desires".[38]

All the dignitary titles, declared he, were invented by the sages
and imposed on others. "If a title can be imposed on others, then
everyone is qualified to assume any title",[39] in other words, everyone
was to have a right to assume the title of kings, princes and others,
because these titles of social distinction were originally something
fictitious in their essence.

His bold attack on despotism deserves to be ranked among the
most valiant ideas in history. But he did not advocate to take up arms
to overthrow the despotic rule. He found sustentation only in his
illusion of returning to the primitive society in which there would be
neither the sovereign nor the subjects, an illusion which was contrary
to the trend of historical development.

The Thoughts of Tan Qiao

Tan Qiao (dates unknown), a native of Quanzhou (now Nanan
in Fujian), was a Taoist scholar in the time of the Five Dynasties
(first half of the 10th century). His writings were collected in his
Book of Transformation.

In his conception of nature, he took Void or Emptiness as the
source of the world. He taught that the Void transformed into the
Spirit, the Spirit transformed into ether which begot all things; and
that all things would finally resolve again into the Void. In one
important aspect, he broke away from the traditional Taoist teaching
that all things originated from quietude. He paid special attention to
the changing of things and taught that all things were generated and
transformed through "the mutual grinding of motion and rest".[40]
Therefore, all natural phenomena, such as the changes of fire, water,
cloud, snow, rainbow, were merely the result of the mutual actions

and reactions of the two phases of the material world: motion and rest. "The mutual grinding of motion and rest transform into fire, the mutual steaming of the dry and the wet transforms into water, the mutual clash of fire and water transforms into clouds",[41] etc., so went on the process of nature. But it was to the cyclic process of transformation that he gave priority. He described the cycle of human life in the same way: "When one is dead, he transforms again into the Void, the Void transforms again into the Spirit, the Spirit transforms again into the ether and the ether transforms again into all things. This incessant transformation goes on just like along an endless circle."[42] Thereon the naive dialectical elements in his thoughts were entangled within a mechanic cyclism. All things and their variations, in the last analysis, were subject to the dominance of the Void.

In his social and political views, there was also much worthy to be recommended. He forcefully revealed the suppression and exploitation of the peasants who were under "seven plunders": "First, the sovereigns plunder them; second, the officials; third, the armed forces; fourth, the wars; fifth, the artisans; sixth, the merchants; and seventh, the Buddhists and the Taoists".[43] The peasants were thus extorted to the last drop of their blood. He compared the exploiters to the rats in the grain depot. Under the endless extortions, the peasants were compelled to resort to no other means than an armed uprising. He was full of sympathy for the peasants and explained in details how they were driven by the ruling class to the way of rebellion. He wrote in one of his poems:

> Be careful not to blame the robbers,
> because you have invited them;
> and be careful not to complain about the rebels,
> because they follow only your own teachings.[44]

But in front of the existing social crisis, he made no breakthrough beyond his predecessors. He only appealed to the frugality on the part of the ruling class.

It was noteworthy that he advanced the idea of equalizing food, claiming that by this measure the world would be brought to good order. This view was a continuation of the tradition of the primitive Taoism which propagated similar ideas amongst the uprising peasants. Obviously, it exaggerated the role of this measure to meet the social problems, but it did reflect the desires of the populace struggling on the brink of death.

Still more noteworthy was his vision of an ideal society. He alluded to the life of the ants in these words: "The ants have their sovereign who shares the tiny palace together with the populace, enjoys the tiny terrace together with the populace, preserves a grain of food together with the populace and eats the meat of a worm together with the populace."[45] With this allegory, he showed that in the kingdom of ants the ruling order even looked superior to that in human society. It seemed to him that when the superior and inferior would cherish their common life together in an intimate relationship between each other, then the world would dispense with all disputes. This illusion of his, though utopian in nature, reflected more or less the peasants' longing for a society of equality.

Chapter 12

ECONOMIC THOUGHTS
IN THE TANG PERIOD

In the Tang period, the most prosperous epoch in the Middle Ages, the outstanding representatives in the field of economic thoughts were Liu Yan and Yang Yan. But both of them lived at a time when the reign of the Tang Dynasty was turning from the peak of peace and prosperity to civil wars and decline, so that their economic thoughts were directed predominantly to provide a remedy for the financial reforms as well as for the corruption of the officialdom.

1. THE ECONOMIC THOUGHTS OF LIU YAN

Liu Yan (718-780), a native of Caozhou (now Dongming in Shandong) was generally acknowledged as one of the two foremost financiers in the Middle Ages, the other being Sang Hongyang of the Han Dynasty. For more than twenty years Liu was in charge of the imperial finance and economic affairs.

The main points of his economic thoughts lay in his brilliant handling of the relation between the national economy and the financial income. He realized that the development of production and the security of the people's livelihood constituted the basis of financial income. Thence his famous proposition: "Taking good care of the people should always be the prerequisite of financing."[1] When the population multiplied, the number of the labourers as well as the tax-payers would increase correspondingly; and this would lead to the increment in tax income, or what he said: "When there is a steady increase in population there would be a much wider resource of tax income."[2] On this ground, he paid his main attention to the recovery and development of the economy, taking special care not to aggravate the burden of the peasants. He succeeded Sang Hongyang's financial principle of increasing the income by means of tapping more tax resources and, in the meanwhile, diminishing the forced exaction of taxes. But he differed from Sang in that he took the management of commerce and trade as the chief measures of financial income instead of the government's policy of monopoly. Herein is shown the characteristic feature of his ideas.

In his salt policy reform, he abolished the former practice of the production and sale of salt by the government, and in its stead appointed officials to collect the salt from the salt producers and sell it to the merchants who would transport it to all places for sale. When the supply was not sufficient and the price of salt was rising, the government would sell it out from its storehouses. This measure was conducive both to the circulation of goods and to the financial income as well. In the salt area of the Huai valley were instituted thirteen official agencies in charge of salt affairs. Through this reorganization, the amount of salt income was raised sixty-folds; and "half of the government's income was furnished from the sale of salt upon which the court expenses, the military expenditures and all the officials' salaries depended",[3] so was it recorded in history.

The government's grain storage was also run on commercial principles. Since the Western Han, the government's storages had, as a rule, aimed at the regulation of the market prices of grain and at the preparation for natural disasters. Liu made a great change. What he stored was not only grain but "all kinds of goods". He aimed not only at adjusting and balancing the good and bad harvests and stabilizing the grain prices, but also at arranging all commodities so as to bring about good profits. This, of course, would require a timely mastery of the fluctuations of market prices; so he instituted local agencies for market investigations and information together with the establishment of specific transportation posts for couriers. The function of the government storage was then sufficiently enlarged so as to guarantee both the supply on the market and the financial income of the imperial treasury. Thus the record in history reads: "All the differences of prices in various localities, even in the remotest regions, were known within a couple of days ... [and so the government] was enabled to keep all commodities at reasonable prices and to get hold of the surplus resources and wealth of the whole country in support of the military expenses; hence the people were under no burden of ever increasing exactions and enjoyed their lives in sufficiency, though the wars had been going on for decades".[4] Liu's reform was really an innovation in the history of financing in the Middle Ages, for he had come to realize the role of the development of commerce and trade in promoting economic prosperity as well as in increasing the government's income.

Another principle of special significance in his management was the adoption of wage labourers. In the past, grain transported from the Yangtze Valley to the capital were by corvées of the local people. It had always been a heavy burden to them, while causing much loss of grain on the way and taking much longer time in transportation. Liu carried out his reform by hiring wage labourers to take charge of the grain transportation and paying them with the income from the salt tax. The forced corvée system was substituted by the wage labour system with the result that this transportation on a tremendous scale was accomplished "without enlisting the corvée labourers or exacting the localities".[5] Originally it took eight to nine months for the transport of grain from one place to another, but after his reform it was shortened to only forty days. And "with the opening to traffic of boats and carts, the merchants and tradesmen were in a constant flow of coming and going",[6] and the economic prosperity was greatly facilitated. The historical significance of his reform, "unprecedented since the ancient times", consisted in its abrogation of the feudal corvée system. Since Liu, people began to have a clearer knowledge of the backwardness of the obligatory and gratuitous system of forced corvée.

Liu's reform was carried further by Yang Yan whose job it was to rearrange the already collapsed taxation system of the early Tang period.

2. THE ECONOMIC THOUGHTS OF YANG YAN

Yang Yan (727-781), a native of Fengxiang (in Shaanxi), was a prominent financier for his innovation of the two-taxation system. Ever since the revolt of An Lushan and Shi Siming, the population, the land properties and the social conditions in general as well as the farmland distribution system and the taxation system of the former days had suffered great violations which resulted in the disorders of the imperial finance and the miseries of the people. With this background in view, Yang proposed to Emperor Dezong (775-805) his two-taxation programme.

In 780, his proposal was adopted and promulgated by the emperor in an edict. Its main contents consisted in the levying of only two kinds of taxation: the farmland taxation and the assets taxation, being collected respectively in summer and autumn. It was declared that with the enactment of this new taxation system, all the previous ones were abolished. The categories of the tax-payers was much more broadened than before, with all landlords and tenants, merchants and tradesmen and the nobilities and officials included, while in former days the last two were exempted. With the introduction of this two-taxation system, the financial income got better and the burden of the people considerably lightened. So reads the record in history: "The whole country enjoyed it [the new taxation programme].... Since then the power of regulating the taxes was in the control of the imperial court."[7] No doubt, this new taxation reform had alleviated the financial crisis and stabilized the rule of the Tang regime, at least for the time being. It also laid down the basis of the taxation system for a long time to come which lasted from the late Tang (late 8th century) to the mid-Ming (early 16th century).

The innovations of his programme consisted of the following aspects:

1. In contrast to the traditional financial principle of "expenditure in proportion to income", he proposed his new idea of "income in proportion to expenditure".[8] He professed that all taxes should be levied according to the need of expenditure, or in other words, the government should arrange its financial income with a view of its indispensable expenses. Compared with the traditional principle, this new one was designed to meet the financial crisis with more flexibility, though it also paved the way for the government to make more exactions.

2. Simplification of taxation and its procedure constituted one of the peculiarities of this new programme. In previous days, there were numerous items of taxation to be levied at different times and

places and on different occasions. The people were too frequently troubled by the exactions of the government. Yang Yan categorically abolished the much complicated taxation system of the former days and substituted them by a simplified measure. It was a timely reform which showed his good knowledge of the advantage of simplified taxations.

3. The idea of taxing in accordance with the tax-payers capability was conspicuous in his reform. His new taxation system rested on the principle of "gradation according to the wealth of different people",[9] a principle which adapted better to different financial conditions of the people than any of the previous ones. Taxes in the Han Dynasty were levied on the basis of the number of the people and the area of the farmlands; taxes in Western Jin were levied on the basis of the quality and quantity of the labouring forces; whereas this new two-taxation system made a still further progress by taxing with a view of different capabilities of the tax-payers. It rested not on the basis of labouring force but on that of property. It marked the demarcation line of the early and the late periods of feudalism in mediaeval China, and hence bore an epoch-making significance in the progress of history.

4. It stipulated the payment of taxes in money, though not realized completely. At any rate, this stipulation represented some new elements and new ideas in the development of social economy. It showed that Yang had embraced some premonitions of a new type of economy in germination, the money-economy. By the mid-Tang, there were already instances indicating the transition from rents in kind to rents in money. It was just along this direction of transition that the development of history was heading. Here the new ideas in the two-taxation system once more signalled the historic turning from the early stage of feudal society to the late.

Though from the viewpoint of economic development, the two-taxation system had its progressive bearings, it meant nevertheless the strengthening of the feudal rule and feudal exploitation in a easier way. Since it did not and could not remould the very nature of feudalism, so the people were soon subjected again to extortions and reduced to the same miserable state as before.

Chapter 13

SCIENTIFIC, HISTORIOGRAPHIC AND LITERARY IDEAS IN THE SUI AND TANG DYNASTIES

The Tang Dynasty reached one of the high peaks of social and economic prosperity in mediaeval history, which in its turn facilitated the advancement of science and technology. Among the achievements of this period, the most noteworthy were the inventions of gunpowder and printing. When they were introduced to the West, the former prepared the way for the newly rising bourgeoisie to destroy the castles of the feudal seigneurs and the latter facilitated the advancement of learning which eventually led to the Renaissance. They were outstanding contributions of Chinese learning to the history of world civilization.

1. SCIENTIFIC IDEAS

Concerning the concepts of the universe, the vaulted theory of heaven and the global theory of heaven marked two stages of the Chinese knowledge of the cosmos. Zhang Heng in the Han period founded the global theory of the cosmos which signified a milestone in the early history of the knowledge of the earth. This global theory, which took the earth as global rather than plane, was further proved in the Tang period by the works of Yi Xing and since then became dominant in the study of cosmogony and astronomy.

Yi Xing (also known by his original name Zhang Sui, 683-727), a native of Weizhou (now Nanle in Henan), was a prominent astronomer and a Buddhist monk (known by the name of Yi Xing). In the early years of the 8th century, he was placed in charge of calendar reform. For the accuracy of the calendar, he presided over large-scale measurements on the different latitudes of Huaxian, Kaifeng, Fugou, and Shangcai respectively, and found out that the length of one degree in the meridian equalled to 351 *li* plus 80 strides (or 129.22 kilometres in terms of modern measurement). This was the earliest measurement of the meridian in the world. It contributed to the verification of the global form of the earth and to disproving the vaulted theory of heaven. Thenceforth the global theory of the earth was confirmed as the guiding principle in the field of cosmogony.

In the year 724, Yi Xing and others made measurements and observations on the movements of the sun, the moon and the planets and found that the locations of the fixed stars were not really fixed but in motion—a discovery about one thousand years earlier than Halley's in the West. He remeasured the locations of certain stars upon which he worked out the Dayan Calendar in the year 727. This calendar, more advanced than the previous ones, furnished a more scientific foundation for all later calendars.

The remarkable advancement in astronomy pushed forward the mathematical learnings. Owing to the requirement of locating the accurate positions of the celestial bodies, the question of how to compute their locations between two separate measurements was brought to the fore. Prior to Yi Xing, Liu Zhuo, the famous astronomer and mathematician of the Sui period, in the year 600 had already worked out a new method of solving that problem. The method was known as the equi-distance quadratic interpolation. On the basis of Liu, Yi Xing innovated the unequal distance quadratic interpolation, thus providing an advanced method in studying the mysteries of the universe.

As regard to the conception of the evolution of the cosmos, the finest works of that time were Liu Zongyuan's *A Treatise on Heaven* and *Answers on Heaven* and his friend Liu Yuxi's *Treatise on Heaven* which we have dealt with in Chapter 11.

2. HISTORIOGRAPHIC IDEAS

In view of the rapid downfall of the Sui Dynasty under the blow of the peasants' uprisings, the early Tang regime was much concerned with the study of the past experiences of the preceding dynasties from which it compiled various historical works under official editorship, such as the histories of Jin, Liang, Chen, Northern Qi, Northern Zhou and Sui. Alongside with the official compilations of the histories of the former dynasties, there emerged a large number of private historical writings, such as *The History of the Southern Dynasties* and *History of the Northern Dynasties* by Li Yanshou, *A General Treaties on Historiography* by Liu Zhiji and *The Classified History of Institutions* by Du You. Thus the Tang Dynasty witnessed the flourish of historical studies of the Middle Ages. It innovated a new style in historiography, especially in setting the example of the official editorship of histories for the later generations. Among the historical writings of that time, we shall content ourselves in commenting only two works, one by Liu Zhiji and the other by Du You, the former being the first systematic treatment on historiography, the latter on the history of institutions.

Liu Zhiji's Historiographic Ideas

Liu Zhiji (661-721), a native of Pengcheng (now Xuzhou in Jiangsu), was one of the foremost historians and ideologues of the age. For many years he had served as an official historian and accumulated broad knowledge in historical studies. Among his works, *A General Treatise on Historiography* was the only one that was handed down to us, all others being lost.

One of his basic points was his theory of the correlation of knowledge and faithfulness in historical writings. He was the first historian who advanced a comprehensive study of historiography, demanding that a historian should be equipped with three indispensable merits: the talent, the scholarship and the insight. Once being asked why there were always more good literary writers than good historians, he replied that a good historian ought to possess the three qualifications: If he had scholarship without talent, he would be just like a foolish merchant who did not know how to make profits with his money; if he had talent without scholarship, he would be like a skilful craftsman who had no materials and instruments to get his works done; and when he had both talent and scholarship, he was still in need of a penetrating insight for guidance. So he claimed:

"The scholars learned broadly only for the sake of making a correct selection"; but for this, "of no avail would the scholarship be, no matter how abundant it might prove".[1] Before Liu, these three qualifications had been discussed by his predecessors, but none had treated them so comprehensively and so definitely as he did. Of course, we should not expect that his "insight" would result in a breakthrough of the feudal ethical code, but his synthesis of the three qualifications for historians with "insight" as the most important one was of creative significance in the theory of historiographic ideas.

Besides these three qualifications, a historian, he considered, ought to be inspired by his faith in and his faithfulness to truth. He proclaimed: "A good historical writing is to be valued for its faithfulness in recording the truth."[2] This theory of his succeeded the tradition of Sima Qian and constituted one of his guiding principles in historical study and research. His whole book was permeated with this spirit of faithfulness to truth which he held as a criterion in passing judgments on all historical works, ancient and contemporary. It was for this reason that he shunned to make any eulogy to the sacred classics of the ancients or to any contemporary authority. This spirit inspired him to hold a sceptical attitude towards the age-old traditions and to expose the internal contradictions within the ruling camp.

Liu had been at the post of the official historian in the royal court under five succeeding emperors and witnessed personally the frequent coup d'etats in the court and the sharp political strifes within the ruling class. The reality of the present helped to deepen his understanding of the past. While paying homage to the progressive ideologues of the past who launched their critiques on the orthodox ideology, he professed himself in the direct line of Yang Xiong, Wang Chong, Huan Tan and Liu Xie in criticizing the traditional classics.

In particular, he singled out the faults and falsities in the *Book of History* and *Spring and Autumn Annals* both of which were generally held sacred since Han. He questioned the Confucian classics by pointing out that in the *Spring and Autumn Annals* there were twelve misunderstandings and five false euphuisms and that it had concealed some facts of the ruling dignitaries, thus "confusing truth and falsehood".[3] He even found that the Confucian version of the

five classics were self-contradictory. He pointed out that the traditional classics were sanctified only because they had been maintained
so by the dignitaries and scholars of the past. He did not admit the
existence of any perfect sage and criticized severely the blind admiration of the age-old traditions.

The historiographic practice of concealing the facts for the
ruler's sake, he pronounced, had become a prevailing mode in historical writings since old, so that "the unfaithfulness to truth might be
found in historical writings of each generation".[4] He openly declared
that some of his contemporaneous historians did not record the facts
as they really were. He even made severe critique of the *History of
the Jin Dynasty*, a history under the imperial editorship of Emperor
Taizong of Tang personally. His condemnation on the falsification of
history by way of concealing the facts, together with his sceptical
attitude towards the traditional classics, struck a forcible blow
against the orthodox ideology and contributed much to the liberation
of the people's ideas from the bondage of the superstitions in what
was antique and traditional.

Inseparably connected with his progressive conception of history
that the present surpassed the past, was his general ideological
tendency. It might be clearly seen from his book that his ideas were
under the influence of the pre-Qin thinkers who taught people "to
follow the later kings" on the ground that since history was ever in
progress, one should never stick to "the ways of the ancient kings".
It was interesting to note that in various places of his book he
employed the terms "the ancient", "the mediaeval" and "the modern", roughly equivalent to the pre-Qin period, the Qin and Han
period and the period of Wei and Jin respectively. This schema of
periodization showed that he had already embraced a definite idea
of the stages of development in history, though still in an embryo
form. In Europe, as is well known, it was not until the early 18th
century that G. Vico (1668-1744), the founder of modern historiography, had formulated a definite schema of the ancient, the mediaeval and the modern. In many aspects, including the periodization of
history. Liu might be compared to Vico in their positions of laying
down the foundation of the science of historiography, one in China
and the other in Europe; but Liu preceded Vico by one thousand
years and more.

In addition to his demand of accuracy and truthfulness in historical writing and to his belief in the progress instead of the retrogress of history, Liu made still another valuable proposition that the study of history should "take the human affairs as its main object".[5] thus excluding all kinds of superstitious theological preachings. He attributed all natural phenomena and natural disasters, so often supposed to bear mystical connotations with human affairs, to the sphere of changes in natural world having nothing to do with human affairs at all. The idea of the interaction between Heaven and man were thus being banished out of the scope of historiography.

But in his concept of nature, Liu was still imprinted with certain dross of traditional theology, not daring to repudiate all the mystic absurdities in classical writings. In spite of that, his book was nonetheless the most important work in the history of Chinese historiography and his ideas inspired later progressive ideologues such as Liu Zongyuan and Liu Yuxi.

Du You's Historiographic Ideas

Du You (735-812), a native of Wannian (now Xi'an in Shaanxi), had been an official holding several important administrative posts and was experienced in political and financial affairs and well acquainted with the knowledge of all institutions, past and present. In more than thirty years' time, he compiled his monumental work *A General Record of Institutions* in 200 volumes. His book classified all institutional records in history under the following nine headings: economy, selection of personnels, officials, rites, music, army, jurisdiction, prefectures and frontiers. By his systematic and comprehensive studies on institutions in history, Du accomplished the first work on the specific topic of the history of institutions. Not confined to the traditional historiography which took the study of the individuals as its main task, his book opened a new field in historical research and created a new style in historiography which was followed as a model by later historians.

One of the salient features of his ideas was the priority he gave to the material basis of history. The reason he put economy in the first place of his book was: "The foundation of culture consists in the sufficiency of food and clothes."[6] This was perhaps one of the finest

insights underlying all historical writings. Sima Qian had already
touched the economic basis of history, but it was Du who provided
an over-all model of the study of political, economic and social
institutions in history.

In opposition to the popular mode of "rejecting the present and
admiring the antique", Du's idea of history led him to recommend
"to build up institutions with a view to the changes of the times and
to vary them with a view to the requirements of the circumstances".[7]
He studied history not for the sake of returning to the antique but
for that of rearranging the present; and the compilation of his
General Record of Institutions aimed at finding the solutions for the
political and economic problems of his day. Though a rather great
part of his book was propagating the traditional ethical code which
limited his own thoughts and field of vision, his whole work was
inspired throughout by a realistic spirit to serve his time.

3. LITERARY IDEAS

In the realm of literary activities, the Tang period was well-
known for the flourish of poetic writings as well as poetic theories.
It was in the course of their fighting against the formalistic style of
the Six Dynasties (3rd-6th century) that the Tang poets elaborated
their literary ideas. The foremost figures in this field were Chen
Ziang of early Tang who first raised the banner of poetic renovation,
followed then by the great poets Li Bai, Du Fu and Bai Juyi in
succession. Echoing it, there was the movement of returning to the
classical style of prose heralded by Han Yu and Liu Zongyuan who
were in essence striving for a literary renovation under the pretext
of "back to the classical". It was by the mid-Tang that the main
literary current took a definite turn from the formalistic style of the
rhythmical prose characterized by parallelism to the plain style of
prose as well as from the ornate euphemism to the expression of
substantial contents.

Chen Ziang and the Poetic Renovation

Chen Ziang (661-702), a native of Shehong (in Sichuan), had

served as an official at various posts in the royal court. He was put into prison for attacking the social evils of his time and died therein. Though Chen lived at a time of prosperity of the early Tang, he was very sensitive to the political corruption and social unrest. In the sphere of poesy, he was inspired by a longing for the realistic reflection of social reality. Hence it was he who first started the poetic renovation against the age-old reign of formalism in literature.

In the ancient classic *Book of Odes* there were many passages that praised or satirized the real political and social life of the time. But during the Southern Dynasties, literary writings were indulging more and more in mere rhetorical ornament and embellishment to the total oblivion of their social bearings. So Chen asked a return to the spirit of the Jian'an period when poetic works were conscientiously concerned about the sufferings of the people written in a simple and plain style. His ideal had always been the unity of artistic skill and intellectual content through their reflection of social reality. In this respect, he was the successor to the poets of Han and Wei down to Liu Xie and Zhong Rong of a later period. Under the banner of returning to the classical, he was in fact demanding for poetic renovation. Based on this principle, he had written many poems in deep sympathy of the people in sorrow and distress. In some of his finest verse, such as *Ascending the Youzhou Terrace* and *On Being Moved with Sorrows*, there was a vein of deep sensation and genuine sensibility never seen in the early Tang echoes of the effeminate artificiality of the Six Dynasties.

Li Bai and Du Fu

Li Bai (701-762), undoubtedly the greatest romantic poet in Chinese literature, was born in Suiye (near Tashkent in Central Asia, as some scholars asserted) but brought up in Sichuan. He was under the influence of Chen Ziang and openly professed in his poem: "The ornate works since the Jian'an period, are not worthy to be honoured",[8] and "For returning to the classical ways, who will it be but me?" He took the poetic renovation by way of returning to the classical as his vocation. He advocated the natural and simple style of the Jian'an poets and urged the sweeping away of all kinds of ornament and artificiality, demanding vehemently for a spiritual liberation from the restraint of the courtly poetic practice. With Li's poetical works, poetry was freed from the formalism of the courtly style and given an outlet for the genuine aspirations of the common folk.

Du Fu (712-772), generally known as the equal of Li Bai by the name "Li and Du", was the greatest realistic poet in Chinese literature. A native from Gongxian (in Henan), he experienced the most tumultuous years during the revolt of An Lushan and Shi Siming and spent his later years in exile, wandering from the capital to Sichuan where he wrote a great part of his finest poems.

The poetic ideas as expressed in his poetical writings were most closely affiliated with the social reality of his time. He highly praised the poetic works of Chen Ziang, thinking that they were permeated with a poet's worry about the country and the people. It was also the concern of social reality that constituted the main theme of Du's poetical works. So much was his involvement in the sufferings and sorrows of the people that his poems earned him the title of "the poet-historian". Historical events of his own time were profoundly reflected in his poetical works in their full variety. With him, the Chinese realistic poetry reached its culmination.

Bai Juyi's Literary Ideas

Bai Juyi (772-846), a native of Xiagui (now Weinan in Shaanxi), was the most noted realistic poet after Du Fu. In his poetry he had painted the panorama of the social life of mid-Tang Dynasty which was then falling into rapid decline. His poetical works promoted greatly the development of poetry along the realistic line.

Bai's literary position might be found in his thesis: "Essays should be written for the sake of the age and poems for the sake of the issues",[9] a thesis which ran contrary to the aesthetic formalism devoid of any social content. He was of the opinion that poetry should serve the society by depicting the real life of the people and thereby criticizing the political measures of the time. In line with this argument, he advocated the tradition of the *Book of Odes* in its description of the political and social evils as well as its reflection of the desires and the longings of the people. "It was through these poems that the prosperity and decline of a country might be seen, the gain and loss of political measures learned, and the happiness and the misery of the people known."[10] With the social role of poetry in view, he demanded that a piece of poetry ought to exercise certain social function and to achieve certain social effects. For him, poetical writings should never be empty words, but instead they should help to criticize social reality in various ways. In social criticism by means of poetic forms, a poet "should sing solely for revealing the social evils"[11] and "lament over the sufferings of the people".[12] Since the duty of a poet should in no time be anything but the reflection of the people's miseries and desires, so most of Bai's poetical works were aimed at exposing and criticizing the evils of the time. The combatant character of his poems signalled the most important development of literary ideas in mid-Tang period.

Han Yu, Liu Zongyuan and the Classical Style Movement

Here by the term "the classical style movement" was meant the literary reform movement in the mid-Tang, which took the pre-Han classical writings as the model of prose writings in form and the traditional Confucian ideology as its guiding principle in content. As early as in the Sui period, Wang Tong and others had already stressed the primacy of Confucian ideology in literary writings and anticipated in a certain way the classical style movement in Tang. Prior to Han Yu and Liu Zongyuan, there were writers in the early Tang, such as Chen Ziang, Li Hua and others who by proposing that literary writings ought to "venerate the classics" and "to bear the Tao (the Confucian Way)" might be regarded as the forerunners of this movement. But it was Han Yu who formally laid down the foundation of this movement.

What Han Yu emphasized was still "to venerate the classics" and "to bear the Tao", but he amplified this idea into a systematic theory. In his *Treatise on the Tao*, he upheld an orthodoxy from the legendary sage-kings Yao, Shun, Yu and Tang through the Duke of Zhou, Confucius and Mencius down to himself. He proclaimed that he learned the classical style and wrote in that style with no other purpose than propagating the Tao, or as what he said of it: "Literary writings for the sake of bearing the Tao."[13] The Tao was the end and the literary form the means to that end. The means should always serve the end. Starting from this view, Han opposed strongly the age-old style of rhymed writings so prevalent since the Six Dynasties which with all their ornate dictions had nothing to do with the Tao after all. Consequently, he gave priority to the moral content in literary writings and considered the moral cultivation the prerequisite of a writer. The relation between morality and literature was compared to that between the roots and the fruits or between the fuel and the light. As a result, he rejected the rhymed style of writing since the Six Dynasties and urged a return to the classical style of Han and before.

His literary theory as directed against the superficial and florid style of writing since the Six Dynasties, had a positive impact on his time. His propagation of the classical style was not for a mere return to the ancients, but for the renovation of literature on the basis of the ancients. Hence he taught that in learning the classical style one should "learn its spirit, not its diction", and "all the cliches ought to be got rid of"[14] and "all literary dictions should be one's own creation".[15] The ancient classical style was thus revived and reinforced with a new vitality. In addition, he took literature as a product of the expression of the people about their feelings and emotions, claiming: "Where there is injustice, there will be an outcry."[16] By such an argument, literature was integrated with the reality of social contradictions, a rather keen insight in the history of literary ideas.

Liu Zongyuan was a co-founder of this classical style movement and his literary theory had much in common with Han Yu's. Yet in some aspects they differed from each other. Both upheld the credo: "Literature for the sake of the Tao"; but Han stressed the Confucian orthodoxy against Buddhism and Taoism so much so that he concerned himself only with the maintenance of the orthodoxy with its ruling orders and was indifferent to the political reform movements of his time, while Liu never advertised any orthodoxy but urged strongly "to carry the Tao into practice",[17] i.e., to engage in activities of social and political reforms. Hence Liu joined the political reform movement of his time and wrote many works in deep sympathy with the misery of the people against the injustice of the ruling class—a career which Han hardly dreamed to touch upon.

Part III

IDEOLOGY IN THE LATER MIDDLE AGES

GENERAL SKETCH OF
THE LATER MIDDLE AGES

The later Middle Ages in China comprised a period of nearly nine centuries from the founding of the Song Dynasty in 960 to the Opium War in 1840. In comparison with the early period of the Middle Ages, there were obvious developments in every field of human activities: but viewed from the inner structure of the feudal society itself, the main historical tendency was heading towards an irretrievable decline which could be seen in every phase of the intellectual history.

(1)

The feudal society was founded upon its economic basis of feudal land property. The system of the distribution of land practised under the Tang regime was carried out on the presumption that the shares of land were periodically returned to the community. But the ever-increasing landlord ownership of large land properties prevented the land distribution system of the Tang regime from being realized on a universal scale. Here lay the intrinsic and irreconcilable contradiction of feudalism which led irreversibly to its own decadence. For the remedy of the disintegration of the land distribution system, the two-taxation system sponsored by Yang Yan, as mentioned in Chapter 12, afforded a moderate measure of compromise. This new two-taxation system made possible for the peasants to become small land proprietors and thus to possess, as tax-payers, an independent status in the government's census instead of their former status of personal dependence on their seigneurs. The exploitation then assumed, for the most part, the form of rents in kind instead of in corvée practised in the former days. This measure alleviated relatively the personal bondage of the peasants to their land and landlords. However, this did not prevent the land annexation on a large scale on the part of the bureaucrat-landlords through channels other than the privileges inherent of their social strata.

With the establishment of the Song Dynasty, there emerged a large number of bureaucrat-landlords who were officially exempted from being taxed. Thus the imperial taxes fell upon the middle and lower strata of the landlords (the non-privileged landlords), and especially upon the small land-holding peasants. As for those peasants who lost their land, they could not find a livelihood but to become the clients of the large landlords and were excluded from the the tax census of the government. But on the other hand, the privilege of tax exemption enjoyed by the upper landlords greatly reduced the financial income of the imperial government. It was under this historical background that Wang Anshi initiated his reform movement which somewhat ameliorated the sharp social contradictions. But before long, it suffered a complete failure under the counter-offensive of the higher bureaucrat-landlords' group.

Wang's reform did not change the status quo of the upper landlords' ownership, since the imperial government was no longer in a position to possess and to distribute land as it did in former times. This showed that the irresistible tendency of land annexation was already out of control of the imperial government. With the social contradictions sharpened, economic stability was at stake. The failure of Wang was not that of an individual but rather a reflection of the general decline of the feudal society which was beyond the power of any reformer to repair. This irresistible trend continued throughout the Ming and Qing dynasties when large land properties increased in number under various names and pretexts to the erosion of the very basis of the feudal society itself.

(2)

Simultaneous with this declining tendency of feudalism was the strengthening of the monarchical despotism which of necessity led to political corruption.

The Song Dynasty at the very beginning of its foundation was motivated by a monarchical despotic spirit much more than ever before. According to the view of Zhao Kuangyin, the first emperor of Song (960-975), the tumults and disorders of the late Tang and the Five Dynasties were due to the fact that "the local magistrates were too powerful, causing the weakening of the sovereign and the strengthening of the vassals"; so he adopted a policy of weakening the local powers and concentrating all administrative and military functions to the royal throne. The administrative and military functions were subdivided to the heads of various governmental branches who were directly responsible to the throne instead of the cabinet headed by a prime minister.

This was a major change on the powers and functions of the centralized government since Qin and Han. The power of the prime minister was given over to the emperor who became an absolute autocrat in the fullest sense of the word, with no check or balance on him by either the legislative power and the jurisdiction or the prime ministers and the imperial censors. Later, Zhu Yuanzhang, the first emperor of Ming (1368-1398), even utterly nullified the traditional institution of premiership. Then the whole political framework was run by the sole volition of one person. The officials in authority were selected from among the personal confidentials of the emperor, so that even the eunuchs and secret agents were given the power to rule over the officialdom. The well-known dictum of Lord Acton, "Power corrupts, absolute power corrupts absolutely", may find one of its best models in the history of Chinese despotism.

(3)

Since the Song Dynasty, the feudal society was stepping into its later stage, the stage of decline, while the germination of capitalist elements in late Ming accelerated this process of decline. But the germination of capitalist elements in China suffered its serious setbacks first by the invasion and the rule of the Manchu tribes and then the Western Powers, a historical fact which impeded China to step into a capitalist society. Yet these new elements brought forth a new phase in social struggle, for the emerging bourgeoisie was becoming more and more an important factor with which the opposition party of the landlord class formed a political alliance. In this respect, the opposition party of the later feudal period differed in nature from the earlier ones. All these complexities of the political and social changes found their expressions in the realm of ideology with their characteristic features which were at variance with those of the former times.

In general, Neo-Confucianism which emerged in the Song period was in essence an official ideology in defence of both the feudal order and its despotic rule. In particular, it developed the ideas of Zi Si-Mencius School of the pre-Qin Confucianism, emphasizing the speculative role of the subjective spirit. To most of the Neo-Confucianists, the objective world was an embodiment of the feudal ethical code while the spiritual substance, i.e., *li* (or the Principle), as the source of the objective world, was everlasting and unchangeable.

In the history of the development of Chinese idealism, this theory of ontology marked a new stage which succeeded the theory of teleology for the former times. In the Han period, there was the polemic between Dong Zhongshu's teleological theory and Wang Chong's naturalistic theory. Dong's theory was further developed by Wang Pi and others during the period of Wei and Jin, and later inherited by the Cheng-Zhu School in the Song period which by absorbing some of the essential elements of Buddhism and Taoism recast it into the Neo-Confucian ideology. This Neo-Confucian ideology was further pushed to its extremity by Wang Yangming in the Ming period. But thenceforth it ceased to thrive with any new idea or new content.

On the other hand, the naturalistic view was striding forward as an antithesis to Neo-Confucianism. This naturalistic tradition was remoulded by Zhang Zai into an ether theory of ontology which, though still appeared as an opposition within the camp of Neo-Confucianism, far exceeded the naturalistic ether theory of Wang Chong in that it afforded a better explanation on such important issues as substance versus function, mind versus nature, and knowledge versus practice. It was upon the basis of this theory that the foremost ideologues of Ming and Qing like Wang Fuzhi and Dai Zhen were able to reach the culmination of naturalistic philosophical thinking in the history of China.

(4)

This attribute of the later feudal society found its expression also in all the other fields of intellectual activity. Generally speaking, all kinds of ideology were in the last analysis still feudalistic in nature, their ways of thinking being restricted by narrowness and simplicity conditioned by the scale of mere reproduction of the mediaeval natural economy.

It was only with the germination of capitalist elements that there emerged the earliest modern ideas in the strict sense. It was then that the upsurging of the peasants' uprisings was able to give an unprecedented impetus to the intellectual world, which resulted in an enlightenment movement comparable to the flourish of the Hundred Schools in the pre-Qin period. In a certain sense, the progressive ideologues of the early enlightenment movement, though stepping out of the landlord class, were aspiring after a new world in the future with their prophetic visions. It was no other than a new society of the bourgeoisie. Hence sharp critiques of the feudal order and its despotism had always been an integral part of the progressive ideologies of the time, in spite of the fact that those enlightenment thinkers were fond of expressing their new visions under the clock of antiquity. It was an intellectual liberation by way of resorting to the ancients. It was by this time too that we find the earliest hint of modern scientific thinkings in China as shown in the works of Xu Guangqi.

It was really a pity that all these progressive factors in intellectual history were dealt a deadly blow by the savage rule of the Qing regime. Through a series of complicated intellectual struggles, the Qing royal court finally succeeded in turning the early Qing study of Sinology (which originally aimed at the preservation of the national culture against the Manchu rule) into the mid-Qing study of Sinology (which consciously engaged in mere textual criticism of ancient learnings). The Sinology since mid-Qing, though contributed much to the work of editing and compiling the ancient classics, had nevertheless brought forth few ideas of intellectual significance. But at the same time, outside of the academic studies and theoretical speculations, there were other indications anticipating the coming downfall of the feudal society such as one might readily read in such literary works as *A Dream of Red Mansions.*

Chapter 14

PHILOSOPHICAL AND RELIGIOUS THOUGHTS IN THE SONG AND YUAN DYNASTIES

1. NEO-CONFUCIANISM OF THE CHENG-ZHU SCHOOL

Since the Song period, the relations of production of the feudal society had entered the stage of descendancy. The nobility households of the foregoing epochs were greatly diminished, but there emerged large numbers of politically privileged bureaucrat-landlords who with their insatiate greed for land annexation came into conflict with the middle and lower strata of the under-privileged landlords as well as with the tenant-peasants. In order to stabilize the feudal rule, the Song Dynasty resorted to the measure of strengthening the autocratic despotism, which in its turn required an ideology as a theoretical basis. This was the historical background of the birth of Neo-Confucianism.

With regard to its emergence, Neo-Confucianism came into being as a theory in opposition to the New Learnings of Wang Anshi (1021-1086). During its first stage, the pivotal figure in the formation of Neo-Confucianism was Sima Guang (1019-1086), who worked for bringing about a setback to Wang's reform. In succession to Sima, the most prominent figures of Neo-Confucianism were Zhou Dunyi, Shao Yong, Cheng Yi and Cheng Hao who were all political followers of Sima in their concert against Wang's reform and its ideology. Intellectually they derived their ideas from the Zi Si-Mencius School of the ancient Confucianism.

The Buddhist and Taoist thoughts had had their days, but after all their other-worldliness with all its underlying principles was not in conformity with the requirements of the feudal ethical code and the feudal ruling order. Hence they suffered severe attacks from the orthodox Confucians among whom Han Yu was the most outstanding representative. The orthodox Confucians intended to develop the traditional Confucianism, especially that of the Zi Si-Mencius School, so as to accommodate it to the long changed social conditions. This new orthodox ideology was branded by Han Yu and the Neo-Confucianists as the Orthodoxy of the Tao, or the Orthodoxy of the Way of Confucius and Mencius. It was said that this orthodoxy had fallen into oblivion long since Qin and that it was their historical vocation to restore this long obliterated orthodoxy. Those who professed this orthodoxy were called the Neo-Confucianists. In appearance they were repudiating the Buddhist and Taoist thoughts, but in reality they absorbed into their theories a lot of the world views of both Buddhism and Taoism. It was a historical imperative that a comprehensive system of the three teachings, with Confucianism in command, would best suit the rule of the feudal landlords.

In their philosophical speculations, the Neo-Confucianists were mainly concerned about the issues of the Principle, the Ether, the mind, the human nature, etc. Since there were various groups and strata within the landlord class, so Neo-Confucianism.differentiated into various schools. Roughly speaking, there might be found three main schools in it: the school of objective idealism headed by Cheng Yi and Zhu Xi, the school of subjective idealism headed by Lu Jiuyuan and later by Wang Yangming, and the school of naturalism and utilitarianism headed by Zhang Zai, Chen Liang and Ye Shi. We shall begin with a few words on the forerunners of Zhu Xi.

It was generally acknowledged that Zhou Dunyi (1016-1073) was the founder of Neo-Confucianism whose main writing was the *Explanation of the Diagram of the Supreme Ultimate*. He proclaimed that the origin of the world was the Supreme Ultimate which being soundless and formless and having no beginning nor end, was also termed the Ultimateless. By the motion of this Supreme Ultimate were begotten Yin and Yang, the combination of which begot the Five Elements which in turn begot the world with all things in it. Zhou reduced all existences to an indescribable spiritual entity, called the Supreme Ultimate which bore an implication of Tao (Way) or Principle (*Li*). To him, Tao and Principle were essentially identical, but the former was more applied to cosmogony while the latter to social ethics.

Of all existences begotten by the Supreme Ultimate, it was only the human being that was the most receptive of the principle of the Supreme Ultimate. Since the principle of the Supreme Ultimate was perfect honesty, so human beings were born with innate goodness. But owing to their contacts in different ways with the outside world, people differed. Some were good and others evil. As regards the evils in human nature, Zhou recommended people to cultivate their perfect honesty for the sake of restoring their inborn good and thus becoming a sage. Here Zhou touched upon many important categories in the philosophy of Neo-Confucianism, such as the principle, the ether, the mind, the human nature, the Supreme Ultimate and the Ultimateless, around which the Neo-Confucianists of later generations unfolded their inquiries and their polemics.

Among Zhou's disciples, the Cheng Brothers were the most noteworthy in the course of the development of Neo-Confucianism, Cheng Hao (1032-1085), or Cheng the Elder, and Cheng Yi (1033-1107), or Cheng the Younger, were natives of Luoyang and hence their learnings were called the Luoyang School. Both of them elaborated systematic expositions on the idea of *Li* (Principle) which was venerated by later Neo-Confucianists às the orthodox explanation.

Li (Principle) as a philosophical category appeared long before the Song period, but it was raised to the height of the Heavenly Principle, or the supreme philosophical category, only by the Cheng Brothers. The Elder Cheng once said: "The term Heavenly Principle was worked out by no other than myself."[1] According to them, *Li* was the supreme principle governing both the natural world and the human society, and it was everlasting without beginning or end. So it was asserted: "There is but one and the same Principle in the world",[2] and "all things are coming into being by this Heavenly Principle".[3] This Heavenly Principle manifested itself at all times and all places, in natural world and in the ethical code of social life. The feudal ethical code was thus sanctified under the name of Heavenly Principle. This Principle or

Heavenly Principle was a Heavenly Mandate which was incarnated in human mind as well as in human nature. Consequently there was the communion between Heaven and Man. Once Cheng the Younger told the emperor a story: One day after Liu Xiu had ascended the royal throne as the first emperor of Eastern Han, he invited his old friend Yan Kuang to his palace and late at night they slept together on the same bed. The next day it was reported that "a guest star was intruding upon the Royal Constellation yesternight".[4] This kind of far-fetched analogy between natural phenomenon (a shooting star) and human affair (Yan Kuang sleeping with the emperor) showed the mystic element in his ideas.

Then, how were people to know the Heavenly Principle? The Elder Cheng persuaded people to keep their mind in a state of honesty and veneration. And the Younger Cheng taught people to engage in "the investigation of things" through the process of which the innate Heavenly Principle might be restored and the human desires expelled. But the sages and the ordinary people differed in proportion to their different grades of inborn gifts, so they also differed in their respective shares in their ability to know the Heavenly Principle: The ordinary people could only hope to attain the sagehood of the lower degree. Here the Cheng Brothers inherited the theory of the three grades of human nature expounded by Han Yu and Li Ao.

In the main, both the Cheng Brothers were the same in their expositions of the Principle. But as to their respective approaches, there were some differences. The Elder Cheng laid more emphasis on the inner meditation of the mind than on the studying of the outside world, so he insisted that "the scrutiny into the Principle, the fulfilment of human nature and the realization of the vocation, all the three should be accomplished simultaneously".[5] Later, Lu Jiuyuan and Wang Yangming followed his approach and developed the Neo-Confucianism along the line of subjective idealism, commonly known as the School of the Study of the Mind. The Younger Cheng laid more emphasis on the knowledge of the outside world in its role of attaining the inner knowledge, or to use the Confucian terms, the process of extension of knowledge through the investigation of things. Later, Zhu Xi followed his approach and elaborated the system of the Study of the Principle, commonly known as the Cheng-Zhu School of Neo-Confucianism.

2. ZHU XI AND LU JIUYUAN

Zhu Xi (1130-1200), a native of Wuyuan (in Anhui), was brought up in Fujian, so his school was known as the Fujian School. A disciple of the fourth generation of the Younger Cheng, Zhu was the most prominent figure of Neo-Confucianism who epitomized the thoughts of the Song Neo-Confucianism and played the most important role in the ideology of the later middle ages. Some of his followers even compared him with Confucius.

Zhu lived at a time when the northern part of the country had fallen under the rule of the Kin tribe and the impending problem confronting the Southern Song regime was whether to appease the Kin or to make war against them. Zhu was one for making war, proclaiming: "The policy at present is but to improve the political situation so as to be able to drive out the barbarians." He condemned Qin Hui, the leader of the appeasement camp, and praised Yue Fei, the leader of armed resistance. In his later years when he was disappointed with the political situation, he turned exclusively to academic and speculative activities. Among his voluminous works, the most noted were his *Summary of Systematic Thought, Collected Annotations on the Four Books, Detailed Outline of Siam Kuang's "History as a Mirror"* and others on the study of ancient classics as well as on the study of the Luoyang School.

The world view of Zhu Xi was based on the synthesis of Zhou Dunyi's idea of the Supreme Ultimate and the Younger Cheng's ontology. Zhou made but a very faint and ambiguous interpretation about the Supreme Ultimate. The Younger Cheng then attributed the Principle (*Li*) to the metaphysical realm and the Ether (*Qi*) to the physical. As to the question of how could the two different worlds act upon and communicate with each other, the Younger Cheng gave no definite answer. On the basis of Zhou and the Younger Cheng, Zhu formulated a more coherent theory. He claimed that the entity of the world was the Supreme Ultimate which consisted of both the Principle (*Li*) and the Ether (*Qi*), the former being prior to the latter. And the Supreme Ultimate in the last analysis was the Principle too, i.e., the Principle that synthesized all principles of the world.

The Supreme Ultimate as the Principle, differed from the principle that was in contrast with the ether, because the former was wholly transcendental and perfect, while the latter the concrete principles governing concrete objects in the world (hence being called the principles instead of the Principle). Since the latter was derived from the former, so he remarked: "All things have their principles which are all originated from one and the same source [the Principle]."[6] In other words, the Principle of the Supreme Ultimate was the synthesis of all principles.

It was obvious that in the above argument Zhu derived his ideas from the Huayan (or Garland) sect of Buddhism which taught that varieties were comprehended in the entity. What the Younger Cheng taught as "the variegated things sharing in one and the same Principle",[7] Zhu interpreted as "all principles originating from one and the same source".[8] Zhu even borrowed the Buddhist allegory that all waters reflected one and the same moon to illustrate that all principles shared in the Principle of the Supreme Ultimate. "There is but one Supreme Ultimate from which all things take their shares and hence have their own Supreme Ultimate",[9] said he. As a consequence of this, "everyman has his own share in [the Principle of] the Supreme Ultimate".[10] All men and all things were thus said to be the manifestations of the Principle (or the Heavenly Principle). And since the Principle (or the Heavenly Principle) dwelt within the minds of human beings, so "the mind comprehends all principles, and all principles consist in the mind".[11]

It is interesting to note that this Heavenly Principle or the Supreme Ultimate was literally nothing else than the philosophical incarnation of the feudal ethical code and the feudal order. The logical corollary from this was the assertion of the Neo-Confucianists that all the three cardinal guides and the five constant virtues were but "the expression of this Principle". Human nature by Heavenly Mandate was perfect, because it came directly from the Principle of the Supreme Ultimate. But human beings in their daily life were unavoidably infected by various actions of the ethers, some cleaner and some dirtier. Thus came into being what he termed "the human nature by temperament" which were sometimes good and sometimes evil, just like the water which was originally clean and clear might be turned dirty in a dirty pot. The sages were said to be endowed with cleaner temperaments that were harder to be infected by the dirty while always inclining to manifest their innate goodness; but the common people were said to be on the contrary. So taught Zhu's theory of human nature.

In ancient times there had been the polemics on the innate goodness or evil of human nature. Zhu proclaimed that Mencius' theory about the goodness of human nature referred to the human nature per se or the human nature by Heavenly Mandate, while Han Yu's theory of the three grades of human nature to that by temperament. Zhu tried to make a synthesis of the two with the purpose to bring forth a solution to the age-old polemics.

For those whose temperaments were said to be dim or muddled, Zhu advised them to remould or to renovate their temperaments. But he laid down a limit to the possibility of the remoulding: one's lot could not be recast and what was capable of being remoulded was only the degree of their clearness and dimness. This idea reflected the socially hierarchical character of his theory. He proposed two ways by which the temperament could be remoulded: by "keeping earnestness" and by "exhaustive study of the Principle". The essence of his theory was after all just to bring the people into the channel of the feudalistic norm which was transformed by him into a shrine of the Heavenly Principle with his intoxicating metaphysical argumentations. In the last analysis, the feudal ethical code—the three cardinal guides and the five constant virtues—formed the substantial nucleus of the everlasting Principle which should hold its reign for ever and ever.

When applied to the interpretation of history, Zhu's theory taught that the course of history was determined by the minds of the sovereigns. The ancient sage-kings, so he argued, practised the Heavenly Principle while the emperors of the later ages the human desires; hence the former reigned in a kingly way while the latter in a coercive way. For him, history was ever retrogressing.

Zhu's theory met the oppositions from Lu Jiuyuan (1139-1193), a native of Fuzhou (in Jiangxi) who was Zhu's contemporary and his chief opponent. Lu also admitted the Principle as the entity of the world, but disagreed with Zhu in that he insisted that the Mind was the Principle while for Zhu the Principle lay outside of the Mind. Lu criticized Zhu's method of investigation of things outside of the Mind by a process of gradual cultivation as frivolous and trivial. Lu asked people to become sages simply by cultivating their own minds.

In the year 1175, the renowned meeting between Zhu and Lu took place at Goose Lake (in Qianshan of Jiangxi), presided over by Lu Zuqian. On the topic of education and cultivation, Zhu recommended the approach through learning while Lu insisted the finding out of the mind from within at the very start. Zhu considered Lu's method too simple and easy, while Lu thought Zhu's too trivial and fragmentary. As was well-known, Lu developed Neo-Confucianism along the line of searching for the mind which was later elaborated into the Idealistic School by Wang Yangming in the Ming period. However, it was Zhu's doctrine, generally known as the Rationalistic School, that held the reign of the Confucian orthodoxy; and his *Annotations on the Four Books* was honoured as an official textbook in later ages.

Zhu was by no means a superficial idealist. In many of his propositions, he brought forth ideas that were of lasting value in the history of thinking. It was he who made "the discernment of the subject and the object" in epistemological studies, i.e., the relationship between the subject and the object in the process of knowing.

The term Principle, though a metaphysical embodiment of the feudal ethical norm at its bottom, sometimes implied in it the connotation of natural laws. On the relation between learning and knowing, his well-known remark: "When we have exerted ourselves for an enough long time, then an enlightenment would eventually come when perfect understanding will open before us",[12] though full of the Zen flavour of sudden enlightenment, did touch upon the issue of the relationship between the quantitative aspect and the qualitative aspect of human knowledge and did imply in it an element of rationalism. Problems like this, distorted as they might be by his idealistic system, helped to deepen the philosophical inquiries for the later ages, including some of the advanced thinkers like Wang Fuzhi and Dai Zhen.

Zhu Xi himself was a scholar with versatile scientific knowledge, a topic which will be dealt in Chapter 16. Though his investigation of things aimed at proving or experiencing the transcendental Heavenly Principle, he never repudiated the reality of the objective world which, however, was said to be derived from the transcendental noumenon called the Principle. And he was also the earliest noteworthy scholar on classical criticism. Of the *Book of Odes*, he stripped off many distortions and prettifications imposed on it by the traditional Confucians. Of the *Book of History*, he doubted the authenticity of the old text version. Of the *Spring and Autumn Annals*, he did not agree with the prevailing opinion that all the records were the words put down by Confucius himself. It was sure that Zhu had no intention of nullifying the traditional classics, but he did make a big step forward on the way of criticism in classical studies which initiated a new spirit in academic learnings, the critical spirit, for centuries to come.

3. ZHANG ZAI AND THE GUAN SCHOOL

Zhang Zai (1020-1077), a native of Changan (in Shaanxi) had lived for the most part of his life in Maixian (in Shaanxi) and his teachings were generally called the Guan School (literally the School within the Passes, i.e., the middle part of Shaanxi). He was a contemporary of Wang Anshi and an elderly relative of the Cheng Brothers. Having been in governmental posts for sometime, he returned to his native place where he gave lectures to his disciples, mostly from Shaanxi, and wrote with them a series of works. His school enjoyed equal popularity with the Luoyang School. Among his main works were *The Correct Discipline for Beginners*, *Sayings of Master Zhang* and *Comments on the "Book of Changes"*. During the Ming period, most of his works were collected into the *Complete Works of Master Zhang*.

Zhang Zai's Philosophical Ideas

The Guan School stressed the learning of "that which is valuable for practical purposes"[13] in contradistinction to the speculative tendency of the Luoyang School. Zhang had a very good mastery of astronomical and mathematical knowledge. He affirmed the theory of the motion of the earth which was a great breakthrough of the traditional theory of the moving heavens and unmoving earth and constituted an integral part of his view of nature.

Zhang taught an ontology based on the theory of Ether, claiming that all existences and their phenomena were but the modifications of the Ether by which he meant the subtlest material substances, very akin to the notion of the atom. This theory was an antithesis to the Luoyang School which took the spiritual substance, the Principle, as the basis of the world.

The earliest notion of Ether dated back to the pre-Qin period. But it was not until Zhang that the notion of it was clearly explained. Zhang maintained that Ether was the matter or the substance which was shapeless when dispersed and took form when condensed. All that were capable of being perceived were but modifications of Ether. He proclaimed: "the Great Void (the ultimate state of the world) cannot subsist without the Ether. The Ether cannot but condense into all things which in their turn cannot but disperse again into the Great Void.... The Great Void which is formless is full of ethereal substance which condenses into and disperses out of the forms of all changings and all changeables."[14] In other words, the Great Void was but the world of the primeval Ether before its modification, and the perceptible world but the momentary condensation of the Ether.

According to him, things could never vanish into nothingness but only disperse into their ethereal state. Hence there could never have been a world of emptiness without any substantial reality. In this way the traditional conception of Ether was turned by him into the conception of matter or substance with which he refuted the age-old proposition that being came out of non-being. Life and death of human beings were also attributed to the condensation and dispersion of the Ether. This led Zhang to assume a critical position towards the prevailing religious belief in the immortality of the soul.

As to the question why there was the condensation and dispersion of the Ether, Zhang proposed a theory of motion which might be roughly summed up like this: The world was unified by Ether and in Ether which was in perpetual motion, being caused by the action and reaction of the two opposites, or in his own words: "What makes up the Ether is the unity of the two opposites."[15] The unity comprised the two opposites and the two opposites combined into the unity. Without the contradiction of the two opposites, nothing whatever could come into being at all. What he termed the two opposites referred to the motion and rest of things or the condensation and dispersion of Ether. He compared the two opposites to Yin and Yang, or male and female, the interaction between which resulted in perpetual motion. Motion was but the process of nature by itself, not being caused by anything external. It had neither volition nor purpose. Zhang explained the motions and changes of the world in his peculiar terminologies such as Moment and Delicacy, which though imbued with a somewhat mystic tone, represented nonetheless his endeavour to reduce all movements to their internal causes instead of the action of external forces. Such was the scientific elements in his outlook on the changes of the world.

As for the course of movements, Zhang characterized them with two correlative stages: transforming and becoming. "Transforming refers to what is abrupt and becoming to what is gradual."[16] Or in other words, transforming was roughly equivalent to sudden changes, and becoming to gradual changes. When gradual change reached a certain degree, a sudden change would be induced. And after a sudden change, the gradual change would again ensue. This view of his enriched greatly the conception of nature in mediaeval times. And in his notion of movement there was also implied a sense of progress which broke out the age-long theory of cyclism.

Though the change of Ether might seem incomprehensible at first sight, it obeyed certain necessary laws which he termed *Li* (Principle) or "the Principle of Change". When he claimed that "all things were endowed with principles", what he really meant by principle was not anything spiritual, his basic thesis on the relation of the Principle and the Ether being: "Principle consists in the Ether."[17] For him, the existence of the objective world was the primary while the principle the secondary—a reverse of what was professed by the Luoyang School.

Zhang Zai's Theory of Human Nature

Perception, Zhang argued, had to have its roots in the objective existence, or in his words: "Perception depends on the object: where there is an object, there is perception. If there is nothing in existence at all, then what is there that is to be perceived?"[18] It was from the "combination of the internal and the external"[19] that knowledge was given birth. In other words, knowledge was originated by the sense organs in touch with the external world. As to the process of obtaining knowledge, he divided it into two stages: knowledge by perception and knowledge by reasoning.

But on the issue of how to obtain rational knowledge, Zhang was more or less puzzled. He knew well that one could never hope to know all of the world through mere perception. Perception only enabled one "to know a small part of the world, then how can it exhaust the knowledge of all things?"[20] Perceptive knowledge was indeed very much limited in its scope as he would willingly admit, but thencefrom he was led to think that only by rejecting it one could hope to attain the knowledge of all things through rational thinking. Thus perceptive knowledge and rational knowledge were mistaken by him as mutually exclusive. He did not teach people to acquire rational knowledge on the basis of perceptive knowledge, but on the contrary he preached to find it out by "scrutinizing the principle" within one's inner heart wherein, so he urged, lay the innate knowledge. It seemed to him that by giving up the knowledge of the external world one could hope to get genuine knowledge through mere internal cultivation. In this respect, he was very close to the orthodox doctrine of the Luoyang School.

This innate knowledge was born with all men, but, so he asserted, only the sages who were superior to the ordinary people were capable of developing it to its fullest extent. Here was another point where Zhang came very close to the Luoyang School. There had been polemics on the issue of human nature ever since old, but all the polemists talked idly about the inborn nature of man disregarding its relation to social practice. Even Wang Chong and Fan Zhen were no exception to this, because they tried to explain human nature barely in physiological terms. And so did Zhang Zai.

Zhang Zai concluded that all things in the world, human beings included, were formed by Ether, the sole source of the universe. Before the emergence of all things and all human beings, there was only one and the same nature in common, called "the cosmic nature" which was pure and perfect. But once human beings emerged, the sages among them were gifted with the cleaner Ether, while the ordinary people the more turbid. This resulted in the difference in the degrees of human nature, called "nature by temperament". Some belonged to the higher degree, and others to the lower.

But "nature by temperament" was in essence not nature. It was only the cosmic nature that deserved to be rightly so called. For the sake of obtaining genuine nature, Zhang advised "the transformation of temperament" through learning. One should be earnest in learning the traditional ethical code while persistently getting rid of the evils or the dirty Ether in him. By digging out strenuously the innate knowledge, one was able to attain his cosmic nature. In the process of "transformation of temperament", the sages (rather those who embodied the feudal ethical code) would be faster in returning to their cosmic nature than the ordinary people. Herein was exposed Zhang's prejudice in favour of that social class to which he himself belonged.

Since the Ether prior to its condensation (into all things as well as into human beings) was pure and perfect, but after that it became variegated as people were affected by different degrees of purity of the Ether, so Zhang put forward his thesis: "Principle is but one, yet the parts of it are different".[21] This was the answer to the problem of the relation of the one and the many, or the universal and the particular. From this he drew one of his ethical conclusions that since all people were originated from the same source, they should regard others as their fellow folks. It was for this aspect of his theory, but not for his materialistic interpretation of nature, that he was honoured as one of the foremost representatives of Neo-Confucianism. Zhu Xi said of him that "he contributed much to the Confucian teaching",[22] and the Cheng Brothers praised his writing *The Western Inscription* as "unexcelled ever since Mencius".[23]

However, it should be kept in mind that in his view of the natural world he was fundamentally different from the orthodox Neo-Confucianists, and in his view of nature he was also not the same with the Luoyang School. For the Cheng Brothers and later for Zhu Xi, the relation between nature by Heavenly Mandate and that by temperament was one between the Principle and the Ether with the former always prior to the latter; while for Zhang both were the Ether, the relation between the two being that between the universal and the particular. Hence his cosmic nature was in essence not the Principle in the sense of Cheng and Zhu but "the nature of the Ether".

The fact was that Cheng and Zhu accepted the notion of "nature by temperament" from Zhang but remoulded it into the pattern of the Neo-Confucian orthodoxy. So it is only by a concrete analysis of the concrete issues that a better understanding of the different tendencies within Neo-Confucianism can be reached. Thus it might be seen that alongside with the general current of Neo-Confucianism with the Cheng-Zhu School as its orthodoxy, there were also the naturalism of Zhang Zai as well as the utilitarianism of Chen Liang and Ye Shi.

4. UTILITARIAN IDEAS OF CHEN LIANG AND YE SHI

The thoughts of Chen Liang and Ye Shi were evaluated in the comments of their contemporaries as something "that had never been so expounded by scholars for centuries".[24] They shed a new light on the arena of intellectual history at a time when the Southern Song Dynasty (1127-1279) while exercising its sovereignty over only the southern part of the country was heading rapidly to collapse within and being seriously menaced by the invasion of the Mongols from without. Both Chen and Ye came from the lower strata of the landlord class and upheld the feudal rule, but they strongly demanded political reforms and armed resistance. Therefore on many cardinal points they were opposed to the uselessness and vanity of orthodox Neo-Confucianism with their own utilitarian doctrines stressing practical effects on society.

The Thoughts of Chen Liang

Chen Liang (1147-1194) was a native of Yongkang (in Zhejiang) and his school was generally known as the Yongkang School. He wrote few works on philosophy proper and his philosophical ideas can only be found in his political and historical writings as well as in his debates with Zhu Xi. He talked about Tao, Principle, mind and human nature at random. According to him, Tao or Principle dwelt in things and in things only. "Tao always dwells in things" and "can be grasped";[25] it was not something outside of things nor independent of things. It was but the law that regulated all things.

Of human nature, he made a naturalistic interpretation by which it was identified with human desires in daily life. He reinterpreted the ancient proposition of Mencius that "all things are within me", to the effect that the daily requirements of everyone "are to be furnished by hundreds of craftsmen".[26] The necessities in daily life could not be satisfied by merely searching the Heavenly Principle from within as taught by the orthodox Neo-Confucianists.

Chen concentrated his concerns on the political and social issues of the day. He severely criticized the indifferent attitude of the Neo-Confucianists towards the practical problems of society, especially their inactivity in face of the impending invasion of the enemy. He blamed them as only good at talking idly about their vainglorious terminologies while "discarding all the practicalities of the world ... with no due regard to anything that is in need".[27] In opposition to them, Chen advocated "to solve the problem of the day practically", in order that "all the evils may be eliminated and all the people may enjoy a peaceful life".[28] This ideal of his formed a sharp contrast with the pedantic way of the Neo-Confucianists of the day. Inspired by such an ideal, he wrote many works and used to submit his proposals to the emperor, refuting the opinions of the defeatists and the capitulators. For this reason, he was put in prison three times.

His utilitarian ideas came nowhere else more vividly than in his debate with Zhu Xi over the issue of "the rule by benevolence versus the rule by force", or "the righteous versus the utilitarian". In the year 1184 when Chen was forty-two, he met Zhu for the first time. Later on, within a course of three years they held a series of debates in their correspondences.

Zhu maintained that the Heavenly Principle fell in the category of the righteous while the human desires in that of the utilitarian; the two were antagonistic and mutually exclusive. In consequence of this, history in the times of antiquity was dominated by the Heavenly Principle which was, however, gradually replaced in later ages by human desires. Therefore the present fell short of the benevolent rule of the antiquity, and the course of history was ever retrogressing.

Conversely, Chen maintained that human desires existed everywhere at all times, and that righteousness existed nowhere else than in its utility, i.e., in its maximum satisfaction of the requirements of the people; the two were inseparable from each other and in harmony with each other. The often too much idealized society of the antiquity, just like the Han and the Tang of the later ages, was dominated by human desires, and their difference lay only in their respective degrees of satisfying the human requirements. The ancient sage-kings had satisfied the desires of the people to the maximum degree, so they fulfilled the righteousness and the Heavenly Principle to the utmost. The Han and the Tang had done just the same, but only to a lesser degree.

As to the question why the Han and the Tang were inferior to the antiquity, Zhu's reply was that the ancient sage-kings followed the Heavenly Principle, so that there was then the rule by benevolence; but the rulers of Han and Tang were dominated by human desires, so that there was then the rule by force. The distinction between them lay in the different motivations of the rulers. As a result, it would only be through a process of moral cultivation "to preserve the Heavenly Principle and to banish the human desires"[29] that the benevolent rule of the antiquity could be restored. To this, Chen put forward his opposite argument that there was no contradiction between the Heavenly Principle and human desires, or the righteous and the utilitarian, and hence between the rule of benevolence and the rule by force. To Zhu's criterion of motivation, Chen substituted that of effect. Therefore there was no essential distinction between the rule in antiquity and that of Han and Tang. In his stress of the practical effect of human motivation, Chen was in direct confrontation with Zhu's viewpoint.

In Chen's theory there were some aspects which were nothing short of a progressive ideology. But in other aspects, one may easily find fault with him. He accepted some basic points of the traditional theory of Heavenly Mandate, conceding the sovereign's power of punishing the people in order to withhold their human desires. This power of the sovereign was said to be endowed by Heaven. In comparison with Chen, his contemporary Ye Shi held some ideas that were more penetrating and unique in the history of utilitarian thoughts.

The Thoughts of Ye Shi

Ye Shi (1150-1223), a native of Yongjia (in Zhejiang) and the dean of the Yongjia School, was a friend of Chen Liang. Like Chen, Ye was an advocate of the armed resistance against the Kin invaders. After being framed by the capitulators' camp, he stayed in recluse at home, lecturing and writing.

In his philosophical views, Ye held that the world was made of Ether which manifested itself in various fashions, such as the five elements and the eight diagrams. All came out of the Ether and returned to the Ether. With this theory which, like Chen Liang's, was drawn from Zhang Zai's ethereal ontology, Ye criticized the Rationalistic School of Neo-Confucianism which professed that the world originated from the Supreme Ultimate or the Ultimateless.

Ye explained emphatically that the Tao dwelt in things: "Whenever and wherever there are things, there is the Tao"; therefore Tao could never antecede the objective reality as preached so much since ancient times. Everything, so he held, was the unity of the opposites of Yin and Yang, by the interaction of which the world was set in perpetual motion. This was called by him "the nature of things".

Consequently in his epistemological theory, Ye maintained that knowledge could never be "separated from its object even for an instant". Just like a craftsman had to start his work with his materials and instruments, so in the same way human cognition had to start with the perception of sense organs in contact with the external world. And only after that, correct knowledge would ensue by the employment of the thinking organ or the mind. But the Rationalistic School of Neo-Confucianism confined themselves only within the realm of the thinking mind, then how could it be that the principles they drew were not absurdities? The so-called "investigation of things" of the Rationalistic School was thus turned upside down by

Ye. For him, knowledge was but the correspondence of the subject and the object. The criterion of truth should only be derived from "the scrutiny of all things in the world", and hence "all that are not verified by facts are false assertions".[30]

Dong Zhongshu in the Han period had announced his famous dictum: "Act to follow the righteous while paying no consideration to its utility". But Ye criticized this age-long famous dictum as high-sounding but empty and vain, for the content of the righteous existed nowhere else but in its utility. And since the righteous existed only in its utility, one should at no time "suppress the utility with the righteous".[31] He propounded that the search for truth should be correlated with "the scrutiny of all things in the world". By "all things in the world", he meant "all the facts that will prove either profitable or harmful to the age".[32] Hence his utilitarianism was one which was enhanced by the criterion of the social utility instead of the individual utility.

Chen Liang had refuted Zhu Xi's doctrine of the benevolent rule and righteousness. Ye went even further as to criticize the Neo-Confucianism itself professed by Zhu Xi (as well as by Lu Jiuyuan). This made his anti-orthodox ideas the more forcible and his utilitarian ideas the more characteristic. He was bold enough to question the Neo-Confucian way of venerating the ancient sages and their classics by saying that there had already been sages before Confucius and that Confucius' teachings were not all his own originality but the legacy of the ancient classics. He criticized Mencius' teaching as empty and not necessarily in the line of Confucius. He found faults with the *Doctrine of the Mean* which, said he, was not what Confucius taught. As to the doctrine of the Cheng Brothers on the Supreme Ultimate and the Ultimateless, he attributed it to a derivation from *The Ten Wings* which was in fact not the work of Confucius but the notes taken by later scholars in their study of the *Book of Changes*. Hence the Confucian orthodoxy professed by the Neo-Confucianists was almost utterly incredible.

The Cheng-Zhu School proclaimed a succession of the orthodoxy from Confucius to Zeng Zi, then to Zi Si and Mencius, and boasted themselves in the direct line of this orthodoxy. Ye was of the opinion that the Cheng-Zhu School succeeded partly the Zi Si-Mencius' doctrine on mind, but had no relation at all with Confucius.

Confucius appreciated a handful of his disciples such as Yan Yuan and others but had never mentioned Zeng Zi who deviated from Confucius' teaching of an all-pervading principle by taking the self as the basis. The myth of orthodoxy fabricated by the Neo-Confucianists was thrown into confusion by Ye who blamed their learnings as empty and void and good for nothing. It was also Ye who keenly revealed the Buddhist substance in the Neo-Confucian doctrine.

Ye exposed relentlessly the absurdity and perniciousness of those teachings of the Neo-Confucianists which would, as he strongly asserted, eventually lead to the disintegration of society and the downfall of the nation. So it was no wonder that Zhu Xi said of him as well as of Chen Liang that their ideas made him much more irritated and anxious than those of Lu Jiuyuan. In fact, both Chen and Ye belonged to the feudal landlord class and their theories served the benefits of that class; but their criticism on the hypocrisy and uselessness of the Rationalist Neo-Confucianists as well as their ardent patriotism were among the valuable legacies in the intellectual history of mediaeval China and left their irradicable imprints on the progressive ideologues of the later ages.

5. TAOIST THOUGHTS IN SONG AND YUAN

Since its emergence in the Han period, Taoism had lasted many eventful centuries. Down to the Song period, Buddhism was declining but Taoism was becoming more prosperous than ever before, especially under the reigns of Zhenzong (998-1022) and Huizong (1101-1125) when the Taoist temples spread all over the country and the Taoist clergymen sometimes even became royal advisers to the imperial court.

Of the Taoist sects the most influential were the Jindan Sect (literally the Golden Pellet Sect) in Song and the Quanzhen Sect (literally the Nature-Preserving Sect) in Kin and Yuan. After the unification of the whole country by the Yuan Dynasty in the late 13th century, the former was called the Southern Sect and the latter the Northern Sect.

Taoism had its own classics and documents. Under the reign of

Taizong of Song (976-997) was compiled the monumental Taoist collection *The Taoist Patrology* containing 1464 Taoist works in more than seven thousand volumes. Later, *The Taoist Patrology* was supplemented many times and numbered nearly ten thousand volumes in the existing editions. In it were collected a great many of magic figures and incantations as well as alchemy and other superstitious practices, but there were also parts in it which provided important materials on the study of the history of both Taoism and natural sciences.

As for their guiding principle, the Taoists held "the unity of the three teachings", absorbing the ideas of Confucianism and Buddhism while exercising in its turn the intellectual influences on the other two teachings. The unity of the three teachings showed the fact that Taoism had no coherent and independent theory of its own, a fact that led to the exhaustion of its intellectual originality. After the Ming period, Taoism began to assume the role of a mere popular belief in magics and necromancy and lost any significance in creative ideas.

Taoism in the Song Period

With the close of the turbulent period of the Five Dynasties (907-960), Taoism reasserted itself again. The most renowned among the Taoists of that time were Chen Tuan and Zhang Boduan.

Chen Tuan (fl. mid-10th cent.), like all other renowned Taoists, had been much mystified by legends. This even led some scholars to doubt the very existence of the man. But according to historical documents, he had been received by Emperor Taizong of Song. According to Huang Zongxi, *The Explanation on the Diagram of the Supreme Ultimate* by Zhou Dunyi, the founder of Neo-Confucianism, was derived from Chen Tuan.

In Huang's opinion, the Diagram of the Supreme Ultimate was created by He Shang Gong, being originally called the Diagram of the Ultimateless, and finally passed on to Zhou. At the beginning it was a method of the Taoist practices. From Zhou's work it might be known that Chen was concerned with the formation of the cosmos and the origin of all things. This was indeed in the tradition of the Taoists who in their seeking for immortality had to resort to the study of the changes of the cosmos with all things in it. Thus a set of theory "from the Ultimateless to the Supreme Ultimate" was worked out. It taught that the cosmos originated from "quietude" and the world came out of non-being. The Neo-Confucianists of the Song period were very much interested in the study of cosmogony and readily accepted this theory from the Taoists. Few Confucians before Song had dealt in detail with such topics. In this respect, the emergence of Neo-Confucianism was under the strong influence of Taoism.

Another leading Taoist of the Northern Song period was Zhang Boduan (fl. 3rd quarter of the 11th century), the initiator of the Golden Pellet Sect. In his work *A Treatise on the Understanding of Truth*, it might be seen that he was the earliest Taoist influenced by the Zen Buddhism. He advised people to undergo three stages of cultivation: first, longing for immortality; second, mastering the Buddhist essence; third, reaching the perfect enlightenment with complete expulsion of all illusions. There was a strong vein of Zen ideas permeating through his whole work. As an initiator of one of the Taoist sects, Zhang took "the unity of the three teachings" as his main doctrine which surpassed his predecessors in that he criticized both traditional Taoism and Buddhism while accepting many of their ideas. Zhang's theory became the main Taoist theory since the Song period.

In the Southern Song, The Taoist leader succeeding Zhang was Bai Yuchan (dates unknown) who was much honoured in the imperial court and founded the Southern Sect of Taoism, retroactively recognizing Zhang as its original initiator and upholding his doctrine of the unity of the three teachings.

Both in doctrine and in practice, Bai was basically following the Confucian theory of "knowing where to rest". For those who engaged in cultivation, Bai taught: "Once the point of where to rest being known, the object of pursuit is then determined; when that being determined, the state of a calm unperturbedness would be attained. Once this state is attained and persists long enough, the wisdom would become perfect; then the celestial brightness would enlighten within and the mind would be purified by Tao and become in one with Tao." And "this is what is called the Supreme Tao".[33] This preaching was literally but a reprint of the Confucian classic *The Great Learning* as well as Zhu Xi's doctrine on "the investigation of

things" and "the extension of knowledge". In reality, he accepted the
distinction of the mind of human beings and the mind of the Tao
preached by the ancient Confucians, or that of the nature by Heavenly Mandate and the nature by temperament preached by Zhu Xi,
Bai admired Zhu Xi very much and once wrote an eulogy before the
statue of Zhu.

After Bai, the most renowned Taoist was Yu Yan in the last
years of the Southern Song. Yu wrote a work entitled *An Exposition
of the Accordance of the "Book of Changes"*. *The Accordance of the
"Book of Changes"* was written by Wei Boyang, a Taoist of the
Eastern Han, dealing with topics on spiritual practice and alchemy.
This book was much treasured by Zhu Xi who revised and annotated
it. But in order to assume the appearance of an orthodox Confucian,
Zhu never dared to admit that he had any affiliation with either
Buddhism or Taoism; so his work was put forth under a pseudonym.
Later, Yu the Taoist copied Zhu's version and recast it into his
Exposition. It was natural that by being revised and annotated to and
fro between the Taoists and the Confucians, books like the *Accordance* were transformed into semi-Confucian and semi-Taoist works,
a fact which showed the tendency of the integration of the Confucian
and the Taoist ideas.

Taoism in the Jin and Yuan Period

When the Southern Song regime reigned in the south, the
northern part of the country was under the rule of the Kin Dynasty
(1115-1234). Among the various Taoist sects in Kin, the most influential was the Quan Zhen (Nature-Preserving) Sect, its founders
being Wang Zhe and his disciple Qiu Chuji (or Qiu Changchun, after
his Taoist name The Master of the Everlasting Spring). This sect was
generally known as the Northern Sect of Taoism.

In the beginning, this sect emerged from amongst the populace
under the oppression of the Tartar invasions, and even some of the
patriotic intellectuals found their refuges in it. Therefore it was
inspired by a spirit against national oppressions. Its founder Wang
Zhe had intended to learn from Zhang Liang in overthrowing the
tyranny of the Tartars. After having realized the impracticability of
his intention, he dug a grave for himself to live in, professing himself

"a living dead man". Many his followers took an attitude of non-cooperation with the Kin regime and led a retired life on farms on their own labour.

This sect, owing to its origin from amongst the populace, was becoming renowned for leading their hard and earnest living which resulted in a reform of the Taoist tradition with its abuses and corruptions. They had few connections with the magics, alchemy, necromancy and other fantastic practices of the old times. But once it surpassed the other sects and assumed the ruling position, it soon turned away from its original style and became a religion in close connection with the upper classes; and many of the prominent Taoists of this sect enjoyed their luxurious life in the imperial capital.

Its doctrine as expounded in their main theoretical writing *The Fifteen Treatises* dealt primarily with the method of detaching from the worldly life and preserving the true nature endowed by Heaven, hence this sect was also known by the name of Nature-Preserving Sect.

Its basic teaching was non-activity through "the control of the mind"; or in their own words: "Tao takes the non-existence of the mind as its substance and the forgetfulness of the speech as its function."[34] When one got rid of all thoughts, one would attain a state of perfect enlightenment of the mind and of the human nature as well. As might easily be seen, there was a strong Buddhist element in it. Nature as they understood it, was namely the Tao which coming out of chaos was eternal, prior to the cosmos and outside of all things. It was in reality no more and no less than Deity. When a man dies, "his nature never dies", because "what is nature is but Deity".[35] Therefore human body was regarded as a mere corporeal shell and only the spirit was genuine, and "what is the genuine is the Supreme Deity".[36] The purpose of learning the Tao was to get the spirit liberated from the worldly body, "bursting out of its corporeal shell", just like a fish getting out of the net.

In order to attain such a state of life, one was required to realize that "there are always emotions affecting the mind and dusts polluting the nature";[37] therefore one should constantly see to it that these emotions and dusts had to be kept away, or one could not hope to get liberated. This was essentially a reprint of the theory of "recovery of the human nature" proposed by the Confucians. What the Taoists claimed as Nature or Tao that was said to be "prior to the cosmos" and "outside of all things", was in reality but the Principle or Li of the Neo-Confucianists. That was why the Nature-Preserving Sect also adhered to the doctrine of the unity of the three teachings.

Indeed, few of the thoughts of the Song Taoists were original. With the unification of the whole country by the Yuan Dynasty (1279-1368), the fantastic and superstitious elements in the tradition of Taoism reasserted themselves once more. It was then that the Taoist ideas ceased to develop any more, and what was continued was only their indulgence in oracular and necromantic practices in consequence of which there was no more significant place for the Taoists in the intellectual history of Ming and Qing periods.

Chapter 15

SOCIAL THOUGHTS IN
THE SONG AND YUAN PERIOD

1. SOCIAL THOUGHTS OF LI GOU AND DENG MU

In the long course of middle ages, there were progressive ideas among the landlord elements and the revolutionary ideas of the peasants; but lying between them there were also the opposition factions within the landlord class whose ideas were more radical than those of the landlord progressive reformers yet distinct from those of the peasants. They were generally known as the heretics. In the Song period, there were the progressive ideas of Wang Anshi on the one hand and the peasants revolutionary ideas of Li Shun and Wang Xiaopo on the other; but lying between them there was an opposition faction within the landlord class like Li Gou (and later Deng Mu in Yuan). Their ideas constituted an integral part of the intellectual treasures in the history of China.

Their ideas were emerging at a time when the despotic autocracy was being strengthened and the social contradiction sharpened. They went so far as to advocate the ideal of "no sovereign" and "equalization of farmland". They raised a much stronger protest against the existing social order than the moderate reform ideas of Wang Anshi. Deng Mu lived under the racial oppression of the Yuan regime and his ideas sounded more "violent" than his predecessor Li Gou's.

The Thoughts of Li Gou

Li Gou (1009-1059), a native of Nancheng (in Jiangxi), was contemporaneous with Wang Anshi with whom he had contact. Li came from a family of the common folk and worked on the teaching staff of the Royal Academy.

In his discontent with the social realities, Li wrote a series of works, starting from the topic of the origin of the state. His political theory may be roughly summed up as follows. Human beings were born with natural desires, so the essence of the "Rites" existed in the satisfaction of their natural desires. Herein lay the origin of all institutions, political and social. All that belonged to the natural desires of human life was rational. Hence he concluded: "Men cannot subsist without resorting to utility"[1] and "desires are in the nature of man".[2]

Mencius was opposed to utility; but Li asked: Where could one find benevolence and righteousness while discarding utility? Zhou enlarged its reign from a territory of seventy *li*'s to the whole China, "was it not a great utility?" Even Confucius was not without desires, only he had not allowed them to overstep the normal boundary. In The *Book of Odes* edited by Confucius himself, there were passages full of human emotions and desires which "accommodated themselves most appropriately to human nature".[3] When Mencius came forth to oppose utility and desire, he was against human nature and consequently not in conformity with the teachings of the ancient sages.

In the beginning, so he argued, the sovereign was instituted for the sake of the people, but not vice versa. Therefore the country was never the private property of any one. But in course of time, this relation was upturned and the people was at the mercy of one man. This was the cause of all mischiefs in the society. Li's idealized antiquity was much different from the tradition as propounded in *The Evolutions of the Rites*, because he took the state as originated from natural desires and the essence of human nature as consisted of self-interests.

Li was keen in his criticism of the social realities. In his work *The Hidden Book*, he pointed out that the cause of people's disparity in social position was due to the irrationality of land ownership. Why the labouring people, asked he, who were ploughing and spinning could not help from starving? The answer to this was: "The land was not owned by them",[4] while the rich people who neither ploughed nor spinned were enjoying their products. As a remedy for this, Li proposed "the employment of the nine-square system" by equalizing the land properties. Under the pretext of returning to "the kingly way of the ancients", Li worked out his plan which was partly a reverie of the agrarian commune of the antiquity and partly a reflection of the peasants' demand for land during his own age.

So far as the land problem was concerned, Li was much more radical than the reformers of his time and had something in common with the peasant rebels such as Li Shun (and Wang Xiaopo of a later age). But as to the realization of his ideal, Li was a step backward by placing his hope on the reform from above by the sovereign; in this respect he shared the common idea of the reformers of the landlord class. Especially in his later years when he was defending the middle and lower strata of the landlords against the injustices of the privileged landlords, his position came even more close to that of Wang Anshi.

At any rate, Li's emphasis on self-interests as the essence of human nature as well as on the institution of the sovereign for the sake of the people was no less than a forcible critique of the feudalistic ideology based on feudal land ownership and autocratic despotism. On the basis of Li's ideological legacy, Deng Mu in the Yuan period went even further.

The Thoughts of Deng Mu

The time in which Deng lived was characterized by cruel racial discriminations in addition to all kinds of social evils Li Gou witnessed and suffered, so that Deng's social critique appeared more violent and his vision of an ideal society in the future more radical than Li's.

Deng Mu (1274-1306), a native of Hangzhou (in Zhejiang), was born in a family of lower intellectuals. In his youth, the Southern Song Dynasty was destroyed by the invading Mongols. He never served the new reign of the Yuan Dynasty. Withdrawing into the mountains, he lived the life of a recluse. His main writing *The Harp of Boya* was considered by later ages as a book "inspired by a strong emotion which naturally led to radical speeches".[5]

His book began with a violent attack on the tyranny of despotism. "Heaven instituted a sovereign," he stated, "not for the sake of the sovereign himself but for the sake of the people; then why is it that the whole country should support the expenses of this one man?"[6] The sovereigns "become dignitary only by their ranks and honourable only by their positions".[7] "They exhaust all the wealth of the country to provide the enjoyments for themselves".[8] Hence it was the sovereign who was the greatest plunderer. "In case when they were defeated, they were robbers; but in case when they were successful, they were the sovereigns";[9] hence the robbers and the sovereigns were basically one and the same. The sovereign did not come from another world, and in no respect did they differ from the common folk. "The sovereigns do look just the same as other people, so it is within the capacity of everyone to become a sovereign."

Under the tyranny of despotism, "numerous officials, high and low, spread all over the country; they were ever more extorting and the people were ever more suffering".[10] They proved themselves even more mischievous than the robbers, because they plundered officially and legally under various pretexts, "making the people complaining to themselves but daring not to cry out, infuriated but daring not to start a war against them".[11] This was the reason that led to social disorders ever since Qin. That Deng traced back the despotic rule to Qin showed a keen insight on the course of history.

Deng proclaimed that the autocratic monarchy with all its ruthless rules existed only in later ages, and that the case in antiquity was fundamentally different. With this idea in mind he began to describe the antiquity in an utopian hue. He proclaimed that the sovereigns and officials in the antiquity were obliged to assume their offices only involuntarily. The royal throne was forced upon a certain person who could resort to no means to refuse such an obligation. The sovereigns never enjoyed a luxurious life; they were always under the burden of worrying about the daily necessities of the people. It was a time when the sovereign entertained the idea: "The world is in need of me, whereas I am in no need of the world."[12] The sovereigns used to go among the people and to take care of them instead of only promulgating his decrees from the depth of his strictly guarded palace. Under a reign as intelligent as this, the officials were few in number but highly efficient. Everyone earned his living by his own labour, while engaging in different occupations. Since every one was destined to be a gentleman in such a society, so all the people were enjoying their life of happiness and prosperity.

Yet Deng realized that the current social panorama was full of evils and corruptions and the utopia he depicted could only be "floating somewhere in dreamland".[13] As he was unable to find a way out, he was obliged to resort to an anarchical measure of "dispensing with the royal court and the officialdom and letting the world go by in its own way".[14] Apparently, he differed from Li Gou in that he did not lay his hopes in the reforms from above by the sovereigns, nor did he agree with the violent measures of the peasants' revolution. The way out left for him was only "to let the world go by in its own way". Herein he found the last den of retreat for his utopian ideal which was actually no more than the wishful thinking of the weak.

After all, the social critique of Li and Deng with their utopian visions reflected the dissatisfaction and protest of the people against the social realities as well as their longings for an ideal future. This utopian expression of their ideas and ideals signified the progressive current in history. When the historical conditions were ripe for the emergence of the bourgeoisie with their theory of human nature, then Huang Zongxi formally proposed self-interests as the core of human nature. Obviously Huang was in the direct line of Li Gou. But what remained a fancy in dreamland with Li and Deng was turned into the starting point of the Enlightenment ideas of Huang under different historical conditions.

2. WANG ANSHI AND HIS IDEAS OF REFORM

Throughout the long reign of the Song Dynasty, the regime had ever remained in a state of poverty and weakness, witnessing none of the prosperous epochs of Han or Tang. With the centralized despotism strengthened, there came into being a large number of privileged bureaucrat-landlords who with their political status were given preferential treatment by the government as the "official households"; and the burden of taxes and corvées fell naturally upon the landholding peasants and the middle and lower strata of the ordinary (unprivileged) landlords, or the "self-subsistent households".

Once the self-subsistent households were bankrupt under the annexations of the official households or the exactions of the government, they were compelled to seek refuge under the patronage of the privileged bureaucrat-landlords and became their clients who were subordinated to the patrons and hence were exempted from any obligation to the government. Thus there was a strong current of annexation of lands and labourers by the official households. Sou Che, one of the most renowned literary writers of the time, once said of it: "The land of the emperor is now turned into the possessions of the powerful" and "the peasants of the emperor are now becoming the peasants of the wealthy"[15] With their personal attachment to the official households, the peasants under the direct control of the government greatly decreased. This necessarily led to the financial crisis of the imperial government.

Since the strengthening of the autocratic monarchy was of necessity accompanied by the expansion of the bureaucratic group, which in its turn injured the political and economic basis of the state, so the two always went together in an endless vicious circle.

In order to free itself from this crisis, the imperial government had to make effort to maintain the productive forces of the self-subsistent households and to protect them from bankruptcy. This was considered by many as the only way out. Lü Dajun, a noted states-man of the age, once remarked: "For the sake of the nation, nothing was more urgent than the protection of the people, and the essence of the protection of the people consists in giving reliefs to the self-subsistent households."[16] He even worked out a plan for "attract-ing" those tenants attached to the official households by way of "allocating farmland to them so as to change their status into self-subsistent households. And when the self-subsistent households are multiplied, the foundation of the nation will naturally get strengthened".[17] But to realize such a plan, the interests of the bureaucrat-landlords would unavoidably be injured. It was under such circumstances that Wang Anshi proposed his large-scale re-forms.

Wang Anshi's Theory of Reform

Wang Anshi (1021-1086), a native of Linchuan (in Jiangxi), was promoted from a local official to vice prime minister and entrusted by Emperor Shenzong (1067-1085) with the task of reform. Wang's reform, characteristic of the late middle ages, was based on a set of new theories.

Wang claimed that the Tao was the primeval ether which could be known by perception and thinking. From this starting point he drew the conclusion: "There is nothing in the world that cannot be thought or cannot be done."[18] Hence there was always the possibility of change and reform by substituting the new for the outdated. Upon this idea of change and reform, he proposed a series of new laws and new institutions concerning mainly "financial arrangements". Quan Zuwang, the noted scholar of Qing, considered Wang's new laws originated from the *Book of Rites*; and another scholar Cai Shangxiang held the similar view, saying: "Most the new laws of Wang were derived from the *Book of Rites*."[19]

Indeed, Wang himself had annotated the *Book of Rites* minutely as one of the basic readers for his New Learning. But this did not mean that his ideas came entirely from that book. His intention was only to carry out his reform under the pretext that it was in line with "the policies of ancient kings". Actually, he drew from that book only those parts which came to his help for strengthening the centralized monarchy. He pretended to show that his economic ideas were in compliance with the traditional Confucian view on righteousness and utility. So he claimed that the management of financial affairs was a political issue, i.e., a matter of righteousness; or as he put it: "Politics deals with the management of financial affairs and the management of financial affairs constituted what is called righteousness."[20] This idea was amplified in his annotations on the *Book of Rites* which on the one hand reflected the profound Confucian tradition in him and on the other showed his resolution to cope with the opposition party against his reform.

It was not until the Qing period, i.e., almost eight centuries later, that scholars made more truthful comments on his writings. *The Summary Catalogue of the Complete Collection of the Four Categories of Books* had it in these words: "Wang's intention was to make the enfeebled Song regime wealthy and strong; but on the alert of being attacked by the Confucian scholars, he had given strained interpretations on the ancient classics for the purpose of withstanding their criticisms. The fact is that he never believed in the practicality of the *Book of Rites*."[21] This comment came very much to the point.

It was impossible for Wang not to have studied the failure of Wang Mang's reform modelled on the *Book of Rites*. In his reform, he had actually made use of many foregoing economists from Sang Hongyang, Li Anshi, Li Chong down to Liu Yan and Yang Yan (see relevant sections in preceding chapters). He even derived some of his measures from Wang Mang. With all of them, he worked out his new theory and his proposal of reform.

Wang's Economic Ideas and Policies

The main contents of his new laws and new policies consisted basically in preventing the privileged bureaucrat-landlords from encroaching on the land of the farm-holding peasants and of the landlords of the middle and lower strata. In his reform were included the following measures:

> *The prohibition of usury;*
> *Loans to be provided by the government;*
> *Market-control and price-regulation by the government;*
> *Limiting of the amount of land occupied by the bureaucrat-landlords;*
> *More equal distribution of taxes at the expense of the privileged bureaucrat-landlords;*
> *Compulsory military service instead of the mercenary system;*
> *Reorganization of the social units in the countryside.*

The spearhead of his reform was directed towards the annexation of land by the bureaucrat-landlords by giving some rein to their unbridled privileges. By these reform measures, it was expected that the government might have a firm hold of the basic agrarian households under its direct control so as to guarantee the sources of taxation. This was what Wang stated: "Let the power over all taxations and spendings be held by the government"[22] and "let the local incomes be stored in the royal treasury".[23] Undoubtedly Wang's reform, if realized, would effect the protection of the agrarian productive forces.

But the progressive significance of Wang's reform was very limited. Under the feudal mode of production, the development of social economy was always accompanied with its inherent contradictions and its frequent outbursts of crisis. Therefore Li Anshi in the

Northern Wei (5th century) had come to acknowledge that the secret
of social crisis lay in the unequal occupation of land, though he did
not yet come to see that it lay in the landlord ownership itself. Li's
idea was typical of the early middle ages. But Wang was even a step
backward from Li in that while trying to limit the occupation of land
he did not even touch the fact of the bureaucrat-landlords ownership
of large estates and farmlands. Once when Emperor Shenzong in an
outburst of fury was about to apply sanctions against the land
annexation of certain big landlords, Wang even came to oppose it on
the ground that one was powerless to do anything about it, saying:
"Those who are annexing land are all the powerful and the influential.... Now since all legal institutions are still in compliance with the
expediency of human affairs but not in a position strong enough to
check the annexation, I am afraid Your Majesty are also not in a
position to overcome the opinions of the multitude".[24]

Wang conceded that the annexation of land was a *fait accompli*
and the government needed only to ask the big landlords to pay taxes
in proportion to the amount of their land without further interfering
in their land occupation. This was the reason why his reform had
made no provisions for the grant-and-return of land and the maximum amount of land to be possessed. What he aimed at was only to
prevent the evading of tax payments. Thereupon took place the
transition from the idea of a reasonable distribution of land in the
early middle ages to that of reasonable taxation in the late middle
ages. Ever since then, this latter idea had constituted the essence of
the economic thoughts of almost all the statesmen and scholars. This
transition should rather be regarded as a retrogress in the intellectual
history, though it was affiliated with transition from rent in kind to
rent in money.

This was indeed the main cause of the failure of Wang's reform.
The national income of Song rested predominantly on the shoulders
of the self-subsistent households which were divided into five classes:
the upper two classes included the middle and lower landlords (being
called the upper households), and the lower three classes included
the farm-holding peasants or owner-peasants (being called the lower
households). Wang's reform measures were for the benefits of the
upper two classes. Even Zhang Dun, a renowned supporter of the
reform once remarked: "With the new laws being carried out, the old

evils of corvées though eliminated, the new evils of exemptions succeeded to thrive.... "Those who approve the reform are mostly from the upper three households, while those who disapprove it are mostly from the lower households."[25] Su Che also said of it: "The upper households favour it, while the lower do not."[26]

In measuring the farmland, as a result of the corruption of the officialdom and the malpractices, the amount of the big landlords' possessions was greatly concealed while the taxes on the lower households greatly increased. The benefits of the reform fell to the upper strata rather than the lower. It provided no effective means to recover the original status of the self-subsistent household who had after their bankruptcy become attached to the official households. Wang tried to elude the issue at the core, i.e., that of land ownership, but it was just there where the reform suffered its complete failure. Consequently with Sima Guang coming to power, the reform was easily abrogated.

Wang's reform represented the struggle of the middle-small strata against the big within the camp of the landlords rather than that of the peasants against the bureaucrat-landlords. From its very start, it was unfolding in the midst of contradictions amongst the three contending forces: the imperial power, the bureaucrat-landlords and the middle-and-small landlords. What Wang concerned most was the consolidation of the autocratic monarchy of the Song Dynasty rather than the improvement of the daily life of the common folk.

The failure of Wang's reform was also due to his resorting to administrative compulsion in the field of economic affairs. The capricious intervention of the government on economic affairs only helped to upturn the natural order of things. Wang tried to place the government in a position of issuing orders to control the course of events that were beyond the power of human volition, while the fact was that the sovereign was in no time capable of changing the course of things by a mere sheet of edict. It might be said that when the political measure was enforced with no regard to economic laws and economic conditions, it would be doomed to failure, not to speak all kinds of abuses and corruptions that accompanied it. By giving predominance to administrative powers over economic courses, Wang was putting the cart before the horse.

Wang's reform ideas, though not sticking to the age-old conventions, had had little originality of his own and, though absorbing his predecessors into his own system, lacked in theoretical depth. His failure was not due to the insufficiency in his resolution and courage, for he was well known in history as an outstanding statesman who was inspired by the spirit that "heavenly disasters are not so much as worthy to be daunted, ancestors are not so much as worthy to be followed and public opinions are not so much as worthy to be taken care of".[27] But like all reformers coming from the class he belonged to, Wang was entirely powerless to make a shift of the irretrievable decline of the late feudal society and to rejuvenate it. It was just because of this that Wang was unable to confront the historically given situation with any new practical plan. What he could do was only to make a compromise which might serve as an expediency for finding a way out of the entanglement of the current crisis. Later, the reform of Zhang Juzheng in the Ming period belonged also to the same category. It was until the turn from Ming to Qing when the capitalist elements were in germination that new ideas of an Enlightenment genre were given birth.

Polemics Between Sima Guang and Wang Anshi

Wang's reform was confronted by many opponents among whom the foremost representative was Sima Guang (1019-1086), a native of Xiaxian (in Shanxi) and the leader of the conservative party. In the field of historical studies, Sima made great contributions, but in political and economic thoughts he reflected the decadent tendency of the later feudal society. While Wang was resorting to reform, Sima stuck to the convention of the old ways.

The polemics between Sima and Wang reflected not only the different interests of the different strata of the landlords, but also the intellectual divergences within the Confucian tradition.

Among the ancient Confucians there had been those who were for the reform and the renewal, such as the Gong Yang School that placed its ideal society in a golden age of the future, though under the guise of returning to the antiquity. As late as the last years of Qing, the Chang Zhou School and Kang Youwei still succeeded this tradition to which Wang Anshi belonged. Indeed Wang never denied the Confucian idea of "the rule of man", but he laid more emphasis on "the rule of law". Wang represented the active and aggressive aspects of the Confucian teaching, while Sima the passive and conservative ones of it. Wang emphasized the political and judicial factors for a good government, while Sima the moral and ritual ones for it.

For Sima, the Confucian ethical code was what was essential for a lasting reign of peace and security, while the rule of law was only secondary or accidental for a good government. He was of the opinion that the First Emperor of Qin had brought about his own fall by his frequent changes of laws and that Jia Yi and Guan Zhong were but historical personal of the moment's luster. The distinction between Wang and Sima lay in their different emphasis on the relative importance of the rule of man versus the rule of law. It by no means bore the character of the struggle between the Confucians and the Legalists of the pre-Qin period as some people asserted. Both knew well that each of them was a genuine Confucian. In a letter to Sima, Wang once remarked: "[You and I] have often been at variance with each other ... only because the methods we adopted are always different." And Sima in his letter to Wang also said: "Though you and I take different approaches, our main tendencies are always the same."[28]

Within the camp of the Confucians, the rule of law tended to renovation and the rule of man to conservatism. This was shown in their polemics over the relation of righteousness and utility. Sima insisted "the strict discernment between the righteous and the utility", which, however, by no means implied that he aimed at the expulsion of all that was of utility. What he meant was only that utility should never be identified with righteousness and that it was, after all, righteousness that served the basis of a good government. But Wang identified righteousness with utility. For Wang, what was of utility was righteousness and therefore his financial reform was righteous. Sima held righteousness preponderant over utility, while Wang took them as mutual inclusive. The substance of their polemics lay not in the necessity of utility but in its relation to righteousness.

Sima was never ignorant of the importance of good financing. He openly claimed: "The economic life is the key issue to be well treated in the life of a nation.... From antiquity down to the present day, money and food have ever been the cardinal concern of the prime ministers."[29] But he was obsessed by the idea that the material wealth at any given time and place was of necessity to be limited, and it was either in the possession of the people (the privileged landlords) or in that of the government. Hence there was no need to make any interference on it, as Wang did. But Wang was unwilling to give up his view to such a passive position, so he adopted the policy of active interference in economic matters.

Sima did catch sight of the seriousness of land annexation and of the disparity between the wealthy and the poor, but he professed that they were necessitated both by the existing social ranks and by the different gifts of people's natural intelligence. From the stand-point of moral determinism, he took the social inequalities as pre-ordained by Heaven or lot. If people were to insist to change their lots and their positions, then the social order would fall into chaos. For the sake of keeping society in good order, what should be relied upon was the ethical cultivation but not the exactions on the wealthy who were supposed by Sima to be the patrons of the poor and the main supporters of the imperial government. Wang took an opposite view to this, claiming that the financial income of the imperial government was seriously menaced by the increment of the privi-leged wealthy who had to be brought under control so as to guarantee the imperial income and the social order.

Besides the theoretical debates, Wang's reform measures were carried out with much malpractice. It resulted in no success what-soever. Consequently under the fierce attacks of the conservatives headed by Sima, Wang was eventually compelled to give up his premiership. Of this contention first about intellectual issues and then about political issues, there have ever been different opinions and comments. Perhaps it seems safe to say that Sima represented the passive side of the mentality of the declining landlords in the later feudal society. Wang, though active in his reform, could not escape from the fate of a complete failure. But it was rather the failure of the feudal society which was heading towards irretrievable decline than the personal tragedy of Wang himself. Hence the author of the "Biography of Wang Anshi" in the *History of the Song Dynasty* lamented: "Alas, it was the misfortune of the reign of the Song Dynasty as well as that of Wang personally."[30] And Li Guang-zuo in Ming period also said: "It was Wang's personal misfortune, but it was also the misfortune of the Song epoch."[31] These writers seemed to have an obscure presentiment that the failure of Wang's reform was connected with the decline of the Song Dynasty. They touched more or less the social cause of its failure.

3. PEASANTS' REVOLUTIONARY IDEAS IN SONG AND YUAN

With the farmland system of Tang already shaken, most of the land and the peasant households were falling under the patronage of the "powerful people" in the Song period, i.e., the newly arising bureaucrat-landlords. More and more peasants were rendered bankrupt and became their clients or tenants who were attached to the lords and to the land of the lords. The unbearable conditions of the life of the peasants caused a large number of them to flee their home villages to lead a vagabond life. Later, under the reign of the Yuan Dynasty, the Mongol nobilities with their racial discriminations imposed upon the peasants even more backward enslavement. These complicated social contradictions gave impetus to peasants' uprisings of this epoch.

In the Northern Song, there were the uprising of Wang Lun in Shandong and the Huai Valley, the uprising of Li Shun and Wang Xiaopo who once captured Chengdu and assumed the title of kings and the uprising of Fang La in Zhejiang under the religious clock with hundreds of thousands in its armed forces. In the Southern Song, there were the uprising of Wang Chongshi in Jiangxi in the form of the Munist Sect (a Chinese variety of Zoroastrianism), the uprising of Li Dongzhi who fought his way from Jiangxi into Guangdong, the uprising of Zhang Fu under the name of "The Troop of the Red Kerchiefs" in Sichuan and the uprising of Zhong Xiang and Yang Yao in Hunan with a multitude of hundreds of thousands in their army. By the end of Yuan, the large-scale peasants uprisings finally succeeded in overthrowing the reigning dynasty. Suffice it to enumerate only some of the main aspects of their ideas.

The Equalitarian Ideas of the Peasants

The peasants' uprisings in Song had forwarded the slogan: "Equalizing the dignitary and the humble, the wealthy and the poor" and those in Yuan: "Crash the rich to supplement the poor."[32] They did take some measures in getting the farms of the landlords equally divided, but these were only particular cases, not the main stream, Judged by their practices, the equalitarian idea as they understood it, referred primarily to the liberation from the burden of heavy taxes and the equal distribution of the movable properties of the landlords.

Against the heavy burden of taxes and corvées, Fang La adopted the measure of "plundering the wealthy households", while Yang Yao promised his followers: "There will be no more taxes and corvées."[33] They confiscated all treasures and movable properties in the stores of the government and the wealthy households. The peasants' uprisings in late Yuan were everywhere plundering the treasures and granaries of the landlords. From those practices, it might be seen that their equalitarian ideas were basically a continuation of the peasants' revolutionary ideas of the early feudal society without being conscious of the demand of the equalization of the land property itself. Nevertheless, it was a step forward as they linked economic equalization between the wealthy and the poor with the political equalization between the dignitary and the humble, for such definite demands had never appeared in the early feudal society.

Chen Sheng in the Qin period had demanded: "Perchance some day any one of us becomes wealthy and dignitary, let him not forget all his fellows."[34] Compared with this, the slogan in Song "equalizing the dignitary and the humble, the wealthy and the poor" outshone the slogans of the former ages. Chen Sheng, the slave labourer, being not content with his own lot, was longing for wealth and dignity—a fact which challenged the privileges of the wealthy and the dignitary. It was revolutionary in its nature. But it did not aim at the abolition of the distinction between the wealthy and the poor, the dignitary and the humble, nor at equality between the superior and the inferior. In the Tang period, Huang Chao had assumed a somewhat unspecified title: "Heavenly Supplement for Equality" in a very ambiguous sense.

But in Song and Yuan, the slogan of equality and equalization upheld by the peasants' uprisings became a vivid banner of revolution. Furthermore, this idea brought with it a strong lash to Neo-Confucianism which taught that one's dignitary or humble status and wealth or poverty was an outcome of his share (or participation) in "the purity of the Ether" and hence an irrevocable lot. To support it, they had worked out even a much sophisticated philosophical theory. But the peasants with their revolutionary practices taught differently. They claimed that the dignitary and the humble or the wealthy and the poor should and could be equalized. This was nothing less than a severe blow on the Neo-Confucian ideas. It was for this reason that Wang Yangming strongly proposed "to annihilate the rebels within the human hearts".[35]

The shortcoming of all these revolutionary ideas was that they failed to correlate the causes of dignity and humbleness or wealth and poverty to the land property system itself. Herein lay the ideological limitedness of the mediaeval peasants.

The Religious Ideas of the Peasants

It was a historical fact that the mediaeval peasants universally resorted to religious superstitions and mystical forebodings as a means for their intellectual mobilization and revolutionary organization. Fang La professed himself "having received magic spells from Heaven"[36] which foretold that he would become the king, so that he was accused by some of his contemporaneous literati for "alluring the people with magic and mysteries".[37] Zhong Xiang professed himself to be "The Master" and "The Great Sage from Heaven" and his disciples were required to join his sect through a ritual of "worshipping the Master". Yang Yao called himself "The Heavenly Master". In the late Yuan, the peasants' uprising headed by Han Shantong and Liu Futong engaged in esoteric activities under the guise of the White Lotus Sect, prophesying that Buddha Mitreya (the Buddhist Messiah) would come to earth and the Bright King would be born. Along the Yellow River they spread the prophetic folksongs inciting the river labourers to take up arms to rebel, and all of a sudden the long suppressed hatred against the Mongol rulers was fomented. After the large-scale uprising burst out, Han Lin'er, son and successor of Han Shantong, assumed the title of the Small Bright

King who came forth in response to the prophesy.

Apparently, these religious and mystical prophesies served a powerful means to inspire and to organize the peasants, and their leaders always assumed the appearance of a demigod in whom the peasants found their political and spiritual sustenance. In the long course of Chinese feudal society, there had been neither the church nor the systematic theology as found in the West. But there was in China the theory of the divine rights of kings in service of the autocratic monarchy. It was asserted that there were premonitions and forebodings indicating the Mandate of Heaven. The sovereigns as a rule were wrapped up in an inviolable sanctity. This idea was often intermingled with the traditional Confucian teachings and thus formed, so to speak, a specific religion of the Chinese genre. It forged one of the heaviest spiritual chains on the Chinese minds, the influence of which was even more lasting than the Buddhist and Taoist religions.

The uncultured peasants under long oppression and exploitation easily and readily accepted this tradition of the theocratic ideas. In order to realize their own hopes, the peasants during their uprisings would naturally direct their spearheads towards the theocratic ideas upon which the feudal despotism rested. But this was not enough to prevent them from being nourished by the same idea once they came to power. It was but convenient for their leaders to adopt those elements from the past religious sects which accommodated to their immediate needs. They assumed the form of the theological heresies and hid the interests of the peasants under a religious cloak. Therein the peasants would find their own Heaven and their own gods.

Throughout Song and Yuan, the peasants had made use of the names and terminologies of various sects, but substantially all of them belonged to the pattern of ideas as mentioned above. They placed their hopes and faith in their own Heaven and their own Masters of Heaven. It was necessary for them to have their own spiritual forces in smashing the existing theocracy. And it was easy to advocate their ideal of equalization under the guise of a ready-made religious or mystical cloak.

Before Song, most rebelling peasants in taking the religious forms had maintained many of the original ideas and organizations of Buddhism and Taoism. Among them were the Taoism of the Great

Peace preached by Zhang Jiao in late Han, the Taoism of the Heavenly Master by Sun En and Lu Xun in late Eastern Jin and the Mahayana Sect Uprising by the Buddhist monks in Northern Song. Just because of this, the three teachings of Confucianism, Buddhism and Taoism were in the habit of accusing each other for favouring the rebels. But down to the turn of Song and Yuan, the peasants became more inclined to build up their own sects while absorbing the equalitarian ideas from the traditional religions. Hence they were under severe attacks from all the three teachings. This fact showed that the peasants were going ahead on their way of groping about for an independent ideology of their own.

Though the religious ideas served the peasants in their revolutionary organization as well as in their spiritual mobilization, representing their equalitarian aspirations and demands, they could not help from being characterized by the backward elements which in course of time exercised their passive influences on the peasants themselves. In them were invariably mingled the reactionary ingredients which the peasants were unable to get rid of, as shown in the peasants' uprisings throughout Chinese history.

The Imperial Ideas of the Peasants

Many of the peasants' uprisings in the Song and Yuan period had formed their temporary regimes, assuming royal titles and instituting their governments with a system of officialdom and administration. During the time of war, such a kind of regime was in its nature the military dictatorship of the peasants. And what is most noteworthy is the fact that although the peasants advanced their equalitarian ideals, equalitarian social system had never reigned predominantly under their temporary rule. Never had the peasants established a state really run by the peasants themselves. On the whole, there had never been a stabilized regime founded by the mediaeval labourers.

The military dictatorship of the peasants was only a transitory phase in the evolution of their regimes. It was destined either to vanish altogether with their defeats or to transform into another feudal regime after their triumphs. The cases of Li Shun, Zhong Xiang and Fang La belonged to the former while Zhu Yuanzhang to the latter. In the course of his triumphant overthrow of the Yuan Dynasty, Zhu had simultaneously turned the military dictatorship of the peasants into a feudal state apparatus and himself a feudal emperor.

This transformation reflected the imperial ideas inherent in the minds of the peasants. Again, take the case of Zhu. In his youth, Zhu was so poverty-stricken as scarcely being able to keep himself from starving. At the time he was obliged to join the uprising army, one could hardly expect him to have embraced the slightest idea of ever becoming the emperor. Like the multitude in the uprising, he was dominated by the equalitarian idea of the small peasants. But with the ascendancy of his position in the army, he developed an independent force of his own and established his regime, assuming the throne of the King of Wu. It was by this time that he began to accept the proposals of the Confucian scholars such as Li Shanchang, Feng Guoyong and others who advised him to take Liu Bang as his model in winning over the whole country by advocating benevolence and righteousness. Since then, Zhu employed quite a large number of Confucian scholars from among the landlords. With the eventual unification of the whole country, Zhu ascended the royal throne as the first emperor of the new feudal dynasty. And the process of transformation from a peasant regime into a landlord regime was completed.

In appearance it seemed that this transformation was connected with the intellectual influences of the Confucians as well as with the personal traits of Zhu himself. But in fact the very cause of it should be found in the peasants' ideas. Under feudalistic rule, the peasants were no representative of new productive forces, therefore one could never expect them to build up new social orders outside of the old framework of feudalism. And their equalitarian ideals were doomed never to succeed. They were capable of overthrowing an old dynasty, but they were totally powerless to build up a new state in the interests of the peasants. In the history of mediaeval times, there could never have been a government of the peasants, by the peasants and for the peasants.

Since the peasants were unable to form new social relationship, they were consequently unable to form their independent ideology. Their visions were limited by the narrowness of the economy of the small peasants. When under the ruthless oppressions and exploitations and on the verge of bankruptcy, they might be inspired by the equalitarian ideas of the small peasants with the impetus of which they founded their temporary military dictatorship. But once when they triumphed over their enemies, the ideas inherent in the very nature of the private ownership of the small peasants swelled rapidly and then they began to entertain the hope of the benevolent rule of a good emperor. And when a certain stage of historical development was reached, leaders of the peasants like Zhu would naturally become new emperors. The peasants were only thinking of a new patriarch who would bring them refreshing rains. So was the origin of the imperial idea of the peasants.

One should not mistake the imperial idea and the equalitarian idea as contradictory or mutual exclusive. Both co-existed in the minds of the peasants. They manifested the dual character of the mediaeval peasants: their historical progressiveness as well as their historical limitedness. Just because of their progressiveness, they often succeeded in dealing deadly blows at the dying old dynasties. And just because of their limitedness, the peasants' uprisings were either suppressed by the landlord regime or transformed into it. In either case they failed to build up a new peasant regime.

Chapter 16

SCIENTIFIC, HISTORIOGRAPHIC AND LITERARY IDEAS IN SONG AND YUAN

1. SCIENTIFIC IDEAS IN SONG AND YUAN

Achievements in natural science, as the theoretical formulations of human experience and knowledge, signal the stages of development of social productive forces. On the basis of the long development of the early middle ages, scientific knowledge and scientific ideas reached a new height in Song and Yuan. In the Song period, except the world famous inventions of gunpowder, campass and printing, there appeared in the realm of astronomy the earliest written record of the supernova and the star chart; in the realm of mathematics the Yang Hui's method of extraction and the Qin Jiushao's solution of the cubic equation, both being centuries earlier than that in the West; in the realm of geology Shen Kuo's observation of fossils leading to the earliest theory of the evolution of the shell of the earth and in the realm of meteorology Zhu Xi's interpretation of the rainbow and the dew. In the Yuan period, Guo Shoujing and Xu Heng worked out highly precise astrometric instruments, Wang Zhen summed up agricultural technology and Huang Daopo popularized the technique of spinning and weaving. All of them contributed their achievements to the treasury of world civilization.

The advancement of scientific knowledge in various branches of learning paved the way for an over-all speculation with regard to their contexts, and consequently new scientific ideas were elaborated. Thus a new current of comprehensive understanding of the world, natural as well as human, was given birth.

Shen Kuo's Scientific Ideas

Shen Kuo (1031-1095), a native of Qiantang (now Hangzhou in Zhejiang), had taken charge of the royal observatory and had participated in Wang Anshi's reform. In spite of his long service in the officialdom, he was a scientist par excellence of his age. In his later life of retirement, he summed up his life long career of scientific studies in the form of a notebook entitled *Dream Stream Essays* in which were recorded more than six hundred articles of his scientific observations and ideas. This work should deserve to be valued as one of the most precious legacies in the history of science, not only of China but of all the world. So Dr. Joseph Needham rightly called it "the coordinate of the history of science in China".[1]

In astronomy, it was Shen who, earliest in the world, measured the distance between the North Star and the North Pole and explained the cause of the light of the moon as well as of its waxing and waning. In the study of calendar, he eliminated the leap month and worked out a solar calendar with twelve months determined by the solar terms which dated eight centuries earlier than similar ones in the West. In mathematics, he developed the arithmetical series into a higher one applicable to the operation of summation. In geometry, he improved the method of the inquiry on the length of an arc. In physics, he discovered the magnetic inclination (another discovery far ahead of the West), the refraction of light and the resonance of sound. In geology, he found out the phenomena of the changes of land and sea and of the climates on the basis of his fossil studies. The term petroleum in Chinese (meaning literally stone-oil) was first used by him who predicted that it would be the main fuel-resource in the future. And at the meantime, he was also an outstanding engineer in irrigation, armament and some other fields. He was indeed a Renaissance man.

The rich and broad scientific achievements of his were inseparable with his scientific ideas which might be summed briefly as follows:

1. At a time when Neo-Confucianism and other religious superstitions were prevailing, Shen insisted a scientific attitude, claiming that the natural world was dominated by its inherent laws, or in his own words: "The causes of Yin and Yang or the actions and reactions

are all grounded on nature itself and never dominated by human wills.... The changes in heaven and on earth, the climatic variations and the natural disasters such as drought, flood and locusts, are all following their natural laws."[2] As for the causes of natural phenomena, there were the internal (the subjective) ether and the external (the objective) ether which under certain conditions might transform into the opposite side with each other. This caused the various combinations of "constancy" and "variation". The idea that all things followed their laws was the most valuable among the theoretical formulations of his scientific studies.

2. Shen not only acknowledged the objective laws governing the natural world, but also asked people to develop their subjective capability of controlling the objective world, or "harmonizing the subjective and the objective"[3] for the benefits of the people. For instance, agricultural production was conditioned by the climate and the soil, but on the same piece of soil, the manured parts would sprout first; because here "human labour" could effect "the nature of things". Once people came to know the laws of the natural world, they would be in a position to rule over it by appropriate means. Therefore he opposed the passive attitude towards the outside world.

3. Shen studied natural phenomena with a view to their interconnections. As to this respect, his geological research furnished a fine example. It was carried out under the guidance of his keen scientific insight. When he was visiting the Yandang Mountains and holding sight of the towering cliffs, he considered them to be caused by the lashings of the torrents in the valley which carried away with them the muds and the sand, leaving only the tremendous rocks aloft. He then compared this landscape with that he saw on the loess plateau in Shaanxi and arrived at the conclusion that the large ravines and the towering blocks on the loess plateau were "but what happened to the Yandang Mountains (by the erosion of the water) only in a smaller scale",[4] the only difference between them being that the one was the loess and the other the rocks. Once during his travel in the Taihang Mountains, he observed there were layers of spiral shells and pebbles embedded in the cliffs, so he concluded that this place had once been a seashore in antiquity and became a part of the continent only through long years of deposits of silt brought by the rivers. This was the earliest scientific observation on the evolution of

land which dated eight centuries before Lyell and seven centuries before Hutton.

Before Shen, Yan Zhenqing in the Tang period had suggested similar ideas about the fossils of the spiral shells, but they were only capricious imaginations and lacked the scientific depth and exactness as those found in Shen's. Shen also made research on the fossil of the plants. When he travelled in Yanzhou (now within the area of Yan'an in Shaanxi), he discovered fossilized bamboo shoots lying deep underground and reasoned that the weather there had to be much warmer and wetter in antiquity so as to make possible the growth of the bamboo shoots which were completely out of sight in his day. It was also there that he saw the people in the habit of using an inflammable liquid from the underground which he gave the name stone-oil (petroleum), a name still in use at present. He found that petroleum "was stored underground in immeasurable quantity"[5] and predicted that some day it would be in wide use. All this knowledge of his was acquired in close connection with his innovative method of research which marked a significant development in scientific ideas. Ever since Qin, natural sciences in China had made their progress along different and independent branches. Shen threaded them up in the light of their universal connections, which afforded a new approach in scientific thinking and methodology and thus promoted greatly the knowledge of the natural world. Down to the eighteenth century, scientists in the West were still in the habit of taking the natural world as something rigid and invariable, but long before them Shen had already forwarded the idea of viewing it as a process of evolution in which nothing should be regarded as rigid and unchangeable. Such an idea helped to expel the traditional teleological and voluntaristic view out of the natural world.

4. Shen insisted on the view that scientific knowledge was ever progressing with the later generations always surpassing the previous ones. This view was clearly shown in his work on astronomy and calendar reform. The study of astronomy and calendar had ever been at the core of ancient and mediaeval sciences. But since it dealt with cosmogony, it was of necessity concerned with Heaven that in its turn was regarded as related to the divine rights of the emperors who were supposed to be the sons of Heaven and to assume their reigns "by grace of Heaven". Therefore the study of astronomy and calendar

had always been taken as a political matter of the state. Just because of this, every step forward made in this field was always confronted with obstacles from the traditional ideology and even political persecutions, such as in the case of Zhang Heng in Han who, like Copernicus and Bruno, had suffered much for the cause of scientific truth. Shen was no exception to this, but he fought stubbornly to the last moment of his life.

At the age of thirty-six, Shen was appointed to take part in remoulding the astronomical apparatus. In his research on the horological apparatus, he found faults with the old conventions and broke through their confines. In the course of more than ten years' research, he finally formulated his experience and knowledge in his writing *The Horological Apparatus of Xining* in four volumes which "did not follow the line of his predecessors". And as late as Qing, his method was still in use. Later on when he was in charge of the Royal Observatory and presided over the revision of the calendar, he employed the results of his long-time astronomical studies while at the same time promoting young talents to the fore and discharging a group of officials who were superfluous and good-for-nothing. But his measures were fiercely attacked by the conservatives, and his new calendar after being in effect for a short time was eventually abrogated.

Shen never gave up his ideal and faith. In his later years when he was writing his *Dream Stream Essays*, he still prophesied: "Some day my doctrine will certainly avail."[6] His prophesy came true when the calendar of Guo Shuojing in Yuan and that of Taiping in Qing were all based on the work of his. And the modern calendar in the West was essentially the same as his.

Shen firmly believed that in scientific studies the late comers, as a rule, would surpass the old-timers. It was because on the one hand, people's knowledge of the natural world was a process of gradual accumulation and deepening in which no one was qualified to presume the discovery of the ultimate truth, and on the other hand, nature itself was ever changing which could not be foreseen by the previous generations. For instance, the Taihang Mountains once being a seashore became a part of the continent with the climate changing from warm and wet to cold and dry. The late-comers should not lightly affirm or negate the old-timers' achievements at will, but the old-timers had to make room for the late-comers who were destined to surpass their predecessors. This view of his advanced one of the keenest insights in the history of scientific ideas in China which might be compared to Pascal's expounded in his famous Preface to the *Traité du Vide* in the West.

As a scientist of the Middle Ages, Shen was of course subject to the limitations of his own time. He lacked the foundation of scientific experiments for the formulation of his ideas. And in company with it, he had no knowledge of, and hence made no use of, the inductive method so important in modern experimental sciences. His scientific ideas were naive and intuitive in nature, characteristic of all ancient and mediaeval sciences.

Zhu Xi's Scientific Ideas

Zhu Xi was predominantly a philosopher, but as a versatile scholar, he also possessed a wide knowledge of natural sciences, sometimes with penetrating ideas which were characteristic of the interrelations between Neo-Confucianism and scientific learning.

In the main Zhu embraced all the scientific knowledge of his time, especially those of Shen Kuo's. In his writings, those among his statements which dealt with concrete issues in the sphere of natural science were basically sound.

As regards cosmogony and cosmic structures which had always been at the core of natural knowledge, Zhu agreed with Zhang Zai in supporting Zhang Heng's theory which was still the most advanced one by that time. Some of his statements about the universe deserve to be mentioned. Zhu taught that the celestial bodies "are constantly in motion and revolution day and night ... rotate endlessly and rise and fall unceasingly".[7] He took the earth as the centre of the universe, and declared that the earth was formed by the dregs of Ether and was always floating in the cosmos which was filled with Ether all over. It revolved with the revolving Ether and would never cease. Zhu further amplified Shen's view of the relative positions of the sun and the moon as well as on the waxing and waning of the moon. There were, to be sure, many unscientific conjectures in him. For example, like Shen Kuo, he considered the sun and the moon to be ethereal with no substance at all, though with a definite form.

In the sphere of geology, Zhu had proposed some brilliant hypotheses: "In the primeval chaos when heaven and earth had not yet differentiated, there were probably only fire and water. The dregs of the water formed the earth. When one ascends the height, one would find the mountains rising and falling just like the waves of the flood. We do not know when was it solidified, but we know it was soft at first and then solidified."[8] Here his guess was mingled with true scientific insights.

Before Zhu, people like Kong Yingda and Sun Yanxian had talked about the causes of the rain, the dew and the rainbow, but Zhu's interpretation was more scientific. He claimed that the rain and the dew were formed by vapour and that the rain when cooled was turned into snow and the dew when cooled was turned into frost. This explanation distinguished him from those who affirmed that the dew was the ether of the moon and the stars. As for the rainbow, there had been various mysterious interpretations. Some said the rainbow could stop the rain. Shen Kuo even said erroneously that the rainbow could dip into the stream to sip the water. Zhu refuted all these statements by affirming that the rainbow was formed by the emission of the sun-light through the thin clouds and light showers. With these views, Zhu deserved to be ranked among the foremost scientists in mediaeval history, although in the manipulation of his natural knowledge he adopted a methodology of reasoning which fell short of Shen's.

In contrast with the idealist Neo-Confucianists Lu Jiuyuan and Wang Yangming, Zhu did pay more attention to knowledge about the objective world and asked other people to learn it. Consequently in making himself acquainted with the natural knowledge he assumed an attitude more clear-minded and more serious which enabled him to render a more realistic description and explanation of certain natural phenomena than those made by the Idealistic School. But beyond that scope, Zhu identified the idea of the entity of the natural world with the Principle or the Supreme Ultimate. He went even so far as to assert that only the Principle was the substance of the objective world. The Principle existed in itself and was made known to men only through their earnest "investigation of things". Thus knowledge of the natural world was only made to serve a ladder leading to the comprehension of the Principle. The Principle constituted a transcendental world of which the natural world was but a physical embodiment. So for Zhu, it was not the existence from which ideas were derived but it was the idea from which the existence was derived. Reality was reduced by him to a specific function of speculation. It was in this way that he made his natural knowledge serve his philosophical system as a stepping stone. Different from him, Shen Kuo, in formulating his scientific abstractions, never repudiated the objective world in all its liveliness, nor turned it into an absolute idea. In this respect, Shen was much more scientific than his late-comer Zhu.

Scholars who embraced both the Confucian ideals and a wide range of natural knowledge as was seen in the case of Zhu, were not seldom found in the mediaeval history. Jia Kui in Eastern Han had discovered the obliquity of the ecliptic and the change in the motion of the moon and its perigee. Kong Yingda in Tang had proposed an explanation of the rainbow, Lü Zuqian in Southern Song advocated the observation of insects, birds and plants in the light of climatic studies—the earliest phenological innovation in the world. All of them were noted scholars in the Confucian tradition, yet their scientific contributions could by no means be denied. Just as Ruan Yuan, the famous scholar of Qing, said of it: "[The Confucian scholars] either worked on astronomical measurements and computations which were verified at their own times, or wrote mathematical treatises which were handed down to the later generations; and all those who belonged to the Confucian School were generally capable of doing such work."[9] Ruan's statement was basically in conformity with historical facts. Since the economic foundation of the landlords was agricultural production which was in close connection with the studies of astronomy, calendar, agronomy, hydraulics, biology, herb medicine, etc., the landlord scholars as a matter of course often had to pay much attention to them for their own benefits.

In view of this, one can never oversimplify historical truth by saying that the development of natural science was only connected with the advanced ideologues in the Middle Ages and had nothing to do with the conventional Confucians. We should properly acknowledge the fact that many of them did have a good mastery of certain knowledge of the natural world and did contribute their knowledge to the progress of natural science. Indeed, many of them failed to elaborate a more advanced system of scientific ideas. This, however, provides a most delicate and complicated issue in the study of intellectual history which requires further researches.

2. HISTORIOGRAPHIC IDEAS IN SONG AND YUAN

During the Song period, the feudal society was taking its turn from prosperity to decline. In such a transitional period, there were statesmen, like Wang Anshi, who stepped forth with their reform proposals to meet the social and political crisis, and philosophers and ideologues, like the Cheng Brothers and Zhu Xi, who worked out their Neo-Confucian doctrines to remould the ideology of the later feudal society. And there were also historians, like Sima Guang, Zheng Qiao and Ma Duanlin, who wrote their historical works with their views centred on the topic of good or bad governing in history in order to furnish a mirror to the sovereigns who aimed at strengthening the imperial power.

Sima Guang's Historiographic Ideas

Sima Guang (cf. Chapter 16, Section 2), the leader of the conservative party, was contemporaneous with Wang Anshi. When he was appointed to the post of prime minister in the year 1085, all Wang's reform measures were abrogated. And his historical viewpoints were closely connected with his political positions.

Ever since his youth, Sima had been very much fond of historical studies. Later on, under the sponsorship of Emperor Yingzong (1064-1067) he engaged in the compilation of a general history which was given the name *History as a Mirror* by Emperor Shenzong. When Wang Anshi was in power, Sima was relegated to Luoyang where he finally finished his work in the year 1084. It started from the beginning of the Warring States (early 5th century B.C.) and ended with the close of the Five Dynasties (mid-10th century), comprising all the important political events of more than thirteen centuries in chronological order. In the Preface, he confessed: "I have exhausted all my energy in preparing this book."[10] The richness of his materials and the exactitude of his scholarship have been highly praised by all later historians.

The aim of his book was "to collect those facts which concerned the prosperity and decline of the nation and the ease and hardship of the people, with their merits worthy to be modelled upon and their evils worthy to be guarded against",[11] in order the rulers might draw the necessary lessons therefrom. It was due to this reason that his comments on history were concentrated on the criticism of the merits and defects of the statecraft of the sovereigns rather than on the objective laws which governed the development of history. What it was in want of was historical perspective rather than political viewpoints.

The spirit of truthfulness led him to assume a realistic attitude in studying history. In exposing the evil-doings of all the previous rulers, he was almost unexcelled in the history of historical writings. For example, Emperor Taizong of Tang was generally acknowledged as one of the most outstanding sovereigns in history; but in the narration of his career, Sima at the same time recorded the ruthless aspects of his rule realistically. As warnings to the sovereigns, Sima often stressed the fact that it was the political misbehaviours that led to the peasants' uprisings.

Sima was a follower of the conventional creed: "Heaven does not change, nor does the Tao", so that in the course of historical evolution he missed what was essential in its development. It seemed to him that history was always repeating itself, so to speak, in an endless circle, just like the revolution of the sun year after year. The present moved just in the same way as in the past. Since the Tao of Heaven never changed, so the question left was but how to master the statecraft for the sovereigns and how to obey the orders mandated by Heaven. Herein lay the most serious of Sima's shortcomings. For this reason he was handicapped from finding out the historical development in the light of evolution, as did Zheng Qiao.

Zheng Qiao's Historiographic Ideas

Zheng Qiao (1104-1162), a native of Putian (in Fujian), was famous for his life long work the *General Records* in two hundred volumes, a monumental writing of comprehensive historical knowledge which was called by Ma Duanlin "the great summing-up of all learnings under heaven".[12] Zhang Xuecheng, the noted scholar of Qing, said of it: "Zheng's *General Records* excelled in its keen insight in a way unique and unparalleled."[13] In the field of historical writings, Zheng's ideas had made great progress over all his predecessors.

Among the historians of the past Zheng admired Sima Qian and Liu Zhiji for their treatment of history in an unbroken line. He did not appreciate Ban Gu on the ground that Ban's *History of the Han Dynasty* had cut off the thread of historical continuity. According to him, it was only from the general history which covered both the past and the present that one could expect to learn the significance of the causation and evolution in historical events from a historical point of view. Herein showed the keenness of his historical insight. This approach in historical studies contributed much to the progress of historiography.

Before Zheng, Liu Zhiji had stressed the importance of comprehensive understanding for the study of history. But Liu paid his attention mostly to the extensive collection and the careful examination of historical sources, while Zheng laid more emphasis on the full-scale comprehension of history as a whole and the discovering of its laws of change through the causation of succeeding events. Starting from such a standpoint, Zheng went against any record of supernatural or superstitious explanations of historical events in historical writings, such as the action of the Yin and Yang and the Five Elements, the propitious auspices and disastrous omens so frequently recorded in many historical works.

Another noteworthy idea of his was found in his criticism of Neo-Confucianism prevailing in his day. The doctrine of the Neo-Confucianists, he announced, "though sounds profound, is just like to grasp the echoes in an empty valley",[14] and one could never hope to get anything substantial from it.

In his search for causation in the continuity of historical evolution, Zheng was much concerned with the economic life of the society, the treatment of which occupied a large portion of his *General Records*. And his historiographic ideas which was more far-sighted than the previous historians, was carried still further by

Ma Duanlin.

Ma Duanlin's Historiographic Ideas

Ma Duanlin (fl. in late 13th century during the turn of Song and Yuan), a native of Leping (in Jiangxi), continued and developed the historiographic tradition of Du You and Zheng Qiao. Ma's monumental work *General Collection of Historical Documents* covered a span of time from the earliest antiquity to his own age, totalling 348 volumes. He classified all historical events under twenty-four headings: farm rents, grain markets, institution of officials, rites and music, defence and jurisdiction, books and documents, geography, etc. He took Du You as his model but his own work was much more detailed than Du's. It was not a mere classification of historical events, but an inquiry into the causation of historical evolutions and changes with regard to different classes of facts. And in this respect, he was a follower of Zheng Qiao.

In the study of history, Ma gave priority to the material life of the people and proceeded from the economic activities to the political and the cultural. In comparison with Du You's work, the account of royal genealogies and sacrificial rites was greatly reduced and that on economic and political affairs greatly enlarged. This represented a shift in historical viewpoints—a shift which promoted the progress in historiography by attaching more importance to the study of the basic factors in the evolution of history.

One of the novel ideas advanced in his book was his view on the periodization of history. Prior to him, there had been various schemes on the periodization of the historical stages, but he was the first who made the historical periodization in the light of the changes in economic institutions. He proclaimed: "In ancient times, the nation had never been the private properties of the sovereigns, but with the abolishment of enfeoffment by Qin, the whole country was rendered to serve the sovereign in person. In ancient times, the farmland had never been the private properties of any one, but with the abolishment of the nine-square system, the farmlands fell into the hands of the people.... Since Qin conquered the six nations, the whole country was run by an imperial prefecture system, it was then that each inch of land and each person began to be owned by the sovereign."[15] Here the periodization of history was demarcated in the light of land ownership (common or private) and to the nature of sovereignty (by the community or by the royal house). Though still entangled with many conventional ideas, there were nevertheless implied in it some elements which were novel and scientific.

About the history since Qin, Ma paid particular attention to the issue of how autocratic despotism had been strengthened. He found that the ministerial power became ever decreasing in proportion to the ever-increasing royal power. As a consequence to it, the ministers were more and more reduced to the personal subordinates of the emperor. And with it, the ancient "tradition of selecting the good and the talented has gone forever".[16] In company with the strengthening of despotism was the ensuing corruption of the officialdom and the regime. With the whole country becoming the private property of the sovereign, the sovereign was more and more prone to squander all the treasures of the country for his own enjoyment. Under such a sovereign, it became possible for the officials to find their easy ways to high ranks and large wealth. Then the time would come when "the officials treat the people as their preys" and "the people regard their officials as robbers".[17]

In his study of the trend of historical evolution, Ma not only touched the inherent abuses and corruption of the despotism, but also observed the fact that the process of this historical evolution was a necessity which could never be changed or reversed. Consequently, it was entirely impossible to return to the supposed golden age of antiquity so passionately longed for by many scholars. For this reason, although he conceded the defects in the reforms of Shang Yang in ancient times and of Wang Anshi in Song, he nevertheless acknowledged that they were, after all, the appropriate measures to meet the demand of their respective ages which "could no more be ruled by keeping to the institutions of the old". This progressive view of the evolution of history was one of his most significant contributions to historiography.

Ma lived at a time when the course of history was taking its turn from the early feudal society into its later stage. This incited many historians to make efforts to look beyond the narrow scope of a short span of history in their endeavour to attain at an over-all comprehension of the main trends and general laws of the universal history.

Sima Guang tried to draw lessons of the political experience from history for the sovereigns, while Zheng and Ma to find out the rules and laws that governed the evolution and changes in historical development.

3. LITERARY IDEAS IN SONG AND YUAN

Of the fact that literature, as an expression of the social life of the age, consisted of both artistic form and intellectual content, the ancient literary critics were already well conscious. The polemics over the priority of the literary skill or of the Tao, was in reality that of artistic form or of intellectual content. In this respect, literary works were never limited to the realm of literature proper, but always involved the whole range of intellectual activities. So in the Song period, not only literary writers such as Su Shi, but also statesmen such as Fang Zhongyan and Wang Anshi and philosophers and scholars such as Zhu Xi, were all engaging in the discussion on the notion of the Tao. So far as this topic was concerned, literary works were always correlated with political and philosophical implications. Their mutual interactions afforded one of the main issues in the study of intellectual history.

Literary Ideas in Northern Song

The unification of the whole country by the Northern Song put an end to the turbulences of the late Tang and the Five Dynasties, and a centralized autocracy was finally established. And with it there was the demand for unification in the cultural and ideological fields as well. As historians forwarded the theory of the orthodoxy of sovereignty in the field of historiography, so the Cheng Brothers and Zhu Xi forwarded also their theory of the orthodoxy of the Tao in the field of philosophy. Together with them, there was the theory of the orthodoxy of literary writings in the field of literature.

This theory of literary orthodoxy was at first just the same as the Neo-Confucian theory of the orthodoxy of the Tao. In the early Northern Song, Liu Kai, an upholder for the returning to antiquity, once remarked: "My Tao is no other than that of Confucius, Mencius, Yang Xiong and Han Yu, and my writings are the writings of Confucius, Mencius, Yang Xiong and Han Yu." For him, both literature and philosophy originated from the same orthodoxy, so he followed Han Yu's creed of "literary writings for the sake of bearing the Tao". This led to the priority of the Tao—the embodiment of the Confucian ethical code—over the literary art.

Yet there were those such as Ouyang Xiu (1007-1072) who though admitted the orthodoxy of the Tao, made a rather liberal interpretation of it. On the whole, they were more or less against the Neo-Confucian literary ideas which, they claimed, only taught people "to keep silence the whole day long just like a fool".[18] Ouyang proclaimed that literary writings ought to be valued by their social effects. The introduction of this new spirit into literature was in conformity with his reform ideals in politics and brought a liberating effect against the Neo-Confucian restraint. Under the slogan of "returning to the ancients" of the Northern Song, there was indeed a renovating spirit which resulted in two consequences: Firstly, it swept away the florid and ornate style in literature since the late Tang and brought in an air of freshness and naturalness in its stead; and secondly, it tended to reflect the social reality in place of the vain and empty artificiality of the former days. This new spirit was clearly shown in the writings of Ouyang Xiu, Wang Anshi and the Su Brothers (Su Shi and Su Che).

Su Shi (1036-1101, or better known by his courtesy name Su Dongpo), a native of Meishan (in Sichuan), was the son of the renowned writer Su Xun (1009-1066). He was a man with a strong Confucian inclination, but in his literary view he deviated from the Neo-Confucianists and never took the Confucian ethical code as the core of literature. In his opinion, literature consisted in the expression of the vivid vitality of the world in which the Tao dwelt. So the Tao rested nowhere else but in social life. By upholding this view, he kept a distance from the teachings of the Neo-Confucianists. "All the beauty of the landscapes, the simplicity of customs and manners and the legacy of the bygone personages that come to my mind through my eyes and my ears," he remarked, "I'd like to give expressions in my verse."[19] Therefore many of his writings were characterized with a vivid emotion and a broad vision as well as a forcible attack on the social injustices. This was especially so in his early writings. Many of his well-known and often-quoted lines (e.g., "Eastward flows the Great River"—to the tune of Nian Nu Jiao) became the banner of literary renovation against the decadent and ornate tendency ever since the late Tang. And his literary influence was widely spread by his followers, the noted poet Huang Tingjian being one of them. But in his later years Su Shi vacillated between the reformers and the conservatives, and suffered political setbacks. His disappointment was reflected in some of his works in a dejected vein.

Another outstanding figure in literary renovation of the time was Wang Anshi, the indomitable leader of the reform movement. Inspired by his reform ideal, Wang demanded literature to take up its social responsibility of "raising the people out of their bitterness and curing the nation of its maladies".[20] According to him, the function of literature was "to come to help the world", so it "should take practicality as its target" and "should never seek after artificial and florid style".[21] In this exposition of the relation between literature and real life was implied his viewpoint of the relation between the literary art and the Tao. Tao, as he understood it, consisted in the political measures rather than in the exegesis of the Confucian classics as taught by the Cheng Brothers. With this theory he renovated both the idea of literature and that of Tao.

In comparison with Su's, his writings impressed the readers by its more advanced ideas and broader social content. In some of his verses, such as *Thoughts on Current Affairs* and *The People in Hebei*, while describing vividly the sufferings of the people, he exposed before the readers a pitiful panorama of society in urgent need of reform. His literary ideas represented the current of renovation against both the fashion of the ornate style in literature and the Neo-Confucian creed of "literature for the sake of bearing the Tao".

In the history of Chinese literature, Su and Wang were two of the Eight Great Writers of Tang and Song, the other six being Han Yu, Liu Zongyuan, Ouyang Xiu, Zeng Gong, Su Xun and Su Che.

Patriotic Literary Ideas in Southern Song

In Southern Song, Zhu Xi as the dominant figure in Neo-Confucianism, exercised a great influence also in the sphere of literature. He taught that through the proper internal cultivation of the mind, the Principle would be brimming within and literary works would come out by itself spontaneously. The Tao' was the essential and the literary art the subordinate in the same way as the Principle was the essential and the Ether the subordinate. "The Tao," proclaimed he, "is the root of literature and literature the branch of the Tao; and just because it is rooted in the Tao, literature is but an expression of the Tao or the Principle."[22] Literature was thus attached to Tao but segregated from the real life of the people. In the Northern Song, the Neo-Confucianists preached "literature for the sake of bearing the Tao", conceding that the propagation of the Tao was dependent on the literary writings. But Zhu went even further as to oppose this dictum by declaring: "Since all literary writings are the spontaneous outflows of the Tao, how can it be that they are to bear the Tao in reverse?"[23] By stressing the predominance of the Principle, Zhu denied entirely the value and function of literary art. On the other hand, alongside with him there was the Jiangxi School of poesy which indulged so much in the skill of poetic diction as to neglect totally the social reality.

The grim reality confronting the Southern Song regime was the fact that the royal court, small and weak, could hardly maintain the sovereignty over the southern part of the country which was under the constant threat of the Kin Dynasty of the Tartars from the north. Under this impending menace, most writers were inspired by a strong aspiration for armed resistance and their patriotism influenced greatly the literary ideas of the age. They carried on the tradition of literary renovation of the Northern Song, with Lu You and Xin Qiji as their foremost representatives.

Lu You (1125-1210), a native of Shaoxing (in Zhejiang), was never a pedantic scholar of the Neo-Confucian sort. In his middle age, he came to recognize the fact: "When one wants to learn the poetic art, he has to learn it outside of poetry itself".[24] By "outside of poetry itself", he meant social life and activities. He was much inspired by the patriotism of the ancient poet Qu Yuan, and joined the army in the anti-Kin campaigns. His combatant experience gave birth to many pieces of his majestic verse with patriotic ardour. While on his death-bed, he was still thinking of the recovery of the land occupied by the enemy. The active spirit as expressed in his poetic works, was in sharp contrast to the dumb and morbid mentality of the Neo-Confucianists of his time.

Xin Qiji (1140-1207, or better known by his courtesy name Xin Jiaxuan), a native from Jinan (in Shandong) had joined the armed uprisings against the rule of the Kin regime in his native place when still a youth. After coming to the Southern Song, he had, through the long years of his frequently frustrated life, composed numerous pieces of verse of which more than six hundred were handed down to the present day. In his writings, he developed the robust and vigorous tradition of Su Shi and formed his own heroic style of verse, unique in the history of the Song literature. The patriotic excitement in his verse, similar to Lu You's, was a protest against both the delicate and decadent tendency in literature and the pedantry of the Neo-Confucianists of his time.

In the sphere of literary thoughts, Lu and Xin represented the opposition current against the ideological rule of Neo-Confucianism, just as what Chen Liang and Ye Shi did with their utilitarianism in the sphere of social thought.

Anti-Racist Literary Ideas in the Yuan Period

By the thirteenth century the Mongols were arising in the farther north; and after annihilating consecutively the Kin Dynasty in the north and the Southern Song Dynasty in the south, they founded the Yuan Dynasty. Social contradictions were further aggravated by the most ruthless form of racial discrimination and oppression. Against this background, the traditional culture of the nation was seriously jeopardized and a strong anti-racist current was given birth. Many intellectuals did their utmost in keeping up their national integrity and behaved themselves in strong protest against the rule of Yuan. Of them, Deng Mu with his work, as mentioned in the preceding chapter, was an example. The main trend of literary activities in Song was the renovation current to break loose from the restraint of Neo-Confucianism, while that in Yuan the liberation from the yoke of racial oppression. Among the foremost Yuan writers were Guan Hanqing, Ma Zhiyuan, Ji Junxiang and others.

Guan Hanqing (1230-?), a native of Dadu (now Beijing), in his famous play *Going to Conference with a Single Sword* had remoulded the famous general Guan Yu of the Three Kingdoms period into a national hero in whom he found the best expression of his patriotic aspiration.

Ma Zhiyuan (?-1321), also a native of Dadu, in his famous play *Autumn in the Han Palace* described the well-known story of Wang Zhaojun. In the past, Wang was merely treated as a tragic personage being sent to the Huns for a political marriage; but Ma found in her the best model of a patriotic heroine under the racial oppression of the barbarian rulers. In his play, when Wang was on the point of leaving her motherland, she prayed for her and then suddenly committed suicide to show her resolution never to submit to the enemy. The plot was not true to historical fact, but it inspired the patriotic sentiment against the rule of the Mongol regime.

Ji Junxiang (in early 14th century), also a native of Dadu, in his famous play *The Orphan of Zhao* told the story of a righteous man who preserved the descendent of his friend under the hardest circumstances. It expressed the intention of preserving the national strength in its struggle against the rule of the barbarian tribes. The longing of recovering national independence and taking revenge on the enemy by way of innuendo were the prevailing theme of many patriotic plays during the Yuan period. It is interesting to add that Ji's *Orphan of Zhao* when introduced to Europe served as the archetype of Voltaire's renowned play *L'Orphan de la Chine*.

Chapter 17

PHILOSOPHICAL THOUGHTS IN THE MING AND QING DYNASTIES

1. WANG YANGMING AND HIS SCHOOL

From the Northern to the Southern Song, Neo-Confucianism had developed a systematic and highly sophisticated philosophy. which in many ways might be compared with the scholastic philosophy of the high Middle Ages in the West. And Zhu Xi held a place in intellectual history rather similar to that of St. Thomas Aquinas.

Within the camp of Neo-Confucianism, there were the Rationalistic School headed by Zhu Xi and the Idealistic School headed by Lu Jiuyuan. It was upon the basis of Cheng the Elder's teaching: "The scholar should take the recognition of benevolence [i.e., the mind] as the starting point",[1] that Lu developed his systematic philosophy that might be summarized in his well-known proposition: "The world is my mind and my mind the world."[2] Zhu and Lu had held some debates with each other. But compared with Zhu's, Lu's school at that time seemed to be a much smaller one. It was not until the time of mid-Ming that Wang Yangming had perfected Lu's ideas into a systematic philosophy as sophisticated as Zhu's. This school gave priority to the "cultivation of the mind" and was hence called the Idealistic School (literally the study of the mind) in contradistinction with the Rationalistic School of Zhu.

By the time of mid-Ming, with the imperial reign in rapid decline, the political and social contradictions were ever more sharpened. As an imperial official, Wang had personally commanded an army to suppress the uprising peasants. From his personal experiences he came to realize that the uprising might be suppressed for the time being but the seeds of dissatisfaction and rebellion could never be annihilated. Hence he was led to the conclusion: "It is easy to extinguish the robbers in the mountains, but it is hard to extinguish the robbers in the mind."[3] By "the robbers in the mind" he meant what the Neo-Confucianists called "the human desires" previously. And in contrast with Zhu's over-elaborate scholastic way of learning, Wang worked out a more simplified way of thinking by "pointing directly to the mind". It afforded a more efficient ideological weapon which would more readily meet the needs of the time. This explains the vogue of Wang's idealistic doctrine since mid-Ming.

Wang Yangming's Idealistic Doctrine

Wang Yangming (1472-1528), a native of Yuyao (now Hangzhou in Zhejiang), was born in a family of high rank official. He passed the highest level of imperial examination and later assumed the post of Defence Minister in Nanjing (a kind of shadow cabinet in nature). In his youth he followed Zhu's teaching on "the investigation of things". Once he investigated the reason why there were knots on the stem of the bamboos. In front of the bamboos he meditated continually for seven days without being able to arrive at any conclusion, and thereupon he fell ill seriously. Later, he was exiled to Guizhou, because politically he belonged to the opposition party against the eunuch clique in the court headed by Liu Jin then in power. Once in the middle of the night during his exile, he was all of a sudden enlightened by an intuitive awareness that the world was simply within his own mind and there was no need at all at seek the Reason or the Principle outside of it. Thereupon his idealistic doctrine took its definite shape. Fundamentally it was based on the ancient teaching of the Zi Si-Mencius School of "exercising the mind to the utmost" and the Zen Sect's teaching of "instantaneous enlightenment".

The basic proposition of his world view reads: "There is nothing outside of the mind"[4] and "there is no Principle outside of the mind",[5] meaning that everything in the world was but the product of the mind. Once on a trip to the mountains, a follower of his asked him: You say there is nothing outside of the mind, but the flowers on the trees in the mountains blossom and fall by themselves, what relation do they have with my mind? To this, Wang replied: So long as you do not perceive them, they and your mind are both quiescent;

but as soon as you perceive them, their colour and form at once become clear to you; and from this you may come to know that they are not outside of your mind. Such an argument reminds us of George Berkeley's well-known proposition: "Esse est percipi", of which Wang seemed to have provided a succinct explanation almost three centuries ahead. The common sense of everyone taught that the existence of the external world does not depend on human perceptions. But Wang exaggerated the role of human perception to its extremity by taking it as an absolute term. Hence his conclusion that to be is to be perceived—a Berkeleian proposition that predated Berkeley. By him perception was identified with the mind (the cognitive subject) from which the external world was said to be derived. As a logical conclusion, this led to solipsism.

For a better understanding of the role of his theory in history, we may fairly put his question in the reverse way: Suppose there be something, say X, which exists but of which we have no perception at all; then on what ground are we qualified to affirm that this X exists? Is there any meaning at all to say that something exists of which we neither have nor can have any perception whatsoever? In this sense and in this sense only, human knowledge is indeed limited within the sphere of possible perception (or possible experience as Kant held it). Sometimes wrong answers are valuable in that they set people's ideas free from the conventions and prepared the way for the innovated ones. Wang gave the wrong answer, but at any rate his theory lent the issue a depth which was never so penetratingly treated before and without the baptism of which human knowledge could never expect to arrive at a higher level.

What, then, is meant by the mind? Wang's answer was: It is but my spirituality or consciousness, or in other words, the activeness of the cognitive subject. So he asserted: "My spirituality is the ruler of the heaven, the earth and the spirits.... If the heaven, the earth, the spirits and all things are separated from my spirituality or consciousness, they would cease to be. And if my spirituality or consciousness is separated from them, it would also cease to be."[6] Further he went on to say: Without this spirituality or consciousness, who would care how high is the heaven or how deep is the earth and who would care for any fortune or disaster? Hence outside of the spirituality, there would be nothing whatsoever of the external world. It was in this way that Wang interpreted his proposition "there is nothing outside of the mind".

There is still another implication in the theory mentioned above. Not only there is nothing outside of the mind, but the thing-in-itself was the spirituality or consciousness itself. Since both the mind and the external world belonged to the spirituality, so the external world "is in one with me". By this inference, his notion of the things in the external world was thickly wrapped up in all its ambiguity—though his world view basing on the unity of the external world and the cognitive subject far surpassed all his predecessors both in its minuteness and in its sophistication.

With this idealistic philosophy, Wang proceeded to argue that the ethical code was given a priori. The Heavenly Principle was but the Propriety (or rites) or the ethical code which as a transcendental existence was of necessity perfectly good. As for the human desires which were in pursuit of material welfare, they were said not in conformity with the Heavenly Principle. Mencius had spoken of "the innate knowledge" and "the innate capability", and *The Great Learning* had taught "the extension of knowledge by the investigation of things". These paved the way for Wang's theory of "the extension of innate knowledge". The so-called innate knowledge was said to be the Heavenly Principle inborn in the human mind which was perfect goodness without the slightest evil in it. This innate knowledge pervaded the whole world and all things in it. Just because human beings were inborn with this innate knowledge, so they would be moved by compassion when they saw a baby being about to fall into a well or heard the birds and animals moaning mournfully, etc. In this respect, human beings and all other things were said to be in one; for they all shared "the benevolence of co-existing in one".

But many of the human beings, predominantly the vulgar and the low-graded, were tinged with evils whenever their minds were engaging in intentional activities; and this was what Wang called: "The presence of good and evil characterizes the intention in action."[7] In other words, the evil would be present when the innate knowledge was hoodwinked by human desires. Hence in order to get rid of these desires, one had to resort to "the investigation of things". Here by investigation, he meant the rectification; and by things, what was intended, i.e., the desires. "The investigations of things" meant but the rectification of the unrighteous desires. In other words, it was "to extinguish the robbers in the minds" so as to reveal to light the innate knowledge and thus "to unite the mind and the Principle in one".[8] In short, Wang's "extension of the innate knowledge" was a process of self-cognition (or discovery) of the transcendental ethical code within one's own mind.

The extension of the innate knowledge constituted the main theme of Wang's philosophy. But in his early years he had propounded a theory of "the unity of knowing and action" of which a few words of explanation shall suffice. Zhu Xi had once treated this topic without much success. Dissatisfying with Zhu's explanation, Wang manipulated it in his own way. Here what we should keep in mind is the fact that knowledge, for Wang, always referred to and only to the innate knowledge which was self-evident and self-conscious. It was not produced by any practice outside of human minds. And action, for Wang, always referred to and only to the motivation which was in essence the activity of the consciousness. Both knowledge and action fell within the realm of spirituality. For the sages, their intentional activities were in perfect conformity with the innate knowledge, and hence there was in them "the unity of knowing and action". The substance of this theory implied that any motivation not in conformity with the ethical code had to be extinguished in its cradle. By this, the human mind would attain a state "perfectly in correspondence with the Heavenly Principle without the least of human desires".[9]

Wang took the mind, i.e., the embodiment of the feudal ethical code, as the substance of the world. The mind was both the subject and the object of cognition. In this ways, all the contradictions ad antagonisms in real life would be melted in the mind and unified by the mind. When the robbers in the mind were annihilated, the feudal ruling order would secure a lasting stability. When Zhu Xi spoke of the mind, he taught that the Principle was outside of the mind, therefore one should pursue the Principle not in the mind but in things outside of the mind. This would require a rather tedious and over-elaborate procedure. But Wang's teaching sounded easy and ready-made. For Wang, "the mind is the Principle", so one needed not to go a long way but could find the Principle right within one's own mind. And this was the reason why time and again Wang was accused as an offspring of the Zen Sect.

Both Zhu and Wang upheld the basic position of "preserving the Heavenly Principle and extinguishing the human desires" as well as of identifying the Heavenly Principle with the feudal ethical code. Zhu Xi, though advocated the investigation of things outside of the mind, professed that "once an all-pervading understanding will open before us", then "every exercise of our mind will be marked by complete enlightenment".[10] Here his last resort was still the mind (and hence was also accused as an offspring of the Zen Sect). The divergence between the two schools was rather one of methodology than that of the world view. Of this, Huang Zongxi in the 17th century remarked: "Both Zhu Xi and Lu Jiuyuan were upholding the ethical code and supporting the Confucian teachings; both took Confucius and Mencius as their models; even when they held different opinions, they were no more than the different approaches towards the same goal."[11] And Huang's son Huang Baijia likened them to two persons entering the same house through different doors. This judgment holds valid, too, for the divergence between Zhu an Lu's follower Wang.

Wang's Followers and Their Schools

The intellectual influence of Wang Yangming in the late Ming period was tremendous, and it was said there were seven schools among his followers, each with its specific interests. Of them the most prevailing were the Central Zhejiang School headed by Wang Ji (or Wang Longxi 1498-1583) and Qian Dehong (1497-1574) and the Taizhou School headed by Wang Gen. Huang Zongxi said of them: "It was with the emergence of the Taizhou School and Wang Longxi that the doctrine of Wang Yangming prevailed over the whole country."

The Central Zhejiang School was much appreciated by Wang Yangming himself. In Wang's later years, Qian Dehong when discussing with Wang Longxi, formulated his master's teachings in these words: "The absence of good and evil characterizes the substance of the mind, the presence of good and evil characterizes the intention in action, the innate knowledge is that which knows the good and the evil, the investigation is that which strives for the good against the evil."[12] This had been known as "the teaching in four propositions" which was approved by Wang Yangming himself. Though there were polemics over its truthfulness to Wang's doctrine, it was so frequently quoted that it became an authentic résumé of both Wang Yangming and the Central Zhejiang School.

The Taizhou School was founded by Wang Gen (courtesy name Wang Xinzhai, 1483-1541), a native of Taizhou (in Jiangsu), used to be a tradesman in salt. He admired his master so much that after becoming his master's disciple he took the task of spreading his master's doctrine to be his own vocation. On his trip from Jiangxi (where he learned after his master) to Beijing, he professed his master's teaching all the way and greatly promoted the popularization of it. Following his master, he interpreted "the investigation of things" as "the rectification of the self" the aim of which was "to bring security to the people and peace to the world."[13] Wang Gen's disciple Han Zhen preached the ideal of a self-contented life which, he taught, would enable everyone to participate in the nature of Heaven and Earth and of the mind of the sages.

The Central Zhejiang School prevailed among the upper strata of the society, while the Taizhou School was popular among the lower. Just because the latter prevailed among the lower strata, "the peasants, the craftsmen and the merchants, though engaging in different occupations, all came to learn it";[14] so that it naturally tended to be linked with the daily life of the common people. The bounds of the original doctrine of Wang Yangming was largely broken by those disciples of the younger generation, such as He Xinyin (1517-1579) and Li Zhi (better known by his courtesy name Li Zhuowu 1527-1602). Into it were introduced more and more radical ideas, so that the bondage of the traditional ethical code could hardly be maintained any more. This group belonged to the left wing of Wang's followers.

Wang Yangming's doctrine started from those points in Zhu Xi's theory which were logically incoherent or insufficient, such as Zhu's teaching on mind and matter or on knowing and action; and its emergence marked an important stage in the development of intellectual history. It treated in details some of the cardinal issues with a searching insight and an unprecedented depth. For all their mistakes and fallacies, philosophical or logical, many of them had enriched the treasury of the history of ideas; and perhaps no later thinker could ever keep aloof from them, whether he was for or against it. The questions he raised stimulated the development of philosophical thinking in a great variety of ways.

While following Wang in the idealistic study of the mind, people were led more often than not to deny the external authority or dogma. This spirit contributed much to the intellectual liberation from the bondage of the age-old conventions. This was clearly shown in his theory of education in which he advocated educating children with the elicitation method in accordance with their natural inclinations so as to ensure their vigorous growth. Besides, their talents and merits should be induced to develop with a view to their peculiar gifts. Among others, this educational theory of his should be accepted as one of the most precious legacies in the history of ideas.

2. THE PHILOSOPHY OF WANG FUZHI

Neo-Confucian idealism was brought to its culmination by Zhu Xi in Song and Wang Yangming in Ming, and not much room was left for its further development. Since then it was the turn for the anti-Neo-Confucian thoughts to come to the fore. In the Ming period, there were thinkers like Luo Xinshun (1465-1574) and Wang Tingxiang (1474-1544) who succeeded and expounded the naturalistic idea of the Ether. But lacking in theoretical innovations, they were incapable to cope with Neo-Confucian idealism then much in vogue. It was not until Wang Fuzhi and Dai Zhen that new philosophical systems were worked out against the Neo-Confucian current. The emergence of the new philosophies were conditioned by the decline of feudalism as well as by the sharp racial contradictions under the new historical situation.

Wang Fuzhi (or Wang Chuanshan, 1619-1692), a native of Hengyang (in Hunan), joined the armed resistance against the rule of the newly founded Manchu Dynasty of Qing but failed. In his later years he retired to his native place engaging in his writings which totalled no less than one hundred titles. Among them the most well-known were *The Annotations to Zhang Zai's Correct Discipline for the Beginners, Commentaries on the "Book of Changes", Interpre-*

tations on Zhuang Zi, Discourses on Sima Guang's "History as Mirror", Discourses on the History of Song and others. As an advanced ideologue with keen insight and novel ideas, Wang on the one hand inherited the naturalistic tradition from Wang Chong to Zhang Zai, and on the other hand criticized Taoism, Buddhism and Neo-Confucianism while absorbing their rational elements. In his philosophy there might be found a configuration of many of the previous schools.

The ideas of Ether, as is well known, dated from the ancient times, but it was later remoulded and wrought into the Neo-Confucian system. Zhu Xi admitted that the objective world was made of Ether, but he made an abstraction of it into an absolute term and placed it side by side with the Principle or the Supreme Ultimate. The world of reality was unified and governed by the Principle to which all things, as the products of the Ether, were subordinated. In the last analysis, the Principle was prior and superior to the Ether. Before Wang Fuzhi, all philosophers in the naturalistic tradition from Zhang Zai to Luo Xinshun and Wang Tingxiang had failed to render a logically coherent theory in their explanation of the reality by the unitary function of the Ether.

Wang Fuzhi developed Zhang Zai's idea of Ether as the substance of the world as well as his idea that "motion is not caused by external forces". Wang claimed that the world and all things in it were but various forms of the existence of the Ether, so the world was uniform in the Ether and unified by the Ether without which "there would be neither any thing nor any empty void".[15] According to him, all motions and transformations were the intrinsic attributes of the Ether, and "the void is also the Ether which is ever in motion".[16]

The world is in motion by itself spontaneously without being caused by any external force or action. Wang characterized the changes and motions of all things in the world as "the vital evolution through the process of emanative interaction".[17] The term "the emanative interaction" was borrowed by Zhang Zai from the Book of Changes to denote the contrariety and transformation of Yin and Yang. But Wang employed it by lending it a new connotation. By this term Wang meant not only the contrariety and the motions produced thereby, but also that those unceasing motions were simultaneously "the ever renewing transformations" instead of the simple repetition in cyclic movements as conceived by his predecessors. In this sense, it was not simply a process of evolution but a process, so to speak, of creative evolution.

In this unceasing process of creative evolution, "the winds and the thunders of today are not those of yesterday, nor the sun and the moon of today those of yesterday";[18] everything was in a process of ever renewing evolution, always "weeding through the old and bringing forth the new".[19] The world is the Ether in eternal motion in its various modifications, but it was never created nor will be extinguished. With this reasoning, Wang tried to argue the eternity and infinity of the world by the unifying role of the Ether in which he believed to have found a solution for the opposition between what is the particular and what is the universal.

The Ether and its manifold manifestations were in a state of "mutual implications" of the substance and its function. Substance and its function correlate with, yet differ from, each other; and one should never, as did the Neo-Confucianists, "stick to the substance while discard its function",[20] i.e., to isolate the universal from the particular. The Cheng-Zhu School segregated the Principle and the Ether, but Wang held that the Principle and the Ether "can never be bifurcated", "each of them is the substance of the other reciprocally; outside of the Ether there is no Principle, nor is there the Ether outside of the Principle".[21]

In Wang's opinion, the Principle was manifested in the Ether but not independent of it. The two consisted in their unity and the unity consisted in the two. This thesis of Wang ran contrary to that of Zhu who claimed: "The Ether exists in subordination to the Principle."[22] It is interesting to note that this polemic reappeared in a new way at the end of the nineteenth century when the conservative camp insisted that Chinese Learning was the substance which never varied while Western Learning the function which might and even should be implanted in China; but the progressive camp insisted that the substance and the function were inseparable so that one could never learn the function while discarding its substance.

As early as in the fifth century, Fan Zhen had advanced a theory of the relation between the spirit and its form in a crude fashion, entangled with his fatalistic ideas. Later on, the Buddhists had forwarded the contrariety of the subject and the object in human cognition and made their specific contributions to the study of epistemology. But the Buddhists reversed the true relation between them by claiming that the object was derived from the subject. Wang reversed again their standpoint by asserting that cognition on the part of the subject was derived from the existence of the object, or more specifically, perception originated from the combination of the sense organs, consciousness and the object. Hence he proclaimed that the correct cognition dwelt in the conformity of the subject and the object. Over-emphasis on the subjective role in human cognition, he pointed out, would lead to the repudiation of the objective world, that is, to the affirmation of the Principle solely by the mind.

The most outstanding feature of his philosophical ideas was found in his dialectical treatment of movement and motion. Above all, he affirmed that all the movements in the world were "in obedience to the intrinsic nature of things".[23] Both motion and rest dwelt in the very nature of things. And the laws governing them were called the Tao. Most philosophers of the past took the state of rest as the end of all things while motion a temporary phenomenon. But Wang took motion as eternal, because the material world from which all motions came was in perpetual motion but not at rest. Motion succeeded one by one without beginning or end. The state of rest was but a relatively special case in the infinite process of eternal motion. The cause of motion was explained by Wang thus: All things and phenomena were composed by the contradiction of Yin and Yang (or Qian and Kun, the terms being borrowed from the *Book of Changes*) which "interacted with each other through their differences" "with their frictions and lashings".[24]

Therefore, according to Wang, materiality, contradiction and motion, being simply various expressions of the same entity, are all intrinsic in the nature of things. All things are in a state of ceaseless motion which is at the same time a progression from the simpler to the more complicated and from the lower to the higher—a process of weeding through the old and bringing forth the new instead of the mere cyclic repetitions. Hence in the sphere of human affairs and history, Wang also opposed to conservatism and stuck to the view of an ever-renewing evolution. Different from almost all his predecessors, Wang set forth a philosophy unique in the history of China.

Never before had any other thinker carried this line of materialistic reasoning so far and so thoroughly as he did.

But for all that, Wang still belonged to the opposition party of the landlords of the late feudal period when modern science had not yet come into existence in China, therefore both his social affiliations and his historical background had inevitably left their imprints upon his thoughts. He had confined himself so much to the mediaeval pattern of languages and conceptions which prevented him from elaborating an utterly new model of thinking in response to the calling of the new age. For the task of formulating a naturalistic philosophy in the modern sense, he was so much in want of the necessary scientific and logical equipment. After all, he was more an epitomizer of the traditional ideology rather than a creator of the new. It was a historical misfortune that he did his work in an epoch when the philosophy of nature had not yet given birth to modern science and modern scientific methodology.

3. THE PHILOSOPHY OF DAI ZHEN

If Wang Fuzhi is said to have attained outstanding achievements in his philosophy of nature, he appeared pale and weak in his criticism of the Neo-Confucianism. He was unable to break the bonds of the creed of "preserving the Heavenly Principle and banishing the human desires". It was in this respect that Dai Zhen, a century later, became the anti-Confucian standard-bearer of the late Middle Ages. Dai lived at a time when the great turbulences, political and intellectual, were already past and the reign of the Qing regime in prosperity and peace was at its zenith. Like a shooting star breaking the dark night, Dai, with his anti-Neo-Confucian ideas, pierced through the intellectual world and wrote the most brilliant pages in the history of the eighteenth century.

Dai Zhen (courtesy name Dai Dongyuan 1723-1777), a native from Xiuning (in Anhui) was one of the most noted scholars of his time. As the dean of Han learning of the age, he contributed much both to the study of astronomy and calendar as well as to that of traditional classics in the light of phonetics and textual criticism. But the aim of his study was to arrive at a philosophical understanding through the scholarly researches, or to use his own words: "It is to proceed from the words to the diction and then from the diction to the Tao."[25] Therefore among his voluminous writings, he valued most of all the philosophical work of his later years *An Explanation on the Meanings of Mencius*, saying: "Above all the works in my whole life, I take my book *An Explanation on the Meanings of 'Mencius'* as the foremost."[26] Prior to this work, Dai had written a book entitled *On Goodness* in three volumes which formed the archetype of his *Explanation*.

In his interpretation of Tao, Dai surpassed all his predecessors. There had been since ancient times various interpretations of the Tao which constituted a focus of polemics in the intellectual history. Some took it as the noumenon or the Principle, others as the general law of the physical world; but all of them were rather ambiguous as to the relation of Tao with the Principle and the Ether. Particularly, whether the Tao was one and the same with the Principle? or, did the two differ from each other; and if so, in what manner and in what respect? Wang Fuzhi developed Zhang Zai's view, but without much success.

Concerning this issue, Dai elaborated a theory by far superior to his forerunners. In the Preface to his book *An Explanation*, he made the best possible definition of the Tao, the Principle and the Ether by forwarding his proposition: "Tao as professed by the ancients comprised both the Principle and the Ether."[27] Here under the pretext of "the ancients", it was really Dai himself who professed so. According to him, Tao, the source of the world, was composed of both Ether (materiality) and Principle (the laws inherent to the Ether). The relation between them was that the Ether was "the substance of the Tao" and the Principle "its inalterable laws". Hence the term Tao referred to actuality but not to any transcendental spirituality.

Dai went on to explain that since the substance of Tao was the Ether, it comprehended the Yin and Yang and the Five Elements. Therefore the essence of the world consisted in its materiality with all movements and changes in it. So he declared: "Tao is precisely what is meant by motion. The Ether evolves; it produces and reproduces without cease. That is the reason why it is called the Tao."[28] In this way, the Tao was identified with the evolution and movement of the Ether in which was comprehended all that was in the natural and human world. It was by "its reference to the actual objects and events" that the Tao manifested itself; and consequently there was nothing mysterious or supernatural in it. As to the relation between the Tao and the Instrument or Qi (or matter of separate objects), Dai did not agree with Zhu Xi's bifurcation by attributing the one to the transcendental world and the other to the physical. Dai took them as two phases, the one before it taking shape (hence formless and imperceptible), the other after it taking shape (hence with a definite form and perceptible). It was not the difference between spirit and matter or between the transcendental and the physical (which were supposedly segregated from each other).

As to the Principle, Dai claimed: "The Tao reigns comprehensively and the Principle individually",[29] meaning that the Principle dwelt with the concrete laws governing the concrete items. Therefore in contrast to Zhu Xi's assertion that the Principle was superior and anterior to the Ether, Dai asserted that the Principle dwelt nowhere else but in the Ether. As to the Ether, Dai in the main followed Wang Fuzhi's exposition.

Since Tao was but the evolution of the Ether of which human beings were of necessity a constituent part, only of a higher order, so the source of human cognition "rests on the object rather than on the subject".[30] In the process of evolution, the human beings gradually formed their sense organs through which the external objects were recognized by the human mind, so that all knowledge and intelligence depended on learning. This was an antithesis to, as well as a critique of, the doctrine of innate knowledge held by the Neo-Confucianists. The epistemological fallacy of the Neo-Confucianists, Dai found in their exaggeration of the Principle into an independent and absolute existence which was said to be abstract, transcendental and omnipresent. But the truth, he urged, was that the Principle (the transcendental world) always went along with the Ether (the physical world) and could never be in any way segregated from it. With this, Dai hinted the earliest idea of modern philosophy in its germination by pointing out that all epistemological fallacies were the offspring of a partial exaggeration of one aspect of human cognition.

The most brilliant components in Dai's thoughts were his social and ethical views which carried on the Enlightenment spirit of the early seventeenth century (at the turn of Ming and Qing) and launched the sharpest critique on the Neo-Confucian doctrine of the opposition and antagonism of the Heavenly Principle and human desires. Dai worked out his theory of human nature by turning the table on the Neo-Confucian creed of "preserving the Heavenly Principle and extinguishing the human desires".

Men, proclaimed Dai, were born with desires which were the natural expressions of human nature and could never be dispensed with. The material desires in daily life were natural demands of men which, far from being evils (as taught by the orthodox Neo-Confucianists), were goodness so far as they were rightfully handled. To satisfy human desires to the optimum was the ideal of benevolence. Natural desires could not be suppressed nor extinguished, and what made up evils was only its improper exercises which led to selfishness, ignorance and partiality. So the question lay only in how to adjust them to the best possible accommodation with nature; and this meant no other than the Principle itself. In other words, human desires were but the constituent parts of the Principle in its natural development which embodied itself in the demands of the people in their daily life and no more than that. So Dai blamed the Cheng-Zhu School for "talking idly about the principle, regardless of the human beings".[31] This was the main argument of his anti-Neo-Confucian theory. In the elaboration of this theory, he divided human nature into three categories, i.e., intelligence, emotion and desire—a classification which predated Kant's (in the beginning of his *Critique of Judgment*) half a century.

The Cheng-Zhu School bifurcated human nature into the nature of the Principle and that of the Ether (or temperament). They preached moral obligations apart from natural desires. Dai conversely affirmed that all moral obligations drew their origin from natural desires, and refuted the Neo-Confucianists by asking: "Without desire and without motivation, how can there be any Principle?"[32] Hence the Way (or the Tao) of the sages "lay precisely in the maximum satisfaction of human desires" so as "to enable all people to enjoy life".[33] With arguments like these, Dai was drawing near to the proposition of modern times: The "greatest happiness of the greatest number" as enunciated by Jeremy Bentham and others. In all these, there shine the sparkles of the ideology of modern times in its embryo, though still wrapped up in mediaevalistic terminology.

To him, the Neo-Confucianist creed of "preserving the Heavenly Principle and extinguishing the human desires" was exactly against both the Heavenly Principle and the human desires; it was but the age-long Buddhist selfishness under a new dress with the aim "to satisfy their own selfishness by extinguishing the desires of others".[34] Under their Principle against human desires, "the dignitary exacted the obedience of the low-graded with the Principle"; and the outcome of it was to enable the dignitary "to throw all the restraints on their greeds to the wind, and to do what the robbers do", and "all the country would become the victim of it".[35] When the people were suffering, Dai went on to argue, even on the verge of death, the Neo-Confucianists would come forth to blame them that their demands were all human desires that ought to be utterly extinguished. And he raised his protest bitterly: When people died under the swords, they were pitied by others; but when they died under the Principle, who would come to have pity on them? The Neo-Confucianists, he pointed out, "are murdering the people with their Principle". So he advocated the slogans: "Comply with the emotions of the people" and "satisfy the desires of the people"[36] as his creed against the Neo-Confucian preachings.

So fiercely and firmly was his challenge to the Neo-Confucianism that just one month before he deceased he still openly declared that he was "completely at variance [with the Neo-Confucianism] and has nothing in common with it in the slightest degree". His clear-cut stand as well as his penetrating theory marked a new height of the anti-feudalistic spirit with its faint tincture of modern ideology. In this respect he was indeed the worthy forerunner of the modern spirit in China.

Chapter 18

POLITICAL AND SOCIAL THOUGHTS IN THE MING AND QING DYNASTIES

1. HUANG ZONGXI AND TANG ZHEN

Among the advanced ideologues of the early Enlightenment at the turn from Ming to Qing, the most famous were Huang Zongxi, Gu Yanwu, Wang Fuzhi, Fang Yizhi, Tang Zhen, Yan Yuan, Li Gong and others. Their ideas were much varied and their intellectual interests were directed each to his own specific field. Wang Fuzhi characterized himself in the field of philosophy; Gu Yanwu in that of academic researches, Yan Yuan and Li Gong in that of practicality, and Huang Zongxi and Tang Zhen in that of political and social theories.

Huang Zongxi's Enlightenment Ideas

Huang Zongxi (1610-1695), a native of Yuyao (now Hangzhou in Zhejiang), was born in a family of bureaucrats. In his youth he took part in the activities of the Fu She, an association of the progressive intellectuals in succession of the Dong Lin as an opposition party against the eunuch clique then in power. After the downfall of the Ming Dynasty, he organized an armed resistance against the Qing regime, but failed. In his later years he retired to the countryside as a recluse engaging in his writings among which were the well-known *School of the Ming Philosophers* and *A Treatise on Government and Politics* (literally *The Dawn of Good Politics Awaiting Inquiries*), the former being generally acknowledged the best work on the intellectual and philosophical history and the latter a concentrated exposition of his progressive social and political ideals.

His Enlightenment ideas were directed predominantly against

autocratic despotism, attacking severely the theory of the divine rights of sovereigns. The keynote in his theoretization was his conception of human nature that human beings were by nature self-interested and self-profiting; thus he argued "in the beginning, every one was self-interested and self-profiting" and even the sages were no exception to this trait "which was universally valid for every one".[1] It was upon this individual self-interest that the public interest of the community had come into being. Then there was the need of someone to take care of the community. This was the origin of the sovereign and the sovereignty. So in the antiquity, held he, the sovereigns were but public servants.

But in course of time, the individual self-interests of the sovereigns were step by step differentiated from that of the public; and then the sovereigns began to take the whole community or the nation under their rule as their private properties which were turned to be inherited. Then it happened that people began to compete for the throne of the sovereign. This was the origin of all kinds of evils and disasters, social and political. Not only the ambitions and luxuries of the sovereigns had to be satiated at the burden of the whole country, but also the laws which were at first instituted for the purpose of harmonizing the public interests and welfares were turned into the personal decrees of the sovereign himself. Since these personal decrees ran contrary to the nature of laws, they were but the "unlawful laws" or "lawlessness", the consequences of which could be no other than abuse, corruption and all that sort of things. Huang was dauntless enough to raise the question: "Is it that the heaven and the earth with all their magnitute are destined only in favour of one person or one family among all the people?"[2] In a society in which all were under the absolute power of the sovereign, Huang's doctrine appealed to the intellectual circle like a thunder heralding the coming of a new age with his brand-new ideology.

What struck the readers most was the fact that the standpoint from which he started differed at the bottom from nearly all the previous ones. Prior to him, there had been many descriptions of the enchantingly intelligent rules in the antiquity. But all of them founded their ideals on the supposition that men were born altruistic, as we might see from the *Book of Rites* to the wide-circulated stories of the *Peach Bloom Stream* and the *Land of Gentlemen*. At variance with all of them, Huang held that men were by nature self-interested. Just because the sage-kings of antiquity took into account the self-interests of everyone, they were capable of bringing about their golden rules. This theory of Huang anticipated clearly the ideology of the emerging bourgeoisie in their embryo. In the past, critiques of feudalism were confined to the sphere of social evils and political abuses, but Huang directed his critique directly on the sovereign and his despotism. In questioning the legitimacy of the despotic autocracy, Huang dealt a fatal blow on the traditional Confucian teaching of the divine rights of the sovereigns. His viewpoint that the sovereign was originally one from among the populace was signalling the idea of equality of the bourgeoisie. In these respects, Huang was the representative of those advanced ideologues trying to break the madiaeval traditions.

The germination of the bourgeois ideology was shown still more clearly in his design for a new society to come in which the political institutions and social orders were based on the inviolability of the individual rights. First of all, he demanded that the legislation should serve for the nation instead of the royal house ("one family"). Once the rule of law was instituted, all the administration should be handed over to a "Council of the State", more or less a sort of modern responsible cabinet, under the titular reign of an emperor. Alongside with the administration, there should be instituted an advisory and supervisory organ by the name of "School", more or less akin to the modern parliament, to which the premiers were obliged to render reports and to subject to questions regularly. The emperor, the premier and the ministers were all the pupils of the master of the "School" who was endowed with the right to make frank critiques of them. So was it also in all localities. The districts and prefectures were given the right to rule over their own affairs, more or less in a fashion akin to modern federalism. All the officials and bureaucrats should be educated by the School in which practical courses were required such as military science, mathematics, medicine and others. As to the selection of personnels, he advised the principle of "liberal in enrolling but strict in assessment",[3] meaning that all who were gifted with specific abilities should be enrolled, but in appointing them to official posts they had to undergo a procedure of strict check and examination beforehand.

In the economic field, Huang advocated the measure of distributing farmland to the peasants with the ownership remaining in the hands of the state, while the surplus land was left to the free occupation of "the rich people". The most noteworthy in his economic ideas was his advise of "taking the crafts and the commerce as the essential".[4] He proposed to issue a unitary currency and to institute a national bank in control of the currency. In military sphere, he advised the system of compulsory service instead of the conventional mercenary system.

All these visions of his for a future society reflected not only his critical spirit against feudal despotism at its very root, but also an obscure longing for a bourgeois republic. In spite of all the antique form of language he made use of, he was, after all, the foremost representative of the naive ideas of the emerging bourgeoisie; and his theory served as the starting point of modern ideology in China. Within the ideological dungeon of mediaeval despotism, it threw a new light on the coming of a new age. His ideas based on the "sacro egoism" of human beings and his stress on the rule of the law heralded the theory of natural rights of modern times. His *Treatise on Government and Politics* predated John Locke's *Two Treatises of Government* by half a century and Rousseau's *Contract Social* by a whole century. It is interesting to note that both Huang's book and Rousseau's had given an immense intellectual impetus to the democratic current of the late 19th and early 20th centuries in China —from the Reform Movement of 1898 to the Revolution of 1911. the proposal of "a republic under the titular reign of the emperor" which Kang Youwei and Liang Qichao advanced was a reprint of Huang's idea, and in the same way the Provisional Constitution of 1912 was modelled upon Rousseau's theory of natural rights.

In Huang's later years, the Qing regime was gradually stabilized. Under the high pressure of its intellectual despotic policy together with its large-scale literary inquisitions and its veneration of the Neo-Confucian orthodoxy, the high-tide of the Enlightenment current during the turn from Ming to Qing was then drawing to a close. But there were still persons in succession of this progressive tradition among whom the most salient figure was Tang Zhen who was twenty years Huang's junior.

Tang Zhen's Enlightenment Ideas

Tang Zhen (1630-1704), a native of Dazhou (in Sichuan), was known by his life-long work *The Hidden Book* in which he launched his critique on feudal despotism much more radically than Huang. Tang pointed out: "The emperors with all their dignities are not in any way superhuman, they are after all but human beings."[5] He then went on to assert that the emperors were not the common folk but robbers: "Ever since Qin, all the emperors have been robbers....[6] They have murdered [the people] for two thousand years without a pause."[7] He argued with an analogy like this: If one was murdered on the way, his possessions being plundered, all others would unanimously demand the punishment of the robbers. But the fact was just that the emperors were murdering the people and plundering their possessions. What cruelty and suffering they would bring on the people and render them miserable only for the squanderings and enjoyments of the emperors themselves? Hence the real robbers were no other than the emperors.

Tang came to the conclusion that few of the despots were really good or intelligent, proclaiming that "of all the royal dynasties, the well-ordered reigns numbered only one or two out of ten, while the other eight or nine were all disordered"; so "in each dynasty in the course of dozens of reigns, good rulers were but rare" and in most cases the emperors were "either tyrannic or ignorant".[8] The sources of all these evils lay in the despotic rule of the emperors. "Millions of people within the realm are under the control of one man; if he happens to take good care of them, they might be leading a peaceful life; but if he does not, then they are doomed to perish",[9] so that "it is left only to the emperor to run the nation in good order, and it is left only to the emperor alone to run the nation in disorder".[10] But unfortunately all the emperors were blind and deaf, because as a rule they were "up on high and far from the masses". When the emperor on high "reigns over ten people", his intelligence would be sure "below the general level of that of the ten"; and when he "reigns over the whole nation", his intelligence would be sure "below the general level of that of the whole nation".[11] Consequently it was seen that the emperors were destined to be much inferior to the common folk.

In Tang's view, the evils inherent in despotism was due to the fact that what the emperors did always ran counter to human desires. But different from Huang, Tang took the human desires as the essence of human nature which Huang identified with self-interests. Huang considered that men were born self-interested and therefrom derived his conception of natural rights, whereas Tang taught that men were born with desires and therefrom derived his idea of equality which came very near to the modern sense of the word. In his demand of equality—"equality is the way of the world",[12] were included that between men and women as well as that between different classes and strata. For the satisfaction of the human desires of all people, he advised the rulers to lend their ears to public opinion, claiming that "with public opinion in mind when making plans, all plans will accommodate to the circumstances appropriately; and with public opinion in mind when acting, all actions will suit the cases properly."[13] According to him, public intelligence was the most reliable guide which was in its turn conditioned by public desires, the relation between them being that public desires could only be best satisfied by developing public intelligence to its fullest.

As to the wealth of the nation, Tang advocated to have it stored among the people instead of being kept in the royal treasury or in the rich and dignitary households. The vocation of the officials and bureaucrats was "to nourish the people", and it was with reference to their achievement in this respect that their merits and defects should be judged. By the notion of "the people", Tang referred primarily to the craftsmen and merchants who were, generally speaking, the predecessors of the modern bourgeoisie. For the benefits of them, Tang stressed that wealth should be encouraged to circulate in the market rather than to be accumulated and stored up in the royal treasury as all the emperors had been so often prone to do. This idea was also an obvious reflection of the characteristic feature of the modern bourgeoisie. Tang advised a laissez-faire policy in economic affairs by which, he contended, the society might be enriched "tenfolds" or even "hundredfolds". It would benefit both the rural and the urban areas. He was so persuasive with his economic views and policies that he should rightfully by regarded as one of the foremost representative in calling the bourgeois society to come, though, like Huang Zongxi, still in a very crude and naive form. Above all, both of them did bring forth in the late mediaeval times a set of novel ideas completely new which signalled the advent of a new historical age.

As to the constitution of the state, Tang did not propose straight-forwardly the abolition of the monarchy, but he did advise the adoption of a responsible cabinet under the reign of a titular emper-or, proclaiming: "When the state is run by an intelligent premier, there will be of certainty a wise rule of the law and an honest practice of jurisdiction."[14] His proposal resembled that of Huang Zongxi's Council of the State, and both of them conceived the state and the government in the light of the germinal bourgeoisie.

2. GU YANWU, YAN YUAN AND LI GONG

The ideas of Gu Yanwu, Yan Yuan and Li Gong were charac-terized by their practicality which was affected by the reaction against the ruling ideology of the orthodox Neo-Confucianism. And Gu's methodology in academic research directly contributed to the formation of the eighteenth century Han learning.

Gu Yanwu and His Doctrine

Gu Yanwu (courtesy name Gu Tinglin 1613-1682), a native of Kunshan (in Jiangsu), had in his youth witnessed the historic catas-trophe of the downfall of the Ming Dynasty and the rise of the Qing Dynasty of the Manchus. With ardent patriotism he participated in the armed resistance movement in the south of Yangtze valley against the rule of Qing. After the defeat of the resistance movement, he travelled widely through the whole country, devoting himself to academic investigations and studies. The Qing regime had induced him to join the government but he refused to stoop.

Deeply grieved with the downfall of the Ming Dynasty, Gu studied the social evils, political corruptions and intellectual deca-dence of his day through his personal experiences. He thought that the Idealistic School of Wang Yangming had helped to cause the ruin of the Ming Dynasty both by its emptiness and impracticability and by its vanity. It neglected the real problems of the day and the sufferings of the people. On the basis of his academic researches as well as of his social investigations, he strongly demanded social reforms and the free expression of public opinion about political affairs. He favoured the practice of bestowing political powers to the local authorities instead of the imperial centralization. In economic affairs, he advocated the making of an all-round plan for both the national expenditure and the people's livelihood against the one-sided view of increasing the royal income. Priority should be given to the wealth of the people rather than to the wealth in the imperial treasury. He stressed the study of irrigation for agricultural production and the necessity of alleviating the over-exploitation of the people. All these showed the democratic elements in his thoughts. But his basic position was: "It is in the unchanging that changes reside",[15] or in other words, reforms should be carried out only within the boundary of not changing the feudalistic system. In this respect, he lagged behind the Enlightenment ideas of his contemporary Huang Zongxi.

To reform the corrupted society, Gu asked for a change of the prevailing social manners and customs. With this in view, he advocated learning for the sake of practicality. Against Wang Yangming's thesis "the mind is the Principle", Gu proposed: "The study of the ancient classics is the study of the Principle."[16] (The study of the Tao is generally translated as Neo-Confucianism, but it is also known by the term "the study of the Principle"). In Gu's opinion, the study of classics should chiefly concern with the political and economic problems of the day in which the study of the Principle should reside. Gu also discussed the mind, saying "the Principle resides in my mind";[17] but what he really meant was only that human understanding (the Principle in the mind) should be verified by "the test of things and events".[18] Here Gu remoulded some of Zhu Xi's ideas which he often mentioned in his works. And his notion of "the tests of things and events" was in the main drawn from the utilitarian teachings of Chen Liang and Ye Shi. In explaining "the investigation of things for the extension of knowledge" in the text of *The Great Learning*, he taught that the "things" here referred predominantly to "the task of top priority" and he asked the learners to put their knowledge into practice.

In his academic works, Gu had advanced many novel ideas. Firstly, he maintained that all kinds of learning should be aimed at the learner's own understanding in his own view instead of a mere copy of the ancients. And the study of ancient classics should be aimed at their practicability to meet the present reality. It should never be the ancient products dished up only in a new form. Secondly, he demanded broad collection and research on evidence and verification both in books of the ancients and through the test of the social realities. He insisted his scrutinizing and critical studies with all possible evidence, positive as well as negative, against the blind followers of the ancients and all kind of their subjective conjecture. This academic discipline together with his emphasis on the importance of practicability pointed to a new direction in the academic world of the Qing period.

Yan Yuan and Li Gong

Yan Yuan (1635-1704), a native of Boye (in Hebei), in his stress of practicability and in his critique of Neo-Confucianism, was even more radical than Huang Zongxi, Gu Yanwu and Wang Fuzhi. Gu and Wang still retained parts of the Cheng-Zhu Rationalistic Neo-Confucianism and Huang parts of Wang Yangming's Idealistic Neo-Confucianism; but Yan denounced bitterly all Neo-Confucianism without exception. He declared that both schools of the Neo-Confucianism were just "playing games with empty conceptions" and belonging to the sort of learning of "killing the people".[19] They talked idly about the mind and human nature, leading people to exhaust their whole life in it without any use to society. It was but a "void learning" in which "empty words followed one after another and written papers accumulated page after page".[20] Yan taught that the Heavenly Principle was no other than the principle (or reason) of the external world which had nothing to do with any transcendental ethical code in eternity. The Principle resided exactly in concrete things outside of which one could never hope to find any other principle.

A widely circulated story may help to show his ideological features. Once in a discussion with a Buddhist monk who boasted to Yan the Buddhist teachings in lavish talks, Yan refuted him by saying: The Buddhist teaching, say what you may, falls short of the way of women. Upon being asked by the monk what was meant by the way of women, Yan replied: Sakyamuni, the founder of Buddhism, had not only a father but also a mother; if you had only a father but no mother, then wherefrom could you ever come into this world? Therefore without the way of women, there could be no Buddhism at all. Thereupon the monk bent down his head. While openly ridiculing the sanctity of the Buddhist religion, Yan declared that the clerical life of the monks was against human nature. He advised the monks to return to secular life and thereby to human nature.

Against "the void learning" of Neo-Confucianism, Yan advanced "the practical learning" in which, he claimed, the true function of the Six Liberal Arts of Confucius dwelt. Learnings should never be segregated from the reality, just like playing a harp, one could never know how to play it by simply reciting the musical notes instead of playing it oneself over and over again. What one learned had to be put to the test of practice. Yan lived at a time when modern science and industry were still beyond the vision of the Chinese scholars, so it was no wonder that in searching for practical learning Yan turned his eyes to the traditional Six Liberal Arts. The only language he could make use of was still the traditional language.

After the downfall of the Ming Dynasty, Yan refused to submit to the new regime of Qing and led a life of lecturing in his native place. Among his disciples the most noted was Li Gong (1659-1733), a native Lixian (in Hebei), and hence their school was known as the Yan-Li School. Sometimes Yan still resorted to the authority of the ancients such as the Duke of Zhou and Confucius, but Li definitely proposed: "There is no need to follow the steps of the ancients."[21] Li taught that the first thing a benevolent government should do was the equalization of land property so that all tenant farmers might have their own land. He proposed to adopt the measure of election of the officials by way of which the low-graded might be duly and equally eligible for being elected. Li was already aware of the fact that science and technology in China was lagging behind the West, so he demanded "to absorb the Western methods of the age"[22] and to break the narrow bonds of racial prejudice.

In his later years, under the influence of Yan Ruoqu and Mao Qiling, Li gradually turned away from the path of practicality as taught by his master Yan as well as from the radical ideas of his early years, and took refuge in the study of classical criticism once so severely condemned by his master Yan. This intellectual transformation of Li was no isolated phenomenon of the age. His later years were approaching the reigns of Qianlong (1735-1796) and Jiaqing (1796-1820), commonly known as the epoch of Qian-Jia, when the academic spirit and interests were turning away from the height of the Enlightenment of the seventeenth century to the era of the over-elaborate pedantry of textual criticism of the eighteenth century, or the era of Han learning of which Li afforded one of its earliest examples.

3. THE HIGH TIDE OF HAN
LEARNING IN THE QING PERIOD

The textual criticism of the ancient classics, especially in the Qian-Jia epoch, was generally known by the name of Han Learning. Its origin might be traced back to Gu Yanwu and it closely synchronized with the beginning of modern times, that is, from the late 17th century to the mid-19th century. Owing to its enduring and wide-spread influence, it was often juxtaposed with Neo-Confucianism in the intellectual history as the two main currents in academic disciplines: the Han Learning and the Song Learning.

With the germination of the capitalist elements in the late Ming period, there emerged the earliest ideology with a visible bourgeois tendency. This was followed by the great peasants' uprisings of Zhang Xianzhong, Li Zicheng and others, and later the founding of the new dynasty of Qing by the Manchu. The whole nation experienced a catastrophe of what Huang Zongxi called "the heaven broken and the earth collapsed".[23] In close connection with the sharpest and the most complicated social and political struggles, stepped forward a group of the early Enlightenment ideologues like Huang Zongxi, Gu Yanwu, Wang Fuzhi and others who were all prominent scholars in the field of classical studies. But the classical studies had never been the aim of their academic research. They were inspired by a much higher ideal and a much broader vision, aiming at the betterment of the whole society through the practicality of their academic learning. For this reason, their academic researches were subordinate to a higher level of intellectual activity and did not belong to the proper realm of Han learning in the strict sense.

Later in the Qian-Jia epoch, the cultural and intellectual despotism of the Qing regime was strengthened and the imperial rule stabilized. Anti-Qing currents were gradually sinking low. The royal court had repeatedly carried out literary inquisitions, and at the same time tried hard to attract many recluse scholars from among the people to the capital to write a history of Ming and to take part in the compilation of the *Complete Collection of the Four Categories of Books*. The scholars were thus being drawn further away from social realities and political struggles. They were more and more attracted to engage their energies in classical studies, their patriotic ardour being melted and their aspiration for practicality vanished. It was upon this historical background that Han learning became the main academic concern and activities of the age.

This textual criticism of the ancient classics was called Han learning because it started with the opposition to the emptiness of Song Learning (Neo-Confucianism). Still in the late Ming, the Idealistic School of Wang Yangming was already blamed for being abstruse and mysterious with a ruinous effect both on the social customs and on the academic discipline. Some scholars turned away from Wang Yangming to Zhu Xi who at any rate taught people to study and to investigate all things in the external world and looked more realistic than Wang. But others came forth to oppose Zhu, blaming Song Learning too for being void and useless, because Zhu's doctrine came to no help to the disasters of his time. It was then Han learning, i.e., the phonetic and textual criticism on ancient classics by Xu Shen, Cheng Xuan and other Han scholars who came to their stead. As mentioned above in Part Two, there were in the Han period various schools contending one another. It was only the habit of the Qing scholars to call the classical criticism of Xu and Zheng the Han learning in contrast to the philosophical speculations of the Song (Neo-Confucianist) learning.

The two predominant schools of Han learning were the Suzhou School headed by Hui Dong and the Anhui School headed by Dai Zhen with whose ideas we have dealt in the preceding chapter. Of the two, the more influential was the Anhui School with Dai and his disciples Duan Yucai, Wang Niansun and his son Wang Yinzhi as its foremost representatives, generally known as "Dai, Duan and the Wangs". But in regard to its depth and width as well as to its interests and approaches, the Qing study of Han learning was rather different from that of the Han scholars. For a better understanding and evaluation of it, concrete analyses should be given in regard to concrete issues.

Strictly speaking, the forerunners of the study of Han Learning in the Qing period were Yan Ruoju, Hu Wei and Mao Qiling rather than their predecessors Gu Yanwu and Huang Zongxi. Yan's *Annotations on the Old Text of the "Book of History"* and Mao's *Corrections to the Texts of the Four Books* were already textual criticism in the proper sense of the term. Their works contributed much to the academic studies by discovering the errors, faults and fabrications in the classics, and, as a matter of course, shook the very foundation upon which Neo-Confucianism rested. But they lacked the spirit of anti-racial oppression and social enlightenment of their seniors Gu and Huang.

Later the Suzhou School was much limited to the confines of the Han scholars, and the Anhui School was pedantic and scholastic, though Dai himself as an anti-Neo-Confucianist ideologue did not "stick entirely to the doctrine of the Han scholars"[24] nor adhere to textual criticism for the sake of textual criticism itself. Dai's disciples Duan and the Wangs were good at critical scholarship and achieved much in the field of phonetics, philology and etymology, but they developed the textual criticism of ancient classics into a mere academic discipline along a narrow scholarly path and lost the anti-Neo-Confucianist spirit of their master—a turning which accommodated to the requirement of the cultural despotism of the Qing regime.

At first, the rise of the study of Han Learning was a reaction against Neo-Confucianism for the purpose of providing practical learning for the benefits of society through earnest and strenuous studies in place of the idle talking about the mind and human nature. But later it tended more and more to get into minute techniques in research, entirely losing sight of the world of reality. Such was the case of the study of Han Learning at its zenith during the mid-Qing period.

The ever-narrowing approaches in Han learning incited strong reactions from the mid-Qing scholars like Zhang Xuecheng, Wang Zhong and Jiao Xun and later from Gong Zizhen, Wei Yuan and Kang Youwei who, confronting the serious situation of internal strife and foreign invasions, were led to think Han Learning impractical and useless to solve the problems facing them. Many of them turned to the New Text School of Gong Yang as an ideological foundation for their reform movements. It was thus that since the mid-19th century the Gong Yang School stepped forward to dominate the intellectual and academic world, replacing the Qian-Jia Han learning. But we have to admit the academic legacy of Han learning in mid-Qing. It was by their diligent studies that the ancient classics were rearranged into a readable form roughly as they had been. Ruan Yuan compiled most of their works into several monumental collections which provided the most important resources for the study of ancient classics.

In the main, Gu Yanwu's academic discipline was full of vigour with its emphasis on practicability, but by the Qian-Jia period, Han learning had gradually fallen into a state of mental impotence by indulging themselves in the ivory tower of mere textual criticism far from the world of reality in which they lived. This fact was a reflection of the rapid decline of the feudal society.

4. ECONOMIC THOUGHTS IN MING AND QING

The Enlightenment ideologues by the turn from Ming to Qing demanded a more equal, more democratic and more enlightened atmosphere in politics while criticizing autocratic despotism. At the same time, they proposed their economic measures based on taking the crafts and commerce as the basis, stressing the importance of the circulation of currency and the equalization of land properties. Their economic ideas proceeded from their theoretical premise that the self-interest of human beings was both natural and rational. Though most of their works appeared antiquated both in form and in language which looked at first sight like a returning to antiquity, their intellectual contents were in fact orientated to the future instead of the past. The modern substances in their theory were dressed in a mediaeval cloak. In spite of the residues of traditional ideas, the essence of their works complied with the interests of those who were initiating a new society. Different from Wang Anshi whose reform aimed only at the continuation of all things mediaeval, they played the role of the forerunners of the modern age. This great historical turning left its irradicable imprint on the economic thoughts of that time.

The Idea of Taking the Crafts and Commerce as the Basis

The idea of taking agriculture as the basis had ever been in the tradition of the economic thoughts of the middle ages, characteristic of the natural economy of the feudal mode of production. Crafts and commerce were regarded as subordinate professions, and the slogan of "venerating the basis and checking the subordinate" had always been in fashion. Indeed, there were persons like Sang Hongyang who attached importance to commerce for increasing the wealth of the nation, and Sima Qian and Han Yu who placed similar emphasis on both agriculture and crafts and commerce. But what they stressed was substantially only the importance of the division of professions within the pattern of natural economy beyond the boundary of which they never exceeded. They aimed rather at the increase of the government's income than at the development of crafts and commerce. They never approached the question with a view to the production and exchange of commodities. Fundamentally their ideas belonged to the category of natural economy and differed from the idea of taking the crafts and commerce as the basis in the theory of the Enlightenment ideologues at the turn from Ming to Qing.

Huang Zongxi censured severely the measure of "venerating the basis and checking the subordinate" which, he claimed, rendered the merchants dependent on the supply of luxuries to the royal court, the nobilities and their followers. This state of things was not conducive to social development. He urged the necessity of dispensing with this practice. Fang Yizhi (cf. next chapter) in the work of his later years *A Treatise on Trade and Commerce* blamed the extra-economic exploitation by subordinating crafts and commerce to the rule of feudal powers and advanced the motto: "Let the crafts and commerce thrive" in their own independent way. To the Enlightenment ideologues, the craftsmen and the merchants were no longer the low-graded (often the lower two among the four ranks of the people: the intellectuals, the peasants, the craftsmen and the merchants), but the dignitary "rich people". Wang Fuzhi asserted; "The big merchants and the rich people are those on whom the fate of the state is dependent", and urged the government "to punish the corrupt officials and relieve the rich people".[25] Tang Zhen demanded a laissez-faire policy so as to let "everyone develop his talents to his utmost and all commodities circulate without any restraint", and "to give free rein to their profits in accordance with the natural course of things without the slightest interference".[26] Here the "rich people" in their terminology denoted the germinal bourgeoisie who were striving for liberation out of feudal bondage for their own free enterprises. Their demands were in essence the Chinese laissez-faire theory in its premature form of what Adam Smith expounded in *The Wealth of Nations* more than a century later in the West.

The Idea of Circulation of Currency

Almost all the Enlightenment thinkers had brought forth their ideas of currency with a modern hue. Huang Zongxi bitterly pointed out the fact that money were coined and controlled by the imperial court merely as a means to strengthen its rule. Since all taxes had to be paid in money, people were obliged to seek after money everywhere. This led to the decrement of prices of agrarian products. And along with it went the poverty of the peasants and the social crisis. He elaborated a theory of the origin of money thus: Gold and silver were at first just ordinary treasures like other articles, but in course of time they gradually assumed the function of balance as a means of credit; this was what he called: "to circulate the useful articles by means of the useless objects (i.e., gold and silver)."[27] Their functions being so regulated, they ought not to be monopolized and stored up merely as a means for strengthening political powers. They should be made "to circulate infinitely so as to be able to render continuous profits".[28] The more they circulated, the more they would serve as "the source of profits, public as well as private". Here again we see in it the modern elements which differed from the traditional ones that mixed up the notion of money with that of wealth.

Huang Zongxi also pointed out that money when not in circulation was but "dead storage". And Gu Yanwu described it in these words: "To enrich the nation with silver is no more than to appease one's hunger by drinking only liquors."[29]

The distinction of money and wealth and the opposition against the storage of money marked the new economic ideas on the eve of a new age. More than a century later, Adam Smith expounded essentially the same thesis that it was extremely erroneous to identify money (the precious metals) with wealth itself.[30] He attacked many of the current economic ideas of the time and laid down the theoretical foundation of capitalist development in Britain. In the same way was the monetary theory of Huang and others leading to the emergence of the "rich people", the predecessors of the modern bourgeoisie.

Further, Huang proposed to issue the unitary paper-money on a nationwide scale, with gold and silver as its reserve which would guarantee the credit of the paper-money in circulation. With the issue of the paper-money as a convenient means, the crafts and commerce would be much more facilitated than ever before, or as Adam Smith said of it: in promoting the trade and commerce, paper-money in place of precious metals was what a new wheel would do for the carriage in place of the worn-out.

The Idea of Equalization of Land

The liberation of the mediaeval peasants from their attachment to the land and their seigneurs was the prerequisite of the origin and development of capitalism. It went hand in hand with the economic demands of the new-born bourgeoisie as well as with the democratic and humanistic ideals of the early modern times. Under the pretext of returning to antiquity, the Enlightenment ideologues revived the advice of equalizing land ownership proposed more than once by their predecessors. But their predecessors held it only as a measure to prevent annexation of land and to ameliorate the social contradictions, in other words, for the purpose of a better maintenance of the feudal system; while the Enlightenment ideologues linked it with the substitution of the hereditary monarchy by a democratic parliamentarism.

Huang Zongxi in his *Treatise on Government and Politics* asked for the abolition of feudal despotism. Under this guiding principle, he exposed the evils and disasters of the feudal land ownership, pointing out that three tenths of the land in the country were the official land and the rest were plundered by the royal house and the landlords. Besides, the peasants had to pay innumerable taxes and to do their corvée, legal and illegal. In revealing the sufferings of the peasants, Huang's intention was to show that the current land system was already beyond remedy and the only way out was the equalization of land. He proposed that all land, public and private, should be divided into nine-square farmland and distributed equally to the peasants, and the rest be left to the free occupation of the "rich people", with the land taxes being levied on the basis of the quantity of their occupation.

Wang Fuzhi repeated Zhang Zai's proposal of the nine-square system on the ground that the land was not the personal property of the emperor. In his historical works, Wang made an analytical narration of the evolution of land ownership like this: in antiquity there was no idea of ownership of the land, but in course of time there took place the division of the land into the nine-square system with the sovereign above and the people below. It was then that wealth was combined with power on the basis of the principle of heredity. But since the Qin and Han period, the wealth began to fall into the hands of the intelligent, and so the difference in wealth was effected by the difference in intelligence rather than by birth. This was due to the fact, so he argued, that "Providence intends to achieve his great unselfishness through the selfishness of the individual"[31]—a notion which reminds us of Kant's notion of "unsocial sociability"[32] so eloquently expounded in his *Idee zu einen allgemeinen Geschichte in weltbürgerlicher Absicht* and of the similarity in their respective arguments.

This view of his might seem at first sight to apologize for the rationality of the feudal ownership, but in reality Wang half-consciously and half-unconsciously defended the economic ideas of the new-born bourgeoisie, approaching the modern notion of private property on the basis of free competition; although his theory was far from being systematic and heavily wrapped up under the cloak of antiquity. What he described here as the evolution since Qin and Han was but his personal ideal for social reform and reorganization. He yearned for a society based on the difference of intelligence instead of the current hereditary system. His economic idea complemented Huang's, both representing the tendency towards a modern society of the bourgeoisie.

Self-Interest as the Essence of Human Nature

The Enlightenment ideologues in China, like Adam Smith, based their economic theory on the premise that man by nature was self-interested and self-profiting, as propounded in Huang Zongxi's well-known argument (cf. Section 1). On this basis of the individual self-interest was formed the public interest of society. For the union and the unity of the individual and the public, the state and the sovereign came into being. The sovereign, though also self-interested as a human being, was primarily the public servant by vocation. But with the change of time and circumstance, the sovereign succeeded in turning the public interest to his own benefit and the state to his own private property. Thenceforth the sovereign became "the greatest harm-doers of the nation".[33] And then only the abolition of autocracy of the sovereign could it become possible for each to take care of his own interests and for the human nature to develop fully without restraint. Such was Huang's theory of the origin of the state —a theory of social contract of the seventeenth-century China.

With his critique of the Neo-Confucianist idea of the antagonism between the Heavenly Principle and human desires, Huang proclaimed that all men were born with desires in which the Heavenly Principle dwelt. Since human desires were in human nature, they were as natural as the Heavenly Principle. When one had no desire for material and physiological life, there would be no reason for him to live on at all. So it would be an act against nature to suppress the natural desires of human beings. Once human desires were suppressed, life itself would be strangled and goodness in nature destroyed. Then society as a whole would be doomed to ruin.

In this sense, natural desires were the natural rights upon which the Enlightenment ideologues elaborated their new ways of thinking. This furnished the starting point of the earliest Chinese bourgeois ideology which was of epoch-making significance in the progress of history. What differentiated them from Rousseau, Adam Smith and other representatives of the modern age in the West was the fact that they were still tightly entangled with the mediaeval traditions both in the content of their ideas and in the forms of their expressions.

This was a historical fact conditioned by the backwardness of social development in China in comparison with the West, though their theory provided a new starting point in the intellectual history.

5. PEASANTS' REVOLUTIONARY IDEAS IN LATE MING

The Ming Dynasty founded by Zhu Yuanzhang was still a feudal one in nature. Although in its early years, it adopted certain measures trying to sweep away those backward policies of the Yuan Dynasty such as racial discrimination and to promote social productivity, it was nevertheless doomed to move along the feudal routine based on the antagonism between the landlords and the peasants. The unceasing annexation of land and increases of taxes led once more to the outbursts of the peasants' uprisings. In the mid-Ming there were the peasants' uprisings headed by Wang Sen and Xu Hongru, and in the late Ming the much greater uprisings headed Zhang Xianzhong and Li Zicheng burst out first in Shaanxi where the exiled emigres and frontier soldiers swarmed together and natural disasters occurred repeatedly. In about a decade's time, the uprisings of Zhang and Li overwhelmed a large part of the country and eventually brought about the downfall of the Ming regime. During their uprisings they raised the motto of "equalization of land and exemption of grain taxes".[34]

Li Zicheng's army in Henan declared their program of "equalization of land among all regardless of their social positions"[35] and "equalization of land and exemption of grain taxes". Zhang Xianzhong's army in Hunan and Hubei also raised their outcry: "Let the land seized by the powerful be returned to the common folk", "equalization between the wealthy and the poor" and "three years' exemption of taxes in money and in kind".[36] Some of their slogans were inherited from the uprisings of the past, but the most significant of them, "the equalization of land", was their own creation. It shook the very foundation of the feudal society, i.e., the landownership, and showed the fact that the peasants in the uprisings were more or less conscious of the reason of their enslavement.

The peasants in the Song period had gone only so far as to raise the slogan of "equalizing the rich and the poor", not yet embracing the idea of equalizing the land. Through long experience of their social struggles, the peasants were led to realize that the differentiation in social status was rooted in landownership. Therefore, the slogan "equalization of land" might be as well regarded as a deepening of the idea of equalization inherent in the small landholders. Like all their predecessors, the late Ming peasant uprisings were substantially acts of spontaneity. Bred up in the feudal mode of production, they were incapable of understanding their own historical missions; though compared with the obscure and indefinite idea of the equalization of fortunes, the demand for "the equalization of land" did reflect the progress in the social awareness of the peasants. But they remained on the level of a rather vague slogan and went no farther than that. In historical documents, we can find no record of its definite program or procedure of realization.

Chapter 19

SCIENTIFIC, HISTORIOGRAPHIC
AND LITERARY IDEAS
IN MING AND QING

1. SCIENTIFIC IDEAS AND THE INTRODUCTION
OF WESTERN KNOWLEDGE

The social Enlightenment current at the turn from Ming to Qing manifested itself also in the field of natural sciences. Outstanding scientists followed one after another, including Li Shizhen, Xu Xiake, Song Yingxing, Fang Yizhi, Xu Guangqi, Li Zhizao, Mei Wending, Wang Xichan and many others. Some of them summed up the scientific knowledge of the past, while others probed new approaches to modern science. The new scientific spirit of the time was characterized by the mid-Qing scholar Jiao Xun's proposition: "The knowledge of the world starts from one's self."[1] This new spirit coincided with Descartes' famous starting point: I think, therefore I am.[2] They were heralding the coming of a new age, with a new awareness in observing both the world and the self in a new perspective, while totally discarding the conventional dogmas. Down to the late Ming period, scientific knowledges in China had already in many aspects lagged behind the advanced level of the world, but the Chinese scientists never gave up their effort in formulating a new and more advanced natural philosophy and methodology for a better understanding of the natural world. Of them, we shall name only a few.

Fang Yizhi's Idea of Nature

Fang Yizhi (1611-1671), a native of Tongcheng (in Anhui), was in his youth a leader of the Fu She, a noted association of progressive intellectuals in late Ming. After the defeat of the Ming forces in the south against Qing, he retired as a recluse, engaging himself in his writings among which the most well-known were the *General Encyclopaedia* and *Notes on the Nature of Things*.

Fang made extensive studies on many scientific topics with the purpose "to gather the wisdom of all times".[3] He did not stick to what the ancients had said but took them as the foundation to make new progress of his own. He befriended Adam Schall von Bell (1591-1666), the famous Jesuit missionary in China, from whom he learned Western knowledge. He admitted its superiority in certain aspects but did not admire it blindly.

His main scientific contribution lay in his outlook on nature, especially in his idea of the motion of matter which hinted more or less the notion of the conservation of energy. "The sun and the moon are in constant motion,"said he, "and there is nothing at rest, even the heaven and the earth."[4] Since the whole world was in a state of constant motion, so "the celestial bodies are in constant motion, and the human beings too".[5] He proclaimed that the state of constant motion was "the nature of things". But sometimes he inclined to take all motions as merely mechanical, either in equilibrium or in inequilirium, in obedience to a pre-arranged relation of figures and numbers in the tradition of what was called the study of diagrams and numbers. By assigning the attribute of constant motion to the natural world, he broke through the previous ideas of taking the world in an eternal state of rest and rigidity. In connection with the Enlightenment current, it marked the historical transition from the mediaeval outlook of the world to the modern.

On the relation and interconnection of facts and theory, he expounded his ideas by the two terms "observation" and "generalization", the former denoting the study of concrete phenomena, while the latter the universal principles. He taught: "Generalization dwells in observation" and "observation is hidden in generalization",[6] meaning that scientific studies had to deal with philosophical principles. This idea was an extension of the tradition "the Tao dwells in things" to the scientific field. It tried to explain the relation of the hows and the whys in scientific research. Fang taught that because the ancients often disconnected the two, so the general principle was often fictionalized into God or Deity. In view of this, he urged the unity of the two: one should not talk about general principles regardless of the facts, nor should make observations regardless of the general principles. Or in terms of modern expression, science should be guided by philosophical principles which in their turn should be substantiated and regulated by science. They were inseparable from and mutually promoting to each other, hence he concluded: "One should not discard generalization by mere observation, nor observation by mere generalization."[7]

In his natural philosophy, Fang singled out "fire" as the primum mobile of the natural world. He succeeded Zhang Zai but brought Zhang to a new height. Zhang took the Ether as the substance of the world but failed to provide an explanation on the causes of its motions and changes upon which all things and events in the world depended. So, above the Ether Zhu Xi superimposed the Principle and placed the Ether in the framework that "the Principle is prior to the Ether". Fang elaborated his monist theory of the Ether by proclaiming that the world "originated from the Ether" and "was substantiated by the Ether".[8]

Fire seemed to be the most active element in the material world which was ever activating all motions and changes. So he introduced fire into his natural philosophy, asserting: "All motions of the Ether are but fire" or "the action of the fire", and "all motions are caused by fire".[9] The fire was not something outside of and external to the Ether; it came from the very Ether, and hence "the fire and the Ether are but one and the same".[10] Since the cosmos was composed of the Ether, one might fairly say that "heaven and fire are one".[11] Since the Ether is everlasting, so the fire will transmit forever without an end, that is, the activity of the fire will exist in the world to eternity. In this fashion, fire was endowed by him with the implication of energy and motion by means of which he provided a better solution on the idea of motion than Zhang Zai did. Motion was said to be generated from the intrinsic nature of things and "was not caused by any external action".[12] In this respect, Fang was similar to the ancient Greek philosopher Heraclitus who identified the substance of the universe with fire which was always in motion and change. Their reasonings and arguments bear a striking resemblance to each other.

As the germination of modern science, Fang's doctrine broke through the mediaeval conception of a rigid nature which was forever invariable and at rest. Though it was not a product of modern scientific experiments, nor belonged to the category of modern scientific thoughts or methodology; it nevertheless possessed its enlightenment bearings at the rise of modern science in China.

Jiao Xun's Scientific Ideas

Jiao Xun (1763-1820), a native of Yangzhou (in Jiangsu), was one of the most noted Qian-Jia scholars. He mastered a good knowledge of the classics and mathematics. In the field of mathematical science, Dai Zhen was a follower of Mei Wending, the foremost mathematician of early Qing; and Jiao was a follower of Dai. Ever since the Western (and essentially mediaevalistic) mathematical and astronomical knowledge was introduced by the Jesuit missionaries into China, the study of them had become a vogue among the Chinese academic circles. Nearly all the scholars of the Qian-Jia School were well trained both in classical textual criticism and in mathematics and astronomy. After all, the Qian-Jia School was not so narrow as people were apt to imagine, and their textual criticism was even affected by their mathematical studies and methods. Jiao himself was a representative of those versatile scholars who had a good training in mathematics as people of that time thought they should have. Jiao was known at his time as one of "the three friends in astronomy", the other two being Li Rui and Wang Lai, and his mathematical works were admired as "a formulation and an outline of all the previous works", including both the traditional Chinese mathematics and the Western mathematics which had been introduced into China earlier.

As a result of his mathematical studies, he worked out a set of philosophical principles by means of which mathematical deductions and frameworks were applied to the natural world as well as to social phenomena. This was indeed a perfectly novel approach which "elaborated what the ancients had never done".[13] There was, so he found, always a mathematical stipulation or norm in figures and numbers of all things. So he extended this in the explanation of the natural world, thinking that all things with definite forms might be explained by the formless mathematical principles. It seemed to him that the natural world was regulated or manipulated by an invisible hand, the mathematical principle, from the rule of which nothing could ever escape. Perhaps Sir James Jeans (1877-1946) would rejoice at finding an 18th century Chinese scholar who preceded him in affirming "the Great Architect of the Universe now begins to appear as a pure mathematician", or in "thinking the designer of the universe as a mathematician".[14]

A step further, the mathematical principle was considered permeating the human society. It seemed that all social phenomena might be also comprehended in the light of their mathematical stipulations and norms. In his philosophical studies, Jiao tried hard to interpret the *Book of Changes* in terms of mathematical notions. The method of mathematical deductions was carried by him to its farthest possible extent from the natural world to principles in philosophy and human affairs, so that Ruan Yuan said of him: "Without mathematical interpretation, one cannot make clear the functions [of his philosophy]; without mathematical interpretations, one cannot reach his conclusions; and without mathematical interpretation, one cannot grasp the essence of things."[15] So enchanted by mathematics was Jiao that he was ever obsessed with the idea that underlying the objective world there had to be the mathematical principles which had to be comprehended in their transcendental models. In doing so, he allowed himself to be carried away to the extremity by taking the mathematical method as the sole method for the study of both nature and man. In view of the fact that modern experimental sciences were then not yet given birth in China, Jiao's obsession with his mathematical ideas was indeed surprising, if not entirely applausible.

Whatever might be said of Jiao, at least in one cardinal point, his effort was really applausible. The main tendency of modern science in its early stage was aiming at finding out *The Mathematical Principles of Nature Philosophy* (so reads the title of Newton's immortal work). Galileo, the founder of modern science, held that the "Book of Nature is ... written in mathematical characters";[16] and Newton tried to sum up the natural laws by mathematical formulae. Descartes took the mathematical method as the sole method of certainty in science. In founding modern science, these masters by introducing mathematical reasoning into the realm of knowledge and science, had contributed greatly to the sweeping out of the theologi-

cal teleology on the way to the *Advancement of Learning* (so reads
the title of Francis Bacon's immortal work). Science and scientific
thoughts, once emancipated from the bondage of conventional superstitions, would open up the possibility of a vigorous growth of
science. The development of science in China followed a path essentially not different from this. Thus Xu Guangqi in late Ming probed
for such a mathematical approach exactly in its modern sense,
proclaiming that only mathematics could serve as the basis for all
scientific studies. A century and half later, Jiao innovated a large
amount of mathematico-philosophical terms in his strenuous endeavour to interpret the natural philosophy by mathematical ideas in an
unprecedented way. Herein lay the progressive significance of his
thoughts in sweeping away the mediaeval tradition and taking a new
direction toward a new age.

Introduction of Western Knowledge into China

The introduction of Western Knowledge into China since late
Ming (late 16th century) by the Jesuit missionaries gave an immense
impetus to the scientific studies of the Qing scholars. But what
scientific Knowledge, after all, was then introduced from the West
into China?

The missionaries who came to China were at first exclusively the
Jesuits who stood for the cause of the counter-Reformation in Europe
against the modern ideology of the rising bourgeoisie (the Reformation) and, together with it, the modern scientific revolution which
accompanied the birth of capitalism. Therefore, what they introduced into China was destined to be the antiquated mediaevalistic
ideology rather than the advanced scientific knowledge and scientific
ideas of the age. As a matter of fact, the new science of Galileo and
Newton and the new scientific thoughts of Francis Bacon and Descartes were never formally introduced into China. This was the basic
historical fact that ought to be mentioned emphatically during the
first phase of the intellectual intercourse between China and the
West.

Since the very beginning, the missionaries were appreciated by
the imperial court for their knowledge of astronomy and calendar,
map-drawing and cannon-making. But in the sphere of ideology,

what they brought to China was the mediaevalistic world view, such as scholastic logic, teleological metaphysics (Thomas Aquinas in fragments), the Ptolemaic theory of the universe and much more religious preachings, all of which, though something new for the Chinese scholars in a certain sense, belonged after all to the mediaeval ideology rather than to the modern. And since they were something new—though surely not the advanced knowledge of the time and deeply tinted with a religious hue—the scientific parts in them were still welcomed by the Chinese intellectuals, because they added something new to the Chinese traditional knowledge. For instance, there had never been systematic geometric deduction in China, it was only by then that Euclid's book was translated into Chinese. Hence many Chinese scientists of the time, while summing up the ancient and mediaeval scientific knowledge of China, were earnestly learning from the West. Fang Yizhi advised people to take the West as the teacher. Xu Guangqi, Li Zhizao, Mei Wending, Dai Zhen, Jiao Xun, Ruan Yuan and many others were all well versed with the mathematical and astronomical knowledge of the West within the limited bounds the missionaries allowed them. In contrast with the conservatives who stood against all things foreign, they were broad-minded people with no racial prejudice. They were bold enough to admit the fact that science in China in many respects was lagging behind the West and that much of the Western knowledge "has never been found in the land of China",[17] "a rather large part of them surpasses by far the teachings of our previous scholars".[18] Xu Guangqi forwarded the slogan: "Let us first have a thorough knowledge of both the Western science and the Chinese".[19] And later, Jiao Xun advocated: "To learn both the Western and the Chinese with no prejudice nor preference".[20] In this spirit, they were the worthy representatives of the Chinese intellectuals in search for scientific truth.

In learning Western knowledge, they embraced a rather sound and balanced attitude. Fang Yizhi commented it: "During the reign of Wan Li [1573-1619], Western knowledge was introduced into China which was good at observation but poor at generalization; and hence the wise people would reason that there must still be inperfections in their observation".[21] Xu Guangqi, the foremost representative in the learning of Western knowledge, recommended people to study both the Chinese and the Western "in order to surpass the

West".[22] He was not satisfied with merely following the steps of others. In general, the advanced scholars of China in their learning from the abroad showed that they were both earnest and good at that.

Indeed, there were things in Western knowledge that were really modern at the time, but not much. Of these, we may enumerate the use of the telescope in astronomical observation, a very rudimentary and even obscure introduction of logarithm, a by-passing mention of the name of Copernicus, and by a much later time when the modern science held its reign unshakably in the West, the introduction of Kepler's ecliptical method in co-existence with the Ptolemaic epicycles. But so far, the Jesuit missionaries had never formally introduced the theory and methods of the Galilean-Newtonian system, the core of modern science at that historical epoch.

However, it was upon this intellectual background that the Chinese scholars were given an unprecedented impetus in their study of the traditional science as well as in their preparation for the new scientific ideas with a brand new vision. It was then that the methodology of science began to divorce itself from the intuitional and conjectural way of thinking and turned to the path of observation and experiment together with mathematical abstraction and deduction. Xu Guangqi in his work of revising the old calendar, had given priority to the employment of observatory apparatus and in his agricultural study made intensive experiments on seed selection and breeding. Fang Zhongtong, son of Fang Yizhi, interpreted the traditional teaching of "the investigation of things" as: "To investigate a thing is to investigate the mathematical model of that thing."[23] And Wang Xichan remarked: "To be precise and exact, one has to employ the mathematical reasoning."[24] In this current, Ruan Yuan observed the fact that the scholars of the Qing period had changed the traditional view of taking mathematics as a sort of magic or divination and "dared no more to talk lightly about mathematics".[25] The emphasis on experiments and observations as well as on the formulation of the data obtained from them into a mathematical model, constituted the characteristic feature of the early modern science. It was but obvious that China was then just about to take that path too.

With the feudal society tottering into its last stage, the development of science was slowly preparing for modern scientific ideas which in turn were inevitably to exercise their influence on other

fields of intellectual activities. It was by that time that the Chinese
intellectual world had their first contacts with Western knowledge.
This new knowledge from the West introduced some new elements
into China, but nothing of the modern Galilean-Newtonian system.
On the Chinese part, we find nothing that afforded serious obstacles
on the way to modern science. Conversely, leading Chinese scientists
from Xu Guangqi to Jiao Xun were doing their best in probing a new
scientific outlook and methodology which pointed to modern science.

But since the germination of capitalism in China was then still
too weak to induce a social and economic revolution, so in correspondence with it the new scientific spirit and idea from Xu Guangqi
to Jiao Xun was also too feeble to induce a scientific and intellectual
revolution. And their advanced scientific thoughts served only as a
prologue to the enlightenment of modern thoughts rather than the
real beginning of a mature modern ideology.

2. HISTORIOGRAPHIC IDEAS
IN MING AND QING

Different from the historiographic ideas in Song and Yuan
which were in the main dominated by the orthodoxy of the feudal
rule, the thoughts of the prominent historians during the turn from
Ming to Qing were closely connected with their social enlightenment
ideas. As a rule, they took an evolutionary view in their comprehension of history. Therefore, though in the expression of their ideas
they often assumed the form of venerating the antiquity and followed the traditional practice in their exegeses of the ancient classics,
they, nevertheless, worked out some completely new comments on
things past in order to convey their new ideas on history. In this field,
the most outstanding figures were Huang Zongxi and Zhang Xuecheng. Zhang being more than a century later than Huang, belonged
to the next historical epoch posterior to the turn from Ming to Qing,
but he evidently succeeded the intellectual tradition of Huang. They
lived in different epochs and each had his own intellectual experiences, so the historiographic ideas of each possessed their own peculiarities. Generally speaking, Huang opened a new phase in the
historical research of the Eastern Zhejiang School; while Zhang,

though less radical than Huang in social and political ideas, provided many penetrating ideas in historical studies which surpassed Huang in many respects and exercised great influences on the historians of the later generations.

Historiographic Ideas of Huang Zongxi

In his *Treatise of Government and Politics*, Huang attacked dauntlessly the despotic monarchy and proposed a vague design of a future society. But in his academic thoughts, he laid more emphasis on the doctrine of Wang Yangming, as he had in his youth learned after Liu Zongzhou, a noted scholar of the Wang School. Later, being dissatisfied with its emptiness and idle talks, Huang made critiques on the learning of Wang. To counterbalance the emptiness and uselessness of the Wang School, he advocated the study of history, Quan Zuwang, his noted disciple, said of him: "Since the mid-Ming, the academic discipline had fallen into decay, scholars with books closed and unread indulged themselves in idle talks about human nature and the Way. The better of them were but pedantic, and none of them were deeply rooted in any solid and sound study. It was Master Huang who began to teach that only learnings that started from the classics would not lead one astray into vainglory and only learnings that had evidences in history would suffice the need of practicability."[26] With these words, Quan made a very good comment on the intellectual world of that time. Apparently, Huang's historical studies aimed at practicability against the defects of the Wang School, and this was in conformity with his political and social ideals.

Huang concerned himself particularly with the Ming Dynasty as its downfall was witnessed by him personally. Among his historical writings, the most significant were his *Philosophical Schools of Ming* and *Philosophical Schools of Song and Yuan*, the latter being posthumously accomplished by Quan Zuwang. These two works dealt with almost all the thinkers from the beginning of Song (late 10th century) to the end of Ming (mid-17th century) by tracing their origins and evolutions with a view to their interrelations and connections. He broke through the boundary between the orthodoxy and the heresies, professing that "any prejudicial viewpoint or any polemical argument"[27] ought to be treated carefully. And the divergence of different schools was just the point "which is worthy to be scrutinized by the historians".[28] To study the various aspects of different doctrines—herein consisted the right way of learning. In his opinion, to treat the orthodoxy simply from the orthodox point of view was just like "keeping the water from overflowing by pouring more water into it, how then could it be worthy of the name of learning?"[29] "The Tao", he asserted, "never dwells merely in the teaching of one school; the blood veins of the sages were dispersed in a hundred schools".[30] Consequently, he opposed the study of history "by taking any single approach". As a matter of course, this view led him to put the Confucian classics on the same level with all other schools; sometimes Huang compared the relation between Confucianism and other schools to "one root with multiple branches"[31]—a view by which the Confucian orthodoxy was depreciated and the heretical ideas of the hundred schools were enhanced. Under the supremacy of the Confucian orthodoxy at that time, this was really a progress in the study of history which anticipated the new intellectual trend of the late Qing period.

In his treatment of the history of antiquity, he never separated himself from the reality of his own time and his enlightenment ideal, though his progressive conception of history was still far from being a scientific one in the modern sense. In his *Treatise on Government and Politics*, he criticized the autocratic despotism in the light of the democratic spirit in the antiquity, "the rule of one man" in the light of the rule of the law in the antiquity and the extra-economic exploitation in the light of the safeguarding of the individual rights in the antiquity. In appearance, the conclusion was a return to the ideal state of the antiquity, but in reality it was not a state characterized by the retrogress of history back to the primitive society as preached by Lao Zi but by the progress of history towards a new society of the greatest happiness of the greatest number in a Benthamite sense. His proposal was still crude and vague but it responded to the trend of the historical development of his time. It was this idea of his which became a tremendous stimulus to the Reform Movement as well as to the democratic current of the late Qing period.

The progressive ideas in the historical writings of Huang opened a new phase in historiography along the line of practicability of the

Enlightenment current. He and his disciples Quan Zuwang and Wan Sitong, generally known as the Eastern Zhejiang School, were taken as the models in historiography by most historians of the Qing period.

Historiographic Ideas of Zhang Xuecheng

Zhang Xuecheng (1738-1810) lived more than a century later and had no direct contact with Huang, but he admired Huang and was influenced by Huang. A native of Kuaiji (now Shaoxing, in Zhejiang), Zhang lived at the prime of the Qing regime when the imperial rule was relatively stable and the feudal society was undergoing its last stage of prosperity. Among the intellectual circle, it was the high time of Han learning of the Qian-Jia period, and Zhang's historiographic ideas started from his critique on the Qian-Jia Han learning. His main work was *A General Treatise on Literature and History*.

Zhang criticized the scholars of Han learning of his time that they "only recite the dead words of the ancient kings and know nothing about the institutions of the later kings".[32] They spent their whole life in the study of the antiquated words and phrases; but "they are ignorant of their own time while boasting their knowledge of the ancients".[33] In short, what they taught had nothing to do with real life. On the contrary, in intellectual tendency Zhang succeeded the practical spirit of the Enlightenment thinkers a century ago.

Han learning of the Qian-Jia period venerated the Six Classics as sacred and inviolable, but Zhang advanced his basic thesis: "All the Six Classics are history",[34] taking the Confucian classics as historical sources. This was an idea of lasting significance in the intellectual history. Prior to him, Wang Tong in Sui and Wang Yangming and Li Zhi in Ming had already taken the Confucian classics as historical sources in a certain sense. But they applied such ideas only to certain paragraphs in the classics, not (like what Zhang had done) as a whole from their contents to their form and style. By the thesis: "All the Six Classics are history", he meant that the traditional classics were no more than historical products of their own times, or what he called the records of "the political affairs of the ancient kings"; because "in ancient times there was no distinction between the classics and history",[35] they were but one and the same.

So for the later generations, all the ancient classics were but historical sources of the ancient times.

Since "the ancients were never in the habit of engaging themselves in writing their own works", so "the ancients had never talked about the Principle [the theory] apart from the facts".[36] Therefore, the Six Classics, so much venerated by the later generations, had never been sanctified at their own times as sacred dogmas, they were records of plain facts. Here Zhang brought forward the antithesis between the methods: the method of studying the classics and the method of studying history. The former took what was said in the classics as indisputable truth, while the latter took all that as products of certain historical situations and conditions. Roughly speaking, the former was the dominating way of thinking in the Middle Ages. In order to break through the intellectual bonds of mediaevalism, it was necessary to repudiate the sanctity of the traditional classics. This was what Zhang had done that helped much to encourage modern ideas in the field of historiography. Since the classics were but the historical records of political affairs of the ancient time, they could be no other than the loci of changes in different periods; and therefore people of the later ages should never be obliged to take the ancient records as the inviolable norms, and what they should do was to make their own progress in conformity with the requirements of their own times. This thesis of his dealt a blow at the Confucian classics as well as at the scholars of Han learning of the Qian-Jia period whose job it was to scrutinize the ancient classics as their life-long careers.

The thesis "all the Six Classics are history" broadened considerably the scope of historiography and transformed profoundly its concepts. From this, Zhang went even further as to assert that all writings in existence might be regarded as parts of history, though not all of them were worthy of the name of historiography but were only raw materials for it. What made a writing historiographic was "not only the narration of events in an orderly way with a well-arranged style" but also its "comprehension" or "interpretation" by which the historian was enabled "to make his exposition on the Tao" "into his own independent doctrine through a thorough understanding of history in its totality".[37] For this purpose, the historians were required to have "the capability in passing judgments by his own understanding". Only by such a historiography, "what the former historians had dealt with only briefly could be made clear; what the former historians had not thought of could be worked out and what the former historians were accustomed to could be renovated".[38] In fact, it was demanding to break away from the old tradition by way of setting up the new one. The interpretation of history was to know not only the how but also the why. "The Tao," said he, "is just the reason why things are what they are"; and historiography should do its duty by explaining and illustrating "the trend which cannot be otherwise".[39] This was called in historiography: "To find out the truth."[40]

Zhang made a great deal of comments on historical writings of the past. He considered the *Book of History* and the *Spring and Autumn Annals* worthy of the name of history, because "they never talked about the Principle apart from the facts"; while many others only served as historical documents and materials. As to the pre-Qin non-Confucian thinkers and scholars who had always been regarded as heretics, Zhang affirmed that each of them had his share in certain aspects of the Tao which was generally thought to be comprised only in the Six Classics. Of course, Zhang's opinion that they all derived their origins from the Six Classics was no truth, but by his affirmation the Hundred Schools were all placed on a parity with the Confucian; and in this way Confucianism was deprived of its supremacy and the Neo-Confucianist theory of the Confucian orthodoxy was seriously shaken.

Zhang valued the study of general history, such as the works of Du You, Sima Guang and Zheng Qiao, which were higher than those on specific topics, his reasoning being that only through the study of the universal history one was qualified to learn "the course of evolution from the ancient times to the present".[41] This was an amplification of Ma Duanlin's view that historical studies should keep in view the causations of evolution. Besides, Zhang advocated the study of local history as a constituent part of the general history, the former providing the materials for the latter—a view which echoed Huang Zongxi's idea of local autonomy and belonged to the Enlightenment tradition.

Liu Zhiji in Tang had enumerated three prerequisite qualifications of being a historian; the talent, the scholarship and the insight;

but above all these Zhang particularly elaborated and advocated the historiographic virtue as the most essential. He stressed, "Those who possess historical insights have to know what is historiographic virtue"[42] without which a historical writing was doomed to be deceptive and untrue. Hence in his book he devoted a specific chapter to historiographic virtue. By the term historiographic virtue, he meant "the intention of the writer", or the truthfulness and conscience of the historian who ought never to be subject to the vogue of the age or any personal preference as "to go contrary to the impartiality of the Tao [the truth]".[43] In another chapter entitled "Beware the Love of Fame", he remarked: "Those who are anxious for fame are destined to speculate after the vulgar fashion", and so "their intentions have to be carefully examined".[44] His notion of historiographic virtue was in close connection with his opinion about historical interpretation. In ancient historiography of China, there had been indeed a tradition of truthfulness in historical records which demanded the historians an objective attitude neither to exaggerate the good nor to cover up the evil. But in addition to this, Zhang, while stressing historiographic virtue, demanded that the historian always be inspired by an aspiration for the search of the Tao (truth) and for the benefits of society which could only be brought forth by an impartial intention. It was obvious that the historiographic ideas of Zhang, though more than a century after Huang's, were in the direct line of the Enlightenment current; and in their width and depth they even surpassed Huang's in many respects.

3. THOUGHTS IN THE LITERARY WORKS OF MING AND QING

The Enlightenment current of Ming and Qing manifested itself in various fields of cultural and intellectual activities of that time. And literary writings were no exception.

The Bourgeois Ideology in the Middle and Late Ming Novels

Since the mid-Ming, the young leftists of the Wang Yangming School such as Li Zhi (Li Zuowu) set off an anti-dogmatic and sceptical upsurge against the Confucian tradition, and under its direct influence there appeared in literature the Gongan School headed by Yuan Hongdao (1568-1610), a native of Gongan (in Hubei) with his two brothers. They stood for the cause that literature should be "the expression of human sentiments only, regardless of any literary rule or norm". Yuan professed that he was under the intellectual influence of Li Zhi for his literary liberation movement, blaming the Six Classics as not genuine literary writings. He and his circle asked for the full expression of the sentiments or individuality —a tendency which showed clearly the bourgeois ideology in its demand for breaking the feudal restraints.

The most prominent dramatist of the age was Tang Xianzu (1550-1616), a native of Linchuan (in Jiangxi), who learned from his master Luo Rufang, another young leftist of the Wang Yangming School, and was on intimate terms with the Yuan brothers. Tang praised Li Zhi, and in his famous dramatic works (The Four Dreams, or the four plays each of which with the title of a Dream) he sang the eulogy of romantic love, the central theme of them being the antagonism between personal sentiments and the restraint of the Neo-Confucian Principle and the longing for individual liberation. It echoed in dramatic form what the Yuan brothers demanded in essays and belles-lettres and what Li Zhi demanded in his theory of human nature.

This was especially so in the case of popular novels and short stories of the age in which the lives and characteristics of the declining feudal landlords and the new-born bourgeoisie found their most vivid reflections. Often they told about how a maid of the feudal nobility fell in love with a petit-bourgeois youth, or how a man gave up taking the imperial examination and became enriched by running business instead. Sometimes even adventurous enterprises were idealized and romanticized. Most of the motives in these writings were expressions of the ideas and longings of the germinating bourgeoisie. Their authors as a rule launched severe attacks on the corruption and hypocrisy of the landlords who were suppressing and murdering the vitality of human life. In their forecasting of the decline of the feudal ruling class, they were more representative of the spirit of the age than the romances of the Tang and Song periods.

Literary Thoughts in Early Qing

The armed intrusion of the Manchu and the downfall of the Ming regime caused the emergence of large amounts of nationalistic verses. They expressed the reverie of the Ming Dynasty, laments on those who died in the struggles against the Manchu and longing for the recovery of the Ming. In line with the Enlightenment ideology, the Enlightenment thinkers cultivated a new creative spirit in literary ideas and theories.

Gu Yanwu claimed that literary works should be valued by their originality; hence a writer should not depend upon the outdated language of the ancients, i.e., the Confucian ethical dogmas. In opposition to the theory of "literature for the sake of conveying the Tao" since Han Yu, Gu advertised that literature should express "what the ancients failed to express".[45] Otherwise, it would only be an inferior copy of the ancient model without its own life. Huang Zongxi expounded a theory of spontaneity, asserting that literary works were the spontaneous outflow of human emotions and sentiments. "No literature," claimed he, "does not deal with what is within one's own heart."[46] His emphasis on the individual sentiment ran parallel with his demand for the liberation of the individuality so earnestly propounded in his *Treatise on Government and Politics*.

Wang Fuzhi held that all literary works were based on the intentions of the author. Here the term "intention" meant an antithesis to the ideological bondage at the cost of the free expression of the individual sentiment which, he claimed, ought to be the starting point of poesy, or in his own words: "Wherever the sentiments lead, the poesy will follow."[47] This was directed towards the Neo-Confucianists who took the literary creation simply as a vehicle to convey ethical teachings and so reduced poesy to a rhymed lecture on Neo-Confucian doctrine. In his philosophy, Wang professed that the Tao dwelt in things, or the Heavenly Principle in human desires; so he advocated people "to follow nature" and "to venerate life", taking human desires and human emotions as an integral part of the Heavenly Principle. Therefore, his literary theory affirmed that human intentions originated from human desires in opposition to the Heavenly Principle which asked people to extinguish their human desires.

With his literary theory directed against the orthodox preach-ings, he urged that the writer's intentions should be in communion with social realities. Social realities referred to "what one experienced personally and what one witnessed with one's own eyes";[48] therefore a writer "ought not to stick to the old ways" as a means of propagat-ing the teachings of the ancients, but ought "to keep contact with the will of the world".[49] In confrontation with the ruling ideology of the time, Wang upheld the banner of the liberation of the individuality in the field of literature and launched more forcible attacks than any other on various literary schools which followed the Neo-Confucianist teaching and maintained the return to the ancients as the sole model. These advanced literary ideas together with the social Enlightenment ideas constituted the progressive intellectual current of the age.

Literary Thoughts in the Mid-Qing

Zhang Xuecheng in his *General Treatise on Literature and History* embraced many of the traditional Confucian ideas, but at the meantime he taught people "to be good at learning Confucius" and "to be good at applying Confucius' teaching", that is, "to vener-ate Confucius with one's innermost intentions" and not to treat his teaching as inviolable dogmas. So he proclaimed: "One should not serve the ancients but should let the ancients serve."[50] Hence the Tao (the intellectual contents) of literature should not be confined to the teachings of the Six Classics but should be connected with all that were in the world. This literary view in company with his historio-graphic ideas threw a new light of social progress on the stagnant intellectual world of his time.

Literary works characteristic of the spirit of the age were the novels in the Qing period. During the reign of Qianlong, there was a resurgence of the current for the emancipation of individuality after a century of low tide under the high pressure of political and intellectual despotism of the Qing regime. And this resurgence was taking place under the shadow of the coming collapse of the feudal society itself. Such was the historical background upon which the best novels of Qing (even of all times) were created. Together with the *Outlaws of the Marsh* and *Journey to the West* of Ming period,

The Scholars and *Strange Tales of Liaozhai* and others have been among the most popular ever since their creation. In them one find satiric passages revealing the cruelty of the ruling class, the decadence and hypocrisy of the Confucian scholars, the moral corruption of the society and the darkness of the officialdom side by side with stories of young people in search of love and life with a spirit longing for the liberation of individuality. All of them forecast the impending fall of the feudal ruling system. And, above all, it was in *A Dream of Red Mansions* that we find the most profound reflection of the age in a most admirable artistic form.

The author of *A Dream of Red Mansions*, Cao Xueqin (?-1763 or 1764), also known as Cao Zhan, came from a family of high bureaucrats affiliated to the imperial house; but in his later years, after the fall of his family, he could hardly keep himself from starving. From the prosperity and the ruin of his own life, he experienced the bitterness of life and various kinds of social ways. In his immortal works, he took the tragic love story of two young lovers as its main thread around which he described the rise and fall of a nobility household upon a broad social background and exposed all kinds of tricks and treacheries and the hypocrisy and irrationality of the social morality, legality and ideology of the age. With deep sympathy and affection, he created some of his heroes and heroines who were charming and upright and tragically dauntless in their rebellion against their lots. They were striving for freedom in the hope of a better life against the chains of the traditional ethical code, but all in vain. By exposing the darkness in social life, he sang the elegy over the fate of the whole social mansion which was on the verge of total collapse.

The tragedy was caused by the ruthless rule of the orthodox ideology which served a butchering knife over the innocent people. Cao's contemporary Dai Zhen had in his philosophical theory blamed the Neo-Confucianists as "killing people with their Principle", and Cao raised the same bitter protest in an artistic fashion. With his work, the author showed his rebellious spirit against the age-old creed "literature for the sake of conveying the [Confucian] Tao". And on the other hand, the sympathy and admiration he paid to his heroes and heroines were in essence a condemnation on the Neo-Confucianist preaching of "extinguishing the human desires".

The author deliberately and consciously created his characters with his aspiration to pay homage to human nature and human sentiments along the line of the advanced ideas of the main current of Enlightenment. Hence his work, in the form of literature, was also a product reflecting the general intellectual trend since late Ming.

Part IV
CHINESE IDEOLOGY
IN MODERN TIMES

PRELIMINARY REMARKS ON MODERN SOCIETY AND MODERN IDEOLOGY

In the year of 1840 the Opium War broke out and Great Britain, then by far the most advanced among the capitalist nations, with her gunboats forced open the front door of the ever-closed and self-satisfied Celestial Dynasty of China. The Opium War marked the beginning of the modern history of China as well as that of her modern intellectual history. Thenceforth, China was gradually reduced from an old feudal society to a semi-feudal and semi-colonial society.

In the long course of her ancient and mediaeval history, China had accomplished brilliant contributions to the civilization of mankind. Judged from the prolongation and the richness of her cultural legacy, these should be acknowledged as rare and unique in the world. It was only by the time of Renaissance in the fifteenth-sixteenth centuries that China began to lag behind the advanced culture then emerging in Western Europe. There the capitalist mode of production was flourishing and, together with it, modern sciences and their corresponding ideologies.

But in China, the antiquated feudal mode of production was unable to give impetus to the development of modern science and industry, and the semi-feudal and semi-colonial regime was unable to catch up with the advanced achievements of the West. Under this historical situation, being backward meant always being defeated, humiliated and subjugated by foreign powers. For a whole century after the Opium War, the imperialist powers, large and small, all waged wars of aggression against China, each time leading to a new defeat for China and the conclusion of a new humiliating peace treaty.

In the West, Galileo laid down the experimental foundation of modern classical mechanics at the beginning of the 17th century and then Newton completed its theoretical formulation. They were generally acknowledged as the most important achievements of modern science; but it was not until two centuries later, in 1860s and 1870s, that the Newtonian system was finally and formally introduced into China. Not only in this respect was China lagging behind, but also in relation to a long series of the most important accomplishments of modern science. Contemporary Chinese intellectuals were completely unaware of such theories as that of the cells on the 1830s, the law of transformation of energy in the 1840s, the theory of biological evolution in the 1850s, the spectrum analysis, the hereditary experiments and the periodic table in the 1860s, the study of curved space and the theory of groups in the 1870s, the discovery of germs and advancement in microbiology in the 1880s and the discovery of radioactive elements and the measurement of free electricity in the 1890s. In China, the reactionaries, domestic and foreign, collaborating in their cultural despotism and obscurantism, blockaded the Chinese intellectuals from access to the wide world, and sharply handicapped their share in the scientific efforts of mankind. The corrupted feudal productive relations had severely obstructed the development of social productive forces and of science and technology. Without a scientific revolution, capitalism and the bourgeois democratic culture were denied a chance for vigorous growth.

In close connection with backwardness in science and culture was the backward state in China's industry. In the West, the scientific revolution took place in the sixteenth and seventeenth centuries and the industrial revolution followed in the eighteenth century. This provided the material basis that enabled the Western powers to come flock to China after her front door was forced open by modern gunboats. The decisive step in improving the steam engine was accomplished by the end of the eighteenth century and the appearance of the railroad train and steamer heralded a new "era of iron and steel", iron and steel becoming the main industrial materials, and coal the main source of energy. In order to compare China with the West, some data might be cited as an indicator. The four main industrial countries, whose production amounted to more than 70 per cent of the world total, had coal and iron figures as follows:

		1800	1850	1900
Coal (millions of tons)	Gt. Britain	11.8	50.0	228.8
	U.S.	0.1	3.6	244.7
	France	0.2	4.4	33.4
	Germany		6.7	149.8
Iron (thousands of tons)	Gt. Britain	160	2,290	9,100
	U.S.	40	570	14,010
	France		410	4,240
	Germany		210.	8,520
Railroad (km.)	Gt. Britain		10,650	38,000 (1910)
	U.S.		14,500	311,100
	France		3,230	36,800
	Germany		6,000	49,900
Vessels (thousands of tons)	Gt. Britain		3,565	9,304
	U.S.		3,206	4,865
	France		688	1,038
	Germany			1,942

Compared with the above figures, railroad mileage in China was 15 km. in 1876 and increased to 364 in 1894. The tonnage of vessels in China was 22,100 in 1882 and 36,800 in 1892, roughly about 1 per cent of that of Great Britain. As for coal and iron, the foundation of modern industry, as late of as 1900 China's iron output was only 26,000 tons and her coal output had never reached the level of Great Britain in the 18th century (9 million tons in China compared to 10 million tons in Britain in 1795).

With such a backward economic basis, it was unavoidable that in modern science and culture China would be unable to catch up with the advanced West. The Westerners had already successfully built up modern capitalist states and were using their advanced sciences and industries to wage wars of aggression on the backward nations, including China. And this was the reason why the Chinese progressive intellectuals at that time were so eager to learn from the West. They were thirstily learning from the West how to get their country enriched and strengthened and how to transform their backward social institution so as to get China out of backwardness and subjugation. Yet, at just that time the Western powers (including

Japan), taken as models by the Chinese intellectuals, were entering a historical stage when they were in urgent need of an alliance with the reactionary elements in China for the sake of holding colonial control over China. Thus it was a historical fact that the predominant focus of the modern history of China (and hence her modern intellectual history) was the anti-imperialist and anti-feudal revolution.

Facing this historical situation, the camp of the feudal intelligentsia began to split. A group with more enlightened views and more realistic sense of the contemporary world emerged. They sensed rather acutely that China was confronting a new situation and that she should do her utmost to learn about the world so as to compete for her own survival among the modern nations. It was clear for them that the closed world in which China had held supremacy, politically as well as ideologically, was gone forever. But since this part of the intelligentsia were by birth closely related to the feudal forces, they were virtually incapable of carrying out a thorough-going democratic revolution. For about half a century, they had incessantly demanded the development of capitalist relations, first vaguely and then more and more consciously and conscientiously. They were ever more realizing and propagating that only a reform upon a new (i.e., Western) model could make the country rich and strong. What differentiated them from the reactionaries, domestic and foreign, was this: whereas the feudal diehards clung to the corpse of feudalism, and the imperialists (with their lackeys) attempted to turn China into their colonies, the progressive intellectuals, on the contrary, aimed at turning China into an independent state, rich and strong.

Overall, the struggle on the intellectual and cultural battlefield was essentially one between the new bourgeois culture and the feudal culture, or in other words, between the Chinese Learning and the Western Learning or between the Old Learning and the New Learning. In fact, the main intellectual current of modern times, from its forerunners (such as Lin Zexu, Gong Zizhen and Wei Yuan) in the 1840s and 1850s, through the early New Learning School (such as Guo Songtao, Feng Guifen, Xue Fucheng, Ma Jianzhong and Zheng Guanying) in the 1860s, 1870s and 1880s, down to the Reformists of the 1890s (such as Kang Youwei, Liang Qichao, Tan Citong and Yan Fu), should be viewed from two aspects. Politically as reformists, they were against the revolution of the masses, and as dependents of the feudal regime they fancied a reform by an enlightened autocratic monarch. But culturally and ideologically they did contribute much in emancipating the minds of the people by their earnest search for truth from the West. Nevertheless, because of China's backwardness in science and due to the feebleness of their character, it was impossible for them to identify exactly and penetratingly the real issues of their time, and hence few effective solutions resulted.

The situation on the part of the masses proved to be quite otherwise. In the 1850s and 1860s, the great peasants' uprising, known as the Taiping Movement, set a widespread conflagration over the greater part of the country and dealt a severe blow to the already shattered and shaken Qing regime. However, for lack of a right line in politics as well as in ideology, the movement was eventually suppressed by the imperial Qing government with the help of the imperialists, who preferred a submissive and corrupted imperial government rather than a new independent peasant regime in China. Then followed the Nian Uprising in the 1870s, a series of anti-foreign-religion movements succeeding one another in the 1880s and the Yi He Tuan Movement in the 1890s. Though they assumed unavoidably backward forms and were finally strangled by the combined forces of the reactionaries, domestic and foreign, they played a tremendous historic role. They fiercely hit the Qing regime at its core, smashed the imperialist dream of partitioning China and established the basis of the democratic revolution that came later under the guidance of Sun Yat-sen.

In the first decade of the twentieth century, i.e., from the Yi He Tuan Movement to the Revolution of 1911, the upsurging democratic revolution reached its high tide. The establishment of the Tong Meng Hui (China Revolutionary League) signalled that the Chinese bourgeoisie had formed its own political party and was working out a rather mature programme. But the Chinese bourgeoisie, suffering from its inherent weaknesses, was incapable of carrying the anti-feudal and anti-imperialist democratic revolution to the end. The Revolution of 1911, though having overthrown the monarchy and forcing the last emperor of China to abdicate, had by no means brought to an end the rule of feudalism and imperialism over the Chinese people. It was not until the May Fourth Movement in 1919 that the bourgeois democratic revolution entered a new phase in its history—the transition from the old democratic revolution to the new democratic revolution. The banner of "science" and "democracy" held high by the May Fourth Movement initiated a new upsurge in the anti-imperialist and anti-feudal movements. New doctrines including Marxism began to spread in China and a new era in the history of modern China dawned.

In what follows we shall give a brief review of how modern Chinese ideology developed and evolved.

Chapter 20

IDEOLOGY IN THE TIME OF THE OPIUM WAR AND THE TAIPING REBELLION

1. IDEOLOGICAL TRENDS IN THE TIME OF THE OPIUM WAR

In the eighteenth and the first half of the nineteenth century, Chinese scholars for the most part dared not confront real life issues; being under pressure of the country-wide suppression and cultural despotism of the feudal monarchy, they could only try to escape from contact with the social reality and find retreat in the dead documents of the age-old classics. This led to the so-called Han Learning or textual criticism, which flourished during the reigns of Qianlong (1736-1799) and Jiaqing (1796-1819). But as China entered the modern era, this kind of learning, segregated from the social reality, became more and more inadequate in relation to the complicated new situations of a new and troublesome era. From the rank of the feudal intelligentsia there began to emerge a group of persons who were acutely sensitive to their epoch and courageous enough to face the darkness of the feudal social and political realities. They were no longer satisfied with the narrowness of the traditional classical learning and expressed their longings for a change toward reality, though at first in a tentative manner. Thus the academic discipline of the Qianlong and Jiaqing periods gradually began to divert its course, and in contrast with the convention of textual criticism of the ancient classics, a new stress on the practicality of academic learning for the betterment of the political and social reality appeared at last. Among the representative figures who took the lead in the trend were Lin Zexu, Gong Zizhen and Wei Yuan. An enlightened intellectual camp now began to take shape in opposition to the orthodoxy of the traditional intellectual gentry.

Lin Zexu (1785-1850), a native of Fuzhou in Fujian, had been the governor of Canton and in command of the Chinese forces during the Opium War. As a prominent representative of the camp upholding the war against the invaders, he was obliged to focus his view on the living world, instead of confining himself to the dead documents of the ancient classics as did the old-fashioned intellectuals. He was the first in modern times who made serious and systematic efforts to study the outside world and compiled a book under the title of *A Record of the Four Continents*. He took the lead of the new wave and of the group of advanced intellectuals who gradually enlarged their visions and emancipated themselves from the bondage of the old classics, turning instead to learning about the wide world and the place of their country in it. To know the world and to know the place of oneself in it; this was the first step in modern times towards China's ideological emancipation.

Gong Zizhen (1792-1841), a native of Hangzhou in Zhejiang, was born in a bureaucratic family. Though a bureaucrat too, he was never in power. He was a little younger than Lin and died during the time of the Opium War. Although active in the time prior to the Opium War, in many aspects he deserved to be ranked as one of the earliest modern ideologues. Meanwhile, he was also a recognized poet. In his many widely circulated poems, there might be perceived a deep sense of dissatisfaction with the social reality and a clear call for a brighter future. He was undoubtedly worthy to be ranked high on the list of forerunners who opened a new way of thinking in a new epoch. Speaking about the historical role of Gong, Liang Qichao remarked: "In recent decades it was Gong who took initiative to make the intellectuals turn the focus of their learning on the lively discussion of current affairs in the world by studying history and by scrutinizing the past."[1] History was then moving from the mediaeval to the modern, and so also did the learning and ideas of the intelligentsia. And Gong's writings were the cutting-edge of this historic transition. As an outstanding literary writer, Gong Zizhen exercised immense influences on the intellectual world of the late Qing period, especially on the New Learning School.

While in the later half of the 18th century, Zhuang Cunyu and Liu Fenglu in Changzhou and Song Xiangfeng in Suzhou undertook to study anew the teachings of the Gong Yang School of the Han

Dynasty. They added and elaborated some ideas from the traditions of the New Text School. In the study of the ancient classics, they were looking for a sense of the so-called "great meanings within the delicate expressions", literally the esoteric teachings in the Confucian classics outside of the annotations and commentaries of the Old Text School. In his youth, Gong had learned after this school, which provided him with a ready-made mode of expressing his own thoughts vis-a-vis both the textual approach of the Han School and the speculative approach of the Song School. Gong adopted the antiquated form of "a theory, extremely strange and queer," to criticize the political and social reality of his time while tortuously expressing his demand for reform. With poems and essays in an entirely fresh and brilliant style he opened a new field of thought independent of both the Han School and the Song School and forcibly moved the minds of the progressive intellectuals of the late Qing period. To quote again the words of Liang Qichao: "As soon as the modern idea of freedom of thought was spoken of, the foremost figure of it was undoubtedly no other than Gong Zizhen. All modern intellectuals who had in one way or another shed light upon the intellectual emancipation, had as a rule admired no other than Gong from the start."[2] The prevailing mode of learning at his time was textual criticism along the line of the Han School, but Gong commented profusely on various current affairs topics. The prevailing literary style at his time was the classical style of the Tongcheng School which officialdom employed as a tool for expressing the orthodox ideology of the Neo-Confucianism preached by the Cheng brothers and Zhu Xi; but Gong stood forth in opposition to this orthodox ideology with his literary style by employing the rhymed form of essay writing in his comments on current affairs.

In his writings, Gong exposed the serious social crisis and condemned the corruption of officialdom. He sensed that the political and social structure of his time was rapidly declining and provoking "a strong protest from the people in the mountains".[3] He had proposed some measures of reform upon the model of Wang Anshi, the famous reformer of the 11th century, and even designed a system for the official distribution of farmlands in an attempt to moderate the sharp contradictions between the rich and the poor. But all were no more than visions and were of no practical avail at all. Neither did he ever think of overthrowing the age-old institution and the feudal regime, nor of embracing the coming capitalism. The historical contribution of his ideas lay mainly in the fact that by criticizing the darkness of the waning society he threw the earliest light upon the arrival of a new epoch.

The articles and pieces that Gong wrote dealt with various aspects, political, social, academic and literary; but as a whole they did not form a systematic theory. His basic political position was that of a reformist. The criticism he directed at the traditional idea of Heavenly Mandate and of human nature, though bearing political and social significance, was far from being penetrating.

At the pivotal moment when feudal society was falling headlong into its dying stage, the feudal apologists were trying their utmost to propagate their retrogressive interpretation of history, asserting that each generation was a step backward of the former one and that the course of history should be kept unchanged within the pattern of antiquated feudalism. Against this current of thought, Gong Zizhen proposed his evolutionary interpretation of history. He taught that history was in constant progress and each epoch had to be succeeded by a new one; and that this was an irrevocable trend dictated by the necessity of history. This progressive conception of history, professed at that time, was a valuable contribution to modern intellectual history as well as to the theoretical foundation of his own demand for political and social reform. But just as his idea of reform did not touch the very basis of feudal institutions, so his evolutionary concept of history did not exceed the basic boundary of feudal institutions. In the later years of his rather short life, he was obssessed with a sense of perplexity and desperation and turned more and more to Buddhism for consolation in order to escape the reality which he found himself incapable of coping with.

Wei Yuan (1794-1857), a native of Shaoyang in Hunan, was born in a landlord family. Being an intimate friend of Gong Zizhen, he and Gong were known together as "Gong and Wei" by their contemporaries. Wei had served successively as an aide on the staffs of Tao Shu and Lin Zexu, both well-known governors of the age, and was renowned for his study of practical learning. His works were collected posthumously into the *Writings from the Guwei Hall*. He was also a famous ideologue and historian. Such works as *A Record of the Imperial Expeditions, An Illustrated Record of the Oversea Countries* and *The Essence of Lao Zi* were circulated widely.

The span of his activities was a little later than Gong Zizhen's. He witnessed the whole course of the Opium War and was frustrated by the bitter experience of this hard time; so it was natural that his thought was motivated by an urgent longing for reform. He pointed out serious social and national crises and advocated plans for domestic reform and resistance to foreign aggressors. The old routine practised in the feudal way was obviously incapable of meeting the new situation of the new epoch, so he called for reform on a large scale. He postulated: "There is no institution that can have no fault for centuries nor can forever remain unchanged";[4] and he propounded: "As to all the old things, the more thoroughgoing changes are made, the more convenient they would be for the people."[5] This was the earliest theory of reform summarized in modern times. The Opium War impressed him deeply with the backwardness of China in regard to modern scientific culture, and he came to the conclusion that in order to get a secure footing in the modern world, China had to catch up rapidly with the outside world, while discarding her antiquated conventions. Thus he put the idea in his slogan: "To learn the merits of the foreign nations for the sake of defending against them",[6] that is to say, China had to learn scientific culture from the West in order that she might resist the Western invaders. This was the earliest theory of learning from the West formally expounded in the modern era. All these ideas had a positive bearing on antifeudalism, intellectual emancipation and the demand for progress.

Wei Yuan was one of the earliest founders of the modern Western Learning School in China. He supplemented and augmented Lin Zexu's *A Record of the Four Continents* into *An Illustrated Record of the Oversea Countries*, which became the first book dealing with world knowledge and world affairs in modern China and reflected a change in the vision of the advanced intellectuals.

At bottom, Wei Yuan's world view was an idealistic one; he never thought of, nor asked for, a fundamental transformation of the traditional feudal institutions. He seemed too simple in supposing that the issues of the age could be met merely by enlarging the range of the people's knowledge and by some revisions of the corrupt links in the conventional political and social chains. It might be perceived

that modern reformists from Gong Zizhen and Wei Yuan in the
Opium War period down to Kang Youwei and Liang Qichao in the
Reform Movement of 1898 had continuously held the same view in
an unbroken line.

Yet some materialistic elements could also be found in Wei's
philosophical ideas, especially when he was laying emphasis on social
reform. Directed towards problems concerning social reality, his
ideas were bound to come into contact with objective reality and thus
break away from his idealistic restraint. In theory of knowledge, he
stressed the importance of learning, as opposed to the idealistic
preaching that knowledge was something inborn in men (and in
particular in sages). He advocated the theory that "one knows only
through one's own experiences and one learns to know the difficulties
only through one's own practices".[7] This was a valuable thesis in its
acknowledgement of the importance of practice to human knowledge; and it went along in unity with his idea that learning should
aim at practicality for the betterment of the real world in which
people lived rather than the useless vainglory of the Han School or
the Song School; and that China should learn from the West in view
of its merits rather than being satisfied with the obscurantist convention of her past.

Like Gong Zizhen, Wei Yuan made use of his progressive view
of history as an ideological weapon to fight against the rule of the
Neo-Confucian orthodoxy, which idealized the ancients and professed a retrogressive view of history, and which by asserting that
each generation was a degradation of the former one, endeavoured
to negate entirely the progress of history. Upon this topic Wei Yuan
argued that in the history of mankind each generation was moving a
step forward beyond the preceding one; and this progress was a
historically necessitated process and could never be reversed by any
individual, including the sage-king. Thus in early modern Chinese
history, there were the polemics between the ancients and the moderns, or Chinese Learning and Western Learning, very much akin to
what had happened between the ancients and the moderns in the
early modern stage of the West, or between the Slavophils and the
Westerners in the 19th century Russia. Indeed, these phenomena
might be regarded as parallel and similar from the perspective of a
comparative study of history.

Wei Yuan affirmed: "Even the ancient sage-kings could not bring a world of arms back to a world without arms, nor a world of criminal punishment to a world without criminal punishment, nor a world of singing and dancing to a world without singing and dancing."[8] This thesis, when applied to political and social reality, meant that China should abandon its old position and should make efforts to progress incessantly; this was necessitated by history itself. Like those of his friend Gong Zizhen, the progressive ideas of Wei Yuan were far from being thoroughgoing; at bottom they did not break through the feudal limitedness. This led to serious weaknesses and shortcomings in his theory. Like Gong, the ideology of Wei in his later years began sinking more and more into decadence and inactivity, and finally he sought consolation in Buddhism, another example of how the reformist way in modern China turned out to be an impasse without exception.

From the above-mentioned forerunners of modern ideology, one may well depict some of the main characteristics in modern history of China as reflected in the intellectual world.

The opium issue and the Opium War, instead of bringing somnolence, had quickened the birth of modern China; it awakened not only the progressive intellectuals among the gentry but also the peasant class, a populous multitude that formed the basis of Chinese society.

2. IDEOLOGY OF THE TAIPING MOVEMENT

The Taiping Movement was the last and the greatest of a long series of the peasant uprisings during the course of feudal society in China. Like all other peasant uprisings, it ended finally in failure; but it hit the feudal regime so severely and shook the very foundation of feudal rule so violently that the Qing Dynasty under the impact was never able to reassert itself, and after tottering for some time the imperial power was definitely and desperately headed for its final collapse.

The defeat in the Opium War and the subsequent humiliating Nanking Treaty brought China into a new depth of suffering, and sharpened an already existing social crisis. The dumping of imported commodities from abroad caused the bankruptcy of the rural manu-facturers, and the opening of foreign trade ports crushed the tradi-tional manufacturing and commercial activities in inland China and led to mass unemployment of transportation labourers. These social turbulences in turn accelerated the annexation of farmlands in the countryside. Now all the conditions were ripe for an outburst of a great revolutionary storm to clean up the old society; and the spark of the great peasant uprising, first kindled in Guangxi in the year 1851, soon swept over half the country. With the momentum of an avalanche, the Taiping army starting from Guangxi and Guangdong, thrusted into Hunan, then occupied Wuhan, the pivotal stronghold in the middle Yangtze valley, and then marched on along the river and captured Nanjing, which was immediately made the capital of the new Taiping regime. A vanguard group of the Taiping army dashed forward as far as the environs of Tianjin, about a hundred kilometres from the imperial capital Beijing.

Hong Xiuquan (1814-1864), the leader of the Taiping Move-ment, came from a peasant family in Guangdong. Like doctrines of all mediaeval peasant uprisings, which for lack of a clear ideological guideline were obliged to adopt some form of religion, Hong's doc-trine was dressed in a religious cloak. In studying it, due valuation should be attributed both to the role of the religious superstructure and to the temporal interests under that religious cloak. Since the early years of the 19th century, the Chinese translation of the Holy Bible and other Christian brochures and pamphlets began to circu-late in some coastal regions of China. Before his armed uprising, Hong had read a Christian pamphlet entitled *Good Words for Ex-horting the Age* published in Hong Kong, from which he capriciously quoted some paragraphs for the purpose of propagating his own ideas. Soon afterwards, he founded the Society for the Worship of God. In 1845-1846, he wrote three apocalyptic religio-political essays with a strong similarity to primitive Christian equalitarianism. He propounded in a prophet-like tone that all the people were the children of one and the same God, so they were all brothers and sisters among themselves, and that in one and the same family of the world all people should eat in common what there was for their meal and dress in common what there was for their clothes. He called for the people to rise up in unity and to annihilate the monsters and devils (referring in his religious terminology to the feudal ruling class) in order to build a new society in which the supreme peace (i.e., Taiping) would reign. This doctrine reinforced in a simple way the protests of the masses against feudalism and rapidly won support from them.

In the cause of overthrowing the feudal rule, it was necessary not only to carry forward an armed revolution, but also to smash the spiritual bonds imposed on the masses by the feudal ruling class, that is to say, to elaborate a theory of revolution. And a revolutionary critique of the existing order was an indispensable constituent of the whole revolutionary movement. Since all the official doctrines of the feudal rulers were invariably incarnated in the worship of the idol of Confucius and his teachings, it was only natural that the doctrine of the Taiping Movement directed its spearhead at Confucius and his teachings. In his essay, Hong declared: "In search of the evils committed by the monsters and devils, we may always find that they were caused by the faults in the teachings of Confucius."[1] This rebellious spirit against the supreme sage reflected an important aspect of the anti-feudal position of the Taiping ideology.

The Taiping Movement demanded the people to crush the old society and to replace it by a new one which might embody the simple ideals of the peasants; and the blueprint of that ideal was presented by the programmatic document the *Heavenly Land System*. It provided regulations for the abolishment of feudal private land property and the distribution of farmlands among the population. All people were to be organized in a military ration system, its ideal being a society in which "all people plow in common, eat in common, have their dress in common, have their expenses in common, and there is no place where there is found inequality and there is no one who is without food to eat and clothes to wear", and "everywhere under the heaven, all people are rationed equally and are well-fed and well-clad".[2] Since the feudal private land property system formed the basis of the feudal society, the Taiping Movement not only revived the slogan "equalization of the farmlands" of Li Zicheng in the 17th century, but also attacked even more fiercely the feudal land property system. With the proclamation of the *Heavenly Land System*, it attracted multitudes from the peasant masses to join its army; and all of a sudden the Taiping Movement rolled into an overwhelming torrent.

But in feudal ages all the ideas aimed at an equal distribution of farmlands were doomed to failure. After all, what was regulated by political coercion in the last resort had to give in to the objective laws of the material world. The Taiping *Heavenly Land System* adopted the measure of equal distribution of farmlands to the people and organized them into a military establishment (the basic unit of which was called Liang,) supported by the public treasury on a rationing system. Being a reflection of the equalitarian idea of the small peasants, it might have satisfied for the time being the land demands of the masses, but it could not and did not conform to the objective laws of historical development in the long run, therefore it was destined to survive only a short time. For a backward society, the way out dwelt in modernization, not in mere equalization among the small proprietors. The Taiping Movement, to avoid the failure of its predecessors on this basic issue, i.e., the issue of land propriety, would have had to elaborate a set of higher and more advanced guidelines in its theory fundamentally different from the utopias of the previous peasants' revolutions. Since the Taiping regime failed to create a more advanced ideology than its predecessors, the same destiny awaited it.

As to the issue of the replacement of an old society by a new and advanced one, practical ideas were contained in the works of Hong Rengan (1822-1864), an important leader of the Taiping Movement in its later stage. He was a distant cousin of Hong Xiuquan and came from Hong Kong to Nanjing to join the movement in 1859 when the Taiping Movement suffered severe setbacks. In 1864 when Nanjing, the capital of the Taiping, was taken by the Qing army, he was captured and killed. During the years of his stay at Hong Kong he had learned something about Western capitalism which enabled him to bring a new element into the ideology of the Taiping Movement. His main work, *New Guide to Government*, written in 1859 (the same year Darwin published his *Origin of Species*), summarized his political ideas and was indicative of the level that a revolutionary intellectual could attain in his search of truth from the West under the historical conditions of that time. In addition to his criticism of the traditional feudal culture and his proposal for revising and strengthening the Taiping regime in regard to a series of current problems,

Hong Rengan went further designing such capitalistic measures as protection of private capital and investments, development of mining industries, establishment of banks, promotion of trade and transportation and advancement of scientific and technological research. But his programme was never put into practice, for the Taiping regime by then had become corrupted and seriously weakened by internal dissensions and military defeats.

After the Taiping regime took Nanjing as its capital, it began gradually losing its original revolutionary ardour and momentum. Towards its later stage, the leaders were blockaded within a besieged city and indulged only in their own illusions with no more force to push the movement forward. Ideologically, they could find no way out except by repeating their superstitious dogmas. Eventually the Taiping Movement, once so dynamic and full of vigour, ended in a complete failure under the attack of the combined forces of domestic and foreign enemies. But added to these external pressures were the fundamental faults committed by the Taiping leaders themselves, ideologically as well as politically, that helped to hasten the downfall of their regime and afforded opportunities for their enemies.

External causes always function through inner causes. The Taiping Movement was typically a peasant war, and as such it carried at its core the weaknesses and limits of all peasant rebellions. To analyse in detail the reasons of its failure is beyond our present scope. But so far as ideology is concerned, one point ought to be emphasized, that is , all superstitions are spiritual opium serving only to anaesthetize the minds of the people. In order to emancipate themselves, the people must struggle by their own efforts, not on the grace of any deity or emperor. In order to overthrow a theocracy, they must not rely on the goodwill of an emperor; to overthrow an emperor they must not rely on any deity or his temporal agent or his oracles. A progressive movement can only be possible when it is under the guidance of a right ideology which meets the demand of its age. The Taiping Movement succeeded and flourished not by the help of God (as they so often professed), but by granting the peasant a piece of farmland; and it failed not due to the loss of the grace of God but to its own mistakes in building up its new hierarchy. In the last analysis, all the illusions born from superstitions could only play one role: to deceive the people. No deity could ever be so well reformed as to meet the need or to serve the interests of the people. Superstitions, as far as they do not reflect the reality of the objective world, can only play a negative role in the progress of human society. To preach that Jehovah was the Heavenly Father, Jesus the Heavenly Brother and Hong Xiuquan himself the Younger Brother who came to the world to propagate their doctrines—all these myths were mere absurdities that ran contrary to any common sense. The Taiping leaders professed that their truth came from their mystic power of conveying heavenly revelations. In its later history the Taiping Movement proved by its bitter failure how seriously the stereotyped and decadent superstitions had bound the initiatives of the masses in their ideas and actions while at the same time had corrupted the Taiping leaders.

The Taiping Movement was a summarization of the long history of peasant revolutions in China, and so it was unavoidably full of the serious limitedness of all the previous peasant revolutions, including equalitarianism, superstition, asceticism and strict hierarchy. The peasant class in the middle ages, as a rule, was incapable of building a brand-new socio-political institution; consequently the peasant uprisings would result either in failure or in the creation of a new dynasty in place of the old one. Under specific conditions, superstition might expediently and conviently serve as a means of propaganda, but it could never last long because it was based on fiction, not on facts. While playing the part of the leader of the peasant uprising, Hong Xiuquan did triumph over his enemy rapidly; but as he was transforming himself into a theocratic sovereign and acting contrary to the interests of the people and the current of history, he hastened his own end. The more he felt he was going to fail, the more he resorted to self-deification, in a desperate need to deceive the people as well as to deceive himself. When the hope for a bright future was relegated to a Saviour and his temporal agent (Hong Xiuquan himself in the case of the Taiping Movement) instead of depending on clear-minded realistic measures, it could only hasten the end of the movement and his own doom. The bondages of superstitions exercised only a disintegrating role for the later Taiping Movement. Within the span of a little more than a decade, the Taiping Movement came to its close; the reasons were manifold, but elements inherent the ideology of Hong himself undoubtedly had a share in it.

All the peasant uprisings inspired by the belief in a divine power, from the Taiping Movement down to the Yi He Tuan Movement, ended in failure; all the reformist movements inspired by the belief in an enlightened royal power, from the early reformists down to the reformists of 1898, ended in failure too. Next in turn were the bourgeois democratic revolutionaries, advancing to the forefront of the historical stage. It was the natural logic of history.

Confronting the Taiping Movement stood the domestic feudal ruling class as well as the foreign aggressors. This counterrevolutionary alliance simultaneously employed two hands: on the one hand, brute force to suppress the people, and on the other hand deceptive preaching to fool the people. From the beginning of the Taiping Movement, the Western aggressors had tried to insinuate themselves into the Taiping regime with their Christian masks in the hope of bringing the new regime under their control. Face to face with the foreign aggressors, the Taiping Movement succeeded in maintaining solemnly the national sovereignty and independence. It was the Qing government that servilely bartered away the national interests to foreign lords in a plot to extinguish the revolutionary flames. In his collusion with the foreign aggressors and in the employment of these two hands simultaneously, Zeng Guofan should deserve the rank of past master.

Zeng Guofan (1811-1872), a native of Xiangxiang in Hunan, was born in a landlord family; during the Taiping uprising, when he was a vice-minister temporarily retired in his native town, he hastened to organize an armed force based on local affiliations for the suppression of the Taiping forces. In comparison with other dominant figures in the ruling camp, he was outstandingly skilled in playing at sanctimonious preaching of feudal orthodox doctrines. Since his youth, he had assumed himself an orthodox Neo-Confucianist as well as a devout follower of the Tongcheng School, that is, an incarnation of the orthodox feudalistic culture. In the year 1854, as he headed his native Hunan army into the battlefield, he issued a proclamation whose central theme was a combination of defending royal power and orthodox ideology.

The proclamation lamented bitterly that orthodox Confucian ideology was threatened by the revolutionary storm and called for the intelligentsia to come to the rescue of the feudalistic ethical code

(Ming Qiao). He declared: "Ever since the archaic times of Tang and Yu, sages of each generation upheld the ethical codes and promoted human relationships", but "the rebels from Guangdong (i.e., the Taiping army) plagiarized foreign teachings to honour a Heavenly Lord ... and the intellectuals were allowed no more to read the Confucian classics, and all of a sudden all the rites and ethics and all the classics and codes were swept away without a trace. It was not only a catastrophe for the Great Qing Dynasty but also an entire break-up of the ethical codes since the creation, which would even make Confucius and Mencius burst into tears in the underground. How is it permissible for all the intellectuals to sit comfortably aside and not to make any effort for some actions?"[3] Zeng based his argument on the long-standing appeal of the traditional "ethical code" with the hope of uniting the old-fashioned intellectuals for his cause. In fact, many intellectuals, including a large number of the New Learning School, were persuaded to follow him against the Taiping Movement. This might be partly attributed to the fact that the Taiping policy, owing to its sensitivity to the valuable and democratic elements in the traditional culture, had committed serious faults ideologically and politically. These made it possible for Zeng to assume the role of a defender of the historical culture rather than as a mere royalist partisan for the imperial regime of the Qing Dynasty, at least in the eyes of a large group of the intellectuals.

With the closure of the Taiping Movement, the period of domestic armed conflicts came to an end, but the ideological conflicts still went forward. Some of the Taiping revolutionary ideas were absorbed by the later revolutionaries into their ideology, while the thought of Zeng Guofan was taken as a model by the ruling class down to the twentieth century.

Chapter 21
IDEOLOGY IN THE 1870S AND 1890S

1. BIRTH OF THE EARLY NEW LEARNING SCHOOL

The course which China took while emerging into the modern period of her history was one in which she fell into a semi-feudal and semi-colonial status. An advanced group of intellectuals sensed the portent of this epoch-making moment and demanded a change of the age-old China attitudes to meet the new situation. Most of them came from the feudal intellectual gentry, but they realized the unrealistic and useless features of the feudal culture and began to advocate the learning of the Western culture from abroad which was then called Western Learning or New Learning in contrast with Chinese Learning or the Old Learning. They proclaimed that only the New Learning could save China from the impending crisis and make her wealthy and strong.

From the failure of the Taiping Movement to the Sino-Japanese War, namely in the thirty years from 1864 to 1894, the collusion of domestic feudalism with foreign imperialism had been hastening the process of driving China into colonial status. Companies run by foreign capitalists in China monopolized her foreign trade and her transportation on the sea; and through their industrial and commercial enterprises they were ruthlessly exploiting resources and labour forces in China. The financial life-line of China was in the hands of a few foreign banks such as the Bank of Shanghai, Hong Kong and Singapore (Great Britain), Syokin Bank (Japan) and the First City Bank of New York (U.S.A.). The natural economy of the feudal agricultural society and the traditional manufacture of China was disintegrating under exploitation and suppression by the domestic and foreign ruling classes. The social crisis of semi-feudal and semi-colonial China became ever worsening.

After the fall of the Taiping Movement, the Nian Army in the valleys of the Yellow River and the Huai River continued their armed struggle for years against the Qing government. As world capitalism turned toward imperialism, the partitioning of China was fully under way; and China was facing an unprecedented crisis of national existence. It was during this period that some Chinese merchants, landlords and officials began to invest in modern enterprises and industries—something brand new in the history of China. At the same time, capitalist production emerged; but neither the Chinese bourgeoisie nor the Chinese proletarians had yet come forward as an independent political force.

At that time the Yangwu (literally "the foreign affairs") faction, emerged as a result of the collusion of feudalism and imperialism. Depending on the arms and munitions of the imperialists, they succeeded first in suppressing the Taiping Movement and then the Nian Army. This experience led a group of the bureaucrats in power to realize the importance of the role of Yangwu and they began to pursue the Yangwu practice, i.e., to deal with the imperialists. This trend was headed by Yi Xin, Prince Gong (1833-1898), and Wen Xiang (1818-1876) in the court and by Zeng Guofan, Li Hongzhang (1823-1901) and Zhang Zhidong (1837-1909) in the key provinces. The Yangwu Movement marked the transformation of the feudal bureaucratic class into the compradore bourgeoisie while maintaining feudal privileges. Also, a conservative group of the ruling class was forming a diehard faction. There were slight differences in their respective views and rules and hence a certain degree of contradiction, but in regard to their basic policies, domestic and foreign, these two factions were fundamentally in conformity with each other.

The appearance of the Yangwu faction was a historical necessity following the decline of the feudal regime and the intrusion of the imperialist invaders. Since the 1860's, a group of the so-called "eminent magistrates of the Tongzhi Resurgence", such as Zeng Guofan, Zuo Zongtang (1812-1885), Li Hongzhang and others, undertook to run modern factories and enterprises, mainly in the field of armament production and transportation. Among the most notable were the Jiangnan Manufacturers, Fuzhou Shipyard, and the Tianjin Manufacturers. Later on, a number of coal mining, iron mining, textile and transportation industries developed. They were run by the bureaucrats; hence bribery, corruption and incompetence greatly hampered the development of science, technology and production. It was not until a much later period that private capitalist enterprises began to grow up on a small scale.

The diehard faction invariably stuck to the core of feudalism tightly, while the Yangwu faction tried to rely on the imperialist powers for support of the royal regime, which was in rapid decline. The ideological banner raised by the diehards was still the orthodox feudal dogma that "Heaven does not change, so the Way also does not change." By the Way was meant the traditional feudal ethical codes such as the three guiding principles and the five constant virtues. The Yangwu faction, while keeping the feudal ethical codes intact, added to it elements of "foreign affairs" or "current affairs" or "new policy". The ideological banner upheld by the Yangwu faction was the well-known motto: "Let Chinese Learning be the substance and Western Learning the function." But under the pretext of "self-strengthening" and "striving for wealth", what it meant in reality was only a colonial economy of manufacture-processing. The diehards boasted blindly and presumptuously and refused to learn anything from abroad, and indeed rejected any advanced culture or idea from any source whatever. The New Learning School aptly said of them: "They resent the mere mention of foreigners, and resent much more to hear of getting rich and strong by adopting machinery from abroad",[1] and "they assume themselves to be the only honourable people ... and are proud not to mention foreign affairs at all. Whenever they find anyone in search of Western Learning, they denounce him as a criminal against the Confucian ethical code".[2] Such was the mental state of the diehards. On the other hand, the Yangwu faction was the result of the defeat of feudalism by capitalism, hence they proposed to maintain the feudal ruling order by the application of techniques drawn from abroad. In an attempt to strengthen their own rule, they launched a programme of "army training" and "armament production". Externally they gave in to the imperialists and internally they definitely repudiated any demand for social and political reform. On this basic standpoint, they were in agreement with the diehards and at variance with the New Learning School or the Reformists.

The diehards and the Yangwus were a pair of twin brothers born from the marriage of feudalism and imperialism. The diehards had to make use of some of the "foreign affairs" from opium to artillery, and the Yangwu faction needed the continuance of the feudal royal power. Their basic doctrines were essentially the same. The diehards proclaimed that to learn from abroad meant "to take the foreigners as teachers"—an act by which "what is the fundamental would be neglected at the price of what is the incidental" and consequently "the populace of China would be driven over to the side of the foreigners".[3] Hence they advocated that people "have to learn well Confucius, Mencius, the Cheng brothers and Zhu Xi, the Four Books and the Five Classics as well as textual criticism and their moral and political teachings as fundamental requirements, ... and let these be the substance; then and only then people may proceed to learn foreign languages and arts and to make them function".[4] Such was the idea of the substance (or essence) vs. the function (or incident) in the eyes of the diehards. The Yangwu faction advocated that pupils "should take loyalty to the throne and filial piety to the parents as the essence and Chinese Learning of the Confucian classics and history as the foundation, so that the pupils' minds might be brought to purity, and then and only then they are allowed to irrigate their knowledge and train their crafts with Western Learning",[5] for "the Chinese Learning constitutes the inner learning, while the Western Learning the outer.... The Chinese Learning cultivates the minds and the behaviour, while the Western Learning deals with current affairs";[6] this was what made up the thesis on the substance and the function of the Yangwu faction. As to their basic notions and approaches, there was no difference in regard to the issue of "substance" vs. "function" between these two factions. *An Exhortation on Learning*, composed by Zhang Zhidong, summarized the theory of the Yangwu faction, the central theme of which was aimed at nothing less than the maintenance of the feudal ethical code and the feudal ruling order.

But besides the diehards and the Yangwus, still another faction sprang out of the feudal intellectual gentry. This faction followed the patriotic ideological tendencies of Lin Zexu, Gong Zizhen and Wei Yuan and prepared the way for the ideology of the Reform Movement of 1898. In the political field they advocated reforms and in the ideological sphere they earnestly propagated Western Learning. They belonged to a group of those intellectuals who had recently broken away from the landlord class and embraced some preliminary bourgeois tendencies. Among the main representatives of this New Learning School were Feng Guifen (1809-1874), Wang Tao (1828-1897), Xue Fucheng (1838-1894), Ma Jianzhong (1844-1900), Chen Zhi (?-1899) and Zheng Guanying (1841-1920).

The common features of this early New Learning School were that all of them came from the ranks of the feudal intelligentsia and were trained from their youth by traditional education; but compared with their contemporaries they had more acquaintance with the outside world. Moreover, they were all inspired by a patriotic ardour and the demand for reform, longing in various ways to learn from the West for the sake of transforming their backward country into an advanced one; though their social positions and experiences varied and the points of emphasis in their doctrines were not all the same. They studied Western Learning and demanded the adoption of sciences and technologies as well as some social reform measures after the pattern of the West. In them, there already were some elements of the new bourgeois culture in contrast to the old feudal culture. They expressed in various ways their dissatisfaction with the Western Learning provided by the Yangwu faction in power. They denounced the total dependence of the Yangwu faction on the imperialists which, they taught, could never be capable of bringing any real progress for China. They asked for a breakup of the barriers laid on Western Learning by the imperialists and the Yangwu faction. They had more or less perceived the difference between the capitalist and feudal institutions. They proposed reforms of the old institutions and thus in a certain degree demanded the development of capitalism, in spite of the fact they had not yet formulated their political programme in a completely definite and integrated sense.

The theoretical formula of the Yangwu faction was "let Chinese Learning be the essence and Western Learning its function", a formula which was denounced by the New Learning School as "seeking its function while discarding its essence".[7] On the contrary, the proposition of the New Learning School was: "For a well-governed country, it is its wealth and strength that constitutes the essence, and in search of the way of getting strengthened it is always the way of getting wealthy that takes the lead";[8] and they further asserted: "In their course of getting wealthy and strengthened, the Western nations have given priority to their industry and commerce".[9] Therefore, they insisted that in addition to sciences and technologies, China should learn about the ways and manners by which a country could be well governed and a society well developed. It seemed to them that herein lay the essence of the Western Learning after which they were so eager to pursue.

These arguments concerned political and social institutions. For the first time in modern China the problem of civil rights was touched upon, though in a germinative state with no exposition in full. At the most, they asked nothing more than the institution of a parliament as an advisory rather than a legislative organ, representing more or less the opinions and interests of the bourgeoisie. Even this mild claim was not made manifest by all of them. Generally speaking, the early New Learning School made only some preliminary critical remarks on the feudal institutions and on the Old Learning, and favoured Western Learning. Their criticisms were very much limited both in depth and in width. They had not yet been able to elaborate a systematic theory that could hit the very core of the feudal institution and its ideology, the Old Learning. They played only the role of forerunners for the reformers of the next generation, more mature in form and in content, i.e., the reformers of 1898.

2. GUO SONGTAO AND THE NEW LEARNING SCHOOL

The Yangwu faction had itself undergone a process of differentiation. A part of it was making contact with Western Learning earlier than others; they were motivated by an enthusiastic patriotism and were possessed in various degrees with knowledge of the world and a world vision. They were eager to reform the old society in order to make China wealthy and strong. Such was the genesis of the early New Learning School under the specific historical conditions of that time. Of the upper Yangwus, Guo Songtao was a remarkable personality in whose works might be perceived the first revelation of a wisp of new light.

Guo Songtao (1818-1891), a native of Xiangyin in Hunan, had been the governor of Guangdong and later the Chinese minister to Great Britain and France. In spite of the official posts he held, as a member of the upper Yangwu faction, he embraced his own views on learning and on the world, which ran contrary to that of such other Yangwu leaders as Li Hongzhang and Zhang Zhidong. With these views, he became the enlightened dean of the New (or Western) Learning School.

Guo made very sharp criticisms of other dominant figures of the Yangwu faction. "Nowadays," he remarked, "in managing the Yangwu (foreign affairs), the first thing they do is to learn how to win the battle, but as to the fundamental issue concerned they do not dare even to utter a single word".... "The second thing is to muddle along with the matter as long as possible, and no one dare to speak of any reform about the political institution or social customs, so far as there is no immediate trouble for the time being."[1] The "fundamental issue" postulated here was namely that of the substance vs. the function, or the essence vs. the incident. The issue concerned, in its reality, was no less than the reform of political and social institutions, which the Yangwu leaders never dared to touch upon. Again he remarked: "The old-fashioned intellectual gentry, being ashamed of studying the foreign nations, looked down upon everything foreign and resorted to harangues in pompous words", and "so far as I know, no one who is known for his knowledge of foreign affairs ... knows both the essential and the incidental of it".[2] With this assertion, he cancelled at one stroke all significance of the undertakings managed by the Yangwu faction, and thus opened the vision of a new direction. He criticized the Yangwu faction by pointing out that the emphasis they laid on armament production was definitely "the incidental among the incidentals". And he further explained: "Concerning the wealth and the strength of the Western nations, there is also the issue of the essence vs. the incidental, and all the machinery employed in production are the incidental among the incidentals."[3] Thus on the polemics of the substance vs. the function, or the essence vs. the incidental, he parted company with the Yangwu faction and opened an ideological current of another type, the theme of which might be formulated in the following proposition of his: "Armed forces are the incidentals while legislation and institutions are the substances upon which a nation really rests."[4]

It was noteworthy that many predominant figures of the New Learning School from Xue Fucheng to Yan Fu and Tan Citong had all admired him greatly and agreed with him. Tan Citong had repeatedly praised him to justify Tan's own opinions. When Yan Fu was a naval cadet in Britain, Guo was the Chinese minister there; they became intimate friends and "discussed day and night incessantly on the similarities and differences between the Chinese and Western Learning."[5] Upon the death of Guo, Yan wrote an elegiac couplet, saying in effect that "in the course of my whole life I had been looked upon by you as a national élite" and "in your activities in the world you had been involved by being far too clear-minded"; this referred to the fact that Yan himself was appreciated by Guo and that Guo's ideas were incompatible with the Yangwu faction. From the standpoint of the polemics between Chinese Learning and Western Learning in modern times, the thought of Guo had some basic ideas which differed from those of his predecessors and contemporaries of the ruling camp but which were later taken up and developed by the reformers of the New Learning School. In truth, his ideas sketched in rough outline the ideology of the later reformers from the 1870s to the 1890s.

With Guo Songtao, the views and visions of the progressive intellectuals began breaking away from learning to make steam engines and artillery and began focusing on the political and social institutions as well as the ideology and culture of the West. Guo declared: "All the wealthy and strong nations have to rest on a foundation which is no more than the cultivation of their ideas, mentalities and political institutions."[6] By this thesis, not only did he break away from the dominant diehards and the Yangwus but also affirmed that the wealth and strength of a nation are rooted in its social institutions and ideology. It thus marked the origin of the main currents of the later New Learning School. Guo used to make comparisons between Chinese and Western Learning, pointing out that "the Westerners stick to practicality" while "the Chinese stick to vainglory".[7] All these ideas were later absorbed into the thought of Yan Fu.

Guo Songtao possessed a first-hand knowledge of the West which was rare in his contemporaries and which helped him in the formation of his own ideology. After he stayed some time in Britain, he came to realize that "what contributed to the constant renewal of the politics and manners here" lay in the fact that "for more than a hundred years the officialdom and the people have studied their politics together and carried it out in the name of the king, hence they go day by day towards a well-governed state". In comparison with Britain, "the Chinese intellectual gentry are always prone to count on their own selfish motives, endeavouring to withhold the momentum of the world, and so they are doomed to fail".[8] Here the "momentum of the world" was interpreted by him as "the natural motive of self-interest in society with which all people are endowed and through which all are able to manage by themselves with no need of supervision at all on the part of officials".[9] This was plainly asking for a laissez-faire capitalism in place of the bureaucratic capitalism under the supervision of the Yangwu bureaucrats. The Yangwu faction was in reality colluding with the diehards in strangling the vitality of the germination of capitalism, whereas behind all the doctrines of the New Learning School there was a drive for the birth of national capitalism. It was on this point that Guo became the earliest spokesman for capitalism.

Emphatically Guo pointed out: "The cause of the wealth and strength of the Western nations dwell with their civilian business-men" and "What makes them wealthy and strong are the abundant accumulations of the civilian businessmen".[10] What he termed the "civilian businessmen" meant the private capitalists in contrast to the bureaucratic capitalists from the Yangwu faction. The implication of his doctrine was that China might become wealthy and strong only by the development of the capitalism of the national bourgeoisie instead of the bureaucrats. "Is there any such thing in the world," he asked, "that a state seeks after wealth and strength for herself, while leaving her people in poverty? Those who talk profusely about wealth and strength nowadays seem to consider that the basic policy of the state has nothing to do with the common people. They do not understand that the wealth of the Western nations dwells with the people but not with the state."[11] Here "those who talked profusely about wealth and strength" referred to the bureaucratic capitalists of the Yangwu faction, and he affirmed that the path they took could only result in forming a bondage to the development of capitalism, without ever reaching the goal of getting wealthy and strong.

Since the development of capitalism would make China wealthy and strong, he thought, there was an urgent need to introduce a set of political and social reforms to accompany the development of capitalism. Guo had extensively discussed the political and social institutions of the Western nations, such as the institution of parliament; but he laid most of his emphasis on "learning", stressing its special importance. This position of his became, later on, one of the important theses which brought the New Learning School in antagonism with the Yangwu faction. Since the time of Guo, the cardinal importance of "learning" was without exception stressed by all the New Learning School from the earliest ones down to the reformers of 1898.

Many Western missionaries advertised that the Western religion (Christianity) was the root of getting wealthy and strong, while the diehards and the Yangwus tried their utmost to uphold the feudalistic royal orthodoxy and ideological orthodoxy as the root. The polemics over the issue of the substance vs. the function, or the essence vs. the incidental, constituted the demarcation line in the ideological battlefield of that time. And what defined the New Learning School was that it sought Western Learning (instead of the art of steam and artillery) as the truth that might serve to save their country and their people. It was in this respect that Guo Songtao stood out as the foremost representative of the early New Learning School.

"What the foreigners deal with in China," remarked Guo, "consists in: first, trade; second, religion; third, armed forces. These three go in inter-dependence but each in its own way."[12] But besides these three, there was also Western Learning (in the sense the New Learning School understood it). Hence Guo proposed: "Nothing would be more urgent than the learning of what concerns the basic policy of a nation and her talents."[13] He criticized the old-fashioned intellectuals with these words: "They read all day long without ever knowing about what it is for. They think that if they could learn the vainglorious writings quite well they might eventually pass the civil examinations and earn themselves official ranks and wealth, then the task of their readings would be accomplished." He recalled the days when he himself "went to the West and saw there some remnants of the ancient schools; but they were in general strictly regulated with exacting studies and aimed at practicality, not at vainglorious writings". So he came to the conclusion that "it is appropriate now to establish schools in the port cities to foster practical knowledge for the benefits of society".

The idea and the spirit of the early Qing scholars in favour of practical knowledge for the benefit of society, once buried underground by the Han Learning of the Qianlong and Jiajing period, was now reasserted with emphasis. Western Learning as advocated by Guo Songtao was obviously much at variance with that of the Yangwu faction, who in running their organization and institutions put Western Learning within a very narrow scope and in a state of vassalage to orthodox Chinese Learning. Now the current started by Guo began to become the opposite of the Chinese Learning upheld by the diehards and the Yangwus, and signalled the key moment of transition in the polemics between the Old and the New Learning Schools. Guo had engaged almost his whole life in the study of the basic issues of institutions and learning, Chinese and Western. He declared: "The Western nations subsist by relying on both the substance and the incidental, and both the governing and the governed are in unity in finding the ways and means of their own subsistence. It is important for us to scrutinize their conditions and tendencies so as to know their merits and defects."[14] This conviction became the goal and the direction of the emerging New Learning School.

In addition, Guo Songtao created a rather systematic theory of the causes relating to the rises and declines in the long history of China. He put forth repeated discussions on the political strategies of the Han and Tang dynasties, the principles of which (so he taught) were forgotten and understood no more by the later generations. "Since the Southern Song Dynasty (12-13th century)," he remarked, "the intellectuals were accustomed to the hypocritical phraseology, and so the loci of the right vs. the wrong, of the gains vs. the losses and of the well-governing vs. the bad-governing for the past thousands of years were vanishing into oblivion."[15] This remark, of course, implied criticism of Song Learning. His demand for real learning of practical knowledge for the benefit of society, his opposition to the uselessness and vanity of the traditional Han and Song

Learning, his urge to learn after the West, not only to learn their sciences and technologies, but (what was more important to him) to learn their ideologics and institutions; all these showed that Guo had taken another path quite different from the Yangwu faction and opened the way for the New Learning School in the late Qing Dynasty. Though he professed himself to be a Yangwu, the contents of his teachings were in reality no longer Yangwu in the sense of the Yangwu faction, but were Western Learning in the sense of the New Learning School.

Concerning his own Yangwu ideas, Guo made a self-criticism as follows: "What I have learnt in my whole life was all of the vanities, to no effect of practicality.... Yet in studying the ancient history for the sake of testifying to the happenings in the modern times, I did know something about the political strategies in governing the country and winning over the foreign countries, from the history of Han and Tang up to the antiquity, as well as something about the keynotes of the whereabouts of the unity and the diversity of the merits and defects of the respective epochs. And I know all of them to their depth. I am of the opinion that since the time of the Southern Song Dynasty these principles had been neglected and fallen into oblivion for more than seven hundred years, and in this I have confidence in myself and ought not to be too moderate to confess it."[16] In his moderation, we may decipher a sense of satisfaction in himself. He criticized the conservative tendency of the ruling class that "none of them has a sense of being guilty"[17] in smoking opium or enjoying foreign commodities, but "on hearing the proposals of building the railroads and telegraphs they would all rise in objection with bitter hatred".[18] He did not agree with Li Hongzhang's way of "striving merely for arms and armaments", but advised that China should, above all, build up modern industries of her own in order to avoid the situation in which "all the privileges are left to the side of the foreigners, while China is left with no means to support herself".[19]

Guo Songtao made a comparison between Chinese autocracy and British constitutionalism, saying: "In China, there is too wide a gap between the officials above and the people below; and moreover, the officials make it a usual practice to harbor one another for their own selfish interests. As the sight and hearing of the sovereign is covered, so the wishes and emotions of the populace are always smothered before coming to the throne." The building of railroads, posts and telegraphs, so he recommended, would let "the rich do their duties for the utility of the nation. It would move all to cheers. The railroad would pass the whole country just like the circulation of the blood would do naturally with the human body. Under this condition, all the good and all the bad in politics cannot lie hidden, and then there would be no need to worry about the corrupt officials who would for their own profits withhold the people's desires.... The prosperity of the antiquity would exist nowhere else than in the officials doing their duties and the people expressing their opinions".[20] Such was Guo's naive political ideal, which subsequently became the common programme of all the later reformers.

In what follows we shall make a brief survey on a series of the prominent figures of the New Learning School, contemporary with Guo or a little bit after him. All of them possessed social status far inferior to him, but their basic ideas were mainly the same as his.

3. IDEOLOGY OF THE EARLY NEW LEARNING SCHOOL

Since China entered her modern era, she has been confronting "a situation of great change unprecedented in the course of two thousand years". Lashed by the new historical torrent, the antiquated ideology was obviously becoming entirely inadequate in coping with the new realities. Yet the age-old social institutions and ideologies were so deep-rooted that it was hard, if not impossible, to pull them down lightly and in a short time. New ideas were germinating but were still packed with the old label.

The reason that China was defeated again and again by the invasion of foreign nations might be summed up in two ways: first, the decadence of her traditional institutions; second, her backwardness in modern science and industry. Exactly here lay the central context to which the progressive intellectuals were to address their answers on how to make China wealthy and strong.

The Yangwu faction blew also its trumpet about "self-strengthening". But since it was beyond their capacity to launch any fundamental reform of traditional institutions, their views were of necessity limited to the realm of armament production and other related enterprises of a compradore nature. Unlike the Yangwu faction, the New Learning School began to turn its eyes to the learning of the Western ideologies, together with basic science in a more general sense. They demanded development of the industrial and commercial enterprises of the bourgeoisie and of political and ideological measures to complement it. They differed from the Yangwu faction in their basic views, but the earliest group of the New Learning School grew just out of the Yangwu faction; because it was only in the Yangwu camp that they were provided with conditions for contact with the earliest Western Learning.

The guiding formula of the Yangwu faction (and later on, the diehards as well) might be summed up as the feudal ethical codes plus the colonial processing industry; and that of certain Western missionaries, theological preaching plus the Yangwu formula. Both were obstinately opposed to the basic reforms of the feudal institutions. But the New Learning School came forth to profess that for the sake of making China wealthy and strong it was necessary to master Western Learning, by which they meant not only science and technology, but what is more important, the political and social institutions of the West and their related doctrines.

Members of this New Learning School for the most part came out of the middle social stratum; their ideas were similar, with only minor variations. They demanded chiefly such reforms as the abolishment of the old-style imperial examination system based on ancient classics, the convening of a parliament, and the promotion of civil industries and of Western Learning. Once Western Learning was fully mastered, they expected the Chinese nation would be wealthy and strong. One among their ranks described the rising of Western Learning in their time in these words: "Since the reigns of the Emperors Daoguang [1821-1850] and Xianfeng [1850-1861], China had been more than once defeated by the Western nations, and then envoys were sent abroad engaging in diplomatic intercourse. Among the intellectual gentry, those who took interest in current affairs, observing the orderliness regulated by the statutes [in the Western nations], the skill of their manufactures and crafts, the refinement of their armies and navies and the prosperity of their trade and transportation, began being ashamed of their own poverty and weakness. Thereupon Western Learning flourished exuberantly, and all people [the progressive intellectuals] began racing in competition to talk about their [the Western] books and their institutions in order to transform the old customs and manners [of China]."[1]

A forerunner of the early New Learning School contemporaneous with Guo Songtao was Feng Guifen (1809-1874), a native of Suzhou and a pupil of Lin Zexu. Feng followed the Han School in the interpretation of the ancient classics and studied intensively on philosophy, textual criticism and mathematics. His ideas and doctrines were put forth in his theoretical work "*Discourses in the Xiaobin House*", the preface to which reads: "I had studied ten years and then experienced the hardship of the worldly life for thirty years, so that my personal opinions could not help from being intermingled with the thoughts of various schools and biased by my prejudices and even mixed with foreign doctrines, but I'll not allow my intentions go astray, running contrary to the teachings of the ancient sages."[2] These words showed that he embraced in a certain degree a discontent with the orthodox learning and tried to introduce some of the Western Learning; but at the basic points he kept himself within the very boundary of the traditional old learning and ideology. The relation of the Chinese and Western Learning was defined by him as that between the main and the auxiliary, or as he put it: "Take the Chinese ethical codes as the essential and the foreign ways of getting wealthy and strong as the auxiliary."[3] His statement represented the New Learning School's diffident voice calling for Western Learning and signalled a deviation from the orthodox Chinese Learning. It can't be equated with Zhang Zhidong's proposition "let Chinese Learning be the substance and Western Learning the function". Here the difference lay in the fact that Feng's proposition was directed against the monopoly of the orthodox Chinese Learning and ethical codes, hence was striving for a room for Western Learning; whereas the Yangwu faction's proposition, like that of Zhang Zhidong, was directed against "the theory of civil rights and equality" of the New Learning School, and hence was striving for the rule of the feudal orthodoxy. Despite their verbal similarities, they implied very different historical connotations.

Feng Guifen advocated: "Learning is that out of which the practical utility is derived. Sima Qian in his discussion on statecraft said: Follow the later kings, because they were nearer to and similar in manners to the present, and their proposals were easy to realize. And I think it appropriate today to say: Take the foreign [the Western] nations as mirrors. They are contemporaneous with us in our neighbourhood; but they are capable of getting wealthy and strong, while we are not. Are they not the better and the more evident among what are similar to us and easy to follow?"4 Again he proclaimed: "In that there is no talent wasted, China is inferior to the foreign [the Western] nations; in that there is no land not utilized, China is inferior to the foreign nations; in that the teachings conform with the practices, China is inferior to the foreign nations"; therefore it was necessary for China to learn "why they are smaller yet stronger and why we are bigger and weaker?" and then "to strive to be their equal".5 This implied that China ought to learn from the West and to make reforms on her own institutions. Feng's ideas were among the most advanced of his time and also the earliest refutation of the position of the Yangwu faction.

Moreover, in advocating Western Learning, he taught that: "All Western learning comes from mathematics", and thus paid special attention to the significance of basic science. This view obviously ran contrary to that of the Yangwu faction, who thought and taught that Western Learning existed nowhere else than in their gunboats and artillery.

A bit later after Feng was Xue Fucheng (1839-1894), a native of Wuxi in Jiangsu who came forth out of the staff of Zeng Guofan and then that of Li Hongzhang, and went to Europe as the Chinese envoy to Britain and France. His works were published under the title of *The Complete Works of Yong'an*. On the issue of substance vs. function, or the essence vs. the incidental, Xue advised that people should "employ the practical sciences (of the West) for the purpose of defending the Chinese ways inherited from antiquity"; but at the same time he advocated the "unification of all learnings, Chinese and Western, old and new,"6 and thus he allocated to Western Learning a higher position than before. On the following two issues Xue expounded his views in a more definite mode than his predecessors. One of them was which way China should follow in getting herself wealthy and strong. He taught: "In striving for wealth and strength, the Western nations put industries and trades above all others.... As to their ways of getting wealthy, it is industry that leads to the development of trade, hence it is industry that constitutes the substance and trade is function."[7] Again he taught: "In recent times the leadership and the rank and file of the British are of one mind in managing their policies deliberately, and thus bring their industries and trades up day by day. Therefore Britain now holds a position superior both in wealth and in strength to all other nations which are in their turn following Britain and scrambling for wealth and power. It is this situation that leads the Western nations to an unprecedented prosperity."[8] Xue's intention was only too clear: For the sake of getting wealthy and strong it was necessary for China to develop a capitalist economy following the path of Great Britain.

Another issue of both theoretical and practical importance was the problem of change vs. inertness, or whether China should change or not. In opposition to the feudal apologists' theory: "Heaven does not change and so the Way does not change too", Xue put forward his proposition: "The Way of Heaven changes slightly within hundreds of years and enormously within thousands of years", and "when the world changes slightly, the Way of governing a state changes with it slightly; and when the world changes enormously, the Way of governing a state changes with it enormously".[9] This proposition carried epoch-making significance. Since there was no eternally unchangeable and unchanging Way of Heaven, so there was also no eternally unchangeable and unchanging political and social institution; China was just on the turning point "when the world changes drastically", so it fell to her to change drastically together with the world. Xue asserted: "The reason why the Western nations change lies not in that they are taking interest in changing but that they are obliged by the situation to do so. The world changes so rapidly at the present time that I am led to the conclusion that the Way of no change should serve the cause of changing the present for a return to the ancient, while the Way of continuous change should serve the cause of changing the ancient for the expediency of the present."[10] The theory he elaborated, though not thorough-going nor fully amplified, had nevertheless presented clearly the polemics between the two lines; i.e., the return to the ancients held by the Old Learning School and the renewal for the present by the New Learning School. His theory of change, thus formally put forward, was full of realistic significance in the intellectual history of modern China; it pushed forward the ideology of the New Learning School and enriched its content. It afforded theoretical ground for demanding reform and essentially heralded the demand for changing the putrefied feudal society into a modernized capitalist society. Soon afterwards, the representatives of the New Learning School brought Xue's theory of change to its apex on the eve of the Reform Movement of 1898.

Another outstanding figure of the New Learning School in the same context but of a much later date was Zheng Guanying (1841-1920), a native of Xiangshan in Guangdong, whose social experiences differed considerably from the above personalities and whose views represented that of the enlightened intellectual gentry. Having witnessed the aggressive war of the Anglo-French forces in China, Zheng determined to give up taking the traditional imperial examination for entering into officialdom, and turned away to engage himself in trade. Such an action itself furnished an example of the transition of the feudal intelligentsia into the bourgeoisie. With a direct knowledge of the capitalist countries, he formulated his ideas in a book entitled *Frightening Words to a Prosperous Age*. Like many others of the New Learning School, Zheng was dissatisfied with the Western Learning taught by the Yangwu faction, denouncing it by saying: "The strength of the Western nations exists in their learning but not in their talents. Therefore in order to compete with them, the point does not lie in arms and warships only.... Those who nowadays learn after them, have learnt no more than a superficial knowledge of their languages with the sole purpose of earning a living with it. How can they ever come into contact with even the slightest idea of the profundity and variety of Western Learning?"[11] Here Western Learning was elevated to the status of being the only way to save the Chinese nation.

On the issue of the substance vs. the function, or the essence vs. the incidental, Zheng preached: "Let Chinese Learning be the essence and Western Learning the incidental", or "Chinese Learning is the essential and Western the auxiliary". Furthermore, he even argued that sciences were the physical "means" while the traditional ethical codes the metaphysical "Way"; and tried to bring science into the framework of the feudal orthodoxy. Hence he asserted: "The Way is the essential and the means the incidental, the means changes but the Way does not; therefore we may well recognize that what changes is only the expedient means to become wealthy and strong, but not the constant Way of Confucius and Mencius."[12] In this respect, his theory sounded rather backward when compared with those of other members of the New Learning School, and might be assigned no progressive meaning whatsoever. As to another issue, i.e., how wealth and strength came about in the Western nations, he summed it up in "learning", just as others of the New Learning School did. He taught: "The strength of the Western nations lies in their learning", so that for the sake of getting China wealthy and strong it was necessary "to learn what they have learnt", or to learn "what makes them so wealthy and strong",[13] i.e., to learn Western Learning. In spite of his talks about the Way vs. the means, or the essential vs. the incidental, he laid his emphasis, above all, on Western Learning; and it was in this respect that he distinguished himself from the Yangwu faction. And his emphasis on basic scientific knowledge also reflected his critical attitude towards the Yangwu view which was limited to the mere utility or function of the gunboats and artillery.

The progressive elements in his ideas were manifested mainly in his political and social doctrines. He spoke of his experience in learning from the West in these words: "I could not help getting angry at the avarice of the foreign nations and being filled with pity at the faults committed by the Chinese government; so I began to learn foreign languages and went abroad to get personal acquaintances with their peoples, to examine their ways and manners, to study their political doctrines and to investigate the reasons of their merits and defects and of their prosperity and declines. It was only then that I came to know that the way of their governing and the basis of their wealth and strength did not lie in their gunboats and artillery but in the unification of their leadership with the rank and file as shown in their parliament, as well as in their ways of good education and good care for the people. All their people are led to realize their talents by the establishment of schools, the enlargement of universities and the study of techniques and specialities; all their lands are made to realize their utility by the cultivation of agricultural and irrigational arts and by the transformation of barren lands into fertile farms; and all their commodities are brought into full circulation by the building of railroads and telegraphs, the rational regulation of taxation and the protection of trade."[14] This viewpoint led naturally to the demand for the development of a capitalist economy as well as for the reform of the political and social institutions.

The idea of "commercial warfare" with a strong mercantilist tendency became the prevailing view among those in the New Learning School. Zheng Guanying justified his theory of commercial warfare by saying that in the last analysis, "the decisive battle is to be waged on the front of the commercial war", and for the purpose of restraining the Western nations and getting China self-strengthened, there is no better way than the promotion of commerce".[15] He went on to say: "So long as our trade and commerce do not flourish, the avaricious tricks and intrigues of the foreign nations would never cease", and moreover, "to engage in armed warfare pays not so much as to engage in commercial warfare. Commercial warfare constitutes the essential and armed warfare the incidental".[16] In this way he gave priority to the development of the capitalist economy, not of armament production as did the Yangwu faction. But the realization of such ideas required a series of political institutions, primary among which, he thought, should be the institution of a parliament, or a representative system after the Western model. Therefore he proposed: "For the strengthening of a nation's power, no measure is more important than winning over the hearts of the people; and for winning over the hearts of the people, no measure is more important than the leadership keeping close contact with the rank and file; and for the leadership keeping close contact with the rank and file, no measure is more important than instituting a parliament."[17] This doctrine was virtually a direct request on a part of the sovereignty of the royal dynasty, though still in a form of petitioning.

Zheng had held that the means was changing while the Way did not. But when the problem concerned the impending interests of the immediate present, he turned abruptly away from his original stand and went as far as to profess: "The Way varies together with the time", and "it is urgent for China to reform her old institutions and customs and to learn from abroad in order to taste the fruits of becoming wealthy and strong".[18] As to the issue of the substance vs.

the function, he also put forward a new proposition: "To cultivate talents in the schools, to discuss policies in the parliament with the Sovereign and the people in unity, the upper and the lower in one mind—all these constitute the substance. Steamers, cannons, rifles, torpedoes, railways, telegraphy—all these constitute the functions."[19] What constituted the essence was now not the ethical codes but the modern parliamentary system. This view came into direct contradiction with his own former theory concerning the Way and the means as stated above, which looked rather like a copy of the Yangwu doctrine. It also reflected sharply the weakness and the vacillating character of the Chinese bourgeoisie, who were wandering between capitalist institutions and feudal orthodoxy. In another place, he even went so far as to warn that "the wise people should be heedful never to stick to the antiquated manners so as to run against the Way of Heaven, casting easily the die that concerns the lot of the nation";[20] this implied that in his views the Way of Heaven was always changing, and it would run contrary to the Way of Heaven to stick to the old institutions and thus to endanger the future of the nation. And the mottoes he advanced: "Let all people render their talents, let all lands render their utilities, and let all commodities be in full circulation" were later on accepted by Sun Yat-sen as one of the ideological components in Sun's early thought.

Yet with all these ideas of Zheng Guanying, as well as those of others of the New Learning School, all they could do was to base their trust in the goodwill of the emperor, hoping he would adopt some benevolent reform measures from the above; they themselves lacked a social basis strong enough to realize their ideals. They had never thought of any realistic way to arouse the masses of the people into a persistent and resolute struggle against the corrupt regime.

Since the 1860s, the New Learning School, though not moving into a face-to-face clash with the feudal regime and the feudal ideology, had in their Western Learning taken a line quite different from that of the Yangwu faction, in their direction as well as in their content.

In the ranks of this school there might be listed many others, such as Ma Jianzhong, Wang Tao and Chen Zhi. Their thoughts were basically of the same pattern. They all demanded the development of capitalist industries and trades and the institution of a parliament transmitting the feelings and thoughts of the lower to the upper; and they put special emphasis on the cardinal importance of Western Learning. Politically they were reformists without the slightest intention of overthrowing the rule of the royal throne; but they were patriots and demanded to learn the merits of their opponents for the purpose of reforming the old rotten institutions. It was for this reason that they distinguished themselves from the reactionary ruling group, who pursued nothing else except the maintenance of their own privileged position.

With the Yangwu in bankruptcy, the aspiration for political and social reform among the people became stronger and stronger. But a more direct confrontation and clash between Chinese Learning and Western Learning, or the Old Learning and the New Learning, did not appear until the middle of the 1890s, that is, on the eve of the Reform Movement of 1898. By that time modern ideology was formally coming forth to the stage and the New Learning School was transforming into a political programme ready for political action.

Chapter 22
IDEOLOGY OF THE REFORM MOVEMENT OF 1898

1. THE REFROM MOVEMENT AND THE THOUGHT OF KANG YOUWEI

The Sino-Japanese War of 1894 ended with the defeat of China and the peace treaty signed the following year was a deep humiliation to China. The failure sounded an alarm to the country: the national crisis to her own survival was becoming unprecedentedly serious, the disaster of being partitioned was impending; and in order to save herself from such a destiny, China had to change through a thorough reform, or she would be doomed to be subjugated. The stimulus of all this to the progressive intellectuals was exceedingly keen. Under these circumstances the Reform Movement emerged, headed by the leading reformers as the spokesmen of those among the intellectual gentry who were on their way of transition into modern bourgeoisie. As the natural economy of feudal China further disintegrated under the suppression and exploitation of the imperialist powers, the social crisis of the semi-feudal and semi-colonial condition was further deepened. The reformers, as a result, developed the reform demands of the early New Learning School into a large-scale political and ideological movement for national emancipation.

Japan, originally a small nation and as backward and closed to the outside world as China, after undergoing a process of reforms, was capable of defeating the Celestial Dynasty of China at one blow in the War of 1894; this not only smashed the arrogance of the diehards at its core, but also signalled the complete bankruptcy of the system run by the Yangwu faction so painstakingly for decades. The path of the diehards was thus at an impassé, and so also was that of the Yangwu faction. In their stead a reform current surged amid the storms of domestic turmoil and foreign invasions. The spread of the news of the peace treaty of 1895 aroused nationwide bitterness and indignation. Thereupon Kang Youwei, uniting 1,300 candidates for the imperial examination in Beijing, presented a petition to the emperor appealling for reform to save China. This was known in Chinese history as the *Petition of Provincial Graduates* of 1895. The long-developing ideology of the New Learning was now bursting into a political and ideological upsurge.

In the same year Kang organized in Beijing the Society for Self-Strengthening, which as an organization for political propaganda and agitation contributed much to the ideological mobilization of the Reform Movement. Kang ran also a periodical *The Chronicle of China and the World*, which introduced to the public current affairs, domestic and foreign, while advocating ideas of reform. Meanwhile the Society for Self-Strengthening was founded also in Shanghai, with its newspaper *Self-Strengthening News* echoing to Beijing from the south. Most members of the society came from the upper and middle strata of the enlightened bureaucrat intelligentsia. As to the more radical youths of the lower strata, they had not as yet formed an independent political force.

In the following year was published Yan Fu's translation (or rather his rewriting) of T. H. Huxley's *Evolution and Ethics*, in which the ideas of natural selection and the survival of the fittest ("the fittest" often read "the most excellent" in Yan's terminology), with ways of thinking unheard of in China. This shook the intellectual world like a bomb. In a series of articles, Yan introduced to the Chinese public the theory of evolution and other brand-new doctrines which served as powerful weapons for the New Learning School and brought it to a new height. In the same year Liang Qichao began to run the *Bulletin of Current Affairs* in Shanghai; and with his fluent and brilliant writings he promoted the idea of reform into an overwhelming torrent. Also by this time, Tan Citong elaborated his *Treatise on Benevolence*, which by arguing against feudal bondages raised the outcry "breaking through the traditional traps."

In the year 1897 the publication of Kang Youwei's *An Inquiry into Confucius' Reform* provided the ideological and historical ground for the Reform Movement. And in Hunan, the reformers organized their Society of the South, together with their periodical the *Hunan Report* or later the *New Report of Hunan*. They ran also the School of Current Affairs with Liang Qichao presiding. Their propaganda for reform was lively and colourful, making Hunan a stronghold for the Reform Movement. In the mean time Yan Fu ran the newspaper the *National Reports* in Tianjin, which published many of his important articles. Various societies were then founded throughout the whole country, newspapers and periodicals poured forth in large quantity, patriotic intellectuals vied in their calls for reform and pushed the Reform Movement to a climax. The propaganda work on the eve of the Reform Movement of 1898 promoted an unprecedented ideological emancipation which quickened the awakening of the Chinese people.

In early 1898, Kang Youwei presented to Emperor Guangxu (1875-1908) his writings on Peter the Great's Reform in Russia and Meiji's Reform in Japan, asking for a reform in China similar to that in Russia by Peter the Great and that in Japan by Meiji. Then Kang organized the Society for National Preservation and raised the slogan: "Preserve the nation, preserve the race, preserve the culture." It attracted a large number of intellectuals from various fields and soon became a political body with a strong influence, or rather a society in name but in fact already an opposition political party after the pattern of the West. In the summer of 1898, Emperor Guangxu adopted Kang's proposals and promulgated a series of reform edicts, including the abolishment of the old-style imperial examinations, the establishment of modern schools, the promotion of industries and transportation, the lifting of the restrictions on the freedom of speech, the reform of the bureaucratic organizations and the appointment of new personnel. But under the obstruction of the reactionary forces of the privileged class headed by the Empress Dowager, these reform edicts remained empty words on paper. In the autumn, the reactionary group headed by the Empress Dowager started a coup d'état in which Tan Citong and five other reformers were imprisoned and killed, and Emperor Guangxu himself was practically dethroned. Kang Youwei and Liang Qichao, by far the most important leaders of the Reform Movement, were exiled abroad. Thereupon, the "Hundred Days' Reform" of 1898, like a momentary flash, vanished in a complete failure. This dramatic episode was known in the Chinese history as the coup d'état of 1898.

The predominant leader of the Reform Movement was Kang Youwei (1858-1927), a native of Nanhai in Guangdong. Kang came from a landlord family and was trained in his youth by traditional feudalistic education on the ancient classics, but later came into contact with Western Learning. While lecturing in Guangdong, he wrote his main works: *Forgeries in the Classics of the Confucian Canon* and *Confucius' Reform* along the line of the New Text School, both for the purpose of offering the Reform Movement a theoretical basis. After he came to Beijing, he presented many reform proposals to the emperor, asserting: "No conservative nation on earth can help the lot of being partitioned", and "all nations on earth become strong by carrying out reform and decline by keeping to conservatism".[1] Therefore he urged a "great change", a "rapid change", a "complete change". Kang laid his hope solely on the throne, dreaming that it could grant beneficial reforms from above and adopt certain capitalist policies after the Western mode. Kang failed to make a proper valuation of the reactionary forces, nor was he able to effect efficient measures for reform. After all, the outcome of the struggle between the contradictory forces in society was not dependent on the will of any individual, not even on that of the emperor himself.

Yet one can never undervalue the immense emancipating effect of the Reform Movement of 1898 led by Kang Youwei, and the new ideas it brought into the hearts of the people. The appearance of his two books, in particular, dealt the intellectual world a shock and aroused outcries and condemnations from the reactionary camp. As a political movement, it eventually failed in its attempt to secure power from the regime. As a reformist movement, it never demanded a thorough change of the very foundation of the feudal institutions. It only demanded in a certain degree some protective measures for the development of capitalism and the participation of the bourgeois intellectual gentry in the regime, at least of that part of the intellectual gentry who were on their way of transformation into the new-born bourgeoisie. But in their heart of hearts, they were, just like the royal dynasty, afraid of the masses rising up in rebellion against the royal dynasty, so they preferred to depend blindly on the kindheartedness of the emperor who might, as they would like to imagine, grant them certain benefits and satisfy more or less some of their wishes. In their view, the determining factor in the development of history was reduced to the goodwill of a certain superior being. This limitedness in their views was of necessity reflected in their theories.

First of all, in the core of their minds they were incapable of breaking up thoroughly with the old ideology. Most of them were satisfied with borrowing one old tradition (e.g., the New Text School of classical studies) in opposition to another on the major premise of not upturning the root of the feudal regime and its ideology. This tendency was most vividly manifested in the doctrine of Kang Youwei, the dean of the Reform Movement. Indeed, Kang made proposals to change the autocracy into a constitutional monarchy, declaring that "the strength of all the powers, Eastern and Western, depends without exception on their constitutions and their parliaments", and "the parliament is where the sovereign discusses the policies and laws with the people", and that "in all nations, East and West, which practise this political system, their sovereigns are united with the multitude of the people in one; and in this case how can their nations be not strong? But our nation is run by an autocracy under which the nation is governed by a sole sovereign with a few ministers; in this case how can our nation not be weak?"[2] Yet his ideal of reform was dressed up with the language of the antiquated New Text School in its interpretation of ancient classics, holding the traditional dogmas as the sole ideological authority. His *Forgeries in the Classics of the Confucian Canon* attacked some Confucian classics violently, declaring that they were fabricated by Liu Xin for the reign of Wang Mang (A.D. 9-22), and Kang branded them as the Xin Learning. In his book, Kang upheld the New Text approach of study in opposition to the Old Text approach. Under the historical conditions of that time, such a theory meant a violation of the age-old sanctity of the inviolable classics and hence a violation of the theoretical foundation of the feudal institutions. Though possessing anti-feudal and anti-orthodox significance, it was after all not a scientific theory in itself, nor had it set itself free from the routine of the feudalistic teachings. In this respect, Kang might be compared to Wang Anshi, the reformer of the 11th century.

This line of thought, when manifested in his political position, led Kang on the one hand to refute certain teachings of the feudal traditions, but on the other hand to still uphold earnestly the highest synthesis of the feudal tradition embodied in the royal authority. His *Confucius' Reform*, published on the eve of the Reform Movement, by adopting the doctrine of the "three ages" as preached by the Gongyang New Text School, had made a false analogy with Confucius' "reform in resorting to the ancients" so as to provide a theoretical and historical ground for Kang's own reform. The Gongyang School in the Han Dynasty preached the "theory of the three ages" by professing that the history of mankind evolved or progressed from the "Age of Disorder" to the "Age of Approaching Peace" and finally to the "Age of Universal Peace". The "three ages" idea was interpreted by Kang as the universal law of the evolution of history from monarchy to constitutionalism and then finally to republicanism; thus the ancient "great significance covered up in delicate expressions" (i.e., the esoteric teachings in the classics) was interpreted by him in the light of the Western concepts, reflecting the reform demands of his time. There were many far-fetched analogies in his books which proved only the fact that since Kang was unable to find anything for working out a theory of a more or less modern character, he was therefore obliged to resort to theological preaching with Confucius as the pontifex maximus so as to facilitate Kang's own reform activities.

It seems that historical phenomena always appeared not uniquely but in pairs; in the West, as history entered its modern stage, the anti-feudal Reformation and the Peasants' War broke out in the 16th century when there were on the one hand the middle-class reformers headed by Martin Luther and on the other hand the peasant revolutionaries headed by Thomas Münzer. As history entered its modern stage in China, there was also the same vivid contradistinction between these two lines: on the one had, the Reform Movement of the reformers and on the other the peasants' revolution of the Taiping Movement. Kang assumed himself the stature of a pontifex maximus, proclaiming: "Never had there been a pontifex maximus who has not legislated for the sake of reform." So it was no wonder that he assumed himself to be a Martin Luther—both he and Luther taking the same hostile attitude toward peasant rebellions. From its very beginning, the Reform Movement possessed a dual character: on the one hand it emancipated people's minds and demanded progress, and on the other hand it feared and opposed the masses rising up in revolution. The reformists were afraid of the people much more than of the reactionaries; and as a result, at the key moment when social contradictions sharpened, the reformers retreated to the side of the reactionaries and reduced themselves to the status of the royalists. And with it, their ideologies were also deteriorating and retrograding.

With the failure of the Reform Movement of 1898, the progressive elements in the thought of Kang Youwei began fading into historical relics while the reactionary elements in his thoughts went from bad to worse. The coup d'état of 1898 marked the demarcation line in the transition of his thought; before it he resorted to the ancient tradition for his reform and laid his hope on the emperor to carry out a liberal reform from above. After it he fell to the royalist camp and upheld Confucius for a wholesale rule of feudalism. As a pontifex maximus, he was eventually self-intoxicated (somewhat in the same way as Hong Xiuquan) and fell from a reformist to a royalist.

Two other works of his later years, *Lectures on the Heavens* and *Book of Cosmopolitanism,* he declared emphatically to be his early writings. Nevertheless, not only were they published for the first time in his later years, but also they had contained in them many historical facts and ideological materials of obviously a much later date; hence there is no reason whatsoever to believe that they were actually written as early as he claimed them to be. There were some topics in the *Book of Cosmopolitanism* which might be regarded as belonging to an early date, but at any rate the whole book was a composition of a much later date. He claimed that as early as 1884 when he was composing his *Axioms of Mankind*, he was meditating about the principles of a society of Cosmopolitanism, but the fact was that he never showed his manuscript to anybody, nor had anybody ever read it. The book as presented in its present form, though dressed up here and there with some seemingly new ideas, was on the whole contrived in a mythical manner, describing intentionally and sophisticatedly a colourful earthly paradise with all possible kinds of luxuries and enjoyments, the sole purpose of which was to boast that his utopia appeared more alluring and much earlier than all the ideals of the democratic revolutionaries, with whom Kang had engaged in bitter antagonism since he took exile abroad after the failure of the Reform

Movement in 1898.

His *Lectures on the Heavens* was not a book on astronomy as its title seemed to suggest. In this book Kang stood in direct opposition to science and crazily preached a new form of religion, i.e., that of Confucianism of the Kang brand. He created in his wildest fantasy a race of fairy-like superhuman beings who looked like no mortal creature. What he discussed untiringly in both books was how those imaginary fairy-like creatures indulged eternally in their fantastic sensual enjoyments. Both books paid lip service to the ideal of Cosmopolitanism; but it should be kept in mind that so long as the real world consisted of various political and social contradictions, it was apparently impossible to realize any kind of Cosmopolitanism until the fundamental contradictions were settled effectively. The more sharp the social contradictions were in antagonism, the more the reactionaries were prone to employ their preachings of "Cosmopolitanism" to blunt the people's fighting will by lulling them with a ready-made utopia. This might explain why the study of Cosmopolitanism, being essentially something of a spiritual opium in nature, became much in vogue in the early 20th century. It was then that some highly-placed philistine missionaries in China were energetically preaching their Cosmopolitanism. It was also then that the domestic reactionaries were energetically preaching their Cosmopolitanism, together with their activities for reviving the Confucian cult. In mutually singing the same tune with each other, they formed a chorus of a hymn of Cosmopolitanism in the midst of which Kang's book came forth as a model of teaching the Chinese people to get into relations of Cosmopolitanism peacefully and willingly with both the foreign imperialism and domestic feudalism. The more Kang elaborated the details of his utopia, the more he betrayed the hypocrisy and fictitiousness of his teaching.

Genuine Cosmopolitanism could never be realized by a mere self-hypnotization leading to mirages. The masses of the people, when not enlightened enough, might dream of a pretty new world in their fancies; but the good wishes of the people could by no means be identified with the preaching of Cosmopolitanism of the reactionaries, which was nothing more than a means of deception for keeping the people in ignorance. The fact that Kang in his later years fell to the position of a myth-teller was inseparable from his political

standpoint as a royalist in front of the coming storm of the democratic revolution. If anyone is to believe that Kang, the royalist,
could produce a genuine blueprint of a genuine Cosmopolitanism for
the new-born republic, that would be equivalent to believing that
Santa Claus could really bring Christmas gifts.

2. THE THOUGHT OF TAN CITONG

The foremost philosopher or, to use the words of Liang Qichao,
"the shooting star" of the Reform Movement period was Tan Citong
(1865-1898); a native of Liuyang in Hunan, who was born in a family
of a provincial governor and was trained in his youth in the Old
Learning. The Sino-Japanese War of 1894 was a great shock to the
intellectual world; after it Tan turned from the Old Learning to the
New and followed Kang Youwei, engaging actively in the Reform
Movement. It was in this period that he wrote his main philosophical
work, *Treatise on Benevolence*, and organized the Society of the
South, waging relentless polemics with the feudal apologists and
diehards. In the coup d'ètat of 1898, a group of the reformers known
as "The Six Gentlemen" were killed, including Tan.

In attacking the feudal autocracy and the teachings of the feudal
"ethical codes", the *Treatise on Benevolence* put forth many audacious criticisms, the acuteness of which reflected vividly the spiritual
image of a fighter who aimed at "breaking through the traditional
traps". He severely condemned all the monarchs for being "great
robbers" and the whole intelligentsia for being "hypocrites" in the
history of China for more than two thousand years; and he proclaimed that the hypocrites by their nature flattered the robbers and
the robbers made use of the hypocrites—"they were ganging up and
bartering with each other".[1]

Furthermore, he advanced his own theory of the origin of the
state, declaring: "In the beginning, there were neither the sovereigns
nor the subjects; all of them were the common people. As the people
were too much occupied to engage in governing themselves, they
began to choose one among them as their sovereign. Since the
sovereign was chosen by the people in common, so it was not the
sovereign who chose his people, but the people who chose their

sovereign", and "since the sovereign was chosen by the people in common, so it was a matter of course that the people were prior to the sovereign; the sovereign was the incidental and the people the substantial".[2] Such a doctrine was full of the flavour of the modern contract theory of the state in opposition to the feudalistic theory of the divine rights of kings, a theory which might strike the readers by its similarity to those in the modern West.

Tan blamed the feudal ethical codes for the "catastrophes and disasters" it had brought upon the people "in the course of the past thousands of years".[3] Among the five traditional ethical categories, he laid stress only on that of friendship to the utter negation of the others. Again this was full of the flavour of the modern idea of civil rights in opposition to the feudal idea of personal dependency and signalled the historic transition "from status to contract".[4] Hence he was regarded by the feudal apologists as a heretic engaging in professing a doctrine of "no patriarch, no sovereign." What he asked was in fact to break through the feudal barriers between men and men and to change to a laissez-faire (or free circulating, in his terminology) bourgeois society. In his *Treatise* he affirmed: "Benevolence takes the free-circulating as its primary principle", and "there is nothing more benevolent than free-circulating, and nothing more unbenevolent than no free-circulating".[5] This philosophical idea reflected clearly the abstraction or generalization of the relations in a capitalist society where all things were expressed in relationship to the commodity-money circulation.

His attack on the feudal ethical codes and the feudal autocracy was a progress in history and a great step forward beyond Wang Fuzhi and Dai Zhen. It was indeed one of the preludes to the Democratic Revolution of 1911. In this respect, he exceeded by far both the early and the later New Learning Schools. But what appears ironic was that he himself became an official in the royal court, joined the reformers' group, was looked upon with favour by the emperor, and even more, stuck stubbornly to the hope that through a sheet of paper of a royal edict issued by a wise and benevolent emperor, new features in the history of China might be expected. This strange phenomenon showed the inherent self-contradictions in his political ideas. And this self-contradiction also manifested itself in his philosophical theories.

There were too many imaginary and fantastic elements in his thoughts to let him make any exact analysis of reality. What was rational in them lay mainly in his view that the whole world existed in and only in a process of eternal movement, variation and development; it provided thereby a philosophical ground for the Reform Movement. Historically, he went beyond the materialistic thesis: "The Way dwells nowhere else outside of the events" and proceeded with his own proposition: "As the events change, how can the Way remain unchanged?"[6] and "the universe is renovating day by day",[7] a proposition which while refuting the transcendentally unchanging entity of the Way as presented by the feudal apologists, provided a theoretical ground for "Reform and Renovation". In addition, he combined the Heavenly Way and human desires in one, claiming that the Heavenly Way existed nowhere else than in human desires; this was a view on human nature in an enlightened way. But Tan had never thrown away the teachings of Confucius and Mencius, and later on he was engrossed in Buddhism and even influenced by certain teachings of the philistine missionaries (including such absurdities as the theory of the response of mental electricity and the cure of disease by cultivating the mind). Especially after he made acquaintance with Kang Youwei, he worshiped Kang and his doctrines. Therefore the course of his thoughts did not go straight towards progress but on the contrary wandered in zigzag fashion back again to an idealistic position.

For the objective world, he fictionized a spiritual substance called Benevolence which he identified with the essence of the universe and all things in it, while the world was thought to be the outward representation of Benevolence. Particularly, he borrowed an outdated and fictitious concept in natural science in his endeavour to illustrate the material world. It was called the "ether" which he identified with Benevolence. Tan was in the habit of quoting capriciously scientific terms which he did not really understand. He gave a free rein to his imagination for the unrestrained exposition of his views. For instance, when he discussed "force", he enumerated as many as eighteen mutual exclusive forces in coordination, while according to the scientific knowledge of his time, there was only one force unique in nature, i.e., the universal gravitational force. This doctrine of his turned out to be a game of playing with concepts and apparently was influenced by the Buddhist way of thinking.

As to the notion of ether, it was originally a conception in physics which was taken by certain early modern physicists as an all-permeating medium in the physical world. In the 1870s, a series of well-known experiments carried by Michaelson and Morley had proven definitely its non-existence. Even before that, when Maxwell in the 1860s measured the velocity of the electromagnetic waves as being about the same as that of light, it was already concluded that light was but an electromagnetic phenomenon, hence there was no longer any necessity to presuppose on ether. Tan's thesis on ether reflected characteristically the limitation of his age as well as of himself. His effort to combine ethical and theological conceptions with the material and natural conceptions was described by a contemporary of his as imbued with an air of Pantheism. Pantheism it was, in the sense that it dissolved the deity in nature and possessed in a certain degree a materialistic tendency. But the philosophical system of Tan was eventually led to a subjective idealism wrapped in a mystic cloak. This could be explained not only by the weakness of the social class he belonged to, but also by the backwardness of the intellectual level of his age; these were factors characteristic of the modern intellectual history of China. Even the democratic revolutionaries of a later period were no exception to this.

Just like many other members of the New Learning School, Tan got a large amount of his knowledge about Western Learning from second-hand dealers, the missionaries; so it was no wonder he admitted certain conceptions, outdated and unscientific, swelling in his mind into a universal truth. Hence Tan believed in the myth that Benevolence or ether might result in a great "mental force" that would carry the Reform Movement and even determine the whole course of history. Therefore he took the goodwill on the part of the emperor as the guarantee for the realization of his ideal. The personal tragedy of his untimely death was but a historical witness of the bankruptcy of the reformist movement.

3. THE THOUGHT OF LIANG QICHAO

The most outstanding young propagandist in the Reform Movement was Liang Qichao, who was at first a pupil and the chief assistant of Kang Youwei, but soon became famous enough to rank with his master, so they were commonly called "Kang and Liang" in China. Liang Qichao (1873-1929), a native of Xinhui in Guangdong, followed Kang in participating actively in the Reform Movement. In 1896, as the editor-in-chief of the *Bulletin of Current Affairs*, he wrote his famous article "A General Treatise on Reform"; in 1897 he assumed the post of the dean of the School of Current Affairs in Hunan, organized with Tan Citong and others the Society of the South and ran the journal *The New Report of Hunan*. Writing in a new style of brilliance and freshness, he made the ideas of reform and renovation a fashion of the time. The awakening intellectuals found his ideas fresh and new. The School of Current Affairs, with Liang as its dean, had waged a tit-for-tat theoretical struggle in Hunan against the feudal diehards headed by Wang Xianqian, Ye Dehui and Su Yu. It was an exciting part of the ideological battles on the eve of the Reform Movement of 1898.

In the School of Current Affairs, Liang and his followers discussed among other things the ideas of "civil rights" and "equality", and expressed sorrow for the fact that in China "the rule of the monarchy has lasted too long". In the eyes of the diehards, Liang and his group, by professing the theories of "civil rights and equality", were running wild to the point of becoming willingly "the criminals of the ethical codes". The diehards in Hunan then proclaimed the following verdicts on the reformers: "The spreading of the heretical theory and the growing unrest in the minds of the people began with Kang Youwei"[1] and "what Kang and Liang employed in misleading the world was the theory of civil rights and equality. But if sovereignty were to shift into the hands of the masses, then who would govern the nation? If the people were to rule themselves, then of what use would it be to have a sovereign? This can lead to disorder in the whole country"; and again: "Kang's disciple Liang is the dean of the School of Current Affairs who professes his master's doctrine, and regardless of the teachings of the ethical obligations, even many among the well-educated admired them as though they were the orthodoxy. Their doctrines rest mainly on Kang's *Forgeries in the Classics of the Confucian Canon* and *Confucius' Reform* and are further supplemented by such absurdities as civil rights, equality and the chronicling dated from Confucius. To falsify the ancient classics means to destroy the sacred dogmas, to credit reform means to discard the established regime, to profess equality means to ruin the ethical codes, to promote civil rights means to abrogate the Sovereign, and to chronicle from the date of Confucius means to deny our Qing Dynasty."[2] Against these theories of the reformers, the reactionary camp, the diehards and the Yangwu alike joined in this position: "Let Chinese Learning be the substance and Western Learning the function." For them, Chinese Learning meant the feudal ruling order and its ethical codes, Western Learning the applied sciences and technology. By that time, the diehards and the Yangwu faction, having held similar positions, came into confluence. Their common position was made well-known by Zhang Zhidong's formulation: "If the doctrine of the civil rights were to be advanced, the befooled would be encouraged and the rebels would rise up, the social and ethical codes would cease to work and great disasters would follow all over the country."[3] For them, the doctrine of the reformers appeared to lead to the destruction of feudalism in its entirety.

Actually, the theories propagated in the School of Current Affairs by Liang and his circle—though they launched certain criticisms on the traditional ethical codes and hence might be regarded as a progressive movement for intellectual emancipation—were nevertheless by no means directed at the complete negation of the feudal institution and its ideology. There was still a great gap between their theory and that of the natural rights and equality of the democratic revolution of the bourgeoisie. The Chinese reformers of the late 1890s were themselves endowed with a strong feudalistic character, so that what they advocated never went further than the demand for freedom of speech and for certain reform measures. But the reactionary camp, out of its instinctive consciousness, sensed rather keenly that this would be the beginning of what would shake the very foundation of the feudal ethical codes upon which they maintained their ruling order. These polemics created a tournament of strength on the ideological front between the two antagonistic camps on the eve of the Reform Movement.

After the coup d'état of 1898, Liang Qichao was exiled to Japan, where he ran the *Forum of Public Opinion* and later the *Journal of the Renovated People* in which he continued to propagate his revisionist theory of constitutionalism, but his intellectual influence was shrinking. With the failure of the reformist movement, the ideology of the democratic revolution under the leadership of Sun Yat-sen and his group was spreading. In this new historical moment, the focus of the contradictions began to take a new turn. Kang and Liang, who then formed a royalist group under the banner of constitutional monarchy in opposition to the democratic republic of the revolutionaries, had already moved to the opposite side of the progressive historical current.

Also the gap between Kang and Liang widened. When Kang retreated from the stage of history, playing no substantial role except that of an awkward clown, Liang was still active in the intellectual arena for a rather long time and with considerable influence, though politically he was in retrogression. In the early years of the 20th century, Liang in his exile in Japan published a series of articles propagating various modern Western ideas such as those of Hobbes, Rousseau, Kant, Bentham and others; as to the variety of their topics, the vastness of their contents and the intensity of their influences, they were almost unparalleled in the history of Western Learning in China. Even some ideological sources of the democratic revolution were directly or indirectly drawn from these writings. They represented a significant enlargement and deepening of the New Learning in contrast to the old feudal ideology; and their contribution to the widening of the vision of the Chinese intellectuals and the emancipating of their minds should never be undervalued. Of course, in propagating the Western theories, Liang did not forget to convey his own reformist ideas. But at any rate, his works, judged from their broad influences, should have to be ranked among the main ideological sources of the later New Learning.

After the Qing Dynasty was overthrown and the Republic established, Liang in addition to his practical political activities (he had been a member of the parliament as the leader of the Progressive Party and twice a minister in the cabinet of the Republic), had written many scholarly works, chiefly in the field of historical study, which were collected in his *Complete Works of the Yinbing Hall*. As to these, we shall give a short narration in the last chapter of the present book.

4. THE THOUGHT OF YAN FU

Another representative of the Chinese progressive intellectuals in their quest for truth from the West was Yan Fu. What separated Yan from Kang and Liang and others was that organizationally Yan did not join the direct political activities of the Reform Movement of 1898, yet ideologically he made the most remarkable contribution to that movement.

Yan Fu (1853-1921), a native of Fuzhou in Fujian, was almost the only one among the students sent abroad by the Yangwu faction in decades to ever become an important figure in modern ideological activities. In the 1870s Yan was sent to Britain for naval studies. He acquired, as a result, first-hand knowledge about this oldest, wealthiest and most powerful of the capitalist nations. During his stay in Britain he witnessed the prosperity of the Victorian period and came to the hope that China should follow the path of Britain. The basic experiences of the Western nations (and specifically of Britain) in building up their modern states were summarized by Yan Fu into two items: "In the world of learning, they dismiss the falsity and advocate the truth; and in political society, they give up the self for the sake of the public."[1] The former referred to natural science, the latter to the capitalist institutions of the West. These were considered to be the model of the wealthy and the strong. It might be fairly said that these ideas of Yang Fu marked the earliest mention of "science" and "democracy"—later the watchwords of the New Culture and May Fourth Movement. In contrast with other members of the New Learning School, Yan had a better mastery of the knowledge of the West. Kang Youwei continued the ideology of traditional learning, while Yan Fu began an entirely new approach in contrast to the old. It was only in the hands of Yan that Western Learning attained its definite theoretical form and content.

Strongly stimulated by the defeat of China in the Sino-Japanese War of 1894, Yan wrote some famous political articles which created a furor over the whole country, such as "On the Urgency of the Present Transformation", "On the Causes of Becoming Powerful", "A Definitive Exposition on the Salvation of the Nation" and "The Refutation on Han Yu". In them, he fiercely attacked feudal learning and ideology as well as the traditional imperial examination system, pointing out that they were utterly "impractical" and "useless" (a view he inherited from Guo Songtao). He termed the work of the Yangwu officials utter "physical superficialities"; and in contrast, he proposed a programme of "encouraging the people's forces, cultivating the people's intelligence and renovating the people's morality".

As to the controversial issue of the substance vs. the function, Yan denounced the motto of the Yangwu faction "Let Chinese Learning be the substance and Western Learning the function" as a vain effort in "seeking its function while discarding its substance", something which was neither an ox nor a horse. He proclaimed that an ox, as endowed with the substance of an ox, had the function of an ox; and a horse, as endowed with the substance of a horse, had the function of a horse. This implied that the function of something was nothing else but the function of its substance, and the substance but the substance of its function (incidentally, Yan was the first to introduce some of the ideas of Hegel to China). To him, substance and function were inseparable from each other; or as he put it, there could never be a thing having the substance of an ox and at the same time the function of a horse, or vice versa. Chinese Learning had its substance as well as its function; and so also did Western Learning. He came to the conclusion that in order to make China wealthy and strong, Western Learning, both its substance and its function, ought to be employed. Defining the substance and the function of Western Learning, he remarked: "The Western nations are superior to us both in their lawfulness and out of their lawfulness simultaneously"; and again in another place: "if we scrutinize that, it is because they take liberty as substance and democracy as function".[2] But he stopped there without any further explanation or amplification.

The polemics over the issue of the substance vs. the function between Chinese Learning and Western were in reality over which of the two paths China should follow: whether to stick to the traditional feudal institutions, or to learn after the West for a reform, capitalistic in nature? The position of Yan was completely opposite to that of the reactionaries, who were advertising "the indispensable trinity of the Confucian ethical teachings, the literary style and the textual study of the ancient classics",[3] the perfection of the traditional learning and the imperial examination system. On the eve of the Reform Movement, the controversy between the Chinese Learning and Western, between the Old Learning and the New, between the modern school system and the traditional imperial examination (based on ancient classics) reached a climax in which Yan played the role of the most outstanding spokesman of the Western Learning camp.

Now, a few words about the polemics between Chinese Learning and Western which constituted the centre of gravity in the modern intellectual history of China. As we have mentioned above, the Yangwu leaders strongly advocated "self-strengthening". Among them, Yi Xin, or Prince Gong, asserted that "for self-strengthening, it is of the utmost importance to train the armed forces, and to train the armed forces the armament production should take the lead".[4] In a similar vein Li Hongzhang asserted additionally that "if China wishes to get herself strengthened, there is no better way than to learn about the powerful armaments of the foreign nations".[5] They all laid their stress predominantly on arms and armament, a proposition which ran contrary to that of the New Learning School. In addition to learning science and technology from the West, the Western Learning group asked further and foremost to learn the Western political and social theories so as to enable the people to reform the old feudal institutions. While both the diehards and the Yangwu faction asked to learn from the West with the sole purpose of maintaining the feudal regime and old institutions, the New Learning camp aimed at reform. Here lay the basic difference. While the motto of Zhang Zhidong "let Chinese Learning be the substance and Western Learning the function" was directed against "the doctrine of civil rights and equality" of the New Learning School, Yan naturally proceeded to refute it. Yet it should also be noted that the idea of "let Chinese Learning be the substance and Western Learning the function" had never been really and entirely discredited; it held its sway in the ideological sphere for a rather long time as a maxim of all the reactionary forces. Even a considerable part of the enlightened intellectuals did not completely free themselves from this ideological bondage. Among those who suffered defeat on the ideological front and finally surrendered to the feudal conviction of "returning to the ancients", Yan himself was a notable example.

In the year 1896, i.e., two years after the Sino-Japanese War of 1894 and two years before the Reform of 1898, Yan Fu translated the first part of T. H. Huxley's (1825-1895) *Evolution and Ethics* under the Chinese title *Evolution*. Historically, the impact of the original work on the West probably might not be as strong as that of its translated version (of course, Yan's translation) on China. A book on the intellectual history of Britain might well slur over Huxley's work, but it would be an unpardonable mistake not to stress its immeasurable impact on China in any account of the intellectual history of China.

By introducing the evolution theory, Yan in his work showed the truth to the Chinese public that struggle for existence, natural selection and survival of the fittest were the fundamental laws governing the world, so that unless China could readjust herself to the natural laws, striving to become strong in order to survive in the world, she would be doomed. This was the main topic of his book, in which he "repeatedly paid attention to the issue of self-strengthening and self-preservation of the Chinese nation".[6] To the Chinese public, such a theory of evolution was something entirely new and unheard of, and the publication of his book was like a bomb bursting amidst the intellectual circles of China; and the ideological repercussions it brought to the public were unparalleled in the history of China. Never had there been any doctrine that sounded such a strong alarm to the whole nation: the world was in constant progress, and if China wanted to survive in it she should have to make constant reforms to institute the new in place of the old. Henceforth the idea of progress as a necessary and objective law, both of the natural world and of human society, was firmly rooted in the very heart of the Chinese public. The feudal ideas calling for return to the ancients, standing still within the traditional norm and refusing to make any change, suffered a fatal blow and lost decisively the dominant place they had held in the past. The eventual establishment of the idea of progress and the necessity of change and reform—herein lay the incomparable value of Yan's introduction of the theory of evolution. A bit later, a considerable part of the ideological weapons of the democratic revolutionaries were derived from the works of Yan Fu and Liang Qichao, among which the most important were the theory of evolution and the theory of natural rights. The revolutionaries differed from the reformists in employing these ideological weapons, the former aiming at justifying a democratic republic and the latter at that of a constitutional monarchy. *The People's Journal*, the organ of the Chinese Revolutionary League, once remarked: "Ever since the publication of Yan's work, the principles of struggle for existence and natural selection have gone into the hearts of the people and the mood of the Chinese has greatly changed. The people professed openly the unity of the community, the repulsion of the foreign aggressors and the expulsion of the Qing Dynasty. All these were of course inspired by the torrents of the age, yet Yan contributed no small part in it."[7] This statement was a truth, though not necessarily corresponding to Yan's own intention.

In addition, Yan through his translation of Adam Smith's *The Wealth of Nations* introduced to the Chinese public the classical theory of laissez-faire, and through his translation of Montesquieu's *L'Esrit des Lois* (or *The Spirit of Laws*, for Yan's translation was from English not from French) introduced the theory of the division of state power into three branches: legislative, judicial and administrative. Through his translation of J. S. Mill's *System of Logic*, he introduced the empirical induction of modern science. All of them represented modern Western ideology in some of its most significant aspects and helped greatly in building up the theoretical system of the New Learning School. Yan made use of these theories in criticizing the traditional Chinese ideology as a kind of idealistic apriorism with no ground of verification in facts. These assertions by Yan embodied the theoretical essence of the New Learning School of his time. They contributed to the criticism of the feudalistic Old Learning not only in their world views but also in their methodology and ways of thinking.

But even before the Reform of 1898 when Yan was playing a positive role on the ideological front, his thought contained a great many negative elements. He did introduce and propagate some new ideas full of progressive significance, but at the same time he also advanced the views of a vulgar sociology. He was especially fond of quoting H. Spencer's arguments to justify his own reformist position. Again and again he praised Spencer, saying: "True were the remarks of Spencer that the people were capable of being cultivated infinitely towards the ideal, but it could never be expected to become realized with great speed";[8] that is to say, the problem of China could only be dealt with bit by bit through a process of gradual transformation instead of sudden change, or in other words, through reform instead of revolution. In his early political programme as well as in the thought of his whole life, he was permeated from beginning to end with the basic viewpoint: "Never expect any sudden leap." Yan's philosophical views were of a dualistic nature: on the one hand there was a vein of mechanistic materialism, trying to interpret the world by mere material principles, but on the other hand they contained a strong element of idealistic agnosticism. As early as in his notes to the translation of *Evolution and Ethics* there were such statements as "any reasoning when carried to its extremity would lead necessarily to the unthinkable".

The bourgeoisie of modern China as a class was congenitally deficient and post-natally malnourished, so that they were deprived of the background to create their own ideology and obliged to copy stiffly the various schools of the variegated thought of the Western bourgeoisie from different nations under different historical conditions over a course of several centuries. From these various schools, the Chinese bourgeoisie picked over a heap of fragments and mixed them up to satisfy their urgent need. And in this respect, Yan was typical. In his theoretical works, there might be found a medley of thoughts separately drawn from Descartes, Rousseau, Montesquieu, Kant, Adam Smith, Darwin, T. H. Huxley, J. S. Mill, Spencer and even Bagehot. Generally speaking, the elements of evolution, parliamentarism and mechanistic materialism were conspicuous during the period of the Reform of 1898. But after that time, the elements of vulgar evolutionism, vulgar sociology and idealistic agnosticism were gaining the upper hand more and more. In his translations of Adam Smith's *The Wealth of Nations*, J. S. Mill's *Logic* and Montesquieu's *The Spirit of Laws*, his fighting spirit as well as his ideological vision were both deteriorating in comparison with the period of his translation of Huxley's *Evolution and Ethics*. Although Yan's works and translations opened an inspiring new world of ideas outside of the traditional Confucian teachings, the more the revolutionary atmosphere (indeed partly inspired by him directly or indirectly) surged, the more Yan became afraid of and bitterly hostile to the revolution.

When Yan was translating J. S. Mill's *On Liberty*, he deliberately changed the title of the book into *On the Boundary Between the Community and the Individual* in order to avoid the term "liberty" which sounded too appalling for him. In his later works he even changed the Chinese term liberty into a synonym to show that his idea of liberty differed from that taught by the democratic revolutionaries. Many a time he stressed that social progress could only be achieved step by step, but "never by overleaping the gradations". By gradations he meant the political process of development from the primitive society to the monarchy and then to constitutionalism and finally to the republic, his standpoint being definitely antagonistic to the impending revolution. It is interesting to note that in like manner the *Journal of the Renovated People* run by Liang Qichao also remarked: "The progress of the world could only be accomplished by the accumulation of piecemeal reforms, but never by overleaping the gradations".[9] It was clear that with the defeat of the Reform Movement and the subsequent surge of the revolution, Yan was falling into a retrogressing path day by day. By that time the ideological weapons of the theory of evolution and the theory of natural rights were already transferred into the hands of the revolutionaries.

After the Revolution of 1911, the Western Learning of Yan Fu had already suffered its final failure. Lagging far behind his time, Yan was unable to find a way out, so that he turned back and surrendered to the feudalistic teachings against which he had fought so valiantly in his former days. Hence it was no accident that when Yuan Shikai (1859-1916) was plotting to assume the throne of the emperor, Yan Fu became one of the six members of the Society for Planning the Peace, an organization manipulated by Yuan in preparation for his ascendancy to the royal throne. In this respect, Yan acted as Kang Youwei did in the restoration of the dethroned Qing emperor Puyi. It was not without a sense of repentance that Yan confessed: "In the last years of my life, I look upon the Way roughly in the same manner as Kang Youwei, and I think that the old ways and manners of our nation should never be questioned."[10] The thought and activities of Yan in his later years, just like that of Kang, were finally spurned by his contemporaries.

The modern history of China changed so rapidly and so drastically that the representative ideologues of each generation seldom had time enough to elaborate their own theoretical systems. They only felt and reflected for a given moment the pulse of the age, and then, after a short-lived appearance, were swept rapidly into oblivion by the currents of the age. This feature manifested itself most remarkably in the representatives of the Reform Movement of 1898. The failure of the Reform Movement signalled the bankruptcy of the reformers and their reformism. The modern history of China then entered its next stage: democratic revolution.

Chapter 23
THOUGHT AT THE TIME OF
THE 1911 REVOLUTION

1. DEMOCRATIC REVOLUTIONARY IDEOLOGY
BEFORE THE REVOLUTION

The reformist movement, from the early New Learning School down to the 1898 reformers, had been a failure. Similarly, the peasant movement, from the Taiping Revolution down to the Yi He Tuan (Boxer) Uprising, had failed. Next to mount the stage of history was the democratic revolutionary movement of the bourgeoisie. The first decade of the 20th century, or rather the ten years between the Yi He Tuan Uprising (1900) and the 1911 Revolution, were the high tide of the bourgeois democratic revolutionary movement. Sun Yat-sen was the movement's most outstanding leader with whom the bourgeois democratic revolutionary movement formally began. As a great pioneer in revolution, he influenced not only China but many oppressed peoples of the world, particularly those of the East.

Sun Yat-sen (or Sun Zhongshan, 1866-1925) was born into a peasant family in Xiangshan (now Zhongshan) of Guangdong. He spent part of his youth in Hawaii, then returned to China and studied medicine in Hong Kong where he received a relatively systematic training in modern natural sciences. Following this, he pursued a medical career, while at the same time continuing his secret organizational work. At first, his thought had not yet broken out of the bondage of reformism, as evidenced by his petition to Li Hongzhang requesting Li to carry out reforms. Only after China's defeat in the Sino-Japanese War of 1894 did Sun realize that China's despotic monarchy was essentially moribund, and that reform was a dead-end path. In 1895 he founded the headquarters of the China Revival

Society, and launched his first armed uprising in Guangdong. Following the failure of the uprising, he continued his revolutionary activities overseas, and formulated the initial concept of his Three People's Principles. The bourgeois democratic revolutionary movement led by Sun Yat-sen began to grow as an independent political force in the wake of the bankrupt reformist effort of 1898. It throve vigorously, winning the support of progressive intellectuals whose numbers were growing daily.

The oppression of the late Qing government drove a great many Chinese youths and intellectuals of the bourgeoisie and petty bourgeoisie to flock to Japan. The number of Chinese students there increased to ten thousand and Japan became an active centre for their ideological and political activities. In 1905 Sun's China Revival Society joined in Tokyo with the Society for the Revival of the Chinese Nation led by Huang Xing, Chen Tianhua and Song Jiaoren, and the Restoration Society led by Zhang Taiyan, Cai Yuanpei and Tao Chengzhang to form the China Revolutionary League. The establishment of the China Revolutionary League marked the birth of a political party of the Chinese bourgeoisie and petty bourgeoisie in preparation for carrying out a democratic revolution to seize political power and establish a bourgeois republic. It expanded rapidly, and within a year had reached a membership of ten thousand.

In 1906 it began publishing its own official organ *Minbao* or *People's Journal* which promoted revolutionary ideology and opened up a heated debate with the *Journal of the Renovated People* of the reformists, who advocated constitutional monarchy. This was one of the greatest ideological debates of the early 20th century China. The *People's Journal,* under Zhang Taiyan's editorship, served as the most important battlefront for revolutionary opinion of the time. And suddenly, various other revolutionary publications appeared at this same time, adding momentum to revolutionary thought.

The band of reformers around Kang Youwei had already organized themselves into a royalist party. This group opposed any revolution, and sought to frighten people with such statements as "revolution means chaos, and chaos invites foreign intervention."[1] In short, revolution meant the carving up of China by foreign powers, China's extinction as a nation and extermination as a people. The difference between the royalist (literally the Emperor Protection) party and the reactionary ruling group of the royal court lay in the fact that not long before, the former had had to flee overseas to avoid arrest by the latter after the failure of their reform effort. This allowed them to attract people in supporting them. For a time, they were even able to contend against the democratic revolutionaries for the leadership of the multitude and the overseas Chinese.

The year 1903 marked the dividing line between the revolutionaries and the reformists. In that year, in response to the royalist party's position that revolution would bring about national extinction, Sun and his revolutionary group set forth their position that revolution would bring about national salvation. Sun drew a distinct line between protecting the emperor and revolution, asserting that they were utterly incompatible. Those wanting revolution could not protect the emperor, and vice versa. The ensuing debate between the revolutionaries and the reformists focused around whether or not it was possible to realize a revolutionary leap, or whether a process of step-by-step reforms was advisable; and likewise, whether to support the Qing regime or to overthrow it.

Both in his editorial for the inaugural issue of the *People's Journal* and in his speech to the meeting welcoming him to Tokyo by the Chinese students there, Sun pointedly rejected the royalist assertion that China at that time was only capable of a constitutional monarchy but not able to skip beyond that. Sun, on the contrary, insisted upon the idea that China could and should definitely carry out a revolution and establish a democratic republic. Sun's stand in this debate became the banner for China's revolutionary democratic forces.

The revolutionary programme presented by Sun in 1903 read: "Drive out the Tartars (i.e., the Qing Dynasty) and revive the Chinese nation, establish a republic and equalize land property." By the establishment of the China Revolutionary League in 1905, Sun had formally developed these ideas into a relatively comprehensive doctrine of the Three People's Principles. The principles of nationalism, democracy and people's livelihood, collectively known as the Three People's Principles, served as the political programme of the revolutionary bourgeois democrats during China's early democratic revolution. Nationalism called on the Chinese people to rise up in revolt against the Qing (Manchu) Dynasty as well as their bosses, the imperialist powers. Democracy demanded the establishment of a bourgeois democratic republic. And the principle of people's livelihood postulated that it was possible to realize "equalization of land property" and thus avert some of the abuses of capitalist society, or what was called "accomplishing the whole task of political revolution and social revolution at one stroke."[2]

The China Revolutionary League particularly stressed "citizens' revolution" or "commoners' revolution" so as to distinguish itself from the peasant revolutions of the past, which had resulted merely in one dynasty being replaced by another. Naturally, owing to the level of their knowledge, this theory also had its deficiencies and weak points, and was incapable of being thoroughly anti-imperialist and anti-feudal. Nevertheless, it far surpassed the level of the previous two ideological emancipation movements, those of the Taipings and of the New Learning School. But it was still the old Three People's Principles, an historical product born out of the specific conditions of the old democratic revolutionary period. At any rate, Sun, as the leader of the revolutionary democrats, and his thought should be highly valued.

In the sharp ideological debate between the revolutionaries and the reformists, an important role was played by Zhang Taiyan. Zhang Taiyan (1867-1936) was from Yuhang in Zhejiang. As a youth, he studied the Han School of classical learning under that school's famous scholar Yu Yue. In political thought, Zhang moved from reformism towards anti-Manchu revolution. Following the 1898 Reform Movement, he went to Japan where he came in contact with a number of New Learning ideas, as well as with German philosophy, Indian Buddhism and others. He took the various schools and tried to combine them into a single new system, while at the same time he energetically promoted revolution. Zhang typically reflected the mode of thought of his time. His studies of Chinese thinkers, of Buddhism and of Western philosophy were all in the service of criticizing the Confucian tradition, and were hence noteworthy in their anti-feudal significance.

The first ten years of the 20th century were those in which Zhang was most active, energetic and progressive as an ideologue and propagandist. In this period he published one article after another rejecting the reformist position of Kang Youwei and Liang Qichao, and supporting revolution. He provided the Preface for Zou Rong's *The Revolutionary Army*, and was imprisoned. He organized the revolutionary Restoration Society with others and then edited the *People's Journal*, the organ of the China Revolutionary League, and wrote many incisive political commentaries for it, greatly influencing the intellectuals of the time.

The basic theory of the reformists at this time was that China was capable only of going the route of constitutional monarchy, because the Chinese people were still backward in their thinking and were unable to skip beyond constitutional monarchy; and that revolution would only lead to bloodshed and to the carving up of China. Zhang Taiyan not only refuted this argument point by point, but advocated that under the corrupt Qing court, the path of reform was out of the question. Revolution alone, though a bitter medicine, would awaken the people. Though blood might be shed, this was a historical inevitability.

At the same time, Zhang Taiyan advocated the slogan: "Equal distribution of land." This reflected the sympathy that the bourgeois democrats had for the peasants. Zhang also criticized the various irrational social phenomena and shortcomings in the Western capitalist countries, subjectively hoping to avert the same disastrous road of capitalism. In his memorial essay "Some Recollections on Zhang Taiyan", Lu Xun recalled: "To my mind, his [Zhang's] contribution to the history of revolution is actually greater than that to the history of scholarship." And again: "I heard about China's Mr. Zhang Taiyan not because of his studies on the Confucian classics and ancient philology, but because he attacked Kang Youwei, wrote a preface to Zou Rong's *The Revolutionary Army*, and was imprisoned in the jail of the International Settlement in Shanghai.... I liked this paper [*People's Journal*], not because of his old-fashioned and difficult prose style ... but because of his campaigns against Liang Qichao. His work was really gallant and inspiring."[3] As a classical scholar, Zhang made use of the Old Text classics to propagate the anti-Manchurian doctrine in the name of racial revolution against Kang's New Text classics in service of Kang's reformist and royalist position. And the broad ideological influence Zhang exercised on the public was "not because he was a good scholar but because he was at the same time a revolutionary". Lu Xun pointed out specifically: "those polemic essays are the greatest and most lasting monument to his life."[4] This evaluation of Zhang's historical role is very much to the point.

Yet in the last analysis, Zhang Taiyan was characteristic of the Chinese intellectuals, who were inherently weak and fragile themselves. And because the feudal ideological ties that bound him were so great, his revolutionary idea was quite incomplete. There was in it a strong vein of the antiquated discernment of the Chinese and the barbarians. He possessed both the narrowness of the peasants and small producers. His outlook was bound too much by the past; it lacked a broad view toward the future. Basically, he simply stopped at the stage of anti-Manchu revolution. His theories were not nearly as thorough nor his revolutionary vision as bold as those of Sun Yat-sen. Along with the *People's Journal*, anti-Manchu revolution was the most notable feature in his ideology. And the tool he used was traditional Chinese classical studies of the Old Text School. At that time, he promoted the notion of "national essence", intending to encourage nationalism and patriotism. But a large portion of feudal rubbish was inavoidably mixed up in this concept.

With the Qing Dynasty overthrown and the banner of anti-Manchu revolution becoming outdated, Zhang's ideology lost its clear target and its former splendour. At a loss and confused, he gradually retreated. By his later years, he had completely fallen behind the times, locking himself within an ivory tower of ancient classical studies. In the above-quoted article, Lu Xun pointed out penetratingly that Zhang in his later years "was dressed up under the splendour of an academic vestment and became a Confucian scholar" and "though Mr. Zhang Taiyan first became known as a revolutionary, he later retired to live as a quiet scholar cut off from the age by means of a wall built by himself and others".[5] On this point, too, Zhang was unlike Sun; on the contrary, he had looked more like certain reformists whom he had opposed in the past.

Like other bourgeois democratic revolutions in history, the ideological movement in China was much more active and energetic prior to the 1911 Revolution than after it. In the first decade of the 20th century, a large number of advanced young students and intellectuals threw themselves into the high tide of revolutionary activities. Concentrated primarily in Tokyo and Shanghai, they organized a number of revolutionary groups under various names. In 1905, most of these joined together to form the united China Revolutionary League. These revolutionary groups issued many periodicals to publicize their revolutionary ideas and to communicate with their revolutionary comrades.

The theories of evolution and of natural rights had first been introduced from the West and adopted by the reformists, and used by them as ideological weapons in their struggle against the Old Learning School. These ideological weapons had been passed to the revolutionary democrats, first by the reformists of the generation of the 1898 Reform. Later, these weapons came from their place of origin directly or via Japan. Whereas the reformists used the theory of evolution to defend gradual change (reform) and oppose revolution (skipping over historical stages), the revolutionary democrats simply and directly took revolution itself to be progress, and raised the slogan: "Revolution is the evolution of the 20th century."[6] And whereas the reformists used the "theory of civil rights and equality" to demand the expansion of gentry rights, the revolutionary democrats had already declared "freedom and equality" as their battle cry against the despotic feudal regime. What particularly distinguished their position from the reformists' advocacy of constitutional monarchy was that they openly called for a bourgeois republic. It was the early Zhang Taiyan who first employed the term "the Republic of China."

Many outstanding revolutionary ideologists and propagandists emerged from this group. Zou Rong and his *The Revolutionary Army*, Chen Tianhua and his *Sudden Awakening* and *The Alarm Bell*—all reflected the revolutionary ideological trend of the time. In 1903, Zou Rong (1885-1905) at the age of eighteen, wrote *The Revolutionary Army*, which clearly endorsed the democratic principle of natural rights, and demanded the overthrow of the despotic Manchu (Qing) regime and the establishment of a democratic republic where freedom and equality would be the guiding principles. Zou looked for a time when "never again would there be a despotic monarchy". Zhang Taiyan wrote a preface for Zou's work which was carried in the *Su Bao*. Because of these writings, both men were arrested and imprisoned. Zou died in jail. In *Sudden Awakening* and *The Alarm Bell*, Chen Tianhua (1875-1905) employed popular propaganda forms to enthusiastically spread nationalistic and democratic revolutionary ideology. These men with their revolutionary works and activities heightened the ardour of the democratic revolutionary movement.

2. THE DEVELOPMENT OF SUN YAT-SEN'S THOUGHT

As the foremost leader of the current of democratic revolution, Sun Yat-sen's thought merits our special attention. Like most advanced intellectuals of the time, Sun borrowed the theories of evolution and of natural rights from the West, and combined them with the needs of the democratic revolution. In the inaugural issue of the *People's Journal* in 1905, he formally set forth his Three People's Principles. Sun regarded evolution as an immutable law of nature, and revolution as a stimulant to hasten the evolutionary process. He rejected outright the reformist position of gradualism—that is, a gradual step-by-step advance with no possibility of skipping the orderly stages of history. This, he said, ran counter to the universal truth of evolution. He pointed out that as civilization progresses, "the newcomers would surpass the old-timers". He concluded by extension that not too long after China undergoes a revolution, she will be able to catch up with and surpass the advanced countries of the West.

This argument clearly reflected the vigour and spirit of the revolutionaries. In ideological theory, Sun Yat-sen was certainly not a thorough-going thinker. In particular, he was unable to solve satisfactorily China's basic problem—the land problem of the peasants. This led to the failure of the revolution and enabled feudal rule to drag on. In philosophical terms, and in terms of social history, Sun's views often vacillated between materialism and idealism, finally settling on a dualism of the two. His world view belonged to that of an old-fashioned democratic revolutionary.

Although the Revolution of 1911 overthrew the two-thousand year-old imperial and monarchical system, the government simply changed names and hung up a signboard that read "Republic". Political powers fell into the hands of Yuan Shikai and various other great and small warlords, and the reactionary alliance of imperialists and feudal forces continued to control China. There was no fundamental change in the nature of Chinese society. The suffering and powerlessness of the masses remained as before, unchanged.

The democratic revolution had not succeeded, and a good many former democratic revolutionaries fell into an ideological haze, aimlessly groping in the dark for a path to take. Under these conditions, Sun's thoughts advanced a step further. He worked energetically to strengthen the revolution, organizationally and ideologically. He called his ideological reconstruction "the psychological construction". In 1918, he wrote *The Doctrine of Sun Yat-sen*, in which he introduced his new theory "to know is difficult, but to do is easy", as an ideological weapon to spur on those in the revolutionary party. He considered that the revolutionary party had failed because of its embrace of the traditional ideological dogma that "to know is not difficult, but to do is difficult"; that is, it is not knowledge or understanding that is difficult, rather the real difficulty lies in the actual doing. Sun's opposite view that "to know is difficult, but to do is easy" was proposed to counter the conservative trend of thought which traditional habits continued following as if stuck in a rut and unable to get out. This view was also a summing up of his theory of revolutionary practice garnered over long years of experience. He was the first among Chinese thinkers to examine the relationship between knowing and doing, or between knowledge and action, from the standpoint of revolution, and also the first to criticize the hitherto generally accepted view regarding the knowledge-action dichotomy of the idealists, and hence there were in his views certain rational elements. Yet this theory was incapable of getting at the basic ideological and material contradictions between the revolutionaries and counter-revolutionaries. It was also burdened by a heavy metaphysical lop-sidedness by separating knowledge and action and placing them in opposition. This should be borne in mind while affirming the basically positive historical significance of his doctrine.

A similar dual character might also be discovered in Sun Yat-sen's view of social history, that is, it contained both positive elements and very serious limitations. Sun accepted the notion of evolution that regarded human history as one continuously advancing developmental process, going from lower to higher stages, and believed it was an objective law that could not be obstructed by any man. Beyond this, he advocated the necessary use of revolutionary means to hasten this process, and the need to fight for the early realization of his ideal of nationalism, democracy and people's livelihood. Sun's activities in his early years laid particular stress on overthrowing the despotic regime of the Qing Dynasty. Following the 1911 Revolution, he placed greater stress on the issue of "people's livelihood". The concept "people's livelihood" summed up his views on human society. Sun believed that "people's livelihood"—that is, how man resolves the issue of finding the means for substance—was a motive force in historical development, the so-called "central point of history". Actually, this "people's livelihood" view of history had a dualistic taint, too. On one hand, Sun tried hard to explain the laws of social development in historical movement in terms of physical human needs; this bore a materialistic colour. He stressed the importance of material production and the material life of the masses in the course of history, and thus proposed an antithesis to the traditional idealistic conception of history, i.e., the doctrine of the creation of the sages (including that of Kang Youwei). Yet on the other hand, he departed from material laws and human relationships in social development by summing up human needs into certain abstract concepts—such as the desire of and the instinct for existence—and thus fell into an abstract historical sermonizing. This abstract view of history led him towards other abstract ideas and principles, such as "the love of mankind" and the like.

Idealistic views also determined his attitude toward Marxism. He asserted that the evolution of society came about not from the struggle between men, but through their cooperation and accord. Actually, this theory took the nation as a cooperation of classes. He regarded class struggle as a sort of abnormal state of society, and Marx as merely a social pathologist. He also accepted the theory of "mutual aid" and proclaimed that "competition is the fundamental law in the animal kingdom, but cooperation is the fundamental law of mankind".[1] So in his view, the propelling force in the development of social history was not class struggle, but mutual aid and cooperation between classes. Although he admitted that class conflict existed in the capitalist countries of the West, he taught that there was no class conflict in China. Allegedly, China had no wealthy class, but only a difference between "great poverty" and "small poverty". Sun was under the illusion that China could avert class conflict, and asserted confidently that since China's industry was undeveloped, there was no need to speak of class conflict and the dictatorship of the proletariat. This theory of class reconciliation, based on the theory of universal human love, reflects a distinctive feature of the Chinese intellectuals under historical conditions that prevailed at that time. The wishful thinking out of his goodwill as well as his magnificent ideals of national construction, as embodied in his *Programme of the Construction of the Nation* and *The Outline of the Construction of the Nation*, all failed to be realized completely.

In the decade following the 1911 Revolution, a whole series of Sun's efforts ended in failure, one right after the other, and he was unable to find an outlet, ideologically. Only with the October Revolution in Russia and the establishment of the Chinese Communist Party was Sun able to acquire new ideological life and lift himself out of the depth of his despair. Sun welcomed both of these events, which stimulated his thought into an entirely new stage of development; that is to say, he developed his Three People's Principles of the old democratic revolutionary period into the new Three People's Principles of the new democratic revolutionary period. In collaboration with the Chinese Communist Party, Sun formulated his Three Great Policies: uniting with Russia, uniting with the Communists and assisting the peasants and workers.

At the First National Congress of the Kuomintang (the Nationalist Party) held in 1924, Sun explained anew the revolutionary principles of his revised Three People's Principles which were basically the same as the Communist programme in this stage of democratic revolution except on the issue of leadership. The revised Principle of Nationalism stressed the cardinal importance of anti-imperialism for the people of China. The new Principle of People's Rights (or Democracy) rebuked "the so-called democratic system" of Western capitalist countries as "usually monopolized by the few and therefore become simply an instrument for oppressing the common people". And it stressed the need to establish the kind of democracy that would be "shared by all the common people and not privately owned by the few".[2] The new Principle of People's Livelihood developed further the idea of "equalization of land property" by advocating "the distribution of land to the tiller" and support for the peasants' demand for land. But Sun imagined that these demands could be realized through peaceful reforms. The new Three People's Principles also proposed "control of capital", which was intended to protect the national capital of the people while opposing the economic aggression of foreign imperialism. It was also meant to prevent private capital from controlling the national economy and the livelihood of the people. In his later years, Sun Yat-sen went further toward recognizing the power of the worker and peasant masses, and formulated the policy of "assisting the peasants and workers". In his will, he still exhorted his followers that "we must arouse the masses of the people and unite in common struggle with those nations of the world which treat us as equals".

One of Sun Yat-sen's great historical achievement lies in developing his Three People's Principles into a new Three People's Principles. Yet his world outlook, in the final analysis, was that of a bourgeois democratic revolutionary. In his view, the task of "assisting the peasants and workers" and of "arousing the masses" could only be taken on by the national bourgeoisie and the petty bourgeoisie. But in reality, in a semi-feudal and semi-colonial nation like China, and in an imperialist age, the national bourgeoisie and petty bourgeoisie were not yet powerful enough for leading a revolution.

Sun drew up his Three Great Policies and the new Three Peoples' Principles after the May Fourth Movement, and so they do not properly belong within the scope of the present book. But it was necessary to deal with them here briefly in order to provide a relatively complete introduction and evaluation of Sun's thought as it developed throughout his whole life.

3. SCHOOLS OF THOUGHT AND IDEOLOGICAL STRUGGLES FOLLOWING THE 1911 REVOLUTION

The 1911 Revolution overthrew the emperor of an old despotic system that had ruled China for over two thousand years, but it only overthrew one emperor and did not get at the root of this age-old monarchic system. The 1911 Revolution was unable to solve land problems for the peasants nor to fight effectively against the domestic and foreign enemies of the revolution. The semi-feudal and semi-colonial social base remained untouched, and political power fell into the hands of Yuan Shikai and other local warlords.

The regime of Yuan in Beijing took the place of the Provisional Government in Nanjing which represented the revolutionary forces. Soon afterwards Yuan planned the assassination of Song Jiaoren (1880-1912), one of the foremost leaders of the revolutionary party, who was devoting himself to the task of instituting parliamentary democracy, party politics and a responsible cabinet. Then, Yuan Shikai began to suppress the revolutionary camp in the south, dissolved the parliament and flagrantly tore up the Provisional Constitution, which in a considerable degree was the fruit of the revolution and democratic in spirit. Finally Yuan rigged a farce of monarchic restoration, proclaiming himself the new emperor. Within a hundred days, the royal dynasty of Yuan ended in bankruptcy under nationwide denouncement. Nevertheless, the whole country still remained under the combined rule of imperialism and feudalism. The outcome of the 1911 Revolution proved that the feeble intellectuals of China was still too weak to lead the Chinese people in a thorough-going democratic revolution. The model of a Western republic, combined with the theories of evolution and of natural rights in their Chinese version, was finally proven to be an impasse.

Upon this occasion, a feudal, back-to-the-ancients Confucian Association was formed, headed by Kang Youwei and controlled by feudal warlords, great and small. Local Confucian Associations were set up around the country. These societies colluded with local forces of restoration, fanning up a counter-current which promoted worship for Confucius and revival of ancient ways. They even openly called for the "establishment of Confucianism as the state religion", asserting that even though the given form of the state had already been changed, the obligations of ethics and morality were eternal and unchanging. Yet no matter how they tried to explain it, their theory still amounted to nothing more than the old feudal cliché that "Heaven does not change, and so the Way does not change too", and did not say anything new. But it did glaringly express the fact that the corrupt forces of feudalism were not going to withdraw willingly from the stage of history.

The ideological standoff of the previous period continued under a new guise. In this period, a group of imperialists energetically participated in this counter-current of the "worship of Confucius and revival of ancient ways", because they believed that this counter-current could serve the benefits of imperialist aggression better.

The imperialists had once comfronted the ideological resistance by China's feudal literati. But this resistance had been extremely weak. Feudalism was quickly brought to its knees by imperialism, and the Qing Dynasty was transformed from the Celestial Kingdom despising all things foreign to the cringing servant of imperialism. And now, imperialism changed course, shielded the feudal revival of ancient ways and censured the New Learning. Because, at its root, the New Learning served the purposes of China's democratic revolutionaries, and it was the democratic revolutionaries who opposed feudalism and the imperialists who now propped it up. The imperialists and the reactionaries needed not only someone to play the role of an executioner for them in their oppression of the people, but also someone to play the role of a pastor to deceive the people. They found both in the feudal system. And precisely for this reason, imperialism and feudalism formed an intimate ideological and cultural reactionary alliance.

The worship of Confucius and the return to the ancient ways was but one of the ideological chains employed by this reactionary cultural alliance for enslaving the people's minds. Another measure of their obscurantist policy was their preaching of so-called "Cosmopolitanism". They founded organizations and ran periodicals to preach the gospel of an ecumenical harmony to the suffering multitude, urging them to give up their national and democratic revolutionary ideals, to cultivate a mutual love for imperialism and feudalism so as to replace their resistance and struggle through an illusion of universal love. The propaganda on "Cosmopolitanism" was much in vogue for a time, but its content extended no further than attempting to persuade the Chinese people to abandon the cause of revolution, to accept hypocritic preachings and to submit willingly to the reactionary rule of imperialism and feudalism. These sorts of clichés about harmony were sung not only by the domestic feudal elements but also by the imperialist propagandists. Their chorus showed that feudal class had now rendered itself into lackeys of imperialism. Kang Youwei's *Book of Cosmopolitanism*, as mentioned in the preceding chapter, was an example.

Contemporaneous with this, the advanced intellectuals continued to seek and to apply various ideological weapons from the West. But because there were many different ideological trends among the Chinese intellectuals, the ideological weapons they sought and the methods they applied were varied as well. In the period between the 1911 Revolution and the May Fourth Movement, many Western ideologies were in vogue for a while. Kantian philosophy, anarchism, neo-idealism, pragmatism, individualism, certain types of utopian socialism—each had its own adherents in the ideological circles of the time.

From the reformists Yan Fu, Liang Qichao and also Wang Guowei, all the way to the revolutionaries Zhang Taiyan and Cai Yuanpei, all either vigorously promoted, or at least were influenced by, the Kantian philosophy from the modern West. But that part of Kant's thought of most positive significance—its method of dialectical thinking—had not been given due attention by the representatives of China's intellectuals.

Cai Yuanpei (1868-1940) was born in Shaoxing in Zhejiang. At the time of the 1898 Reform Movement, Cai advanced the theory of evolution, advocated people's rights and women's rights, and opposed the traditional concept of respecting the sovereign and humbling the subjects. In 1904, he organized the democratic revolutionary group, The Restoration Society, which was incorporated the following year with the China Revolutionary League. That same year, too, he published an article, "Exposition on the Hostility to the Manchus" which called for people's rights and attacked feudal privileges. Later he went to Germany to study philosophy, and it was the theory of the German philosopher Kant that formed the basis of his own ideology. Kant's theory was formed under the strong ideological influence of the French Enlightenment and democratic revolution. Yet this philosophy also reflected the peculiar weakness of the German bourgeoisie of that time. Cai Yuanpei's thought bears the same feature. He stressed the slogan "liberty, equality and fraternity" of the democratic revolution and believed that these formed the moral foundation needed for establishing a new-born republic.

Moreover, to establish what he called "civic morals", he advocated "world-view education" which meant for him "a philosophical course by adopting the pre-Qin (non-Confucian) masters, Indian philosophy and European philosophy (and synthesizing them) in order to break the two-thousand-year habits of hidebound Confucianism".[1] He openly criticized Dong Zhongshu's policy of rejecting the Hundred Schools and revering only Confucianism. During his tenure as President of Beijing University, Cai was well known for his "tolerance and broadmindedness". This was extraordinarily significant under the situation of the time, because it created the conditions in which the New Culture Movement of the upsurging democracy struggled against the ideological system of the old feudal culture. This same tolerant atmosphere enabled Beijing University to become a major centre during the coming high tide of the New Culture Movement and of the May Fourth Movement.

Cai Yuanpei was particularly interested in Kant's aesthetics and taught that the aesthetic sense was something transcending all times, places and material advantages. Accordingly, he proposed the slogan "replace religion by aesthetic education". This proposal of aesthetic education, though not without value, was nevertheless a manifestation of the attempt of China's weak intellectuals to escape reality and to erase social conflict. Because of Cai's position first as the Minister of Education and then as the President of Beijing University during the period between the 1911 Revolution and the May Fourth Movement, his views contributed to the influential ideological trends in the cultural, educational and ideological circles of the period.

Before the 1911 Revolution, the *People's Journal* and certain other publications had already introduced to the Chinese public a few anarchist theorists such as Stirnir (1806-1856), Proudhon (1819-1865), Bakunin (1814-1876) and Kropotikin (1842-1912). This interest in anarchism reflected the immature state of naivete of China's intellectuals, wanting as they did to study any new theory from the West that came along, since they themselves were still without a fully mature theoretical system or an accepted standard. Even the *People's Journal* was not immune to this. Anarchism denied the objective laws of historical development of society. Proceeding from the wishful thinking and fantasies of a desperate individualism, it vainly attempted to rely on individual action to bring about a paradise on earth overnight. This kind of thinking appealed in particular to the inherent weaknesses and the vacillating nature of the Chinese intellectuals so that a good many among them readily fell into the embrace of anarchism. Some even believed that the history of society could be regulated by their own individual wills and wishes, and yearned to employ radical actions, such as assassination, to overthrow the Manchu regime. There were among them even a few, like the renowned politician Wu Zhihui who took part in the democratic revolutionary camp while pronouncing himself to be anarchist. By proclaiming the obscurantist view that life was "utterly a pitch-dark muddle", Wu attempted to corrupt and subvert the ideology of the democratic revolution by asking the people to be content with their bitter fate. Anarchism, however, was never able to hold an important place in the ideological circles of the time.

Before the 1911 Revolution, the principal element of the reactionary cultural alliance between imperialism and feudalism was the combination of Western theology and Chinese feudal ideology. After the revolution, there was found no "walk into a bright future" as the democratic revolutionaries had once assumed there would be. Rather, the dark reactionary politics and society remained unchanged. Because of this, many revolutionaries fell into a sort of ideological wilderness and did not know which way to turn. They had lost the drive and the spirit that possessed them during the preparatory propaganda work for the revolution. Then the obscurantist trend of thought of the modern West were ready to take advantage of this situation by injecting new elements into the old cultural mix and thus giving it a new guise. The domestic reactionary class and its representatives then depended on the import of these new goods to numb the minds of the people, while strongly resisting the revolutionary trend. Between the 1911 Revolution and the May Fourth Movement neo-idealism of various sorts created a stir for a while, in particular the anti-rationalism of Bergson (1859-1941) and Eucken (1846-1926), Machism (empirical criticism) and pragmatism. Among them it was the popular influence of pragmatism that lasted longest in China. Modern pragmatism originated in America. It was introduced to China by Hu Shi, an intellectual representative of China's upper class scholars, as a weapon for guiding the ideological trends of the Chinese people.

During the democratic revolution, Hu Shi at first had assumed a place in the frontline of the New Culture Movement, by then he did really support the cause of democracy and science. But, he preferred the idealism of pragmatism to science and at the same time professed the ideal of Cosmopolitanism which he valued much more than nationalism. Later, during the new democratic revolutionary period, Hu Shi proposed the slogan "sort out our nation's past" to call people to concentrate interest on historical criticism and preached a bit-by-bit reformism to oppose the spread of Marxism.

4. THE NEW CULTURE MOVEMENT ON THE EVE OF THE MAY FOURTH MOVEMENT

History's tortuous route following the 1911 Revolution acceler-ated the deepening ideological awareness of advanced intellectuals. Why had the theory of evolution, the theory of natural rights, and the programme for a bourgeois republic all failed in China? Bit by bit they realized that the reason for this failure lay predominantly in the fact that their efforts had not in any fundamental way touched the old ideological system, represented by Confucianism. And the outbreak of World War I gave them an additional intellectual shock. Beginning in 1915, a strong intellectual movement was well under way, known as the New Culture Movement. The banners upheld by this movement were "science" and "democracy" which forcefully represented the most vivid aspirations and ideals of the democratic culture. Since "for the cause of democracy and science the people of the Western nations had undergone many disturbances and shed much blood so that finally Mr. Democracy and Mr. Science were step by step coming to their rescue in the darkness"; they declared: "we are firmly convinced that only Mr. Democracy and Mr. Science can come to our rescue and lighten up all our darkness—political, moral, academic and ideological. For the cause of Democracy and Science, we do not mind suffering all kinds of suppression from the govern-ment, the attacks and abuses from the society and even the blood-shed of being beheaded."[1] It is quite right that they believed the backwardness of China was due to the lack of modern science and democracy. But what reason made her lack modern science and democracy? For this, many of them failed to find a good answer.

Imbued with zeal and courage, they stridently called out "down with the house of Confucius" to counter the reactionary trend, since the time of Yuan Shikai, of worship of Confucius and revival of ancient ways. In their pursuit and promotion of science and democracy, they did indeed liberate the Chinese people ideologically to a great degree, thus making a lasting historical contribution. But for a very long time after the New Culture Movement, these two things —science and democracy—were still unable to put down roots in China's soil, let alone sprout, flower and bear fruit. The New Culture Movement was a necessary step toward a new stage in Chinese history, but it was far from being sufficient.

Opposing the house of Confucius comprised a great ideological revolution. It was as if China was actually aroused out of a deep, deep sleep. Of course, prior to the 1911 Revolution, the democratic revolutionaries had in various degrees criticized the Confucian ideology of feudal China. Going back even further, the Western Learning sought by the New Learning School was essentially no more than modern Western science and, to a certain extent, Western bourgeois democratic culture as well. Because of this, it too constituted an assault on traditional learning. The New Culture Movement was a continuation and development of the struggle between Western Learning and Chinese Learning in the 19th century. Yet neither the New Learning School nor later the democratic revolutionaries carried out a direct, fierce and large-scale assault on the feudal ideological system the way that the New Culture Movement did by making it its main target.

In 1915, Chen Duxiu (1880-1942) founded the *Youth Magazine* in Shanghai, later changing its name to *La Jeunesse* (*New Youth*) and moving operations to Beijing. There it became an important battleground in the spread of the New Culture Movement. At the same time a great many other publications appeared one after another throughout the country, spreading the new ideological tide and forming a surging ideological revolution. Li Dazhao (1889-1927), Wu Yu (1871-1949) and Chen Duxiu each engaged in anti-Confucian activities during the New Culture Movement. At the same time, Lu Xun (1880-1936), with his incisive pen, wrote a series of articles and literary works impassionately exposing and sharply attacking the hypocritical preachings of feudal morality. His *A Madman's Diary*, a novel against the cannibalistic nature of the traditional ethical code, was one of the most notable among them. In many respects, the ideological ingredients of the New Culture Movement retained many ideas from the theory of evolution, the theory of natural rights and the programme for a bourgeois republic. It still used the Western ideological theory to oppose feudal ideology, and was basically still an integral part of the tide of democratic revolution. Yet within it there began to percolate a few new ideological elements, a few things that had never been seen before. The New Culture Movement occurred just as World War I was going on in Europe and just at the outbreak of the October Revolution. It was the ideological overture to the May Fourth Movement.

The New Culture Movement developed into the May Fourth Movement in 1919; and from that time on, Chinese history entered into a brand new stage, the stage of a New Democratic Revolution. It was then that Marxism among others began to be formally disseminated in China and, with them, the course of the Chinese history began to take a fresh new look.

Chapter 24

MODERN SOCIAL, ECONOMIC, SCIENTIFIC, HISTORIOGRAPHIC AND LITERARY THOUGHTS

1. MODERN SOCIAL AND ECONOMIC THOUGHTS

During the period of the great historical upheaval at the end of the Ming and the beginning of Qing dynasties, ideological circles appeared very active and lively. But as the Qing regime's political power, after its establishment, was becoming relatively stable, the emperor and his court encouraged Song Learning, whereas the majority of scholars from among the populace had been following the path of Han Learning. At the very start, there were some subtle signs of diversity that could be detected between them. Later, when men spoke of Han Learning, they often understood it as simply limited to textual research and critical interpretation of ancient texts; but this is a misunderstanding of the facts. During the height of its prosperity in the Qianlong and Jiaqing period, the fact that the representative scholars of Han Learning, from Dai Zhen to Ruan Yuan, were nearly all at the same time outstanding mathematicians, might serve to disprove this prevailing belief. Although Han Learning was not as narrow as certain later people were prone to imagine it, it was after all primarily a kind of academic trend of thought—searching into the past and honouring courtly learnings—that adorned a peaceful and prosperous age of the royal reign.

Upon entering the modern age, a succession of domestic troubles and foreign invasions compelled Chinese intellectuals to turn their sights from their stacks of books to the grim social reality before them. Thereupon the dispirited Qing social thought which lasted one hundred to two hundred years suddenly took on a dynamic appearance again. This ideological transformation was caused by an unprecedented historical momentum; and the process was rather long and complicated. Confrontations between the Old Text School and the New Text School, between the Tongcheng orthodoxy and the rhythmical and parallel style of prose writing, between the syntactic and semantic analysis of ancient texts and the knowledge of current affairs, between the understanding of the world and the narrow study of the sacred classics and their commentaries by ancient scholars, between the teachings of the Confucian orthodoxy and the study of the ancient non-Confucian writers and of Buddhism; all of them had prevailed for short or long periods in modern times. Little by little the fossilized intellectual barriers of the textual criticism of Han Learning and the speculative argumentation of Song Learning were broken down. But it was the idea of Western Learning that was decisive. And it was on the eve of the 1898 Reform that the bourgeois new culture in confrontation with the old feudal culture finally gained its own relatively clear-cut ideological form and content.

The first to extricate himself from the bonds of feudal academics —always a life-long pursuit—and to advance in the direction of practical knowledge for worldly utility, was none other than Gong Zizhen, whose ideas, as mentioned above, opened a fresh new era. He said of himself: "Even though I opened a new age, I don't assume myself to be a master." His works sounded bitter protests against the decadent feudal academic thought of the age. Not only his studies along the line of the Gongyang School, but also his essays, always written in rhythmic paralleled style, and his exquisitely fresh poetical works as well, all made a tremendous impact to the entire generation. He was an important forerunner of the late Qing New Learning School. In social thought, Gong stressed change and openly advocated "self-interest" and "wealth". By proposing the formulas "do not oppose self-interest"[1] and "there is no shame in speaking of wealth",[2] he began to reveal the germination of modern individualism. The acceptance or non-acceptance of the concept of an individual's "sacred egoism" or "self-interest" has been one of the demarcation lines in the struggle between Chinese and Western Learning. For the most part, the conservative camp supported the preaching of the ethical code of traditional virtues, while the progressive intellectuals fought for individual rights. Yet Gong's theory of "change" lacked philosophic depth, and hence not well suited to the immediate needs for social change or reform.

Yu Zhengxie (1775-1840), slightly before the time of Gong, was another thinker and propagandist for the enlightenment of people's ideas who had hitherto received little attention. Yu was born in Yixian in Anhui, and his works were compiled into *The Classified Manuscripts of Guisi* and *The Collected Manuscripts of Guisi*. One of his outstanding features was his bold advocacy of equality between the sexes in a feudal society where male superiority was an age-long practice. His thought directly influenced the later democratic revolutionary Cai Yuanpei, and became one of the integral parts of the social liberation movement.

To sum up, the progressive intellectuals of the enlightened gentry were a positive force. They opposed foreign invasion while criticizing the dark, reactionary aspects of the feudal system. But in their basic position, they still supported the feudal dynasty and opposed peasant revolution. (In his later years, Lin Zexu took part in suppressing the Taiping Movement.)

The Taiping Movement was the greatest mass revolutionary movement of the early modern period. Although a basic Taiping revolutionary programme, the "Land System of the Heavenly Kingdom", contained the ideal of abolishing the feudal land ownership system, the equalitarianism of the small peasant economy that it reflected did not in any way correspond to the direction of the development of social history. Nor did the small peasant represent the new social forces of production, and therefore it was unable to liberate itself or to liberate the rest of mankind. Precisely because of this kind of narrowness, the thought of Hong Xiuquan himself, from start to finish, included a thick layer of religious superstition. Basically speaking, it was theocratic and ran against the tide of history. It was only in the final moment of the Taiping Movement that another of its representatives, Hong Rengan, set forth a fairly complete programme for the development of capitalism. But by that time the Taiping Revolution was already on its deathbed. So his plans remained on paper and were never put into practice.

After the Taiping Movement, two separate currents appeared in ideological circles. One was the Yangwu faction, the mandarin bureaucrats whose job it was to deal with the foreigners or things foreign; and the other, the New Learning group. At that time, both had already begun to have some contact with modern science and technology, and both were in touch with certain modern Western political and social ideas—these were fundamentally different from the indigenous ideological components that had been carried down from the ancient and middle ages in China. But these two currents had different attitudes and different methods in dealing with the new ideas. The Yangwu faction which bartered itself away to the patronage of imperialism, focused its attention only on such things as sturdy gunboats and powerful arms. Their goal was merely to strengthen their own conservative controlling apparatus. A number of the enterprises they initiated were actually in the service of the rule of the bureaucratic compradore class. "Self-strengthening" and "search for prosperity" in their vocabulary were only synonyms for bureaucratic compradore monopoly. And their principal aim was merely to run their colonial processing industry, particularly armament manufacture. Moreover, under the slogan of "government supervision and merchant operation", they tried hard to bring national capitalism into the channel of bureaucratic capitalism. *An Exhortation of Learning* was the representative work of the ideological theory of Zhang Zhidong. At bottom, the purport of the entire piece was the necessity of relying on imperialism to support the moribund feudal ruling order.

In parallel with this, the opposition party within the landlord class at that time transformed into the New Learning School. While carrying on the traditions of the enlightened literati of the previous period, they studied at the same time the thoughts and institutions of the Western bourgeoisie (the New Learning or Western Learning in the sense they understood it). During the final one-third of the 19th century they were the representatives of the progressive current of thought. But politically, they were reformists. Their anti-feudal stand was by no means thorough, bearing a strong tendency toward compromise and concession. They sought to study Western Learning to achieve national prosperity and strength, their goal being to develop national capitalism in China and to establish China as a modern independent capitalist nation as the West. They not only promoted "wealth and strength" but also advocated "wealth first and then strength".[3] This was diametrically opposed to the thesis of the

Yangwu faction, whose ideas placed primary emphasis on the arms and armament industry. In tune with the demands for the development of national capitalism, the early New Learning School put pressure on the feudal monarchy to carry out a number of appropriate political reforms so as to facilitate the development of capitalist relations.

An important point in the social thought of the early New Learning School was their theory of "commercial war". They summed up the relations between the modern capitalist nations as commercial war, and believed that in order to carry out commercial war, it was first necessary to develop science and national industry. They put forth China's own theory of mercantilism. Xue Fucheng advanced the view that "it is the merchants who hold the key to the four classes (scholar, peasant, worker and merchant)". Consequently Xue demanded that China too ought to study and emulate the Western nations' "reliance on merchants as the life-line for creating the nations' material and spiritual success".[4] From Ma Jianzhong to Wang Tao and Chen Zhi, all these men embraced similar ideas of "prosperity through commerce". On the essential issue concerning the confrontation between feudalism and capitalism, Wang Tao clearly stated the necessity of "relying on commerce as the foundation of the nation".[5] This was developed further in the writings of Zheng Guanying, who professed: "Military aggression brings disaster to the people which is easy to recognize, but commercial invasion drains the nation invisibly", and consequently, in addition to "the tangible preparation for war to treat China's symptoms", it was more important that China should "learn from the West learnings of their scholars, peasants, workers and merchants and use an invisible war to consolidate China's foundation". Zheng Guanying asserted that "manufacturing is crucial for the flourishing of commercial affairs, and machines are a prerequisite to methods of manufacture"; and "if scholars were without merchants, then the study of science would not flourish; if peasants were without merchants, then the types of cultivation would not be broad; if workers were without merchants, then the items they produced could not be sold. This is how the merchants provide the great path for creating wealth, and how they hold in their hands the guiding principle for the four classes. The significance of merchants is great indeed!"[6] This is a typical thesis of the New Learning School, completely turning upside down the traditional feudal concept of merchants as nonessential.

Unlike the Yangwu faction, these men demanded that China develop a capitalist mode of production geared to the needs of a capitalist nation in competition with others, or as Xue Fucheng said: "If China produces one unit of goods, then foreigners will earn one unit less of profit, and thus our people will gain the benefit on one unit more for self-sufficiency; to seize foreign profit in order to benefit our people—there is nothing better than this!" This view is fundamentally different from the Yangwu's strangulation of national capitalism. In *The Manifesto of the Communist Party*, Marx said: "The cheap price of its [bourgeoisie's] commodities are the heavy artillery with which it batters down all Chinese walls, with which it forces the barbarians' intensely obstinate hatred of foreigners to capitulate. It compels all nations, on pain of extinction, to adopt the bourgeois mode of production."[7] This could well be a portrait of the tendency of the social thought of the early New Learning School.

The New Learning School of the 1898 Reform period carried the "commercial warfare" ideas of the early New Learning School a step further by opposing such feudal theories as "emphasizing the essential (agriculture) and restraining the nonessential (commerce)" and "rejecting extravagance and upholding frugality". Their economic thought was progressing from mercantilism toward the laissez-faire stage. Such major figures of Reform as Tan Citong, Yan Fu and Liang Qichao all paraded the idea of upholding extravagance and opposed the idea of upholding frugality. One cannot deal with this issue of upholding extravagance or frugality abstractly, but should relate it to the concrete historical background of the time. In the hands of the feudal diehards, the slogans "restrain the nonessential" and "uphold frugality" had already become pretexts for opposing the developing of modern science and industry, and the reformers' position of upholding extravagance was actually their advocacy of stimulating capitalist production on an ever-enlarging scale and opposing the feudal mode of production.

On the issue of the essential and accidental, Yan Fu, based on his understanding of the world at that time, pointed out that modern Western nations had all achieved wealth through commerce and industry, while certain countries of Eastern Europe "had nearly no other trade aside from agriculture, but none was rich; moreover, their progress was extremely slow".[8] Yan Fu viewed frugality as a necessary condition for capital accumulation, and thus, as a positive thing. In this sense, both extravagance and frugality might produce the same effect: stimulating capitalist production.

An outstanding figure in transmitting Western learning and theories, Yan introduced not only a new world view based on the theory of evolution (which provided people with a new tool for observing the destinies of nations and societies). He also introduced the classical theory of laissez-faire capitalism more systematically than any other of his time (in his translation of Adam Smith's *The Wealth of Nations*) as well as the liberal doctrine of the state (in his translation of Montesquieu's *The Spirit of Laws*). In all they comprised one of the most important components in the high tide of the ideological struggle between Chinese Learning and Western Learning at the turn of the 19th and 20th centuries. Yan Fu's translations were using others' works to express what he himself hoped for; therefore in the course of the translation of *The Wealth of Nations* "whenever and wherever I (Yan) read some paragraphs that touched my heart and might be correlated to the current affairs, I would put down my own ideas in my notes time and again without being conscious of the elongation and vehemence of my words".[9] His intention in translating *The Wealth* of Nations was clearly to promote laissez-faire capitalism.

Yan also prepared notes and comments for a new edition of *The Book of Lao Zi*, interpreting it as laissez-faire thought. He proclaimed: "What is called wealth and strength, plainly speaking, is nothing other than benefiting the people. But if the government wishes to benefit the people, the people must first be able to benefit themselves. And for the people to benefit themselves, it is necessary, first, that they gain their freedom."[10] The principle set forth here is none other than the fundamental tenet of laissez-faire capitalism: the best society is that which allows the greatest degree of individual freedom (for the bourgeoisie, that is). But the concept of freedom of such thinkers of the Enlightenment as Adam Smith, Montesquieu and Rousseau with whom Yan agreed was aimed against the feudal system, while Yan's concept of freedom was aimed not only against the feudal system, but also at the fetters of imperialism and of the bureaucratic compradore class as well. And precisely because of this difference, the ideas and principles of the 18th century West did not work in the 19th century China.

The thought of Tan Citong was unparalleled in its time for the remarkable spirit it directed at "smashing the (feudal) bonds". But the true nature of his philosophy "Benevolence is but to communicate with each other" was in its very essence only a kind of refracted view of the circulation of capitalist goods and currency. He declared that "with wealth, you can establish factories; poor people can rely on them for support, products can rely on them for plenty, currency can rely on them for circulation, and one's own wealth can rely on them to expand and to become even richer".[11] This is simply a bare-faced manifesto for capitalist free competition. Another prominent thesis of Tan's was his active opposition to the feudal concept of "rejecting extravagance and upholding frugality". He advertised that only by following the exact opposite course, that is by upholding extravagance and rejecting frugality, would one be able to break away from the conservative, complacent social relationships of the habit-bound past. This thesis was one of the most important of his social thought.

While Kang Youwei was more moderate than either Tan, Yan or Liang on this point, his advocacy of "complete change" and "rapid change" also included the advice: "In planning self-strengthening, and in preparing for ten thousand generations of peace, you must thoroughly change the old ways or there will be no way to do it; as for methods of change, enriching the nation is the first."[12] "Enriching the nation", as set out here, actually implied adopting capitalist relations to replace the old feudal social relations.

Because of their reformist position, these men of the New Learning School did not think of overturning feudal rule, nor were they able to do so. They only imagined they could improve certain corrupt social practices within feudalism, and thus achieve social progress. With the upsurge of the democratic revolution movement, reformist thought dragged steadily towards an impasse. Among the later reformists who found themselves in this dilemma, we can point to Zhang Jian as an example of those who preached "save the nation through practical enterprise (industry)".

Zhang Jian (1853-1926) was born into a feudal bureaucratic

family in Nantong of Jiangsu Province and had close political connections with the reactionary ruling class. Later, he successfully managed cotton mills and engaged in capitalist management in other fields as well. These activities included the formation of one of the powerful financial groups in southeast China. He thus represented a typical case of feudal gentry turned bourgeois. He professed the belief that practical enterprise (industry) could save the nation, asserting that "common men all say foreigners founded their nations through commercial affairs. This is a superficial observation. They do not understand that the source of foreign nations enriching their peoples and strengthening their countries lies in industry".[13] Industry was then generally called practical enterprise. He also said: "The only way to aid the poor is through practical enterprise, and the only way to achieve wealth, too, is practical enterprise."[14]

But politics is always conditioning the mode of economics, and if anyone is divorced from this central issue of political power and boasts of saving the nation through mere practical enterprise; then it is just the same as various other theories that were popular for a time, such as "save the nation through education" or "save the nation through science", and in the end simply disintegrated into impractical, empty talk. Politically, Zhang opposed the democratic revolution. Following the 1911 Revolution he sought the patronage of the Beiyang warlords, but the practical enterprises that he managed eventually went bankrupt. This fact furnishes evidence of the bankruptcy of his theory of saving the nation through practical enterprise.

Along with the spread of Western Learning, the concepts of the rights and of the rule of the law, which went against feudal social relationships, began to appear on the agenda of the day. At the last moment of its reign, the tottering Qing Dynasty was forced to adopt a few modern ideas of jurisprudence as ornaments to decorate its facade. In 1902, Shen Jiaben and Wu Tingfang were among those who were appointed to revise statutes with reference to the laws of the Western nations. In 1908, a new penal code was enacted, abolishing certain parts of the old that were too deeply tainted by feudal brutality. Although this code remained only on paper and was never actually carried out, it still conveyed the fact that the democratic tide of the time could not be stopped.

Under assaults by the new ideological tide, the old laws, which were an important part of the feudal ideological system, had already began to crumble. Following the 1911 Revolution, part of the revised laws were retained by the Republican government. At the time when the Republic was established, the first "Provisional Constitution", which contained the general principles borrowed from the West, affirmed that sovereignty abided with the people, affirmed the freedom and rights of the people and affirmed the equality of the people before the law. This series of basic democratic stands embodied to a certain degree the ideals and principles of the democratic revolutionaries. But before long the gains of the 1911 Revolution were usurped by Yuan Shikai, who turned the "Provisional Constitution" into a piece of waste paper and tore it to shreds.

By the beginning of the 20th century, Chinese ideological circles began to have some contact with socialist theory, but their understanding of socialism was often fragmentary and lacking in scientific depth. For instance, the *People's Journal* introduced socialism and anarchism at the same time, putting them on a par with each other. Of those who introduced subjective socialist thought in this period, Zhu Zhixin was typical. Zhu Zhixin (1885-1920) was born in Fanyu, Guangdong. In 1904 he went to Japan to study. The following year, he joined the China Revolutionary League, becoming one of its radical propagandists. At that time the revolutionaries and the reformists were engaged in a great polemic debate, and Zhu actively promoted a programme of nationalistic and democratic revolution, expounding in particular on Sun Yat-sen's Principle of People's Livelihood. In the inaugural issue of the *People's Journal*, Sun introduced the slogan: "Carry out the political and social revolutions at one stroke." Zhu followed this up with an article entitled "On the Need to Carry Out Political Revolution and Social Revolution at the Same Time". He believed that private ownership inevitably led to a social disparity between the rich and the poor, and that this disparity created the causes of social revolution. Consequently, it was necessary to carry out social and political revolutions at the same time.

But Zhu did not come to know that private ownership inevitably brings class differentiation and struggle. He merely stressed the equalization of land property, subjectively hoping through this to avoid the calamities of capitalism. He thought that by merely carrying out land nationalization it would be possible to achieve the socialist ideal. This subjective understanding of socialism was typical of the time and formed an integral part of the democratic revolution of the period. It thus represented a first step in the development of the radical democrats' thought towards a socialist concept.

In 1906 Zhu introduced some fragments of Marxism in the *People's Journal*, and also translated several excerpts from the *Manifesto of the Communist Party*, asserting "the principal part of the social revolution is the masses". He also believed that "henceforwards, the power of the revolution ... will come not from the wealthy but from the common people."[15] At the same time, Liao Zhongkai (1878-1925) of the China Revolutionary League, under the pen-name of Tu Fu (literally "Slaughter the Rich") wrote along the same line. These were the men who made the earliest introduction of socialist ideas. But their understanding could only be incomplete and abstract and could not reach to the genuine nature of class struggle or the dictatorship of the proletariat.

In the course of his study of the West, Sun Yat-sen did perceive a number of internal contradictions in capitalist society. He consequently produced his own subjective socialist ideas, hoping that China would be able to avoid taking the same disastrous course as Western capitalist societies. This kind of thinking was later distilled into a relatively clear and definite theory, the Principle of People's Livelihood in his Three People's Principles. In his later years he even formulated a grand plan for China's industrialization, as embodied in the works *Programme of National Construction* and *Outline of National Construction*. At that time, too, he summed up his Principle of People's Livelihood in two main points, i.e., "equalization of land property" and "control of capital". These together represented the height of understanding that a democratic revolutionary attained in social thought at this period.

Although the Revolution of 1911 overthrew the feudal dynasty, the basic nature of Chinese society did not change. The democratic revolutionaries that ascended the stage of history at the beginning of the 20th century were the political representatives of the bourgeoisie and the petty bourgeoisie. And because of the weakness of this group as a class, their leaders did not and could not set forth a thoroughly anti-imperialist and anti-feudal programme, nor had they the power to solve, in time, the most fundamental social problem, i.e., the land problem of the peasants. What is more, they were unable to mobilize the broad masses of the people and to organize them into a revolutionary army, and with this revolutionary force, to smash the counter-revolutionary forces. Indulging in fantasy, they followed along a path of compromise with the reactionary forces in order to establish a bourgeois republic.

In this respect, Song Jiaoren might be considered a typical example. Song Jiaoren (1882-1913) was born in Taoyuan of Hunan Province. After the 1911 Revolution, he vigorously promoted a republican-style parliament and responsible cabinet after the Western pattern. But he was murdered by an assassin sent by Yuan Shikai because of his views and activities. It might be said that after the 1911 Revolution, the history of the Republic of China—which existed in name only—was also a history of the bankruptcy of the bourgeois republican plan in China. After this, the democratic revolutionaries groped about in the dark for a period, unable to find an ideological outlet. Only with the New Culture Movement on the eve of the May Fourth Movement did their social thought again shed some rays of hope.

2. MODERN SCIENTIFIC THOUGHTS

In the modern period, Chinese scientific thought witnessed three great events, or rather three high tides. The first was the system of classical mechanics publicized by the early New Learning School. The second was the theory of evolution propagated by the reformers on the eve of 1898 Reform Movement. And the third was Mr. Science—scientific attitudes and scientific methods—publicized at the time of the May Fourth Movement. Each of these high tides was accompanied by a sharp battle between the old and the new thought. Modern scientific thought was established in China by progressive Chinese intellectuals in the long course of their ideological struggle against the corrupt culture of the old society.

As was mentioned above, the Western missionaries who came to China at the end of Ming and the beginning of Qing did not really bring modern science with them, or modern classical mechanics as started by Copernicus and completed by Newton. The reason was that, historically speaking, the birth of modern natural science was thoroughly revolutionary in nature and consequently aroused religious and theological hostility. For a very long time, fundamental scientific principles known in China did not extend beyond premodern statics. Liu Shizhong said: "The distinguished foreign guest Matteo Ricci [1552-1610] first transmitted the study of the epicycles, and then Ferdinand Verbiest [1623-1688] and Sebastian de Ursis [1575-1620] who followed him, took his work even further." Ricci, Verbiest and Ursis were among the Jesuit missionaries who came to China at that time.

Science is the formulation of the natural laws of the world, it deals with the issue of truth vs. falsity but not with the Chinese vs. the Western. Most of the Chinese scientists made their approaches through a unified comprehension of both the Chinese and the Western. When the Chinese scholars were in their first contacts with the Western scholars, Xu Guangqi advocated early in the 17th century the principle that "in order to surpass the West, it is necessary to have a unified comprehension of both the Chinese and the Western". The tradition formed by such an attitude towards science helped, in the last analysis, to break through the barriers of the old learning, although modern science in its strict sense had not yet been known in China at that time.

The first man in China to lay down the foundation of modern science was Li Shanlan (1810-1882). Li was born in Haining of Zhejiang Province, served in the staff of Zeng Guofan and later headed the Mathematics Department of Tongwen College. Eventually modern classical mechanics, after being established in the West for about two centuries, was born in China only through the hands of Li. He also formally introduced modern astronomy, calculus and others, and translated Newton's *Principia Mathematica*, which was later completed by Hua Hengfang. He continued the work left unfinished by Xu Guangqi, completing Xu's translation of Euclid's *Elements of Geometry*. It was he who introduced to China modern science which differed from the science of antiquity and the middle ages.

Half a century before Li, lived Ruan Yuan (1764-1849) of Yizheng in Jiangsu, the last and the greatest of the Han Learning scholars during the Qianlong and Jiaqing period, and also the last man of science in the middle ages. Although Ruan Yuan knew a few names of modern Western scientists, his scientific knowledge did not go beyond the statics of antiquity and the middle ages. Because they were hoodwinked for a long time by Western missionaries, the Chinese scholars throughout the period were unclear about exactly what modern science was. Ruan Yuan professed: "New scientific methods in the West have gone through continuous changes, schools broke off from the old path and formed new approaches, and their teachings were different from each other; Johann Schall von Bell [1591-1666] devoted himself especially to the operation of the epicycles; Smogolenski [1611-1656] had his concepts of heavens with different centres; in the translation of Ignatius Kögler [1680-1746], the heavens go round; and Michael Benoist [1715-1774] affirmed that the sun stands still and the earth moves. Their teachings were too confused and difficult to be reconciled into one."[1] It is clear from Ruan's remarks on the teachings of these missionaries that 19th century Chinese scholars were still unclear and baffled about the distinction between the science of antiquity and middle ages and that of modern times, and so felt much confused in the face of the approaching modern scientific revolution, all at a loss about where to go.

Methodologically, Ruan Yuan summed up an idealistic theory of scientific knowledge. He taught that the truth or falsity of a scientific theory lay not in whether or not it reflected accurately the laws of change of the objective world, but rather whether or not it more conveniently served or suited a subjective hypothesis. Ruan proclaimed: "If a hypothesis serves only to meet the requirements of a mathematical principle, then it would be as well to suppose (that) the earth moves and the sun remains stationary."[2] Consequently he concluded: "Instead of saying that when Westerners speak of heavens they are able to comprehend the reason why things are the way they are, it would seem forever much safer to say simply that something appears so and not to say the reason why."[3] In his views it did not matter whether you said that the sun moves and the earth remains stationary, or that the earth moves and the sun remains stationary. Both statements are scientifically equivalent. This kind of thinking actually negates the objectivity of scientific truth and amounts to an obscurantist teaching. As he put it: "The Way of Heaven is too mystical to be fathomed by human understanding."[4]

Li Shanlan advocated a mechanistic theory of knowledge based on modern science, which was aimed primarily against the agnosticism represented by Ruan Yuan. Li emphatically pointed out: "The writer [Ruan Yuan] said that 'this [Kepler's laws] was but a mere hypothesis. Actually it was assumed only in order to meet his mathematical operations. Really there is no such thing as what the hypothesis tends to show'. I would rather remark that the writer had not observed it carefully, but restricted himself to the teachings of the ancient classics and ran wild in his arguments; and it is all extreme nonsense. Since ancient times up to the present, among those who spoke about the heavens, there had been no better expression than Ziyu's: 'You must carefully find out the reasons.' And the gentlemen of the West [Copernicus and Newton] were among those who excelled at finding out the reasons."[5]

In the preface to his book, Li explained and described the two opposing lines of scientific research as clearly as possible. One was that of modern science, running from Copernicus to Newton. The other was that of the obscurantists' agnosticism, running from Matteo Ricci to Ruan Yuan. And Li put himself in opposition to the mediaeval idealistic theory of knowledge, substituting a rather naive scientific mechanistic position based on modern science. In the early Western Learning camp, Li was the most outstanding figure in the field of scientific thought during the struggle between Western and Chinese Learning.

As early as Li's time, another outstanding mathematician, Hua Hengfang (1833-1902), a native of Wuxi in Jiangsu, had already pointed out that Li's theory of scientific knowledge was one of "following heavens in order to seek their conformity (with the motions of heavens)" and not the idealistic views of Ruan Yuan which sought to "create conformity in order to regulate the motion of heavens".[6] In other words, Li employed a mechanistic theory of reflection to oppose idealist apriorism. Though on the basic issue of scientific knowledge, the sharp contrast between these two lines had existed ever since antiquity, it was only with the formal establishment of modern science in China that the mechanistic theory of knowledge and the corresponding materialist methodology received a relatively clear theoretical form.

This controversy marked the first round by the two opposing scientific lines of thought in modern China. Since then, new scientific ideas became one of the sources of Western Learning that inspired later reformers at the time of the 1898 Reform Movement. Liang Qichao, in recalling the tremendous thirst for knowledge of the New Learning School on the eve of the 1898 Reform Movement, said that at that time "there were still some twenty to thirty translated scientific works published by the Jiangnan Manufacturers. Li Shanlan, Hua Hengfang and Zhao Zhonghan were responsible for translating them", and "during the Guangxu period, those of the so-called New Learning School wishing to seek knowledge beyond the national borders considered these works to be like secret alchemy formulas".[7]

It is already a fact generally known that "what really pushed them [the philosophers] forward was above all the powerful and increasingly rapid and impetuous progress of natural science and industry".[8] Originally, the appearance of modern science in China was accompanied by modern industry (for example, the Jiangnan Manufacturers, from which came the first group of modern Chinese scientists). But the combined oppression of imperialism, feudalism and bureaucratic capitalism made it difficult for Chinese industry and science to develop. Therefore the scientific ideas lacked the material driving force to push them forward. So even after individual scientists like Li Shanlan appeared, progress in science and scientific thought was unable to swell to a surging ideological revolution as it did earlier in modern Western Europe.

Li Shanlan advanced the thesis that "today the daily increase in the power and wealth of the various nations of Europe causes much trouble on the borders of China. In tracing the reason, we find it is because they are skilful in making machines; and they are skilful in making machines because they mastered mathematics".[9] This idea might be said one of the earliest example of modern "save the nation through science" theories. But the development of science, too, requires its own objective material conditions; otherwise, even the best of intentions would falter when faced with social reality. Unfortunately, this was what happened in late 19th century China.

At the end of the 19th century, a great ideological liberation surged hand in hand with the Reform Movement. The greatest contribution of the reformers in the field of science and scientific thought was their introduction of the idea of evolution. On a theoretical level, the idea of evolution dealt a mortal blow to the feudal metaphysical dogma that "Heaven does not change, and so the Way also does not change". Since the natural realm and the human world were both in constant and continuous progress, the feudal theory advocating the return to ancient ways and respect for antiquity definitely lost its theoretical basis; and with each passing day it lost more of the audience for its ideology. On the eve of the 1898 Reform, Yan Fu published his well-known series of political articles which emphatically introduced the theory of evolution to China, providing the progressive intellectuals with a most important theoretical weapon.

Yan's translation of T. H. Huxley's *Evolution and Ethics* has been mentioned above. The section of the book dealing with evolution in the biological world is materialistic, while the section dealing with social ethics is idealistic. Yan Fu's purpose in translating this book was to promote a theory that documented and expounded the inevitability and necessity for change and progress in Chinese society to get rid of the bondage of the old ways. This can be plainly seen in the voluminous commentaries that he provided for his translated version. For half a century, Chinese society had been in constant ferment, awaiting a tremendous metamorphosis, but her progressive intellectuals seemed unable to find an appropriate ideological theory with which to arm themselves. The publication of Yan's translation *Evolution and Ethics* provided them with a new world outlook and a new ideological methodology to serve as a window for observing the fate of nations and peoples.

Liang Qichao, after reading it, wrote to Yan Fu, saying: "Master Nanhai (Kang Youwei) on reading your great work said that he had never imagined such a man. Suiqing (Xia Zengyou) is unstintingly admiring it."[10] Wu Yuzhang recalled this work, too: "The ideas in the book of *Evolution and Ethics*, such as natural selection and survival of the fittest, profoundly stimulated a good many of our intellectuals at the time. The book seemed to sound an alarm for us and made us acutely and painstakingly aware of the danger of being subjugated. We had to fight hard to ensure our survival.... Indeed, in early 20th century China, the idea of evolution played a positive role."[11] At this time, the young Lu Xun had just come to Nanjing to study. When he heard about this book, he sought it out and read it from cover to cover. Then all of a sudden, he learned that "in this world there actually are men like Huxley, sitting in their studies thinking. And thinking such fresh new thoughts. Reading along, the terms 'struggle for living' and 'natural selection' jumped out at me".[12] These are only a few samples showing how popular the idea of evolution was and how it influenced that time.

The Chinese bourgeoisie did not have enough time to create its own ideological system, so the only thing it could do was to bring in a ready-made product from the West. On this point, *Evolution and Ethics* provides a good example. Due to the reactionaries' cultural despotism and their policy of keeping the people ignorant, "prior to 1894 [the Sino-Japanese War], those of our literati who spoke of Western Learning thought that the strong points of the Westerners were simply their sturdy gunboats, powerful artillery and clever machines, and the like. Therefore, those who studied Western Learning limited themselves to arms, machinery and ships".[13] Yan Fu himself had originally been a naval cadet in England. The loss of the Sino-Japanese War of 1894 stimulated a great transformation among Chinese intellectuals, and threw the progressives into a mood of extreme distress and indignation. The threat of national subjugation and genocide was right before them, and they ran about for help, demanding a way to save the nation from subjugation and to ensure survival, demanding survival of the nation and the race, demanding new (Western) learning, demanding reform and modernization, and demanding human rights and equality. They founded associations, kept contacts with their comrades and ran newspapers and periodicals to inspire the people. "Since 1894," said a contemporary, "newspapers began prevailing.... periodicals of various kinds were edited and published, mostly by the elite of the intellectual circle, moving the people to tears and crying."[14]

Under these conditions, Yan Fu came to assail what he termed the "vulgar, coarse material aspects" of previous Western learning that had been transmitted to China by the foreign missionaries and the domestic bureaucrats, and translated *Evolution and Ethics* in the literary style of the pre-Qin philosophers. He introduced what he thought to be the theory which formed the "lifeline" of Western learning. It included not only scientific thought, but social and political doctrines as well. His translations and articles marked an intellectual highlight in the ideological conflicts between the old and the new. The theory of evolution also furnished an important theoretical ground for the later democratic revolutionaries, even though their political positions were fundamentally different. The reformists and the revolutionaries of the period each understood and used this theory in accordance with their own needs. This point should not be neglected.

At that time, the works of Darwin had not yet been translated into Chinese, but his evolutionary theory (or rather the evolutionary theory as propounded by Yan Fu) had brought an unprecedented impetus to the intellectual world of China. In Darwin's Origin of Species, one reads: "As natural selection acts solely by accumulating slight, successive, favourable variations, it can produce no great or sudden modification; it can only act by very short and slow steps. Hence the canon of Natura non facit saltus, which every fresh addition to our knowledge tends to make truer, is on this theory simply intelligible."[15] Yan did not quote this passage word by word, but the basic standpoint from which the reformists came into antagonism with the revolutionaries—i.e., the so-called "there is no leaping over the gradations" (that is, no revolution)[16]—was essentially along the same theoretical line. Yan himself had never taken the theory of evolution solely as natural science; on the contrary, he was always employing it in explaining the social phenomena and moulding it to his reformist views. As his anti-feudal spearhead lost more and more of its lustre, the more pronounced his anti-revolutionary tendency became. The theory of evolution was essentially a biological doctrine and could not be applied to the social and historical sphere in a ready-made fashion, because social phenomena differ essentially from the biological and are governed by the laws of social development.

Yan Fu's evolutionary theory had its positive historical effects. It spread patriotism. It called for progress. It called for the abolition of the old and the unfolding of the new. It gave rise to ideological emancipation. And it stirred up popular sentiment. Nevertheless, his evolutionary idea was no serious science. He poured into it other elements. He took from Adam Smith the concept of universal human nature and made perpetual selfishness the nucleus of it. He also took from Spencer that society is an abstract and mechanical summation of human nature, and proclaimed: "Those who do not know division cannot know unity.... Therefore, those who do not know about human nature cannot speak of society."[17] This is simply taking human nature, which is itself a product of society, and turning it on its head into a presupposition of society, and then attempting to demonstrate the rationality of capitalist relations from innate human nature. With the further intensification of social contradictions and with the fear of and the opposition to the great wave of the democratic revolution, the reformists thought it best to throw in their lot with the reactionary forces. So they turned around, ideologically as well as politically, and went in the opposite direction. This is why Yan Fu in his later years surrendered himself to feudalism and abandoned his early views on Western Learning.

In the early 20th century, the weapons of natural science that were available to the democratic revolutionaries did not go much beyond the scope of evolution. Because of the backwardness of Chinese society, the series of basic conceptual changes in science that had begun taking place by the late 19th century did not have enough time to create an echo within Chinese ideological circles. Tan Citong's borrowing of the outdated concept "ether" was an example. It was only with the New Culture Movement that the two great banners of "democracy" and "science" were formally raised. Only then was science again taken seriously, and scientific thought developed further. Science and democracy became the trend of the times, and the number of people who consciously began to publicize science far exceeded that of the previous era. Lu Xun was one of the most outstanding among them. The May Fourth Movement does not belong within the scope of our book, so we shall satisfy ourselves with a brief introduction of Lu Xun's contribution in the area of scientific thought in the pre-May Fourth period.

From the beginning, Lu Xun's evolutionary idea was saturated with dialectical elements, that is, he was able to engage in thought from the standpoint of development and transformation of things. In 1907, he wrote "On the Demoniac Poets" in which he professed: "There is nothing peaceful within mankind, even if one were to insist on speaking of peace, it could merely mean antagonisms having just ceased or being just about to begin. The outer appearance may resemble peace, but within, the current of hostilities remain submerged, and at the right moment will be set into motion again." This was a brilliant proposition with which Lu Xun saw movement as absolute and being stationary as relative; the whole objective world, including mankind, was in constant process of continuous transformation and development.

Modern science from the 16th to the 18th century, while taking great strides forward, was still shrouded by a rigid metaphysical concept of nature. In the West, it was the philosopher Kant who first broke a hole in it. In his *Universal History of Nature and Theory of Heavens* (1755), Kant denied constancy in the physical world, and described the entire cosmic realm as a developmental process. The first to introduce this theory to China was none other than Lu Xin. In 1903 he wrote *An Outline of Chinese Geology* in which he introduced the Kant-Laplacian theory of nebula. In his article, Lu Xun said: "The theory of nebula advanced by the German philosopher Kant, as followed by the French scholar Laplace, takes the earth to be part of what was once a large gaseous body in the universe, that separated out and revolved in space for untold thousands of aeons before congealing into liquid. Later, while cooling off, it contracted, the outer surface solidified and is now what we call the earth's shell." This explanation used modern scientific concepts to demonstrate that the physical world was itself in a process of development, and subsequently this concept smashed a hole in China's rigid traditional concept of the Way of Heaven. Slightly before Lu Xun, Yan Fu and Liang Qichao had discussed Kant's thought, but that part of classical German philosophy which was richest in scientific value—the dialectic method of thinking— was introduced by Lu Xun. Here we see reflected the differences in the ways the reformists and the revolutionaries borrowed and transplanted Western ideology.

From the very beginning, natural science was an important source and component of Lu Xun's thought. In 1903, he wrote "On Radium" in which he introduced the greatest scientific advance at the end of the 19th century, the discovery of radioactive elements. He also wrote *A Record of China's Minerals*, and translated *From the Earth to the Moon* and *Vogage to the Centre of the Earth* by the French science fiction writer Jules Verne (1828-1905), who became since then well-known to many Chinese readers. In 1904, Lu Xun translated *Exploration of the North Pole*. In 1907, he wrote *A History of Man*, *A Textbook of the History of Science*, and other writings on scientific topics. In *A History of Man*, Lu Xun reintroduced the theory of evolution, this time as applied to biology, a task Yan Fu had failed to do. *A Textbook on the History of Science* pointed out the significance of science and the great role it played in the process of human civilization. It was not only an important document in the Chinese study of the history of science and scientific thought, but also conveyed the author's aspiration for change and progress. Scientifically, the young Lu Xun was a materialist full of combattant spirit, who worked hard to spread scientific thought and introduce scientific achievements. These ideas based on natural science were among his most powerful weapons in assailing the old ideology and culture.

Of course, in the early 20th century, Lu Xun was still too young and too immature to be a conscious and thorough-going materialist. But his scientific thought reached a new historical height. And since modern science was closely related to modern industry, he began to realize the interdependency between science and industry, asserting: "Much did industry owe to science, but science was by no means less indebted to industry."[18] The relationship of their interdependence meant also, in a certain sense, that a similar one existed between the theoretical and the practical. In his exposition that science itself was a tremendous productive force, he argued that it was due to the advancement of science that "the safety lamp was invented, the steam engine was worked out and the mining industry prospered", in short, "all the equipment and means in industry, all vegetation and reproduction of the plants and all the stock-rearing were benefited by science".[19] Here he made a penetrating analysis of the topic of the social significance and function of science and the relation of science to society. Plain and simple as it might look at first, it dealt with a truth that few had touched upon in China.

By the May Fourth period, Lu Xun's scientific thought had developed along with the times. He already clearly appreciated the fact that science itself was an extremely important factor in the democratic revolution, in the liberation of mankind and in the progress of society. In 1918, on the eve of the May Fourth Movement, Lu Xun wrote: "Now the 606 has been discovered [meaning

the discovery of Salvarsan by the German doctor Paul Ehrlich]
which can cure physiological illness; and I hope there will be also a
discovery of 707 to cure ideological illness. Of course, this medicine
has already been discovered. It is no other than science."[20] The
following year, the year of the May Fourth Movement 1919, Lu Xun
stated even more clearly: "It would be good if every issue of the *New
Tide* will have one or two articles on pure science.... And no matter
what, we must keep stabbing at the old illness of China.... Now we
are bent on talking about and discussing science, on and on, in order
to make them [the representatives of the putrefied old culture]
off-balance. Then no one can blame us that we did not do what we
possibly could."[21]

It was quite apparent, then, that Lu Xun placed great importance on science. To him, science was frankly and honestly concerned
with the truth, and so was able to lay bare the lies spread by the
reactionaries. He understood this principle well, and he explained it
equally well. It was no accident that science became one of the two
main standards of the May Fourth Movement; and it was also no
accident that science became an integral part of Lu Xun's thought.
As a foremost representative of the New Culture Movement, Lu Xun
was at the same time the foremost representative of the third high
tide of modern scientific thought in China.

3. MODERN HISTORIOGRAPHIC THOUGHT

In the early Qing period, most historians under the high pressure
of the Manchu regime engaged themselves in research on the history
of the late Ming dynasty, in which they found sustenance for the
nostalgia of a conquered people. Then the Qing regime, to strengthen
the rule of its cultural despotism, carried out literary inquisitions
time and again which drove most scholars to retreat into the den of
textual studies of the ancient classics far away from the reality of the
age. This was what was generally called Han Learning, which flourished during the reigns of Qianlong and Jiaqing and was hence
termed "the Han Learning of the Qian and Jia period". At first the
royal court advocated Song Learning (the New Confucianism of the
Song period), while most scholars without official affiliations en-

gaged themselves in Han Learning; between them there might be perceived some very delicate differences. But down to the reigns of Qianlong and Jiaqing, Han Learning had already became an academic adornment of the prosperity of the royal reign and lost the last spark of the Enlightenment ardour and the practical spirit of the progressive ideologies of its founders in the late Ming and early Qing period.

With the great historical change in modern times, people had their minds gradually emancipated from the restraint of musty old books; and the ideas of history changed. Because foreign aggression forced open the gate to China and pushed China onto the world historical stage, the attention of historiography gradually shifted from critical research on ancient texts which were far removed from the present reality, in the direction of practical statecraft founded on a broad world view, despite the fact that their knowledge of the world at that time was still quite limited. Such early modern historical works as Wei Yuan's *Illustrated Record of the Oversea Countries*, He Qiutao's *Historical Sources of the Northern Regions* and Tu Ji's *History of the Moguls*, no longer adhered to the Han Learning tradition of stodgy textual scholarship, but began to face the vast real world of the present and the past. And the scope of historical materials accordingly expanded. Excavated archaeological evidences began to occupy an important place, along with other modern scientific discoveries. By the turn of the century, both reformists like Kang Youwei and revolutionaries like Zhang Taiyan were bound up in the historico-cultural spirit growing out of the real needs of the time, and proceeded to break with the Han School of textual criticism. Thus at one and the same time they consciously pursued history in the spirit of the age and embodied that spirit through their historical research.

Liang Qichao's incomparable influences on modern times can hardly be overvalued. Politically, Liang followed Kang's royalist line after 1898, but in the cultural and ideological sphere he was still an important representative of Western Learning by any standard. The sources of his Western knowledge were multifarious, but a great part was copied indirectly from the Japanese; he confessed that "all my writings are no more than the exposition of the lectures of my teachers and friends, picked up here and there from fragments from the Western thinkers. I am only summing up the thoughts and words of others".[1] Yet, introducing Western ideas on such a large scale as he did, he is worthy of specific attention.

The modernized historiographical thought of Liang occupies an important place in modern intellectual history. His historical writings were voluminous, and in his later years he concentrated even more of his energies on historiography. Some concise comments that illustrate his historiographical thinking follow.

The governing idea in feudal historiographical thought was the set of feudal ethical teachings or commandments that served as guiding principles. Feudal historiography employed moral norms such as "good and evil, worthy and unworthy" to achieve its view of how the past mirrored the present. Liang Qichao, as the spokesman for the new modern historiography, liberated it from the bondage of ethical judgment and vested it with the task of seeking objective laws. This was a major transformation that brought historiography out of the middle ages into the modern era. Liang's work in 1901, *An Introduction to Chinese History*, already deviated in style from feudal principles. The following year he wrote an article "The New Historiography" in which he openly called for new historical thinking and censured the old historiography for knowing only about dynasties and individuals, but not about nations and social groups. He declared: "This subject of study [historiography] has developed now for over two thousand years, yet it still follows the same rut, and now I have yet to hear of anyone opening up new ground in historiography."[2] This plainly shows that Liang personally rejected the old historiography and hoped to establish a new historiography.

Towards this end, Liang offered some new formulations relating to historiography. He set forth a brand new definition for history: "The historian is to record phenomena relating to progress", followed by "the historian is to record phenomena relating to progress of social groups", and "the historian is to record phenomena relating to progress of social groups and to find out the general rules and patterns in them".[3] This was in direct opposition to the respect for the old and the cyclical theory of feudal historiography. It clearly set forth a view of social progress. Moreover, this view directly opposed the highly trumpeted good-and-evil, praise-and-blame feudal historiography. It clearly gave a concept of objective law—Liang's so-called general rules and patterns. Particularly since the *Outline of General History* of the Neo-Confucian Zhu Xi, which was so tightly bound up in the "criteria of recording", history had become jacketed by such orthodox fallacies as political legitimacy, the lawful reign and orthodox thinking.

That same year, Liang wrote his *On Legitimacy* in which he pointed out specifically: "The absurdity of the traditional historians was nowhere more manifest than in their claim for the legitimate orthodoxy. They professed that since there could not be a day without a sovereign, there should be orthodoxy; and since there could be no two suns in the heaven and no two sovereigns over the people, there should be only a sole legitimate orthodoxy. What was termed orthodoxy by them was presumably what was erected by Heaven and worshipped by the people. And what was termed legitimacy was presumably that among different rulers only one could be the genuine sovereign and all the rest were false. For more than two thousand years, the vulgar scholars have been arguing minutely over all this; they were confronting one another with sophisticated polemics, drawing false analogies and making irrelevant comparisons incessantly. In short, they were under the restraint of their slavishness, by which they in turn were to foster the slavishness of others, and nothing else than that. This is exactly what has to be discriminated."[4]

He further sharply rejected the definition of legitimacy in feudal historiography for being no more than the six criteria of "the amount of territory under control ... the length of time of the reign ... the kinship in blood lineage or pedigree ... location of the capital on the site of the previous dynasty ... the forefather of the later dynasties" and "being of the Han stock".[5] Liang showed these six criteria to be demonstrably "self-contradictory". He cited proofs that the leaders of both aristocratic revolts and peasant uprisings could also, with any luck, become the founding emperors of new dynasties; and he went on to say that in terms of these men being exalted as legitimate emperors there was not the slightest sense of "disrespect" or "impropriety". Having discredited the old feudal historiographical rut, he proclaimed that there had never really been any such thing as "legitimate orthodoxy" since times of old. This theoretical work of his was significant in liberating historiographic thinking and greatly cleansed China of its moribund historical concepts.

Following that, he wrote two treatises entitled "On Historical Recording" and "On Chronicling", and both stood in direct opposition to the feudal historical recording method, such as praising the good, condemning the evil and upholding the "orthodox calendar". All these treatises by him, together with another article "On the Main Trends of Transition of the Ancient Chinese Learning and Ideology", written at the same time, aimed at an objectivistic analysis of the origin and development of ancient thought, helped greatly in broadening the field and bringing forth new ideas and concepts of history, thus sweeping away the pedantic and unscientific style of historical study of the feudalistic methodology. Meanwhile, he also wrote *On the Principle of Succession of the Monarchy by the Democracy* which explained the history of the polity of China in terms of Western political ideas. And in his *The Main Features of the Geography of China*, he tried to explain cultural phenomena in history (such as the differences of the north and the south with respect to their scholarship and their teachings) through the perspective of geographical factors instead of the traditional ethical preaching. He even wrote a paper on the history of science, "An Examination on the Development of Physical Sciences", a topic generally neglected in the traditional historiography.

Liang's historical writings of this period all centred around his Western learning concepts, which he used to elucidate and criticize the old historiography and historical thought. They became the leading works of his time in bringing about a renewed appraisal of both Chinese history and Chinese historiography from a modern standpoint. Yet they also embodied Liang's idealistic view of history with its exaggeration on the role of the spirit. Though he cast off the bonds of feudal "ethical" historiography and brought a fresh outlook, he basically ignored the material base of history and the decisive role of the masses in the development of history. The masses, in his eyes, were little more than the common herd.

What reflected most clearly the negative elements in his idea of history was his view that the historical arena of China was but "a great slaughter-house" and all the historical writings were but the "records of men killing men".[6] He felt great pity for the fact that China had never had a powerful middle class in her history. It was the reason, so he held, why the revolutions taking place in the history of the West always resulted in progress, while the revolutions in the history of China resulted in retrogress. Therefore in the same year he wrote *An Interpretation on Revolution* in which he emphatically advocated peaceful reform against violent revolution. This idea constituted one of the main threads in his historical thought. In 1904, when the demarcation between the Reformists and the Revolutionaries had already become clear, he wrote *A Study on the Revolutions in the History of China* in which he characterized Chinese history in these words: "In China there had been revolutions by the upper and the lower classes but never a revolution by the middle class", and this was due to the fact that "the initiatives for the revolutions in the West rested mainly in the middle class; for the upper class was the object of revolution while the lower class had neither the ideas nor the ability to start a revolution."[7] Consequently, a representative of the Western Learning camp though he was, Liang nevertheless held a deep suspicion as to whether China might "get entry into the rank of the Western revolutions". From this he drew his conclusion that since China had never had a powerful enough middle class, she was destined to follow the path of reform instead of revolution.

It was at this time that Liang wrote a great many historical biographies, and the dominant theme throughout was the "great man" idea in history, or the belief that the force that propelled or changed history was ultimately a function of the individual heroes' subjective will. A whole series of Liang's historical works, from *The Coup d'Etat of 1898* to the *Method of Studying the Chinese History*, all stressed the predominant role of the spiritual or psychic factor in the development of history.

His heroic conception of history was systematically amplified in his book *Method of Studying the Chinese History*, which was the first book dealing with historical methodology in modern China and the sole one on that topic since Zhang Xuecheng's *General Treatise on Literature and History* in the 18th century. The definitive version of this book appeared at the much later date of 1920, but its content was a theoretical summarization of his historical thinking since 1898. "Perhaps I have overrated myself," he professed, "in undertaking the study on this topic in a course of twenty years and more. So even though the accumulated manuscripts piled high, I have not been convinced of myself in a condition to put it forth."[8] Therefore it might be affirmed that the original idea of the book should be dated as early as 1898, finally put in its finished form in 1920.

The heroic conception that the course of history was determined by a few heroes while the masses played only a passive role formed the thesis of his book. He declared: "Try to think it happened that such persons as Confucius, the First Emperor of Qin or Emperor Wu of Han had never appeared in the history of China ... then what would become of the Chinese history?"[9] And he agreed with Bertrand Russell that the history of the world would be totally altered if only a handful of historic figures were taken out of it. Here the historic figures were identified, or rather confused, by Liang with the development of history itself, of which these historic figures were but the representatives. It looked to him as though in the absence of certain historic figures there would be no historical development at all. This reasoning must be regarded as a sophism of the idealistic conception of history. Just the contrary is the fact. The course of development of history itself never depends on any individual, no matter how great he might prove to be. Suffice to say, if there had been no Columbus, the new continent was still destined to be discovered by somebody else. The heroic figures thus highly idealized by him were termed by him "historic personages". "Why were they," he asked, "termed historic personages? Because they initiated, at least partly, a group of historical events taking place then and there, and their statures were raised almost to a level high enough to overshadow the whole society."[10] Going a step further, he took the will of the individual as the determining factor in the whole course of history, asserting: "The totality of history might change its course if only once the psychic moments of these figures somewhat slightly deviated from their original tracks. This principle holds valid not only for a dictatorial system but also for a democracy."[11]

With regard to the task and method of historical research, in Liang's hands this ultimately meant merely how to "recognize the important personalities in a given historical circle" in given circumstances, because each set of historical circumstances "necessarily has some personalities as its backbone". He cited the Paris Peace Conference ending World War I as an example: "In the small group at the Paris Peace Conference, one recognizes Clemenceau, Lloyd George and Wilson as the leading personalities."[12] Even such a personality as Yuan Shikai was regarded as being able to determine the fate of China; and "there is no way to know whether the situation of the past ten years of the Republic of China might have been completely different, had Yuan's character been slightly more upright, or conversely, had it been slightly more mediocre".[13]

In his later years, Liang Qichao dabbled in the historical thought of the German neo-Kantian philosopher Heinrich Rickert (1863-1936) which saw history as a product of "mental vigor". This type of mental force was both unpredictable and without discernible laws. Liang asserted categorically that "history is the creation of man's mental vigor, and this mental vigor is utterly free and cannot be predicted".[14] This view was a great step backward from Liang's early seeking of the general rules and general patterns of history. It also indicates that although Liang made a major contribution by smashing the bones of feudal historiographic concepts, his idealistic view of history was in the final analysis essentially little different from the old ideas viewing the development of history as a product of kings, generals, ministers and eminent men.

Another man who played an equally important role in modern historiography was Wang Guowei. Liang proclaimed that history was created by the mental vigor of man, Wang proclaimed that the world was created by the mind. Wang Guowei (1876-1927) was born in Haining of Zhejiang, and earned his reputation in modern intellectual history primarily as a historian. In his early period (1898-1907) he studied philosophy, in his middle period (1907-1912), literature, and in his later years (1912-1927), historiography. He was successful in all three phases of his career, particularly in his later years when he made numerous discoveries in the course of his research on ancient history. Wang's philosophical and esthetic ideas, which fell within the Western Learning camp of that period (he introduced Kant, Schopenhauer and Nietzsche to China), were historically significant in their opposition to China's old feudal culture. But his idealistic thinking was saturated with a heavy sentimentalism.

After the Revolution of 1911, he accompanied Luo Zhenyu (a mediocre official of the Qing Dynasty, then an adherent of the dethroned emperor and finally one of the greatest national traitors) to Japan, where he fell in with a group of the adherents to the former Qing Dynasty, and involved in an impasse ideologically. Thereupon he turned and escaped into the ivory tower of ancient history and ancient documents, becoming an unfortunate comic figure of the time. But the historical thinking and method of his later years were by no means entirely controlled by the reactionary political concepts of the Qing diehards, just as the philosophical thought of his early years was not entirely in extricably tied to the structure of the pessimism of Schopenhauer or to the voluntarism of Nietzsche. He achieved impressive results by proceeding from an attitude and method of "seeking truth from facts" in his studies of ancient data.

In saying all this, one must bear in mind that Wang Guowei benefited greatly from objective conditions, that is, from the tremendous historical discoveries dating from the late 19th century. Wang was one of the earliest scholars to come into contact with these materials and to undertake their systematic research. And these massive discoveries of new materials since the late 19th century were made possible only in the modern historical era. Among the most important finds were: 1. the oracle bones in the Yin tombs; 2. the Han and Wei dynasty bamboo slips from the shifting deserts; 3. the Tang Dynasty scrolls from the Dunhuang caves; 4. the Ming and Qing documents from the Archives of the Grand Secretariat; and 5. the ancient writings of non-Han border peoples.

Wang used these materials to re-examine ancient history and ancient records. His historical methodology was refined by the use of these materials, resulting in what he called the "double verification method", that is, to verify written records with reference to archaeological excavations and vice versa. Of the achievements and deficiencies of the Qing historians, Wang commented: "Their skeptical attitude and critical spirit had something to recommend it, but unfortunately these were never fully applied to ancient historical finds." The reason that the contemporary historians surpassed their predecessors was simply because "scholars born in the present generation are blessed by having newly excavated materials to verify the written materials. Because of these new materials, our own generation can form a reliable picture of the past by verifying a certain portion of ancient works through these supplementary proofs and by testifying what part of the works of ancient writers about their own times are truth. This double verification method has become possible only in the present day".[15] On the whole, the application of Wang's method in sorting out historical data, just like Liang's propagation of new historical theories and concepts, must be regarded as representative of historical thoughts in this period of breaking with the old and establishing the new.

In the preface to his *Examination on the Dramas of the Song and Yuan Period*, Wang Guowei wrote: "All the materials therein were collected by me, and the explanation about them were mostly my original ideas"; a remark which reflected his high self-valuation and which might appropriately be applied to his manifold contributions in the study of ancient history. For instance, the authenticity of the ancient book *The Bamboo Chronicles* had always been a much disputed topic in the field of ancient history. The book was first unearthed from the tombs in Ji at the end of the 3rd century, but was later lost in the Song period; and the current version of it was a collection made from various sources. Some scholars considered it a fabrication in the Jin period, others thought that both the original and the current versions were genuine; and still some others assumed that the original was true while the current one was false. After scrutinizing examinations, Wang worked out his *Commentaries on the Current Version of "The Bamboo Chronicles"* in which he came to the conclusion that there were in it fragments of the original version from the tombs in Ji but not the entirety of the original text. Ever since the Qianlong and Jiaqing period the Han Learning scholars had made extensive textual criticisms on it, but Wang's was generally accepted as the last and the most precise.

On the one hand, Wang's historical research had inherited the tradition of the Han Learning in the Qing period; and on the other hand, he had broken through it by bringing in modern methodology, the most important of which was the comparative method of study, or the "method of double verification". For example, some of his main works concerning the institutions of the Yin and Zhou and of the early kings of the early Yin Dynasty were all prepared by a searching comparison of the unearthed relics with the ancient written documents. Indeed, they made valuable academic discoveries. This led his historical methodology to the forefront of modern historiography—though still not without a trace of the outdated and outworn reverence for the ancients in it.

"Two factors," in the words of Liang Qichao, "account for the progress in historical research. One is the systematic organization of the objective data ... the other is innovations in subjective concepts."[16] The important contribution of Wang Guowei to modern historical study lay mainly in the systematic organization of objective data, whereas that of Liang lay in the innovation in subjective concepts. Neither man could avoid the serious limitations of his own world view, yet their legacies must be regarded as important in the field of modern historiography.

4. MODERN LITERARY THOUGHTS

Literature and art are important components in the fabric of a nation's superstructure. When history enters an age of great transformation, the awakening of a modern consciousness will inevitably be expressed in literary thought. Resisting foreign aggression, unmasking the darkness and decadence of feudal authority and of the feudal society, and seeking the independence, wealth and strength of the nation—these desires formed the intellectual themes of the broad masses of the Chinese people and of the progressive intellectuals of the time. They were also the main themes of the literary thought of the time.

The literary expression of feudal thought in the Qing period was the classical style of writing (or literary writing) of the Tongcheng School, so called because its chief members Fang Bao, Yao Nai and others were from Tongcheng in Anhui Province. The "orthodoxy of the Way" of Confucius, Mencius, the Cheng Brothers and Zhu Xi was synthesized by them with the "orthodoxy of writing" of Han Yu, Liu Zongyuan, Ouyang Xiu and Su Shi. In the modern period, the ruling cultural clique headed by Zeng Guofan worshipped this school of orthodoxy. Though within the arena of classical or traditional Chinese learning of that time there were polemics between the so-called Han Learning and Song Learning, that was not where the main current dwelt. The main current revolved not around traditional differences, but around Chinese or Old Learning versus Western or New Learning. From the early New Learning group to the 1898 reformers and down to the democratic revolutionaries, literature and art were employed as important weapons in their ideological and cultural struggles. But all of them were burdened with serious limitations and narrowness. Not until the May Fourth Movement did a relatively thorough anti-imperialist and anti-feudal literary thought appear.

With the dawn of China's modern history, Gong Zizhen took his pure, fresh literary brush to criticize and protest the corrupt old feudal society. Certain of his poetic and prose writings expressed his call for a new era. The new style prose from Gong down to Liang Qichao was essentially a revolt against the classical literary style of the Tongcheng School and hence a new intellectual tool for expressing new ideas and demand for change. Wei Yuan went far beyond the scope of literature in his use of the Gongyang approach in his essays on current affairs. His eyes were focusing on the future rather on the past. He embodied consciously the historical view that the later surpasses the earlier and the present surpasses the past. His suggestion that merchants should run factories for industrial production was China's earliest call for the development of capitalism.

In most respects, however, the Tongcheng School representing China's conservative cultural forces still dominated the literary world of the period. Zeng Guofan, who was venerated as the legitimate heir of the Tongcheng School, was grouped with Fang Bao and Yao Nai as "great men of their age". Li Shuchang said of him: "[Zeng] enlarged Yao, unified the feats, virtues and teachings in one, embraced the merits of all others, overshadowing Gui and Fang, standing high above the schools, outstripping the Han and going back to the ancients.... He was really the only one since Ouyang Xiu."[1] Even Xue Fucheng praised him as: "A great man of the age who in his literary writings developed his Neo-Confucian conviction and showed his ability to run the state.... He was worthy to rank with Fang and Yao and in his sublimest moments was even about to surpass his predecessors."[2]

Echoing the literary style of the Tongcheng School, but in the field of poetry, was the School of the Song Poetry. The leading members of this group were chiefly of the feudal literati. They enjoyed expressing their hallowed and decadent sentiments in obscure poetic diction. Since this style gained popularity for a time during the Tongzhi and Guangxu periods, it was generally called the "Tong-Guang style".

In direct opposition to these were the reformers of the 1898 period, who carried forward the tradition of Gong Zizhen and Wei Yuan and advocated not only political reform but literary reform also. Huang Zunxian (1848-1905) of Meixian in Guangdong province, attempted his so-called "poetic reform" under the motto: "My hand writes as my mouth speaks." In the preface to his 1891 *Poetic Works of the Renjing House,* he declared: "Outside of poetry there are always the events and inside poetry there are always the people. The world of today is different from that of old, so why should the people of today be the same as those of the old?" These words reflected the fact that the reformers of this period were turning away from the old tradition to face reality, seeking the new and seeking change. And in the realm of literature, they opposed the empty feudal preference for the doctrine of "back to the ancients".

Huang himself participated in the Reform Movement. A number of other noted reformers wrote poetry—Liang Qichao also wrote novels—as a means of expressing their hopes for reform. Tan Citong in 1896 wrote a poem entitled "With Emotions" to the effect that: There is nothing in this world to relieve my spring sorrows; I have but to turn toward the Heavens and weep. The tears of the four hundred million people fall together; Where in the vast horizon is the China of our ideals? Four hundred million people referred to the population of China at that time. The poem soberly expressed the patriotic cry over injustice suffered by China's progressive intellectuals of that time. But the inherent weakness of the reformers was clearly visible in the life of the famous poet Chen Sanli (1852-1937), from Yining of Jiangxi, who was the son of the Hunan governor Chen Baozhen. He participated in the Reform Movement in Hunan. Yet after it failed, he became dispirited and in his later years even thought of himself as one of those left from the former overthrown dynasty. He wrote in one of his poems: "Leaning on the railing as I watch the coming storms, I put my hands in my sleeves, a bystander, merely observing China's fortune." This reflected the character of those intellectuals from the ranks of China's literati, so feeble as to be unable to withstand the slightest blow. Even Liang Qichao expressed a sense of pity and regret over Chen with a critical attitude by asking: "How can it be that in front of the coming storms you stand with your hands in your sleeves, a bystander, merely observe

China's fortune and do nothing more?"[3]

In the year 1909, on the eve of the coming Revolution, some poets with democratic revolutionary tendencies formed the Southern Society. They made poetry the conscious weapon of their struggle. But their ideological content was exceedingly narrow, and their artistic style was still far from being liberated. Consequently, the end for most of them was what Lu Xun pointed out: "The members of the Southern Society were mostly very revolutionary at their very first, but they embraced a fancy that once the Manchu regime was expelled, all would return to the glory and splendour of the Han institutions.... The case turned out to be entirely otherwise after the Manchu emperor was dethroned and the republic established; hence they fell into disappointment, and part of them even became opponents to the new movement."[4] This judgment passed on the Southern Society in a considerable degree also held valid for the weaknesses generally existing among a large sector of the progressive intellectuals of that time.

Liang Qichao at that time was using something approaching a vernacular literature to spread Western Learning ideas, which he interspersed liberally with new terms and concepts. With such expressions as "my brush tip abounds with feeling" and "once in writing my brush cannot stop itself," his so-called "renovated people's style" became a very influential new writing style for a time. This new style of writing suited well his propaganda on new thoughts and ideas, for the antiquated archaic Tongcheng style could not appropriately express new ideas in a new era. This new style of writing, from Gong Zizhen to Liang Qichao, in its comprehensiveness embracing topics from antiquity all the way to current affairs, was attacked by Wu Rulun (a close follower of Zeng Guofan and a native of Tongcheng himself) as "writings of political strategy". Beneath the polemics over the literary style, there was a real controversy between Chinese Learning and Western, the Old and the New, the feudalistic and the bourgeois.

Using this new literary form, Liang introduced a great many Western ideas to China, and moreover, critically summed up some aspects of China's traditional history and culture. His writings were widely circulated and made a great impact on the public. Guo Moruo assessed Liang Qichao in this way: *"The Forum of Public Opinion* [ran by Liang] was easy to read, and though quite shallow in content, it exhibited a new spirit and a new manner of expression. By that point, Liang had already joined the royalist [Emperor Protection] party. Though we despised him in our hearts, we still enjoyed his writings." And again: "[His works] written in an elegant and charming style, telling how patriots were in exile and heroes engaged in building up their nation, were really fascinating. They led me, besides admiring Napoleon and Bismarck, to admire also Cavour, Mazzini and Garibaldi [the heroes in Liang's writings]." And further Guo commented: "In all fairness, Liang's position in his time ought after all to be regarded as a representative of the revolutionaries. He lived at a time when feudalism was giving way to capitalism. Carrying out the historical mission of his time, he advertised freedom of thought, fighting against the split forces of feudalism. Facing his dashing speeches, almost all the old ideas and the old ways and manners were suddenly stripped of their splendour, like withered leaves in the midst of a hurricane. There was hardly any one of the younger generation twenty years ago [i.e., the first decade of the 20th century], in other words, of the bourgeois youngsters of that time, who had not been baptized by Liang's ideas and writings, whether they were with or against him. He was the most authoritative spokesman in the time of the bourgeois revolution, and his feat was indeed by no means inferior to Zhang Taiyan or any other. The difference between Zhang and Liang was only that Zhang advocated the racial revolution in a narrow sense, which Liang deemed as an act of unnecessary destruction. Both of them longed for capitalism and were admirers of the capitalist institutions."[5] This judgment comes so penetratingly to the point as to exclude the need for any more amplification. In the post-1898 period, Liang should not be valued on the same scale with Kang Youwei. A large part of Liang's intellectual activities after 1898, including his pounding on the old feudalistic culture, his propagation of so much Western learning and ideas, and his providing of so many new ideological sources (among which a considerable amount was absorbed by the democratic revolutionaries), should be given due credit.

Novels, particularly social novels, are often the most exact historical records of social life, even more exact than history books. By this time, the representatives of the New Learning School had come to realize the social function and the social responsibility of literature. Liang Qichao stated that "the novel is the soul of a people", and wrote an article entitled "On the Relation of Novels to the Community" in which he proclaimed: "In order to renovate the people of a nation, always renovate their novels first ... for novels hold an unthinkable sway over humanity.... Therefore the desire today towards a democratic rule must begin with a revolution of novels, and the desire for a renovated people must begin with renovated novels."[6] These views showed what importance the New Learning School placed on literature as a weapon. Its members made a number of attempts in this direction but with limited results.

Raising the position of the novel meant at the same time raising the position of the vernacular literature, because modern novels constantly widened the use of the spoken language as a means of expression. Thus, along with the popularization of the novel came the popularization of vernacular literature. This was an important new facet of the cultural trend of the time. Qiu Tingliang, in his essay "On Vernacular as the Root of Reform", went so far as to say: "As a tool for making the people of the empire stupid, nothing matches classical [literary] writing; as a tool for making the same people wise, nothing surpasses the vernacular.... With the rise of classical writing, practical studies declined; but without practical studies, there could be no people."[7] To treat the vernacular as important enough to arouse the culture of the entire nation indicated the strength of the cultural awakening of the period.

Owing to the corruption of the Manchu regime, the darker aspects of the society grew ever more severe with each passing day. A great number of satiric and exposé-type social novels thereupon sprang into being. Their shortcoming was in their failure to display much ideological and artistic depth. They were simply like reports of social news that disclosed from an onlooker's viewpoint the ugly side of contemporary society, and that was it. They were what Lu Xun referred to as "novels of denunciation". In his description Lu Xun remarked: "After 1900, there was a rich crop of novels of exposure", the reason was that "Two years after the failure of the 1898 Reform came the Yi He Tuan Movement, a result of the people's complete loss of faith in the government. The trend in fiction was to expose social abuses and lash out at contemporary politics, sometimes at social conventions as well. Though this attack on abuses has something in common with novels of satire, the criticism was made openly without innuendo, sometimes even exaggerated to suit the popular mood, and the spirit of these works is intolerant."[8] Some of the better known novels of this type are *Exposure of the Official World* by Li Baojia (penname Nanting Tingzhang, or the Chief of the Southern District) and *Strange Events of the Past Twenty Years* by Wu Woyao (under the penname of A Foshan Man). Another contemporary writer had written the preface to the *Exposure of the Official World,* saying: "Unafraid of the officials, unafraid of the executioner's block, his pen lashes out and his words punish, calling out in a loud voice to extend justice to the world; making the officials not dare to go against public opinion. We can still say that the power of the *Spring and Autumn Annals* continues to exist today. Now who would say that the poor cannot save the nation!" This expressed, to some extent, a positive critical attitude about society. At the same time similar works like *The Travels of Laocan* by Liu E and *Flower in an Ocean of Sin* by Zeng Pu and others depicted social lives, all permeated with the same denunciatory implications.

Up to the Revolution of 1911, Wang Guowei continued to engage in literary and artistic theories from within the camp of Western Learning. Just as his historical research does, his position in these other fields warrants serious attention. Among his important works were *Critique of "A Dream of Red Mansions", Renjian Notes on Poesy* and *An Examination of the Song and Yuan Dramas.* He commented on and amplified the aesthetic thoughts of German philosophers Kant, Schopenhauer and Nietzsche, and elaborated some rather representative modern literary theories of his own. His *Critique of "A Dream of Red Mansions",* based on the pessimism of Schopenhauer, was the only critical study of this work during this period which was wholly a theoretical exposition, i.e., neither textual research nor tracing its hidden meanings; and because of this it can be regarded as an attempt to break away from old-style studies of the work. Wang criticized earlier textual researchers and those who attempted to find hidden meanings in their studies for having robbed the artistic life from the work through their textual approach. In fact, the two were entirely different things. "But what our people debated about", he remarked, "was not this [its artistic value] but that [examination of historical details with no relation to art]"; and even "those who are reading the novel, are reading it in the light of finding out the hidden historical details.... This is really something incomprehensible".[9] It should be admitted that his view stood high above the prevailing vulgar level of study, which focused its interests solely on historical background while leaving aside the art itself. His effort, consciously or unconsciously, lay in pounding feudalistic culture with the idealistic ideas derived from Western philosophy.

It should also be pointed out that Wang's thought embraced not just the idealism of Kant and Schopenhauer but also elements of his own clear-headed, sober realism. So with his Renjian Notes on Poesy —a very short gem-like work full of insight—he reached new heights among the literary and artistic theories of his time.

In terms of the history of modern literary and artistic theory, what is worth stressing is that Wang Guowei was the first to set forth a relatively systematic theory of aesthetics. This theory had three aspects to it. First, the nature and theory of Wang's aesthetics were derived primarily from Kant, that is, human reason consisted of three integral parts: knowledge, emotion and volition. Hence what is aesthetic beauty is that which transcends science and transcends gain and loss. "The nature of beauty," so he asserted, "is, in a word, that it can be cherished and enjoyed but not used." Second, his ideas on the theory of the function of art came chiefly from Schopenhauer, that is, that art serves to free life from human desires and sufferings, or from what he called "the trinity of desire, life and suffering". Third, Wang's own standard of art criticism put forward the "naturalness" criterion. For example, traditional Chinese drama had always been disdained as something not fit to be enjoyed in the biased traditional view of arts. But Wang researched into Chinese drama, praised it, and explained that its high artistic achievement resulted from its being nothing more than "entirely natural".[10]

Wang Guowei possessed a strong nihilist tendency toward life. However, this must be understood in the context of the concrete historical setting of his time, with its demand for enlightenment and reform. One of the central tasks on the modern ideological front was to oppose feudal cultural despotism. Wang's thought, which at its bottom belonged to the Western Learning School, forsook and resisted China's feudal culture of the time. But because of the bonds of his pessimist world outlook, his thinking failed to progress and ultimately reached an impasse. Yet the fresh rational elements which now and then spontaneously appeared in his thinking are nonetheless worthy of praise.

Another figure, representative of the Western Learning literary camp, is Lin Shu (1852-1924) of Fuzhou in Fujian Province. The large amount of Western literature introduced by him at the end of the Qing period was unequalled in that time. Whether in the richness of their intellectual content, or in opening up men's visions and minds or in smashing the chains of the narrow and degenerated feudal cultural despotism, they all abounded in historical significance. Yet Lin Shu himself came from a feudal literati background and was a member of the Tongcheng School, and after the 1911 Revolution even became a Qing adherent. At the time of the May Fourth Movement, when he opposed the vernacular movement, he became a target of public criticism. But we have to honour the true face of history and not to allow Lin's later actions to obscure his earlier contributions or his political attitudes to wipe out his artistic achievements. Strange to say, Lin "never knew any foreign language, yet over the course of nineteen years he had translated 123 works of Western novels in twelve million words".[11] Among these were some of the most popular books of the time: *La Dame aux Camelias* by Alexandre Dumas fils (from which came the popular expression of the day: "The book of the young lady Camelia moved the Chinese youngsters to burst into tears"); Charles Dickens' *David Copperfield* and *The Old Curiosity Shop,* all consciously propounding social change. In the preface to his translation of *Oliver Twist,* he claimed: "A hundred years ago, the political corruption in Britain was not much different from present-day China.... Britain was able to become powerful because she was able to reform and to follow the better way. It would not be hard for China to get herself reformed. Would that there but be a Dickens in China who should reveal to the public the social evils in his novels." And again in the preface to his translation of *David Copperfield,* he said: "This work of Dickens described various aspects of the lower classes. Would that the Chinese public after reading it be enough cultivated and the Chinese society be as well reformed.... If it be so, then it would be not in vain for me to translate the novel." In particular, his translation of Mrs. Stowe's

Uncle Tom's Cabin, which keenly described the miserable life of the American Black, became a deeply and bitterly felt appeal to a China on the brink of national subjugation and racial extinction. While working on the translation of it, he "wept while translating and translated while weeping, not only lamenting over the suffering of the Blacks but also over the 400 million Chinese people following the steps of the Blacks".[12]

The ideological influence of Lin's literary translations on the public was immeasurable. The idea that literature should both serve and reform society was clearly expressed in a number of his translations. The best of Lin's translations can be favourably compared with some of the most outstanding political and literary works of the time with respect to their social impacts. They were by all means an integral part of modern intellectual history. Hence Guo Moruo recalled: "The novels translated by Lin Qinnan [Lin Shu] were extremely popular at that time and were among my most favourits books.... Some years ago when we were fighting for the dominance of the vernacular literature, Lin was one of the chief opponents in confrontation with us. At that time, people tended to deny his worth entirely, but his literary contributions were just like Liang Qichao's cultural criticism. Both men were representative figures of the capitalist system's revolutionary period, and, moreover, are men of considerable attainment."[13] Guo regarded Liang's achievements as no less than those of Zhang Taiyan, and went on to mention Lin and Liang in the same breath. This is a just historical appraisal. To highlight Zhang Taiyan, deprecate Liang Qichao and totally ignore Lin Shu—such an attitude is unfair in the face of the truth of China's modern intellectual and cultural history.

By the end of this period, the main current of advanced literary thought came to be represented by Lu Xun. His essay "On the Demoniac Poets" is the earliest and relatively most complete introduction to China of the modern Western Romantic School. "I borrowed this term," said Lu Xun, "which meant Devil in China and Satan in the West, from India. Originally, this term was applied to all those who intended to rebel, aiming at some action not pleasing the world." Here his rebellious spirit against feudalism stood out in a clear-cut way. This essay prominently displayed the militancy of the revolutionary democratic elements of the time: learning the truth according to the West and demanding the liberation of the individual and individuality from under the feudal bondage. This ideological emancipation of his was not that kind of lonely, empty, individual emancipation which breaks away from the mainstream of the masses, but rather an integral part of the democratic revolutionary upsurge of the broad masses, representing their voice. The essay mentioned Byron many times, and actually used the spirit of Byron to criticize the decrepit old feudal tradition. It also introduced Shelley and publicized the unconquerable spirit of resistance in his "Prometheus Unbound". Lu Xun praised his indomitable spirit of rebellion and said that Shelley "made Prometheus the spirit of mankind, who because of his love of justice and freedom, did not relieve his hardships, but forcibly resisted the suppression of Jupiter, stole fire and gave it to man; he was therefore imprisoned on a mountain top where a fierce eagle came daily to eat his flesh; but he never surrendered". He claimed further: "The old ways and manners being broken up, what remained would be only the new spirit of reform. It was on this that the new momentum of the 19th century rested." Here the author borrowed the terminology from Western literature in expressing his own heart-felt need to try to pour the reform spirit of romanticism into China and to rejuvenate her life. The entire work overflowed with patriotism and national democratic enthusiasm. It wound up calling for the appearance of new spiritual warriors: "Searching throughout China today, where is such a spiritual warrior?"[14]

Later Lu Xun cited many times the ideological teachings of modern Western individualists such as Ibsen and Nietzsche. But their language and ideas were transformed in the hands of Lu Xun into ideological weapons opposing the bonds of feudalism and calling for the people's awakening. The same language, under different historical conditions, can bear different historical implications.

Seldom had the contemporaries of Lu Xun ever made demands as intense as his for ideological emancipation and individual libera-tion. It was only for this purpose that he energetically introduced and highly praised such poets and thinkers as Byron, Ibsen and Nietzsche. The language he employed could only be understood in the context of the concrete historical setting of his time in its opposition to the customs and traditions of the old. In literary thought, Lu Xun represented a peak in the old democratic revolutionary period. His vision was never limited to narrow individualistic confines. His thought always responded to the flavour and pulse of the time and people. And because of this, we do not find in him the usual despondent and sad mentality of so many of the intellectuals of this period. He had instead a unique fervour and zeal that pressed forward indomitably in search of light. This was Lu Xun's most commendable trait.

"On the Demoniac Poets" urgently called out: "If you encounter a slave, you should be sad and incensed; sad so as to mourn his misfortune, incensed so as to rage at his failure to struggle." In nearly all of his works, this yearning for the salvation of the nation and its people and the democratic revolutionary struggle are intimately intertwined. Although Lu Xun's thought in this period was still enveloped in a layer of idealism and unable to free itself from evolutionary theory, it was nevertheless poles apart in its essence from the gradualism of the reformists and the superman philosophy of Nietzsche. It was the ideological preparation and yeast for the new age. Despite the fact that Lu Xun's thought of this period still retained vestiges of the old Western Learning, the seed of a new ideology that was to break through the confines of the old Western Learning had begun to gain the upper hand in his thinking. And later, having embraced the brand-new world view to arm his own thinking, he became one of the most prominent figures of China's cultural history.

*   *   *

In the preceding chapters we have made a brief survey on some of the main trends of the ideology from the 19th to the early 20th century. The New Culture Movement prepared the way for the May Fourth Movement. During the May Fourth period, China as well as the world was facing a new historical situation.

During World War I, the Western powers were incapable of interfering in the affairs of the East. It was under this circumstance that capitalism developed considerably in China, and with it appeared the Chinese proletariat. The Socialist October Revolution in Russia in 1917 sent the message of Marxism to China.

By the end of 1918, World War I came to an end, and in the next year the Peace Conference was convened in Paris. From its very start, the Conference was controlled by a few Western powers and turned to be an imperialist conference for sharing the spoils. China had participated in the war and was, as a matter of course, one of the victorious nations; but the Peace Conference flagrantly delivered the former German privileges in China to Japan. On hearing the news, the whole country was thrown into bitter frustration and anger. On May Fourth, 1919, students in Beijing rose in a patriotic demonstration to which people all over the country, especially the young intellectuals, responded vehemently. Thus began the May Fourth Movement. It was then that a group among China's advanced intellectual ranks began to employ Marxism as a means for observing the fate of the nation. And from that point onward, the Chinese revolution began to be brought into the orbit of Marxist ideological leadership. It was thus that the face of the Chinese revolution began to take on a new look, moving away from the channel of the old democracy into that of the new democracy. And this new historical stage awaits a new book on contemporary intellectual history to describe it.

THE IDEA OF NATURAL RIGHTS IN CHINA: A HISTORICAL PERSPECTIVE

by He Zhaowu
Institute of History
Chinese Academy of Social Sciences

1

The idea of natural rights in its modern sense was established in the West from the seventeenth and eighteenth centuries and in China as late as the turn of the nineteenth and twentieth centuries. But some of its earliest origins in China might be traced to the pre-Qin philosophers, just as in the West they might be traced back to the ancient Greek philosophers. The ideal of a beneficial government taught in the original teachings of Confucius was based on humanity; Confucius stressed the value of human beings. Mencius' assertion, "The people are supreme," "the sovereigns are insignificant," afforded a most important source for the tradition of democratic thought in China. The Taoists, focusing on the nature of human beings and their values, propounded rule by inactivity. In a certain sense all of this might be regarded as the earliest germination of the idea of natural rights. This humanistic tradition has permeated the whole course of Chinese history, so much so that even some among the sovereign emperors came to realize the importance of taking the lives of the people as the essential factor in their rule. For example, the famous Emperor Taizong of the Tang Dynasty made many remarks along this line which are recorded in historical documents. In other words, their views implied a basic presupposition that men were born with a proper right to their life and living, though this did not yet assume a definite form of argumentation.

The Renaissance of the sixteenth century marked a turning point in the civilization of the West. It might be noted that in the seventeenth century, Chinese history witnessed a similar process. In the pivotal moment of transition from Ming to Qing there emerged a new intellectual awakening of humanity and humanism, and in the sphere of political thought it manifested itself in the formation of democratic ideas with a distinctly modern hue. Progressive ideologues of this period like Huang Zongxi and Tang Zhen put forward political theories in which the state was considered no more than a mutual relationship between man and man, not a divine ordinance of Heaven. This might be regarded as the earliest Chinese version of natural rights in the modern sense of the term, a development predating Locke and Rousseau.

What Huang affirmed was not the sanctity of the rule of the sovereign but the sanctity of human self-interest—a view bold enough to afford in philosophical theory an antithesis to the mediaeval scholastic Neo-Confucian teaching and in political doctrine an antithesis to mediaeval theocracy and royal sovereignty. It reflected the demands of the early Chinese bourgeoisie. Inheriting and developing Mencius' idea that the people should be held supreme, Huang elaborated his view: "The people are the master, while the sovereign is their employee." He proceeded to affirm: "What results in great harm to the people is none other than the sovereign." He taught that the relation between the sovereign and his subjects, or between government and the governed, should be one of mutual agreement and cooperation. He asserted that, "Governing the world is like the hauling of great logs. The sovereign and his subjects are log-haulers working together." This viewpoint suggested that China was undergoing a great progressive social movement, or, in the words of H. Maine, "a movement from status to contract".

Tang Zhen, not so well known as Huang, was roughly contemporaneous with Huang, but a bit later. Tang spent his whole life under the pressure of the Manchu rule. In his works he made the bitter accusation: "All sovereigns are robbers." That is to say, the coercion exercised by the ruling sovereign is but robbery of the right which once belonged naturally to the people. Differing from Huang, Tang upheld human "feeling" and employed his theory of human feelings in opposition to the Neo-Confucian notion of the necessity of overcoming human desires. He concluded that, "Everyone will get his due when equality prevails." It might be said that, in their explanations of the origin of the state, the seventeenth-century enlightenment philosophers Huang and Tang embraced a view that all political rule ought to presume the consent of the governed.

As a form of orthodox feudal scholasticism, late mediaeval Neo-Confucianism always played the role of an ideological hindrance to individual demands and desires. Therefore, democratic ideologies demanding individual human rights generally assumed a fighting stance against Neo-Confucianism. And what constituted the basis of the struggle between Neo-Confucianism and anti-Neo-Confucianism at that time was the inexorable historic movement from status to contract. This is a fact which appears quite akin to the main current of thought in the West since the Renaissance with its urgent demand to break free of the spiritual bondage of mediaeval clericalism and asceticism. Thus the outstanding philosopher of the Qing period, Tai Zhen, taking human desires as nature or human nature, evolved his famous proposition: "*Li* (principle) exists in human desires." This represented the legitimacy of the natural right to life and living, an important contribution to the pre-modern idea of natural rights. Given a traditional background in which the basic human right of life and living had no guarantee whatever, it is easy to comprehend why the idea of natural rights in China always gave priority to the right of life and living. If we recall that it was only a few years ago that the so-called Gang of Four, in order to push their feudal-fascist obscurantism, was still trying their utmost to propagate the replacement of "the self" by "the public", that is, to suppress the right of life and the desires of the individual in the name of "the public", we may well see that the past history of the struggle between heavenly principle and the human desires has never died out. It still lives on in the present.

In the history of the development of the idea of natural rights, one may come to be aware that there were between China and the West some parallel and synchronic developments. Yet there were also some significant differences between them which should not be neglected. First, ideological features in China were stipulated by the characteristics of Chinese society. China was a patriarchal society; Chinese social relationships were, since antiquity, bound up with blood lineage more than those of the West. This historical characteristic of China, in my opinion, comes under what Marx termed the Asian mode of production, which differed from the classical mode in the West. Hence, the process of theoretization in the West often proceeds from the individual, taken as the substance or the Leibnizian monad, in contrast and contradistinction to the community, the society, and God. In China, by contrast, the individual generally has no value or independent existence of his own; he is regarded primarily as a member of the blood-bound community, his personality being subordinated to, or even dissolved into, a greater communal life. People in the West believe in religion, seeking for individual immortality, whereas in China there has never been a strong rule of religion because people believe in the greater life of the community, individual immortality flowing and merging into the life of the community. Since the individual is not the final substance or monad, he ceases to be an end in himself. He has no ultimate being of his own and serves only as an instrument of the community to which he belongs. For example, he is first of all an instrument in fulfilling not his own personal aims but those of his family or his clan, and his life and its value exist only insofar as he serves as such an instrument. This is prescribed by moral obligations. Indeed, Huang Zongxi confirmed self-interest and attacked monarchical autocracy, but his starting point was "the benefit of the people", not any right indispensable and inalienable to the individual in the sense professed by the Bill of Rights. Consequently, when the interests of one's community require it, he should engage in military exploits in the name of filial piety. He should go to battle valiantly because "it is not in conformity with filial piety when one behaves without valour on the battlefield".

Such reasoning would sound strange from the point of view of any ideology with the individual life and personality as its end. So it is with all intellectual and artistic activities, which are considered as having no value of their own. Art for art's sake or truth for truth's sake never held any place of importance in the history of China. When Leo Tolstoy in his book *On Art* proclaimed that a work of art should be judged by the criteria of its ethical values and functions, this sounded strange to many Western readers, but what he professed was only a plain way of reasoning generally taken for granted in the East. The doctrine of the "docile instrument"—a doctrine severely criticized not very long ago in the Cultural Revolution—which taught that an individual should strive absolutely and unconditionally to become an instrument of the community, was in its essence an offspring of an age-old ideological tradition in China. While the starting point in the West was the opposition between the individual and the community, the Chinese took the individual as only a constituent part of a super-individual community for the sake of which all individual activities were motivated. Hence in the intellectual tradition of China there could hardly be any ideology based merely on the monadic individual. All of his ideas about human rights were heavily enshrouded in a feudalistic ethical dress. There was no ideology defending the right of the individual in a clear-cut fashion in the manner seen in the West. Chinese arguments on natural rights, as a rule, assumed the form of scholastic exegeses which attempted to explain the ancient sages and their classics. This was true down to the end of the nineteenth century when Kang Youwei elaborated his reforms through resort to the esoteric meaning of the Confucian classics. The apology for Kang's plan of reform had to make its last resort to the ancients—here lies the characteristic Chinese feature so much at variance with the modern West. Before the end of the nineteenth century no important Chinese ideology was ever able to separate itself from the attachment to antiquity.

Consequently, much of the waywardness and tragedy in the modern history of China may perhaps be explained by this fact: in the endeavour of Chinese society to modernize, the awakening of the individual and the self-consciousness of individual rights were destined to come into an irreconcilable clash and antagonism with the super-individual community. An ideology based on the individual was incompatible with that based on the super-individual community. While entering into the modern epoch, China to a great degree accepted Western arguments and a Western sense of value, including liberalism and Marxism, among other views, but they were often accepted only insofar as they were represented literally or verbally. Behind the words and phrases, what mattered was still the hidden traditional spirit which lay deep-rooted in the cultural history of the nation. Hence the words they employed were modern or Western, but their essence and practice were traditionally Chinese. If one is to understand the secret of modern Chinese ideology, the key is perhaps to be found in this.

Secondly, in the history of China down to the late nineteenth century, there never emerged a scientific revolution of the kind that took place in modern Western history. In each age, scientific ideas have always dominated or influenced world views and modes of thinking, and this was especially true in the case of modern Western intellectual history. This aspect of the history of China was, however, unduly neglected by many scholars. Modern science, or specifically the Newtonian system, was formally introduced to the Chinese public by Li Shanlan in the 1870s, though Xu Guangqi as early as the beginning of the seventeenth century was already in eager search of an approach to science along the road of probing the mathematical principles of natural philosophy. Modern science in the West gave birth to the idea of iron laws in nature. Human nature, as a matter of course, is a part of nature; hence it is, as a matter of course, natural; concomitantly, the right to human nature and to all that belongs to human nature is also natural—this reasoning is but natural, logically as well as politically. But in China there had never been a strong idea of natural law derived from natural science (as Descartes had put it, even God had to observe natural law); correspondingly there had never been the idea of natural rights in close connection with it. Down to the present day, the term "natural" in "natural rights" is dichotomous in Chinese terminology, as seen in the terms themselves). Hence from the immutable natural law to the indubitable natural rights there could be found no logical inference as natural as that in the West. This is no place for a detailed discussion of the ideological consequences of the absence of modern science in China; what I want to call to the reader's attention is that, both in her view of society and in her view of nature, China's background was quite different from that of the West. There was in her history, too, her own idea and theory of natural rights; but the argument that these rights were natural (or endowed by heaven) was merely based on the requirement of humanity or human feelings of compassion rather than on a close connection with the idea of natural law in its modern scientific sense.

2

As China was entering her modern stage, not only was her traditional social structure disintegrating, she was also at the same time accepting modern science. It was also then that the doctrine of natural rights and the contract theory of the state were formally introduced into China. Beyond any doubt, these involved an unprecedented challenge to the age-old monarchical autocracy and its underlying principles. In the great polemics between the Western Learning School and the Chinese Learning School, or between the New Learning School and the Old Learning School, the theory of evolution and the theory of natural rights represented the most important ideological contents of the Western (or New) Learning School. Nevertheless, this Western Learning School was by no means committed to wholesale Westernization; its adherents still succeeded to traditional Chinese culture. It might well be said that when modern Chinese ideology was transferring to Western channels, the idea of natural right in China drew its origin simultaneously from two sources: one was the humanistic ideas which had evolved from Mencius to Huang Zongxi and Tai Zhen; the other was the theory of human rights exemplified in the American and French Revolutions. Yet the ideology of the Western Learning camp was further stamped with the specific brand of its own age, differentiating itself from both the ancient and the Western views. The characteristic feature of the age being that China was suffering from chronic foreign aggression and confronting the crisis of being partitioned or annexed by foreign powers, the issue of national survival now became the impending problem of the age. Hence it was inevitable that all her ideas and ideologies had to meet this urgent condition of the time; all had to be subordinated and correlated to this requirement.

In the year 1896 (that is, two years after the Sino-Japanese War and two years before the Reform Movement) Yan Fu published his *Theory of Evolution*, being a translation of the first part of T. H. Huxley's *Evolution and Ethics*. Meanwhile, Liang Qichao was lecturing in the College of Current Affairs in Hunan, energetically propagating the "doctrine of human rights and equality". An ideological torrent calling for the arrival of a new age was thus upsurging. By that time, Liang had not yet been able to get in touch formally or systematically with the theories of the modern West—a fact which might readily be apparent from his compilation of *The Catalogue of Western Learning* or his much later work, *Intellectual Trends of the Qing Period*. The main source of his ideas came from Huang Zongxi's political theory, Kang Youwei's doctrine of social evolution based on the Kongyang School's teaching of the three successive historical epochs, and Yan Fu's introduction to the theory of evolution. But with them he was able to meld his own knowledge of the world and his own view of the age, preaching his "doctrine of human rights and equality" against the age-old doctrine of the divine right of emperors. His activities aroused the fanatic opposition of the Old Learning camp whose polemical works were compiled into the *Anthology in Support of Orthodoxy*, from which one may get a glimpse of how violently the battle between the upholders of royal rights and hierarchy and those of human rights and equality was being waged. Attacking the doctrine of human rights and equality, the Old Learning camp resorted to the importance of honouring the emperor and honouring Confucius and laid emphasis on the sanctity of the Orthodoxy and its ethical codes of hierarchy (the three guides and the five virtues, etc.). They were supported by the imperial court and by various levels of authorities. Zhang Zhidong, the leading magistrate of the Yangwu faction, in his widely circulated work, *An Exhortation on Learning*, remarked, "As soon as the doctrine of human rights prevails, the discipline of the ethical codes will certainly fall to the ground, and great social tumult will ensue all over the country." There is real irony to be found in the fact that this viewpoint has in its various forms persisted ever since. It shows how deeply rooted are the social forces that it represents.

At that time, Yan Fu also introduced certain theories of human rights from the West. In his essay "On the Urgency of Changing the World," Yan declared, "It is really an endowment of nature that all men are born free, and hence everyone ought to be free." "To encroach on the liberty of other persons means to run against heavenly [natural] principle." Here the natural right of liberty was raised by Yan above the ethical codes of hierarchy. Yan, among others, advanced Rousseau's doctrine of "upholding the people and degrading the sovereign". These had become the main ideological resources for the Western Learning School as well as for the democratic revolutionaries later on.

As is well known, the focus of the polemics between the Western Learning School and the Chinese Learning School lay in the debate over what should be regarded as the substance and what should be regarded as its function. The watchword of the conservatives was: "Let Chinese Learning be the substance and Western Learning be the function." Yan Fu came forward in opposition to this, criticizing it as "neither an ox nor a horse". He held that substance is insepa-rable from its functions, and in his *Inquiry on the Causes of Self-Strengthening*, he put forward his watchword: "Let liberty be the essence and democracy the function." But his use of the term "people", applied only to a small group of enlightened intellectuals, while the peasants who constituted the dominant majority of the population remained outside of his field of vision. Here lay the great fallacy of the Western Learning School both in its views and its practices.

During the Reform Movement of 1898 Kang and Liang were always named together, while after its failure their approaches were differentiated from each other step by step. Kang took the royalist position and achieved nothing important in either the political or the ideological sphere. At the same time Liang worked out a series of articles and essays propagating Western Learning and ideas, the influence of which was almost unprecedented in the intellectual history of modern China. In the period of his exile in Japan, Liang was able to read many modern Western theories and introduced Hobbes, Rousseau, Bentham, and many others to the Chinese public. He earnestly professed that men "are born with equal rights, and hence they are born for enjoying liberty; these are endowed by nature with no distinction of rank, high or low". Such a conception of natural rights greatly broadened the vision of Chinese intellec-tuals, leading them away from the channel of traditional ethical principles and toward modern Western ideology. Many began to realize that a man should dedicate himself not to the cause of Confucian ethical preachings but to the cause of liberty. It was through the writings of Liang and Yan that a large number of democratic revolutionaries came to be enlightened in their early years.

The ideology based on natural rights was later expounded more fully by the democratic revolutionaries and through them was im-planted in the hearts of the people as a generally acknowledged maxim. People like Cai Yuanpei, the great modern liberal, and Chen Duxiu, the founder of Marxism in China, all expounded the idea of human rights epitomized in the watchwords: liberty, equality, frater-nity. For a whole generation these watchwords had replaced the traditional ethical codes and teachings as a national creed.

I remember personally the days when I was a schoolboy, before the reign of the Kuomintang. One could see almost everywhere the words "liberty, equality, fraternity"—in books, in newspapers, in pamphlets, in songs, and on wall posters. A couplet which hung in my school read: "Humaneness, righteousness, decorum, wisdom, and honesty" and "Democracy", representing the idea of the concurrence of the Chinese tradition with Western ideas.

The formative contribution of Liang Qichao in propagating "the doctrine of human rights and equality" deserves more attention. Not long ago, under the control of the so-called Gang of Four, there blew in China a wind of exalting the merit of Zhang Taiyan, the exponent of Legalism, as the foremost ideologue in modern history. But I prefer to agree with Guo Moruo's evaluation of Liang, which seems to me to come nearer to the truth in history. In his memoir, *My Youth*, Guo remarked, "To be fair, Liang in his time was no less a representative of the revolutionaries." In pointing out that few among the intellectuals of that time were not under the strong influence of Liang (and Guo himself was one among them), he went on to say, "Liang was a forceful spokesman in the age of bourgeois revolution. His contribution was by no means inferior to that of Zhang Taiyan or any other." This, I think, is a fair evaluation.

If it may be said that the pre-modern idea of natural rights expressed itself in ways traditionally Chinese, then it may also be said that in modern times it tended more and more to Western ways of expression. The democratic revolutionaries took directly from the West as their cardinal (or even their sole) ideological weapon the theory of natural rights. Zou Rong, one of their outstanding representatives, called on the Chinese people to learn from Montesquieu, Rousseau, Mill, and the Declaration of Independence in carrying out a revolution against monarchical autocracy in order that "everyone may be able to enjoy his natural rights". Another outstanding representative, Chen Tianhua, proclaimed that "China ought to institute a democracy", arguing that the twentieth century was a "civilized age" in which "to restore our natural liberty and equality". And this spirit of the age was manifestly embodied in the Provisional Constitution following the Revolution of 1911, the guiding principle of which was modelled on that of the American and French Revolutions. Its main point was to affirm the right of liberty and to provide for a form of state and of government which would ensure that right. In a certain sense it was a condensation of the ideals and aspirations of the advanced intellectuals of modern times. However, ideas transplanted from abroad could neither endure nor thrive if indigenous conditions were not such as to allow for their vigorous growth. The democratic revolutionaries failed to take due notice and measure of the old social forces in their native land. And Yuan Shikai with but a slight stroke assassinated Song Jiaoren, the most vehement propagandist for parliamentary democracy, throwing the Provisional Constitution into the garbage heap like so much waste paper. As a Chinese proverb has it, no law in the world can be brought into effect by itself. The realization of any theory and ideal necessarily requires the material conditions of the time and the place.

Since that time more than one constitution has been drafted and promulgated in China. Although each of them contains a magnificent list of the rights and freedoms of this or that, none of it has ever finally been fulfilled. It is indeed a tragedy of history to see that the codification of natural rights and the popularization of democratic ideas have been so short-lived, enduring no more than two decades in the early twentieth century. It is well known that the principle of democracy, or literally human rights, constituted one of Sun Yatsen's Three Principles of the People. But it is also well known that it has never been carried out. At the same time it signalled a further penetration of the idea of human rights because Sun was able to observe the fallacies of democracy in the West and to ask for a democracy "which would be accessible to all the populace in common and not be subject to the ownership of a few persons". From the end of the nineteenth century to the beginning of the twentieth century, there had emerged three great emancipation movements, i.e., the Reform Movement 0f 1898, the Revolution of 1911, and the May Fourth Movement of 1919. As ideological movements, the achievements of the Reform Movement and the May Fourth Movement were historic and lasting. But the Revolution of 1911 as a political event succeeded in nothing except the dethroning of the royalty. The journey of China in entering the modern age was just commencing, and the journey was destined to be long.

Confucians and Neo-Confucians, assuming themselves to be the orthodox successors of the ancient sages, were mostly patrons and upholders of the rule of hierarchy based on distinctions of social status. When modern democratic rights were demanded, it was necessary to break the ideological chains forged under the pretext of Confucian ethical codes. In the intellectual sphere the anti-Neo-Confucian trend had become manifest since the period of the Ming-Qing transition. In this sense the Han Learning which prevailed since the early Qing among scholars outside of the official circles might be regarded as a sort of passive resistance against the hypocrisy of official Neo-Confucianism. This tendency becomes clearer when one considers that both the imperial court of the early Qing and the famous magistrates of the Restoration in the middle and late nineteenth century were all actively responding to the teachings of Orthodox Neo-Confucianism. The struggle between the heavenly principle and human desires had been turned into a struggle between the traditional super-individual social forces and the newly awakened consciousness of the individual, or, in the political field, between the divine right of the emperor under the traditional monarchical autocracy and the natural rights of man under the institutions of a democratic republic. This ideological polemic was fervently developing by the end of the last century with the introduction of the theory of evolution and the idea of natural rights. In studying the course of it, one cannot help experiencing the strong pulse of the age: China was transforming "from status to contract". And the natural yet necessary result of it turned out to be the outburst of the May Fourth Movement.

The slogan of the New Culture and May Fourth Movement —"down with the Confucian House"—was the culmination of the historically progressive movement from status to contract. It was almost unavoidable that this movement should be subject to some faults of childishness and simple-mindedness, especially with respect to such a complicated issue as how to deal with cultural legacies. But it is not difficult to find in examining the representative documents of this period that the main current of the movement can be summed up under the two well-known banners: democracy (Mr. D.) and science (Mr. S.). Upholding these two banners, the movement waged its historic battle against feudal autocracy and obscurantism. Ever since 1915 when Chen Duxiu declared formally "for the sake of science as well as for the sake of human rights", the implications of the idea of democracy throughout the May Fourth Movement had been almost a literal copy of the theory of natural rights in the modern West. It was a copy so over-simplified that it failed to render itself indigenous—that is, to respond to indigenous surroundings and conditions. Viewed retrospectively, even from the standpoint of today, the ideological battle waged by the May Fourth Movement against the age-old rule of feudalistic ethical teachings was in conformity with the historical trend of the age in its main directions. One may find fault with it in its failure to be more thoroughgoing —after all, the old social forces were too great. It was impossible to attain its aim by resorting merely to the ready-made ideas borrowed from abroad. This is a historical lesson worth remembering.

What deserves to be noted specifically is that, due to the continued deepening of national crisis in modern times, the cause of national survival came to assume the foremost place as the central theme of the entire nation. The May Fourth Movement burst forth under the direct stimulus of the Paris Conference of 1919 which conceded to Japan the German privileges in China. There was no movement in modern China which was not predominantly patriotic in nature. The December Ninth Movement in the mid-thirties, the most widespread student movement following the May Fourth Movement, was the prologue of the national war against Japanese aggression. It was only in terms of the larger imperative of resistance to Japan that it came to demand the abolition of one-party rule and the adoption of certain democratic measures. In modern China nearly all democratic demands for human rights had to be correlated with the patriotic demand for national salvation. (Of course, this took a new turn in the forties, a discussion of which would be beyond the scope of the present essay.)

Thus was the concrete historical background of the Chinese idea of natural rights at variance with that in the West. It was always dominated by a greater and more imperative national demand. As early as the Reform Movement of 1898, the doctrine of human rights and equality expounded by Liang and Yan was defended on the ground that it would be conducive to the final goal of "self-strengthening and national preservation". It was argued that it would be only through a process of democratization and restoring to the people their natural rights that the nation could become strong enough for her own preservation. Modern democratic revolutions in the West were directed against the *ancien regime* under which people were deprived of their rights of freedom and equality; but, above and beyond this, there was in modern China the greater and more urgent issue of national preservation and resistance to foreign aggression. The democratic rights of the people had to serve the end of national survival. Such was the historically defined condition under which the idea of natural rights strove to assert itself in China. Natural rights and national survival were not necessarily mutually exclusive, yet in the final analysis the former was doomed to be a means to the latter. What was held to be primary in the case of the West could only be secondary in the case of China. After all, the existence of the nation was valued above all else.

It is only after this context is comprehended that one is able to understand the course of development of the idea of natural rights in China in all of its complexity. In a situation of war the democratic rights of the individual were often ruthlessly curtailed. Moreover, the traditional feudal forces in China always took advantage of the wartime atmosphere intentionally to curb or to deprive the people of their rights. Human rights were often abruptly abrogated under the pretext of coping with enemies. The long course of the suffering of the Chinese people, with their human rights trampled upon from the time of the late Qing to the Gang of Four, may well show how long a journey China still faces ahead.

For the task of modernization, the present authority in China has proposed the rule of law. It goes without saying that the rule of law presupposes the respect for human rights; this may show that the significance of the idea of rights, without which modernization would default on one of its most important political tasks, is now once again assured. China, too, will learn from her historical lessons; perhaps she will no longer simply copy a ready-made ideology from abroad, be it the Western, the Soviet Russian, or any other model, as a ready-made means to build a modernized nation. She will, let us hope, learn how to absorb better the intellectual and cultural legacies of all nations, including their theories of human rights, as nourishment to enrich her own ideology. At the same time these must be adjusted and incorporated in terms of her own conditions and based on her own realities.

3

Ideology has no history in its own existence. It is always related to and, in the final analysis, determined by social reality. This being so, perhaps some preliminary conclusions may be drawn from what has been said above.

In the pre-modern period, Chinese ideology was strongly conditioned by her specific patriarchal clan system. Therefore the idea of human rights in China, though it had a long history, always assumed a more non-individual or communal form. This characteristic has left its apparent and ineradicable traces down to modern times. Its theory started not from the individual versus the community but from the individual for the sake of the community. The community was not perceived to have been established on the basis of monadic individuals, as Western ideologies were always prone to assume. Here the presupposition was that an individual was first of all not a natural man but a member of a community. Therefore it would be difficult to find in Chinese intellectual history the idea of the indispensable and inalienable rights of the individual as advocated in the West. What prevailed was rather the idea that an individual should absolutely and unconditionally submit to, or even merge himself into, a much greater entity. This tradition in Chinese history was different from the basic sense of the value of the individual in the West.

Down to modern times the imperatives of national survival became an overwhelming theme in history, and the newly imported idea of natural rights could only be made readjusted to this major premise. The demands made on the individual in the name of national survival, together with the traditional communal spirit, made the political authority a real Leviathan which threatened to devour, or had already devoured, the rights of the individual which in the West were considered indispensable, indivisible, and inalienable. And thus it was seen that, for the principle of consent of the governed, there was substituted, in practice as well as in theory, the traditional paternalistic principle of herding the people. Then it was seen that the sovereigns, despite the pretext of being all for the nation and for the people, have never cared for the wishes and wills of the governed; their capricious behaviour being categorically identified with the interests of the governed, they deemed any such concern utterly unnecessary.

If it can be said that in the pre-modern period the starting point of the idea of natural rights in China differed from that in the West, it may also be said that in modern times the goal or end of natural rights differed also, in spite of the fact that the idea was transplanted directly from the West. In light of this, it would be inappropriate to place and to measure the Chinese idea of natural rights on the same coordinate framed by Western ideas and backgrounds. Otherwise, in comprehending the role of Chinese ideas of natural rights in the historic movement from status to contract, there would be a risk of undervaluing traditional trends and overvaluing the foreign impact, or of undervaluing the forces in real life and overvaluing the role of ideas. Of course, China neither would nor could set herself alone apart from the general current of the history of mankind at large, but she will join it through a course of her own.

CHRONOLOGICAL TABLE OF CHINESE DYNASTIES

Xia   c. 2000 B.C.-c. 1520 B.C.
Shang (Yin)   c. 1520 B.C.-1030 B.C.
Zhou
   Western Zhou   1030 B.C.-722 B.C.
Spring and Autumn   722 B.C.-480 B.C.
Warring States   480 B.C.-221 B.C.
Qin   221 B.C.-207 B.C.
Han
   Western Han   202 B.C.-A.D. 9
Xin   9-23
   Eastern Han   25-220
Three Kingdoms
   Shu (Han)   221-264
   Wei   220-264
   Wu   222-280
Jin
   Western Jin   265-317
   Eastern Jin   317-420
Southern and Northern Dynasties
   Song   420-479
   Qi   479-502
   Liang   502-557
   Chen   557-587
   Northern Wei   386-535
   Western Wei   535-554
   Eastern Wei   534-543
   Northern Qi   550-577
   Northern Zhou   557-581
Sui   581-618
Tang   618-906

The Five Dynasties   907-960
Song
   Northern Song   960-1126
Kin   1115-1234
   Southern Song   1127-1279
Yuan   1260-1368
Ming   1368-1644
Qing   1644-1911
The Republic 1911-1949
The People's Republic 1949-

SELECTED BIBLIOGRAPHY

Feng Youlan (Fung Yu-lan), *History of Chinese Philosophy*
Hou Wailu, *A General History of Ideas in China*
Zhang Dainian, *Outline of Chinese Philosophy*

Book of Changes
Book of Rites
Confucius, *Analects*
Mo Zi, *The Book of Mo Zi*
Lao Zi, *The Book of Lao Zi*
Zhuang Zi, *The Book of Zhuang Zi*
Mencius, *The Book of Mencius*
Xun Zi, *The Book of Xun Zi*
Gongsun Long, *The Book of Gongsun Long Zi*
Sun Zi's Art of War
Han Fei, *The Book of Han Fei Zi*
Zi Si, *The Doctrine of the Mean*
Lü Buwei, *Lü's Spring and Autumn Annals*
Zuo Qiuming, *Zuo's Chronicles*

Sima Qian, *Records of the Historian*
Dong Zhongshu, *Exuberant Dew of Spring and Autumn*
Wang Chong, *Critical Essays*
Huan Kuan, *A Treatise on Salt and Iron*
Ban Gu, *History of the Han Dynasty*
Guo Xiang and Xiang Xiu, *Commentaries on Zhuang Zi*
Liu Yiqing, *New Social Discourses*
Jia Sixie, *Important Arts for the Welfare of the People*
Wu Jing, *Essential Political Records of Emperor Taizong of the Tang Dynasty*
The Lotus Sutra
Xuan Zhuang, *The Completion of the Doctrine of Mere Ideation*

The Avatamsaka Sutra
Han Yu, *Works*
Liu Zongyuan, *Works*
Liu Zhiji, *A Treaties on Historiography*

The Cheng Brothers, *Collected Works*
Zhang Zai, *Works*
Wang Anshi, *Works*
Shen Kuo, *Dream Stream Essays*
Sima Guang, *History as a Mirror*
Zhu Xi, *Works*
Lu Jiuyuan, *Works*
Chen Liang, *Works*
Xu Guangqi, *Works*
Wang Yangming, *Works*
Wang Fuzhi, *Works*
Huang Zongxi, *Philosophers of Song and Yuan*
Huang Zongxi, *Philosophers of Ming*
Huang Zongxi, *A Treatise on Government and Politics*
Tang Zhen, *The Hidden Book*
Dai Zhen, *Explanation of the Meaning of Mencius*
Zhang Xuecheng, *A General Treatise of Literature and History*

Gong Zizhen, *Works*
Guo Songtao, *Works*
Kang Youwei, *On the Political Reforms of Confucius*
Kang Youwei, *On the Falsification of the Classics by the Liu's*
Yan Fu, *Selected Works*
Yan Fu, *Evolution* (Tr. of T. Huxley's *Evolution and Ethics*)
Tan Citong, *Works*
Liang Qichao, *Works*
Zhang Zhidong, *Exhortations on Learning*
Sun Yat-sen, *Works*
Song Jiaoren, *Works*
Cai Yuanpei, *Works*
Wang Guowei, *Works*
Lu Xun, *Complete Works*

NOTES

Part I

1 *The Book of Odes*
2 *The Book of History*
3 *The Book of Odes*

Chapter 1

1 *The Book. of Han Fei Zi*
2 Ibid.
3 *Book of Changes*
4 Ibid.
5 *The Book of Huai Nan Zi*
6 *Zuo's Chronicles*
7 *The Book of Huai Nan Zi*
8 *The Books of Lord Shang*
9 *The Book of Zhuang Zi*
10 *Book of Rites*
11 Ibid.
12 *Zuo's Chronicles*
13 *Book of History*
14 Ibid.
15 Ibid.
16 *Book of Rites* in Dai jr.'s version
17 *Book of History*
18 *Book of Odes*
19 *Book of History*, also in the *Zuo's Chronicles*
20 *Book of History*
21 *Book of Odes*

22 Ibid.
23 Ibid.
24 Ibid.
25 *Book of History*, Preface. Cf. also *Records of the Historian*
26 Ibid
27 *Zuo's Chronicles*
28 Ibid.
29 Ibid.
30 Ibid.
31 Ibid.
32 Ibid.
33 *Discourse on the States*
34 *Commentaries to the Book of Changes*
35 *Book of Changes*
36 Ibid.
37 *Zuo's Chronicles*
38 Ibid.
39 Ibid.
40 Ibid.
41 Ibid.
42 Ibid.
43 Ibid.
44 Ibid.
45 *Records of the Historian*
46 *The Analects*
47 Ibid.
48 Ibid.

⁴⁹ Ibid.
⁵⁰ Ibid.
⁵¹ Ibid.
⁵² *Records of the Historian*
⁵³ *Explanations of Characters
    and Interpretations of
    Words*
⁵⁴ *Analects*
⁵⁵ Ibid.
⁵⁶ Ibid.
⁵⁷ Ibid.
⁵⁸ Ibid.
⁵⁹ Ibid.
⁶⁰ Ibid.
⁶¹ Ibid.
⁶² Ibid.
⁶³ Ibid.
⁶⁴ Ibid.
⁶⁵ *Explanations of Characters
    and Interpretations of
    Words*
⁶⁶ Ruan Yuan, *Collected
    Works*
⁶⁷ *Analects*
⁶⁸ Ibid.
⁶⁹ Ibid.
⁷⁰ Ibid.
⁷¹ Ibid.
⁷² Ibid.
⁷³ Ibid.
⁷⁴ Ibid.
⁷⁵ Ibid.
⁷⁶ Ibid.
⁷⁷ Ibid.
⁷⁸ Ibid.
⁷⁹ Ibid.
⁸⁰ Ibid.

⁸¹ Ibid.
⁸² Ibid.
⁸³ Ibid.
⁸⁴ Ibid.
⁸⁵ Ibid.
⁸⁶ Ibid.
⁸⁷ Ibid.
⁸⁸ Ibid.
⁸⁹ Ibid.
⁹⁰ Ibid.
⁹¹ Ibid.
⁹² Ibid.
⁹³ Ibid.
⁹⁴ Ibid.
⁹⁵ Ibid.
⁹⁶ Ibid.
⁹⁷ Ibid.
⁹⁸ Ibid.
⁹⁹ Ibid.
¹⁰⁰ Ibid.
¹⁰¹ Ibid.
¹⁰² Ibid.
¹⁰³ Ibid.
¹⁰⁴ Ibid.
¹⁰⁵ Zhang Xuecheng, *A General Exposition on Literature and History*
¹⁰⁶ *Analects*
¹⁰⁷ *Records of the Historian*

Chapter 2-1

¹ *The Book of Huai Nan Zi*
² *The Book of Mo Zi*
³ *Lu's Spring and Autumn Annals*
⁴ *The Book of Zhuang Zi*
⁵ *The Book of Xun Zi*

6 *Lu's Spring and Autumn Annals*
7 *The Book of Huai Nan Zi*
8 Cf. Wang Zhong's *Preface to The Book of Mo Zi*
9 *The Book of Mo Zi*
10 Ibid.
11 Ibid.
12 Ibid.
13 *The Book of Mencius*
14 *The Book of Mo Zi*
15 Ibid.
16 Ibid.
17 Ibid.
18 Ibid.
19 Ibid.
20 Ibid.
21 Ibid.
22 Ibid.
23 Ibid.
24 Ibid.
25 Ibid.
26 Ibid.
27 Ibid.

Chapter 2-2

1 Liu Xiang, *Garden of Talks*, Notes
2 *The Book of Mencius*
3 *The Spring and Autumn of Lu*
4 *The Book of Mencius*
5 *The Book of Lie Zi*
6 *The Book of Han Fei Zi*
7 *The Book of Lie Zi*
8 Ibid.
9 *Lu's Spring and Autumn Annals*
10 Ibid.
11 Ibid.
12 Liu Xiang, op.cit.
13 *The Book of Han Fei Zi*
14 *The Book of Mo Zi*
15 *The Book of Lie Zi*
16 *The Book of Mencius*
17 *Lu's Spring and Autumn Annals*
18 *The Book of Mencius*
19 *The Book of Han Fei Zi*
20 Ibid.
21 *The Book of Xun Zi*
22 *The Book of Han Fei Zi*
23 *Lu's Spring and Autumn Annals*
24 *The Book of Han Fei Zi*
25 *Lu's Spring and Autumn Annals*
26 *The Book of Mencius*
27 *The Book of Zhuang Zi*
28 Ibid.
29 Ibid.
30 Ibid.
31 *The Book of Huai Nan Zi*
32 *The Book of Mencius*
33 *The Book of Han Fei Zi*
34 Ibid.

Chapter 2-3

1 *The Book of Han Fei Zi*
2 *The Doctrine of the Mean*
3 Ibid.
4 Ibid.
5 Ibid.
6 Ibid.

7 Ibid.
8 Ibid.
9 Cf. *Works of Zhang Tai-yan*, "On the Doctrine of the Five Elements in Zi Si and Mencius"
10 *The Book of Lao Zi*
11 Cf. Pang Pu's Article in *Wenwu* 1977, No. 10
12 *The Book of Mencius*
13 Ibid.
14 Ibid.
15 Ibid.
16 Ibid.
17 Ibid.
18 Ibid.
19 *Records of the Historian*
20 *The Book of Mencius*
21 Ibid.
22 Ibid.
23 Ibid.
24 Ibid.
25 Ibid.
26 Ibid.
27 Ibid.
28 Ibid.
29 Ibid.
30 Ibid.
31 Ibid.
32 Ibid.
33 Ibid.
34 Ibid.
35 Ibid.
36 Ibid.
37 Ibid.
38 Ibid.
39 Ibid.

Chapter 2-4

1 *The Book of Xun Zi*
2 Ibid.
3 Ibid.
4 Ibid.
5 Ibid.
6 Ibid.
7 Ibid.
8 Ibid.
9 Ibid.
10 *The Book of Han Fei Zi*
11 *The Book of Xun Zi*
12 Ibid.
13 Ibid.
14 Ibid.
15 Ibid.
16 Ibid.
17 Ibid.
18 Ibid.
19 Ibid.
20 Ibid.
21 Ibid.
22 Ibid.

Chapter 2-5

1 Sima Tan, *On the Main Dectrines of the Six Schools*
2 *History of the Han Dynasty*
3 Ibid.
4 Cf. *Records of the Warring States*
5 Cf. *The Collected Commentaries on the Historical Records*

6 *Records of the Historcian*
7 Huan Kuan, *A Treatise on Salt and Iron*
8 *Records of the Historian*
9 *Lu's Spring and Autumn Annals*
10 Cf. *Records of the Historian*
11 Ibid.

Chapter 2-6

1 Cheng Qiao, *General Records*
2 Liu Xiang, *Anthology of Anecdotes*
3 *History of the Jin Dynasty*
4 *Records of the Historian*
5 *The Book of Lord Shang*
6 Ibid.
7 *Records of the Historian*
8 Ibid.
9 *The Book of Lord Shang*
10 Ibid.
11 *The Book of Han Fei Zi*
12 *Records of the Historian*
13 *The Book of Han Fei Zi*
14 *The Lost Writings of Shen Zi*
15 Ibid.
16 *Records of the Historian*
17 *The Book of Han Fei Zi*
18 Ibid.
19 Ibid.
20 Ibid.
21 Ibid.
22 Ibid.
23 Ibid.
24 Ibid.
25 Ibid.
26 Ibid.
27 Ibid.
28 Ibid.
29 Ibid.
30 Ibid.
31 Ibid.
32 Ibid.
33 Ibid.
34 Ibid.
35 Ibid.
36 Ibid.
37 *The Book of Lord Shang*
38 *The Book of Han Fei Zi*
39 Ibid.
40 Ibid.
41 Ibid.
42 Ibid.
43 Ibid.
44 Ibid.
45 Ibid.
46 Ibid.
47 Ibid.
48 Ibid.
49 Ibid.
50 Ibid.
51 Ibid.
52 Ibid.

Chapter 3-1

1 *The Book of Lao Zi*
2 Ibid. For "law and decree", the Ma Wang Dui version reads: "law and wealth".
3 Ibid.

4 Ibid.
5 Ibid.
6 Ibid.
7 Ibid.
8 Ibid.
9 Ibid.
10 Ibid.
11 Ibid.
12 Ibid.
13 Ibid.
14 Ibid.
15 Ibid.
16 Ibid.
17 Ibid.
18 Ibid.
19 Ibid.
20 Ibid.
21 Ibid.
22 Ibid.
23 Ibid.
24 Ibid.
25 Ibid.
26 *A Treatise on Salt and Iron*
27 *Records of the Historian*
28 *The Lost Essays of Shen Zi*
29 Cf. Liu Jie, *Essays on Ancient History*, 1943, & Guo Mo-ruo, *The Bronze Age*, 1944
30 *History of the Han Dynasty*
31 *The Book of Zhuang Zi*
32 Ibid.
33 *The Book of Guan Zi*
34 Ibid.
35 Ibid.
36 Ma Zong ed., *Collections of Aphorisms*

37 *The Book of Guan Zi*
38 Ibid.
39 Ibid.
40 Ibid.
41 Ibid.
42 Ibid.
43 Ibid.
44 Ibid.
45 Ibid.
46 Ibid.
47 Ibid.
48 Ibid.
49 Ibid.
50 Ibid.
51 Ibid.
52 Ibid.
53 *The Book of Zhuang Zi*
54 Cf. *Lu's Spring and Autumn Annals*

Chapter 3-2

1 *Records of the Historian*
2 *The Book of Zhuang Zi*
3 Ibid.
4 *Records of the Historian*
5 Ibid.
6 *History of the Han Dynasty*
7 *The Book of Zhuang Zi*
8 Ibid.
9 Ibid.
10 Ibid.
11 Ibid.
12 Ibid.
13 Ibid.
14 Ibid.
15 Ibid.

16 Ibid.
17 Ibid.
18 Ibid.
19 Ibid.
20 Ibid.
21 Ibid.
22 Ibid.
23 Ibid.

18 Ibid.
19 Ibid.
20 Ibid.
21 Ibid.
22 Ibid.
23 Ibid.
24 Ibid.
25 *The Book of Zhuang Zi*

Chapter 3-3

1 Cf. *Records of the Warring States*
2 Cf. Sima Tan, *On the Main Doctrines of the Six Schools*
3 *Lu's Spring and Autumn Annals*
4 *Records of the Warring States*
5 Ibid.
6 *The Book of Zhuang Zi*
7 Ibid.
8 Ibid.
9 Ibid.
10 *Lu's Spring and Autumn Annals*
11 *The Book of Zhuang Zi*
12 Cf. *Records of the Historian*
13 Cf. *The Book of Gongsun Long Zi*
14 Cf. *Lu's Spring and Autumn Annals*
15 *Records of the Historian*
16 *The Book of Zhuang Zi*
17 *The Book of Gongsun Long Zi*

Chapter 3-4

1 *History of the Han Dynasty*
2 Ibid.
3 *Records of the Historian*
4 Ibid.
5 *Wu Qi's Art of War*
6 *Records of the Historian*
7 *Sun Wu's Art of War*
8 *Anthology of Anecdotes*
9 *Sun Bin's Art of War*
10 *Sun Wu's Art of War*
11 *Wu Qi's Art of War*
12 *Sun Bin's Art of War*
13 *Lu's Spring and Autumn Annals*
14 *Sun Wu's Art of War*
15 Ibid.
16 Ibid.
17 Ibid.
18 Ibid.
19 *Sun Bin's Art of War*
20 Ibid.
21 *Sun Wu's Art of War*
22 *Wu Qi's Art of War*
23 Ibid.
24 *Sun Bin's Art of War*

Chapter 3-5

1 *History of the Han Dynasty*
2 Ibid.
3 *Records of the Historian*
4 Ibid.
5 *History of the Han Dynasty*
6 Wang Zhong, *Discourses Weighed in the Balance*
7 *Lu's Spring and Autumn Annals*
8 Ibid.
9 Ibid.
10 Ibid.
11 Ibid.
12 Ibid.
13 Ibid.
14 Ibid.
15 Ibid.
16 Ibid.
17 Ibid.
18 Ibid.
19 Ibid.
20 Ibid.
21 Ibid.
22 *Records of the Historian*
23 *The Book of Han Fei Zi*
24 *Lu's Spring and Autumn Annals*

Chapter 4-4

1 *The Book of Rites*
2 *Discourse on the States*
3 Ibid.
4 *Records of the Historian*

5 Ibid.
6 Ibid.
7 Ibid.
8 Ibid.
9 Ibid.
10 Ibid.
11 Ibid.
12 *The Book of Guan Zi*
13 Ibid.
14 Ibid.
15 Ibid.
16 *The Analects*
17 Ibid.
18 Ibid.
19 *The Book of Mencius*
20 *The Book of Xun Zi*
21 *The Analects*
22 Ibid.
23 *The Book of Mencius*
24 Ibid.
25 *The Book of Xun Zi*
26 *The Analects*
27 Ibid.
28 Ibid.
29 *Zuo's Chronicles* (or, *Zuo's Commentary on the Spring and Autumn Annals*)
30 *The Analects*
31 Ibid.
32 Ibid.
33 *The Book of Xun Zi*
34 Ibid.
35 Ibid.
36 Ibid.
37 *The Book of Mo Zi*
38 Ibid.

39 Ibid.
40 *The Book of Mencius*
41 Ibid.
42 *The Book of Shi Zi,* cited in *The Northern Hall Collection of Books*
43 *The Book of Mencius*
44 Ibid.
45 Ibid.
46 *Records of the Historian*
47 Ibid.
48 *The Book of Lord Shang*
49 *The Book of Han Fei Zi*
50 Ibid.
51 Ibid.
52 Ibid.
53 Ibid.

Chapter 4-4

1 *The Book of History*
2 *The Arithmetical Classic of the Gnomon and the Circular Path*
3 *The Book of Rites, Dai the Elder's Version*
4 *Lu's Spring and Autumn Annals*
5 *The Book of Shen Zi*
6 *The Book of Zhuang Zi*
7 Ibid.
8 Ibid.
9 Ibid.
10 Ibid.
11 Ibid.
12 Ibid.
13 Ibid.
14 *Records of the Historian*

15 *Zuo's Chronicles*
16 *Records of the Historian*
17 *Lu's Spring and Autumn Annals*
18 Ibid.
19 Ibid.
20 Ibid.

Chapter 4-3

1 *The Book of Mencius*
2 *Records of the Historian*
3 *Gong Yang's Commentary of the Spring and Autumn Annals*
4 Ibid.
5 *Zuo Chronicles,* or *Zuo's Commentary of the Spring and Autumn Annals*
6 Ibid.
7 Ibid.
8 Ibid.
9 Ibid.
10 Ibid.
11 Ibid.
12 Ibid.
13 Ibid.
14 Ibid.
15 Ibid.
16 *Discourse on the States*
17 Ibid.

Chapter 4-4

1 *Analects*
2 *Book of History*
3 *Records of the Historian*
4 *Analects*

⁵ Ibid.
⁶ Ibid.
⁷ Ibid.
⁸ Ibid.
⁹ *The Book of Mencius*
¹⁰ Ibid.
¹¹ Ibid.
¹² Ibid.
¹³ *The Book of Xun Zi*
¹⁴ Ibid.
¹⁵ Ibid.
¹⁶ *The Book of Lord Shang*
¹⁷ *The Book of Han Fei Zi*

Part II
General Sketch

¹ Lu Xun, "The Demeaner and Literary Style in Wei and Jin and Their Relations with Medicine and Wine", *Collect Works*

Chapter 5

¹ Sima Qian, *Records of the Historian*
² *History of the Han Dynasty*
³ Sima Qian, *Records of the Historian*
⁴ Lu Gu, *A New Treatise*
⁵ Ibid.
⁶ Ibid.
⁷ *History of the Han Dynasty.*
⁸ Ibid.
⁹ Dong Zhongshu, *Exu-berant Dew of Spring and Autumn*
¹⁰ *History of the Han Dynasty*
¹¹ Dong Zhongshu, op. cit., *Exuberant Dew of Spring and Autumn*
¹² *Exuberant Dew of Spring and Autumn.*
¹³ *A General Treatise from the White Tiger*
¹⁴ *History of the Han Dynasty.*
¹⁵ Huan Tan, *The New Treatise.*
¹⁶ Wang Chong, *Discourses Weighed in the Balance*
¹⁷ Ibid.
¹⁸ Ibid.
¹⁹ Ibid.
²⁰ Ibid.
²¹ Ibid.
²² Ibid.
²³ Ibid.
²⁴ Ibid.
²⁵ Ibid.
²⁶ Ibid.
²⁷ Wang Fu, *Essays of a Recluse*
²⁸ Ibid.
²⁹ *History of the Later Han Dynasty*
³⁰ Ibid.
³¹ *Summary of Books*
³² Zhong Changtong, *The Illuminating Sayings*
³³ Same as ³¹
³⁴ Sima Qian, *Records of the*

Historian.
35 *The Book of Mo Zi*
36 *Canon of Great Peace*
37 Ibid.
38 *History of the Later Han Dynasty.*

Chapter 6

1 *History of the Han Dynasty*
2 Ibid.
3 Ibid.
4 Ibid.
5 Sima Qian, *Records of the Historian.*
6 *History of the Han Dynasty.*
7 Sima Qian, *Records of the Historian.*
8 Huan Kuan, *A Treatise of Salt and Iron*
9 Ibid.
10 Ibid.
11 Ibid.
12 Ibid.
13 *History of the Han Dynasty.*
14 Ibid.
15 Ibid.
16 Ibid.
17 Ibid.
18 Xun Yue, *An Exposition of the Precedents.*
19 Ma Duanlin, *Studies in Ancient Bibliographies*
20 *History of the Later Han Dynasty*

21 Xu Gan, *The Medium Treatise*

Chapter 7

1 *History of the Later Han Dynasty*
2 Ibid.
3 *History of the Jin Dynasty*
4 Zhang Heng, *Annotations on the Armillary Sphere*
5 Zhang Heng, *The Spiritual Constitution of the Universe*
6 *History of the Jin Dynasty*
7 *Canon of Internal Medicine*
8 Sima Qian, *"Letter to Ren Shaoqing"*
9 Sima Qian, *Records of the Historian.*
10 Ibid.
11 Ibid.
12 *History of the Han Dynasty*
13 *Book of Rites*
14 Ibid.
15 Ibid.
16 Ibid.
17 Wang Chong, *Discourses Weighed in the Balance*
18 Ibid.

Chapter 8

1 *History of the Jin Dynasty*
2 *History of Three Kingdoms*
3 Ibid.
4 Ibid.

5 Cao Cao, *Annotations of the "Book of Sun Zi"*
6 Same as 1
7 Cao Cao, *Collected Works*
8 Ibid.
9 Zhuge Liang, *Collected Works*
10 Ibid.
11 *History of the Jin Dynasty.*
12 Ibid.
13 Ibid.
14 Wang Bi, *Explanation on the Analect*
15 Wang Bi, *Commentaries on Lao Zi*
16 Ruan Ji, *Works*
17 Ji Kang, *Works*
18 Ibid.
19 *History of the Jin Dynasty*
20 *Further Collection of Essays on Buddhism*
21 Tan Ji, *On the Six Schools and Seven Sects*
22 *The Analect*
23 Brother Zhao, *Discourses of Zhao*
24 Hui Da, *Commentaries on the Discourses of Zhao*
25 Ge Hong, *Bao Pu Zi*
26 *The Taoist Patrology*
27 *"Biography of Fan Zhen", History of the Liang Dynasty*
28 Ibid.
29 Ibid.
30 Fan Zhen, *A Treatise on the Mortality of the Soul*
31 Ibid.
32 Ibid.

Chapter 9

1 *History of the Jin Dynasty*
2 *Book of Fu Xuan*
3 Ibid.
4 *History of the Jin Dynasty*
5 Shakespeare, *Timon of Athens*, Act 4, Sc 3
6 *History of the Wei Dynasty*
7 Ibid.
8 Ibid.
9 Ibid.
10 Yang Xuanzhi, *Buddhist Temples in Luoyang*

Chapter 10

1 Liu Hui, *Annotations on the "Nine Chapters on the Mathematical Art*
2 *History of the Song Dynasty*
3 *History of the Jin Dynasty*
4 Ibid.
5 Ibid.
6 Ibid.
7 *Zhaoming Anthology of Literary Writings*
8 Jia Sixie, *Important Arts for the People's Welfare*
9 Ibid.
10 *History of the Late Han Dynasty*
11 Cao Pi, *On the Literary Writings*

12 Ibid.
13 Cf. S. B. Coleridge, Biographia Literaria ch 13
14 Cao Pi, *On the Literary Writings*
15 Ibid.
16 Liu Xie, *A Scrutiny of the Spirit of Literature*
17 Ibid.
18 Ibid.
19 Ibid.
20 Zhong Rong, *Judgment on Poesy*
21 Ibid.

Chapter 11

1 Wang Tong, *The Middle Sayings*
2 Ibid.
3 Ibid.
4 Ibid.
5 Ibid.
6 *Essential Political Records of the Zhenguan Period*
7 Ibid.
8 Ibid.
9 Ibid.
10 Ibid.
11 Ibid.
12 Ibid.
13 Ibid.
14 Sima Guang, *History as a Mirror*
15 *Essential Political Records of the Zhengguan Period*
16 *The Metaphysical Essence of Lotus Sutra*

17 *The Doctrine of Completion Through Ideation*
18 *The Hundred Theories in the Sea of Ideas of Avatamsaka Sutra*
19 *Sutra of the Altar*
20 Ibid.
21 Sima Chengzhen, *Treatise on Oblivion of the World by Sitting*
22 Ibid.
23 Ibid.
24 Han Yu, *Complete Works*
25 Ibid.
26 Li Ao, *Essay on the Recovery of Human Nature*
27 Ibid.
28 Liu Zongyuan, *Complete Works*
29 Ibid.
30 Liu Yuxi *Complete Works*
31 Ibid.
32 Ibid.
33 *Complete Tang Essays*
34 *Wu Neng Zi*
35 Ibid.
36 Ibid.
37 Ibid.
38 Ibid.
39 Ibid.
40 Tan Qiao, *The Book of Transformation*
41 Ibid.
42 Ibid.
43 Ibid.
44 Ibid.
45 Ibid.

Chapter 12

1 Sima Guang, *History as a Mirror*
2 Ibid.
3 *New History of the Tang Dynasty*
4 Ibid.
5 Ibid.
6 Ibid.
7 *Old History of the Tang Dynasty*
8 Ibid.
9 Ibid.

Chapter 13

1 Liu Zhiji, *A General Treatise on Historiography*
2 *Old History of the Tang Dynasty*
3 Liu Zhiji, op cit.
4 Ibid.
5 Ibid.
6 Du You, *A General Record of Institutions*
7 Ibid.
8 Li Bai, *Poetical Works*
9 Bai Juyi, *Poetical Works*
10 Ibid.
11 Bai Juyi, *Poetical Works*
12 Ibid.
13 Han Yu, *Complete Works*
14 Ibid.
15 Ibid.
16 Ibid.
17 Liu Zongyuan, *Complete Works*

Part III
Chapter 14

1 Xie Liangzuo, *Quotations from Shang Cai*
2 *Writings of the Cheng Brothers*
3 Ibid.
4 Ibid.
5 Ibid.
6 *Classified Sayings of Zhu Xi*
7 *Works of the Cheng Brothers*
8 Cf Zhu Xi, *Complete Works*, passim
9 *Classified Sayings of Zhu Xi*
10 Ibid.
11 Ibid.
12 Zhu Xi, *Commentaries on "The Great Learning"*
13 *Essential Sayings of the Cheng Brothers*
14 Zhang Zai, *Correct Discipline for Beginners*
15 Ibid.
16 Zhang Zai, *Commentaries on the "Book of Changes"*
17 Cf *Classified Sayings of Zhu Xi*
18 *Sayings of Master Zhang*
19 Zhang Zai, *Correct Discipline for Beginners*
20 *Sayings of Master Zhang*
21 Cheng Hao, *Selected*

Works
22 Classified Sayings of Zhu Xi
23 Writings of the Cheng Brothers
24 Chen Liang, Collected Works
25 Ibid.
26 Ibid.
27 Ibid.
28 Ibid.
29 Ye Shi, Collected Works
30 Ibid.
31 Ibid.
32 Ibid.
33 The Taoist Patrology
34 Ibid.
35 Ibid.
36 Ibid.
37 Ibid.

Chapter 15

1 Li Gou, Collected Works
2 Ibid.
3 Ibid.
4 Ibid.
5 Summary Catalogue of the Complete Collection of the Four Categories of Books
6 Deng Mu, The Harp of Boya
7 Ibid.
8 Ibid.
9 Ibid.
10 Ibid.
11 Ibid.

12 Ibid.
13 Ibid.
14 Ibid.   '.
15 Su Che, Collected Works
16 Literary Examplars of Song
17 Ibid.
18 Wang Anshi, Collected Works
19 Cai Shangxiang, A Research on the Chronology of Wang Anshi
20 Wang Anshi, op. cit.
21 Summary Catalogue of the Complete Collection of the Four Categories of Books
22 Wang Anshi, op. cit.
23 History of the Song Dynasty
24 Li Tao, Supplementary Draft to "History as a Mirror"-
25 Administrative Statutes of the Song Dynasty
26 Su Che, op. cit.
27 Cf Cai Shangxiang, op. cit.
28 Wang Anshi, op. cit.
29 Sima Guang, Collected Works
30 History of the Song Dynasty
31 Cai Shangxiang, op. cit.
32 Local Records of Shaowu
33 Li Gang, Collected Works
34 Sima Qian, Records of the Historian

35 Wang Yangming, *Collected Works*
36 *Genealogy of the Fang Household of Guilin*
37 *History of the Song Dynasty*

Chapter 16

1 J Needham, *Science and Civilization in China*
2 Shen Kuo, *Dream Stream Essays*
3 Ibid.
4 Ibid.
5 Ibid.
6 Ibid.
7 Zhu Xi, *Collected Annotation to Chu Poesy*
8 Zhu Xi, *Classified Sayings*
9 Ruan Yuan, *Collected Works*
10 Sima Guang, *History as a Mirror*
11 Ibid.
12 Ma Duanlin, *General Collection of Historical Documents*
13 Zhang Xuecheng, *A General Treatise on Literature and History*
14 Zheng Qiao, *General Records*
15 Ma Duanlin, op. cit.
16 Ibid.
17 Ibid.
18 Ouyang Xiu, *Complete Works*

19 Su Shi, *Collected Works*
20 Wang Anshi, *Collected Works*
21 Ibid.
22 Zhu Xi, *Classified Sayings*
23 Ibid.
24 Lu You, *Poetical Works*

Chapter 17

1 *Works of the Cheng Brothers*
2 Lu Jiuyuan, *Complete Works*
3 Wang Yangming, *Complete Works*
4 Ibid.
5 Wang Yangming, *Records of Instructions*
6 Ibid.
7 Ibid.
8 Ibid.
9 Ibid.
10 Zhu Xi, *Explanations on "The Great Learning"*
11 Huang Zongxi, *Philosophers of Song and Yuan*
12 Huang Zongxi, *Philosophers of Ming*
13 Wang Gen, *Works*
14 Wang Dong, *Works*
15 Wang Fuzhi, *Annotations on the Correct Discipline for Beginners*
16 Ibid.
17 Wang Fuzhi, *Records of Thoughts and Questionings*

18 Ibid.
19 Wang Fuzhi, *Commentaries on the "Book of Changes"*
20 Wang Fuzhi, *Records of Thoughts and Questions*
21 Wang Fuzhi, *On Reading the "Four Books"*
22 Zhu Xi, *Classified Sayings*
23 Wang Fuzhi, *Commentaries on the "Book of Changes"*
24 Ibid.
25 Dai Zhen, *Collected Works*
26 Dai Zhen, *An Explanation on the Meanings of "Mencius"*
27 Ibid.
28 Ibid.
29 Ibid.
30 Ibid.
31 Ibid.
32 Dai Zhen, *On Goodness*
33 Dai Zhen, *An Explanation on the Meanings of "Mencius"*
34 Ibid.
35 Dai Zhen, *On Goodness*
36 Dai Zhen, *Collected Works*

Chapter 18

1 Huang Zongxi, *A Treatise on Government and Politics*
2 Ibid.
3 Ibid.
4 Ibid.

5 Tang Zhen, *The Hidden Book*
6 Ibid.
7 Ibid.
8 Ibid.
9 Ibid.
10 Ibid.
11 Same as 5.
12 Ibid.
13 Ibid.
14 Ibid.
15 Gu Yanwu, *Collected Essays.*
16 Ibid. and Quan Zuwang, *Works*
17 Gu Yanwu, *Daily Additions to Knowledge*
18 Ibid.
19 Yan Yuan, *Corrections of the Four Books*
20 Yan Yuan, *Notebooks*
21 Li Gong, *Proposal for Perpetual Peace*
22 *Chronology of Li Gong*
23 Huang Zongxi, *Collected Works*
24 Liu Shipai, *Miscellaneous Works*
25 Wang Fuzhi, *The Yellow Book*
26 Tang Zhen, op. cit.
27 Huang Zongxi, *A Treatise on Government and Politics*
28 Ibid.
29 Gu Yanwu, *Collected Essays*

30 Cf Adam Smith, *The Wealth of Nations, On Mercantile System*

31 Kant, *Gesammelte Schriften* (G Reimer, 1912) Bd 8, S 20

32 Huang Zongxi, *A Treatise on Government and Politics*

33 Ibid.

34 Zha Jizuo, *Records of Criminal Thoughts*

35 Ding Yaokang, *Escape from Catastrophe*

36 *A Record of the Subjugation of the Rebellions*

Chapter 19

1 Jiao Xun, *Works*

2 R Descartes, *Discours sur les Methode* Pt. 3

3 Fang Yizhi, *General Encyclopaedia*

4 Fang Yizhi, *Explanation on Zhuang Zi*

5 Fang Yizhi, *Notes on the Nature of Things*

6 Ibid.

7 Fang Yizhi, *Sayings*

8 Same as 5.

9 Ibid.

10 Ibid.

11 Ibid.

12 Ibid.

13 Jiao Xun, op. cit.

14 Sir James Jeans, *The Mysterious Universe*, Cambridge, 1931 p. 134-135

15 Ruan Yuan, *Works*

16 *Le Opere di Galileo Galilei* t. 41, p. 171

17 Li Zhizao, *Works*

18 Ibid.

19 Ruan Yuan, *Lives of Mathematicians*

20 Same as 15.

21 Fang Yizhi, *Notes on the Nature of Things*

22 Same as 18.

23 Fang Zhongtong, *Expositions of Numbers and Measures*

24 Ruan Yuan, *Lives of Mathematicians*

25 Ibid.

26 Quan Zuwang, *Works*

27 Huang Zongxi, *Philosophers of Ming*

28 Ibid.

29 Ibid.

30 Huang Zongxi, *Collected Works*

31 Same as 28

32 Zhang Xuecheng, *A General Treatise on Literature and History*

33 Ibid.

34 Ibid.

35 Ibid.

36 Ibid.

37 Ibid.

38 Ibid.

39 Ibid.

40 Ibid.

⁴¹ Ibid.
⁴² Ibid.
⁴³ Ibid.
⁴⁴ Ibid.
⁴⁵ Gu Yanwu, *Daily Additions to Knowledge*
⁴⁶ Gu Yanwu, *Collected Essays*
⁴⁷ Wang Fuzhi, *A Commentary Selection of Ancient Poems*
⁴⁸ Wang Fuzhi, *Works*
⁴⁹ Ibid.
⁵⁰ Zhang Xuecheng, op. cit.

Part IV -
Chapter 20-1

¹ Liang Qichao, *A Survey of the Learnings in the Qing Period*
² Liang Qichao, *On the Main Trend of Transition of Ancient Chinese Learnings and Ideologies*
³ Gong Zizhen, *Collected Works*
⁴ Wei Yuan, *An Illustrated Record of the Oversea Countries*
⁵ Wei Yuan, *Writings from the Guwei Hall*
⁶ Wei Yuan, *An Illustrated Record of the Oversea Countries.*
⁷ Wei Yuan, *Writings from the Guwei Hall.*

⁸ Ibid.

Chapter 20-2

¹ *The Taiping Heavenly Kingdom*
² *Heavenly Land System*
³ *Complete Works of Zeng Guofan*

Chapter 21-1

¹ Guo Songtao, *Collected Essays of Yangzhi Studio*
² Zheng Guanying, *Frightening Words in a Prosperous Age*
³ *The Yangwu Movement* V. 6, p. 208
⁴ The Reform Movement of 1898 V. 2, p. 485
⁵ Zhang Zhidong, *Exhortation on Learning*
⁶ Ibid.
⁷ Zheng Guanying, *Frightening Words in a Prosperous Age*
⁸ Ma Jianzhong, *Works from the Shike Hall*
⁹ Xue Fucheng, *Proposals for Foreign Affairs*

Chapter 21-1-2

¹ Guo Songtao, *Collected Eassys of Yangzhi Studio*
² Ibid.
³ Ibid.

4 Ibid.

5 Wang Juchang, *A Chronicle of Yan Fu*

6 Guo Songtao, *Collected Eassys of Yangzhi Studio*

7 Ibid.

8 Ibid.

9 Ibid.

10 Ibid.

11 Ibid.

12 Ibid.

13 Same as 1.

14 Ibid.

15 Ibid.

16 Same as 4.

17 Ibid.

18 Ibid.

19 Ibid.

20 Ibid.

Chapter 21-3

1 Shao Zuozhou, *Frightening Warning from Shao*

2 Feng Guifen, *Discourses in the Xianbin House*

3 Ibid.

4 Ibid.

5 Ibid.

6 Xue Fucheng, *Anthology of Physical Sciences, Preface*

7 Xue Fucheng, *Proposals on Foreign Affairs*

8 Ibid.

9 Ibid.

10 Ibid.

11 Zheng Guanying, *Frightening Words in a Prosperous Age*

12 Ibid.

13 Ibid.

14 Ibid.

15 Ibid.

16 Ibid.

17 Ibid.

18 Ibid.

19 Ibid.

20 Ibid.

Chapter 22-1

1 Kang Youwei, "Sixth Memorial to the Throne"

2 Kang Youwei, "Memorial to the Throne Concerning the Constitution and Parliament"

Chapter 22-2

1 Tan Citong, *Complete Works* p. 56

2 Ibid.

3 Ibid., p. 14

4 H Maine, *Ancient Law* Ch. V.

5 Tan Citong, *Complete Works*, p. 1

6 Ibid., p. 391

7 Ibid., p. 317

Chapter 22-3

1 *Anthology of the Essays for the Cause of the Ortho-*

6 Ibid.

7 Ibid.

8 Liang Qichao, *The Method of Studying the Chinese History*, Preface

9 Ibid., p. 203.

10 Ibid., p. 204.

11 Ibid., p. 208.

12 Ibid., p. 215.

13 Ibid., p. 216.

14 Ibid., p. 176.

15 Wang Guowei, *New Evidences on Ancient History*, Chap. 1.

16 Liang Qichao, *Collected Works from the Yinbing Study*.

Chapter 24-4

1 Li Shuchang, Preface to the *Supplementary Anthology of Classified Classical Essays*

2 Xue Fucheng, *Preface to Collected Essays*

3 *Journal of the Renovated People*, 8 No. 3

4 Lu Xun, *Complete Works*

5 Guo Moruo, *My Youth,* pp. 125-126

6 Liang Qichao, *Collected Works in the Yin Bing Hall*

7 Cf *The Forum of Public Opinion,* Vol. 26

8 Lu Xun, *A Brief History of Chinese Fiction,* Foreign Languages Press, Beijing, 1976, pp. 352-353

9 Wang Guowei, *Complete Works,* Vol. 14

10 Wang Guowei, *Examination on the Song and Yuan Dramas*

11 Lin Shu, "Letter to Cai Yuanpei" in *Selected Works of Cai Yuanpei,* pp. 80-81

12 Ling Shi, "On Reading *Uncle Tom's Cabin",* Vol. 1, p. 870

13 Guo Moruo, op. cit., pp. 126-127

14 Lu Xun, *Complete Works*

INDEX

中国思想发展史

何兆武　步近智　唐宇元　孙开太　著

＊

外文出版社出版

（中国北京百万庄路 24 号）

邮政编码 100037

北京外文印刷厂印刷

中国国际图书贸易总公司发行

（中国北京车公庄西路 21 号）

北京邮政信箱第 399 号　邮政编码 100044

1991 年（大 32 开）第一版

（英）

ISBN 7—119—00003—9/B・1(外)

01725(精)

ISBN ▉▉▉▉▉3/B・2(外)

￥19.00

2—E—2114